A GUIDE TO MAGISTRATES

With

Practical Forms

for the

Discharge of Their Duties Out of Court

TO WHICH ARE ADDED,

PRECEDENTS

FOR THE USE OF

PROSECUTORS, SHERIFFS, CORONERS, CONSTABLES, ESCHEATORS, CLERKS, ETC.

ADAPTED TO THE

NEW CODE OF VIRGINIA

By Joseph Mayo

Counsellor at Law, and Public Prosecutor
in the Hustings Court in Richmond

HERITAGE BOOKS
2012

HERITAGE BOOKS
AN IMPRINT OF HERITAGE BOOKS, INC.

Books, CDs, and more—Worldwide

For our listing of thousands of titles see our website
at
www.HeritageBooks.com

A Facsimile Reprint
Published 2012 by
HERITAGE BOOKS, INC.
Publishing Division
100 Railroad Ave. #104
Westminster, Maryland 21157

Originally published Richmond:
Printed by Colin, Baptist and Nowlan
1850

Entered according to Act of Congress, in the year
eighteen hundred and forty-nine, by Joseph Mayo,
in the Clerk's Office of the Eastern District of Virginia.

— Publisher's Notice —
In reprints such as this, it is often not possible to remove blemishes from the original. We feel the contents of this book warrant its reissue despite these blemishes and hope you will agree and read it with pleasure.

International Standard Book Numbers
Paperbound: 978-0-7884-5137-9
Clothbound: 978-0-7884-9273-0

TO

THE JUSTICES OF VIRGINIA,

THE MOST USEFUL BODY OF PUBLIC AGENTS IN THE STATE,

THIS VOLUME,

INTENDED BY ITS AUTHOR TO FACILITATE THE DISCHARGE OF THEIR ARDUOUS DUTIES,

IS

RESPECTFULLY DEDICATED.

PREFACE.

The objects of the following work are explained in a great degree by its title. It professes to aid the Justices of the Peace in Virginia in the discharge of the various and complicated duties connected with their office, which devolve on them *out of Court;* where, unaided by legal advice, they are frequently called to act under circumstances involving the highest degree of responsibility and difficulty. It were unreasonable to expect that a class of citizens, however respectable and intelligent, who have not made the law a study, but who under sudden emergency are often forced to decide on questions involving the most important rights and interests, should, without a competent guide for their action, escape the commission of frequent error. Indeed, considering the great changes which have been made in the law since the publication of the last work on the duties of Justices, it is a matter of surprise, no less than a tribute to their intelligence and uprightness, that so little objection can be urged to the order, regularity and correctness of their proceedings. It may be truly said of them, that there are no public functionaries to whom the community is so much indebted, and none to whom the obligation of gratitude is less acknowledged.

The late revision of the Code has rendered it necessary that the Justices of Virginia should have some practical guide adapted to its provisions. To supply such desideratum, the author has, with no little labour, prepared this book. His principal design has been to make the work what its title purports, a practical guide to Magistrates out of Court, and he submits it to them with the hope that it will be found not inadequate to the end proposed.

The subjects are arranged under their appropriate titles, in alphabetical order, each title containing a full description of the subject matter contained under that head, accompanied by every form necessary to carry into practice all the provisions of the law as explained in each. Where the proceedings are under the statute, as most of them are, great care has been taken to make them conform to the words of the law; and it is believed that the arrangement of the various forms, (as well as the forms themselves,) is so plain and concise, that by adhering to them, error may be avoided. If this anticipation be well founded, the main object of the work will be fulfilled, much valuable time to the Courts, witnesses and parties, as well as expense to the Commonwealth, be saved, and much hardship and suffering to prisoners avoided, which are now occasioned by incorrect proceedings in the incipient stages of criminal proceedings.

To make his labour useful to as many as the subjects of such a work would properly admit of, the author has endeavoured to make it a convenient book of reference to the Bar, by a more copious digest of the Criminal Law than might be thought necessary for the practical purposes of a Justice, and by inserting forms of indictments, pleas, &c., so that there will be found in the small compass of this volume, as he believes, every direction and form of proceeding necessary in a criminal prosecution, from the first complaint before the Justice to the final conviction or acquittal of a party charged with any offence against the laws of Virginia. In its preparation he has availed himself freely of the labour of others, and among American authors he takes pleasure in acknowledging his indebtedness to his late lamented friend, Joseph Tate, Esq., to Mr. Barbour of New York, and to the late learned Solicitor General of Massachusetts, Daniel Davis, Esq.; and now he submits the work to the public, with becoming diffidence, as he trusts; certainly with an earnest desire that it may prove useful to the Magistrates and Bar of Virginia.

INTRODUCTION.

OF CRIMES.

The law does not impute crime indiscriminately to all persons, and it is therefore proper, in a work of this character, to inform the Justice who are incapable of committing crime, either for want of age or from other disability. It is important here, also, to point out to him the leading distinction in the grade of crime, as upon this will depend the tribunal to which a party charged before him with an offence, should be sent for farther prosecution.

I. *Who are incapable of committing Crime.*

Incapacity to commit crime proceeds from want of *will* in the party by whom the act is committed, for where there is no *will* to commit an offence, there can be no reason why a party should incur the penalties of the law. The cases of want or defect of will, seem to be reducible to four heads; 1st. Infancy. 2d. *Non compos mentis.* 3d. Subjection to the power of others; and 4th. Ignorance.([1])

1st. *As to Infancy.* Within the age of seven years an infant cannot be punished for any offence whatever, for in presumption of law he has no discretion whatever, and against this presumption nothing can be heard.([2]) Between the ages of seven and fourteen, an infant is presumed to be incapable of crime, yet this is but a presumption in his favour, which may be rebutted by proof shewing a wicked and depraved discretion, evinced by the particular facts and circumstances of the case. The evidence, however, to repel this presumption,

---
([1]) 1 Russ. 1.   ([2]) Id.

should be strong and clear beyond all doubt and contradiction.(¹)

A boy under the age of fourteen is incapable of committing the crime of rape, upon the ground of impotency, and not for want of discretion, but he may be principal in the second degree, by being present, aiding and assisting in the offence, if it appear by sufficient circumstances that he had a wicked discretion.(²)

On the attainment of fourteen years of age, the criminal *acts* of infants are subject to the same modes of construction as those of the rest of society, for then the law presumes them capable of crime, able to discern between good and evil, and subjects them to punishment as much as if they were of full age.(³) This principle, however, does not apply to misdemeanors arising from *nonfeasance* on the part of infants, for it may be stated as a general rule, (though not without exception,) that persons under full age, (twenty-one years,) are not liable to prosecutions for acts of *omission*, when the offence is a mere misdemeanor only.(⁴)

2d. *Persons non compos mentis.* Every person at the age of discretion is, unless the contrary is proved, presumed by law to be sane and accountable for his actions. But if there be an incapacity or defect in the understanding, as there can be no consent of the will, so the act cannot be culpable. Of persons *non compos mentis*, it is considered that there are four kinds: 1st, an idiot; 2d, one *non compos* by sickness; 3d, a lunatic; and 4th, one that is drunk.

An idiot is one who is of non-sane memory from his birth, by a perpetual infirmity, without lucid intervals.(⁵) One deaf and dumb from his birth, who has had no means of learning or discriminating between right and wrong, or of understanding the penal enactments of the law as applicable to particular offences, is by presumption of law an idiot, and not accountable for his actions. But this presumption may be rebutted by *strong* and *cogent* evidence of the use of understanding. The

---

(¹) 1 Russ. 3.
(²) Id.
(³) Id.
(⁴) 1 Russ. 2.
(⁵) Co. Litt. 247.

humanity of modern times has gone very far to instruct such persons, not only in discerning right from wrong, but in communicating their thoughts by writing and signs; and wherever it appears clearly that he has the use of understanding, he may be tried, and suffer judgment and execution.([1])

From sickness. Insanity from sickness, or adventitious insanity, more technically called *dementia accidentalis*, proceeds from various causes, and is of several kinds or degrees; it is either partial, (an insanity upon some one subject, the party being sane upon all others,) or total; either permanent, (usually called madness,) or temporary, (the object of it being afflicted with his disorder at certain periods and vicissitudes only, with lucid intervals,) which latter is commonly denominated lunacy, from the erroneously supposed influence of the moon, in all disorders of the brain.

Among the causes of this species of insanity may be numbered hereditary predisposition, injuries of the head, certain bodily diseases, a peculiar temperament, habitual intoxication, fever, mercurial medicine improvidently and largely taken, violent passion, grief, terror, degradation, disappointment, the suppression of periodical or occasional discharges, and secretions and childbirth. But from whatever source proceeding, the victim of delusion, whilst under the influence of this disorder, is, by the humanity of the laws, excused from the criminal responsibility of his actions, and accountable for no offence committed during the frenzy.

Where the deprivation of understanding and memory is total, fixed and permanent, it excuses all acts; but the difficulty in these cases is to distinguish between a total aberration of intellect and a partial or temporary delusion, notwithstanding which the party may be capable of distinguishing right from wrong, and of knowing that he was doing a wrong act, in which case he would be amenable for his conduct, and held guilty in the eye of the law. " Partial insanity," says Lord Hale, " is the condition of many, especially of melancholy persons, who generally discover their defects in excessive fear and

---

([1]) 1 Russ. 7.

grief, and yet are not wholly destitute of the use of reason; and this partial insanity seems not to excuse them in the commission of any capital offence. It is very difficult to define the almost invisible line that divides perfect and partial insanity; it must rest upon circumstances, to be duly weighed and considered by the Court and the jury, lest on the one hand there be inhumanity towards the defects of our nature; or on the other too great indulgence given to crimes."[1] It is not every kind of idle and frantic humour of a man, or something unaccountable in his actions, which will shew him to be such a madman as to be excused from punishment; for notwithstanding a party does an act (in itself criminal) under the influence of insane delusion, or with a view of redressing or revenging some supposed grievance, or of producing some public benefit, he is nevertheless punishable, if he knows at the time that he is acting contrary to law; but a person labouring under a partial delusion, must be considered in the same situation as to responsibility as if the facts in respect to which the delusion exists, were real.[2] To entitle a prisoner to be acquitted on the ground of insanity, he must have been, at the time of committing the offence, so insane that he did not know right from wrong.[3] And in all cases of the kind, the jurors ought to be told that every man is presumed to be sane and to possess a sufficient degree of reason to be responsible for his crimes, until the contrary be proved to their satisfaction; and that to establish a defence on the ground of insanity, it must be clearly proved that the party at the time of committing the act, was labouring under such a defect of reason from disease of mind as not to know the nature and quality of the act he was doing, or not to know that what he was doing was wrong.[4]

If a lunatic has lucid intervals, the law presumes the offence of such person to have been committed in a lucid interval,

---

[1] Hale P. C. 30.
[2] M'Naghton's Case, 10 Cl. & Fin.; Arnold's Case, 16 St. Tri. 764; Lord Ferrers's Case, 19 Id. 947, 948.
[3] Reg. v. Higgenson, 1 Carr. & K. 129, by Maul, J.
[4] 10 Cl. & Fin. 200, Bellingham's Case.

unless it appears to have been committed in the time of his lunacy or insanity.(¹)

The statute has pointed out the mode by which the insanity of a party charged with crime is to be ascertained when brought to trial ; but upon the original arrest and examination the Justice must be governed by his own discretion; and unless a case of insanity is clearly made out, he should not discharge for that cause.

Madness proceeding from drunkenness. The vice of drunkenness, which deprives men of the use of reason and throws them into a perfect, though temporary frenzy or insanity, usually denominated *acquired madness*, so far from excusing the commission of any crime, aggravates the enormity of it; and an offender under the influence of intoxication, can derive no privilege from a madness *voluntarily* contracted, but is amenable to the justice of his country, equally as if he had been in the full possession of his senses at the time. Yet, if the primary cause of the frenzy be *involuntary*, or habitual and confirmed, this species of insanity with reference to crimes, will excuse the offender equally as the former descriptions of this malady. Thus, for instance, if a person, through the unskilfulness of his physician or the contrivance of his enemies, take that which may produce a temporary frenzy, he will not be accountable for his actions whilst under the influence of it.(²)

3d. *Subjection to the power of others.* Another case of a want of will, and therefore incapacity to commit crime, proceeds from the matrimonial subjection of the wife to her husband, from which the law presumes a coercion, which, in many cases, excuses her from the consequences of criminal misconduct.

If a felony be committed by a *feme covert* in the presence of her husband, the law out of tenderness to the relation which subsists between them, raises a *prima facie* presumption that she, who was *sub potestate viri*, acted under his immediate coercion ;(³) but this presumption does not arise, unless he were actually present, participating in the transaction ; and therefore, if a *feme covert*, in the absence of her husband,

---

(¹) 1 Russ. 6.   (²) 1 Russ. 7, 8.   (³) 1 Hale 45, 516 ; 1 Haw. c. 1, § 9.

commit an offence, even by his order and procurement, her coverture will be no excuse, and she will be responsible for the consequences of her misconduct.(¹) But even this presumption, which is *prima facie* merely, may be rebutted by evidence; and if it appear clearly, that the wife was principally instrumental in the commission of the crime, acting voluntarily, and not by constraint of her husband, although he was present and concerned, she will be guilty, and liable, equally with him, to criminal punishment.(²) So, by voluntarily inciting her husband to the perpetration of an offence, she becomes an accessary before the fact, and may be indicted and enquired of as such.(³)

But this protection is not allowed in all classes of offences. Those which are *mala in se*, and prohibited by the law of nature, or most heinous in their character and dangerous in their consequences, do not range themselves within the protection presumed from the matrimonial connection; and, therefore, if a married woman be guilty of treason, murder, homicide, or the like, in company with or by coercion of her husband, she is punishable equally as if she were *sole*.(⁴) She will not, however, be answerable for the consequences of his breach of duty, however fatal, though she may be privy to his misconduct, where she acts merely as the servant or agent of her husband. A passive concurrence in his neglect, will not make her amenable to justice, although *in foro conscientiæ* she may be equally guilty.(⁵)

4. *Ignorance.* Ignorance of the municipal law of the State is not allowed to excuse any one who is of the age of discretion and *compos mentis*, upon the ground, that every such person is bound to know the law, and presumed to have that knowledge.(⁶) Though this be the rule, a case has occurred in which it was impossible for the prisoner to have any knowledge of the existence of the law under which he was indicted, as he could not, at the time the offence was committed,

---

(¹) East P. C. 559; R. & R. 27.　(⁴) 1 Hale 45, 47, 48; 1 Haw. c. 1, § 11.
(²) 1 Hale 516.　(⁵) Arch. Cr. Pl. 17; 1 Russ. C. &
(³) Arch. Cr. Pl. 17; 2 Haw. c.　M. 16.
29, § 34.　(⁶) 1 Russ. C. & M. 20.

INTRODUCTION. 15

have heard of the law; and the Court, therefore, recommended him to be pardoned.(¹) In some instances, an ignorance or mistake of fact will excuse for crime, as, if a man intend to kill a thief or house-breaker in his own house in the night, by mistake kills one of his own family.(²) But this rule proceeds upon the supposition, that the original intention was lawful; for if an unforeseen consequence ensue from an act, unlawful and in its original nature wrong and mischievous, the actor is criminally responsible for whatever consequences may ensue.(³)

II. *Of the Grades of Crime.*

We have said that it is important for the practical purposes of a Justice, out of Court, to point out the leading distinction in the grades of crime. This is not to be understood with reference to the different degrees of any particular offence, (as, for instance, in felonious homicide,) but in regard to the division of crimes into felonies and misdemeanors. The different degrees of particular offences, (where any exists,) are noticed under each distinct head of offence. The object now in view, is to guide the Justice in sending on a party charged before him, either with felony or misdemeanor, to the proper Court.

A crime in law is the doing of any act which is forbid, or omitting to do any act which is commanded by public law. So that this general definition embraces all offences against public authority of whatever grade, whether at common law, or by statute.

Crimes at Common Law are divided into two classes, Felonies and Misdemeanors: and so,

BY SEC. 1. CHAP. 199, offences are either felonies or misdemeanors. Such offences as are punishable, when committed by free persons, with death or confinement in the penitentiary, are felonies. All other offences are misdemeanors, except that an offence, which, when committed by a slave, is punishable with death, is as to such slave a felony. It is now useless to

---

(¹) Rex *v.* Bailey, 1 R. & R. 1.   (³) 4 Black. 27.
(²) Levit's Case, Cro. Car. 538.

enquire into the origin of the word *felony*, since it is no longer of practical importance; and as to the mode of proceeding in cases of felony, see titles ARREST and COURTS. The term Misdemeanor, though not so comprehensive as the word Crime, is of very general import, and embraces all offences against public law less than felony. Of these there are many, both at common law and under the statute. For a common law misdemeanor, where the statute has not otherwise ordained, the punishment is by fine and imprisonment; the fine at the discretion of the jury, and imprisonment at the discretion of the Court. In all misdemeanors, where the fine is over twenty dollars, whether the punishment be by fine and imprisonment, or by fine only, the Justice should recognize the offender, if a white person, to answer an indictment for the offence: [See forms Nos. 4 and 5, under the head of RECOGNIZANCE.] Where the fine is twenty dollars and under, the Justice should in all cases try the offender; and so must he, in all misdemeanors committed by slaves, including petit larceny. In the case of a free negro, except in fines under twenty dollars, he may, in his discretion, either try the offender or recognize him to answer as in the case of a white person.

BY SEC. 2, CHAP. 199. No crime shall be punished with death, unless it be so directed by statute.

BY SEC. 3. A common law offence, for which punishment is prescribed by statute, shall be punished only in the mode so prescribed.

BY SEC. 5. No suicide, nor attainder of felony, shall work a corruption of blood.

BY SEC. 6. The commission of a felony shall not stay or merge any civil remedy.

The practice of certifying cases of felony for examination or trial to the regular terms of the Courts, will be found generally more convenient in the country, than issuing warrants for special sessions; and, therefore, the forms under each head of offence, are adapted to that practice; but to meet any case, the forms for special sessions are given under the head of COURTS.

A GUIDE TO MAGISTRATES

OUT OF COURT.

CHAPTER I.

ABDUCTION OF FEMALES AND OF CHILDREN.

[For abduction of white females by negroes, see title NEGROES.]

It seems not to have been an offence at Common Law to take a child, for the purpose of marrying her, from her parents or other person entrusted with her care, unless the taking was by some sinister means, either by violence, deceit, conspiracy or other corrupt or improper means; when done by such means, it is a misdemeanor at Common Law, though she may be consenting to the marriage.(¹)

By SEC. 16, CHAP. 191. If any white person take away or detain against her will, a white female, with intent to marry or defile her, or cause her to be married or defiled by another person; or take from any person having lawful charge of her, a female child under *twelve* years of age, for the purpose of prostitution or concubinage, he shall be confined in the penitentiary not less than three, nor more than ten years.

By the statute, it is felony to abduct a female under the age of twelve years, for either of the purposes mentioned therein, whether against her consent or not; for, a child of that age cannot be said to have any will of her own; and notwithstanding the words, "against her will," used in the statute in reference to females over that age, it has been decided, that although the woman at first be taken away with her consent, yet if she afterwards refuse to continue with the offender, and by force be detained by him, the offence is within the statute.(²) And if a woman be taken away forcibly, and afterwards be mar-

---

(¹) Rex *v.* Seeles, Cro. Car. 557; 2 Str. 1107; 1 East 459; 5 Rand. 627. (²) 1 Hawk. c. 41, § 7; 1 Deac. Cr. Co. 4.

ried or defiled with her own consent, the offence is within the statute; for the offender is not to be exempt from its penalties by having prevailed over the weakness of a woman, whom he originally got into his power by such base means.([1])

Although the woman is taken away, as well as married with her own consent, yet if this be effected by means of any *fraud* practised upon her to induce her to go with the offender, and to consent to marry him, it is said that he is equally within the act; for her mind being in a state of delusion by means of the fraud, she cannot be considered as a free agent to give any consent.([2])

The woman, though married to the offender, may be a witness against him; for though she is his wife in fact, she is not so in law;([3]) and as upon this ground she is admitted as a witness against him, so she is a competent witness for him, though she has cohabited with him from the day of the marriage.([4])

The abduction of a man's wife may be by open violence, fraud or persuasion; though as the wife has no power to consent, the law presumes constraint in every instance; and in the case of a child under twelve years of age, her consent does not mitigate the offence; nor is it any excuse that the defendant made use of no other means than the common blandishments of a lover to induce the girl to elope and marry him, if it was against the consent of the father.([5]) And it seems that where a man, by false and fraudulent representations, induced the parents of the girl to allow him to take her away, such taking is an abduction within the statute.([6])

As to who has the lawful custody of the person of a female child, it has been decided that the taking away a natural daughter under the age of sixteen, (the age prescribed by the English statute,) from the custody of her putative father, is an offence within the statute.([7])

It will be remarked, that to constitute the offence, it is not necessary either that the marriage or defilement in the one case, or prostitution or concubinage in the other, should actually take place. To do the act prohibited, with either of the intents, completes the offence, though the purpose be not accomplished. To constitute the offence, however, the act must be done with one or the other of the intents or purposes specified in the statute.

([1]) Cro. Car. 488; 5 St. Tr. 450; 1 Hale 660.
([2]) Rex *v.* Wakefield, for the abduction of Miss Turner, Lanc. Ass. March 1827.
([3]) 1 Hale 661.
([4]) 1 Russ. 828; 1 East P. C. 454.
([5]) 1 Russ. 579.
([6]) Green *v.* Hopkins, 41 C. L. R. 143, decided upon a similar statute.
([7]) 2 Str. 1162; 1 East P. C. 457.

ABDUCTION—(*Of Females and Children.*)

Besides the injurious consequences to society growing out of these offences when committed, even in the least aggravated form, when done by violence, it is a flagrant breach of the peace, and is peculiarly the subject of a Justice's cognizance; and in such cases he should issue his warrant without delay, that the woman may be liberated from duress, and the offender apprehended and punished.

The abduction of infants for the purpose of extorting money or pecuniary benefit is also felony.

BY SEC. 14, CHAP. 191. If any free person seize, take or secrete, a child from the person having lawful charge of such child, with intent to extort money or pecuniary benefit, he shall be confined in the penitentiary not less than one, nor more than five years.

(No. 1.)

Form of Warrant of Arrest for taking away a female against her will, with intent to marry or defile her.

—— County, to wit:

To all or any one of the Constables of said County:

Whereas, A B. of said County, has this day made complaint and information on oath before me, J. T., a Justice of the said County, that C. D., a white person, on the —— day of —— 18—, in said County, did feloniously take away one E. F., a white female over the age of twelve years, against the will of the said E. F., with intent to marry and defile her, the said E. F.: These are therefore to command you, in the name of the Commonwealth of Virginia, forthwith to apprehend the said C. D. and bring him before me or some other Justice of the said County, to answer the said complaint, and to be farther dealt with according to law. Given under my hand and seal, this —— day of —— 18—.

J. T., J. P. [L. S.]

(No. 2.)

Form of Warrant of Arrest for taking away a female with intent to cause her to be married or defiled.

—— County, to wit:

To all or any one of the Constables of said County:

Whereas, A. B. of said County, has this day made complaint and information on oath before me J. T., a Justice of the said County, that C. D., a white person, on the —— day of —— 18—, in said County, did feloniously take away one E. F., a white female over the age of twelve years, against the will of the said E. F., with intent, unlawfully and feloniously to cause her to be married to (or *to be defiled by*) one G. H.: These are therefore to command you, in the name of the Commonwealth of Virginia, forthwith to apprehend the said C. D. and bring him before me or some other Justice of the said County, to answer the said complaint, and to be farther dealt with according to law. Given under my hand and seal, this —— day of —— 18—.

J. T., J. P. [L. S.]

ABDUCTION—(*Of Females and Children.*)

(No. 3.)

Form of Warrant of Arrest for taking a child under the age of twelve years, for the purpose of prostitution or concubinage.

———— County, to wit:
    To all or any one of the Constables of said County:

Whereas, A. B. of said County, has this day made complaint and information on oath before me J. T., a Justice of the said County, that C. D., a white person, on the ——— day of ———— 18—, in said County, did unlawfully and feloniously take away one E. F., a female child under the age of twelve years, from the said A. B., the person then having the lawful charge of her person, for the purpose of prostitution (or *concubinage* :) These are therefore to command you, in the name of the Commonwealth of Virginia, forthwith to apprehend the said C. D. and bring him before me or some other Justice of the said County, to answer the said complaint, and to be farther dealt with according to law. Given under my hand and seal, this ——— day of ———— 18—.

                                                    J. T., J. P. [L. S.]

(No. 4.)

Form of Warrant of Arrest for taking away the child of another, for the purpose of extorting money.

———— County, to wit:
    To all or any one of the Constables of said County:

Whereas, A. B. of said County, has this day made complaint and information on oath before me J. T., a Justice of the said County, that C. D., a free person, on the ——— day of ———— 18, in said County, did unlawfully and feloniously seize, take away and secrete from J. F., one E. F., the child of the said J. F., he the said J. F. then having the lawful custody and charge of the said child, with intent, feloniously, to extort money from the said J. F.: These are therefore to command you, in the name of the Commonwealth of Virginia, forthwith to apprehend the said C. D., and bring him before me or some other Justice of the said County, to answer the said complaint, and to be farther dealt with according to law. Given under my hand and seal, this ——— day of ———— 18—.

                                                    J. T., J. P. [L. S.]

(No. 5.)

Form of Mittimus where a party is committed for examination or trial for felony in the County Court, for abduction.

———— County, to wit:
    To X. Z., Constable of said County, and to the Keeper of the Jail of said County:

These are to command you, the said Constable, in the name of the Commonwealth of Virginia, forthwith to convey and deliver into the custody of the keeper of the said jail, together with this warrant, the body of C. D., a

ABDUCTION—(*Of Females and Children.*)

white person (or *free negro*, or *a slave, the property of E. F.*, as the case may be,) charged before me J. T., a Justice of the said County, on the oath of A. B., with a felony by him committed, in this that the said C. D., on the —— day of ——— in the year 18—, in the said County, (here describe the offence as in the warrant of arrest.) And you, the said keeper of the said jail, are hereby required to receive the said C. D. into your jail and custody, that he may be examined (or *tried*) for the said offence, by the County Court of said County, and him there safely keep, until he shall be discharged by due course of law. Given under my hand and seal, this —— day of ——— in the year 18—.

J. T., J. P. [L. S.]

(No. 6.)

Form of Certificate of Commitment to be sent to the Clerk of the County Court.

——— County, to wit:

To the Clerk of the County Court of said County :

I, J. T., a Justice of the said County, do hereby certify, that I have, by my warrant, this day committed C. D. (if free negro or slave, state which) to the jail of this County, that he may be examined (or *tried*) before the County Court of the said County, for a felony by him committed, in this that he did, on the ——— day of ——— 18—, in the said County, (here state the offence as in the mittimus.) Given under my hand, this ——— day of ——— in the year 18—.

J. T., J. P.

(No. 7.)

Form of Certificate to the Clerk where party is admitted to bail.

Turn to head of ARREST, and follow No. 6.

(No. 8.)

Form of Recognizance of Bail.

Turn to head of RECOGNIZANCE, and follow No. 1, if person be free; No. 2, if a slave, and state succinctly the offence for which the person is recognized.

(No. 9.)

Form of Recognizance of Witness to appear before the County Court to give evidence upon the examination or trial of a party charged with felony.

Turn to head of RECOGNIZANCE, and follow No. 3.

(No. 1.)

Form of an Indictment for taking away a white female over the age of twelve years, with intent to marry or defile her.

———— Judicial Circuit. \
———— County, to wit: \
In the Circuit Court of said County.
} The jurors of the Commonwealth of Virginia, in and for the body of the County of ————, and now attending the said Court, do upon their oath present, that A. B., on the ———— day of ————, in the year one thousand eight hundred and ————, in the said County, did feloniously take away (*) one C. D., a white female over the age of twelve years, to wit, of the age of ———— years, against the will of the said C. D., with intent to marry her, against the peace and dignity of the Commonwealth of Virginia.

And the jurors aforesaid, upon their oath aforesaid, do farther present, that the said A. B., on the day and year aforesaid, in the County aforesaid, did feloniously take away the said C. D., a white female over the age of twelve years, to wit, of the age of ———— years, against the will of the said C. D., with intent to defile her the said C. D., against the peace and dignity of the Commonwealth of Virginia.

[A count may be added for detaining her.]

(No. 2.)

Form of an Indictment for taking away a child under the age of twelve years, for the purpose of prostitution or concubinage.

Follow No. 1, to the (*) and then proceed thus, "from J. P. her father, (or *guardian*,) one C. D., a female child under the age of twelve years, to wit, of the age of ten years, for the purpose of prostitution, (he the said J. P. then and there having the lawful charge of the person of the said C. D.,) against the peace and dignity of the Commonwealth of Virginia.

And the jurors aforesaid, upon their oath aforesaid, do farther present, that the said A. B., on the day and year aforesaid, in the County aforesaid, did unlawfully and feloniously take away from J. P., her father, (or *guardian*,) one C. D., a female child under the age of twelve years, to wit, of the age of ten years, for the purpose of concubinage, (he the said J. P. then and there having the lawful charge of the person of the said C. D.) against the peace and dignity of the Commonwealth of Virginia.

(No. 3.)

An Indictment for taking away and secreting the child of another, for the purpose of extorting money.

———— Judicial Circuit. \
———— County, to wit: \
In the Circuit Court of the said County.
} The jurors of the Commonwealth of Virginia, in and for the body of the County of ————, and now attending the said Court, do upon their oath present, that A. B., on the ———— day of ————, in the year one thousand eight hundred and ————, in the said County, did feloniously seize, and take away and secrete C. D., the child of T. D., from the said T. D., with intent feloniously to extort money from the said T. D., (he the said T. D. then and there having the lawful custody and charge of the said C. D.,) against the peace and dignity of the Commonwealth of Virginia.

CHAPTER II.

ABORTION.

An infant in its mother's womb is considered by the Common Law as not in being, and, therefore, cannot be the subject either of murder or manslaughter ;([1]) but its destruction, or even the attempt to destroy it by abortion, though unsuccessful, is a misdemeanor.([2])

By Sec. 8, Chap. 191. Any free person who shall administer to, or cause to be taken by, a woman, any drug or other thing, or use any means with intent to destroy her unborn child, or to produce abortion or miscarriage, and shall thereby destroy such child, or produce such abortion or miscarriage, shall be confined in the penitentiary not less than one, nor more than five years. No person, by reason of any act mentioned in this section, shall be punishable where such act is done in good faith, with the intention of saving the life of such woman or child.

The gist of this offence consists in administering the substance with intent to procure abortion, and it does not signify what the substance is; for if a person administer a bit of bread merely, with intent to produce abortion, and the abortion and death of the child are thereby produced, it is sufficient to constitute the offence contemplated by the statute.([3]) But the felony is not complete unless abortion takes place; though, as before stated, the attempt to produce it is a misdemeanor at Common Law, and is now punishable as such by statute. See ATTEMPTS.

(No. 1.)

Form of Warrant of Arrest for abortion.

—— County, to wit:

To X. Z., *Constable of the said County*:

Whereas, A. B. of the County of ——, has this day made information and complaint on oath before me J. T., a Justice of the said County, that E. F. did, on the —— day of —— 18—, in the said County, feloniously administer to, (or *cause to be taken by*) one C. D., then being pregnant with child, a certain medicine, drug or substance, called savon, (or *whatever thing it may be*) with intent to procure the miscarriage of the said C. D., and whereby he, the said E. F., did procure her miscarriage, and destroy the said child: These are therefore to command you, in the name of the Com-

---

([1]) 1 Russ. 424.
([2]) 1 Russ. 553; 9 Mass. R. 287.
([3]) Rex v. Coe, 6 C. & P. 403.

monwealth of Virginia, forthwith to apprehend the said E. F., and bring him before me or some other Justice of the said County, to answer the said complaint, and to be farther dealt with according to law. Given under my hand and seal, this —— day of —————— 18—.

J. T., J. P. [L. S.]

(No. 2.)

Form of Mittimus where a party is committed for examination or trial in the County Court, for procuring abortion.

—————— County, to wit:

To X. Z., *Constable of said County, and to the Keeper of the Jail of said County:*

These are to command you, the said Constable, in the name of the Commonwealth of Virginia, forthwith to convey and deliver into the custody of the keeper of the said jail, together with this warrant, the body of C. D., a white person, (or *free negro*, or *a slave, the property of E. F.*, as the case may be,) charged before me J. T., a Justice of the said County, on the oath of A. B., with a felony by him committed, in this, that the said C. D., on the —— day of —————— in the year 18—, in the said County, (here describe the offence as in the warrant of arrest.) And you, the said keeper of the said jail, are hereby required to receive the said C. D. into your jail and custody, that he may be examined (or *tried*) for the said offence by the County Court of said County, and him there safely keep, until he shall be discharged by due course of law. Given under my hand and seal, this —— day of —————— in the year 18—.

J. T., J. P. [L. S.]

[NOTE.—If the prisoner be a white person, or if he be a free negro, charged with homicide of any grade, or with any offence punishable with death, he must be committed for examination. For all other felonies by free negroes, and in all cases of felony by slaves, the prisoner must be committed for trial.]

(No. 3.)

Form of Certificate of Commitment to be sent to the Clerk of the County Court, for procuring abortion.

—————— County, to wit:

To *the Clerk of the County Court of said County:*

I, J. T., a Justice of the said County, do hereby certify, that I have, by my warrant, this day committed C. D., (if free negro or slave, state which,) to the jail of this County, that he may be examined (or *tried*) before the County Court of the said County, for a felony by him committed, in this that he did, on the —— day of —————— 18—, in the said County, (here state the offence as in the mittimus.) Given under my hand, this —— day of —————— in the year 18—.

J. T. J. P.

ABORTION—(*Indictment for.*)

(No. 4.)

Form of Certificate to the Clerk where party is admitted to bail.

Turn to head of ARREST, and follow No. 6.

(No. 5.)

Form of Recognizance of Bail.

Turn to head of RECOGNIZANCE, and follow No. 1, if person be free; No. 2, if a slave, and state succinctly the offence for which the person is recognized.

(No. 6.)

Form of Recognizance of Witness to appear before the County Court to give evidence upon examination or trial for producing abortion.

Turn to head of RECOGNIZANCE, and follow No. 3.

An Indictment for procuring abortion.

——— Judicial Circuit. ⎫ The jurors of the Commonwealth of Virginia,
——— County, *to wit*: ⎬ in and for the body of the County of ———,
In the Circuit Court of ⎭ and now attending the said Court, upon their oath
the said County. present, that A. B., on the ——— day of ———, in the year one thousand eight hundred and ———, in the said County, did feloniously administer to one C. D., she, the said C. D., then being pregnant with *child*, a quantity of a certain medicine, (*drug* or *substance*,) called ———, with intent to produce the miscarriage of the said C. D. of the child of which she was then pregnant, and whereby the said A. B. did procure the miscarriage of the said C. D., and destroy the said child of which the said C. D. was then pregnant, against the peace and dignity of the Commonwealth of Virginia.

4

CHAPTER III.

ACCESSARIES.

An accessary is one guilty of felony, not as a principal actor, but by participation, command, advice or concealment.

By Sec. 7, Chap. 199. In the case of every felony, every principal in the second degree, and every accessary before the fact, shall be punishable as if he were the principal in the first degree; and every accessary after the fact shall be confined in jail not more than one year, and fined not exceeding five hundred dollars.

By Sec. 8. But no person in the relation of husband or wife, parent or grandparent, child or grandchild, brother or sister, by consanguity or affinity, or servant to the offender, who, after the commission of a felony, shall aid or assist a principal felon or accessary before the fact, to avoid or escape from prosecution or punishment, shall be deemed an accessary after the fact.

By Sec. 9. An accessary, either before or after the fact, may, whether the principal felon be convicted or not, or be amenable to justice or not, be indicted, convicted and punished in the county or corporation in which he became accessary, or in which the principal felon might be indicted. Any such accessary before the fact, may be indicted, either with such principal or separately.

There are three kinds of aiders and abettors: the first are those who are present, aiding and abetting at the commission of the crime; and being present, are for that reason denominated in *law* principals in the second degree. The second are accessaries before the fact, and the third are accessaries after the fact.

I. *Principals in the second degree.*

It is now settled that all those who are present, aiding and abetting when a felony is committed, are principals in the second degree.[1] To constitute presence, they need not be actually and visibly present; for if they accompany the principal to commit the crime, and keep within hearing or upon the watch, ready to assist, if called upon to prevent a surprise, or to favour the escape of those who are more immediately engaged in the commission of the crime, they are all (if the fact be committed) legally present at it.[2] Thus, in the case

---

[1] 1 Russ. C. & M. 21.   [2] 1 Russ. 22; 1 Hale 555; 1 Leach 66.

of stealing in a shop, if several are acting in concert, some in the shop, and some out, and the property is stolen by one of those in the shop, yet those who are on the outside are equally guilty as principals in the offence.(¹) In proceeding against principals in the second degree, the Justice may lay the charge as done by him, as though he were proceeding against a principal in the first degree.(²)

II. *Accessaries before the fact.*

Accessaries before the fact are those who being absent at the time the offence was committed, do yet procure, counsel, command or abet another person to commit a felony, and who are so far absent as not to be able to render any immediate help or assistance in the commission of the offence.(³)

Words that amount to a bare permission only, to commit a felony, will not make an accessary;(⁴) nor will the mere concealment of a felony intended to be committed; for that is only misprision of felony.(⁵) See FELONY.

When a felony is created by statute, though the act mentions nothing of accessaries before or after the fact, yet those who counsel or command the offence, are accessaries before the fact, and those who knowingly receive the offender, are accessaries after.(⁶)

In high treason and petit larceny, (which in Virginia is a misdemeanor,) and in all other crimes under the degree of felony, there are no accessaries, for in these cases all are principals.(⁷)

There are no accessaries before the fact in manslaughter, that offence being in law, sudden and unpremeditated, and therefore admitting of no previous concert.(⁸)

III. *Accessaries after the fact.*

Accessaries after the fact are those who knowing a felony to have been committed by another, receive, relieve, comfort or assist the felon;(⁹) as where one rescues a felon, or voluntarily and intentionally suffers him to escape.(¹⁰) But merely suffering him to escape, when it is a bare omission, will not make the party an accessary.(¹¹)

(¹) R. v. Gogerly, Russ. & Ry. 343; R. v. Owen, 1 Ry. & M. 96.
(²) 1 Russ. C. & M. 29.
(³) 1 Hale 615; 1 Dea. Cr. Co. 11.
(⁴) 2 Hawk. c. 29, § 16.
(⁵) 1 Hale 616.
(⁶) 1 Hale 613-14, 704.
(⁷) 1 Hale 613-16; Fost. 341; 2 East P. C. 493.
(⁸) 1 Deac. C. C. 13.
(⁹) 1 Hale 618.
(¹⁰) 2 Hawk. c. 29, § 27; 1 Hale 619.
(¹¹) Ibid.

A man who opposes or prevents the apprehending of a felon is an accessary at Common Law.(¹) But to this general rule the eighth section of the statute just quoted makes exceptions.

So a man who receives an accessary before the fact, becomes an accessary after the fact, equally as if he had received the principal.(²) Here, again, see the exceptions contained in the statute.

At Common Law, a *feme covert* cannot be made an accessary after the fact for receiving her husband.(³)

If a prisoner has been acquitted as an accessary, and the proof will warrant it, the Justice may commit him as principal; and so if he has been acquitted as principal or as an accessary before the fact, he may commit him as an accessary after the fact.(⁴)

Accessaries, both before and after the fact, may controvert the guilt of the principal, even after the conviction of the principal, and the record of such conviction is not conclusive against the accessary, for a record is conclusive evidence only against those who are parties to it.(⁵)

[No forms are given for aiders and abettors at the fact, or as they are more technically called, principals in the second degree; for as they may be treated as principals, the Justice is advised to proceed against them as such.]

(No. 1.)

Form of Warrant of Arrest against an accessary before the fact, upon positive charge.

——— County, to wit:

To N. O. Constable of the said County:

Whereas, X. Y. has this day made information and complaint on oath before me J. T., a Justice of the said County, that A. B. did, on the ——— day of ——— 18—, at the County of ———, feloniously counsel, aid and abet a certain C. D., feloniously, (*here describe the offence committed by C. D., the principal, according to the fact, as for instance in the case of burglary,* "*to break and enter the dwelling house of the said X. Y. in the night time, with intent then and there and in the said dwelling house feloniously and burglariously to steal the goods and chattels of the said X. Y.,*") which said felony, the said C. D. did accordingly commit: These are therefore to command you, in the name of the Commonwealth of Virginia, forthwith to apprehend and bring before me or some other Justice of the said County, the body of the said A. B. to answer the said complaint, and to be farther dealt with according to law. Given under my hand and seal, this ——— day of ——— 18—.

J. T., J. P. [L. s.]

(¹) 2 Hawk. c. 29, § 27.
(²) Ibid. § 1.
(³) 1 Hale 621.
(⁴) 1 Hale 625, 6; 1 Leach 415; 1 East P. C. 35.
(⁵) 1 Leach 288; Ibid. 290; Foster 365; 3 Esp. 131.

(No. 2.)

Form of Warrant of Arrest for an accessary before the fact, upon suspicion.

—————— County, to wit:
  To X. Y., *Constable of the said County:*

Whereas, A. B. of the said County, has this day made complaint on oath before me J. T., a Justice of the said County, that he has just cause to suspect, and does suspect, that C. D. did, on the —— day of ———— 18—, in the day time, break and enter the dwelling house of him, the said A. B., in the said County, and did then, and from the said dwelling house, feloniously steal, take and carry away one watch of the value of twenty dollars, the property of the said A. B., and that the said A. B. has also just cause to suspect that E. F., of the said County, did feloniously aid, abet and procure the said C. D. to commit the said felony: These are therefore, &c., (conclude as No. 1.)

(No. 3.)

Form of Warrant of Arrest against an accessary after the fact.

—————— County, to wit:
  To X. Y., *Constable of the said County:*

Whereas, C. D. of the said County, is charged before me J. T., a Justice of the said County, on the complaint on oath of A. B., with a felony by him committed in this, that he did on the —— day of ———— 18—, at the said County, feloniously, (here describe the offence, as for instance in murder, "kill and murder one P. K.") And whereas the said A. B. has this day also made oath before me, that he has cause to suspect, and does suspect that E. F. of the said County, since the said felony was committed, has received, harboured, maintained and concealed the said C. D., he, the said E. F., well knowing that the said C. D. had committed the said felony: These are therefore, &c., (conclude as No. 1.)

(No. 4.)

Form of Mittimus where a party is committed for examination or trial as accessary before the fact.

—————— County, to wit:
  To X. Z., *Constable of said County, and to the Keeper of the Jail of said County:*

These are to command you, the said Constable, in the name of the Commonwealth of Virginia, forthwith to convey and deliver into the custody of the keeper of the said jail, together with this warrant, the body of C. D., a white person (or *free negro*, or *a slave, the property of E. F.,* as the case may be,) charged before me J. T., a Justice of the said County, on the oath of A. B., with a felony by him committed, in this, that the said C. D., on the —— day of ———— in the year 18—, in the said County, (here describe the offence as in the warrant of arrest.) And you, the said keeper of the said jail, are hereby required to receive the said C. D. into your jail and custody, that he may be examined (or *tried*) for the said offence, by the County Court of said County, and him there safely keep until he shall be discharged by due course of law. Given under my hand and seal, this —— day of ——— in the year 18—.

J. T., J. P. [L. S.]

[NOTE.—If the prisoner be a white person, or if he be a free negro charged with homicide of any grade, or with any offence punishable with death, he must be committed for examination. For all other felonies by free negroes, and in all cases of felony by slaves, the prisoner must be committed for trial.]

(No. 5.)

Form of Certificate of Commitment to be sent to the Clerk of the County Court in the case of an accessary before the fact.

——— County, to wit:

To the Clerk of the County Court of said County:

I, J. T., a Justice of the said County, do hereby certify that I have, by my warrant, this day committed C. D. (if free negro or slave, state which,) to the jail of this County, that he may be examined (or *tried*) before the County Court of the said County, for a felony by him committed, in this, that he did on the ——— day of ——— 18—, in the said County, (here state the offence as in the mittimus.) Given under my hand, this ——— day of ——— in the year 18—.

J. T., J. P.

(No. 6.)

Form of Certificate to the Clerk where party is admitted to bail as accessary before the fact.

Turn to head of ARREST, and follow No. 6.

(No. 7.)

Form of Recognizance of Bail.

Turn to head of RECOGNIZANCE, and follow No. 1, if person be free; No. 2, if a slave, and state succinctly the offence for which the person is recognized.

(No. 8.)

Form of Recognizance of Witness to appear before the County Court to give evidence upon the examination or trial of a party charged with felony.

Turn to head of RECOGNIZANCE, and follow No. 3.

(No. 9.)

Form of Mittimus where a party is committed to answer an Indictment in the County Court, as accessary after the fact.

—— County, to wit:

To X. Z., Constable of said County, and to the Keeper of the Jail of said County:

These are to command you, the said Constable, in the name of the Commonwealth of Virginia, forthwith to convey and deliver into the custody of the keeper of the said jail, together with this warrant, the body of C. D., charged before me J. T., a Justice of the said County, on the oath of A. B., with a misdemeanor by him committed, in this, that the said C. D., on the —— day of —— in the year 18—, in the said County, (here describe the offence as in the warrant of arrest.) And you, the said keeper of the said jail, are hereby required to receive the said C. D. into your jail and custody, to answer an indictment to be preferred against him for the said offence, in the County Court of said County, and him there safely keep until he shall be discharged by due course of law. Given under my hand and seal, this —— day of —— in the year 18—.

J. T., J. P. [L. S.]

(No. 10.)

Form of Recognizance of Bail of accessary after the fact.

Turn to head of RECOGNIZANCE, and follow No. 4, and state the offence succinctly, for which the party is recognized.

(No. 11.)

Form of Certificate of the Commitment, or Letting to Bail, to be sent to the Clerk of the County Court, in the case of an accessary after the fact.

—— County, to wit:

To the Clerk of the County Court of said County:

I, J. T., a Justice of the said County, do hereby certify, that C. D. was this day committed to the jail of this County by my warrant, (or *was this day admitted to bail by me*, as the case may be,) to answer an indictment to be preferred against him, in the County Court of the said County, for a misdemeanor by him committed, in this, that he did, on the —— day of —— 18—, in said County, (here describe the offence as in the warrant of arrest.) Given under my hand, this —— day of —— 18—.

J. T., J. P.

(No. 12.)

Form of Recognizance of Witness to appear and give evidence to the Grand Jury upon the Indictment.

Follow No. 5, under the head of RECOGNIZANCE.

(No. 1.)

Form of an Indictment against a principal in the second degree in murder.

——— Judicial Circuit. ⎫ The jurors of the Commonwealth of Virginia,
——— *County, to wit:* ⎬ in and for the body of the County of ——, now
In the Circuit Court of ⎨ attending in the Circuit Court of said County,
the said County. ⎭ upon their oath present, that A. B. of the said
County, on the — day of —— in the year ——, about the hour of — o'clock, in the night of the same day, in the County aforesaid, in and upon one C. D., in the peace of God and the people of this Commonwealth, then and there being, feloniously, wilfully and of his malice aforethought, did make an assault; and that the said A. B., with a certain pistol, then and there loaded with gunpowder and one leaden bullet, which pistol he the said A. B. in his right hand then and there had and held, to, against and upon the said C. D., then and there feloniously, wilfully and of his malice aforethought, did shoot and discharge; and that the said A. B., with the bullet aforesaid, out of the pistol aforesaid, then and there by force of the gunpowder and shot, sent forth as aforesaid, the said A. B., in and upon the head of him the said C. D., then and there feloniously, wilfully and of his malice aforethought, did strike, penetrate and wound, giving to the said C. D., then and there, with the bullet aforesaid, so as aforesaid shot, sent forth and discharged out of the pistol aforesaid, by the said A. B., in and upon the head of the said C. D., one mortal wound, of which said mortal wound, the said C. D., from the said —— day of ———, in the year aforesaid, until the —— day of ——— in the year aforesaid, in the County aforesaid, did languish, and languishing did live, on which said ——— day of ——— in the year aforesaid, the said C. D., in the County aforesaid, of the said mortal wound died. And the jurors aforesaid, upon their oath aforesaid, do further present, that E. F., on the day and year first aforesaid, in the County aforesaid, feloniously, wilfully and of his malice aforethought, was present, counselling, aiding, abetting and assisting the said A. B., the felony and murder aforesaid, to do and commit, and so the jurors aforesaid, upon their oath aforesaid, do say that the said A. B. and E. F., the said C. D., in manner and form aforesaid, feloniously, wilfully, and of their malice aforethought, did kill and murder, against the peace and dignity of the Commonwealth of Virginia.

(No. 2.)

Form of an Indictment against an accessary before the fact.

[Draw the indictment as against the principal, leaving out the words, "against the peace and dignity of the Commonwealth," and proceed thus:]

And the jurors aforesaid, upon their oath aforesaid, do farther present, that G. H. of the said County, before the said felony (if it be against an accessary in *burglary,* say "felony and burglary,") was committed in form aforesaid, to wit: On the said —— day of ——— in the year aforesaid, in the County aforesaid, did feloniously counsel, hire, procure, aid and abet the said A. B., to do and commit the said felony, (*and burglary,* if it be for burglary,) in manner and form aforesaid, against the peace and dignity of the Commonwealth of Virginia.

(No. 3.)

Form of same against accessary after the fact.

[Draw the indictment as against the principal, and proceed thus :]
And the jurors aforesaid, upon their oath aforesaid, do farther present, that G. H. of the said County, well knowing the said A. B. to have done and committed the said felony (or *felony and burglary*, if it be for burglary,) in form aforesaid, to wit: On the —— day of ——— in the year aforesaid, in the County aforesaid, him, the said A. B., did then and there unlawfully receive, harbour and maintain, against the peace and dignity of the Commonwealth of Virginia.

CHAPTER IV.

ADULTERY AND FORNICATION.

Adultery is a criminal conversation between two married persons, or between a married and unmarried person. The married person is guilty of adultery, the unmarried of fornication. Fornication is the unlawful carnal knowledge of an unmarried person with another, whether the latter be married or unmarried.

Adultery is no offence at Common Law; nor can an indictment at Common Law be maintained for adultery, by charging it as an offence against public decency,(¹) unless the act is committed in public, or there is a conspiracy to effect it ;(²) but by section 6, chapter 196, of the statute, "If a free person commit adultery or fornication, he shall be fined not less than twenty dollars."

Form of Warrant of Arrest for adultery, by a married man with a married woman.

———— County, to wit:
To X. Y., *Constable of the said County:*
Whereas, A. B. of said County, has this day made complaint upon oath before me J. T., a Justice of said County, that C. D., on the —— day of ———— 18—, in the said County, did commit adultery with one E. F., the wife of one G. F., by having carnal knowledge of the body of the said E. F., he the said C. D., being then a married man, and having a lawful wife living, and she, the said E. F., being then a married woman and the lawful wife of G. F.: These are therefore, in the name of the Commonwealth, to

―――――――――――――――――――――――――――――――――
(¹) 2 Bailey 159.   (²) Anderson's Case, 5 Rand. 627.

command you to apprehend the said C. D. and E. F. and bring them before me or some other Justice of said County, to answer the said complaint, and to be farther dealt with according to law. Given under my hand and seal, this —— day of ——— 18—.

J. T., J. P. [L. S.]

[NOTE.—This being a misdemeanor, the parties should be recognized to answer the offence in the County Court. See Forms Nos. 4 and 5, under the head of "RECOGNIZANCE."]

CHAPTER V.

AFFRAY.

I. *What is an affray.*

The word affray is derived from the French word *affrayer*, to *terrify*. This derivation is strikingly characteristic of the offence. An affray is a misdemeanor at Common Law, and defined to be a fighting of two or more persons in some *public place* to the *terror* of the people.(¹) It is obvious from this definition that every fight between two or more persons, does not necessarily constitute an affray; for if it be in a private place it is no affray, since to fight in a private place out of the seeing and hearing of others cannot be said to be to the *terror of the people*.(²) Such a fight would be nothing more than a simple assault and battery.

That the Justice may not confound affrays and riots, it will be well to remark, that two persons only may be guilty of an affray; whereas three persons at least are necessary to constitute a riot,(³) and moreover a riot is a premeditated offence, so that if a number of persons being lawfully assembled at a fair, market or other public place, suddenly fall to fighting, they would be guilty of an affray and not a riot, because the design of their meeting was innocent and lawful, and the subsequent breach of the peace happened without any previous intent.(⁴)

Words alone, however quarrelsome or threatening, will not amount to an affray; but there may be an affray without actual violence, as in the case of persons going armed with such dangerous and unusual weapons as will naturally cause *terror*

(¹) 1 Russ. on C. & M. 270; 1 Dea. Cr. Co. 26; 4 Black. Com. 144.
(²) 1 Hawk. c. 63, § 1; 1 Dea. Cr. Co. 26.
(³) 1 Hawk. c. 65, § 1.
(⁴) 1 Hawk. c. 63, § 21; 1 Dea. Cr.

to the people, and this is said always to have been an offence at Common Law.(¹)

II. *How an affray may be suppressed.*

A Constable is not only empowered, but bound to suppress an affray which happens in his presence, and for this purpose he may demand the aid of others, and if they refuse to give him their assistance, they are punishable by fine and imprisonment ;(²) but he cannot, without a warrant from a Justice, arrest a man for an affray done out of his own *view or hearing:* for it is his business to preserve the peace only, and not to punish the breach of it.(³) Yet he may carry those before a Justice who were arrested by other persons present at an affray, and who have thus been delivered into his hands.

He cannot lay his hands on those who barely contend with hot words without any threats of personal violence; if however he sees persons upon the very point of entering into an affray, as where one shall threaten to kill, wound or beat another, he may carry the offender before a Justice to find sureties for the peace, and it is said he may imprison him for a reasonable time upon his own authority till the heat be over, and also afterwards detain him until he find such sureties ;(⁴) but the safer course is for the Constable in all cases of arrest forthwith to take the offender before a Justice, unless there is manifest necessity for delay.

A private person, also, who sees others fighting, may lawfully part them and deliver them over to a Constable, to be carried before a Justice ; and he may also stop those whom he shall see coming to join either party. The law so far favours this interference of a private person, that if he receive a hurt in endeavouring to preserve the peace, he has his action against the party, and if he unavoidably inflict one, he may justify.(⁵)

A Justice of the Peace undoubtedly may, and it is his duty to do all things for the suppression of an affray and the arrest of the offenders, which either a private person or Constable is enabled or required to do by law. But he, no more than a Constable, can without warrant, authorize the arrest of any person for an affray done out of his own *view;* yet, in such a case, it is clear that he may make his warrant to bring an offender before him to find sureties for the peace.(⁶)

(¹) 1 Hawk. c. 63, § 2, 4.
(²) Ibid. § 13 ; Regina *v.* Brown, 1 Carr. & Marsh. 314.
(³) Ibid. § 17 ; see 2 Campb. 367 ; Clifford *v.* Brandon, and Regina *v.* Tooey, 2 Ld. Ray. 1296.
(⁴) 1 Hawk. c. 63, § 14.
(⁵) 1 Hawk. c. 63, § 11 ; Burn J. P. 35-6 ; 3 Inst. 158.
(⁶) 1 Hawk. c. 63, § 18 ; 1 Burn J. P. 37.

Indeed, the Justice has much greater power over one who is guilty of an affray than either a private person or a Constable, for, besides his power to arrest or cause the offender to be arrested in all cases of affrays and to find surety for the peace, it seems certain, that where one has *dangerously wounded another* in an affray, the Justice has a discretionary power either to commit him or to bail him until the year and a day be past; and he should be cautious how he takes bail, if the wound be dangerous, lest the party die, and the offender escape.(¹) Moreover, the Justice may require bail of the party to appear and answer an indictment for the offence before the grand jury of the county or corporation court, and on his failure to give such bail may commit him.

An affray was always a misdemeanor at Common Law, punishable by fine and imprisonment.(²)

After giving the form of a warrant to arrest affrayers, that they may be bound to answer in court for the offence, Mr. Hening, in his Justice, remarks, that "when the offender is apprehended for this offence and brought before the Justice, he may admit him to bail or refuse it on due consideration of the nature and circumstances of the case," and to support this opinion, he refers to the statute on the subject of bail. There is but one case in which the Justice is justified in refusing bail to an affrayer, and that is, where a *dangerous* wound has been given by him, and there is good reason to believe that a prosecution for a felonious homicide will result from it. In that case it may be done.(³) It is justified upon the strong probability that the misdemeanor will become merged in a high felony. The principle is not limited to a dangerous wound given in an *affray only*, but equally applies where it is given in any other rencounter. It is the precaution which the law takes to secure the offender to answer, as it were by anticipation, a prosecution for felony, and not to answer an indictment for the affray, which of itself is a misdemeanor only, and for which the Justice is not authorized to refuse bail. The proposition of the author in the terms in which he has stated it, confers upon the Justice a power not given him by law, and is not sustained by the statute to which he refers. By the Common Law, bail was allowed in all cases (even of felony) except for homicide,(⁴) and the statute referred to expressly declared, that those should be let to bail who were apprehended for any crime, not punishable with death or confinement in the public jail and penitentiary, and moreover de-

---

(¹) 1 Hawk. c. 63, § 19; 1 Burn J. P. 37.
(²) 1 Hawk. c. 63, § 2, 4, 20; 1 Dea. Cr. Co. 27.
(³) 1 Hawk. c. 63, § 18.
(⁴) 2 Hale P. C. 127, 129; 1 Dea. Cr. Co. 100.

clared, that if any Justice should refuse to admit to bail any who had a right to be so admitted, he should be amerced at the discretion of a jury.* It has been already stated that an affray is a misdemeanor, punishable by fine and imprisonment only, and therefore one apprehended for an affray is of right entitled to bail. To refuse it would be an offence against the liberty of the citizen, for which the Justice might be called to answer. Dissenting from the opinion thus expressed by the author, we hold that the Justice has no other discretion over the subject than to judge of the sufficiency of the bail when tendered, and is bound to receive it if sufficient; though he may refuse to bail an offender who has given a *dangerous wound*, (whether in an affray, riot, or any other rencounter,) out of which he has good reason to apprehend that a prosecution for a felonious homicide may arise.

(No. 1.)

Form of a Warrant to apprehend affrayers.

———— County, to wit:

To all or any one of the Constables of said County:

Whereas, A. B. of said County, has this day made complaint and information on oath before me J. T., a Justice of the said County, that C. D. and E. F., on the ———— day of ———— in the year of our Lord 18—, at ————, a public place in the said County, did in a tumultuous manner make an affray, wherein the person of the said A. B., was beaten and abused by them, the said C. D. and E. F., without any lawful or sufficient cause given to them or either of them by him, the said A. B. : These are therefore, in the name of the Commonweaith, to command you forthwith to apprehend the said C. D. and E. F., and bring them before me or some other Justice of the said County, to answer the said complaint, and to be farther dealt with according to law. Given under my hand and seal, this ———— day of ———— A. D. 18—.

J. T., J. P. [L. S.]

(No. 2.)

Form of a Common Law Warrant of Commitment for an affray.

———— County, to wit:

To X. Y. Constable of said County, and to the Keeper of the Jail of said County:

Whereas, C. D. of the said County, is now brought before me J. T., a Justice of the said County, and required by me to find sufficient sureties to be bound with him in a recognizance for his personal appearance on the first day of the next ———— term† of the County Court of ————, to be holden for the said County, to answer a bill of indictment, then and there to be preferred against him in the said Court, for an affray by him committed,

---

* Similar provisions exist in the *new Code.*
† The term at which the grand jury is convened.

in making an assault upon, and beating one F. G., at a public place in the said County, on the —— day of ——— 18— ; and whereas the said C. D. has refused, and does now refuse before me to find such sureties: These are therefore, in the name of the Commonwealth, to command you, the said Constable, forthwith to convey the said C. D. to the jail of the said County, and to deliver him to the keeper thereof, together with this warrant; and I do hereby command you, the said keeper, to receive the said C. D. into your custody in the said jail, and him there safely keep until the next term of the said Court, or until he shall be otherwise discharged by law. Given under my hand and seal, this —— day of ——— 18—.

J. T., J. P. [L. S.]

[NOTE.—The party thus committed may be discharged by a Justice, at any time before Court, by his entering into a recognizance to answer the indictment.]

[For the form of this recognizance and the order of discharge, see title RECOGNIZANCE.]

(No. 3.)

Form of Certificate of the Commitment or Letting to Bail, to be sent to the Clerk of the County Court, for an affray.

—— County, to wit:

To the Clerk of the County Court of said County:

I, J. T., a Justice of the said County, do hereby certify that C. D. was this day committed to the jail of this County by my warrant, (or *was this day admitted to bail by me*, as the case may be,) to answer an indictment to be preferred against him, in the County Court of the said County, for a misdemeanor by him committed, in this that he did, on the —— day of ——— 18—, in said County, (here describe the offence as in the warrant of arrest.) Given under my hand, this —— day of ——— 18—.

J. T., J. P.

(No. 4.)

Form of Recognizance of Witness to appear and give evidence to the grand jury upon the indictment.

Follow No. 5, under head of RECOGNIZANCE.

CHAPTER VI.

ANIMALS—(*Cruelty to.*)

[For injury to, or destroying of, see TRESPASS.]
[For poisoning of, see POISON.]

It seems that the maiming of cattle is not held by the English courts to be an indictable offence at Common Law;([1]) but it has been repeatedly held otherwise in this country;([2]) and by section 14, chapter 196, "if a free person cruelly beat or torture any horse or other beast, whether his own or that of another, he shall be fined not exceeding five hundred dollars."

Form of a Warrant of Arrest for cruelly beating and torturing a horse.

———— County, to wit:
  To X. Y., *Constable of the said County:*
  Whereas, A. B. has this day made complaint and information on oath before me J. T., a Justice of the said County, that C. D. did on the ———— day of ———— 18—, in said County, cruelly beat and torture a certain horse belonging to the said A. B.: These are therefore, in the name of the Commonwealth of Virginia, to command you to apprehend the said C. D., and to bring him before me or some other Justice of the said County, to answer the said complaint, and to be farther dealt with according to law. Given under my hand and seal, this ———— day of ———— 18—.

J. T., J. P. [L. S.]

[For commitment and other proceedings after arrest, see from No. 9 to 13, under the head of ARREST.]

APPEALS.

For power to grant an appeal and form of allowing it in prosecutions in the name of the Commonwealth, see FINES and CONVICTIONS.
For authority to allow an appeal in warrants for small claims and for penalties recoverable by warrant in the name of an individual, see WARRANTS—(*Civil.*)

([1]) 2 Russ. 497; Ranger's Case, 2 East P. C. 1074.   ([2]) 5 Cowen 258; 1 Dall. 335; 1 Wheel. Cr. R. 111.

CHAPTER VII.

APPRENTICES.

The manner of binding apprentices, the terms upon which it may be done, as well as who may be bound an apprentice, and the reciprocal duties of master and apprentice, are so fully set forth in the statute, that it is deemed unnecessary to say more in relation to these subjects than to recite it.

By Sec. 1, Chap. 126. Any minor may be bound as an apprentice by his guardian, or if none, by his father, or if neither father nor guardian, by his mother, with the consent entered of record of the court of the county or corporation in which the minor resides, or without such consent, if the minor, being fourteen years of age, agree in writing to be so bound.

By Sec. 2. By the same authority and under the same limitations, any minor may be placed for such time as may be agreed on in writing, in any incorporated association, asylum or school instituted for the support and education of destitute children, which shall thereupon be entitled to the custody of such minor for such time, and may bind him an apprentice until the expiration of that time.

By Sec. 3. Any overseer of the poor of a county or corporation, if allowed by an order of the court thereof, may place in any such incorporated institution or bind out as an apprentice, any minor who is found begging in such county or corporation, or is likely to become chargeable thereto.

By Sec. 4. The term of every such apprenticeship shall be until the apprentice attains the age of twenty-one years if a boy, or eighteen years if a girl.

By Sec. 5. The writing by which any minor is bound an apprentice shall specify his age, and what art, trade or business he is to be taught. The master, whether it is expressly provided therein or not, shall be bound to teach the same, and unless the apprentice be a free negro, shall be bound to teach him reading, writing and common arithmetic, including the rule of three.

By Sec. 6. When a court makes an order allowing a minor to be bound as an apprentice, it shall enquire and direct whether the master, besides maintaining the apprentice and so teaching him, shall pay any thing for his services; and if any thing, how much and for which year or years; the writing by which the minor is bound, shall bind the master to pay what

APPRENTICES. 41

may be so directed. For such payment, bond shall be taken by the overseer binding such minor if the court require it.

BY SEC. 7. The writing by which any minor is bound, and any bond taken from the master, shall within six months from the date thereof be filed in the clerk's office of the court of the county or corporation in which the same may be executed. Unless so filed, the master shall not be entitled to the services of the apprentice.

BY SEC. 8. Such writing may with the approbation of the said court, and on such terms as the court may prescribe, be transferred by the master, or within three months after his death, by his personal representative. The assignee thereof shall succeed to the master's rights and obligations for the future, and shall give bond if required by the court.

BY SEC. 9. The money which the master is to pay for any year, except the last, shall at the end of the year for which it is payable, be paid to the father of the minor, or the mother, or part to each as the court may direct. Or it may be reserved, to be paid to the apprentice at the end of his term, with interest. Such directions may be changed from time to time, on the motion of the overseers of the poor, or of the father, mother or apprentice, on proof of notice of such motion having been given to the adverse party.

BY SEC. 10. The money which the master is to pay for the last year, shall be paid at the end thereof to the apprentice.

BY SEC. 11. Any money to be paid under either of the two preceding sections, may be recovered from those liable therefor, on the motion of the person entitled thereto, or by suit. Any such motion may be in that court in the office whereof the writing or bond of the master is filed.

BY SEC. 12. Such court during the term of apprenticeship, may receive the complaint of such apprentice or any person in his behalf, against the master, for undeserved or excessive correction, want of instruction, insufficient allowance of food, raiment or lodging, or non-payment of what was directed to be paid; or the complaint of a master against his apprentice, for desertion or other misconduct; and after reasonable notice of the complaint to the party against whom it is made, may determine the same in a summary way, making such order as the case may require.

BY SEC. 13. No apprentice shall reside out of that county or corporation, in the office whereof the writing whereby such apprentice is bound, is required to be filed, without the leave of the court of such county or corporation. Whenever such leave is given, a copy of the said writing shall be forthwith filed in the office of the court of that county or corporation wherein the residence is to be; and thereafter, that court may hear and determine any complaint against the said master or apprentice as might have been done by the court giving such leave before the same was given. If without such leave, an apprentice be removed by his master, or with his master's knowledge, out of the first mentioned county or corporation, and remain thereout more than one month, the obligation of the apprentice to serve such master shall be only during the pleasure of the apprentice.

By Sec. 14. If any apprentice who was bound as such beyond the limits of this State, be brought or come within the same, the court of the county or corporation in which he may be, may hear and determine in a summary way any complaint of him or his master, and make such order in the matter as may be right.

By Sec. 15. If any apprentice bound in this State desert the service of his master, he shall be liable to the master, notwithstanding his infancy, and until five years after the expiration of his term of apprenticeship, for all damages sustained by such desertion.

By Sec. 16. If any person shall knowingly conceal or harbour any such apprentice, he shall pay such master three dollars for each day he shall so conceal or harbour the apprentice, in addition to the damages sustained by the master.

Though a person under the age of twenty-one years may voluntarily execute indentures of apprenticeship by signing a formal deed, he is not bound thereby, and no action will lie against him on his indentures, either for desertion or any other breach of his covenant, at Common Law,([1]) but the statute makes him liable for *desertion*. This renders it necessary to get some adult person to become bound for him, and there is nothing clearer than that the father (or any other person) who executes the indentures with the infant, is bound for the performance of the covenants by the apprentice,([2]) and it is no answer to an action brought on the covenant against the adult party, to say that it is in the option of the infant apprentice whether he would serve or not.([3])

A voluntary apprentice, bound when under age, is entitled to be discharged at twenty-one, though the time of service specified in the indentures has not expired; for the indenture is voidable by the infant, and the master must trust to the

---

([1]) Bott 527, and Burn J. P. 122.
([2]) Branch *v.* Ewington, Day 518; 1 B. & C. 469-70.
([3]) Cumming *v.* Hill, 3 B. & Cr. 59.

covenant of those who engage for him,(¹) and who, notwithstanding the discharge of the apprentice, are still liable to the master for any breach of the covenant by the infant, for the courts will not undertake to discharge men from their covenants upon *habeas corpus*.(²)

The apprenticeship may be determined by consent of all the parties concerned.(³) This, we presume, in the case of poor children, includes the consent of the court as well as that of the overseers of the poor.

The assent of two Justices in England, and of the county court in Virginia, is indispensable to the binding of any apprentice by the overseers of the poor. In commenting upon this controlling power of the Justices, Lord Kenyon remarked, in a case before him, "that this appears to be one of the most serious subjects that fall within the decisions of the Justices, for they are empowered by this act (the statute) to take children out of the arms of their parents and to bind them out till they are twenty-one years of age. The law has made them the guardians of those children who have no others to take care of them. And who ought to judge of the fitness of the person to whom the poor children are to be apprenticed? not the overseers; they are frequently obscure people, and perhaps in managing the business of the parish, are not always attentive to the feelings of parents. But the Legislature intended that the Magistrates should have a check and control over them in this instance, and they are called upon to examine with the most minute and anxious attention the situation of masters to whom apprentices are to be bound, and to exercise their judgment solemnly and soberly before they allow or disallow the act of the parish officers." In the same case, Ashhurst, J. said, that "the act of the Justices is in its nature an act of judgment. That they were the guardians of the morals of the people, and ought to take care that apprentices are not placed with masters who may corrupt their morals. The Justices therefore should enquire particularly whether or not they ought to allow the binding by the overseers, and they would be guilty of a breach of duty if they implicitly gave their assent without examining into the circumstances of the case."(⁴) These admonitions are as applicable in Virginia as in England.

(¹) 5 T. R. 715.
(²) Ex parte Gill, 7 East 367; 1 Bott 718.
(³) Burn J. P.
(⁴) Rex *v.* Ridware, 3 T. R. 381.

APPRENTICES.

(No. 1.)

Form of Indenture to bind a boy by overseers of the poor under order of Court.

This Indenture made the —— day of ——— in the year ———, between A. B. and C. D., overseers of the poor of the County of ———, of the one part, and E. F. of the said County, carpenter, of the other part, witnesseth: That the said A. B. and C. D., overseers of the poor as aforesaid, acting with the allowance and approbation of the County Court of ——— County, and in pursuance of an order of the said Court to that effect, made and entered on the —— day of ——— 18—, have put and bound, and do by these presents put and bind G. H., a boy of the said County, (who has to be provided for and assisted by the overseers of the said County,) and being of the age of ——— years, to be apprentice to the said E. F., to learn the trade, business and art of a carpenter and house joiner, and with him to dwell and remain and serve until he the said G. H. shall attain his full age of twenty-one years, during all which time he the said G. H.. his master faithfully shall serve and obey, his secrets keep and his lawful commands willingly do and perform, and shall not absent himself from the service of his said master day or night without his leave, but shall in all things as a faithful apprentice behave himself towards his master and all his family during the said term. And the said E. F., in consideration of the faithful service to be performed by the said G. H., doth hereby covenant, promise and agree with the said overseers and their successors in office, that he the said E. F. his said apprentice in the trade, art and mystery of a carpenter and house joiner, which he now useth, shall and will teach and instruct, or cause to be taught and instructed, in the best manner that he can, and shall and will provide and allow unto the said apprentice during all the said term, competent and sufficient meat, drink, washing, lodging, apparel and all other things necessary for the said apprentice. And the said E. F. doth covenant and agree with the said overseers of the poor and their successors in office during the said term, that he said E. F. shall and will teach, or cause the said apprentice to be taught, reading, writing and common arithmetic as far as the rule of three. And whereas the said County Court by the order aforesaid, did direct that the said E. F. for the services of the said apprentice, should pay, (recite the order,) the said E. F. doth hereby also covenant and agree to and with the said overseers of the poor and their successors in office, that he shall and will well and truly pay the said sums of money to the said overseers of the poor and their successors in office, for the use and objects specified in the said order.

In witness whereof, the said overseers of the poor and the said E. F. have hereunto interchangeably set their hands and affixed their seals, this ——— day of ——— 18—.

[L. S.]
[L. S.]
[L. S.]

[NOTE.—If the apprentice be a free negro, let it be stated after the first mention of his name, as "G. H. a free negro," and in that event, omit the covenant for teaching reading and writing. If the Court make no order for the payment of money, omit the last covenant. Should an order be made and the Court moreover require bond with security to be given for its payment, it may be in this form:]

APPRENTICES.   45

Bond given by master for payment of money directed to be made to minor, or his guardian, father or mother—(under 6th Sec.)

Know all men by these presents, that we A. B. and C. D. are held and firmly bound unto the overseers of the poor for the County of H. in the just and full sum of —— dollars, lawful money of the United States, the payment whereof well and truly to be made to the said overseers of the poor, we bind ourselves, our and each of our heirs, executors and administrators, jointly and severally, firmly by these presents. Sealed with our seals, and dated this —— day of ——— 18—.

The condition of the above obligation is such, that whereas the County Court of H. County, did on the —— day of ——, make the following order: (here recite the order.)

Now, therefore, if the above bound A. B. shall well and truly satisfy and pay the said several sums of money, with interest, at the times they shall respectively fall due, then the aforegoing obligation to be void, else to remain in full force and virtue.

[L. S.]
[L. S.]

(No. 2.)

Form of Indentures by the Father, with the assent of the Court, when the Apprentice is under the age of fourteen years.

This Indenture made the —— day of ——— in the year 18—, between A. B. of the County of ———, the father of J. B., an infant under the age of fourteen years, of the one part, and C. D. of the said County of the other part, witnesseth : That the said A. B. by and with the allowance and consent of the County Court of ——— County, by an order of the said Court, made on the —— day of ——— 18—, in pursuance of the statute in that case made and provided, has put and placed, and by these presents does put and place, the said J. B. (the child of the said A. B.) aged —— years, apprentice to the said C. D., with him to dwell and serve from the day of the date of these presents until the said apprentice shall accomplish his full age of twenty-one years, (or, if a female, eighteen years.) And the said A. B. for himself, his heirs, executors and administrators, does hereby covenant, promise and agree to and with the said C. D., his executors and administrators, that he the said J. B., the said C. D. his master, shall and will faithfully serve in all lawful business according to his power, wit and ability, and honestly, orderly and obediently in all things demean and behave himself towards his said master during the said term of apprenticeship. And the said C. D. for himself, his heirs, executors and administrators, does covenant, promise and agree to and with the said A. B., his executors and administrators, by these presents, that he said C. D. shall and will teach and instruct the said J. B., or cause him to be taught and instructed in the art, trade and mystery of a carpenter and house joiner, in the best way and manner that he can during the said term, and shall and will during all the term aforesaid, find, provide and allow unto the said J. B. competent and sufficient meat, drink, apparel, lodging, washing and all things necessary and fit for an apprentice. (If there be any special or particular covenant here insert it.)

In witness whereof, the parties above mentioned have to these presents interchangeably set their hands and seals, the day and year first above written.

Signed, sealed and delivered
in the presence of

[L. S.]
[L. S.]

(No. 3.)

Form of an Indenture of Apprenticeship when Apprentice is fourteen years old.

This Indenture made the —— day of ——— in the year 18—, between A. B. the father of J. B., a minor fourteen years old, of the County of ———, of the one part, and C. D. of the County of ———, of the other part, witnesseth: That the said A. B. the father of the said J. B., by and with the written consent of the said J. B., given before the sealing and delivery of these presents, and bearing date on the —— day of ——— 18—, hath put and placed, and by these presents doth put and place, the said J. B. aged —— years, apprentice to the said C. D. with him to dwell and serve from the day of the date of these presents until the said apprentice shall accomplish his full age of twenty-one years, (or, if a female, eighteen years.) And the said A. B., for himself, his heirs, executors and administrators, doth hereby covenant, promise and agree to and with the said C. D., his executors and administrators, that he the said J. B. the said C. D. his master shall and will faithfully serve in all lawful business according to his power, wit and ability, and honestly, orderly and obediently in all things demean and behave himself towards his said master during the said term of apprenticeship. And the said C. D. for himself, his heirs, executors and administrators, doth covenant, promise and agree to and with the said A. B., his executors and administrators, by these presents, that he the said C. D. shall and will teach and instruct the said J. B., or cause him to be taught and instructed in the art, trade and mystery of a carpenter and house joiner in the best way and manner that he can during the said term, and shall and will during all the term aforesaid, find, provide and allow unto the said J. B. competent meat, drink, apparel, lodging, washing and all things necessary and fit for an apprentice. (If there be any special or particular covenant, here insert it.)

In witness whereof, the parties above mentioned have to these presents interchangeably set their hands and seals, the day and year first above written.

Signed, sealed and delivered
  in the presence of

                                                  [L. S.]
                                                  [L. S.]

[Written consent of the apprentice to be signed before executing the indenture, and which may be written at the foot of the indentures:]

I, J. B. do hereby consent and agree in writing to be put and bound as an apprentice to C. D. according to the intent and meaning of the foregoing indenture, and do sign this my consent, in pursuance of the statute in that case made and provided, to the said indenture before the same was executed by any of the parties thereto.

[NOTE.—These forms can be easily altered to suit the case of a guardian by leaving out "father" and inserting "guardian."]

CHAPTER VIII.

ARREST.

By Chap. 204, Sec. 1. A Judge of the general court or a Justice may, in vacation as well as in term time, issue process for the apprehension of a person charged with an offence.

By Sec. 2. On complaint to any such officer, of a criminal offence, he shall examine on oath the complainant and any other witnesses, reduce the charge to writing and cause the same to be signed by the complainant, and if he see good cause to believe that an offence has been committed, shall issue his warrant reciting the accusation, and requiring the person accused to be arrested and brought before a Justice of the county or corporation or a Judge therein, and in the same warrant may require the officer to summon such witnesses as shall be therein named, to appear and give evidence on the examination.

By Sec. 3. If a person charged with an offence shall, after or at the time the warrant is issued for his apprehension, escape from or be out of the county or corporation in which the offence is alleged to have been committed, the officer to whom the warrant is directed, may pursue and apprehend him any where in the State; or a Justice of a county or corporation other than that in which it was issued, on being satisfied of the genuineness thereof, may endorse thereon his name and official character; and such endorsement shall operate as a direction of the warrant to an officer of such Justice's county or corporation.

By Sec. 4. An officer arresting a person under a warrant for an offence, shall bring such person before, and return such warrant to, a Justice of the county or corporation in which the warrant issued, or a Judge therein, unless such person be let to bail as hereinafter mentioned, or it be otherwise provided.

By Sec. 5. Where the arrest is in a county or corporation other than that in which the charge ought to be tried, the Judge or Justice before whom the accused is brought, shall by warrant commit him to an officer, that he may, and such officer shall, carry him to the county or corporation in which the trial should be, and there shall take him before, and return such warrant to, a Justice thereof or a Judge.

By Sec. 6. A county or corporation court, or a Justice thereof in vacation, may let to bail a person who is charged with, but not convicted of, an offence punishable with death or confinement in the penitentiary, or of which, if it be so punishable, only a light suspicion of guilt falls on him. If the offence be so punishable, and there is good cause to believe such person guilty, he shall not be let to bail by a Justice or Justices, either in or out of court; and in no case shall a person in jail under an order of commitment, be admitted to bail by a Justice (in vacation) in a less sum than was required by such order. But a circuit court or the general court, or any Judge thereof, may admit any person to bail before conviction.

By Sec. 7. A person charged with an offence not so punishable, and to be carried to another county or corporation, shall, if he request it in the county or corporation wherein he is arrested, be brought before a Justice thereof. In such or any case of a person charged with an offence not so punishable, if he desire it, a Court, Judge or Justice before whom he is brought, may, without trial or examination, let him to bail, upon taking a recognizance for his appearance before the court having cognizance of the case, the fact of taking which shall be certified by the court or officer taking it, upon the warrant under which such person was arrested, and the warrant and recognizance shall be returned forthwith to the clerk of the court before which the accused is to appear; to which court the Judge or Justice who issued said warrant shall recognize or cause to be summoned such witnesses as he may think proper.

By Sec. 8. A Judge or Justice may adjourn an examination or trial pending before him, not exceeding ten days at one time, without the consent of the accused, and to any place in the county or corporation; in such case, if the accused be charged with an offence punishable with death or confinement in the penitentiary, he shall be committed to jail, otherwise he may be recognized for his appearance at the time appointed for such farther examination or trial; or for want of bail be committed to jail.

By Sec. 9. If the person so recognized do not appear at the time so appointed, the said Judge or Justice shall certify the recognizance, and the fact of such default, to the county or corporation court at its next term, and like proceedings shall be had thereon as on breach of a recognizance for appearance before such court.

By Sec. 10. If the accused is committed, it shall be by an order of the Judge or Justice, stating that he is committed for farther examination on a day specified in the order, and on that day he may be brought before the Judge or Justice, by his verbal order to the officer by whom he was committed, or by a written order to a different person.

By Sec. 11. The Judge or Justice, before whom any person is brought for an offence, shall, as soon as may be, in the presence of such person, examine on oath the witnesses for and against him, and he may be assisted by counsel.

By SEC. 12. While a witness is under such examination, all other witnesses may, by order of the Judge or Justice, be excluded from the place of examination, and kept separate from each other.

By SEC. 13. When the Judge or Justice deems it proper, the testimony of the witnesses may be reduced to writing; and the same, if required by him, shall be signed by them respectively.

By SEC. 14. The Judge or Justice shall discharge the accused, if he consider that there is not sufficient cause for charging him with the offence, and when he is not trying him, under chapter 212, shall commit him to jail, if he consider that there is such cause, or let him to bail under the 6th section. He shall require recognizances, with or without sureties, as he deems proper, from all material witnesses against the accused.

By SEC. 15. When a Judge or Justice so considers that there is sufficient cause for charging the accused with the offence, if the accused be entitled to an examining court, the commitment shall be for examination, and the recognizances be for appearance before such examining court, as is provided by chapter 205; and if he be not so entitled, unless it be a case wherein it is otherwise specially provided, the commitment shall be for trial and the recognizances be for appearance in the county or corporation court, at such time as the case can be proceeded in before such court. The Judge or Justice shall return to the clerk of such court, as soon as may be, a certificate of the nature of the offence, shewing whether the accused was committed, or bailed therefor; and the clerk, as soon as may be, shall inform the attorney for the Commonwealth in said court, of such certificate.

By SEC. 16. Every examination and recognizance taken under this chapter, shall, by the Judge or Justice taking it, be certified to the clerk of the court before which the party charged is to appear, on or before the first day of its session. If he fail, he may be compelled to do so, by attachment, as for a contempt.

By SEC. 17. A Justice to whom complaint is made, or before whom a prisoner is brought, may associate with himself one or more Justices of the county or corporation, and they may together execute the powers and duties before mentioned.

By SEC. 18. If a person be in jail or under recognizance to answer a charge of assault and battery, or other misdemeanor, for which there is a remedy by civil action, unless the offence was committed by or upon a sheriff, or other officer of justice, or riotously, or with intent to commit a felony, if the party injured appear before the Judge or Justice who made the commitment or took the recognizance, and acknowledge in writing that he has received satisfaction for the injury, such Judge or Justice, in his discretion, may, by an order under his hand, supersede the commitment, or discharge the recognizances as to the accused and the witnesses.

By Sec. 19. Every order discharging a recognizance shall be filed with the clerk before the session of the court at which the party was to appear, and an order superseding a commitment shall be delivered to the jailor, who shall forthwith discharge the witnesses (if any) and the accused, and against him judgment shall be entered in the said court for the costs of the prosecution.

Most of these provisions affirm principles before well established at Common Law, where many others of primary importance connected with this subject of arrest, may be found, and which equally demand the attention of the Justice, and all others concerned, in the execution of the Criminal Law. They will be noticed in connection with the statute in the order in which they naturally arise, commencing with the complaint, and concluding with the commitment or letting to bail of a prisoner.

I. *Of the complaint.*

The first step to be taken to procure a warrant of arrest is to make complaint to a Justice of the Peace, charging or shewing that a criminal offence has been committed by some certain person, capable in law of committing crime. As a general rule, every person is of common right entitled to prefer a complaint,([1]) and the general presumption is in favour of the competency as well as the credibility of the complainant.([2]) A Justice, however, should in no case receive a complaint upon the oath of persons who are at the time disqualified for being witnesses by insanity or drunkenness,([3]) or want of age; though as to infants, if they understand the nature and obligations of an oath, they may be sworn, no matter how young, and their credit is left to the Magistrate to determine.([4])

Upon the complaint being made, it is the duty of the Justice to examine the complainant and such witnesses, if any, as he may produce, on oath, and to determine whether there is probable cause for proceeding farther. He should not proceed in any case upon the complaint, solely because such complaint has been made, but should endeavour to inform himself of the

---

([1]) 1 Ch. Cr. L. 1.
([2]) 7 Barn. & Cress. 815; 1 Mood. & Ry. 669; 3 Gill & John. 355; Barb. J. P. 465.
([3]) 10 John. 362; 16 Id. 143; 15 Serg. & Rawle 335.
([4]) 10 Mass. R. 225; 18 John. 98; 2 Penning. R. 657; Cowen & Hill's notes to Phil. Ev. 61, note 50.

true nature of it, and if he has good reason to suspect the integrity of the person sworn, he should sift the examination with greater diligence and caution, lest he should be made the instrument of gratifying revengeful feelings. But he should remember that he is not now passing upon the guilt or innocence of the person accused, but merely enquiring into the facts, to satisfy himself whether there is *probable* cause for *arrest*. To this extent, both the credibility and competency of the testimony is submitted to his discretion, and upon the manner in which he exercises it, depends, in a great degree, the good order and well being of society. The amount of evidence necessary to authorize a Justice to grant his warrant cannot be reduced to any definite rule. Evidence that satisfies one mind, may be unsatisfactory to another; but he will still bear in mind that it is the incipient stage of a criminal prosecution, not involving the question of guilt, but *probable cause of arrest*.

A warrant may be granted upon well grounded suspicion; but no warrant of arrest ought to be issued upon the *mere suspicion of a complainant or any witness*, although authority may be found seeming to sanction it. The Justice should not regard mere *allegations* of suspicion, but the grounds of suspicion. The facts, and all the circumstances upon which that suspicion is founded, must be laid before him; he is to be satisfied whether the suspicion that a crime has been actually committed, and that there is probable cause for charging the person complained of with being the offender,([1]) is well founded, and in the language of Lord Hale, "it is then the Justice's suspicion."([2])

It is the duty of the Justice to consider well and impartially what is sworn to, and not to grant a warrant, without such reasonable cause as might lead a discreet and impartial man to *suspect* the party guilty, or that there is *probable cause to suspect him guilty*.([3]) If upon hearing the complaint upon oath, he should think the matter complained of ought to be proceeded in, he should promptly grant a warrant. It is his duty to do so, and when in a case over which he has jurisdiction, he impartially grants a warrant on complaint or information on oath, no mere error of opinion or judgment will render him liable. He is bound to act in such case, and it would be against both policy and justice if the law should suffer him to be punished, or hold him liable for damages because he did not decide correctly.

([1]) 1 Ch. Cr. L. 33; 1 Hale P. C. 210, 582; 4 Blac. Com. 290; 2 Hawk. P. C. c. 13, § 18; 3 Dick. Jus. Warrant 1.
([2]) 2 Hale 79, 80.
([3]) 1 Ch. Cr. L. 34; Hawk. P. C. c. 13, § 18.

Before granting a warrant, the statute requires that the complaint should be reduced to writing and signed by the complainant.

II. Warrant.

A warrant is a precept under the hand and seal of some public functionary having the power to award it, to some officer to arrest an offender, or to seize or distrain upon his goods, to be dealt with respectively in either case according to due course of law ;(1) but in its more limited sense, and as here used, it signifies that *written* authority by which a Justice of the Peace directs a Constable to constrain any person accused of any offence within the cognizance of the Justice, to be brought before him or some other Justice having equal cognizance of the offence.(2)

It is clear that a warrant of arrest may be lawfully granted by any Justice of the Peace for treason, felony or any other offence against the peace, committed within his jurisdiction, in order to compel the person accused to appear before him, and it is well settled, that whenever a statute gives to any Justice jurisdiction over any offence, or a power to require a person to do a certain thing ordained by such statute, it impliedly gives a power to every such Justice to issue a warrant to bring before him any person accused of such offence, or compellable to do any thing ordained by such statute. It would be absurd (as Justice Blackstone expresses it) to give a Magistrate power to examine an offender unless he had also the power to compel him to attend and submit to such examination ;(3) and it would be equally absurd to intend, that a statute giving a Justice jurisdiction over an offence does not mean also to give him the power incident to all courts, of compelling the party committing it to come before him.(4) This power is derived from his commission and the Common Law, and is now affirmed by the statute. But as a warrant deprives a man of his liberty, a summons is the proper process and not a warrant (unless otherwise directed by statute) where the punishment is merely a pecuniary fine.(5) Upon default of appearance on the summons, the Justice may proceed to force his appearance by warrant(6) if necessary ; but it is not proper to arrest a party accused before an indictment is found or presentment made against him, except in cases of felony, breach of the peace, or for misdemeanors

---

(1) 2 Dea. Cr. L. 1368.
(2) 3 Dick. J. P. 501.
(3) 4 Black. Com. 290.
(4) 2 Hawk. c. 13, § 13 ; 12 Co. Rep. 131, b. ; R. v. Simpson, 10 Mod. R.
248 ; Bane v. Matthuen, 2 Bing. 63 ; 1 Dea. Cr. L. 45 ; 5 Burn J. P. 578.
(5) 1 Va. Cases 155, and the Statute.
(6) 5 Burn J. P. 578.

ARREST—(*Warrant for.*) 53

directly tending to produce great and immediate evil, or involving an attempt to commit a felony, unless the Magistrate has strong reason to believe that the accused intends to fly from justice. In cases where the punishment is by fine exceeding twenty dollars, and in ordinary misdemeanors not accompanied by actual violence, the proper practice is to leave the matter to the action of the grand jury, before whom the complainant has a right to appear as the accuser, and if they find an indictment or make a presentment, process as of right must be awarded by the court.(¹) Still it may be proper to issue a warrant in the first instance; as where the party is a non-resident of the State, and likely to abscond.

A general warrant to apprehend all persons suspected, is no less against law than reason. The warrant must specify both a particular person and offence.(²) This principle of the Common Law is re-affirmed by the Bill of Rights and the statute just recited.

It has been already stated, that a Justice may grant a warrant to apprehend a person *suspected of felony*, if the cause of *suspicion in his opinion* be reasonable and well founded; and the reason of it is, that otherwise offenders would escape unexamined; for a man may have a strong and probable presumption of the guilt of a person whom he cannot swear positively to be guilty.(³) But a warrant in a criminal case ought not to be granted upon common rumour and report only of the party's guilt, even where there is danger of his escape before witnesses could be summoned to enable the Magistrate to issue it on oath:(⁴) though general rumour, attended with circumstances of probability, may be relied on;(⁵) nor should it be granted on the oath of an incompetent witness, as upon the evidence of a slave or free negro against a white person, or upon the oath of a convicted felon.(⁶)

In regard to the form of the warrant, the Justice will observe:

1. That a warrant of arrest ought to state the county or city where it is made.(⁷) This is usually done in the margin at the commencement, as thus, "Henrico County, to wit."

2. It must set forth the year and day when it was issued, that it may appear in an action brought upon the arrest by virtue of it, to have been prior to the arrest, and that in cases

---

(¹) Dickenson's Guide by Talford, 76.
(²) 5 Burn J. P. 503; 2 Hawk. c. 13; 2 Hale 111, 114.
(³) 1 Hale 579.
(⁴) Conner *v.* Commonwealth, 3 Binn. 58.
(⁵) See 2 Hawk. c. 12, § 9, 10, 11, 12, 13, 16; 2 H. P. C. 78, 90, 92; 1 H. P. C. 588; 2 Inst. 52, 173; 3 Inst. 158; 2 Ld. Ray. 1300.
(⁶) State *v.* Killot, 2 Bailey 289.
(⁷) 2 Hawk. P. C. c. 13, § 23; 5 Burn J. P. 580; Toone J. P. 771.

where the statute requires the prosecution to be within a certain time, it may appear that the prosecution is commenced within that time.(¹)

3. It ought to be directed to the Sheriff, Sergeant or Constable, though it may be directed to an indifferent person by name, who is not an officer, for the Justice may authorize any one to be his officer whom he pleases to make such.(²) Yet it is most advisable to direct it to an officer, because no private person can be compelled to execute it.(³)

4. It may either be in the name of the Justice, or in the name of the State.(⁴)

5. It should be under the hand and seal of the Justice, by the authority both of Hale and Hawkins.(⁵) But it seems by more modern and equally high authority, that a warrant under the hand of a Justice is sufficient without being under his seal, unless particularly required by an act of the Legislature.(⁶) In this State, it is the practice, and therefore the safest course, to issue it under seal; though it seems a warrant under the hand only of a Justice is sufficient.

6. General warrants, as before remarked, are oppressive and against law, and every warrant ought therefore regularly to mention the name of the party to be arrested, if his name be known, and must not be left with blanks to be filled up by the *party* or officer afterwards.(⁷) If the name be known, it should be accurately stated, and if the name inserted be not the right name, the arrest by virtue of the warrant cannot be justified, unless indeed the party is known as well by the name in the warrant as by his true name.(⁸) But it may be, that the name of the party is unknown, and in such case, the warrant may be issued against him by the best description that can be given of him, or that the nature of the case will allow,(⁹) and should be, to arrest "the body of a man whose name is unknown, but whose person is well known," and then to proceed with the most accurate description of the person that can be given.(¹⁰)

7. Regularly, every warrant of arrest granted by a Justice for a crime or a breach of the peace, ought to comprehend the

---

(¹) 2 Hawk. c. 13; 3 Dick. J. P. 503, 504.
(²) 2 Hawk. c. 13, § 23; 2 Hale 110, 150; 5 Burn J. P. 581; 3 Dick. J. P. 508.
(³) 2 Hawk. c. 13, § 27; 1 Ch. Cr. L. 38; 1 Hale 581; 3 Wend. 350.
(⁴) 1 Ch. Cr. L. 39; 3 Dick. J. P. 503; 2 Hawk. c. 13, § 24; 19 John. R. 279.
(⁵) 1 Hale P. C. 577; 2 Hawk. c. 13, § 21.
(⁶) Ch. Cr. L. 38; Bul. N. P. 83; Toone 450; 5 Burn J. P. 582; Willis R. 411.
(⁷) 2 Hale 114; Dalt. c. 109, p. 402; 5 Burn J. P. 582; 3 Dick. J. P. 583; 1 Ch. Cr. L. 42.
(⁸) 1 Ch. Cr. L. 39; 2 Hale P. C. 114; Foster 312; 8 East 238; 6 Cowen 456; 7 Cowen 332; 3 Wend. 350; 2 Taunt. 400.
(⁹) 1 Ch. Cr. L. 39, 40; 1 Hale 577.
(¹⁰) 1 Ch. Cr. L. 39.

special matter and charge upon which it has been granted.(¹) The cause of the arrest should be shewn with certainty on the face of the warrant, in order to shew the jurisdiction of the Magistrate granting it; otherwise, it would be insufficient.(²) But it is not expected, nor is it necessary, that a Magistrate in framing a warrant should state the offence with the same technical accuracy that is required in an indictment.(³) The statute only requires that the warrant should recite the substance of the offence.

8. The warrant of a Justice is not returnable at any particular time, but remains in force until executed and discharged.(⁴) It fixes no particular time when the party is to be brought before the Justice, because it is uncertain at what time he will be arrested; but it commands the officer *forthwith* to arrest and bring the party before him. It may issue to bring him before the same Justice who granted it, and then the officer is to bring him before that Justice, or it may be to bring him before any Justice, and then it is in the election of the officer to bring him before what Justice of the county he thinks fit, and not in the election of the prisoner.(⁵) But in the exercise of his discretion, the officer must be governed by legal discretion; for he will not be justified in dragging the prisoner to a great distance, when another Justice is near at hand.(⁶)

The jurisdiction of a Justice extends no farther than the limits of his county, city or borough, in issuing warrants of arrest.(⁷) He can, therefore, issue no warrant when beyond the limits of his county.

III. *Arrest—(who liable to, and how made.)*

The term *arrest* applies both to civil and criminal proceedings. It is in the latter sense that it is referred to here, and signifies the apprehending and restraining of the person of an individual, in order to be forthcoming to answer an alleged or suspected crime or offence.

To such arrest all persons without distinction are liable.(⁸) The exemption from arrest in civil cases does not exist here, nor do the various privileges extended to members and officers

---

(¹) Lambard 87; Dalt. 169; 2 Hawk. c. 13, § 25; 2 Hale 111; 3 Dick. J. P. 503; 5 Burn J. P. 581.
(²) Rex v. Dugger, 5 B. & A. 791; 1 Dea. Cr. L. 46.
(³) State v. Killot, 2 Bailey 289.
(⁴) Peake N. P. 234; 3 Dick. J. P. 504.
(⁵) 1 Hale 582; 2 Hale 112; 2 Hawk. c. 13, § 26; 1 Ch. Cr. L. 39; 3 Dick. J. P. 503.
(⁶) 3 Dick. J. P. 503, in note.
(⁷) 3 Dick. J. P. 505.
(⁸) 1 Dea. Cr. L. 45; 1 Ch. Cr. L. 12; 1 Dick. J. P. 152; 4 Blac. Com. 289.

of the Legislature or any others, exempt them from arrest in criminal prosecutions.(¹)

As a general rule, it may be laid down, that every individual before indictment found, may be arrested in every case of treason, felony or actual breach of the peace, and such misdemeanors or offences as subject the delinquent to corporeal punishment.(²)

It may be in any place,(³) in the night as well as in the day, and on Sunday, in order to prevent the escape of the party.(⁴) As to the manner of making an arrest, it is stated by Mr. Chitty, that "to constitute an arrest, the party against whom the process is awarded, must be either actually touched by the officer or confined in a room, or must submit himself either by words or actions to be in custody, and the mere *giving charge* or causing him voluntarily to appear before a Magistrate, without the person's being taken in actual custody, will not amount to an arrest; for bare words will not in this respect be of any avail.(⁵) But no manual touching of the body or actual force is necessary, in order to constitute an arrest and imprisonment. It is sufficient if the party is within the power of the officer, and submits to the arrest.(⁶)

Concerning the authority by which a party may be arrested, it may be, 1st, By a warrant; 2nd, By an officer without a warrant; and 3rd, By a private individual and without a warrant. If it be by warrant directed to a peace officer, as to a Sheriff or Constable, he must with all speed and secrecy find out the party and execute the warrant,(⁷) and in discharge of this duty, he may take of the county (*posse comitatus*) any number of persons that he shall think necessary, to pursue, arrest and imprison the party charged.(⁸) But to do this, there must be apparent and sufficient cause, and if he refuses and neglects to execute the warrant, he will be punishable for such disobedience and neglect. If the warrant be directed to all or any one of the Constables, any one of them may execute it, in any part of the county in which it is issued; his authority in this respect being co-extensive with the jurisdiction of the Justice.(⁹) The officer should attend carefully to the command of the warrant with respect to the person to be arrested, for if he take a different person for the one named in the warrant,

---

(¹) 4 Inst. 24, 5; 1 Blac. 145; 1 Burn J. P. 214.
(²) 1 Ch. Cr. L. 13; 2 Hale 72, 8, 108; Hawk. 2 b., c. 13, § 11.
(³) Bac. Abr. Trespass, (D. 3.)
(⁴) Burn J. P. 23; 1 Ch. Cr. L. 49; 1 East P. C. 324; 3 Taunt. 14.
(⁵) 1 Ch. Cr. L. 47.
(⁶) Russum v. Lucas, 1 Car. & Payne 351; Gold v. Bissell, 1 Wend. 126.
(⁷) Dalt. c. 169, p. 404; 1 Burn J. P. 219; 1 Dick. J. P. 156.
(⁸) Dalt. c. 171; 1 Bur. 290; 1 Dick. 256, and the Statute.
(⁹) Lew. Cr. R. 52.

he will be a trespasser.(¹) So also he should be careful to see that the warrant shews on its face that it is issued by one having competent jurisdiction and authority. The party to be arrested should have due notice of the officer's business and authority to arrest him, unless he is previously acquainted with the business on which the officer comes to him,(²) and therefore the officer serving the warrant should always accompany the service with words of arrest. If the warrant is served by a private individual, he should shew it if demanded, and even officers, if they are not commonly known, should shew their warrant on demand made.(³) But sworn and known officers acting within their jurisdiction need not shew their warrant.(⁴) Yet all persons making an arrest ought to acquaint the party with the substance of the warrant.(⁵) In no case, however, are officers bound to part with the possession of their warrant, for that is their justification, and this rule applies to all persons charged with the service of process of arrest.(⁶) To this rule of the Common Law, the statute makes some exceptions; as under the third section before cited where a party is arrested in one county for a misdemeanor committed in another, and gives bail for his appearance, then the warrant is to be transmitted with the recognizance to the court of that county in which the offence was committed.

It is certainly the safer course in all cases, even of sworn or known officers, to shew the warrant when demanded, though this is not necessary to the validity of the arrest, but will oftentimes prevent resistance. Lord Kenyon, in a case before him in the King's Bench, observed, that he did not think a person bound to take it for granted that another, who says he has a warrant against him without producing it, speaks the truth, and he considers it very important in all cases where an arrest is made by virtue of a warrant, that the warrant, if demanded, should be produced, so as to leave a delinquent no excuse for resistance,(⁷) and it is especially enjoined on all private persons to whom an arrest warrant may be directed, to shew it.(⁸) It has already been stated, that the officer in cases where it is necessary, may summon the *posse comitatus* to his aid, and those thus called, act or refuse to act at their peril.

(¹) 1 Ch. Cr. L. 50; Hawk. P. C. B. 2, c. 13, § 31.
(²) 1 East P. C. 319; Hale 458, 470; Foster 310; Hawk. c. 3, § 49, 50.
(³) 1 Hale 459; Foster 320.
(⁴) 1 Ch. Cr. L. 50, 51; 1 Hale 461, 583; 1 East P. C. 314, 319; 1 Russ. on Cr. 515-6-8; 2 Hawk. P. C. c. 13, § 28; 10 Wend. 514.
(⁵) 1 Ch. Cr. L. 51; 2 Hawk. c. 13, § 28; 1 Russ. 516.
(⁶) 2 Russ. 319, n.; 1 East P. C. 319; 2 Ld. Raym. 1296; Lewin C. R. 53.
(⁷) 8 T. R. 188; 1 T. R. 118; 1 Ch. Cr. L. 51.
(⁸) 1 Ch. Cr. L. 51; 1 T. R. 265; Willis 459.

If the officer is protected in doing the thing in which their assistance is required, they will be protected also, but not otherwise.(¹)

It not unfrequently happens that a party against whom a warrant is issued on a criminal charge, is already in prison in a civil or criminal suit. We are not aware what has been the general practice in such cases in this Commonwealth, but in many cases coming within our knowledge, the English practice has been pursued and no objection taken to it. There, where a party is in custody on civil process, inasmuch as he cannot be taken out and brought before the Justice, the criminal warrant is lodged with the keeper of the place of confinement (the Jailor in this State,) in which the party is. On the termination of the civil confinement, the officer sends for a Constable, who takes the party before a Justice, who proceeds as in ordinary cases.(²)

When the party is already in jail on a criminal charge and fully committed for trial, it is not usual in England to bring him from his first custody before a Magistrate under a subsequent charge; but the examination of witnesses is had as in ordinary cases, and a warrant of detainer is sent to the Jailor in whose custody he remains.(³) This has never been the practice in this State, and the practice here is the same, whether he be in custody under civil or criminal process. It is now the right of the prisoner, by statute in all cases, to be confronted with his accuser before he can be committed for trial, and to examine witnesses against him in his absence while confined would be a violation of this right.

As it regards the duty of the officer after the arrest, his best guide is implicit obedience to the warrant, and to bring the party as soon as possible before the Justice according to the import of the warrant, and if he is guilty of unnecessary delay, it is a breach of duty. But if the time be unseasonable, as in or near night, whereby he cannot attend the Justice, or if there be danger of a rescue, or the party is ill or unable at present to *be brought* before the Justice, the officer, as the case may require, may secure him in a house until the next day or until it may be reasonable to bring him.(⁴)

If an officer having arrested a party under a warrant, suffer him to go at large upon his promising to come again and find sureties, it has been doubted whether he can afterwards be arrested upon the same process, though it would seem that as the public are interested in the offender's being brought to justice, there is no well founded objection to such second

---

(¹) 10 Wend. 128; 12 Mass. R. 561; 3 Wend. 384.
(²) 1 Ch. Cr. L. 63.
(³) 1 Ch. Cr. L. 63.
(⁴) 2 Hale 95, 96, 119, 120; 1 Ch. Cr. L. 59.

arrest.(¹) And it is certain, that if the escape be made without the concurrence of the officer, the prisoner may be re-taken upon fresh suit as often as he flies, although he were out of view or had reached another county.(²) It is also clear, that if, after a departure by the permission of the Constable, the party return into his custody, he may lawfully detain him in pursuance of his original warrant.(³)

In all cases where a prisoner is brought before a Magistrate, he is still considered as being in the custody of the arresting officer until he is discharged, bailed or committed to prison. The person making the arrest, should make a return in writing, stating what he has done under the warrant, and exhibit it to the Justice.

If a felony or other breach of the peace be committed in the presence of a Justice of the Peace, he may in his own person apprehend the offender; and he may by words command any person to apprehend him, and such command is a good warrant without writing; but if the felony or breach of the peace be done in his absence, then he must issue his warrant to apprehend the party.(⁴) Sheriffs also have power to arrest for felony committed in their presence, and for a capital offence, may arrest on a well grounded suspicion, though the guilt of the party suspected is not certain;(⁵) and if the Sheriff is assaulted in the execution of his official duty, he may apprehend the offender and keep him in prison for a reasonable time, to be carried before a Justice of the Peace to be committed or find bail to answer the offence.(⁶) A Coroner is a conservator of the peace in relation to all felonies, and in person may arrest or cause another to arrest any felon. It is safer, however, in all cases to obtain a warrant to arrest for any offence done in the absence of the officer, when time will allow.(⁷) Where the Magistrate is not present when a crime is committed, he ought not upon mere *discretion* to send the party accused to prison, but upon due consideration of evidence adduced before him, and in case he has notice or a particular knowledge that a person has been guilty of an offence, yet it is not a sufficient ground for him to commit the criminal, but in that case he is rather a witness than a Magistrate, and ought to make oath of the fact before some other Magistrate, who should thereupon act the official part by granting a warrant to apprehend the offender, it being more fit that the

---

(¹) 1 Ch. Cr. L. 59; 2 Hawk. c. 13, § 9; Id. c. 19, § 12; 2 Barn. & Cress.
(²) Dalt. c. 169; Dick. J. P. Arrest, III.; 1 Ch. Cr. L. 59.
(³) 1 Ch. Cr. L. 59; 2 Hawk. c. 13; 2 Hale P. C. 120.
(⁴) 2 Hale P. C. 86; 1 Ch. Cr. L. 24, 25.
(⁵) Id.
(⁶) 1 Saund. 77, 78; 1 Taunt. 146; Selw. N. P. 833.
(⁷) 1 Ch. Cr. L. 19, 31.

accuser should appear as a witness than act as a Magistrate.([1]) Nor is a Justice or any officer justified in an arrest without warrant for any offence less than felony committed in their absence.

A Constable is a conservator of the peace, and by the original inherent power which he possesses, may for treason, felony or breach of the peace committed in his view, apprehend the offender by virtue of his office without warrant;([2]) and if any man shall make an affray or an assault upon another in his *presence*, or shall threaten to kill, beat or hurt another, or do any act that has a tendency to a breach of the peace, the Constable may take him into custody, and carry him before a Justice of the Peace to find surety for keeping the peace;([3]) but where the affray is over, and in breaches of the peace less than felony committed in his absence, it is held that a Constable cannot act upon his own authority without a warrant.([4])

A Constable may justify an arrest without a warrant on a reasonable charge of felony made to him by another person, although it turn out that no felony was committed by any one.([5]) But in general, a Constable cannot any more than a private individual, of his own accord, and without *an express charge or warrant*, justify the arrest of a supposed offender *upon suspicion of his guilt*, unless he can shew that a felony was *committed by some one*, as well as the reasonableness of the suspicion that the party apprehended is guilty;([6]) and although he be justified in an arrest founded upon the suspicion and charge alleged by another, he ought scrupulously to enquire into the causes of the suspicion,([7]) and even in all such cases it is advisable to obtain a warrant unless in cases of felony, where the party would otherwise make his escape before the warrant could be issued. In cases where the arrest is made upon the charge of another person, and without warrant, the party suspecting and making the charge should be present at the arrest.([8])

Whenever a felony is committed in the presence of a private individual, the law enjoins upon him the duty of arresting the felon upon pain of fine and imprisonment, if the felon make his escape in consequence of his negligence,([9]) and in such a case the arrest is justified, whether there be time to obtain a

---

([1]) 1 Ch. Cr. L. 25; 2 Wills 158.
([2]) 1 Hale 587; 1 East P. C. 33; 1 Dick. J. P. 155.
([3]) Dalt. c. 1; Ch. Cr. L. 19; 1 Dick. J. P. 479.
([4]) 2 Camp. 367; 1 Dick. J. P. 155.
([5]) Holt C. N. P. 478; Caldecott's R. 219.
([6]) 2 Hale 92, 89, n. f.; Caldecott 291; 2 Hawk. c. 12, § 16; Holt C. N. P. 481.
([7]) 2 Hale 91; 1 Dea. Cr. L. 47; 3 Wend. 350.
([8]) 2 Hale 91; Barb. C. L. 473.
([9]) 2 Hawk. P. C. c. 12, § 1, c. 13, § 7, 8; 1 Ch. Cr. L. 16.

warrant or not.(¹) Although it is the duty of every citizen to aid an officer demanding his help in arresting a felon, yet it seems that he is not bound himself to arrest any person for felony unless the offence be committed in his presence, but it permits private persons to arrest in other cases, as upon an indictment found for felony against a party, a private person may arrest the offender.(²) So he may arrest without warrant upon probable suspicion, *if a felony has actually been committed by some one*, whom he suspects to be guilty.(³) But before he makes the arrest in such case, he must be sure that a felony has been actually committed, and if it then can be proved that there was a reasonable and probable ground for suspicion (against the party arrested,) he will not be liable to an action though it should be afterwards proved that the party charged was innocent.(⁴) But the better course is for a private individual to obtain a warrant in all cases unless the offence be committed in his presence, or unless he is otherwise certain that a felony has been committed by the person arrested, and there is not time before the offender escapes.

A private person will not be justified in breaking doors without a warrant unless the offence was committed in his presence.(⁵) In such a case the offender and offence are certainly known, and to justify him in breaking doors without a warrant, there must not only be a felony committed, but the party arrested must be found guilty; for if he be innocent, although suspected upon reasonable grounds, the breaking will not be justifiable.(⁶) No private person of his own authority can apprehend another for a breach of the peace after it is over, for as an officer cannot justify such an arrest without a warrant, *a fortiori*, it cannot be done by a private person.(⁷) It is every man's duty to interfere for the preservation of the peace or to prevent crime; for this purpose he may lay hold of any individual whom he shall see on the point of committing a felony or of doing an act which will manifestly endanger the life of another; and upon the same principle of *preventing crime*, he may lawfully lay hold of a lunatic who is about to commit mischief, which if committed by a sane person would constitute a criminal offence;(⁸) and thus upon the same principle he may break into a party's house and imprison

---

(¹) 3 Wend. 350; 11 John. 486.
(²) Dalt. c. 170; 1 Hawk. c. 28, § 12; 1 East P. C. 301.
(³) 1 Ch. Cr. L. 15, 16; 1 Cald. R. 291; Doug. 359; 1 Hale 588-9.
(⁴) 4 Taunt. 34; 5 Price 535.
(⁵) 1 Ch. Cr. L. 17, 18; 2 Hale 79, 82, 83.
(⁶) 1 Hale 82; 1 Ch. Cr. L. 54; 1 Deac. 157.
(⁷) 2 Hawk. c. 12, § 21; 1 East P. C. 300.
(⁸) Foster 310; 1 Ch. Cr. L. 18; 2 Hawk. c. 12, § 19; 1 Ry. & Mood. C. C. 93.

him to prevent him from murdering another.(¹) When a private person has apprehended another for felony, he may deliver him to a Constable or take him to jail,(²) but the better course seems to be, to take him, as soon as circumstances will permit, before a Magistrate, to be examined, bailed or committed to prison. And when a private person has apprehended another in the heat of an affray, he may lawfully detain him until the heat is over and then deliver him to a Constable.(³)

As to breaking doors to make an arrest. The law never allows of extremities but in cases of necessity, and it must therefore be remembered, that in every case where doors may be broken open in order to arrest a party, whether in cases criminal or civil, there must be a notification to those within, by the officer or other person making the arrest, of the cause of the coming, and a demand of admittance, and a refusal of such demand, before he can proceed to that extremity,(⁴) and if the Constable have no warrant, a notification of his authority is the more necessary.(⁵) Where *one is certainly known* to have committed treason or felony, or to have given a dangerous wound, and he is pursued by a Constable or private person, either with or without a warrant, doors may be broken open for his arrest, upon proper demand for admittance and its refusal.(⁶)

As to the right of a Constable to break open doors upon a suspicion of felony without warrant, there is a difference of opinion among the writers on Criminal Law. In Lord Hale's Pleas of the Crown, it is held, that where a charge of felony was laid before a Constable, and there was reasonable ground of suspicion, the Constable was justified in breaking open doors, and was punishable for omitting to arrest a party under *such* circumstances.(⁷) Whether the Constable be punishable or not in such case, depends upon the correctness of the position taken by Lord Hale. The law as laid down by him is in direct conflict with other authorities of equal weight. Sir Michael Foster, (who was never favourable to the escape of felons,) in his Treatise on Crown Law, says, " that bare suspicion touching the guilt of the party will not warrant a proceeding to this extremity, though a felony has been actually committed, unless the officer cometh armed with a warrant

---

(¹) 2 Bos. & Pul. 260 ; 1 Ch. Cr. L. 18, 19 ; Selw. 830.
(²) 1 Ch. Cr. L. 20.
(³) 1 Ch. Cr. L. 20 ; 1 Hale 589 ; 2 Hawk. c. 13, § 7 ; Id. c. 16, § 3.
(⁴) Foster 320 ; 1 Russ. 519 ; 2 Hawk. c. 14, § 1 ; 2 Hale 459 ; 1 Dick. J. P. 157.
(⁵) 1 Hale 460 ; Foster 310.
(⁶) 2 Hawk. c. 14, § 7 ; 1 Hale 459 ; Foster 320 ; 1 Ch. Cr. L. 51 ; 14 East 157-8.
(⁷) 1 Hale 583 ; 2 Hale 92.

from a Magistrate grounded on such suspicion."(¹) The law thus stated by Foster is quoted with approbation, and made a part of the text, by the most approved writers on Criminal Law.(²) But Mr. East, after quoting the above passage from Foster, adds, " it will be at least at the peril of proving that the party so taken on suspicion was guilty,"—thereby putting the Constable upon no higher grounds in this particular than a private person, who, as we have already seen, may break open doors when he *certainly knows*, and can *prove* that a felony has been committed, and that the party arrested *is guilty*. In such case, doubtless, the Constable may also justify his proceedings, because in either the party is not acting on mere suspicion, either as to the commission of the felony, or the person committing it, but upon certain knowledge as to both. This qualification still leaves unreconciled this conflict of authority, and we venture to express our concurrence in the rule laid down by Mr. Foster, (which is more in accordance with the Bill of Rights and genius of our government,) and advise that a Constable ought not without a warrant, *upon mere suspicion*, to break open doors to make an arrest. It is certain that he may do it upon the positive information of one who was actually a witness of the felony.(³) A private person without a warrant may break doors and enter the house of another to prevent him from murdering another who is within and cries out for assistance.(⁴)

As to breaking doors under a warrant. It is now clear that in all cases under a warrant for treason, felony, suspicion or actual breach of the peace, or to search for stolen goods, doors may be broken open after notification of the business, demand of entrance and refusal, if the offender cannot otherwise be taken,(⁵) and in these cases the warrant is a complete justification to the person to whom it is directed, acting in good faith *under it*, even though the party accused shall prove his innocence.(⁶)

A writer on Criminal Law, whose work is often cited, after stating that on a warrant for treason, felony or breach of the peace, the doors of the party accused may be broken open, if admittance cannot otherwise be obtained, adds, " but there seems no well founded authority for extending this right to misde-

---

(¹) Foster 321.
(²) 2 Hawk. c. 14, § 7; 1 East P. C. 322; 1 Deac. C. C. 50; Ros. Cr. Ev. 628; 1 Russ. 520; 1 Ch. Cr. L. 51, 53.
(³) 1 Hale 589; 2 Hale 92; 1 Ch. Cr. L. 53.
(⁴) 1 Burn J. P. 321; 2 Bos. & Pul. 260; 1 Ch. Cr. L. 51.
(⁵) 1 Hale 583; 2 Hawk. c. 14, § 7; 2 Hale 117; Foster 130; 1 East P. C. 322; 1 Dick. J. P. 157; 1 Dea. Cr. L. 50; 1 Ch. Cr. L. 54; 1 Russ. 517.
(⁶) 2 Hawk. c. 13, § 11; 1 Ch. Cr. L. 54.

meanors unaccompanied by violence."(¹) With deference, we dissent from this *dictum*, for it is no more, as it is not sustained by the authority quoted. Indeed, on the next page of his work, the author himself cites cases in conflict with his position; for instance, in the case of a contempt of court, or of either House of Parliament, he says, this proceeding may be had under a warrant from the Speaker, and cites for authority a case from 14 East.(²) Now there is no authority which decides that a warrant from the Speaker of either House of Parliament or an attachment issued by a court of record for a contempt, has any extraordinary quality in this respect more than a warrant of arrest issued by a Magistrate. All are alike founded upon a public injury, and the author himself says, " it seems that whenever a *crime* is of a public nature, this may be permitted; that is, doors may be broken open, and cites the same authority.(³) When he here uses the word crime, it is obvious that he includes misdemeanors; for it is used in reference to a contempt of court, which is a misdemeanor, and as such, a crime, but of lower degree than felony. Then, upon *his* authority, the criterion is not the *violence* with which an act is done, but its nature; that is, *if it be of a public nature*. This is just what we believe the law to be; and as a misdemeanor is an offence of a public nature, whether the commission of it be accompanied by violence or not, we maintain that in cases of misdemeanor unaccompanied by violence, doors may be broken open to arrest the offender if he cannot otherwise be taken; and not to mention others, the following cases fully sustain the position. In general, an officer upon *any warrant* from a Justice for a breach of the peace or good behaviour, may by force break open a man's house to arrest the offender.(⁴) So where an injury has been committed by an insult to any of the courts of justice on which *process of contempt is issued*, the officer charged with the execution of such process may in like manner break open doors if necessary in order to execute it.(⁵) So doors may be broken open if necessary upon a *capias pro fine*,(⁶) or on a warrant of a Justice of the Peace for levying a penalty on a conviction founded upon a statute which gives the whole or any part of the penalty to the Commonwealth.(⁷) These authorities and others that might be cited, are in direct conflict with this *dictum*. Most of them are cited by the author as law,

---

(¹) 1 Ch. Cr. L. 54.
(²) 14 East 157, 162; 5 Dow 165; 4 Taunt. 410.
(³) 14 East 116; 1 Ch. Cr. L. 154.
(⁴) 1 Dalt. c. 169; 1 Burn J. P. 221, Lond. edi. 1825; 2 Hawk. c. 14, § 3.
(⁵) 14 East 157; 1 Dea. Cr. L. 51; Cro. Eliz. 909; 1 Rol. Rep. 336.
(⁶) 1 Hale 458-9; 2 Hawk. c. 14, § 4; 1 Dea. Cr. L. 51.
(⁷) 2 Hale 95; 2 Hawk. c. 14, § 5; Dea. Cr. L. 51.

and therefore have his sanction.(¹) There are many misdemeanors, unaccompanied by violence, of a much more atrocious character than others accompanied with violence. An attempt merely to commit a felony, though it should not succeed, is a misdemeanor. If one administer poison with intent to kill, or were to dig a pit-fall in, or set a spring-gun in or near a public highway, with intent to kill a passenger, or if he were to put a keg of powder under the bed of another, and set fire to a slow taper inserted in it, some hours before the occupant retired to bed, so as to kill him by explosion at a late hour of the night,* these, though not successful attempts to murder, are all misdemeanors at Common Law unaccompanied by violence; so is a bare conspiracy to commit murder, although no overt act be done, and yet it can hardly be presumed that the offender would be protected from arrest in such cases by flying within doors, when doors might be broken open in a simple assault and battery, where necessarily there is violence, or in the case just cited upon a warrant for a penalty. The Constable cannot look behind the warrant to ascertain whether the offence charged was committed with violence or not. If the law conferred upon him such authority, it would place him in this respect above the Justice. We have thus noticed this *dictum*, because it is found in a work of very general use and accuracy, and is therefore calculated to throw doubt upon an important branch of a Constable's duty where none should exist. There is no adjudicated authority for it and it ought to be disregarded in practice.

The question as to the power of breaking open doors is confined even in civil cases to outward doors and windows, such as are intended for the security of the house against persons from without, endeavouring to break in. For if the officer find the outward door open, or if it be opened to him from within and he enter that way, he may then break open any inner door if he find that to be necessary to execute the process.(²)

This privilege of a man's castle from an outward breach extends only to those cases where the occupier or some of his family who have their domicil or ordinary residence there, are the objects of the arrest; for if a stranger whose ordinary residence is elsewhere, upon being pursued, take refuge in the house of another, such house is no castle of his, and there-

---

(¹) 1 Ch. Cr. L. 54.
(²) 1 Hale 458; 1 East P. C. 323; Cowp. 1; Leach R. 106, 121.

* This, though put as a supposed case, came under the author's observation. The Commonwealth *v*. Green, before Brockenbrough, Judge, in Henrico superior court. The defendant was convicted and sentenced to two years imprisonment.

fore he cannot claim the benefit of sanctuary.(¹) It must be observed, however, that in all cases where the doors of strangers are broken open upon the supposition of the person sought being there, it must be at the peril of finding him there, unless as it seems where the party acts under a warrant from a Magistrate.(²) And the privilege is also confined to arrests in the first instance; for if a man who is legally arrested escape from the officer and take shelter in the house of another, or even in his own house, the officer may upon fresh suit, break open the door in order to retake him; having given due notice of his business and demanded admittance, and having been refused.(³) If it be not, however, upon fresh pursuit, it seems that the officer should have a warrant from a Magistrate. The officer will not be authorized to break open doors in order to retake a prisoner in any case where the first arrest was illegal.(⁴)

It is to be remembered that all the privileges attendant on private dwellings relate to arrests before indictment; and there is no question whatever that after indictment found, a criminal of any degree may be arrested in any place, and no house is a sanctuary to him.(⁵) In giving notice of the business and authority of the officer, and in demanding admittance into the house before he proceeds to break open doors, no precise form of words is required to be used. It is sufficient if the party be informed that the officer does not come as a mere trespasser, but claims admittance under proper authority, provided the officer in fact had a legal warrant. And where the Magistrate has power to issue the warrant, its legality will never depend upon the truth of the information upon which it was granted.(⁶)

IV. *Examination.*

It has been well remarked by an eminent Justice, "that the duty of examination imposes one of the most arduous of those which a Justice of the Peace has to fulfil, as well as one of the most important to the interest of society." Besides a competent knowledge of the Criminal Code and the law of evidence, it requires great firmness, discrimination and dispassionate investigation.

(¹) Foster 320; 1 Russ. 522.
(²) 1 East P. C. 324; Foster 321; 2 Hale 103; 1 Russ. 522.
(³) Foster 320; 1 St. Tr. 9; 1 Russ. 522.
(⁴) 1 Russ. 522; 1 East P. C. 324; Foster 326.
(⁵) 1 Ch. Cr. L. 58; 11 Coke 121; Inst. 131; 2 Hawk. c. 13, § 3; Dick. J. P. Arrest III.; Burn J. P. Arrest IV.
(⁶) Foster 136-7; 2 Hawk. c. 14, § 1, n. 1; D. Davis J. P. 50.

When an officer has made an arrest, he is within a reasonable time thereafter to bring the party before a Justice, according to the requisitions of the warrant, when it becomes his duty as soon as may be, to examine the complainant and the witnesses to support the prosecution, on oath in the presence of the party charged, touching any matter connected with it, and to discharge him or commit him for farther trial;([1]) but he is allowed a reasonable time for this purpose before he makes his final decision.([2]) It may happen that the examination cannot be immediately proceeded in, in consequence of the non-attendance of material witnesses, or from some other cause. In such case the Justice may commit the prisoner and adjourn the examination until the cause for the delay is removed, provided it be within a reasonable time.([3]) What this reasonable time is, must depend upon the circumstances of each particular case; and as a general rule, he ought not to be restricted to any particular time.([4]) The evidence may not always be at hand, and then a reasonable time ought to be allowed to obtain it. Fifteen days, however, has been held unreasonable, unless there are circumstances to account for it.([5])

During the examination, the Justice may from time to time verbally remand the prisoner into custody;([6]) but if he is detained for examination until another day, the statute requires that it must be by an order under the hand of the Justice, stating concisely that he is committed for farther examination on a future day, to be named in the order, and on the day appointed he may be brought before the Justice by a verbal order to the same officer to whom he was committed, or by an order in writing to a different person. During the examination the prisoner cannot without his consent be committed for more than ten days at any one time, and the case may be adjourned to the same or any other place in the county, and the prisoner (if not charged with felony,) bailed by the Justice from time to time to appear before him at such place for farther examination.([7]) It may be that the examination is held at a distance from the jail, and in that event the prisoner, during the *necessary time for his examination*, may be detained in the custody of the officer or committed to some near and safe place until the examination can be taken;([8]) but when it is at all convenient, it is proper, if the examination cannot be closed in a day, to commit the prisoner to jail by a

---

([1]) 2 Hale 120, and the statute, § 13.
([2]) 1 Ch. Cr. L. 72.
([3]) Id.
([4]) 1 Ch. Cr. L. 73.
([5]) 4 Carr. & Payne 134; 1 Ch. Cr. L. 73.
([6]) 1 Hale 585; 2 Hale 120; Dick. J. P. Examination III.
([7]) Sec. 8, *ante*, p. 48.
([8]) 2 Hale 120.

written warrant. As incident to the power to examine into the nature and circumstances of a criminal charge, the Justice has also the power to compel the attendance of witnesses to testify as well on behalf of the prisoner as of the Commonwealth.(¹)

When the party accused and the witnesses are brought before the Justice, he is to proceed in the presence of the accused, first to examine the complainant and witnesses on behalf of the Commonwealth on oath, and then to examine on oath likewise, the witnesses adduced on the part of the prisoner, who by our statute, is allowed the assistance of counsel to examine the witnesses. When this is done, he is finally to decide whether the prisoner shall be discharged or committed for farther trial. And in the language of the statute, which embodies the Common Law rule upon the subject, if it shall appear to the Magistrate upon the whole examination that no offence has been committed, or that there is not probable cause for charging the prisoner with the offence, he shall be discharged. Let it be here specially remembered by the Justice, that he is not now passing upon the guilt of the accused, but only enquiring whether the offence charged against him has been committed, and whether there is *probable* cause to believe him guilty. Upon the question, what is probable cause, it is impossible to lay down for the government of the Magistrate any precise and invariable rule; but in this Commonwealth, where no one can be committed for more than thirty days without the supervision of at least five Justices, he should commit, (especially in cases of felony,) where there is any real doubt as to the prisoner's innocence. He must act, however, in all cases according to the conscientious dictates of his own judgment; and if he does this with due regard to the responsibility of his station and a proper sense of his oath of office, he has nothing to fear. He may be called upon to sever by his commitment the tenderest ties, but whenever public justice demands it, public duty should be performed firmly, without fear, favour or affection.

If the prisoner be not discharged, he is to be committed or bailed, either for examination or trial before the county or corporation court. Under the statute, as at Common Law, the Justice who examines the prisoner has the power to commit as incident to his office.(²) This is done by a warrant, technically called a mittimus, and in observing its nature and requisites, the Justice has an important duty to perform.

(¹) 1 Ch. Cr. L. 76; Burn J. P. Examination; Dick. J. P. Id.; Roscoe Cr. Ev. 87; 12 Wend. 344.

(²) 1 Ld. Ray. 66; 2 Hawk. c. 16, § 6; and see the opinion of Chief Justice Marshall in Burr's Case.

As we are rather the compiler of a Justice's manual than the author of a treatise on the practice of the Criminal Law, we should exceed the bounds of propriety were we to enter into a consideration of the legal reasons upon which the requisites of a mittimus are founded. It is sufficient for the practical purposes of a Justice, to know that they are legal requisites. For want of due attention to this branch of his duty, it has not unfrequently happened that offenders known to be guilty of felony have been discharged from custody on *habeas corpus*, and finally escaped punishment. To secure, therefore, the final trial of a prisoner, it is important in committing him, that the following requisites of a mittimus be observed : 1st. It must be in writing and under the hand of the Justice,(¹) and shew the time and place of making it.(²) 2d. It may be either in the name of the Commonwealth or in the name of the Justice awarding it, and then it should not only express the name of the Justice, but also his office and authority; in practice the latter is most usual.(³) 3d. The mittimus should point out the place of imprisonment, by being directed to the jailor or keeper of the proper prison, and not be generally to carry the party to prison.(⁴) The proper prison is that of the county, city or borough in which the offence was committed, and where the prisoner is to be tried. In practice it is usual to direct the mittimus to a Constable and to the keeper of the jail, commanding the Constable to convey the prisoner into the custody of the keeper of the jail, and the keeper of the jail to receive and keep him in jail until discharged by due course of law. This is the proper conclusion of a mittimus.(⁵) 4th. It should contain the name and the sirname of the party committed, if known; if unknown, then it should describe the person as exactly as may be, and add that he refuses to tell his name.(⁶) 5th. It is safe, though not absolutely necessary, to set forth that the party is charged upon oath.(⁷) 6th. Although the mittimus need not set forth the cause of commitment with the technical accuracy of an indictment, it is essentially necessary that it should contain the certainty of the cause of commitment; and, therefore, if it be for felony, it ought not to be for felony generally, but to contain the special nature of the felony; as, for felony for the death of J. F.; or, for burglary for breaking into the house

---

(¹) New Criminal Statute.
(²) 2 Hawk. c. 16, § 13; 2 Hale 122; 1 Dick. J. P. 116; 1 Deac. Cr. L. 258.
(³) 2 Hawk. c. 16, § 13; 1 Dick. J. P. 462; 1 Deac. Cr. L. 257, 261.
(⁴) 1 Ch. Cr. L. 109.
(⁵) 2 Hawk. c. 15, § 18; 2 Hale 123.
(⁶) 1 Hale 557; 1 Dick. J. P. 463; 1 Burn J. P. 667.
(⁷) 2 Hawk. c. 16, § 17; 1 Burn J. P. 677; 2 Va. Cases 504.

of J. F. ; or, for larceny in stealing the goods of J. F.(¹) And so in committing for a misdemeanor, the mittimus should state the cause of commitment as in felony.(²)

The proper form for a mittimus for each offence will be found under their respective heads.

V. *Letting to bail.*

Bail is the delivery of a man out of custody who is arrested upon any charge, upon the undertaking of one or more persons for him that he will appear at a day limited, to answer to the charge preferred against him, before some court having cognizance of the offence.(³) This undertaking is technically called a recognizance, and is entered into and acknowledged before a Justice of the Peace or other public functionary duly authorized to take it. See title RECOGNIZANCE.

At Common Law, bail was allowed in all cases except for homicide ;(⁴) but this right is now greatly abridged.

The statute upon this subject is doubtless founded upon the principle that in minor offences bail is equivalent to commitment, but that in the higher grades of crime no security is equal to the custody of the jailor, and therefore, in all capital cases, and cases punishable by confinement in the penitentiary, the power to bail is denied the Justice except in cases of light suspicion of guilt. His authority to admit to bail in such cases depends solely on the weight of evidence, and if more than a slight suspicion is made out, he should for no cause admit to bail. The power to do this for other causes, is not given to him, but confided to others.

It has been said that there is nothing that a man may not be induced to forfeit to save his life, and that it is no satisfaction or indemnity to the public to seize the effects of those who have bailed a murderer, if the murderer himself be allowed to escape with impunity. The improper exercise of the power to bail, has left warning instances in this Commonwealth of the truth of this remark. Upon this subject, Magistrates should act with great caution and firmness, and never be influenced by appeals to their sympathy, (such as are often made,) nor by the censure of others.

In admitting a party to bail, the Justice is to judge of the amount as well as the sufficiency of the bail. Both must necessarily be left to the sound discretion of the Magistrate,

---

(¹) 2 Hale 122 ; 1 Burn J. P. 677 ; 1 Dick. J. P. 463 ; 2 Hawk. c. 16, § 16 ; 2 T. R. 225 ; 1 Dea. Cr. L. 225 ; 3 Pet. R. 208 ; 3 Cranch R. 448.
(²) Young's Case, 1 Rob. Rep. 744.
(³) 2 Hawk. c. 15, § 2, 3 ; 2 Hale 127.
(⁴) 1 Burn J. P. 250 ; 1 Deac. Cr. Co. 100.

and if he should err, and the error be against the prisoner, he has his remedy by *habeas corpus.* Justices need to be admonished that bail means something more than a nominal undertaking, and although excessive bail ought not to be required, and to delay or obstruct it when a party is entitled to it, is a misdemeanor at Common Law, yet it is no less an offence in the Justice to take insufficient bail.(¹) The law demands the trial of every offender against its authority, and " it is manifest that unless proper caution is used by Magistrates upon the subject of requiring such sureties upon taking a recognizance of bail as will be of sufficient ability to respond the sums for which they became bound, the whole object of a public prosecution may be defeated, and the guilty escape and go unpunished." In England the rule is to require at least two responsible sureties in every case of felony,(²) and indeed, the practice in their highest Criminal Court now is to require four. [Rex *v.* Shaw, 6 Dow & Ry. 154.] This case is not referred to for the purpose of giving an invariable rule to the Virginia Justice, but forcibly to impress upon him the necessity of caution upon the subject, for " where the party charged is himself a responsible person *in point* of property, and one surety of unquestionable responsibility is offered, there can be no danger in common cases in accepting him," and not requiring " even" two sureties. But when one surety only is accepted, there ought to be no doubt whatever, of the sufficiency of his property to ensure the penalty of the recognizance.

As a general rule, personal estate is too fluctuating, and may be too easily kept from an officer to be relied on as sufficient, though there may be occasional exceptions to it. In every case the ability and condition in life of the prisoner, and the nature of the crime, should be taken into consideration in determining both the sufficiency of the surety and amount of the recognizance. The proper rule is to require such sureties residing within the State as are possessed, in their own right, of a clear real estate within the Commonwealth, to such amount, that if sold at public sale under an execution, it would certainly realize the full amount of the sum in which the surety is bound; and such sureties should be *severally* of sufficient ability and property to answer the sum in which they are bound. [See Dan'l Davis' J. P. from 96 to 98.]

It is said that the real estate should be within the county where the recognizance is taken. This is not necessary; and if the surety is otherwise sufficient, it ought not to be refused because the person tendered is not possessed of real estate

---

(¹) Hale Sum. 97 ; 2 Hawk. c. 15, § 16.   (²) 1 Burn J. P. 255.

within the county. Such a requisition might amount to a denial of bail in cases where it ought to be allowed. It is sufficient if the estate is unencumbered, and within the reach of process of execution, which extends to every county.

We have already seen that under the statute a Justice may bail a party not charged with felony, to appear before him from time to time during the examination. This power he had at Common Law.(¹)

Whenever a party is arrested for any crime below the degree of felony, he is entitled to bail as a matter of right,(²) except in the case of a dangerous wound given, from which a prosecution for felonious homicide is likely to arise. In that case, the Justice may, in his discretion, refuse bail, and commit the party for a year and a day. [See title AFFRAY.](³)

When a recognizance is taken for the appearance of a party before the Justice himself, the time and place of appearance should be specified with care, and he should punctually attend and have the party called. If the party answers, he is taken into custody, and the bail discharged; and if he fails to answer, his default should be entered on the back of the recognizance, which should then be deposited with the clerk of the county court. [For form, see No. 6, under head of RECOGNIZANCE.]

If a Justice, or any other person authorized to take bail, be in any case so far imposed on as to suffer a prisoner to be bailed by insufficient sureties, it is said that he may require the party to find better surety by entering into a new recognizance with them, and may commit him on his refusal. For, that insufficient sureties are no sureties, and to protect the Justice from such imposition, he may examine the sureties upon oath as to their sufficiency.(⁴) This, however, is only one of the means to which he may resort for that purpose, but he is not bound to receive the surety merely because he has justified. He may still refuse to receive him if he has good reason to believe the surety offered is insufficient.

The bail may, at Common Law as well as under the statute, retake the prisoner and surrender him to a Justice, who should commit him in discharge of the bail, or put him to find new sureties.(⁵)

What has been said upon this subject has more especial reference to admitting to bail by a Justice, and, important and responsible as the duty is, he can seldom err, (taking the sta-

---

(¹) See the statute, and the Commonwealth v. Ross, 6 Serg. & Raw. 427.
(²) See the statute, and Burn J. P. 256.
(³) 1 Burn J. P. 256.
(⁴) 2 Hawk. c. 15, § 4; 2 Hale 125.
(⁵) Hale Sum. 96; 2 Hawk. c. 15, § 23; 2 Hale P. C. 127; 1 Salk. 105; 1 Burn J. P. 250; 1 Ch. Cr. L. 104.

ARREST—(*Letting to Bail on.*)

tute as his sole guide,) and never subject himself to liability, in the firm and impartial discharge of it. Sheriffs also, in particular cases, may admit to bail.

By SEC. 21, CHAP. 207. A person arrested on a *capias* to answer or hear judgment on a presentment, indictment or information, for a misdemeanor other than such as is mentioned in the first section of chapter 198, or on an attachment other than an attachment to compel the performance of an order or decree in chancery, may be admitted to bail by the officer who arrests him; the said officer taking a recognizance in such sum, not being less than two hundred dollars, as he, regarding the case and the estate of the accused, may deem sufficient to secure his appearance before the court from which the process issued, at the time required thereby. The officer shall return the recognizance to said court, on or before the return day of such process. If he fail to make such return, he shall forfeit twenty dollars; and if he take insufficient bail, he shall be fined at the discretion of a jury.

The first section of chapter 198 has reference to exhibitors of faro and games of that character. See GAMING, for form of recognizance under that chapter. For other recognizances of bail under this section, see Nos. 9 and 10, under head of RECOGNIZANCE.

(No. 1.)

General Form of a Complaint to a Justice, of an offence committed.

——— County, to wit:

A. B. upon oath complains, that on the ——— day of ——— 18—, in the County of ———, C. D. did (here state substantially the subject of the charge, as for instance, in the case of larceny, "feloniously take, steal and carry away one silver watch of the value of twenty dollars, of the goods and chattels of the said A. B.,") and he the said A. B. therefore prays that the said C. D. may be apprehended and held to answer the said complaint, and dealt with in relation thereto as the law may require. Dated this ——— day of ——— 18—.

A. B.

——— County, to wit:

——— day of ——— 18—, the said A. B. made oath to the truth of the foregoing complaint before me.

J. T., J. P.

(No. 2.)

General Form of a Warrant of Arrest.

——— County, to wit:

To all or any one of the Constables of the said County:

Whereas, A. B., of the said County, has this day made complaint and information on oath before me J. T., a Justice of the said County, that C. D.

of the said County, on the —— day of ——— 18—, in said County, did (here describe the offence, the particular manner of doing which will be found in the forms under each separate offence:) These are, therefore, in the name of the Commonwealth of Virginia, to command you forthwith to apprehend and bring before me or some other Justice of the said County, the body of the said C. D., to answer the said complaint, and to be farther dealt with according to law. Given under my hand and seal, this —— day of ———— in the year 18—.

J. T., J. P. [L. S.]

(No. 3.)

Form of a Commitment for farther examination.

———— County, to wit:
   To the Keeper of the Jail of the said County:
   Receive into your jail and custody A. B., herewith sent you, he having been brought before me J. T., a Justice of the said County, charged on the oath of E. F., on suspicion of (here describe the offence succinctly,) and him safely keep in your jail and custody until the —— day of ——— 18—, when you are hereby required to bring him before me to be farther examined. Given under my hand and seal, this —— day of ——— 18—.

J. T., J. P. [L. S.]

(No. 4.)

General Form of Mittimus where a party is committed for examination or trial in the County Court for felony.

———— County, to wit:
   To X. Y., Constable of said County, and to the Keeper of the Jail of said County:
   These are to command you the said Constable, in the name of the Commonwealth of Virginia, forthwith to convey and deliver into the custody of the keeper of the said jail, together with this warrant, the body of C. D., charged before me. J. T., a Justice of the said County, on the oath of A. B., with a felony by him committed, in this, that the said C. D., on the —— day of ——— in the year 18—, in the said County, (here describe the offence as in the warrant of arrest;) and you the said keeper of the said jail, are hereby required to receive the said C. D. into your jail and custody, that he may be examined (or *tried*) for the said offence by the County Court of the said County, and him there safely keep until he shall be discharged by due course of law. Given under my hand and seal, this —— day of ——— 18—.

J. T., J. P. [L. S.]

[NOTE.—If the prisoner be a white person, or if he be a free negro charged with homicide of any grade, or with any offence punishable with death, he must be committed for examination. For all other felonies by free negroes, and in all cases of felony by slaves, the prisoner must be committed for trial.]

ARREST. 75

(No. 5.)

Form of a Certificate of Commitment for felony to be sent to the Clerk of the County Court.

———— County, to wit:
To the Clerk of the County Court of said County:

I, J. T., a Justice of the said County, do hereby certify, that I have this day committed C. D. (if free negro or slave, state which) to the jail of said County, that he may be examined (or *tried*) before the County Court of the said County for a felony by him committed, in this, that he did, on the ———- day of ———— 18—, in the said County, (here state the offence as in the mittimus.) Given under my hand, this —— day of ———— in the year 18—.

J. T., J. P.

(No. 6.)

Form of Certificate to the Clerk, where the party is admitted to bail in case of felony.

———— County, to wit:
To the Clerk of the County Court of said County:

I, J. T., a Justice of the said County, do hereby certify, that C. D. has this day been admitted to bail by me, with sureties for his appearance before the County Court of the said County on the first day of the next term thereof, that he may be examined (or *tried*) for a felony by him committed, in this, that he did, on the —— day of ———— in the year 18—, (here describe the offence as in the mittimus.) Given under my hand, this —— day of ———— 18—.

J. T., J. P.

(No. 7.)

Form of Recognizance of Bail.

Turn to head of RECOGNIZANCE, and follow No. 1, if person be free; No. 2, if a slave, and state succinctly the offence for which the person is recognized.

(No. 8.)

Form of Recognizance of Witness to appear before the County Court to give evidence upon the examination or trial of a party charged with felony.

Turn to head of RECOGNIZANCE, and follow No. 3.

ARREST.

(No. 9.)

Form of Mittimus to answer an Indictment for a misdemeanor in the County Court.

―――― County, to wit:

To X. Z., Constable of said County, and to the Keeper of the Jail of said County:

These are to command you the said Constable, in the name of the Commonwealth of Virginia, forthwith to convey and deliver into the custody of the keeper of the said jail, together with this warrant, the body of C. D., charged before me J. T., a Justice of the said County, on the oath of A. B., with a misdemeanor by him committed, in this, that he did, on the ―― day of ―――― in the year 18―, in the said County (here describe the offence as in the warrant of arrest.) And you the keeper of the said jail are hereby required to receive the said C. D. into your jail and custody, and him there safely keep, until he shall be discharged by due course of law. Given under my hand and seal, this ―― day of ―――― in the year 18―.

J. T., J. P. [L. S.]

(No. 10.)

Form of a Certificate of Commitment for a misdemeanor, to be sent to the Clerk of the County Court.

―――― County, to wit:

To the Clerk of the County Court of the said County:

I, J. T., a Justice of the said County, do hereby certify, that I have this day committed C. D. to the jail of this County, that he may be indicted in the County Court of the said County for a misdemeanor by him committed, in this, that he did, on the ―― day of ―――― 18―, in the said County, (here state the offence as in the mittimus.) Given under my hand, this ―― day of ―――― in the year 18―.

J. T., J. P.

(No. 11.)

Form of a Certificate to the Clerk of the County Court, where the party is bailed to answer for a misdemeanor.

―――― County, to wit:

To the Clerk of the County Court of said County:

I, J. T., a Justice of the said County, do hereby certify, that I have this day admitted C. D. to bail for his appearance before the County Court of the said County on the first day of the ――* term thereof, to answer an indictment in the said Court, for a misdemeanor by him committed, in this, that he did, on the ―― day of ―――― 18―, in the said County, (here describe the offence as in the warrant of arrest.) Given under my hand, this ―― day of ―――― 18―.

J. T., J. P.

---

* The term at which the Grand Jury is convened.

(No. 12.)

Form of Recognizance of Bail to answer an indictment for a misdemeanor.

Turn to head of RECOGNIZANCE, and follow No. 4, and state succinctly the offence for which the person is recognized.

(No. 13.)

Form of Recognizance of Witness to appear before the County Court to give evidence upon an indictment for a misdemeanor.

Turn to head of RECOGNIZANCE, and follow No. 5.

(No. 14.)

Form of a Warrant to transfer a prisoner, who has committed an offence in one County and is arrested in another, to the County in which the offence was committed.

———— County, to wit:

To the Sheriff of the said County:

Whereas C. D. has been arrested and brought before me J. T., a Justice of the said County, charged with having on the —— day of ———— 18—, in the County of ————, feloniously (here describe the offence for which the party is arrested as in the warrant.) Now, that the said C. D. may be conveyed to the said County of ————, where the said offence was committed, these are therefore to command you, in the name of the Commonwealth of Virginia, forthwith to convey the said C. D. to the said County of ————, and there carry him before some Justice of the said County, to be there dealt with according to law. Given under my hand and seal, this —— day of ———— 18—.

J. T., *J. P.* [L. S.]

[NOTE.—If the offence be a misdemeanor and the prisoner fails to give bail, this form of a transfer warrant will answer, by leaving out the word "feloniously" and inserting in lieu the word "unlawfully." If the prisoner offers bail for his appearance, follow form No. 4, under the head of RECOGNIZANCE.]

(No. 15.)

Form of Mittimus where a party is surrendered out of Court by his bail.

———— County, to wit:

To A. B., Constable of said County, and to the Keeper of the Jail of said County:

Forasmuch as C. D., who stands bound by recognizance as the bail of E. F., for his appearance before the (here insert the Court before whom the prisoner is to appear,) on the first day of the next term thereof, to answer the Commonwealth for a felony, in feloniously (here state the offence succinctly, as thus, "stealing the goods of G. H.,") has this day taken the body of said E. F., and surrendered him before me J. T., a Justice of the said County, in discharge of his said recognizance: These are therefore to command you the said Constable safely to convey and deliver, together with this precept, the said E. F. into the custody of the keeper of the said jail. And you the keeper of the said jail are hereby required to receive the said E. F. into your custody, and him safely keep, until he shall be discharged by due course of law. Given under my hand and seal, this —— day of —— 18—.

J. T., J. P. [L. S.]

[It is the right of the party to give fresh bail, and for the form of the recognizance in such a case, see No. 11 under head of RECOGNIZANCE.]

(No. 16.)

Form of a Recognizance to answer for a misdemeanor committed in one County, where the party is arrested in another.

—— County, to wit:

Be it remembered, that on this —— day of —— 18—, A. B. and C. D. of the said County, personally came before me J. T., a Justice in and for the said County, and each acknowledged himself to be indebted to the Commonwealth of Virginia in the manner and form following, to wit: The said A. B., in the sum of —— dollars, and the said C. D., in the sum of —— dollars, to be respectively made and levied of their several goods and chattels, lands and tenements, to the use of the Commonwealth of Virginia, if the said A. B. shall make default in the performance of the underwritten condition.

The condition of the above recognizance is such, that whereas the above named A. B. has been this day arrested and brought before me J. T., a Justice of the said County, by virtue of a warrant issued by J. M., a Justice of the County of ——, charged with having on the —— day of —— 18—, in the County of ——, unlawfully (here describe substantially the offence with which the prisoner is charged.) Now if the above bound A. B. shall personally appear in the County Court of ——, (the County where the offence was committed,) on the first day of the next —— term thereof, then and there to answer the Commonwealth touching the said offence, and shall not thence depart without leave of the said Court, then the above recognizance to be void, otherwise to remain in full force and virtue.

Taken and acknowledged before me, this —— day of —— 18—.

J. T., J. P.

(No. 17.)

Form of backing a Warrant to be executed in a County different from that in which it issued.

—— County, to wit:

Being satisfied by the oath of C. D., of the genuineness of the within warrant, I do hereby endorse the same and authorize its execution within this County.

J. T., J. P. of said County.
—— day of —— 18—.

ARREST. 79

(No. 18.)

Form of a Warrant to detain a prisoner, already in custody for another offence.

—— County, to wit:
   To the Keeper of the Jail of the said County:
   You are hereby commanded to detain in your custody in the said jail, the body of C. D., now in your custody there, he being farther charged before me J. T., a Justice of the said County, upon the oath of E. F., with a felony by him committed, in this, that he did, on the —— day of —— 18—, in said County, (here state succinctly the offence as stated in the complaint.) Him, therefore, safely keep in your jail and custody for this cause, until he shall be thence discharged by due course of law. Given under my hand and seal, this —— day of —— 18—.

   J. T., *J. P.* [L. S.]

(No. 19.)

Form of a Warrant to discharge a prisoner from custody who has given bail.

—— County, to wit:
   To the Keeper of the Jail of the said County:
   A. B., now a prisoner in your jail, by virtue of a warrant of commitment signed by me, (or *by F. W. a Justice of said County,*) dated on the —— day of —— 18—, for (here describe the offence briefly as in the warrant of commitment,) having given bail before me to appear and answer for said offence, at the (state the Court in which he is to appear and answer :) You are hereby required forthwith to discharge the said A. B. from your custody in said jail, unless he be detained therein by you for some other cause. Given under my hand and seal, this —— day of —— 18—.

   J. T., *J. P.* [L. S.]

(No. 20.)

General Form of Summons, where the offence can only be punished by fine of twenty dollars or under.

—— County, to wit:
   To X. Y., Constable of the said County:
   Whereas, A. B. has this day made information and complaint on oath to me J. T., a Justice of the said County, that C. D., on the —— day of —— 18—, in the said County, did (here describe the offence, the manner of doing which will be found in most cases under each separate offence noticed in the body of this work. When this is not the case, describe the offence by following the words of the statute as near as may be:) These are, therefore, in the name of the Commonwealth, to command you forthwith to summon the said C. D. to appear before me or such other Justice of the said County, as shall then be present, at ——, in the said County, on the —— day of —— 18—, at the hour of ——, in the —— noon of that day, to answer the said complaint, and to be farther dealt with according to law. And you are moreover required to summon E. F. and G. H. to ap-

pear at the same time and place, to testify as witnesses on behalf of the Commonwealth, touching the matter of the said complaint. And be you then and there to testify what you shall have done in the premises. Given under my hand and seal, this —— day of ——— 18—.

J. T., J. P. [L. S.]

[If the summons be returned executed, and the party do not appear to sustain the complaint, upon being called, the Justice may proceed to force his appearance, by warrant, as without appearance he cannot be committed or recognized to answer for the offence. But this is not the case in prosecutions for fines of twenty dollars and under, and which are within the jurisdiction of the Justice to try, for in all such cases upon the return of the summons executed, he may proceed to trial in the absence of the defendant. See FINES and SUMMARY CONVICTIONS.]

(No. 21.)

Form of a Warrant of Arrest, where a party fails to appear and answer a summons.

——— County, to wit:
  To X. Y., *Constable of the said County*:
  Whereas, A. B. did, on the —— day of ——— 18—, make complaint upon oath before me J. T., a Justice of the said County, that C. D., on the —— day of ——— 18—, in the said County, did (here set out the offence as in the summons;) whereupon I the said J. T., on the —— day of ——— 18—, (the date of the summons,) did issue my warrant, directed to X. Y., Constable of the said County, whereby he was, in the name of the Commonwealth, commanded to summon the said C. D. to appear before me or some other Justice of the said County, at ——— in the said County, on the —— day of ——— 18—, at the hour of twelve o'clock, to answer the complaint aforesaid: And whereas, the said summons was duly executed upon the said C. D., and whereas the said C. D. was, on the day and hour last aforesaid, at ———, in the said County, solemnly called to answer the said summons and complaint, but failed to appear and came not: These are, therefore, to command you, in the name of the Commonwealth, forthwith to apprehend the said C. D., and bring him before me or some other Justice of the said County, to answer the said complaint, and to be farther dealt with according to law. Given under my hand and seal, this —— day of ——— 18—.

J. T., J. P. [L. S.]

[In regard to the arrest of persons charged with crimes against the United States, "the offender may, by any Justice or Judge of the United States, *or by any Justice of the Peace*, or other Magistrate of any of the United States, where he may be found, agreeably to the usual mode of process against offenders *in such State*, and at the expense of the United States, be arrested and imprisoned or bailed, as the case may be, for trial before such Court of the United States, as, by this act, has cognizance of the offence. And copies of the process shall be returned as speedily as may be, into the Clerk's office of such Court, together with the recognizances of the witnesses for their appearance to testify in the case; which recognizances the Magistrate before whom the examination shall be, may require, on pain of imprisonment."—*Act of* 1789, § 33; 1 *Story's L. U. S., p.* 66.]

ARREST—(*For Offences against the U. S.*)

(No. 22.)

Form of a Warrant of Arrest for an offence against the United States.

UNITED STATES OF AMERICA:
Eastern (or Western) *District of Virginia.*

—— County, to wit:

Whereas, information upon oath has been laid before me J. T., one of the Justices of the Commonwealth of Virginia, in and for the said County, by A. B., that C. D., on the —— day of —— in the year ——, in the County and District aforesaid, did, &c. (here state the offence charged in the information, and according to the description given of it in the act of Congress prohibiting the offence, the criminal jurisdiction of the United States being confined to offences created by the act of Congress.) You are, therefore, hereby required forthwith to apprehend and bring before me, or some other Justice in and for the said County, the said C. D., to answer the said charge, and to be dealt with according to the laws of the United States. Given under my hand and seal, this —— day of —— in the year 18—.

J. T., J. P. [L. S.]

To X. Y. *or any other Constable of said County.*

(No. 23.)

Form of a Warrant of Commitment or Mittimus, for an offence against the United States.

UNITED STATES OF AMERICA:
Eastern (or Western) *District of Virginia.*

—— County, to wit:

Whereas, C. D. has been brought before me J. T., a Justice of the Commonwealth of Virginia, in and for the said County, charged upon the oath of A. B. with having (here describe the offence as in the warrant:) I do hereby command you X. Y., Constable of said County, (or the officer or person to whom the *mittimus* is directed,) forthwith to convey the said C. D. to the jail of the said County, and to deliver him to the keeper thereof, together with this precept; and I do also hereby command you the said keeper, to receive the said C. D. into your custody in the said jail, and him safely keep, until he shall be discharged by the due course *of the laws of the United States.* Given under my hand and seal, this —— day of —— in the year 18—.

J. T., J. P. [L. S.]

To X. Y., *Constable of* —— *County, and to the Keeper of the Jail of said County.*

ARSON—See BURNING.

CHAPTER IX.

ASSAULT.

[For assault by a slave or free negro on white person, with intent to kill, rob or to commit rape, see NEGROES.]

I. *Assault.*

An assault is an attempt or an offer to do a personal hurt or violence to another; as, by striking at another with a stick or other weapon, or without a weapon, though the party striking misses his aim: So, drawing a sword or holding up the fist in a menacing manner, or presenting a loaded gun at a person, who is within the distance to which the gun will carry, or any other similar act, accompanied with such circumstances as denote at the time an intention, coupled with a present ability of using actual violence against the person of another, will amount to an assault,[1] although no actual hurt be done; for, an assault does not in law, as in common parlance, necessarily imply a blow. The very attempt or offer, with force and violence, to do a corporal hurt to another, is an assault; but no mere words whatsoever can amount to an assault.[2] Nevertheless, words may aggravate an assault or explain the meaning of equivocal acts of threatening; and, in the language of Dalton, "menacing begins the breach of the peace, assault increases it, and battery accomplishes it."[3] Assaults on highways near populous cities are so common, that it may be proper to notice particularly the case of The People *v.* Lee.[4] The prosecutor was driving his wagon into town and was overtaken by the defendant in a cart. The defendant attempted to run the cart against the prosecutor, who was obliged to stop his wagon in order to prevent being run over, and the cart of the defendant passed before him. The defendant crossed the road several times and came near breaking the wagon. The court were of opinion that the conduct of the defendant in attempting to run against the wagon of the prosecutor was clearly an assault, and that the improper conduct of cartmen and others to travellers upon the road, had demanded and would receive the discountenance of the court. The case was submitted to the jury and they found the defendant guilty.

---

[1] 1 Hawk. P. C. c. 62, § 1; 1 Russ. C. & M. 604.
[2] 1 Russ. C. & M. 604; 1 Dick. J. P. 329.
[3] Dalton c. 121.
[4] 1 Wheel. Cr. Cases 364.

II. Battery.

A battery is *more* than an *attempt* to do a corporal hurt to another,([1]) and in the legal acceptation of the word, includes beating and wounding ;([2]) but any injury done to the person of another in an angry or revengeful, or rude or insolent manner, be it ever so small or trifling, is in làw a *battery*. As, for instance, thrusting him or pushing him in anger ; holding him by the arm ; spitting in his face ; jostling him out of the way ; pushing another against him ; striking a horse upon which he is riding, whereby he is thrown ;—all these, or any other touching the person of another in anger, will constitute an assault and battery : for, the law draws no line between different degrees of violence, but totally prohibits the first and lowest degree of it, and holds that the person of every man is sacred, and that no other has a right to meddle with it in the slightest manner.([3])

The injury need not be effected directly by the hand of the party ; thus, there may be an assault and battery by encouraging a dog to bite, or by riding over a person with a horse, or wilfully and violently driving a cart against the carriage of another and thereby causing bodily hurt to the person travelling in it.([4]) Nor is it necessary that the injury should be *immediate*, as in the case of a lighted squib thrown into a market house, where it was tossed about from one person to another, until it put out the eyes of one of them, it was held an assault by the party who threw it into the market ; and so, there may be an assault by exposing causelessly a child or other person whom a man is bound to protect, (for example, an apprentice.)([5])

If a master take an indecent liberty with the person of a female scholar, without her consent, he is liable to be punished for an assault, though she did not resist ;([6]) and making a female patient strip naked, under pretence that the prisoner, a medical practitioner, could not otherwise judge of her illness, if he assist in taking off her clothes, is an assault.([7])

An unlawful imprisonment is also an assault ; for it is a wrong done to the person of a man, for which the law demands public vengeance, as it is a breach of the peace, a loss which the State sustains by the confinement of one of its members and an infringement of the good order of society.([8])

([1]) 1 Russ. C. & M. 604.
([2]) Arch. Cr. Pl. 346.
([3]) 1 Russ. C. & M. 604-5 ; Arch. Cr. Pl. 346, and the authorities there referred to ; 1 Hawk. c. 62, § 2.
([4]) 1 Russ. C. & M.

([5]) 1 Russ. C. & M. 605 ; R. *v.* Ridley, 2 Camp. 650 ; 1 Dea. Cr. Co. 62.
([6]) R. *v.* Nichol, Russ. & Ry. 130.
([7]) Rosinski's Case, Ry. & Mood. C. C. 19 ; 1 Russ. C. & M. 606.
([8]) 1 Russ. C. & M. 606 ; 1 Hawk. c. 60, § 7.

ASSAULT.

The intent with which the act is done, is a material enquiry; for whether the act shall amount to an assault must in every case be collected from the intention with which it is done. Thus, if one soldier accidentally hurt another by discharging a gun in exercise, it will not be a battery, and it is no battery if by a sudden fright a horse runs away with his rider and hurts another by running against him.(¹)

III. *When justified.*

There are cases in which intentional force used against the person of another may be justified, and will not amount in law to an assault and battery. As if an officer having a warrant against a man who will not suffer himself to be arrested, beat or wound him in the attempt to take him; or if a parent in a reasonable manner chastise his child; or a schoolmaster, his scholar; or a jailor, his prisoner; or if one confine a friend, who is mad, and bind *and beat* him in such a manner as is proper under such circumstances, no assault or battery will be committed by such acts.(²) So, if a man beat, wound or maim one who is making an assault upon his person, or that of his wife, child, parent, or master: or if a man beat one who attempts to kill another;—in these cases, also, the party may justify the assault and battery;—and so may one justify an assault upon another, who wrongfully endeavours by violence to dispossess him of his goods or lands. But no one has a right to revenge himself; and if, when all danger is over, he strikes a blow not necessary for defence, he commits an assault and battery.(³)

Where there is a mere trespass either upon lands or goods, without actual violence, there must be a request to depart or desist, before force is used; but it is otherwise where actual violence is committed, as it is lawful in such cases to oppose force to force; and, therefore, if a person break down a gate or come into an enclosure with force and violence, the owner need not request him to depart, but may lay hands on him immediately.(⁴) But, in general, unless there be considerable violence in the trespass, a party should not, either in defence of his person, or his real or personal property, begin by striking the trespasser; but should gently lay his hands upon him in the first instance, and not proceed with greater force than is made necessary by resistance:(⁵) and, in all cases, where the force used is justified, it must appear that it was no greater than

---

(¹) 1 Russ. C. & M. 607-8.
(²) 1 Hawk. c. 60, § 23; 1 Russ. C. & M. 608.
(³) Regina *v.* Driscoll, 1 Car. & Man. 214.
(⁴) 2 Salk. 641; 1 Russ. C. & M. 609.
(⁵) 1 Russ. C. & M. 609.

was reasonably necessary to accomplish the lawful purpose intended to be effected. Therefore, though an assault merely (as where one man offers to strike another in anger) will justify a battery,(¹) yet it will not justify such battery, if it be excessive and out of all proportion to the necessity or provocation received;(²) and let it be remembered, that no words of reproach, however grievous, are provocations sufficient for an assault.(³)

It has been said, that any touching of the person of another in anger is in law *an assault;* but it does not follow from this, that a Justice is bound upon every complaint, however trivial, to issue his warrant to arrest a party charged with an assault. Experience has taught that this process is often applied for as a mere instrument of gratifying revengeful feelings, when no public good is to be attained by issuing it. In such cases, it is within the discretion of the Justice to refuse the warrant and put the complainant upon his right to appear before the grand jury as a prosecutor; and we advise this course in every case of assault, unless either from its violence, or the manner of making it, or the place where made, or from some circumstance of immoral tendency accompanying it, (as in the case of indecent liberties with females,) the Justice should think that public interest requires his interference.

(No. 1.)

Form of Warrant of Arrest for an Assault.

——— County, to wit:

To all or any one of the Constables of said County:

Whereas, A. B., of the said County, has this day made information and complaint, upon oath, before me J. T., a Justice of the said County, that C. D. of the said County, did on the ——— day of ——— 18—, in the said County, assault and beat him, the said A. B.: These are, therefore, to command you, in the name of the Commonwealth, forthwith to apprehend and bring before me, or some other Justice of the said County, the body of the said C. D., to answer unto the said complaint, and to be farther dealt with according to law. Given under my hand and seal, this ——— day of ——— 18—.

J. T., J. P. [L. S.]

(¹) Arch. Cr. Pl. 347.
(²) 1 East P. C. c. 8, § 1, page 606;
(³) 2 East P. C. 233; 1 Russ. C. & M. 604.
1 Russ. 610.

(No. 2.)

Form of Warrant of Commitment for an Assault.

—— County, to wit:
  To the Jailor of the said County:

Receive into your custody the body of C. D., herewith sent you, charged before me J. T., a Justice of the said County, upon the oath of A. B., with having on the —— day of —— 18—, in the County aforesaid, made an assault upon him the said A. B., and with then and there beating him the said A. B., and him the said C. D., in your jail and custody safely keep, until he shall be thence discharged by due course of law. Given under my hand and seal, this —— day of —— 18—.

J. T., J. P. [L. S.]

(No. 3.)

Form of Recognizance to answer an Indictment for an Assault.

Follow No. 4, under the head of RECOGNIZANCE.

(No. 4.)

Form of Certificate to the Clerk of the Court.

—— County, to wit:

I, J. T., a Justice of the said County, do hereby certify, that I have this day, by my warrant, committed C. D. to the jail of the said County, for want of bail, to answer a bill of indictment to be preferred against him, in the County Court of the said County, for an assault and battery, committed by him in the said County, upon A. B.

J. T., J. P.

(No. 5.)

Form of Recognizance of Witness to appear before the Grand Jury to give evidence.

Follow No. 5, under head of RECOGNIZANCE.

(No. 1.)

Indictment for a Common Assault and Battery.

Commence as No. 1, under head of "INDICTMENTS," and then proceed thus: That A. B. on the —— day of —— 18—, in the County aforesaid, in and upon one C. D., an assault did make, and him the said C. D. did then and there beat, wound and ill treat, and other wrongs to him then and there did, to the great damage of him the said C. D., and against the peace and dignity of the Commonwealth of Virginia.

ASSAULT—(*Indictments for.*)

(No. 2.)

Indictment for an Assault upon a Constable, in the execution of his office.

Commence as No. 1, under head of "INDICTMENTS," and then proceed thus: That A. B. on the —— day of —————— 18—, in the County aforesaid, in and upon one C. D., he the said C. D. being then and there a Constable legally authorized and duly qualified to discharge and perform the duties of said office, and being then and there in the due and lawful exercise of the same, did make an assault, and him the said C. D. did then and there beat, abuse and ill treat; and in the due and lawful execution of his said office did then and there unlawfully and knowingly obstruct, hinder and oppose; and other wrongs to him then and there did, to the great damage of the said C. D., and against the peace and dignity of the Commonwealth of Virginia.

(No. 3.)

Indictment for an Assault with intent to Kill.

Commence as No. 1, under head of "INDICTMENTS," and then proceed thus: That A. B. on the —— day of ——————, in the County aforesaid, with malice aforethought, in and upon one C. D. did make an assault, he the said A. B. being then and there armed with a dangerous weapon, called a knife, and did then and there beat, wound and ill treat him the said C. D., with intent him the said C. D. with set purpose and malice aforethought to kill and murder; against the peace and dignity of the Commonwealth of Virginia.

(No. 4.)

Indictment for a Felonious Assault with intent to commit a Rape.

Commence as No. 1, under head of "INDICTMENTS," and then proceed thus: That A. B., on the —— day of ——————, in the County aforesaid, in and upon the body of one C. D., a female white person, did make an assault, and her the said C. D. did then and there beat, wound and abuse, with intent her the said C. D. then and there feloniously to ravish and carnally know, *by force*, and against her will; against the peace and dignity of the Commonwealth of Virginia.

(No. 5.)

Indictment for an Assault with intent to Rob.

Commence as No. 1, under head of "INDICTMENTS," and then proceed thus: That A. B. on the —— day of ——————, now last past, in the County aforesaid, in and upon one C. D., with a certain dangerous weapon called a pistol, then and there loaded with gunpowder and leaden bullets, with which he the said A. B. was then and there armed, and also with other actual violence, did make an assault, with intent the moneys, goods and chattels of him the said C. D. from the person and against the will of him the said C. D. by force and violence, and by assault and putting him in bodily fear and danger of his life, to steal, take and rob; against the peace and dignity of the Commonwealth of Virginia.

CHAPTER X.

OF ATTACHMENTS—(*In Civil Cases.*)

[For attachments for rent, see RENT.]

Against non-residents.

By SEC. 1, CHAP. 151. When any suit is instituted for any debt, or for damages for breach of any contract, on affidavit, stating the amount and justice of the claim, that there is present cause of action therefor, that the defendant or one of the defendants is not a resident of this State, and that the affiant believes he has estate or debts due him within the county or corporation in which the suit is, or that he is sued with a defendant residing therein, the plaintiff may forthwith sue out of the clerk's office an attachment against the estate of the non-resident defendant, for the amount so stated.

Against a defendant removing his effects out of the State before judgment can be obtained.

By SEC. 2. On affidavit at the time of, or after the institution of any suit, that the plaintiff's claim is believed to be just, and where the suit is to recover specific personal property, stating the nature, and according to the affiant's belief, the value of such property, and the probable amount of damages the plaintiff will recover for the detention thereof, or where it is to recover money for any claim, or damages for any wrong, stating a certain sum which (at the least) the affiant believes the plaintiff entitled to, or ought to recover, and an affidavit also that the affiant believes that the defendant is removing or intends to remove such specific property, or his own estate, or the proceeds of the sale of his property, or a material part of such estate or proceeds, out of this State, so that process of execution on a judgment in said suit, when it is obtained, will be unavailing; in any such case the clerk shall issue an attachment as the case may require. If the suit be for specific property, the attachment may be against the specific property sued for, and against the defendant's estate for so much as is sufficient to satisfy the probable damages for its detention; or at the option of the plaintiff, against the defendant's estate for the value of such specific property, and the damages for its detention. If the suit be to recover money for a claim, or damages for a wrong, the attachment shall be against the defendant's estate for the amount specified in the affidavit as that which the affiant believes the plaintiff is entitled to or ought to recover.

Against debtors removing their effects.

By Sec. 3. On complaint of any person or his agent to any Justice, whether his claim is payable or not, that his debtor intends to remove or is removing, or has removed his effects out of this State, so that there will probably not be therein sufficient effects of the debtor to satisfy the claim when judgment is obtained therefor, should only the ordinary process of law be used to obtain such judgment, if such person or his agent make oath to the truth of such complaint to the best of his belief, as well as to the amount and justice of his claim, and at what time the same is payable, the Justice shall issue an attachment against the estate of the defendant for the amount so stated.

Against vessels, &c. in certain waters.

By Sec. 5. If any person has instituted suit against the commander of any steamboat or other vessel, or against any other person, for any damages sustained by the plaintiff, or any penalty incurred by the defendant, by reason of a slave being assisted to abscond from his owner, or transported or carried out of the State, or out of any county, in violation of any statute, or against the owner of any such vessel, or of any raft or river craft navigating the Ohio river or any of its tributaries, within the jurisdiction of this State, for materials, supplies or labour furnished or bestowed in the building, repairing, equipping, navigating or attending upon the same, or for wharfage, or upon any contract for the transportation of, or for any injury done to, any person or property, by such vessel, raft or craft, or by any person having charge of her, or in her employment, the plaintiff may forthwith sue out of the clerk's office an attachment against the defendant's estate, or against the vessel, raft or river craft, of which he is owner or commander, with all her tackle, apparel and furniture.

Attachment to whom directed and how returnable.

By Sec. 6. Any attachment issued under this chapter may be directed to the Sheriff, Sergeant or Constable of any county or corporation. If issued in a pending suit, it shall be returnable to a term of the court in which the same is pend-

90   ATTACHMENTS—(*In Civil Cases.*)

ing, or to some rule day thereof. Where issued by a Justice it shall, if the claim is over twenty dollars, (exclusive of interest,) be returnable at the option of the plaintiff to the next term of the circuit or county or corporation court of the county or corporation in which the debtor last resided, or in which the leased tenement may be.

How executed.

By Sec. 7. Every such attachment (except where it is sued out specially against specified property,) may be levied upon any estate, real or personal, of the defendant, or so much thereof as is sufficient to pay the amount for which it issues. It shall be sufficiently levied in every case by a service of a copy of such attachment on such persons as may be designated by the plaintiff in writing, or be known to the officer to be in possession of effects of or to be indebted to the defendant; and as to real estate, by such estate being mentioned and described by endorsement on such attachment.

By Sec. 8. But if the plaintiff shall, at the time of suing out such attachment, or afterwards, give bond with security approved by the Clerk or Justice issuing the attachment, in a penalty of at least double the amount of the claim sworn to or sued for, with condition to pay all costs and damages which may be awarded against him, or sustained by any person by reason of his suing out the attachment, the said officer shall take possession of the property specified in the attachment, or where no such property is specified, of any *estate or effects of the defendant*, or so much thereof as is sufficient to pay the plaintiff's claim. When such bond is given the facts shall be endorsed on the attachment, or certified by the Clerk or Justice to the officer, who shall return the said certificate with the attachment; and the bond, when taken by a Justice, shall be returned by him to and filed in the clerk's office of the court to which the attachment is returnable.

By Sec. 9. In either case the officer shall return with the attachment the names of the persons designated as having effects of or owing debts to the defendant; shall summon them to appear as garnishees at the first day of the court to which the attachment is returnable, or if the attachment be returnable at rules, at the first day of the next term after it is returnable, and shall also return a list and description of the property taken (if any) under such attachment; and likewise the date of the service or execution thereof on each person and parcel of property.

By Sec. 10. Such attachment may be issued or executed on Sunday, if oath be made that the defendant is actually removing his effects on that day.

Attachments in equity.

By Sec. 11. When any person claims to be entitled in equity to any money or property from any person against whom, and for which an attachment might be sued out of a clerk's office, if the claim were recoverable at law, upon affidavit, according to the nature of the case, as herein before specified, and filing the same with his bill, he may require the clerk to endorse on the subpœna an order to the officer to whom it is directed, to attach the specific property mentioned in such affidavit, and the estate of the defendant against whom the claim is, in the hands of, or the debts due or to become due to him by, the other defendants. Any such attachment in equity shall be executed in the same manner and shall have the same effect as at law; but the proceeding thereon shall be the same as in other suits in chancery, and the court, or in vacation thereof a Judge of the circuit court, may interpose by an injunction or the appointment of a receiver, or otherwise, to secure the forthcoming of the specified property sued for, and so much other estate as will probably be required to satisfy any future order or decree that will be made in the cause.

Effect of attachment levied.

By Sec. 12. The plaintiff shall have a lien from the time of the levying of such attachment, or serving a copy thereof, as aforesaid, upon the personal property, *choses in action* or other securities of the defendant against whom the claim is, in the hands of or due from any such garnishee on whom it is so served; and on any real estate mentioned in an endorsement on the attachment or subpœna, from the suing out of the same.

How property may be replevied.

By Sec. 13. Any property levied on, or seized as aforesaid, under any attachment where the plaintiff has given bond, may be retained by or returned to the person in whose possession it was, on his giving bond with condition to have the same forthcoming at such time and place as the court may require; or the defendant against whom the claim is may release from any attachment the whole of the estate attached, by giving bond, with condition to perform the judgment or decree of the court. The bond in either case shall be taken by the officer serving the attachment, with security payable to the plaintiff, and in a penalty in the latter case, at least double the amount or value for which the attachment issued; and in the former either double the same, or double the value of the property retained or returned, at the option of the person giving it.

By Sec. 14. Every such bond shall be returned by the officer to and filed by the clerk of the court in which the suit is pending, or to which the attachment is returnable, and the plaintiff may, within thirty days after the return thereof, file exceptions to the same or to the sufficiency of the security therein. If such exception be sustained, the court shall rule the said officer to file a good bond with sufficient security, to be approved by it, on or before a certain day, to be fixed by the court. If he fail to do so, he and his sureties, in his official bond, shall be liable to the plaintiff as for a breach of such bond. But the officer shall have the same rights and remedies against the parties to any bond so adjudged bad, as if he were a surety for them.

By Sec. 15. When any attachment is sued out, either at law or in equity, on such affidavit as is mentioned in the second or third section, although the property or estate attached be not replevied as aforesaid, the interest and profits thereof, pending the suit and before judgment or decree, may be paid to the defendant, if the court deem it proper, and at any time during such period, the court, or a Judge of a circuit court, in vacation, may discharge the attachment, as to the whole of the estate of the defendant against whom the claim is, on his giving bond, with security, payable to the plaintiff in a penalty double the value of such estate, with condition, if judgment or decree be rendered for the plaintiff in said suit, to pay the said value, or so much thereof as may be necessary to satisfy the same.

Property kept, &c., and such as is perishable, &c. to be sold.

By Sec. 16. All property seized under any attachment and not replevied or sold before judgment, shall be kept in the same manner as similar property taken under execution. But such as is expensive to keep or perishable (other than slaves,) may be sold by order of the court, or if it be a circuit court, in vacation thereof, by order of the Judge; such sale to be made in the same manner as if it were a sale under execution, except that where the claim for which the attachment was sued out is not yet payable, or the court or Judge sees other reasons for directing a credit, the sale under this or any other section of this chapter, shall be on credit until the time it is payable, or such other time as the court or Judge may direct, and for the proceeds of sale, bond with good security shall be taken, payable to the officer, for the benefit of the party entitled, and shall be returned by the officer to the court.

Garnishee to be examined.

By Sec. 17. When any garnishee shall appear, he shall be examined on oath. If it appear, on such examination, or by his answer to a bill in equity, that at or after the service of the attachment he was indebted to the defendant against whom the claim is, or had in his possession or control any goods, chattels, money, securities or other effects belonging to the said defendant, the court may order him to pay the amount so due by him, and to deliver such effects to such person as it may appoint as receiver; or such garnishee, with the leave of the court, may give bond with sufficient security, payable to such person, and in such penalty as the court shall prescribe, with condition to pay the amount due by him, and have such effects forthcoming at such time and place as the court may thereafter require.

When garnishee fails to appear.

By Sec. 18. If any garnishee, summoned as aforesaid, fail to appear in an attachment at law, the court may either compel him to appear, or hear proof of any debt due by him to, or of effects in his hands of, the defendant in such attachment, and make such orders in relation thereto, as if what is so proved had appeared on his examination.

By Sec. 19. When it is suggested by the plaintiff, in any attachment at law, that the garnishee has not fully disclosed the debts due by him to, or effects in his hands of, the defendant in such attachment, the court shall cause a jury to be impanneled without any formal pleading, to enquire as to such debts and effects, and proceed in respect to any such found by the jury in the same manner as if they had been confessed by the garnishee. If the verdict be in favour of the garnishee, he shall have judgment for his costs against the plaintiff.

Order of publication.

By Sec. 20. When any attachment except under the third or fourth section, is returned executed, an order of publication shall be made against the defendant, against whom the claim is, unless he has been served with a copy of the attachment or with process in the suit in which the attachment issued.

Defence to the attachment, how and when it may be made.

By Sec. 21. Either the defendant in any such attachment, or any garnishee, or any party to any forthcoming or replevy bond as aforesaid, or the officer who may be liable to the plaintiff by reason of such bond being adjudged bad, may make defence to such attachment, but the attachment shall not thereby be discharged, or the property levied on released.

By Sec. 22. The right to sue out any such attachment may be contested, and when the court is of opinion that it was issued on false suggestions or without sufficient cause, judgment shall be entered that the attachment be abated. When the attachment is properly sued out, and the case heard upon its merits, if the court be of opinion that the claim of the plaintiff is not established, final judgment shall be given for the defendant. In either case he shall recover his costs, and there shall be an order for the restoration to him of the attached effects.

When judgment is in favour of plaintiff.

By Sec. 23. If the claim of the plaintiff be established, judgment or decree shall be rendered for him, and the court shall dispose of the specific property mentioned in the second section as may be right, and order the sale of any other effects or real estate which shall not have been previously replevied or sold under this chapter, and direct the proceeds of sale and whatever else is subject to the attachment, including what is embraced by such replevy or forthcoming bond, to be applied in satisfaction of the judgment or decree. But no real estate shall be sold until all other property and money subject to the attachment has been exhausted, and then only so much thereof as is necessary to pay the judgment or decree.

By Sec. 24. But if the defendant against whom the claim is has not appeared or been served with a copy of the attachment sixty days before such decree, the plaintiff shall not have the benefit of the preceding section unless or until he shall have given bond with sufficient security, in such penalty as the court shall approve, with condition to perform such future order as may be made upon the appearance of the said defendant, and his making defence. If the plaintiff fail to give such bond in a reasonable time, the court shall dispose of the estate attached or the proceeds thereof, as to it shall seem just.

How claim to or lien on property attached may be made.

By Sec. 25. Any person may file his petition at any time before the property attached as the estate of a defendant is sold, or the proceeds of sale paid to the plaintiff under the decree or judgment, disputing the validity of the plaintiff's attachment thereon, or stating a claim to an interest in or lien on the same under any other attachment or otherwise, and its nature, and upon his giving security for costs, the court without any other pleading, shall impannel a jury to enquire into such claim, and if it be found that the petitioner has title to or a lien on, or any interest in such property or it proceeds, the court shall make such order as is necessary to protect his rights; the costs of which enquiry shall be paid by either party at the discretion of the court.

Priority of attachments as to each other.

By Sec. 26. The attachment first served on the same property, or on the person having such property in possession, shall have priority of lien.

How debtor in attachment may appear and open the case.

By Sec. 27. If a defendant, against whom a publication, judgment or decree is rendered under any such attachment, or his personal representative, shall return to or appear openly in this State, he may, within one year after a copy of such judgment or decree shall be served on him, at the instance of the plaintiff, or within five years from the date of the decree or judgment, if it be not so served, petition to have the proceedings reheard. On giving security for costs, he shall be admitted to make defence against such judgment or decree as if he had appeared in the case before the same was rendered, except that the title of any *bona fide* purchaser to any property, real or personal, sold under such attachment, shall not be brought in question or impeached. But this section shall not apply to any case in which the petitioner or his decedent was served with a copy of the attachment or with process in the suit wherein it issued, more than sixty days before the date of the judgment or decree, or to any case in which he appeared and made defence.

By Sec. 28. On any rehearing or new trial had under the preceding section, the court may order the plaintiff in the original suit, to restore any money paid to him under such judgment or decree, to the heir or representative of such defendant, as the same may be the proceeds of real or personal estate; and enter a judgment or decree therefor against him, or it may confirm the former judgment or decree; and in either case adjudge the costs to the prevailing party.

ATTACHMENTS—(*In Civil Cases.*)

Attachments for debts under twenty dollars.

BY SEC. 29. Any creditor whose claim, whether legal or equitable, does not exceed twenty dollars, exclusive of interest, upon complaint on oath in the manner prescribed by the first, second, third and eleventh sections, as the case may be, may obtain from any Justice of any county or corporation in which any property or effects of the defendant may be, or in which any person indebted to him may reside, an attachment against the estate of such defendant, directed to any Sheriff, Sergeant or Constable of his county or corporation, and returnable before any Justice thereof, and thereupon such proceedings may be had before the Justice as would, if the claim exceeded twenty dollars, be had before a court, except that the proceedings shall be in all cases without any formal pleading, and an order of publication need not be published in a newspaper, and the Justice shall try and decide all questions without a jury. All bonds taken under such attachment shall be filed with the Clerk of the court to which the Justice belongs.

If attachment sued out improperly, plaintiff liable to damages.

BY SEC. 30. If upon defence being made in any case, in which property is seized under an attachment, that the attachment was sued out without sufficient cause, it be found either by the court, or by the jury, if one be impanneled, that the defence is well founded, judgment may be entered for the defendant against the plaintiff for the damages sustained by the defendant by reason thereof.

On appeal with security, property discharged.

BY SEC. 31. Where judgment or decree in favour of the plaintiff is rendered in any case in which an attachment is sued out, and on an appeal therefrom an appeal bond is given, with condition to prosecute the appeal with effect, or pay the debt, interest, costs and damages, as well as the costs of the appeal, the officer in whose custody any attached property may be, shall deliver the same to the owner thereof.

Bond may be given by the party, or some one for him.

BY SEC. 32. Any bond authorized or required by any section of this chapter, may be given either by the party himself or by any other person.

ATTACHMENTS—(*In Civil Cases.*)

(No. 1.)

Form of Attachment issued by a Justice for a debt not exceeding twenty dollars, (exclusive of interest,) against a single defendant, who is a non-resident. (Sec. 1.)

———— County, to wit:

To the Sheriff or any Constable of said County:

Whereas, A. B., plaintiff in a certain warrant now pending before a Justice of said County, to recover from C. D. a debt of ——— dollars, and interest on the same, has this day complained and made oath before me J. T., a Justice of the said County, that the said C. D. is justly indebted to him the said sum of ——— dollars, with legal interest thereon from the ——— day of ———, till paid; that the said A. B. has present cause of action against the said C. D. therefor; that the said C. D. is not a resident of this Commonwealth, and that he the said affiant believes that the said C. D. has estate or debts due him within the said County: These are, therefore, in the name of the Commonwealth, to require you to attach the estate of the said C. D. for the amount of the said debt, with interest thereon as aforesaid, and such estate so attached in your hands to secure, or so to provide, that the same may be forthcoming and liable to farther proceedings thereupon to be had, at ——— in the said County, before me or some other Justice of the said County, to whom you are then and there to make return of this warrant, and how you have executed the same. Given under my hand and seal, in the County aforesaid, this ——— day of ——— 18—.

J. T., J. P., [L. S.]

(No. 2.)

Form of Attachment issued by a Justice for a debt not exceeding twenty dollars, (exclusive of interest,) against a non-resident, one of two defendants. (Sec. 1.)

———— County, to wit:

To the Sheriff or any Constable of said County:

Whereas, A. B., plaintiff in a certain warrant now pending before a Justice of said County, to recover from C. D. and E. F. a debt of ——— dollars, and interest on the same, has this day complained and made oath before me J. T., a Justice of the said County, that the said C. D. and E. F. are justly indebted to him the said sum of ——— dollars, with legal interest thereon from the ——— day of ———, till paid; that he has present cause of action against them therefor; that C. D., one of the said defendants, is not a resident of this Commonwealth, and that he the said affiant believes that the said C. D. has estate or debts due him within the said County; (or, "and that E. F., with whom the said C. D. is jointly sued as aforesaid, is a resident of the said County:") These are, therefore, in the name of the Commonwealth, to require you to attach the estate of the said C. D. for the amount of the said debt, with interest thereon as aforesaid, and such estate so attached in your hands to secure, or so to provide, that the same may be forthcoming and liable to farther proceedings thereupon to be had, at ——— in the said County, before me or some other Justice of the said County, to whom you are then and there to make return of this warrant, and how you have executed the same. Given, &c. (as in No. 1.)

(No. 3.)

Form of Attachment issued by a Justice against specific property claimed by plaintiff, not exceeding twenty dollars in value: or against such property and defendant's own estate. (Sec. 2.)

———— County, to wit:
To the Sheriff or any Constable of said County:

Whereas, A. B., plaintiff in a certain warrant now pending before a Justice of said County, to recover from C. D. certain specific personal property, and damages for the detention of the same, has this day made oath before me J. T., a Justice of the said County, that he believes the claim for which he has instituted the said warrant against the said C. D. to be just; that the specific property sought to be recovered by the said warrant, consists of one cow ; that, according to the said affiant's belief, the value of the said cow is ———— dollars, and the probable amount of damages he will recover for the detention thereof, is ———— dollars ; and that he the said affiant believes that the said C. D. is removing (or *intends to remove*) the said cow out of this Commonwealth, [and is also removing (or *also intends to remove*) his own estate, or the proceeds of the sale of his property, or a material part of such estate or proceeds, out of this Commonwealth,] so that process of execution on a judgment upon the said warrant, when it is obtained, will be unavailing : These are, therefore, in the name of the Commonwealth, to require you to attach the said cow, [and also to attach the estate of the said C. D. for so much as is sufficient to satisfy the above stated probable amount of damages for the detention of the said cow ;] and the same (or if specific property sued for and defendant's estate are both attached, instead of *the same* say *the subject*) so attached in your hands to secure, or so to provide, &c. (conclusion as in No. 1.)

[If affidavit do not charge an intent to remove defendant's own estate, or its proceeds, or a material part, but only to remove the specific property, the words in brackets will be omitted.]

———

(No. 4.)

Form of Attachment issued by a Justice for value (not exceeding twenty dollars) of specific property claimed by plaintiff, and for damages for detention of such property. (Sec. 2.)

———— County, to wit:
To the Sheriff or any Constable of said County:

Whereas, A. B., plaintiff in a certain warrant now pending before a Justice of the said County, to recover from C. D. certain specific personal property, and damages for the detention of the same, has this day made oath before me J. T., a Justice of the said County, that he believes the claim for which he has instituted the said warrant against the said C. D. to be just: that the specific property sought to be recovered by the said warrant consists of one cow ; that, according to the said affiant's belief, the value of the said cow is ———— dollars, and the probable amount of damages he will recover for the detention thereof is ———— dollars ; and that he the said affiant believes that the said C. D. is removing (*or*, intends to remove) his own estate, or the proceeds of the sale of his property, or a material part of such estate or proceeds, out of this Commonwealth, so that process of execution on a judgment upon the said warrant, when it is obtained, will be unavailing : These are, therefore, in the name of the Commonwealth, to require you to attach the estate of the said C. D. for the above stated value of the said cow, and the above stated damages for the detention thereof; and the same so attached in your hands to secure, or so to provide, that the same may be forthcoming and liable to farther proceedings thereupon to be had, at ——— in the said County, before me or some other Justice of the said County, to whom you are then and there to make return of this warrant, and how you have executed the same. Given, &c. (as in No. 1.)

(No. 5.)

Form of Attachment by a Justice for a debt not exceeding twenty dollars, (exclusive of interest,) where defendant is removing or intends to remove his estate or its proceeds, or a material part. (Sec. 2.)

——— County, to wit:
To the Sheriff or any Constable of the said County:

Whereas, A. B., plaintiff in a certain warrant now pending before a Justice of the said County, to recover from C. D. a debt of ——— dollars, and interest upon the same, hath this day made oath before me J. T., a Justice of the said County, that he believes the claim for which he hath instituted the said warrant against the said C. D. to be just; that he believes he is entitled to and ought to recover by the said warrant at least the said sum of ——— dollars principal money, and legal interest on the same from the ——— day of ——— until paid; and that he also believes that the said C. D. is removing (or, intends to remove) his own estate, or the proceeds of the sale of his property, or a material part of such estate or proceeds, out of this Commonwealth, so that process of execution on a judgment upon the said warrant, when it is obtained, will be unavailing: These are, therefore, &c. (concluding as in No. 1.)

(No. 6.)

Form of Attachment issued by a Justice where claim (whether payable or not) exceeds twenty dollars, and debtor intends to remove or is removing, or has removed his effects from the Commonwealth. (Sec. 3.)

——— County, to wit:
To the Sheriff or any Constable of the said County:

Whereas, A. B. has this day complained and made oath before me J. T., a Justice of said County, that C. D. is justly indebted to him in the sum of ——— dollars, and that the said sum became payable (or *will become payable*) on the ——— day of ———, and that, to the best of the said affiant's belief, the said C. D. intends to remove (or *is removing*, or *has removed*) his effects out of this Commonwealth, so that there will probably not be therein sufficient effects of the said C. D. to satisfy the aforesaid claim of the said affiant when judgment is obtained therefor, should only the ordinary process of law be used to obtain such judgment: These are, therefore, in the name of the Commonwealth, to require you to attach the estate of the said C. D. for the amount of the said A. B.'s claim above stated: and such estate so attached in your hands to secure, or so to provide, that the same may be forthcoming and liable to farther proceedings thereupon to be had, before the County Court of the said County (or *the Circuit Court of the said County*) on the first day of the next term thereof: And that you then and there have this warrant, and make return to the said Court how you have executed the same. Given, &c. (as in No. 1.)

(No. 7.)

To adapt the foregoing to the case of a complaint by an agent; for A. B. in 3d line, say " E. F. as agent of A. B. ;" line 4 for *him* put " the said A. B. ;" line 10, for *affiant* put A. B.

(No. 8.)

Form of Attachment issued by a Justice on complaint by one member of a firm, where claim (whether payable or not) exceeds twenty dollars, and debtor intends to remove, or is removing, or has removed his effects from the Commonwealth. (Sec. 3.)

———— County, to wit :
   To the Sheriff or any Constable of the said County:

Whereas, D. H., a member of the partnership of D. F., D. H. and R. H., merchants trading in the said County, under the partnership name and style of D. F. and Company, has this day complained and made oath before me J. T., a Justice of said County, that C. D. is justly indebted to the said D. F., D. H. and R. H., as merchants and partners as aforesaid, in the sum of ———— dollars, and that the said sum became payable (or *will become payable*) on the ———— day of ————, and that, to the best of the said affiant's belief, the said C. D. intends to remove (or *is removing*, or *has removed*) his effects out of this Commonwealth, so that there will probably not be therein sufficient effects of the said C. D. to satisfy the aforesaid claim of the said D. F. and Company when judgment is obtained therefor, should only the ordinary process of law be used to obtain such judgment : These are, therefore, in the name of the Commonwealth, to require you to attach the estate of the said C. D. for the amount of the said D. F. and Company's claim above stated ; and such estate so attached in your hands to secure, or so to provide, that the same may be forthcoming and liable to farther proceedings thereupon to be had, before the County Court of the said County, (or *the Circuit Court of the said County*) on the first day of the next term thereof: And that you then and there have this warrant, and make return to the said Court how you have executed the same. Given, &c. (as in No. 1.)

(No. 9.)

Form of Attachment issued by a Justice, where claim (whether payable or not) does not exceed twenty dollars, exclusive of interest, and debtor intends to remove, or is removing, or has removed his effects from the Commonwealth. (Sec. 3.)

This form will be the same as No. 6, except as follows :
Omit all subsequent to the words " thereupon to be had," in 15th line of form No. 6, and in lieu thereof, insert what follows the same words in form No. 1.

Form of Forthcoming Bond taken from defendant or garnishee by officer levying attachment. (Sec. 13.)

Know all men by these presents, that we C. D. (or *G. H.*) and H. I., both of the County of H., are held and firmly bound unto A. B., of the same County, in the just and full sum of * ——— dollars, to be paid to the said A. B., his executors, administrators or assigns; for the payment whereof, we bind ourselves jointly and severally, and our several heirs, executors and administrators. Sealed with our seals, and dated this ——— day of ——— 18—.

The condition of the above obligation is such, that whereas, &c. (as in the bond taken of the plaintiff by the Justice or Clerk, down to the end of the recital there; and then proceeding as follows:) And whereas, the said attachment hath come to the hands of J. K., Sheriff (or *Constable,* or *of L. M., deputy for J. K., Sheriff*) of the said County of H., to be served, who, by virtue thereof, (the said Justice, or the said Clerk, having taken from the said plaintiff such bond and security as the law in that case requires,) hath levied on and seized, in the possession of the said defendant C. D., (or *in the possession of the said G. H.,*) the specific property claimed by the plaintiff as aforesaid,† and the following personal property of the said defendant, that is to say, one bay horse, one dozen mahogany chairs, &c.; and the said C. D. (or *the said G. H.*) desiring to retain in his possession (or if the bond is not given at the time of the levy, but afterwards, say "desiring to have returned to his possession") the property so levied on and seized, hath tendered the above bound H. I. as his surety in such a bond as the law requires for that purpose: Now, therefore, if the said C. D. (or *the said G. H.*) shall have the property so levied on and seized as aforesaid, forthcoming at such time and place as the Court (or *Justice,*) by any order made in the said cause may require, then the above obligation to be void, otherwise to remain in full force.

            C. D. (or *G. H.*) [L. S.]
            H. I.   [L. S.]

BY CLERKS.

(No. 1.)

Attachment issued by Clerk for a liquidated demand in action of debt or indebitatus assumpsit against a single defendant who is a non-resident. (Sec. 1.)

——— County, to wit:

To the Sheriff or any Constable of ——— County:

Whereas, A. B., plaintiff in a certain action‡ of debt upon a note in writing, now pending against C. D. in the County Court of the said County of ———, has this day made oath before me J. T., Clerk (or *Deputy Clerk*) of the said County Court, that the amount of his claim in the said suit is ——— dollars of principal money, with legal interest thereon from the ——— day of ——— till paid; that the said C. D. is justly indebted to him the said

---

* Either double the amount or value for which the attachment issued, or double the value of the property for which the forthcoming bond is given, at the option of the person giving it.

† Where the attachment is not against, or has not been levied on, specific property claimed by the plaintiff, the words "the specific property claimed by the plaintiff as aforesaid, and," will of course be omitted. Where such property alone has been levied on, say "as aforesaid; and the said C. D.," &c. omitting the intervening words.

‡ Or "of debt upon a writing obligatory under seal," or "of *indebitatus assumpsit* for goods sold and delivered by the said A. B. to the said C. D.," or such other description of the action as the writ and endorsement supply.

amount of principal money and interest; that he has present cause of action against the said C. D. therefor; that the said C. D. is not a resident of this Commonwealth, and that he the said affiant believes that the said C. D. has estate or debts due him within the said County of ———, in which the said suit is: These are, therefore, in the name of the Commonwealth, to require you to attach the estate of the said C. D. for the said amount of principal money, with interest thereon as aforesaid, and such estate so attached in your hands to secure, or so to provide, that the same may be forthcoming and liable to farther proceedings thereupon to be had, before the said County Court at the next* term thereof: And that you then and there have this writ, and make return to the said Court how you have executed the same. Given under my hand, at the courthouse of the said County, this —— day of ——— 18—, in the ——— year of the Commonwealth.

J. T., Clerk.

(No. 2.)

Attachment issued by Clerk for a liquidated demand, in action of debt or indebitatus assumpsit against two defendants one of whom is a non-resident. (Sec. 1.)

——— County, to wit:

To the Sheriff or any Constable of ——— County:

Whereas, A. B., plaintiff in a certain action of debt† upon a note in writing, now pending against C. D. and E. F. in the County Court of the said County of ———, has this day made oath before me J. T., Clerk (or *Deputy Clerk*) of the said Court, that the amount of his claim in the said suit is ——— dollars of principal money, with legal interest thereon from the —— day of ——— till paid; that the said C. D. and E. F. are justly indebted to him the said amount of principal money and interest; that he has present cause of action against them therefor; that C. D., one of the said defendants, is not a resident of this Commonwealth, and that he the said affiant believes that the said C. D. has estate or debts due him within the said County of ———, in which the said suit is: (or " and that E. F., with whom the said C. D. is jointly sued as aforesaid, is a resident of the said County of ———, in which the said suit is :") These are, therefore, in the name of the Commonwealth, to require you to attach the estate of the said C. D. for the said amount of principal money, with interest thereon as aforesaid, and such estate so attached in your hands to secure, or so to provide, that the same may be forthcoming and liable to farther proceedings thereupon to be had, before

---

* The statute (sec. 6.) directs, that the attachment issued in a pending suit, " shall be returnable to *a* term of the Court in which the same is pending, or to some rule day thereof." It seems to be most proper, where (as will usually be the case) the attachment issues at or shortly after the time of issuing the writ instituting the action, to make it returnable at the same time with such writ. This can be readily done, both in this and all the other forms of attachments issued by Clerks. If the suit be in a County Court, and the writ be returnable to the next quarterly term, the word "quarterly" will be inserted in the attachment before the words "term thereof." If the suit be in a Circuit Court, (in which case the words "Circuit Court" must be substituted for "County Court" wherever the Court is mentioned in the attachment,) and the writ instituting such suit be returnable at a rule day, the conclusion of the attachment should be as follows: "At the next term thereof: And that you have this writ at the Clerk's office of the said Circuit Court, at the rules to be holden for said Court, on the first Monday in ——— next," (the return day of the writ instituting the suit,) "and then and there make known how you have executed the same. Given," &c.

† This form may be adapted to the other descriptions of action to which form No. 1 applies. See note to that form.

the said County Court at the next term thereof, and that you then and there have this writ, and make return to the said Court how you have executed the same. Given under my hand, at the courthouse of the said County, this —— day of ——— 18—, in the ——— year of the Commonwealth.

J. T. Clerk.

(No. 3.)

Attachment issued by Clerk in action of covenant, debt on bond with collateral condition, or assumpsit for unliquidated damages, against a single defendant who is a non-resident. (Sec. 1.)

——— County, to wit:

To the Sheriff or any Constable of ——— County:

Whereas, A. B., plaintiff in an action now pending against C. D. in the County Court of the said County of ———, to recover damages for the breach of a certain covenant made by the said C. D. with the said A. B. (or "damages for the non-performance of the condition of a certain bond executed by the said C. D. to the said A. B.," or "damages for the non-performance of certain promises and assumptions made by the said C. D. to the said A. B.,") has this day made oath before me J. T., Clerk (or *Deputy Clerk*) of the said County Court, that the claim for which he has instituted his said action against the said C. D. is just; that he believes he is entitled to, and ought to recover in the said action, damages to the amount of ——— dollars at the least;* that he has present cause, &c. (as in No. 1, line 9, down to the words "amount of" in the 14th line inclusive; and then, instead of the words "principal money with interest thereon as aforesaid," say "damages" (or "damages and interest;") proceeding "and such," &c., to the end of the form.

(No. 4.)

Attachment issued by Clerk against a non-resident, one of two defendants in action of covenant, debt on bond with collateral condition, or assumpsit for unliquidated damages. (Sec. 1.)

Follow the above form No. 3, (only substituting everywhere "C. D. and E. F." for "C. D.") down to the words "present cause," in line 13; then say "of action against the said C. D. and E. F. therefor; that the said C. D. is not a resident," &c., as in form No. 2, line 11, following that form thence to the end, except that the words "damages (or *damages and interest*") are to be substituted in the 17th line for "principal money, with interest thereon as aforesaid."

(No. 5.)

Attachment issued by Clerk against specific property claimed in action of detinue. (Sec. 2.)

The form is the same as No. 6, leaving out the words in brackets.

---

* If the case be one in which interest on the damages is claimed, there may be inserted here, the words "with legal interest thereon from the ——— day of ———, until paid."

(No. 6.)

Attachment issued by Clerk against specific property claimed in action of detinue, and defendant's own estate. (Sec. 2.)

As follows, *including* the words in brackets:

——— County, to wit:

 To the Sheriff or any Constable of ——— *County:*

Whereas, A. B., plaintiff in an action of detinue now pending against C. D., in the County Court of the said County of ———, to recover certain specific personal property, and damages for the detention of the same, has this day made oath before me J. T., Clerk (or *Deputy Clerk*) of the said County Court, that he believes the claim for which he has instituted his said action against the said C. D. to be just; that the specific property sought to be recovered in the said action consists of one cow; that, according to the said affiant's belief, the value of the said cow is ——— dollars, and the probable amount of damages he will recover for the detention thereof is ——— dollars; and that he the said affiant believes that the said C. D. is removing (or *intends to remove*) the said cow out of the Commonwealth, [and is also removing (or *also intends to remove*) his own estate, or the proceeds of the sale of his property, or a material part of such estate or proceeds, out of this Commonwealth,] so that process of execution on a judgment in said suit, when it is obtained, will be unavailing: These are, therefore, in the name of the Commonwealth, to require you to attach the said cow, [and also to attach the estate of the said C. D. for so much as is sufficient to satisfy the above stated probable amount of damages for the detention of the said cow:] and the same (or if specific property sued for and defendant's estate are both attached, instead of "the same" say "the subject,") so attached in your hands to secure, or so to provide, &c. (conclusion as in No. 1.)

(No. 7.)

Attachment issued by Clerk against estate of defendant in action of detinue. (Sec. 2.)

——— County, to wit:

 To the Sheriff or any Constable of ——— *County:*

Whereas, A. B., plaintiff in an action of detinue now pending against C. D., in the County Court of the said County of ———, to recover certain specific personal property, and damages for the detention of the same, has this day made oath before me J. T., Clerk (or *Deputy Clerk*) of the said County Court, that he believes the claim for which he has instituted his said action against the said C. D. to be just; that the specific property sought to be recovered in the said action consists of one cow; that, according to the said affiant's belief, the value of said cow is ——— dollars, and the probable amount of damages he will recover for the detention thereof is ——— dollars; and that he the said affiant believes that the said C. D. is removing (or *intends to remove*) his own estate or the proceeds of the sale of his property, or a material part of such estate or proceeds, out of this Commonwealth, so that process of execution on a judgment in said suit, when it is obtained, will be unavailing: These are, therefore, in the name of the Commonwealth, to require you to attach the estate of the said C. D. for the above stated value of the said cow, and the above stated damages for the detention thereof; and the same so attached in your hands to secure, or so to provide, that the same may be forthcoming and liable to farther proceedings thereupon to be had, &c. (concluding as in form No. 1.)

ATTACHMENTS—(*In Civil Cases.*) 105

(No. 8.)

Attachment issued by Clerk where defendant is removing or intends to remove his own estate, or its proceeds, or a material part. (Sec. 2.)

If the action be upon a *contract*, the commencement and description of the action will be as in form No. 1, or No. 3, according to the nature of the case.

If the action be for a *tort*, say, (according to the nature of the case:)
"Whereas, A. B., plaintiff in a certain action of trespass now pending in the County Court of the said County of ———, against C. D., for assaulting and beating him the said A. B."

——— "a certain action of trespass now pending, &c. against C. D., for assaulting and beating a slave of him, the said A. B."

——— "a certain action of trespass now pending, &c. against C. D., for breaking and entering the close of him, the said A. B."

——— "a certain action of trespass now pending, &c. against C. D., for taking and carrying away the goods of him, the said A. B."

(*In ejectment*) ——— "a certain action of ejectment against C. D. now pending in the County Court," &c.

(*In trespass for mesne profits*) ——— "a certain action of trespass now pending, &c. against C. D., for taking the profits of the said A. B.'s land."

——— "a certain action of trespass on the case now pending, &c. against C. D., for slanderous words spoken by him of the said A. B."

——— "a certain action of trespass on the case for trover and conversion, now pending against C. D. in the County Court," &c.

——— "a certain action of trespass on the case now pending, &c. against C. D., for enticing away and harbouring a slave (or *apprentice*) of him, the said A. B."

——— "a certain action of trespass on the case now pending, &c. against C. D. for negligently driving a carriage of him the said A. B., whereby the same was broken and damaged."

And so in each case according to the description of the action in the writ and endorsement.

Then proceed as follows:

has this day made oath before me J. T., Clerk (or *Deputy Clerk*) of the said County Court, that he believes the claim for which he has instituted his said action against the said C. D. to be just; that he believes he is entitled to, and ought to recover in the said action, at least ——— dollars of principal money, with legal interest thereon from the ——— day of ———, till paid (or, if the action be one of those described in form No. 3, say, "damages to the amount of ——— dollars at the least;" or, if interest on the damages be claimed, "damages to the amount of ——— dollars at the least, with legal interest thereon from the ——— day of ——— until paid;" or if the action be for a tort, or ejectment, or for mesne profits, say "damages to the amount of ——— dollars at the least;") and that he also believes that the said C. D. is removing (or *intends to remove*) his own estate, or the proceeds of the sale of his property, or a material part of such estate or proceeds, out of this Commonwealth, so that process of execution on a judgment in said suit, when it is obtained, will be unavailing: These are, therefore, in the name of the Commonwealth, to require you to attach the estate of the said C. D. for the amount of principal money and interest (or *damages and interest;* or *damages*) above specified, and the same so attached in your hands to secure, or so to provide, that, &c. (concluding as in No. 1.)

Form of Attachment Bond (except on attachment in action of detinue) to be taken by Clerk from plaintiff. (Sec. 8.)

Know all men by these presents, that we A. B. and L. M., both of the County of H., are held and firmly bound unto C. D. of the same County, in the just and full sum of ―― dollars, lawful money of the United States, to be paid to the said C. D., his executors or administrators, to which payment well and truly to be made, we bind ourselves, and our heirs, executors and administrators, jointly and severally, firmly by these presents. Sealed with our seals, and dated this ―― day of ―― 18―.

The condition of the above obligation is such, that whereas the said A. B., plaintiff in a certain action of debt, (or *trespass on the case,* or *trespass,* or *covenant,* or *ejectment,* &c. as the case may be) pending against the said C. D. in the County Court of H. County, did, on the ―― day of ――, upon his affidavit made in due form of law before J. T., Clerk (or *Deputy Clerk*) of the said County Court, obtain from the said J. T. an attachment against the estate of the said C. D. for the sum of ―― dollars,* [with legal interest thereon from the ―― day of ―― until paid,] being principal money and interest, (or *damages and interest,* or *damages*) claimed by the said A. B. in the said suit, which said attachment is directed to the Sheriff or any Constable of the County of ――, and is returnable before the said County Court of H. at the next term thereof: Now, therefore, if the said A. B. shall pay all costs and damages which may be awarded against him, or sustained by any person, by reason of his suing out the said attachment, then the above obligation is to be void, otherwise to remain in full force.

A. B. [L. s.]
L. M. [L. s.]

―――

Form of Attachment Bond to be taken by Clerk upon attachment in action of detinue.

If the attachment be against the specific property only, after the words " obtain, &c. an attachment against" in the foregoing form of bond, say " the specific property sought to be recovered in the action aforesaid, consisting of one negro man slave named James."

If the attachment be against both the specific property and the defendant's own estate, after the above words, " the specific, &c. consisting &c. named James," add, " and also against the estate of the said C. D., for the probable damages recoverable for the detention of the said slave, amounting to ―― dollars."

If the attachment be against the defendant's own estate for the value of the specific property, and damages for the detention, after the words " obtain &c. an attachment against the estate of the said C. D.," in the foregoing form, say " for ―― dollars, the value of the specific property sought to be recovered in the action aforesaid, consisting of one negro man slave named James, and also for ―― dollars, the probable damages recoverable for the detention of the said slave."

And then in each case proceed, " which said attachment is directed," &c. to the end of the foregoing form.

―――

* Where no interest is included in the attachment, the words in brackets will be omitted.

Form of Attachment Bond, (except an attachment where specific property is claimed) to be taken by Justice from plaintiff. (Sec. 8.)

Know all men by these presents, that we A. B. and L. M., both of the County of H., are held and firmly bound unto C. D. of the same County, in the just and full sum of —— dollars, lawful money of the United States, to be paid to the said C. D., his executors or administrators, to which payment well and truly to be made, we bind ourselves and our heirs, executors and administrators, jointly and severally, firmly by these presents. Sealed with our seals, and dated this —— day of —— 18—.

The condition of the above obligation is such, that whereas the said A. B., [plaintiff in a certain warrant pending before a Justice of said County of H., to recover from said C. D., a debt of —— dollars, and interest on the same,] did on the —— day of ——, upon his complaint on oath, made in due form of law, before J. T., a Justice of the same County, obtain from the said J. T., an attachment against the estate of the said C. D., for the [said] sum of —— dollars, with legal interest thereupon from the —— day of —— until paid, which said attachment is directed to the Sheriff or any Constable of the said County of H., and is made returnable at —— in the said County, on the —— day of ——, before the said J. T. or some other Justice of the said County: Now, therefore, if the said A. B. shall pay all costs and damages which may be awarded against him, or sustained by any person, by reason of his suing out the said attachment, then the above obligation to be void, otherwise to remain in full force.

A. B. [L. S.]
L. M. [L. S.]

If the attachment is under the 3d section, for a claim on which no proceedings by warrant have been instituted, the words in brackets will be omitted. If the attachment is under the 3d section for a claim *to become payable* at a future day, omit the words " with legal interest, &c., until paid," and in lieu of them insert " to become payable on the —— day of ——." If the attachment is under the 3d section for a claim exceeding $ 20, after the words " is made returnable," say, " before the County Court (or *Circuit Court*) of the said County, on the first day of the next term thereof: Now," &c.

Form of Attachment Bond taken by Justice, where attachment is for specific personal property, or for such property and damages for its detention, or for the value of such property and damages for its detention.

Where the attachment is founded upon a claim of specific personal property, the foregoing form of the bond taken by the Justice will be modified as follows:

If the attachment be against the specific property only, after the words " obtain, &c., an attachment against" in the foregoing form of attachment bond, say, " the specific property sought to be recovered by the warrant aforesaid, consisting of one cow."

If the attachment be against both the specific property and the defendant's own estate, after the above words, " the specific property, &c., consisting of one cow," add, " and also against the estate of the said C. D. for the probable damages recoverable for the detention of the said cow, amounting to —— dollars."

If the attachment be against the defendant's estate for the value of the specific property, and damages for the detention, after the words " obtain, &c., an attachment against the estate of the said C. D.," in the foregoing

form of attachment bond, say " for ——— dollars, the value of the specific property sought to be recovered by the warrant aforesaid, consisting of one cow, and also for ——— dollars, the probable damages recoverable for the detention of the said cow."
And then in each case proceed, " which said attachment is directed," &c., to the end of the foregoing form of attachment bond.

Form of Replevy Bond taken from defendant by officer serving attachment. (Sec. 13.)

Know all men by these presents, that we C. D. and E. F., both of the County of H., are held and firmly bound unto A. B., of the same County, in the just and full sum of * ——— dollars, &c.

The condition of the above obligation is such, that whereas, &c., (as in the bond taken of the plaintiff by the Justice or Clerk, down to the end of the recital there ; and then proceeding as follows :) And whereas, the said attachment having come to the hands of J. K., Sheriff, (or *Constable*, or *of L. M. Deputy for J. K., Sheriff*) of the said County of H., to be served, the following property of the said C. D. hath been attached by virtue of the same, that is to say, one half acre lot of land, with the buildings and improvements thereon, situated on the south side of H. street in the City of R., and now occupied by R. S., being the real estate mentioned and described in the endorsement upon the said attachment, also one negro man slave named John, one bay horse, one dozen mahogany chairs, and a debt of one hundred dollars due to the said C. D. from the said R. S. by his promissory note, executed to the said C. D., payable (or *to become payable*) on the ——— day of ——— 18— ; and the said C. D., desiring to release from the said attachment the estate so attached as aforesaid, hath tendered the said E. F. as his surety in such a bond as the law requires for that purpose : Now, therefore, if the said C. D. shall perform the judgment of the court, (or *Justice*) in case the said attachment be sustained, then the above obligation to be void, otherwise to remain in full force.

C. D. [L. S.]
E. F. [L. S.]

FORM OF JUDGMENTS.

(No. 1.)

Form of Judgment to be rendered by a Justice against specific property and against estate of absent defendant for damages for detention thereof, where specific property is in hand of officer.

A. B. Plaintiff,   At ——— in the County of ———, on the ——— day
against   of ——— 18—.
P. D., Defendant.
On attachment for   Upon hearing, judgment is granted the plaintiff for
specific property.   the cow mentioned in warrant of attachment, and ——— dollars for his damages sustained by him, by reason of the detention of said cow, and ——— dollars for his costs : And I order X. Y. Constable to deliver the said cow to the plaintiff, and that he make sale of

---

* At least double the amount or value for which the attachment issued.

ATTACHMENTS—(*In Civil Cases.*) 109

the estate of the said C. D. attached in his hands, and out of the proceeds of said sale pay the said A. B. the said sum of ——— dollars and the said costs, and that he pay over the surplus, if any, to the said defendant.

J. T., J. P.

(No. 2.)

Form of Judgment to be rendered by a Justice on an attachment levied on effects, and in the hands of the officer.

A. B. } At ——— in the County of ———, on the ——— day of ———
 v.   } 18—.
P. D. }

Upon hearing, judgment is granted the plaintiff for the sum of ——— dollars, with interest from the ——— day of ——— 18—, and ——— dollars costs: ☞ And I order X. Y. Constable to make sale of the attached effects as the law directs, and pay and satisfy the judgment to the plaintiff, and return the surplus to the defendant.

J. T., J. P.

(No. 3.)

Form of Judgment to be rendered by a Justice where garnishee is summoned and is indebted to the defendant.

Follow form No. 2, to the *hand*, and proceed thus: "And E. F., who has been garnisheed in this cause, having appeared and admitted on oath, that he is indebted to the said C. D., in the sum of ——— dollars, judgment is granted the plaintiff against the said E. F., for the sum of ——— dollars, for the use of the said A. B., and for ——— dollars, costs of prosecuting this attachment."

J. T., J. P.

(No. 4.)

Form of Judgment where garnishee has property in his possession, belonging to the defendant.

Follow form No. 2, to the *hand*, and proceed thus: "And E. F., who has been summoned as a garnishee, having admitted on oath, that he has in his possession a horse (or *whatever it may be*,) the property of the said C. D., I order that X. Y. Constable take and sell the said horse, according to law, and from the proceeds of the sale pay and satisfy the said judgment against the said C. D., and return the surplus to the said C. D."

J. T., J. P.

CHAPTER XI.

ATTEMPTS—(*To Commit Crime.*)

A mere intention to commit a crime, unaccompanied by any act, is not an offence, but any *act*, though in itself innocent, yet if it be accompanied with a criminal intent, becomes thereby a misdemeanor at common law, and as such punishable, for the completion of the criminal intent is not necessary to constitute criminality.([1]) So that an attempt to commit any felony, or even a misdemeanor, whether a statutory or common law misdemeanor, is in itself a misdemeanor at common law, and punishable as at common law,([2]) except in cases where the statute has prescribed the punishment. The mere *soliciting* another to commit a felony is a sufficient act or attempt to constitute the misdemeanor; as, for instance, soliciting a servant to steal his master's goods, though the goods are not in fact stolen.([3])

BY SEC. 10, CHAP. 199. Every free person who attempts to commit an offence, and in such attempt does any act towards its commission, but fails to commit, or is prevented from committing it, shall, where not otherwise provided, be punished as follows:

If the offence attempted be punishable with death, the person making such attempt shall be confined in the penitentiary not less than one, nor more than two years.

If it be punishable by confinement in the penitentiary, he shall be confined in jail not less than six nor more than twelve months.

If it be punishable by confinement in jail, or fine, he shall be confined in jail not more than six months, or fined, not exceeding one hundred dollars.

The Justice will see that two classes of cases are embraced in this section. If the offence attempted, be punishable with death, as in murder, then the attempt to commit it is felony; and, in all such cases, he must commit for examination or trial, as in any other case of felony. The attempt to commit any offence not so punishable, is a misdemeanor, and in these the party should be committed, or recognized to answer an indictment. In proceeding for the misdemeanor, it is not necessary, even in an indictment, to negative the actual commis-

---

([1]) Schofield's Case, Cald. R. 397; Higgins' Case, 2 East R. 21; Sutton's Case, Har. R. 370; 2 Str. 1074.   ([2]) 2 East R. 8, by Grose, J.; 6 C. & P. 368.
([3]) 2 East R. 5; 1 Russ. C. & M. 45.

sion of the felony attempted to be committed, for it is for the defendant (if he pleases,) to shew that the felony was committed, and the misdemeanor thereby merged.(¹)

[The infinite variety of expedients resorted to in attempts to commit crime, defy human ingenuity to anticipate a form of legal process for each offence, but we will give one in each class of cases as a precedent, which, without difficulty, may be adapted to any other. In doing so, the Justice has only to state the crime intended to be committed, and the act done by the party in the attempt to commit it.]

(No. 1.)

Form of Warrant of Arrest for maliciously attempting to burn a dwelling house in the night.

——— County, to wit:
To X. Y., *Constable of said County:*

Whereas, A. B. has this day made complaint and information on oath before me J. T., a Justice of the said County, that C. D., on the ——— day of ——— 18—, in the night of that day, in said County, did feloniously attempt, feloniously and maliciously to burn the dwelling house of the said A. B., (he the said A. B. then being in the said dwelling house,) by then and there in the night as aforesaid, setting fire to a quantity of cotton then being in the said dwelling house, with intent thereby maliciously to burn the said dwelling house: These are, therefore, in the name of the Commonwealth, to command you forthwith to apprehend the said C. D., and to bring him before me or some other Justice of the said County to answer the said complaint, and to be farther dealt with according to law. Given under my hand and seal, this ——— day of ——— 18—.

J. T., *J. P.* [L. S.]

(No. 2.)

Form of Mittimus where a party is committed for examination or trial in the County Court for felony.

——— County, to wit:
To X. Z., *Constable of said County, and to the Keeper of the Jail of said County:*

These are to command you, the said Constable, in the name of the Commonwealth of Virginia, forthwith to convey and deliver into the custody of the keeper of the said jail, together with this warrant, the body of C. D., a white person (or *free negro*, or *a slave, the property of E. F.*, as the case may be,) charged before me J. T., a Justice of the said County, on the oath of A. B., with a felony by him committed, in this that the said C. D., on the ——— day of ——— in the year 18—, in the said County, (here describe the offence as in the warrant of arrest.) And you, the said keeper of the said jail, are hereby required to receive the said C. D. into your jail and custody, that he may be examined (or *tried*) for the said offence, by the

---

(¹) By Ld. Mansfield, Cald. Rep. 400.

County Court of said County, and him there safely keep, until he shall be discharged by due course of law. Given under my hand and seal, this —— day of —— in the year 18—.

J. T., J. P. [L. S.]

[NOTE.—If the prisoner be a white person, or if he be a free negro, charged with homicide of any grade, or with any offence punishable with death, he must be committed for examination. For all other felonies by free negroes, and in all cases of felony by slaves, the prisoner must be committed for trial.]

(No. 3.)

Form of Certificate of Commitment to be sent to the Clerk of the County Court.

—— County, to wit:

To the Clerk of the County Court of said County:

I, J. T., a Justice of the said County, do hereby certify, that I have, by my warrant, this day committed C. D. (if free negro or slave, state which) to the jail of this County, that he may be examined (or *tried*) before the County Court of the said County, for a felony by him committed, in this that he did, on the —— day of —— 18—, in the said County, (here state the offence as in the mittimus.) Given under my hand, this —— day of —— in the year 18—.

J. T., J. P.

(No. 4.)

Form of Certificate to the Clerk where party is admitted to bail.

Turn to head of ARREST, and follow No. 6.

(No. 5.)

Form of Recognizance of Bail.

Turn to head of RECOGNIZANCE, and follow No. 1, if person be free; No. 2, if a slave, and state succinctly the offence for which the person is recognized.

(No. 6.)

Form of Recognizance of Witness to appear before the County Court to give evidence upon the examination or trial of a party charged with felony.

Turn to head of RECOGNIZANCE, and follow No. 3.

(No. 7.)

Form of a Warrant of Arrest for an attempt to commit burglary.

—— County, to wit:

To X. Y., *Constable of the said County:*

Whereas, A. B. of the County of ——, has this day made information and complaint on oath before me J. T., a Justice of the said County, that C. D., on the —— day of —— 18—, at the said County, did attempt to commit burglary, by unlawfully and in the night of that day, breaking the door of the dwelling house of the said A. B., with intent then and there, feloniously and burglariously to enter the said dwelling house, and feloniously and burglariously to take, steal and carry away the goods of the said A. B., then being in the said dwelling house: These are, therefore, in the name of the Commonwealth of Virginia, to command you forthwith to apprehend the said C. D., and bring him before me or some other Justice of the said County, to answer the said complaint, and to be farther dealt with according to law. Given under my hand and seal, this —— day of —— 18—.

J. T., J. P. [L. S.]

(No. 8.)

Form of Mittimus where a party is committed to answer an Indictment in the County Court for misdemeanor.

—— County, to wit:

To X. Y., *Constable of said County, and to the Keeper of the Jail of the said County:*

These are to command you, the said Constable, in the name of the Commonwealth of Virginia, forthwith to convey and deliver into the custody of the keeper of the said jail, together with this warrant, the body of C. D., charged before me J. T., a Justice of the said County, on the oath of A. B., with a misdemeanor by him committed, in this, that the said C. D., on the —— day of —— in the year 18—, in the said County, (here describe the offence as in the warrant of arrest.) And you, the said keeper of the said jail, are hereby required to receive the said C. D. into your jail and custody, to answer an indictment to be preferred against him for the said offence, in the County Court of said County, and him there safely keep until he shall be discharged by due course of law. Given under my hand and seal, this —— day of —— in the year 18—.

J. T., J. P. [L. S.]

(No. 9.)

Form of Recognizance of Bail.

Turn to head of RECOGNIZANCE, and follow No. 4, and state the offence succinctly, for which the party is recognized.

ATTEMPTS—(*To Commit Crime.*)

(No. 10.)

Form of Certificate of the Commitment, or Letting to Bail, to be sent to the Clerk of the County Court.

—— County, to wit:
To the Clerk of the County Court of the said County:

I, J. T., a Justice of the said County, do hereby certify, that C. D. was this day committed to the jail of this County by my warrant, (or *was this day admitted to bail by me*, as the case may be,) to answer an indictment to be preferred against him, in the County Court of the said County, for a misdemeanor by him committed, in this, that he did, on the —— day of ——— 18—, in said County, (here describe the offence as in the warrant of arrest.) Given under my hand, this —— day of ——— 18—.

J. T., J. P.

(No. 11.)

Form of Recognizance of Witness to appear and give evidence to the Grand Jury upon the Indictment.

Follow No. 5, under the head of RECOGNIZANCE.

Form of an Indictment for an attempt to commit burglary.

—— Judicial Circuit. ⎫ The jurors of the Commonwealth of Vir-
—— County, to wit: ⎬ ginia, in and for the body of the County of
In the Circuit Court of the ⎨ ——, and now in attendance in the Circuit
said County.   ⎭ Court of the said County, upon their oath present, that A. B., on the —— day of ——— 18—, in said County, did unlawfully attempt to commit the crime of burglary, by then and there attempting, in the night time of that day, feloniously to break and enter the dwelling house of one C. D., with intent the goods and chattels of the said C. D. in the said dwelling house then and there being, feloniously and burglariously in the night time aforesaid, to steal, take and carry away, and that he, the said A. B., did then and there, in the night time as aforesaid, in his said attempt to commit the felony and burglary aforesaid, break the door of the said dwelling house, but did not enter the said dwelling house, against the peace and dignity of the Commonwealth of Virginia.

BAIL—See title ARREST.

CHAPTER XII.

BANKS—(*Unchartered.*)

BY SEC. 16, CHAP. 198. All members of any association or company that shall trade or deal as a bank, or carry on banking without authority of law, and their officers and agents therein, shall be confined in jail not more than six months, and fined not less than one hundred nor more than five hundred dollars.

BY SEC. 17. Every free person who, with intent to create a circulating medium, shall issue, without authority of law, any note or other security, purporting that money or other thing of value is payable by or on behalf of such person, and every officer and agent of such person therein, shall be confined in jail not more than six months, and fined not less than one hundred nor more than five hundred dollars.

BY SEC. 18. If a free person pass or receive in payment any note or security, issued in violation of either of the two preceding sections, he shall be fined not less than twenty nor more than one hundred dollars.

BY SEC. 19. If a free person shall bring into this State, with intent to put the same in circulation, any bank note of less denomination than five dollars, issued in another State, or shall pass or receive such note in payment, he shall be fined not less than twenty nor more than one hundred dollars; but this section shall not apply to a non-resident of this State travelling or temporarily sojourning therein.

BY SEC. 20th, of the same chapter, these provisions are declared to be remedial, and should therefore be liberally construed in suppressing the acts prohibited.

(No. 1.)

Form of a Warrant of Arrest against a member or agent of an unchartered bank, for carrying on banking.

———— County, to wit:

To all or any one of the Constables of said County:

Whereas, A. B., of said County, has this day made complaint and information on oath before me J. T., a Justice of said County, that C. D., on the ——— day of ——— 18—, in said County, he the said C. D. then and there being a member (or *agent*, as the case may be,) of a certain association and company, called (here state the name and style of the company,) did then and there carry on the business of banking without lawful authority, by then and there (state the acts done according to the facts, as proved:) These are.

therefore, to command you, in the name of the Commonwealth of Virginia, forthwith to apprehend the said C. D., and bring him before me or some other Justice of the said County, to answer the said complaint, and to be farther dealt with according to law. Given under my hand and seal, this —— day of ——— 18—.

J. T., J. P. [L. S.]

(No. 2.)

Form of a Warrant of Arrest for unlawfully issuing note with intent to create a circulating medium.

—— County, to wit:
To X. Y., *Constable of said County:*

Whereas, A. B. has this day made complaint and information on oath before me J. T., a Justice of the said County, that C. D., on the —— day of ——— 18—, in said County, did, with intent thereby to create a circulating medium, issue, without authority of law, a certain note, in the words and figures following, to wit: (here set out the note;) purporting thereby, that —— dollars were payable by and on behalf of the said C. D.: These are, therefore, to command you, in the name of the Commonwealth, forthwith to apprehend the said C. D., and to bring him before me or some other Justice of the said County, to answer the said complaint, and to be farther dealt with according to law. Given under my hand and seal, this —— day of ——— 18—.

J. T., J. P. [L. S.]

(No. 3.)

Form of a Warrant of Arrest for bringing into this Commonwealth a bank note of less denomination than five dollars, with intent to put it in circulation.

—— County, to wit:
To all or any one of the *Constables of said County:*

Whereas, A. B., of said County, has this day made complaint and information on oath before me J. T., a Justice of the said County, that C. D., on the —— day of ——— 18—, in said County, did unlawfully bring into this Commonwealth, a bank note of less denomination than five dollars, to wit, of the denomination of three dollars, issued by the Bank of North Carolina, and in the State of North Carolina, with intent to put the same in circulation in this Commonwealth: These are, therefore, to command you, in the name of the Commonwealth of Virginia, forthwith to apprehend the said C. D., and bring him before me or some other Justice of the said County, to answer the said complaint, and to be farther dealt with according to law. Given under my hand and seal, this —— day of ——— 18—.

J. T., J. P. [L. S.]

(No. 4.)

Form of a Warrant of Arrest for passing a note of less denomination than five dollars, issued by a Bank of another State.

―――― County, to wit :

To all or any one of the Constables of said County :

Whereas, A. B., of said County, has this day made complaint and information on oath before me J. T., a Justice of the said County, that C. D., on the ―― day of ―――― 18―, in said County, did pass (or *did receive in payment*) a bank note of less denomination than five dollars, to wit, of the denomination of three dollars, issued by the Bank of North Carolina, in the State of North Carolina: These are, therefore, to command you, in the name of the Commonwealth of Virginia, forthwith to apprehend the said C. D., and bring him before me or some other Justice of the said County, to answer the said complaint, and to be farther dealt with according to law. Given under my hand and seal, this ―― day of ―――― 18―.

J. T., J. P. [L. S.]

(No. 5.)

Form of Mittimus where a party is committed to answer an indictment in the County Court for a misdemeanor.

―――― County, to wit :

To X. Y., Constable of said County, and to the Keeper of the Jail of said County :

These are to command you, the said Constable, in the name of the Commonwealth of Virginia, forthwith to convey and deliver into the custody of the keeper of the said jail, together with this warrant, the body of C. D., charged before me J. T., a Justice of the said County, on the oath of A. B., with a misdemeanor by him committed, in this, that the said C. D., on the ―― day of ―――― in the year 18―, in the said County, (here describe the offence as in the warrant of arrest.) And you, the said keeper of the said jail, are hereby required to receive the said C. D. into your jail and custody, to answer an indictment to be preferred against him for the said offence, in the County Court of said County, and him there safely keep, until he shall be discharged by due course of law. Given under my hand and seal, this ―― day of ―――― in the year 18―.

J. T., J. P. [L. S.]

(No. 6.)

Form of Recognizance of Bail.

Turn to head of RECOGNIZANCE, and follow No. 4, and state the offence succinctly, for which the party is recognized.

(No. 7.)

Form of Certificate of the Commitment or Letting to Bail, to be sent to the Clerk of the County Court.

—— County, to wit:
To the Clerk of the County Court of the said County:

I, J. T., a Justice of the said County, do hereby certify, that C. D. was this day committed to the jail of this County, by my warrant, (or *was this day admitted to bail by me*, as the case may be,) to answer an indictment to be preferred against him in the County Court of the said County, for a misdemeanor by him committed, in this that he did, on the —— day of —— 18—, in said County, (here describe the offence as in the warrant of arrest.) Given under my hand, this —— day of —— 18—.

J. T., J. P.

(No. 8.)

Form of Recognizance of Witness to appear and give evidence to the grand jury upon the indictment.

Follow No. 5, under head of RECOGNIZANCE.

CHAPTER XIII.

BARRATRY, MAINTENANCE AND CHAMPERTY.

These offences are of similar character, and are indictable misdemeanors at Common Law, but they rarely occur in this State, and when they do, prosecutions for them generally originate by indictment or presentment, and not by complaint to a Justice of the Peace. No forms, therefore, for the proceedings of a Justice out of court in relation to either of them will be given. Should a case be presented to him, he is referred, for his warrant of arrest and mittimus, to No. 2 and 4, under the head of ARREST, and to No. 4 and 5, under the head of RECOGNIZANCE, for the proper forms for admitting the party to bail, and for recognizing the witnesses to appear and give evidence against him.

Barratry is the habitual moving, exciting and maintaining suits and quarrels, either at law or otherwise. But a man cannot be indicted as a common barrator, in respect of any number of false and groundless actions brought in his own right, nor in respect to a *single act* in right of another, for this would not make him a common barrator. Nor can an attorney be indicted for this crime merely for maintaining another in a groundless suit.([1])

Maintenance is a malicious, or at least officious intermeddling in a suit in which the offender has no interest, to assist one of the parties to it against the other, to prosecute or defend the action, without lawful authority. But it is not every voluntary interference that will constitute this offence, for there are many acts in the nature of maintenance which are justifiable from the circumstances under which they are done, as where the party has an interest in the subject of dispute, however contingent. So where the parties are of kindred or affinity, as father and son, or husband and wife, or stand in the relation of master and servant, or landlord and tenant. So may an attorney or counsellor justify, but the assistance rendered by him must be strictly professional, for he is not more justified in giving his client money than another man.([2])

Champerty is the offence of bargaining with the plaintiff or defendant to divide the land or other matter sued for between them if they prevail in the suit, the champertor undertaking to carry on the suit at his own expense.([3])

CHAPTER XIV.

BASTARDY.

By Sec. 1, Chap. 125. Any unmarried white woman may go before a Justice of the county or corporation in which she has resided for the next preceding year, and accuse any free person of being the father of a bastard child, of which she has been delivered. The said Justice shall examine her under oath and reduce her statement to writing and sign it. On such examination, unless the child appear to be seven years old, a warrant may be issued, requiring the person so accused to be apprehended and brought before a Justice of the county or corporation in which he may be found, who shall require him to enter into a recognizance, with one or more sufficient sureties, in not less than fifty nor more than two hundred dollars, with condition to appear at the next court for the county or corporation in which the warrant issued, and to abide the order of the court.

([1]) See Bouviers' Dictionary, and the authorities there cited.
([2]) Id.   ([3]) Id.

By Sec. 2. Should the court continue the case at the first or any subsequent term, the recognizance shall continue in force until final judgment, unless the accused, if a new recognizance be required, shall give the same, or be committed to jail.

By Sec. 3. After such accusation shall have been made, proceedings thereupon may be had, either at the instance of the woman or of an overseer of the poor.

By Sec. 4. At the hearing, the woman shall be a competent witness, unless she shall have been convicted of any crime which would render her incompetent in another cause. And if the party accused desire it, he may be examined upon oath, and his statement be weighed along with hers.

By Sec. 5. If the court shall adjudge the accused to be the father of such bastard child, it shall order him to pay to the overseers of the poor of the county or corporation, for the maintenance of the said child, such sums as it may deem proper for each year, until such time as the court may appoint, unless it sooner die. The court shall order the father to give a bond, in such penalty and with such sureties as it may deem sufficient for the performance of the said order, and shall order him to jail until such bond be given in court, or filed in the clerk's office, or the woman and the said overseers consent to his discharge, or he be otherwise legally discharged.

By Sec. 6. As often as the condition of such bond is broken, a motion may be made before the court of the county or corporation, and judgment may be given in the name of the said overseers against the said father and his sureties, and against his and their personal representatives, for the money due, with lawful interest thereon from the time or times when the same ought to have been paid.

By Sec. 7. The attorney for the county or corporation shall appear on behalf of the woman, or of the overseers of the poor, in every case under this chapter.

(No. 1.)

Form of the examination of an unmarried woman, upon complaint against the father of her bastard child.

—————— County, to wit :

The examination on oath of A. B., an unmarried white woman, taken before me J. T., a Justice of the said County, on this —— day of —————— 18—: The said A. B., being by me duly sworn, makes oath and says, that she is an unmarried white woman, who has resided in the said County for one year next preceding this date; that on the —— day of —————— 18—, she was delivered of a male (or *female*) bastard child, and that C. D. of the said County, is the father of the said child.

J. T., J. P.

BASTARDY.

(No. 2.)

Form of Warrant of Arrest against the putative father of a bastard child.

—— County, to wit:
 To X. Y., *Constable of the said County*:
  Whereas, A. B., an unmarried white woman of the said County, has this day upon examination on oath taken before me J. T., a Justice of the said County, accused C. D. of the said County, of being the father of a male (or *female*) bastard child, of which she was delivered in the said County, on the —— day of —— 18—: These are, therefore, in the name of the Commonwealth of Virginia, to command you forthwith to apprehend the said C. D., and to bring him before me or some other Justice of the said County, to be farther dealt with according to law. Given under my hand and seal, this —— day of —— 18—.

J. T., J. P. [L. S.]

[When the party is brought before the Justice, no farther examination is to be had before him, and if the accused fail to enter into a recognizance as required by the first section of the statute, he must be committed to jail to answer the accusation before the court.]

(No. 3.)

Form of Recognizance to appear and answer the accusation of being the father of a bastard child.

—— County, to wit:
 Be it remembered, that on this —— day of ——18—, C. D. and E. F. of the said County, came before me J. T., a Justice of the said County, and severally acknowledged themselves to owe to the Commonwealth of Virginia, that is to say: The said C. D. the sum of —— dollars, and the said E. F. the sum of —— dollars, to be respectively made and levied of their several goods and chattels, lands and tenements, if he the said C. D. shall make default in performance of the condition underwritten.
 The condition of the above recognizance is such, that whereas the above bound C. D. has been arrested and this day brought before me J. T., Justice as aforesaid, accused upon the oath of A. B., an unmarried white woman, of being the father of a male (or *female*) bastard child, whereof she was delivered on the —— day of —— 18—, in the said County: Now, if the said C. D. shall make his personal appearance before the next County Court of the said County, on the first day of the next term thereof, to abide the order of the said Court touching the said accusation, and shall not thence depart without the leave of the said Court, then the above recognizance to be void, otherwise to remain in full force and virtue. Taken and acknowledged before me, this —— day of —— 18—.

J. T. J. P.

(No. 4.)

Form of Mittimus when the person accused fails to enter into the Recognizance.

—— County, to wit:
To X. Y. *Constable of said County, and to the Keeper of the Jail of said County:*

Whereas, C. D. was this day brought before me J. T., a Justice of the said County, accused by A. B., an unmarried white woman, upon her examination on oath taken and reduced to writing by J. M., a Justice of said County, on the —— day of —————— 18—, and by him signed, of being the father of a bastard child, of which she was delivered in the said County, on the —— day of —————— 18—, and was by me, as Justice aforesaid, required to enter into a recognizance with sufficient surety, to appear before the next County Court of the said County, on the first day thereof, to abide the order of the said Court touching the said accusation, and the said C. D. has failed to enter into such recognizance: These are, therefore, in the name of the Commonwealth, to command you, the said Constable, forthwith to convey the said C. D. to the jail of the said County, and there deliver him, with this warrant, to the keeper of the said jail: and you, the keeper of the said jail, are hereby commanded to receive the said C. D. into your jail and custody, and him there safely keep until he shall thence be discharged by due course of law. Given under my hand and seal, this —— day of —————— 18—.

J. T., J. P. [L. S.]

CHAPTER XV.

BIGAMY.

By Sec. 1, Chap. 196. Any white person being married, who, during the life of the former husband or wife, shall marry another person in this State, or if the marriage with such other person take place out of the State, shall thereafter cohabit with such other person in this State, shall be confined in the penitentiary not less than one nor more than five years.

By Sec. 2. The preceding section shall not extend to a person whose former husband or wife shall have been continually absent from such person for seven years next before the marriage of such person to another, and shall not have been known by such person to be living within that time; nor to a person who shall, at the time of the subsequent marriage, have been divorced from the bond of the former marriage, *or whose former marriage shall, at that time, have been declared void by the sentence of a court of competent jurisdiction.*

Under the statute, marrying a second husband or wife out of the State, the first being alive, and cohabiting with such second husband or wife in this State, is as much an offence as if the second marriage had taken place in this State.

In a prosecution for bigamy, the first step is to prove the previous first marriage, and this is done by proof of a marriage according to the rites and ceremonies of the country in which it was celebrated.(¹) Proof of a marriage by reputation merely is not sufficient; an actual marriage must be proved,(²) but to do this, it is not necessary to produce either the register or banns, or license, for the marriage may be proved by a person present at the ceremony,(³) and by other modes that might be suggested; as, for example, the acts, acknowledgments and confessions of a party accused of bigamy, are as good evidence and available and sufficient for his conviction, as they would be in any other case, and when sufficiently strong and clear, will dispense with the production of other testimony.(⁴) But when the acknowledgment is as to the first marriage, and before the second, when the consequences of such acknowledgment would not have been present to the mind of the party, and was made palpably for other purposes at the time, it would seem to be entitled to but little weight.(⁵)

After proof of the first marriage, the second wife is a competent witness, for then it appears that the second marriage was void.(⁶)

(No. 1.)

Form of a Warrant of Arrest for bigamy.

———— County, to wit:

To X. Y., Constable of the said County:

Forasmuch as A. B. has this day made information and complaint on oath before me J. T., a Justice of the said County, that C. D. did, on the ———— day of ———— 18—, at the said County, feloniously marry and take to wife one E. F., he the said C. D. having before married and taken to wife one N. O., and she the said N., the lawful wife of the said C. D., being then living: These are, therefore, to command you, in the name of the Commonwealth of Virginia, forthwith to apprehend and bring before me or some other Justice of the said County, the body of the said C. D., to answer the said complaint, and to be farther dealt with according to law. Given under my hand and seal, this ———— day of ———— 18—.

J. T., J. P. [L. S.]

(¹) 1 East P. C. 469.
(²) Morris v. Miller, 4 Burr. 2057; Birt v. Barlow, Doug. 162.
(³) Rex v. Allison, Ry. & Russ. 109.
(⁴) 8 S. & R. 159; Cayfard's Case, 7 Greenl. 57; Warner's Case, 2 Va. Cases 101.
(⁵) 1 East P. C. 470, 71.
(⁶) 1 East P. C. 469.

BIGAMY.

(No. 2.)

Form of Mittimus for bigamy.

—— County, to wit:

To X. Z., Constable of said County, and to the Keeper of the Jail of said County:

These are to command you the said Constable, in the name of the Commonwealth of Virginia, forthwith to convey and deliver into the custody of the keeper of the said jail, together with this warrant, the body of C. D., a white person charged before me J. T., a Justice of the said County, on the oath of A. B., with a felony by him committed, in this, that the said C. D., on the —— day of —— in the year 18—, in the said County, (here describe the offence as in the warrant of arrest.) And you, the said keeper of the said jail, are hereby required to receive the said C. D. into your jail and custody, that he may be examined for the said offence by the County Court of said County, and him there safely keep until he shall be discharged by due course of law. Given under my hand and seal, this —— day of —— in the year 18—.

J. T., J. P. [L. S.]

(No. 3.)

Form of Certificate of Commitment to be sent to the Clerk of the County Court.

—— County, to wit:

To the Clerk of the County Court of said County:

I, J. T., a Justice of the said County, do hereby certify, that I have, by my warrant, this day committed C. D., to the jail of this County, that he may be examined before the County Court of the said County for a felony by him committed, in this, that he did, on the —— day of —— 18—, in the said County, (here state the offence as in the mittimus.) Given under my hand, this —— day of —— in the year 18—.

J. T., J. P.

(No. 4.)

Form of Certificate to the Clerk where party is admitted to bail.

Turn to head of ARREST, and follow No. 6.

(No. 5.)

Form of Recognizance of Bail.

Turn to head of RECOGNIZANCE, and follow No. 1, and state succinctly the offence for which the person is recognized.

BIGAMY—(*Indictment for.*)

Form of Recognizance of Witness to appear before the County Court to give evidence upon the examination of a party charged with bigamy.

Turn to head of RECOGNIZANCE, and follow No. 3.

An Indictment for bigamy.

—— Judicial Circuit. \
—— County, to wit: \
In the Circuit Court of the said County. } The jurors of the Commonwealth of Virginia, in and for the body of the County of ——, and now attending the said Court, upon their oath present, that A. B., on the —— day of —— in the year one thousand eight hundred and ——, in the said County, did marry one T. C., single woman, and her the said T. then and there had for his wife: and that the said A. B. afterwards, and whilst he was so married to the said T. as aforesaid, to wit, on the —— day of —— 18—, in the County of —— aforesaid, feloniously did marry and take to wife one M. Y., and to her the said M. was then and there married, the said T. his former wife being then alive; against the peace and dignity of the Commonwealth of Virginia.

(*The following may be added as a second count.*)

And the jurors aforesaid, on their oath aforesaid, farther present, that the said A. B., on the —— day of —— 18—, in the said County of ——, did marry one T. C., single woman, and her the said T., then and there had for his wife: and that the said A. B. afterwards and whilst he was so married to the said T., as aforesaid, to wit, on the —— day of —— 18—, in the State of Ohio, did feloniously marry and take to wife one M. Y., and to her the said M. was, in the State of Ohio aforesaid, on the day and year aforesaid, married, the said T. his former wife then being alive; and the jurors aforesaid farther say, that the said A. B. did afterwards, to wit, on the —— day of —— 18—, in the Commonwealth of Virginia, in the said County of ——, and within the jurisdiction of this Court, feloniously cohabit with the said M., he the said A. B. having as aforesaid, before married and taken to wife the said T., and the said T., the lawful wife of the said A. B., being then alive at the time that he the said A. B. did so, on the day and year last aforesaid, in the County of —— aforesaid, in the said Commonwealth of Virginia, feloniously cohabit with the said M.; against the peace and dignity of the Commonwealth of Virginia.

BOAT—(*Adrift*)—See ESTRAYS.

CHAPTER XVI.

BONDS—(*Forthcoming, Indemnifying and Suspending.*)

BY SEC. 1, CHAP. 189. The Sheriff or other officer levying a writ of *fieri facias,* or distress warrant, may take from the debtor a bond with sufficient surety, payable to the creditor, reciting the service of such writ or warrant, and the amount due thereon, (including his fee for taking the bond, commission and other lawful charges, if any,) with condition that the property shall be forthcoming at the day and place of sale. Whereupon such property may be permitted to remain in the possession and at the risk of the debtor.

BY SEC. 2. If the condition of such bond be not performed, the officer, unless payment be made of the amount due on the execution or warrant, (including his fee, commission and charges as aforesaid,) shall, within thirty days after the bond is forfeited, return it, with the execution or warrant, to such court or the clerk's office of such court, as is prescribed by the twenty-eighth section of chapter forty-nine. The Clerk shall endorse on the bond the date of its return, and against such of the obligees therein as may be alive when it is forfeited and so returned, it shall have the force of a judgment. But no execution shall issue thereon under this section.

BY SEC. 3. The obligors in such forfeited bond shall be liable for the money therein mentioned, with interest thereon from the date of the bond till paid, and the costs; the obligee or his personal representative shall be entitled to recover the same by action or motion.

BY SEC. 4. In an action or motion on such bond, when it is taken under a distress warrant, the defendants may make defence on the ground that the distress was for rent not due in whole or in part, or was otherwise illegal.

BY SEC. 5. If any such bond be at any time quashed, the obligee, besides his remedy against the officer, may have such execution on his judgment, or issue such distress warrant as would have been lawful if such bond had not been taken.

BY SEC. 6. No bond, for the forthcoming of property, shall be taken on an execution on a forthcoming bond, nor on an execution on a judgment against a Sheriff, Sergeant, Coroner or Constable, or a deputy of any of them, or a surety or personal representative of any such officer or deputy, for money received by any such officer or deputy, by virtue of his office, or against any such officer or his personal representative, in favour of a surety of such officer, or against a deputy of any such officer, or his surety or personal representative, in favour of his principal or the personal representative of such principal, for money paid or judgment rendered for a default in office; nor on an execution against an overseer of the poor, or his personal representative, for money received by him as such; nor on any other execution on which the Clerk is required by law to endorse that "no security is to be taken."

By Sec. 7. On every execution on which a forthcoming bond is prohibited from being given, the endorsement that "no security is to be taken," shall be made by the Clerk.

To provide for cases of adverse claims to property taken under execution or a distress warrant, and other cases in which persons are in possession of property to which there are conflicting claims, it is declared:

By Sec. 1, Chap. 152. Upon affidavit of a defendant in any action that he claims no interest in the subject matter of the suit, but that some third party has a claim thereto, and that he does not collude with such third party, but is ready to pay or dispose of the subject matter of the action as the court may direct, the court may make an order requiring such third party to appear and state the nature of his claim, and maintain or relinquish it; and, in the mean time, stay the proceedings in such action. If such third party, on being served with such order, shall not appear, the court may, on proof of the plaintiff's right, render judgment for him, and declare such third party to be forever barred of any claim in respect of the subject matter, either against the plaintiff or the original defendant, or his personal representative.

If such third party, on being so served, shall appear, the court shall allow him to make himself defendant in the action, and either in said action or otherwise, cause such issue or issues to be tried as it may prescribe; and may direct which party shall be considered the plaintiff in the issues, and shall give judgment upon the verdict rendered on such trial, or if a jury be waived by the parties interested, shall determine their claims in a summary way.

By Sec. 2. When property, of the value of more than twenty dollars, is taken under a warrant of distress, or an execution issued by a Justice, or when property of any value is taken under an execution issued by the Clerk of a court, and any person other than the party against whom the process issued, claims such property, or the proceeds or value thereof, the circuit court, or the court of the county or corporation in which the property is taken, or the Judge of such circuit court in vacation, upon the application of the officer, where no indemnifying bond has been given, or if one has been given, on the application of the person who claims such property, and has given such suspending bond as is hereinafter mentioned, may cause to appear before such court, as well the party serving the process, as the party making such claim, and such court may exercise, for the decision of their rights, all or any of the powers and authority prescribed in the preceding section.

By Sec. 3. In any case before mentioned in this chapter, the court may make all such rules and orders, and enter such judgment as to costs and all other matters as may be just and proper.

By Sec. 4. If any officer levies, or is required to levy, an execution or a warrant of distress on property, and a doubt shall arise whether the said property is liable to such levy, he may give such plaintiff, his agent or attorney at law, notice that an indemnifying bond is required in the case.

Bond may, thereupon, be given by any person, with good security, payable to the officer, in a penalty equal to double the value of the property, conditioned to indemnify him against all damages which he may sustain in consequence of the seizure or sale of the said property, and to pay to any claimant of such property all damages which he may sustain in consequence of such seizure or sale; and also to warrant and defend to any purchaser of the property such estate or interest therein as is sold.

By Sec. 5. If such bond be not given within a reasonable time after such notice, the officer may refuse to levy on such property, or restore it to the person from whose possession it was taken, as the case may be. If it be given where there has been no levy, within a reasonable time, or after a levy, before the property is so restored, it shall be returned within twenty days to the clerk's office from which the execution issued, or if the execution was not issued by a Clerk, to the office of the court by which such officer was appointed, or in which he qualified.

By Sec. 6. The claimant or purchaser of such property, shall, after such bond is so returned, be barred of any action against the officer levying thereon; provided the security therein be good at the time of taking it. But the sale of any such property shall be suspended at the instance of any claimant thereof, who shall deliver to the officer bond, with good security, in a penalty equal to double the value thereof, payable to said officer, conditioned to pay all persons who may be injured by suspending the sale thereof, until the claim thereto can be adjusted, such damages as they may sustain by such suspension. Upon any such bond as is mentioned in this or the preceding section, suit may be prosecuted in the name of the officer, for the benefit of the claimant, creditor, purchaser or other person injured, and such damages recovered in said suit as a jury may assess. The same may be prosecuted and execution had in the name of such officer, when he is dead, in like manner as if he were alive.

By Sec. 7. When property, the sale of which is indemnified, sells for more than enough to satisfy the execution or distress warrant, under which it is taken, the surplus shall be paid by the officer into the court, to the office whereof the indemnifying bond is required to be returned, or as such court may direct. The said court may take such order for the disposition thereof, either temporarily until the question as to the title to the property sold is determined, or absolutely, as in respect to the rights of those interested may seem to it proper.

(No. 1.)

Form of a Forthcoming Bond taken on a distress warrant for rent.

Know all men by these presents, that we, A. B. and B. F., are held and firmly bound to C. R., in the sum of ―― dollars, to be paid to the said C. R., his executors, administrators or assigns; for the payment whereof, we bind ourselves jointly and severally, and our several heirs, executors and administrators. Sealed with our seals, and dated this ―― day of ―― 18―.

The condition of the above obligation is such, that whereas, C. R. has obtained from J. T., a Justice of the said County, a warrant of distress for rent, againt the goods of the above bound A. B., directed to J. G., Constable of the said County, which warrant, with the legal costs attending the same, amounts to the sum of $――: And whereas, J. G., Constable as aforesaid, by virtue of the said warrant, has taken the following property, to wit: (here specify the property levied on,) belonging to the said A. B., to satisfy the said warrant and costs; and the said A. B. being desirous of keeping the said property in his possession until the day of sale thereof, has tendered the above bound B. F. as his surety for the forthcoming and delivery thereof, on the day and at the place of sale: Now, if the above bound A. B. and B. F., or either of them, do and shall deliver the said property to the said J. G., Constable aforesaid, at the Courthouse of the said County, on the first day of the next ―― term of the County Court for the said County, then and there to be sold, to satisfy the said warrant of distress in favour of the said C. R., then the above obligation to be void, otherwise to remain in full force and virtue.

A. B. [L. s.]
B. F. [L. s.]

(No. 2.)

Form of an Indemnifying Bond taken on a distress warrant for rent.

Know all men by these presents, that we, A. B. and E. F., are held and firmly bound unto J. G., Constable of the County of ――, in the sum of $――, to be paid to the said J. G., Constable, his executors, administrators or assigns; for the payment whereof, we bind ourselves jointly and severally, and our several heirs, executors and administrators. Sealed with our seals, and dated this ―― day of ―― 18―.

130   BONDS—(*Forthcoming, Indemnifying, &c.*)

The condition of the above obligation is such, that whereas, the above bound A. B. has obtained from J. T., Justice of the County of ———, a warrant of distress for rent, for taking the goods of G. M., to satisfy him, the said A. B., the sum of $———, for rent due him from the said G. M., which warrant is directed to the above named J. G., Constable of the said County, who has levied the said warrant on the following property, to wit: (here state the property levied on to satisfy the said rent;) and a doubt arising whether the said property is liable to such levy or not, the said J. G., Constable as aforesaid, has applied to the said A. B. for an indemnifying bond, according to the statute in such case: Now, if the said A. B. and E. F., their heirs, executors or administrators, shall indemnify the said J. G., Constable as aforesaid, against all damages which he may sustain in consequence of the seizure or sale of the said property, on which the warrant aforesaid has been levied, and shall moreover pay to any claimant of the said property all damages which he may sustain in consequence of such sale or seizure, and shall also warrant and defend to the purchaser of the said property such interest and estate therein as shall be sold under the said warrant of distress, then the above obligation to be void, otherwise to remain in full force and virtue.

A. B. [L. S.]
E. F. [L. S.]

(No. 3.)

Form of a Forthcoming Bond, taken under a fi. fa. issued from a County Court.

Know all men by these presents, that we, E. H. and B. F., are held and firmly bound unto C. R., in the just and full sum of $———; to the payment whereof, well and truly to be made to the said C. R., his certain attorney, his executors, administrators or assigns, we bind ourselves, our heirs, executors and administrators, jointly and severally, firmly by these presents. Sealed with our seals, and dated this —— day of —— one thousand eight hundred and ——.

The condition of the above obligation is such, that whereas, C. R. hath sued out of the County Court of H. County, a writ of *fieri facias* against the goods and chattels of the above bound E. H., upon a judgment obtained in said Court; which writ, with the legal costs attending the same, amounts to the sum of $———, and directed to the Sheriff of H. County: And whereas ———, deputy for ———, Sheriff of the said H. County, by virtue of the said writ, hath taken the following property belonging to the said E. H., to satisfy the same, to wit: (here insert the property levied on.) And the said E. H. being desirous of keeping the same in his possession until the day of the sale thereof, hath tendered the above bound B. F. as security for the forthcoming and delivery thereof, on the day and at the place of sale: Now, if the above bound E. H. and B. F., or either of them, do and shall deliver the aforesaid property to the said ———, Sheriff of H. County, or one of his deputies, at the Courthouse in the said County, on the first day of the next ——— term of the County Court for the said County of H., then and there to be sold, to satisfy the said execution in favour of the said C. R., then the above obligation to be void, or else to remain in full force and virtue.

Signed, sealed and delivered
  in the presence of

[L. S.]
[L. S.]
[L. S.]

(No. 4.)

Form of Indemnifying Bond upon levy of a fi. fa. issued from a County Court.

Know all men by these presents, that we, A. B. and C. D., are held and firmly bound unto J. S., Sheriff of the County of H., in the just and full sum of $ ———; to the payment whereof, well and truly to be made to the said J. S., Sheriff as aforesaid, his executors, administrators or assigns, we bind ourselves, our heirs, executors and administrators, jointly and severally, firmly by these presents. Sealed with our seals, and dated this ——— day of ——— in the year of our Lord eighteen hundred and ———.

The condition of the above obligation is such, that whereas, A. B. hath sued out of the County Court of ———, a writ of *fieri facias* against the goods and chattels of G. H., upon a judgment obtained in the said Court, which writ, with the legal costs attending the same, amounts to the sum of $ ———: And whereas ———, deputy for J. S., Sheriff as aforesaid, by virtue of the said writ to him the said Sheriff directed, hath levied the same on the following property, to wit: (here insert the property levied on;) and a doubt arising whether the right of the said property is in the said G. H. or not, the said Sheriff hath required of the said A. B., bond with good security, to indemnify him the said Sheriff, pursuant to the act of the General Assembly, in that case made and provided: Now, if the above bound A. B., shall indemnify the said J. S., Sheriff as aforesaid, against all damages which he may sustain in consequence of the seizure or sale of the property on which the said execution hath been levied; and shall moreover pay and satisfy to any person or persons claiming title to the said property, all damage which such person or persons may sustain in consequence of such seizure or sale, and shall also warrant and defend to the purchaser or purchasers of the said property such interest and estate therein as shall be sold under the said execution, then the above obligation to be void, otherwise to remain in full force.

[L. S.]
[L. S.]

(No. 5.)

Form of Forthcoming Bond taken under a fi. fa. issued by a Justice of the Peace.

Know all men by these presents, that we, E. H. and B. F., are held and firmly bound unto C. R., in the just and full sum of $ ———; to the payment whereof, well and truly to be made to the said C. R., his certain attorney, his executors, administrators or assigns, we bind ourselves, our heirs, executors and administrators, jointly and severally, firmly by these presents. Sealed with our seals, and dated this ——— day of ——— one thousand eight hundred and ———.

The condition of the above obligation is such, that whereas, C. R. hath sued out a writ of *fieri facias* against the goods and chattels of the above bound E. H., upon a judgment obtained before a Justice of the County of H., which writ, with the legal costs attending the same, amounts to the sum of $ ———, and directed to the Constable of the said County. And whereas ———, deputy for ———, High Constable of the County of H., by virtue of the said writ, hath taken the following property belonging to the said E. H., to satisfy the same, to wit: (here insert the property levied on.) And the said E. H., being desirous of keeping the said property in his possession until the day of the sale thereof, hath tendered the above

132   BONDS—(*Forthcoming, Indemnifying, &c.*)

bound B. F. as security for the forthcoming and delivery thereof on the day and at the place of sale: Now, if the above bound E. H. and B. F., or either of them, do and shall deliver the aforesaid property to the said Constable, or one of his deputies, at the Courthouse in the County of H., on the first day of the next ——— term of the County Court for the said County of H., then and there to be sold, to satisfy the said execution in favour of the said C. R., then the above obligation to be void, or else to remain in full force and virtue.

Signed, sealed and delivered
in the presence of
                                              [L. S.]
                                              [L. S.]

(No. 6.)

Form of Indemnifying Bond given upon levy of a fi. fa. issued by a Justice of the Peace.

Know all men by these presents, that we, A. B., C. D., &c. are held and firmly bound unto J. K., Constable of the County of ———, in the just and full sum of $———; to the payment whereof, well and truly to be made to the said J. K., Constable as aforesaid, his executors, administrators or assigns, we bind ourselves, our heirs, executors and administrators, jointly and severally, firmly by these presents. Sealed with our seals, and dated this ——— day of ——— in the year one thousand eight hundred and ———.

The condition of the above obligation is such, that whereas, the said A. B. hath sued out before R. S., a Justice of the County of ———, a writ of *fieri facias* against the goods and chattels of X. Y., upon a judgment obtained before the said R. S., a Justice of the Peace as aforesaid, which writ, with the legal costs attending the same, amounts to the sum of $———. And whereas J. K., Constable of the County of ———, by virtue of the said writ to him directed, hath levied the same on the following property, to wit: (here insert the property levied on ;) and a doubt arising whether the right of the said property is in the said X. Y. or not, the said Constable hath required of the said A. B., bond with good security, to indemnify him the said Constable, pursuant to the act of the General Assembly in that case made: Now, if the above bound A. B., C. D., &c. shall indemnify the said J. K., Constable as aforesaid, against all damages which he may sustain in consequence of the seizure or sale of the property on which the said execution hath been levied; and shall moreover pay and satisfy to any person or persons claiming title to the said property, all damage which such person or persons may sustain in consequence of such seizure or sale, and shall also warrant and defend to the purchaser or purchasers of the said property, such interest and estate therein as shall be sold under the said execution, then the above obligation to be void, otherwise to remain in full force.

                                                       [L. S.]
                                                   [L. S.]

(No. 7.)

Form of Bond for suspending a sale after an indemnifying bond has been given, upon the levy of a fi. fa. issued by a Justice of the Peace.

Know all men by these presents, that we, F. G., L. T., &c., are held and firmly bound unto J. K., Constable of the County of ———, in the sum of $———, to be paid to the said J. K., Constable as aforesaid, his executors, administrators or assigns; for the payment whereof, we bind ourselves jointly and severally, and our several heirs, executors and administrators. Sealed with our seals, and dated this —— day of ———, one thousand eight hundred and ———.

The condition of the above obligation is such, that whereas, A. B. hath sued out before R. S., a Justice of the County of ———, a writ of *fieri facias* against the goods and chattels of X. Y., upon a judgment obtained before the said R. S., a Justice of the Peace as aforesaid, which writ, with the legal costs attending the same, amounts to the sum of $———. And whereas, J. K., Constable of the County of ———, by virtue of the said writ to him directed, levied the same on the following property, to wit: (here insert the property levied on;) and a doubt, whether the said property is liable to such levy or not, having arisen, the said J. K., Constable as aforesaid, required an indemnifying bond, according to the statute in such case; which bond was accordingly given by the said A. B., with C. D. his surety, dated on the —— day of —— 18——. And the above bound F. G., having thereafter claimed the said property, and the sale thereof being thereupon suspended at his instance, according to the statute in such case: Now, if the above bound F. G. and L. T., their heirs, executors or administrators, shall pay to the said A. B. and all other persons who may be injured by suspending the sale of the said property, until the claim of the said F. G. thereto can be adjusted according to law, such damages as he or they may sustain by such suspension, then the above obligation to be void, otherwise to remain in full force.

[L. S.]
[L. S.]

(No. 8.)

Form of Bond for suspending a sale after an indemnifying bond has been given, upon the levy of a fi. fa. by a Sheriff.

Know all men by these presents, that we, F. G., L. T., &c., are held and firmly bound unto J. K., Sheriff of the County of ———, in the sum of $———, to be paid to the said J. K., Sheriff as aforesaid, his executors, administrators or assigns; for the payment whereof, we bind ourselves, jointly and severally, and our several heirs, executors and administrators. Sealed with our seals, and dated this —— day of —— one thousand eight hundred and ———.

The condition of the above obligation is such, that whereas, A. B. hath sued out of the County Court of —— County, a writ of *fieri facias* against the goods and chattels of X. Y., upon a judgment obtained in the said County Court of —— County; which writ, with the legal costs attending the same, amounts to the sum of $———: And whereas, J. K., Sheriff of the County of ———, by virtue of the said writ to him directed, levied the same on the following property, to wit: (here insert the property levied on;) and a doubt, whether the said property is liable to such levy or not, having arisen, the said J. K., Sheriff as aforesaid, required an indemnifying bond, according to the statute in such case; which bond was accordingly given by the said A. B., with C. D. his surety, dated on the —— day of —————— 18—. And the above bound F. G. having thereafter claimed the said property, and the sale thereof being thereupon suspended at his instance, according to the statute in such case: Now, if the above bound F. G. and L. T., their heirs, executors or administrators, shall pay to the said A. B., and all other persons who may be injured by suspending the sale of the said property, until the claim of the said F. G. thereto can be adjusted according to law, such damages as he or they may sustain by such suspension, then the above obligation to be void, otherwise to remain in full force.

[L. S.]
[L. S.]

(No. 9.)

Form of Bond for suspending a sale after an indemnifying bond given upon the levy of a distress warrant.

Know all men by these presents, that we, Z. Y. and X. W. are held and firmly bound to J. G., Constable of the County of ——, in the sum of $——, to be paid to the said J. G., Constable, his executors, administrators or assigns; for the payment whereof, we bind ourselves, jointly and severally, and our several heirs, executors and administrators. Sealed with our seals, and dated this —— day of —————— 18—.

The condition of the above obligation is such, that whereas, A. B. has obtained from J. T., Justice of the County of ——, a warrant of distress for rent, for taking the goods of G. M., to satisfy the said A. B. the sum of $——, for rent due him from the said G. M., which warrant is directed to the above named J. G., Constable as aforesaid, who has levied the said warrant on the following property, (here state the property levied on,) to satisfy the said rent; and a doubt whether the said property is liable to such levy or not, having arisen, the said J. G., Constable as aforesaid, required an indemnifying bond, according to the statute in such case; which bond was accordingly given by the said A. B., with E. T., his surety, dated on the —— day of —————— 18—. And the above bound Z. Y., having thereafter claimed the said property, and the sale thereof being thereupon suspended at his instance, according to the statute in that case made: Now, if the above bound Z. Y. and X. W., their heirs, executors or administrators, shall pay to the said A. B., and all other persons who may be injured by suspending the sale of the said property, until the claim of the said Z. Y. thereto can be adjusted according to law, such damages as he or they may sustain by such suspension, then the above obligation to be void, otherwise to remain in full force.

Z. Y. [L. S.]
X. W. [L. S.]

BOOKS.

For selling books, &c. containing obscene language, see INDECENCY and NUISANCES.

CHAPTER XVII.

BRIBERY AND CORRUPTION.

Bribery is, at Common Law, the receiving of any undue reward, by any person whatever, whose ordinary profession or business relates to the administration of public justice, or who is in any official situation, in order to influence his behaviour in office and incline him to act contrary to the known rules of honesty and integrity. And the person who gives the bribe is as much guilty of the offence as he who takes it.([1]) An attempt, accompanied by an offer of money, to bribe an officer of the government, though it does not succeed, is an indictable offence at Common Law,([2]) as well as under the statute.

On the due execution of public trusts, depends, mainly, the good order of the government and the happiness of the people, and nothing can be more injurious to public weal, than to have places of such high concernment accessible to this means of corruption. The Legislature, therefore, has guarded them by the following provisions of the statute:

By Sec. 4, Chap. 194. Any free person who shall corruptly give, offer, or promise to any executive, legislative or judicial officer, after his election or appointment, and either before or after he shall have been qualified or shall have taken his seat, any gift or gratuity, with intent to influence his act, vote, opinion, decision or judgment on any matter, question, cause or proceeding, which is or may be then pending, or may by law come or be brought before him in his official capacity, shall be confined in jail one year, and be fined not exceeding one thousand dollars.

By Sec. 5. Any executive, legislative or judicial officer, who shall corruptly accept any gift or gratuity, or any promise to make a gift, or do any act beneficial to such officer, under an agreement or with an understanding that his vote, opinion or judgment shall be given in any particular manner upon a particular side of any question, cause or proceeding, which is or may be by law brought before him in his official capacity, or that in such capacity he shall make any particular nomination or appointment, shall be confined in jail one year, and fined not exceeding one thousand dollars, and shall moreover forfeit his office, and be forever incapable of holding any post mentioned in the 1st section of chapter twelve.

([1]) 1 Hawk. c. 67, § 2; 1 Deac. Cr. Co. 155.
([2]) 2 East R. 5; 4 Burr. 2495.

By Sec. 6. If any officer authorized to serve legal process, receive any money or other thing of value for omitting or delaying to perform any duty pertaining to his office, he shall be confined in jail not more than six months, and be fined not exceeding one hundred dollars.

By Sec. 7. Any free person who gives, or offers or promises to give, any money or other thing of value to a commissioner appointed by a court, auditor, arbitrator, umpire or juror, (although not impanneled,) with intent to bias his opinion, or influence his decision in relation to any matter in which he is acting, or is to act; and any such commissioner, auditor, arbitrator, umpire or juror, who corruptly takes or receives such money or other thing, shall be confined in jail six months, and fined not exceeding five hundred dollars.

By Sec. 13. If any officer wilfully or corruptly refuse to execute any lawful process, requiring him to apprehend or confine a person convicted of or charged with an offence, or shall wilfully *and* corruptly omit or delay to execute such process, whereby such person shall escape and go at large, such officer shall be confined in jail not more than six months, and be fined not exceeding five hundred dollars.

By Sec. 22. A Sheriff or other officer, who corruptly, or through favour or ill will, shall summon a juror, with intent that such juror shall find a verdict for or against either party, shall be fined not exceeding five hundred dollars, and forfeit his office, and be forever incapable of holding any post mentioned in the 1st section of chapter twelve.

By Sec. 23. If any free person shall procure a juror to be summoned, with intent that such juror shall find a verdict for or against either party, he shall be fined not exceeding five hundred dollars.

Bribery is one of those offences which may assume such a variety of forms, that it would be impossible to furnish, by anticipation, a precedent for each offence, and the forms given will be limited to one case.

(No. 1.)

Form of a Warrant of Arrest for offering to bribe a Judge.

—— County, to wit:

To X. Y., Constable of the said County:

Whereas, A. B. of the said County, hath this day made complaint and information on oath before me J. T., a Justice of the said County, that on the —— day of —— 18—, in the said County, a certain cause, in which P. S. was plaintiff and P. D. was defendant, was pending and undetermined in the Circuit Court of the said County, before L. P. T., the Judge of the said Court, and that the said P. D., with intent to influence the opinion and judgment of the said L. P. T., as such Judge in the said cause so pending before him, did then and there unlawfully, wilfully and corruptly promise and offer to pay (or *give*) to him the said L. P. T., as Judge aforesaid, a certain sum of money, to wit, the sum of ———— dollars, as a pecuniary reward, to influence and induce him the said L. P. T., as such Judge, to prostitute and betray the duties of his said office, by giving his opinion as such Judge, and deciding the said cause, thus pending in the said Court, in favour of the said P. D.: These are, therefore, in the name of the Commonwealth, to require you forthwith to apprehend the said P. D., and to bring him before me or some other Justice of the said County, to be farther dealt with according to law. Given under my hand and seal, this ———— day of ———— 18—.

J. T., J. P. [L. S.]

(No. 2.)

Form of Mittimus.

Follow form No. 9, under the head of ARREST, and describe the offence succinctly as in the foregoing warrant.

(No. 3.)

Form of Recognizance of Bail.

Follow form No. 4, under head of RECOGNIZANCE.

(No. 4.)

Form of Recognizance of Witness.

Follow form No. 5, under head of RECOGNIZANCE.

(No. 5.)

Form of Certificate to be sent to the Clerk.

Follow form No. 10, under head of ARREST.

Indictment for endeavouring to bribe a Constable.

Commence as No. 1, under head of "INDICTMENTS," and proceed thus: that heretofore, to wit, on the ———— day of ————, one A. B., then and there being one of the Justices in and for the County of ————, duly qualified, appointed and sworn to discharge and perform the duties of said office, did then and there make and issue a certain warrant, under his hand and seal, in due form of law, bearing date the day and year aforesaid, directed to all or any one of the Constables of the County of ————, thereby commanding them, upon sight thereof, to take and bring before him, the said A. B., Justice as aforesaid, (or some other Justice for the said County, if such be the warrant,) the body of one C. D., in the County aforesaid, to answer (as in the warrant) and which said warrant afterwards, to wit, on the —— day of —————— in the year aforesaid, in the County aforesaid, was delivered to E. F. in the County aforesaid, he the said E. F., then being one of the Constables of the said County, duly appointed and qualified to discharge the duties of said office of Constable, to be executed in due form of law. And the jurors aforesaid, upon their oath aforesaid, do farther present, that G. H. of the County aforesaid, well knowing the premises, but contriving and unlawfully intending to pervert the due course of law and justice, and to prevent the said C. D. from being arrested and taken under and by virtue of the warrant aforesaid, afterwards, to wit, on the day and year aforesaid, in the County aforesaid, unlawfully, wickedly and corruptly, did offer unto the said E. F., so being Constable as aforesaid, and having in his custody and possession the said warrant, so delivered to him to be executed as aforesaid, the sum of —————— dollars, if he the said E. F. would refrain from executing the said warrant, and from taking and arresting the said C. D. under and by virtue of the said warrant : and so the jurors aforesaid, upon their oath aforesaid, do say, that the said G. H., in manner and form aforesaid, did attempt and endeavour to bribe the said E. F., so being Constable as aforesaid, to neglect and omit to do his duty as such Constable, and to refrain from taking and arresting the said C. D. under and by virtue of the warrant aforesaid, against the peace and dignity of the Commonwealth of Virginia.

BUGGERY—See SODOMY.

CHAPTER XVIII.

BURGLARY.

[For breaking and entering a dwelling house in the day time, or entering a dwelling house in the night without breaking, and for breaking and entering any other house, or any vessel, with intent to commit felony, see HOUSE BREAKING and SHIPS.]

BY SEC. 11, CHAP. 192. Any free person who shall be guilty of burglary, shall be confined in the penitentiary not less than five, nor more than ten years. If a person break and enter the dwelling house of another in the night time, with intent to commit larceny, he shall be deemed guilty of burglary, though the thing stolen or intended to be stolen be of less value than twenty dollars.

Burglary is defined to be a breaking and entering the mansion house of another in the night, with intent to commit some felony, whether such intent be executed or not.(¹) From this definition it appears, that four things are necessary to constitute the offence. 1st. There must be a breaking and entering.

(¹) 1 Hale 549 ; 1 Hawk. c. 38, § 1 ; 2 East P. C. 484.

BURGLARY.   139

2d. It must be in a mansion house. 3d. It must be in the night time. 4th. There must be a felonious intent.

I. *Breaking and entering.*

There must either be an actual breaking of some part of the house, to effect which, more or less actual force is employed, or else a breaking, by construction of law, as where an entrance is obtained by threats, fraud or conspiracy.([1])

An actual breaking may be, by making a hole in the wall, by forcing open the door, by putting back, picking or opening the lock with a false key, by breaking the window or taking a pane of glass out of it, or drawing or bending the nails or other fastenings out of it, or by putting back the leaf of a window shutter with an instrument. And even the drawing or lifting up of the latch, when the door is not otherwise fastened, the turning the key, where the door is locked on the inside, or the unloosing any other fastening, will amount to a breaking.([2]) To push open folding doors, which remain closed by their own weight, but without any interior fastening, so that those without could, by moderate exertion, open them, is a sufficient breaking to constitute burglary.([3]) And so the lifting the flap of a cellar, usually kept down by its own weight, has been held a sufficient breaking for the purpose of burglary.([4])

Where a window opens upon hinges and is fastened by a wedge, forcing it open by pushing against it, is held to be a sufficient breaking.([5]) So the putting down the upper sash of a window, though it has no fastening and is only kept in its place by the pulley weight, and though there is an outer shutter which is not put to, is held to be a sufficient breaking.([6]) But if the sash of a window be partly open or raised, but not sufficiently to admit a person, the raising it, so as to admit him, is not a breaking of the house, so as to constitute burglary.([7]) It is also a breaking, to get into a house by creeping down the chimney, for it is as much closed as the nature of the thing will permit.([8])

The breaking is not confined to the outer door or the external parts of a house; for if a thief enter a dwelling house

---

([1]) 2 Russ. 2; 1 Deac. 181; 1 Dick. 333.

([2]) 1 Hale 552; 3 Inst. 64; 1 Hawk. c. 38.

([3]) Rex v. Brown, 2 East P. C. 487; 1 Deac. Cr. Co. 184.

([4]) Rex v. George Russell, Moody's C. C. 377; Lewen's Rep. 35, *Note:* Russell's Case settles the doubt raised in Callan's Case, and confirms the opinion of Buller, J. expressed in Brown's Case. But see 19 Eng. C. L. R. 360.

([5]) Rex v. Hall, Russ. & Ry. C. C. 355; 1 Deac. 181.

([6]) Rex v. Haines & al. Russ. & Ry. C. C. 451; 1 Deac. 181.

([7]) Smith's Case, Moody C. C. 178; Lewen's Rep. 34.

([8]) 1 Hale 552; Brice's Case, Russ. & Ry. 450.

in the night time, by an outer door being left open, or by an open window, yet if, when within the house, he turn the key or unlatch or unbolt a chamber door, with intent to commit felony, this will be burglary.[1]

And so, where a servant in the night time, opened the chamber door of his mistress, which was fastened with a bolt, for the purpose of committing a rape, it was held to be a burglary.[2] But whether the opening of an internal door in the night, by a servant, with a felonious intent, amounts to burglary or not, depends upon the question, whether the door might not have been opened *in the course of his trust and employment*. Thus, if a butler or a footman turn a key in the parlour door of his master's house, and steal property out of the room, such opening of the door (being within his trust) is not a breaking. But if he breaks open a door, whether outward or inward, of a closet, study or counting house, with intent to steal goods therefrom, such opening (not being within his trust) will amount to a burglary.[3]

Likewise, it will be burglary, if any lodger in a house or guest at a public inn, open and enter another person's chamber door, with intent to commit a felony.[4] It is not burglary to break open the door of a cupboard let into the walls of a house, or any fixture of this description.[5]

A breaking by construction of law, is, where an entrance is obtained by threats, fraud or conspiracy.[6]

Where, in consequence of violence commenced or threatened, in order to obtain entrance to a house, the owner, either from the apprehension of the violence, or in order to repel it, opens the door and the thief enters, such entry will amount to a breaking, in law.[7] And so, in a case where the evidence was, that the family within the house were forced, by threats and intimidation, to let the offenders in, the learned Judge, who tried the cause, told the jury, that although the door was literally opened by one of the family, yet if such opening proceeded from the intimidation of those who were without, it was as much a breaking, by those who made use of such intimidations, as if they had actually burst the door open.[8]

A breaking may be effected by conspiring with persons within the house, by whose means those who are without ef-

---

[1] 2 East P. C. 488 ; 2 Russ. 6 ; 1 Hale 553.
[2] Strange 481 ; 1 Deac. 186.
[3] 1 Hale 354-55 ; 2 Russ. 10.
[4] 1 Hale 553, 554 ; 2 East P. C. 488.
[5] 1 Hale 523, 527 ; Fost. 109.

[6] 2 Russ. 8 ; 1 Burn 496 ; 1 Dick. J. P. 333.
[7] 1 Hale 553 ; 2 East P. C. 486 ; 2 Russ. 8.
[8] Rex *v.* Swallow & als., before Thompson, B., York assizes, 1813 ; and, upon this direction the prisoners were convicted and executed.

fect an entrance. Thus, if the servant of B. conspire with C., to let him in to rob B., and accordingly the servant in the night time opens the door and lets him in, this is burglary in both.(¹)

Where an act is done in *fraudem legis*, the law gives no benefit thereof to the party, and therefore, if in consequence of any *fraud* or deceit, the owner is induced to open his door to thieves, this will amount to a breaking. As if a man go to a house, under pretence of being authorized to make a distress, and by this means obtain admittance.(²) So, if thieves knock at the door, pretending to have business with the master of the house, and upon its being opened to them, enter the house and rob him, this (if in the night time) is also burglary.(³)

So, where a prisoner met a boy, who had the care of a house, and deluded him to return with her to the house and let her in, upon which she sent him for a pot of ale, and whilst he was gone, robbed the house and went away: it being in the night time, was adjudged to be burglary.(⁴) And not to mention other cases of breaking, it may be stated as a well established principle, that whenever the entrance is obtained, in the night time, by any trick or fraudulent device, it will be burglary; for the law will not endure to have its justice defrauded by such evasions.(⁵)

As to what constitutes an entering.] It is a sufficient entry, if the body or any part thereof, as the foot or arm, is within any part of the house, or if a gun be put into a window, which the party breaks in the night time, (though the hand be not in,) or into a hole of the house, which he makes in the night, with intent to murder or kill, this is an entry and breaking of the house, but if he barely break the house, without any such entry at all, it will not be burglary.(⁶)

Where it appeared in evidence, that a person had cut a hole in the night time, in the window shutters of the prosecutor's shop, which was a part of his dwelling house, and by putting his hand through the hole, took out watches and other things which hung in the shop within his reach, and no other entry was proved, it was held to be burglary.(⁷)

So, putting a hook to steal, or a pistol to kill, within the door or window, though the hand be not in, is an entry,(⁸) and to discharge a loaded gun into a house, is a sufficient entry.(⁹)

(¹) 1 Hale P. C. 553; 2 Str. 881; Roscoe Cr. Ev. 258; 2 East P. C. 486.
(²) 1 Leach 284; 1 Deac. 183.
(³) Kel. 42; 1 Hawk. c. 38, § 1.
(⁴) 2 East P. C. 485; 1 Deac. 383.
(⁵) 1 Hawk. c. 38, § 1; 4 Blac. 227; 2 Russ. 9.
(⁶) 1 Burn 499; 3 Inst. 64; 2 East P. C. 490.
(⁷) Fost. 167; 2 East P. C. 490.
(⁸) Id.
(⁹) 1 Hawk. c. 38, § 7; 1 Burn 500; 3 Ch. Cr. L. 1108; 4 Camp. 220.

In the case of Bailey and Spencer, who were indicted for burglary, it was proved that the house was fastened in the following manner: The sash was drawn down, closed and fastened at the point of division, by a latch on the inside; the inside shutters were closed and fastened by a bar; the pane in the upper part of the window was broken, in order to put in the hand to remove the latch; then the lower sash was thrown up to enable the prisoners to introduce a centre bit, to cut a hole in the shutters; and, while they were engaged in this last operation, and before they had completed it, they were seized. The jury expressly found, that the window was latched, and that the hand of one of the prisoners (both being present) was introduced in order to remove the latch, but the shutter never was actually opened. Upon these facts, the Judges were unanimous that there had been a sufficient entry of the house to constitute burglary.([1])

If divers persons come in the night to commit burglary, and one of them breaks and enters the house, the rest of them standing to watch at a distance, it is burglary in all.([2])

The entry need not be at the same time as the breaking, provided both be in the night; and, therefore, if thieves break a hole in the house one night, with intent to enter another night and commit felony, which they execute accordingly, it is burglary.([3])

II. *The mansion house.*

Every house for the habitation of man, is taken to be a mansion house, wherein burglary may be committed.([4]) Even a loft over a stable used for the abode of a coachman, which he rents for his own use and that of his family, with an outer door, is a place which may be burglariously broken;([5]) and burglary may be committed in a lodging room,([6]) or in a garret used for a workshop and rented together with an apartment for sleeping.([7]) And so, to break in a store, from which there is a communication into a room, occupied for sleeping by a clerk, belonging to the family of the owner of the store, and whose family reside at a separate place, is held to be burglary.([8])

It must, however, actually be a house, and not a booth or tent,([9]) and it must be a place of actual residence.([10]) Where the former tenant of a house had quitted it, and the incoming tenant had put in all of his furniture, and had been frequently

---

([1]) Russ. & Ry. C. C. 341; 1 Burn 499.
([2]) 3 Inst. 64; 1 Burn 500.
([3]) 1 Hale 551; 1 Burn 500.
([4]) 3 Inst. 64; Ch. Cr. L. 1102.
([5]) 1 Leach 305.
([6]) Id. 89.
([7]) 1 Leach 237.
([8]) Wood's Case, 5 N. Y. C. H. Rec. 10.
([9]) 1 Hawk. c. 38.
([10]) 3 Ch. Cr. L. 1101.

there in the day time, but had never slept in the house, nor had his family, it was held that burglary could not be committed therein,(¹) as he had never slept in the house, it had not become his residence; but it is not necessary, to make it a burglary, that any person be actually in the house at the very time the offence is committed.(²) To this rule of actual residence, an exception is made for the protection of churches, to break and enter which, in the night, is held to be burglary.(³)

The mansion house, at Common Law, not only includes the dwelling house, but all other houses within the *curtilage*. This term "curtilage," less defined than any other in law, has given rise to so many legal subtleties and contradictory decisions, that it has been found necessary to declare by statute that "no out house, not adjoining a dwelling house, nor under the same roof, although within the curtilage thereof, shall be deemed parcel of such dwelling house, unless some person usually lodge therein at night." Sec. 3, chap. 192.

At Common Law it is necessary to ascertain to whom the mansion belongs, and to state it with accuracy in the proceedings. But, by our statute, it may be charged to be the house of any one having either the actual or constructive possession of it.

A house, the joint property of partners in trade, and in which their business is carried on, but in which only one resides, may be described as the dwelling house of all the partners.(⁴)

If the house belong to a corporation, and is inhabited by its servants, it may be laid at Common Law, as against the mansion house of the corporation,(⁵) and by the statute it may be charged to be the house of any free person in possession of it.

III. *In the night*.

There can be no burglary in the day time. It must be in the night, and as to what shall be accounted night for this purpose, whatever may be found in the more ancient authorities, it is settled, that if there be daylight enough begun or left, either by the light of the sun or twilight, whereby the countenance of a man may be reasonably discerned, it is not burglary; but this does not extend to moonlight.(⁶)

(¹) 2 East P. C. 498; 1 Burn 503.   (⁵) 2 East P. C. 501; Fost. 38.
(²) 1 Hawk. c. 38.   (⁶) 4 Com. 224; 2 East P. C. 509;
(³) 1 Burn 500; 2 East P. C. 487, 491.   1 Hale 550.
(⁴) Rex *v.* Athea, Moo. C. C. 329.

In a case where it was charged that goods were feloniously and burglariously taken from a dwelling house, without charging it to be done in the night time, the indictment was held to be bad for burglary, and good only as an indictment for larceny.(¹) So, the Justice will see the necessity of charging all the acts done, to constitute the offence, to have been done in the night.

IV. *With intent to commit felony.*

There can be no burglary, unless where the breaking and entering is with intent to commit felony, for if it appear that the offender meant only to commit a trespass, as to beat the party, or the like, he is not guilty of burglary.(²) And the indictment should state accurately the felony really intended to be committed; for if it charge that the entry was with intent to commit one sort of felony, and the fact appear to be that it was with intent to commit another, it will not be sufficient.(³) It is not necessary that the felony should actually be committed; if the breaking and entering is done with intent to commit felony, it is burglary, though the felony be not actually committed.(⁴)

(No. 1.)

Form of Warrant of Arrest for burglary upon a positive charge against a particular person.

——— County, to wit:

To all or any one of the Constables of said County:

Whereas, A. B. of said County, has this day made complaint and information on oath before me J. T., a Justice of the said County, that C. D., on the ——— day of ——— 18—, in said County, did, about the hour of ———, in the night time of that day, in said County, feloniously and burglariously break and enter the dwelling house of the said A. B., with intent the goods and chattels of the said A. B., then and there feloniously and burglariously to steal, take and carry away, and one silver watch of the value of ——— dollars, of the goods and chattels of the said A. B., in the said dwelling house then being, feloniously and burglariously did steal, take and carry away: These are, therefore, to command you, in the name of the Commonwealth of Virginia, forthwith to apprehend the said C. D., and bring him before me or some other Justice of the said County, to answer the said complaint, and to be farther dealt with according to law. Given under my hand and seal, this ——— day of ——— 18—.

J. T., J. P. [L. S.]

(¹) Commonwealth v. Marks, 4 Leigh 568.
(²) 2 East P. C. 509; Commonwealth v. Newell & al. 7 Mass. Rep. 245.
(³) 2 East P. C. 514; 1 Deac. Cr. Co. 195.
(⁴) 1 Deac. Cr. Co. 193; 4 Com. 227; 2 N. Y. C. H. Recorder 45.

(No. 2.)

Form of Warrant of Arrest for burglary, upon belief only.

—————— County, to wit:
To all or any one of the Constables of said County:

Whereas, A. B. of said County, has this day made complaint and information on oath before me J. T., a Justice of said County, that in the night of the ——— day of ———— 18—, his dwelling house in the said County, was feloniously and burglariously broken open and entered, and one coat (or whatever else according to the fact) of the value of ——— dollars, of the goods of the said A. B., was then and there feloniously and burglariously stolen, taken and carried away from the said dwelling house, and that he has good cause to suspect, and does suspect, that C. D. did commit the said felony and burglary: These are, therefore, to command you, in the name of the Commonwealth, forthwith to apprehend the said C. D., and to bring him before me or some other Justice of the said County, to answer the complaint aforesaid, and to be farther dealt with according to law. Given under my hand and seal, this ——— day of ———— 18—.

J. T., *J. P.* [L. s.]

(No. 3.)

Form of Mittimus where a party is committed for examination or trial in the County Court for burglary.

—————— County, to wit:
To X. Z., Constable of said County, and to the Keeper of the Jail of said County:

These are to command you, the said Constable, in the name of the Commonwealth of Virginia, forthwith to convey and deliver into the custody of the keeper of the said jail, together with this warrant, the body of C. D., a white person (or *free negro*, or *a slave, the property of E. F.*, as the case may be,) charged before me J. T., a Justice of the said County, on the oath of A. B., with a felony by him committed, in this, that the said C. D., in the night of the ——— day of ———— in the year 18—, in the said County, (here describe the offence as in the warrant of arrest.) And you, the said keeper of the said jail, are hereby required to receive the said C. D. into your jail and custody, that he may be examined (or *tried*) for the said offence, by the County Court of said County, and him there safely keep until he shall be discharged by due course of law. Given under my hand and seal, this ——— day of ——— in the year 18—.

J. T., *J. P.* [L. s.]

[NOTE.—If the prisoner be a white person, or if he be a free negro charged with homicide of any grade, or with any offence punishable with death, he must be committed for examination. For all other felonies by free negroes, and in all cases of felony by slaves, the prisoner must be committed for trial.]

BURGLARY—(*Indictment for.*)

(No. 4.)

Form of Certificate of Commitment to be sent to the Clerk of the County Court.

—— County, to wit:
   To the Clerk of the County Court of said County:
   I, J. T., a Justice of the said County, do hereby certify that I have, by my warrant, this day committed C. D. (if free negro or slave, state which,) to the jail of this County, that he may be examined (or *tried*) before the County Court of the said County, for a felony by him committed, in this, that he did, in the night of the —— day of ——— 18—, in the said County, (here state the offence as in the mittimus.) Given under my hand, this —— day of ——— in the year 18—.

J. T., J. P.

(No. 5.)

Form of Certificate to the Clerk where party is admitted to bail.

Turn to head of ARREST, and follow No. 6.

(No. 6.)

Form of Recognizance of Bail.

Turn to head of RECOGNIZANCE, and follow No. 1, if person be free; No. 2, if a slave, and state succinctly the offence for which the person is recognized.

(No. 7.)

Form of Recognizance of Witness to appear before the County Court to give evidence upon the examination or trial of a party charged with felony.

Turn to head of RECOGNIZANCE, and follow No. 3.

An Indictment for burglary.

—— Judicial Circuit,
—— County, to wit:
In the Circuit Court of the said County.
}
The jurors of the Commonwealth of Virginia, in and for the body of the County of ——, and now attending the said Court, do upon their oath present, that A. B., on the —— day of ——— in the year one thousand eight hundred and ——, about the hour of ten o'clock, in the night of that day, feloniously and *burglariously* did *break* and *enter* into the *dwelling house* of one C. D., situated in the said County, with intent the goods and chattels of him the said C. D., in the said dwelling house, then and there being, then and there feloniously and *burglariously* to steal, take and carry away, and one silver watch of the value of twenty dollars, of the goods and chattels of the said C. D., in the said dwelling house, in the County aforesaid, then and there being found, then and there feloniously and burglariously did steal, take and carry away, against the peace and dignity of the Commonwealth of Virginia.

CHAPTER XIX.

BURIAL OF THE DEAD.

The Common Law denounces the disinterment of the dead as indecent and shocking to humanity, and will not allow the sanctuary of the grave to be violated, however useful dead bodies may be as a means of instructing the living. It is now well settled, that to prevent a human body from being buried in due time, as well as to disinter it without lawful authority, is a misdemeanor indictable at Common Law, even though it be the body of a capital convict.([1]) AND BY SEC. 13, CHAP. 196, of the Statute. If a free person unlawfully disinter or displace a dead human body, or any part of a dead human body, which shall have been deposited in any vault or other burial place, he shall be confined in jail not more than one year, and fined not exceeding five hundred dollars.

(No. 1.)

Form of Warrant of Arrest for disinterring a dead human body.

———— County, to wit :

To all or any one of the Constables of said County :

Whereas, A. B. of said County, has this day made complaint and information on oath before me J. T., a Justice of the said County, that C. D., on the ———— day of ———— 18—, in said County, did unlawfully disinter and displace from the grave and place in which it had lately before been deposited, a certain dead human body, to wit, the dead body of one E. F.: These are, therefore, to command you, in the name of the Commonwealth of Virginia, forthwith to apprehend the said C. D., and bring him before me or some other Justice of the said County, to answer the said complaint, and to be farther dealt with according to law. Given under my hand and seal, this ———— day of ———— 18—.

J. T., J. P. [L. S.]

(No. 2.)

Form of Mittimus.

Follow form No. 9, under head of ARREST, and describe the offence succinctly as in the foregoing warrant.

([1]) See 1 Leach 497 ; 4 East 465 ; 4 Blac. Com. 236 ; 1 Russ. C. & M. 416 ; Crow. Cr. Comp. 174 ; Russ. & Ry. C. C. 366.

(No. 3.)

Form of Recognizance of Bail.

Follow form No. 4, under head of RECOGNIZANCE.

(No. 4.)

Form of Recognizance of Witnesses.

Follow form No. 5, under head of RECOGNIZANCE.

(No. 5.)

Form of Certificate to be sent to the Clerk.

Follow form No. 10, under head of ARREST.

(No. 1.)

An Indictment for disinterring the dead body of a slave.

—— Judicial Circuit, —— County, to wit: In the Circuit Court of the said County. } The jurors of the Commonwealth of Virginia, in and for the body of the County of ——, and now attending the said Court, upon their oath present, that A. B., on the —— day of —— in the year one thousand eight hundred and ——, in the said County, a certain graveyard in the said County situated, unlawfully did enter, and the grave there, in which the human body of Mary, deceased, who, before her death, was the slave of one E. F., had lately before there been interred, and then was, did dig, open and the said human body of the said Mary, did then and there unlawfully disinter and displace, against the peace and dignity of the Commonwealth of Virginia.

(No. 2.)

An Indictment for disinterring the dead body of a free person.

—— Judicial Circuit, —— County, to wit: In the Circuit Court of the said County. } The jurors of the Commonwealth of Virginia, in and for the body of the County of ——, and now attending the said Court, upon their oath present, that A. B., on the —— day of ——, in the year one thousand eight hundred and ——, in the said County, a certain graveyard, situated in the said County, unlawfully did enter, and the grave there, in which the body of one G. H., deceased, had lately before been there interred, and then was, did dig and open, and the said body of the said G. H. did then and there, and from the said grave, unlawfully disinter and displace, against the peace and dignity of the Commonwealth of Virginia.

CHAPTER XX.

BURNING.

[For the burning of vessels, see title SHIPS.]

Arson, at Common Law, includes only the burning of a dwelling house and houses within the curtilage; but the offence of burning is extended by the statute so as to include all houses and many other kinds of property, and for convenience, the subject is here brought together under the more general head of BURNING, and is divided into two classes: *Felonious burning* and *Unlawful burning*.

I. *Of felonious burning.*

BY SEC. 1, CHAP. 192. If any free person, in the night, maliciously *burn* the dwelling house of another, or any jail or prison, or maliciously set fire to any thing, by the burning whereof such dwelling house, jail or prison, shall be burnt in the night, he shall be punished with death; but if the jury find that at the time of committing the offence, there was no person in the dwelling house, jail or prison, the offender shall be confined in the penitentiary not less than five, nor more than ten years.

BY SEC. 2. If any free person in the day time maliciously burn the dwelling house of another, or any jail or prison, or maliciously set fire to any building or other thing, by the burning whereof such dwelling house, jail or prison shall be burnt, he shall be confined in the penitentiary not less than three, nor more than ten years.

BY SEC. 3. No out house not adjoining a dwelling house, nor under the same roof, (although within the curtilage thereof,) shall be deemed parcel of such dwelling house within the meaning of this chapter, unless some person usually lodge therein at night.

BY SEC. 4. If a free person maliciously burn any meeting house, court house, town house, college, academy or other building erected for public use, (except a jail or prison,) or any banking house, ware house, store house, manufactory or mill of another person, not usually occupied by persons lodging therein at night, or if he maliciously set fire to any *thing*, by the burning whereof any building mentioned in this section shall be burnt, he shall be confined in the penitentiary, when such building with the property therein is of the value of

$1000, not less than three, nor more than ten years; and when it is of less value, not less than three, nor more than five years.

By Sec. 5. If a free person maliciously burn any pile or parcel of wood, boards or other lumber; or any barn, stable, corn house, tobacco house, stack of wheat, or other grain, or of fodder, straw or hay, he shall, if the thing burnt, with the property therein, be of the value of one hundred dollars, be confined in the penitentiary not less than three, nor more than five years; and if it be of less value, he shall be so confined not less than one, nor more than three years, or in the discretion of the jury, in jail not more than one year, and be fined not exceeding five hundred dollars.

By Sec. 6. If a free person maliciously burn any building, the burning whereof is not punishable under any other section of this chapter, he shall, if the building with the property therein be of the value of one hundred dollars or more, be confined in the penitentiary not less than three, nor more than ten years, and if it be of less value, be so confined not less than one, nor more than three years, or in the discretion of the jury, in jail not more than one year, and be fined not exceeding five hundred dollars.

By Sec. 7. If a free person maliciously burn any bridge, lock, dam, or any ship, boat or other vessel, of the value of one hundred dollars or more, he shall be confined in the penitentiary not less than three, nor more than ten years; and if the value be less than one hundred dollars, he shall be confined in jail not exceeding one year, and fined not exceeding two hundred dollars.

By Sec. 10. If a free person wilfully burn any building, or any goods or chattels, which shall be at the time insured against loss or damage by fire, with intent to injure the insurer, *whether such person be the owner of the property or not*, he shall be confined in the penitentiary not less than one, nor more than ten years.

Under these provisions of the statute will be noticed:

1. *The burning of houses.*—Arson is an offence, at Common Law, of great malignity, and described to be the malicious and voluntary burning of the house of another.([1]) Accordingly, there are three things necessary to make out this crime: First, there must be a burning; secondly, the burning must be voluntary and malicious; and thirdly, it must be a burning of the house of another. A *house*, at Common Law, signified a place for the habitation and dwelling of man, and therefore, arson proper, was confined to the dwelling house

---

([1]) 1 Hale P. C. 566; 1 Hawk. c. 39; 2 East P. C. 1014; 2 Russ. C. & M. 486.

and houses within the curtilage; but the statute having included the burning of other houses in the crime, all of these ingredients are necessary to constitute the felonious burning of any house whatever, protected by the statute.(¹)

Burning. There must be an *actual* burning of the whole, or some part of the house; for a mere intention to burn, or even an actual attempt to burn a house, by putting fire into or towards it will not amount to felony, if no part of it be *burned*. It is not necessary, however, that the whole house, or any part of it, be wholly consumed; for, if any part of it be burned, the offender is guilty of felony, notwithstanding the fire be afterwards put out or go out of itself;(²) and it is not necessary that any flame should be visible.(³)

Malice. The firing must be malicious and wilful; otherwise, it is only a trespass; and no negligence or mischance amounts to malice; as, if a man shooting happen to set fire to a house,(⁴) or if he unlawfully shoot at the poultry of another and set his house on fire, it will not amount to arson, unless in the latter case he intended to steal the poultry; for there the intent being felonious, it will be arson, as he must abide all the consequences resulting from an act done with a felonious intent.(⁵)

Malice need not be precisely and positively proved, but may be inferred from such circumstances as must necessarily have been done with intention to injure; and a party who does an act wilfully, necessarily intends that which must be the consequences of that act;(⁶) nor is it any answer to a charge of malicious burning, that the prisoner had no spite or malice to the *real owner* of the property; as, in Solomon's Case,(⁷) where it was in spite and malice to another. Neither is it necessary that the malicious and wilful burning should correspond with the precise intent and design of the party; for, if A. intends maliciously to burn the house of C., and in setting fire to it burns the house of B., this is, in law, the wilful and malicious burning of the house of B.(⁸) So, if one man commands another to burn the house of J. S., and the fire of that house burns another house, he is accessary to the burning of that other house.(⁹)

Though the intention of the party be to burn his own house, yet if another adjoining house be burnt, or one standing in such a situation that the fire must in all probability reach it,

---

(¹) 2 Russ. C. & M. 486.
(²) 1 Hawk. c. 39, § 14; 2 East P. C. 1020; Sarah Taylor's Case, 1 Leach 49; Butler's Case, 16 J. R. 105-9; C. & P. 45; 16 Mass. R. 105.
(³) Moo. C. C. 398; 2 East P. C. 1020; See also 1 Leach 49.
(⁴) 3 Inst. 67.
(⁵) 2 East P. C. 1019; Fost. 258, 9.
(⁶) Rex v. Farrington, Russ. & Ry. 207.
(⁷) Russ. & Ry. 26.
(⁸) 1 Hale 569; 1 Hawk. c. 39, § 19.
(⁹) Plowd. 475; 2 East P. C. 1031.

the intent in this case being unlawful, and the burning of the other house being the immediate and necessary consequence of the original act done, the offence will amount to felony.([1])

The house. Arson at Common Law, as has been already stated, included the burning of any house within the *curtilage.* This undefined term, at Common Law, gave rise, in prosecutions for arson, to great difficulties, which are now removed by the statute.([2])

House of another. Arson is an offence immediately against the possession ;([3]) and therefore, at Common Law, the house or building set fire to or burned, must be described in the indictment to be the house or building of the person in possession,([4]) even though the possession be wrongful ;([5]) and if, in fact, it be the dwelling house of such person, the court will not enquire into the tenure or interest of the occupant.([6]) The strict adherence to this principle of the Common Law, was found inconvenient in practice, and the statute has supplied the remedy by authorizing the house to be charged as the property of any one having either the actual or constructive possession of it. This provision of the statute does not change the nature of the offence, but merely affords a facility in prosecutions which did not exist at Common Law. It is upon this principle of the offence being against the *possession*, that a man cannot be guilty of felony at Common Law, by burning his own house ;([7]) nor can a tenant for years, of a house, be guilty of arson, at Common Law, by burning it.([8]) Upon the same principle, a landlord may be guilty of felony, by burning the house of his tenant ;([9]) for, as to this offence, the possession of the tenant makes it his house against his landlord.

But, though this is an offence against the *possession*, and therefore a tenant may burn the house he occupies and thereby commit no felony, yet it is not a mere residence in a house, without any interest therein, which will bring a party within the principle. The possession must be the possession of the occupant claiming it *suo jure*, (in his own right,) however short that may be ;([10]) as in a case where the prisoner was a poor man, maintained by the parish, and had, for some time before the house was burnt, been put in by the parish officers to live there, and was resident in it with his family at the time of the fact committed, and had the sole possession and occu-

---

([1]) East P. C. 1031 ; Russ. C. & M. 245.
([2]) 3d section of statute.
([3]) 7 Dane's Abr. 131, Burns' Case; Pedley's Case, 1 Leach 277.
([4]) The People *v.* Gates, 15 Wend. 159.
([5]) Willis's Case, 1 Moo. C. C. 344.

([6]) The People *v.* Van Blarcum, 2 J. R. 105.
([7]) 1 Hale P. C. 568; Ros. Cr. Ev. 244.
([8]) Id.
([9]) Fost. 215 ; Ros. Cr. Ev. 244.
([10]) East P. C. 1034 ; Breem's Case, 1 Leach 22.

pation of it without payment of any rent, he was held guilty, for he had no interest in the house, but was a mere servant, so that it was not his house, and the overseers of the parish had the possession of it by means of his occupation.(¹) This principle of possession will not protect a party in setting fire to his own house, with intent, maliciously, to burn the house of another, if the house of that other be thereby burnt.

It is not felony in a wife to burn the house of her husband, with intent to injure him. To constitute the offence, there must be an intent to injure or defraud some third person, and not one identified with herself.(²) But we apprehend, that if she were to set fire to her husband's house, from malice to him, and were thereby to set fire to the house of another person, she would be guilty of felony; for she should not be permitted to shelter herself from punishment, on the ground that the mischief she committed was wider in its consequences than she originally intended.

What has been said as to the necessity of charging the house to be the property of another, does not, of course, refer to buildings belonging to the public generally, but to those belonging either to individuals or to corporations; and, therefore, a jail should not be charged, in the proceedings, to be the house of any one, but laid as the prison and common jail of the county;(³) and so also as to a courthouse.

2. *As to burning of stacks of hay, &c.*—Under the 5th section of the statute, little more need be said than to refer the Justice to the language of the statute, and to the forms which will be found at the end of this title. It may be proper, however, to add, that in this branch of the statute, the word *stack*, alone, is used, in reference to wheat or other grain, fodder, straw or hay, and it must be supposed that the Legislature well knew the meaning of it; and whether this word is to be understood as meaning any thing else than what it imports in common parlance, the Justice, in his proceedings, should adhere to it; for, upon the construction of a similar statute in England, a party who had been committed by eleven Justices, for "setting fire to a *parcel* of unthreshed wheat," was discharged upon *habeas corpus* on the ground that the word "*parcel*" did not bring the case within the statute.(⁴)

3. *The burning of bridges, &c.*—The malicious destruction of, or damaging a public bridge by any means, is a misdemeanor at Common Law;(⁵) and now, under the statute, ma-

---

(¹) East P. C. 1027; 7 Dane Ab. 132.
(²) March's Case, 1 Moo. C. C. 182.
(³) Posey's Case, 4 Call 109; Steen's Case, 4 Leigh 683.
(⁴) Judd's Case, 1 Leach 485; 1 Deac. 56.
(⁵) 2 East P. C. 108; 1 Moo. C. C. 398.

liciously to burn or set fire to any bridge, lock or dam, of the value of one hundred dollars or more, is made felony.(¹)

The word *burn*, in the seventh section of the act, must doubtless have the same construction given to it as in *arson*. In cases arising under it, the Justice must charge, in his proceeding, not only that the burning was malicious, but he should also state that the bridge, or other thing burnt, or set fire to, when burnt, was of the value of one hundred dollars, at the least.

II. *Of unlawful burning.*

By the seventh section of the statute just quoted, it is a misdemeanor, maliciously, to burn any bridge, lock or dam, &c., if the value be less than one hundred dollars. By the eighth section, if any free person unlawfully set fire to any woods, fence, grass, straw, or other thing capable of spreading fire on lands, he shall be fined not exceeding one hundred dollars, and confined in jail not less than two, nor more than twelve months. By the ninth section, if any person intentionally set any woods on fire, whereby damage is done to the property of another, he shall be amerced at the discretion of a jury.

Offences, falling under this division of the subject, are misdemeanors, and the offender should be recognized or committed to answer an indictment in the county or corporation court.

(No. 1.)

Form of Warrant of Arrest for burning a dwelling house in the night time, under the 1st section of the statute.

———— County, to wit:
  To all or any one of the Constables of said County:
  Whereas, A. B., of said County, has this day made complaint and information on oath before me J. T., a Justice of said County, that C. D., on the ———— day of ———— 18—, in said County, did feloniously and maliciously, in the night time of that day, burn the dwelling house of him the said A. B., situated in said County: These are, therefore, to command you, in the name of the Commonwealth of Virginia, forthwith to apprehend the said C. D., and bring him before me or some other Justice of the said County, to answer the said complaint, and be farther dealt with according to law. Given under my hand and seal, this ———— day of ———— 18—.

J. T., *J. P.* [L. S.]

(¹) 7 sec. of Statute.

(No. 2.)

Form of Warrant of Arrest for burning a dwelling house in the day time, under 2d section of the statute.

Follow No. 1, leaving out the word "night," and inserting the word "day" in the place of it.

(No. 3.)

Form of Warrant of Arrest for setting fire to an out building in the night time, whereby the dwelling house is burnt in the night time, under the 1st section of the statute.

———— County, to wit:
  To all or any one of the Constables of said County:

Whereas, A. B. of said County, has this day made complaint and information on oath before me J. T., a Justice of said County, that C. D., on the ——— day of ——— 18—, in said County, did feloniously and maliciously, in the night time of that day, set fire to a certain out house situated in the said County, whereby the dwelling house of one C. D., situated in the said County, was then and there in the night time feloniously and maliciously burnt: These are, therefore, to command you, in the name of the Commonwealth of Virginia, forthwith to apprehend the said C. D., and bring him before me or some other Justice of the said County, to answer the said complaint, and to be farther dealt with according to law. Given under my hand and seal, this ——— day of ——— 18—.

J. T., J. P. [L. S.]

(No. 4.)

Form of Warrant for setting fire to an out building in the day time, whereby the dwelling house is burnt in the day time, under the 2d section of the statute.

Follow No. 3, leaving out the word "night" wherever it occurs, and inserting the word "day" in place of it.

(No. 5.)

Form of Warrant of Arrest for burning a prison or jail, under the 1st section of the statute.

———— County, to wit:
  To all or any one of the Constables of said County:

Whereas, A. B. of said County, has this day made complaint and information on oath before me J. T., a Justice of the said County, that C. D., on the ——— day of ——— 18—, in said County, did feloniously and maliciously, in the night time, burn the prison and jail of the said County of ———: These are, therefore, to command you, in the name of the Commonwealth of Virginia, forthwith to apprehend the said C. D., and bring him before me or some other Justice of the said County, to answer the said complaint, and to be farther dealt with according to law. Given under my hand and seal, this —— day of ———— 18—.

J. T., J. P. [L. S.]

[NOTE.—If the prison or jail be burnt in the day, follow the above form, inserting " day" in the place of " night."]

(No. 6.)

Form of Warrant of Arrest for burning a meeting house, under the 4th section of the statute.

———— County, to wit:

To all or any one of the Constables of said County:

Whereas, A. B. of said County, has this day made complaint and information on oath before me J. T., a Justice of the said County, that C. D., on the —— day of ———— 18—, in said County, did feloniously and maliciously burn a certain meeting house, situate in the said County, erected for public uses, to wit, for the public worship of God, and called ————: These are, therefore, to command you, in the name of the Commonwealth of Virginia, forthwith to apprehend the said C. D., and bring him before me or some other Justice of the said County, to answer the said complaint, and to be farther dealt with according to law. Given under my hand and seal, this —— day of ———— 18—.

J. T., J. P. [L. S.]

[NOTE.—This form with slight variation will answer for any public building mentioned in the 4th section of the statute.]

(No. 7.)

Form of Warrant of Arrest for burning a banking house, warehouse, storehouse, manufactory or mill, of the value of one thousand dollars, under the 4th section of the statute.

———— County, to wit:

To all or any one of the Constables of said County:

Whereas, A. B. of said County, has this day made complaint and information on oath before me J. T., a Justice of the said County, that C. D., on the —— day of ———— 18—, in said County, a certain banking house, (belonging to E. F.,) which, with the property then therein contained, was of the value of one thousand dollars, and was not then usually occupied by persons lodging therein at night, feloniously and maliciously did burn: These are, therefore, to command you, in the name of the Commonwealth of Virginia, forthwith to apprehend the said C. D., and bring him before me or some other Justice of the said County, to answer the said complaint, and to be farther dealt with according to law. Given under my hand and seal, this —— day of ———— 18—.

J. T., J. P. [L. S.]

[NOTE.—This form will answer for a storehouse, warehouse, mill, or any other manufactory or building of the same kind, by leaving out the word " banking house," and inserting the kind of house according to the fact of the case.]

BURNING.

(No. 8.)

Form of Warrant of Arrest for setting fire to any thing, whereby a storehouse, with property therein contained, is burnt, under the 4th section.

—— County, to wit:
To all or any one of the Constables of the said County:

Whereas, A. B. of said County, has this day made complaint and information on oath before me J. T., a Justice of said County, that C. D., on the —— day of —————— 18—, in the said County, did feloniously and maliciously set fire to a certain (here state the thing set fire to,) and that by the burning whereof, a certain storehouse of the said A. B., (then not usually occupied by persons lodging therein at night,) situate in the said County, [and ten pieces of broad cloth, the property of the said A. B., then in the said storehouse contained,] were burnt, and that the said storehouse [together with the said ten pieces of broad cloth] then were of the value of one thousand dollars: These are, therefore, in the name of the Commonwealth of Virginia, to command you forthwith to apprehend the said C. D., and bring him before me or some other Justice of the said County, to answer the said complaint, and to be farther dealt with according to law. Given under my hand and seal, this —— day of —————— 18—.

J. T., J. P. [L. S.]

[NOTE.—If there be nothing contained in the storehouse, leave out what is in brackets, and in either case state the value according to the proof.]

———

(No. 9.)

Form of Warrant of Arrest for burning a barn, cornhouse, boards, stacks, &c., under the 5th section of the statute.

—— County, to wit:
To all or any one of the Constables of said County:

Whereas, A. B., of said County, has this day made complaint and information on oath, before me J. T., a Justice of the said County, that C. D., on the —— day of —————— 18—, in said County, did feloniously and maliciously burn a certain *stable*, the property of the said A. B., situated in the said County, and which was then of the value of one hundred dollars: These are, therefore, to command you, in the name of the Commonwealth of Virginia, forthwith to apprehend the said C. D., and bring him before me or some other Justice of the said County, to answer the said complaint, and to be farther dealt with according to law. Given under my hand and seal, this —— day of —————— 18—.

J. T., J. P. [L. S.]

[NOTE.—This form will answer for the burning of any house or other thing mentioned in the 5th section of the statute, by leaving out the word *stable*, and inserting the thing burnt, as a certain "parcel of wood," or a certain "parcel of boards," or a "stack of wheat," &c.]

(No. 10.)

Form of Warrant of Arrest against a party for burning his own house, with intent to defraud the insurers.

———— County, to wit:
  To all or any one of the Constables of said County:

Whereas, A. B. of said County, has this day made complaint and information on oath before me J. T., a Justice of the said County, that C. D., on the ———— day of ———— 18—, in said County, did unlawfully and feloniously burn a certain dwelling house, the property of him the said C. D., situate in the said County, with intent thereby to defraud the ———— Insurance Company, the said dwelling house being then insured against loss and damage by fire, by said ———— Company: These are, therefore, to command you, in the name of the Commonwealth of Virginia, forthwith to apprehend the said C. D., and bring him before me or some other Justice of the said County, to answer the said complaint, and to be farther dealt with according to law. Given under my hand and seal, this ———— day of ———— 18—.

J. T., J. P. [L. S.]

(No. 11.)

Form of Warrant of Arrest for burning a bridge, lock or dam, of the value of one hundred dollars, under 7th section.

———— County, to wit:
  To all or any one of the Constables of said County:

Whereas, A. B. of said County, has this day made complaint and information on oath before me J. T., a Justice of the said County, that C. D., on the ———— day of ———— 18—, in said County, did feloniously and maliciously burn a certain bridge, then of the value of one hundred dollars, built across ———— river, (or *creek,*) and the property of, (state to whom the bridge belongs:) These are, therefore, to command you, in the name of the Commonwealth of Virginia, forthwith to apprehend the said C. D., and bring him before me or some other Justice of the said County, to answer the said complaint, and to be farther dealt with according to law. Given under my hand and seal, this ———— day of ———— 18—.

J. T., J. P. [L. S.]

[NOTE.—If the bridge, lock or dam burnt, is not of the value of one hundred dollars, the offence is not a felony, but a misdemeanor; so that it is necessary to state the value in the warrant, and if it be under one hundred dollars, the word "feloniously" must be left out.]

(No. 12.)

Form of Warrant of Arrest for unlawfully setting fire to woods, &c. under 8th section of statute.

———— County, to wit:
  To all or any one of the Constables of said County:

Whereas, A. B. of said County, has this day made complaint and information on oath before me J. T., a Justice of the said County, that C. D., on

the —— day of ——— 18—, in said County, did unlawfully set fire to a certain woods, (or *to a fence*, or *to certain grass*, or *straw*,) the property of the said A. B. : These are, therefore, to command you, in the name of the Commonwealth of Virginia, forthwith to apprehend the said C. D., and bring him before me or some other Justice of the said County, to answer the said complaint, and to be farther dealt with according to law. Given under my hand and seal, this —— day of ——— 18—.

J. T., J. P. [L. S.]

[If it be for intentionally setting woods on fire, under the ninth section, say, "did intentionally set on fire a certain woods, (the property of A. B.,) whereby damage was done to the property of the said A. B."]

(No. 13.)

Form of Mittimus where a party is committed for examination or trial in the County Court, for felonious burning.

———— County, to wit:

To X. Z., Constable of said County, and to the Keeper of the Jail of said County:

These are to command you, the said Constable, in the name of the Commonwealth of Virginia, forthwith to convey and deliver into the custody of the keeper of the said jail, together with this warrant, the body of C. D., a white person, (or *free negro*, or *a slave, the property of E. F.*, as the case may be,) charged before me J. T., a Justice of the said County, on the oath of A. B., with a felony by him committed, in this, that the said C. D., on the —— day of ——— in the year 18—, in the said County, (here describe the offence as in the warrant of arrest.) And you, the said keeper of the said jail, are hereby required to receive the said C. D. into your jail and custody, that he may be examined (or *tried*) for the said offence by the County Court of said County, and him there safely keep, until he shall be discharged by due course of law. Given under my hand and seal, this —— day of ——— in the year 18—.

J. T., J. P. [L. S.]

[NOTE.—If the prisoner be a white person, or if he be a free negro charged with homicide of any grade, or with any offence punishable with death, he must be committed for examination. For all other felonies by free negroes, and in all cases of felony by slaves, the prisoner must be committed for trial.]

(No. 14.)

Form of Certificate of Commitment to be sent to the Clerk of the County Court, for felonious burning.

———— County, to wit:

To the Clerk of the County Court of the said County:

I, J. T., a Justice of the said County, do hereby certify, that I have, by my warrant, this day committed C. D., (if free negro or slave, state which,) to the jail of this County, that he may be examined (or *tried*) before the County Court of the said County, for a felony by him committed, in this, that he did, on the —— day of —————— 18—, in the said County, (here state the offence as in the mittimus.) Given under my hand, this —— day of —————— in the year 18—.

J. T. J. P.

(No. 15.)

Form of Certificate to the Clerk where party is admitted to bail, to answer for felonious burning.

Turn to head of ARREST, and follow No. 6.

(No. 16.)

Form of Recognizance of Bail.

Turn to head of RECOGNIZANCE, and follow No. 1, if person be free; No. 2, if a slave, and state succinctly the offence for which the person is recognized. If a Special Court be called, follow No. 3, under head of COURTS.

(No. 17.)

Form of Recognizance of Witness to appear before the County Court to give evidence upon the examination or trial of a party charged with felonious burning.

Turn to head of RECOGNIZANCE, and follow No. 3.

FORMS FOR UNLAWFUL, BUT NOT FELONIOUS BURNING.

(No. 18.)

Form of Warrant of Arrest for burning woods, fence, &c., under 8th section.

Follow No. 2, under head of ARREST, and describe the offence thus: "did unlawfully and maliciously set fire to a certain fence, (or *wood*, or *field of grass*, or *field of hay*, as the case may be,) the property of the said A. B., which then was capable of spreading fire on land: These are," &c.

(No. 19.)

Form of same for intentionally, but not maliciously, burning woods, &c., under 9th section.

Follow No. 2, under head of ARREST, and describe the offence thus: "did intentionally burn a certain woods, the property of the said A. B.: These are," &c.

(No. 20.)

Form of Mittimus where a party is committed to answer an indictment in the County Court for unlawful burning.

——— County, to wit:

To X. Y., *Constable of said County, and to the Keeper of the Jail of said County:*

These are to command you the said Constable, in the name of the Commonwealth of Virginia, forthwith to convey and deliver into the custody of the keeper of the said jail, together with this warrant, the body of C. D., charged before me J. T., a Justice of the said County, on the oath of A. B., with a misdemeanor by him committed, in this, that the said C. D., on the ——— day of ——— in the year 18—, in the said County (here describe the offence as in the warrant of arrest.) And you the said keeper of the said jail are hereby required to receive the said C. D. into your jail and custody, to answer an indictment to be preferred against him for the said offence in the County Court of said County, and him there safely keep, until he shall be discharged by due course of law. Given under my hand and seal, this ——— day of ——— in the year 18—.

J. T., J. P. [L. S.]

(No. 21.)

Form of Recognizance of Bail.

Turn to head of RECOGNIZANCE, and follow No. 4, and state the offence succinctly for which the person is recognized.

(No. 22.)

Form of Certificate of the Commitment, or Letting to Bail, to be sent to the Clerk of the County Court for unlawful burning.

——— County, to wit:

To the Clerk of the County Court of said County:

I, J. T., a Justice of the said County, do hereby certify, that C. D. was this day committed to the jail of this County, by my warrant, (or *was this day admitted to bail by me,* as the case may be,) to answer an indictment to be preferred against him in the County Court of the said County, for a misdemeanor by him committed, in this, that he did, on the ——— day of ——— 18—, in said County, (here describe the offence as in the warrant of arrest.) Given under my hand, this ——— day of ——— 18—.

J. T., J. P.

(No. 23.)

Form of Recognizance of Witness to appear and give evidence to the Grand Jury upon the indictment.

Follow No. 5, under head of RECOGNIZANCE.

(No. 1.)

Form of Indictment for burning a dwelling house in the night.

―― Judicial Circuit. \
―― ―― County, *to wit:* \
In the Circuit Court of the said County.
} The jurors of the Commonwealth of Virginia, in and for the body of the County of ――――, and now attending the said Court, upon their oath present, that A. B., of the said County, on the ―― day of ―――― in the year of our Lord one thousand eight hundred and ――――, about the hour of eleven o'clock in the night of that day, in the County aforesaid, a certain dwelling house of one C. D., there situate, feloniously and maliciously did burn, against the peace and dignity of the Commonwealth of Virginia.

――――

(No. 2.)

Form of Indictment for setting fire to an out building, whereby the dwelling house is burnt, in the night.

Follow No. 1, to the words "a certain," and then say: out building of one C. D., there situate, called a kitchen, did feloniously and maliciously set fire to; and the jurors aforesaid, upon their oath aforesaid, do farther present, that by the burning of the said out building, called a kitchen, so feloniously and maliciously set fire to by the said A. B., as aforesaid, a certain dwelling house of the said C. D., situate in the said County, was then and there, to wit, on the ―― day of ―――― in the year aforesaid, and in the night of that day, in the County aforesaid, feloniously and maliciously burnt, against the peace and dignity of the Commonwealth of Virginia.

――――

(No. 3.)

Form of Indictment for burning a jail in the night.

Follow No. 1, to the words "a certain," and then say: jail, there situate, (the said jail being then and there the public prison and common jail of the said County,) feloniously and maliciously did burn, against the peace and dignity of the Commonwealth of Virginia.

[NOTE.—The foregoing forms will answer where the offence is committed in the day, by inserting the word *day* for *night*, wherever it occurs.]

――――

(No. 4.)

Form of Indictment for burning a meeting house.

Follow No. 1, under head of INDICTMENTS, and say: a certain meeting house, situate in the said County, called ――――, and erected for public uses, to wit, for the public worship of Almighty God, did feloniously and maliciously burn, against the peace and dignity of the Commonwealth of Virginia.

BURNING—(*Indictments for.*)

(No. 5.)

An Indictment for burning a storehouse not occupied by any person lodging therein at night.

Follow No. 1, under head of INDICTMENTS, and say: a certain storehouse of one C. D., situate in the said County, (the said storehouse not then being usually occupied by any person lodging therein at night,) feloniously and maliciously did burn, against the peace and dignity of the Commonwealth of Virginia.

(No. 6.)

Form of Indictment for setting fire to any thing, whereby a mill, with property therein contained, is burnt.

Follow No. 1, under head of INDICTMENTS, and say: a certain (state what) of one C. D., situated in said County, feloniously and maliciously did set fire to; and the jurors aforesaid, upon their oath aforesaid, do farther present, that by the burning of the said (state what) so as aforesaid, then and there feloniously and maliciously set fire to by the said A. B., a certain mill of the said C. D., together with one thousand bushels of wheat, the property of the said C. D., then in the said mill contained and being, was, to wit, on the day and year aforesaid, at the County aforesaid, feloniously and maliciously burnt, (the said mill, with the said wheat then therein contained and burnt as aforesaid, then and there being of the value of one thousand dollars,) against the peace and dignity of the Commonwealth of Virginia.

(No. 7.)

Form of Indictment for burning one's own house with intent to defraud insurers.

Follow No. 1, under head of INDICTMENTS, and say: a certain dwelling house, (or whatever house it may be,) the property and house of the said A. B., situate in the said County, and which said dwelling house then was, to wit, on the day and year aforesaid, insured by the ——— Insurance Company, against loss and damage by fire, did feloniously and wilfully burn, with intent thereby to injure and defraud the said ——— Insurance Company, against the peace and dignity of the Commonwealth of Virginia.

CHAPTER XXI.

CATTLE—(*Distempered.*)

[For cruelty to, see ANIMALS.]
[See also HORSES and POISON.]

BY SEC. 3, CHAP. 102. Every person shall so restrain his distempered cattle, or such as are under his care, that they may not go at large off the land to which they belong, and no person shall drive any distempered cattle into, or through the State, or from one part thereof to another, unless it be to remove them from one piece of ground to another of the same owner; and when any such cattle shall die, the owner thereof, or person having them in charge, shall cause them to be buried (with their hides on) four feet deep. If any person shall offend against this section, in either respect, he shall forfeit four dollars for every head of such cattle.

BY SEC. 4. Any Justice, upon proof before him that any cattle are going at large, or are driven in or through his county or corporation, in violation of the preceding section, may direct the owner to impound them; and if he fail to do so, or suffer them to escape from the pound before obtaining from a Justice a certificate that they may be removed with safety, the Justice giving such direction, or some other Justice, shall order them to be killed and buried four feet deep. with their hides on, but so cut, that none may be tempted to take them up.

(No. 1.)

Form of Summons against a person for suffering distempered cattle to go at large.

———— County, to wit:
To X. Y., *Constable of said County:*
Whereas, complaint on oath has this day been made before me J. T., a Justice of the said County, by A. B., that on the ———— day of ———— 18—, in said County, C. D. did suffer certain distempered cattle, under his care, to wit, (state the number,) to go at large off the land to which they belonged, to wit, off the land of the said C. D.: These are, therefore, in the name of the Commonwealth, to command you to summon the said C. D. to appear at ———— in the said County, on the ———— day of ———— 18—, at — o'clock in the ———— noon, before me or such other Justice of said County as may then be there to hear the said complaint, to answer the same, and to be farther dealt with according to law. Given under my hand and seal, this ———— day of ———— 18—.

J. T., *J. P.* [L. S.]

CATTLE—(*Distempered.*)

[NOTE.—When the offence is for driving cattle into the State, the Justice is advised to issue a warrant instead of a summons, as the party is likely to be a non-resident and disposed to evade the prosecution. If the number of cattle exceed five, the penalty is beyond the jurisdiction of a single Justice, and the party must be recognized or committed to answer an indictment for the offence in the County Court. For form of recognizance of bail, and of witnesses, see Nos. 4 and 5, under head of RECOGNIZANCE, and for the form of mittimus, if he fail to give bail, see No. 9, under head of ARREST.]

(No. 2.)

Form of a Warrant of Arrest against a person for driving distempered cattle into the Commonwealth.

———— County, to wit:

To X. Y., *Constable of the said County:*

Whereas, complaint on oath has this day been made before me, J. T., a Justice of said County, by A. B., that on the ——— day of ——— 18—, C. D. did drive certain distempered cattle, to wit, (state the number,) into this Commonwealth, and that they are now distempered in said County: These are, therefore, to command you, in the name of the Commonwealth, forthwith to apprehend the said C. D., and bring him before me or some other Justice of said County, to answer the said complaint, and to be farther dealt with according to law. Given under my hand and seal, this ——— day of ——— 18—.

J. T., J. P. [L. S.]

(No. 3.)

Form of Judgment for the fine where the number does not exceed five.

It may be endorsed on the warrant or summons in this form: "10th day of August 18—, at ———. Case heard, and judgment against the defendant for $——— fine for suffering ——— distempered cattle to go at large, and for $——— costs of prosecution." For more formal judgment, and appeal therefrom, see FINES and CONVICTIONS.

(No. 4.)

Form of Order directing distempered cattle to be impounded.

———— County, to wit:

To E. F.:

Whereas, upon the complaint and evidence on oath of A. B., it has this day been proved to me J. T., a Justice of said County, that certain distempered cattle, to wit, ten, under your care, are not so restrained by you, as that they may not go at large off the land to which they belong, and that the same are now going at large in the said County: These are to direct you forthwith to impound the said cattle so distempered, and not to suffer them, or any one of them, to escape from the said pound, before obtaining from a Justice of said County a certificate that they may be removed with safety. Given under my hand, this ——— day of ——— 18—.

J. T., J. P.

(No. 5.)

Form of Order of a Justice, to kill distempered cattle going at large.

——— County, to wit:
To X. Y., *Constable of the said County:*

Whereas, on the complaint and proof on oath of A. B., I, J. T., Justice of the said County, did, on the ——— day of ——— 18—, direct E. F. forthwith to impound certain distempered cattle, to wit, ten, then under his care, so that they might not go at large off the land to which they belonged, and not to suffer them, or any one of them, to escape from the pound, before obtaining from a Justice of the said County, a certificate that they might be removed with safety ; and whereas it appears to me by the oath of the said A. B., that the said E. F. [has failed to impound the said cattle, and that they are now going at large in said County:] These are to command you forthwith to kill the said cattle, and to bury them four feet deep, with their hides on, but so cut, that none may be tempted to take them off. Given under my hand, this ——— day of ——— 18—.

J. T., J. P.

[NOTE.—If the cattle were impounded, but not kept impounded according to the statute, change the above form to suit the case, by leaving out all in the brackets and inserting this in place of it, " having impounded the said cattle as required, did afterwards suffer them to escape from the pound, before obtaining from a Justice of said County, a certificate that they might be removed with safety, and that the same are now going at large in said County."]

[The Constable's fee for killing and burying distempered cattle, under the order of a Justice, is one dollar for each head, and he forfeits the like amount for failing to execute it. The fee is to be paid by the owner, if known and able to pay ; if not, by the County or Corporation. Sec. 7, chap. 102.]

CHAPTER XXII.

CHEATS.

[For cheating by selling unwholesome food, &c., see HEALTH : cheats, made felony by statute, will be found under the head of FALSE PRETENCES.]

Such cheats only as amount to misdemeanors will be noticed here. They consist in fraudulently obtaining the property of another by deceitful and illegal practices, and must be effected by means calculated to affect, or which may injuriously *affect, the public.*(¹)

It is a cheat, indictable at Common Law, to evade public justice by any fraudulent means ; as where a person, who was committed to jail under an attachment in a civil suit, counter-

---

(¹) 2 East P. C. 1818.

feited a pretended discharge (as coming from his creditor,) to the Sheriff and Jailor, under which he obtained his release from jail.(¹)

Public officers are also indictable for frauds committed in their official capacity,(²) and, if the fraudulent act be embezzlement, it is felony under the statute.(³)

It is a fraud at Common Law in an apprentice to enlist as a soldier, without the consent of his master, with intent to obtain the government bounty.(⁴)

So, also, any fraud which may be practised on the public by means of false weights or measures, or any false token having the semblance of public authority, and purposely calculated for deceit, and by which the public may be imposed upon without any imputation of folly or negligence, is an offence at Common Law(⁵); as the selling of grain in a bushel short of the statute measure, &c.(⁶) But it is not a cheat affecting the public, and, therefore, not indictable, to sell an article merely under measure, as where, without the fraud of using a false measure, sixteen gallons of liquor were sold as for eighteen gallons. In such cases, the fraud is one from which the purchaser cannot suffer, but from his own carelessness in not measuring the article he buys. His own prudence must protect him in such cases.(⁷) The distinction appears to be this: that where a man sells by *false* weight or measures, though only to one person, it is an indictable cheat at Common Law; but, if without *false* weights or measures, he sells merely *a less quantity* than he pretends to do, though to many persons,(⁸) he is not indictable, but liable only in a civil suit for deceit, unless, indeed, there was a conspiracy to effect the fraud, or it was effected by means of forgery; for these, in themselves, are substantive offences.(⁹)

Nor is it an indictable offence at Common Law to cheat another by telling a mere lie; one man, as was remarked by an eminent Judge, *cannot be indicted for making a fool of another*.(¹⁰) There are many transactions amounting to unfair dealing, and a fraud upon a particular individual, which are not indictable, as where a cheat is practised, which is open to the detection of any man of common prudence; for example, selling an unsound horse, knowing him to be such, with a false affirmation of soundness.(¹¹) But see FALSE PRETENCES.

(¹) 2 East P. C. 862, 952.
(²) 6 East 136; 2 Camp. 268; 4 Burn 2106.
(³) See title EMBEZZLEMENT.
(⁴) 1 Leach 174.
(⁵) 2 East P. C. 820.
(⁶) 2 East P. C. 820.
(⁷) 2 Burr. 1125; 2 East P. C. 818.
(⁸) 3 T. R. 104; 2 Burr. 1130.
(⁹) 1 Deac. C. C. 227.
(¹⁰) Holt, C. J. in Reg. v. Jones, 1 Salk. 379.
(¹¹) R. v. Pywell, 1 Star. R. 402.

(No. 1.)

Form of a Warrant of Arrest for selling by false weights.

—— County, to wit:

To X. Y., *Constable of the said County:*

Whereas, A. B. has this day made complaint on oath before me J. T., a Justice of the said County, that C. D., on the —— day of ——— 18—, in the said County, did in his storehouse, wilfully and publicly keep a certain pair of false scales, for the weighing of goods, wares and merchandize by him sold, in the way of his trade and business, and that he the said C. D., on the —— day of ——— 18—, at his said store, did knowingly and fraudulently sell to him the said A. B., a quantity of sugar, then and there weighed in the said false scales, as and for twenty pounds weight of sugar, whereas in truth and in fact the said sugar so sold then weighed but eighteen pounds, he the said C. D. then well knowing the said scales to be false, and intending thereby to defraud him the said A. B.: These are, therefore, to command you, in the name of the Commonwealth of Virginia, forthwith to apprehend and bring before me or some other Justice of the said County, the body of the said C. D., to answer the said complaint, and to be farther dealt with according to law. Given under my hand and seal, this —— day of ——— 18—.

J. T., J. P. [L. S.]

[NOTE.—This form may be easily adapted to cheats by false measures.]

———

(No. 2.)

Form of Mittimus.

Turn to title ARREST, and follow form No. 9.

———

(No. 3.)

Form of Recognizance of Bail.

Turn to head of RECOGNIZANCE, and follow form No. 4.

———

(No. 4.)

Form of Recognizance of Witness.

See No. 5, under the head of RECOGNIZANCE.

———

(No. 5.)

Form of Certificate to Clerk of the Commitment.

See No. 10, under the head of ARREST.

An Indictment for selling by false weights.

—— County, to wit:) The jurors of the Commonwealth of Virginia, in and for the body of the County of said County.) ——, and now attending the said Court, upon their oath present, that A. B. on the —— day of —— in the year one thousand eight hundred and ——, in the said County, did in his storehouse, situated in the said County, wilfully and publicly keep a certain pair of false scales for the weighing of goods, wares and merchandize, by him sold in the way of his trade and business, and that he the said A. B., on the —— day of —— 18—, at the store aforesaid, in the County aforesaid, did knowingly and fraudulently sell to C. D., a quantity of sugar, then and there weighed in the said false scales, as and for twenty pounds weight of sugar, whereas in truth and in fact the said sugar so sold then weighed but eighteen pounds, he the said A. B. then and there knowing the said scales to be false, and intending thereby to defraud the said C. D., against the peace and dignity of the Commonwealth of Virginia.

CHAPTER XXIII.

COLLEGES.

BY SEC. 1, CHAP. 142. If any money or other thing be directly or indirectly sold, let for hire, lent or advanced to or for the use of any student or pupil under twenty-one years of age, at the Virginia Military Institute, University of Virginia, or any incorporated college or academy in this State, without the previous permission in writing of his parent or guardian, or the authorized officers of such institution, nothing shall be recovered therefor, and there shall moreover be forfeited to the institution twenty dollars and the amount or value of such money or other thing. Where such selling, letting, lending or advancing, is by an agent, such forfeiture shall be by his principal, unless the principal shall, within ten days after he has knowledge or information of the selling, letting, lending or advancing, give notice in writing of the date, nature and amount thereof, to the president or other head of the institution, in which case the forfeiture shall be by the agent. This section shall not apply to a person selling or letting in expectation of immediate payment, if he shall, within ten days thereafter, give notice in writing of the date, nature or amount of the sale or letting, to such president or other head.

BY SEC. 34, CHAP. 198. If a free person so violate section 1, chapter 142, (the above recited section,) as to be liable to the penalties thereby declared, he shall be moreover fined not less than fifty, nor more than three hundred dollars; and, upon conviction, he shall be bound by the court in a sum not less than five hundred dollars, with at least two sufficient sureties, to be of good behaviour for one year, and any subsequent violation of the section aforesaid, shall be held to be a forfeiture of the recognizance.

Form of a Warrant of Arrest for trading with a student of an incorporated college.

—— County, to wit:

To X. Y., *Constable of said County:*

Whereas, A. B. of the said County, has this day made complaint and information on oath before me J. T., a Justice of the said County, that C. D., on the —— day of —— in the year 18—, in the said County, did unlawfully [sell on credit, goods, wares and merchandize, to wit, (state what was sold,)] to one E. F., without the previous permission in writing of G. H., the parent (or *guardian*) of the said E. F., or of any authorized officer of the college of ——, he the said E. F. then and there being an infant under the age of twenty-one years, then attending as a student at the said college: These are, therefore, in the name of the Commonwealth, to command you forthwith to apprehend the said C. D., and bring him before me or some other Justice of the said County, to answer the complaint aforesaid, and to be farther dealt with according to law. Given under my hand and seal, this —— day of —— in the year 18—.

J. T., J. P. [L. S.]

[NOTE.—This form may be altered to suit any violation of the statute, by leaving out all in the brackets and describing the act done by the party, according to the proof; as, for instance, for hiring a horse, say "let to hire on credit a certain riding horse;" or for lending money, "unlawfully did lend and advance money." Upon being brought before the Justice, if not discharged, the party should be committed or recognized to answer an indictment. See RECOGNIZANCE, Nos. 4 and 5, and Nos. 9 and 10, under head of ARREST.]

An Indictment for unlawfully trading with a student of an incorporated college.

—— County, to wit: } The jurors of the Commonwealth of Virginia, in and for the body of the County of ——, now attending the County Court of ——, upon their oath present, that one A. B. was, to wit, on the —— day of —— in the year 18—, a student of —— college, the said college then being an incorporated college in this Commonwealth, in the County aforesaid, and the said A. B. then being an infant under the age of twenty-one years, then and there attending as a student at the college aforesaid: And the jurors aforesaid, upon their oath aforesaid, do farther present, that E. F., of the said County, afterwards, to wit, on the day and year aforesaid, at the County aforesaid, and whilst the said A. B. was attending the said college as student as aforesaid, unlawfully did sell upon credit to him, the said A. B., divers goods and merchandize, to wit, one hat and one pair of boots, without the previous permission in writing, either of G. T. the father (or *guardian*) of the said A. B., or of any authorized officer of the said college, so to do, against the peace and dignity of the Commonwealth of Virginia.

CHAPTER XXIV.

CONSPIRACY.

It has been said "that the offence of conspiracy is more difficult to be ascertained precisely, than any other for which indictment lies, and is indeed rather to be considered as governed by positive decisions, than by any consistent and intelligible principles of law."([1]) True, it is often difficult to conduct successfully a prosecution for conspiracy, but this is to be attributed rather to a failure of proof in the particular case, than a want of fixed legal principles to govern it, for it may now be safely stated as a *consistent and intelligible principle of law*, that the combination of two or more persons to do any act, the doing of which would necessarily tend to prejudice the public, whether the act be done or not; or where the act, if done, would oppress individuals by subjecting them to the power of the confederates, either for the purpose of extortion or mischief, is a conspiracy at Common Law, for which the parties to it may be indicted.([2])

Accordingly, it has always been held, that a confederacy to commit any indictable offence, is itself an indictable offence.([3]) So, any conspiracy tending to obstruct public justice, is a misdemeanor.([4]) And it is under this principle, as necessarily tending to prejudice public interests, that every conspiracy to raise or depress the price of labour beyond what it would be, if it were left without artificial excitement, is a misdemeanor.([5]) And so it is held, that a conspiracy of journeymen workmen of any trade or handicraft, to raise their wages by entering into combinations to coerce other journeymen and master workmen employed in the same branch of industry, to conform to rules adopted by such combination, for the purpose of regulating the price of labour and carrying such rules into effect by other acts, is an indictable offence.([6])

A conspiracy to defraud the public generally is an indictable offence, though no particular persons are made its object;([7]) as, to manufacture spurious indigo with intent to sell it at auction as good, to defraud whoever may be defrauded.([8]) So is a conspiracy to raise the price of public funds by false rumours,

---

([1]) Mr. Talfourd's Edition of Dickinson's Quarter Sessions, p. 200.
([2]) 4 B. & C. 329; 6 D. & R. 345.
([3]) 2 Camp. 229 (n.); 4 Wend. 265.
([4]) 1 Leach 45; 6 T. R. 619; State v. De Wit, 2 Hill's S. C. R. 282.
([5]) Rex v. Bykerdike, M. & Rob. 179.
([6]) Hunt's Case, 4 Metc. 3; and see Fisher's Case, 14 Wend. 9.
([7]) 3 M. & S. 67.
([8]) Comm. v. Judd, 2 Mass. 329.

as being a fraud upon the public ;(¹) and a conspiracy to defraud the public by issuing and negotiating bills in the name of a fictitious and pretended banking firm, is a misdemeanor at Common Law,(²) and if the act be consummated, it will be felony by statute. See FORGERY.

A conspiracy to assist a female infant to escape from her father's control, with a view to marry her against his will or to seduce her, is an indictable offence at Common Law.(³) And a conspiracy to make another drunk, and to cheat him at cards when drunk ;(⁴) to impose pretended wine upon another as and for true and good Portugal wine ;(⁵) to defraud a bank of money by illegal means ;(⁶) to injure a man in his trade or profession ;(⁷) or to charge a man as the reputed father of a bastard, have all been severally held indictable offences. So also it has been held indictable for two or more to conspire for that purpose and destroy a will, with a view to defraud the devisees.(⁸)

A conspiracy to charge a man falsely with an indictable offence, is a misdemeanor at Common Law ;(⁹) but it is not an offence for two or more persons to consult and agree to prosecute one who is guilty, or against whom there are reasonable grounds of suspicion.(¹⁰) A conspiracy to extort hush money, is an offence, whether the charge be true or false.(¹¹)

The offence of conspiracy is complete, by the bare engagement and association of two or more persons to violate the law, without any act being done in pursuance thereof by the conspirators ;(¹²) and it is indictable even to conspire to make use of illegal means to effect an object not in itself illegal, as where a conspiracy fraudulently to seduce and carry off a female over sixteen years of age, though the seduction and abduction was not in itself an indictable offence.(¹³)

If the object of the conspiracy be to commit a felony, and the felony be actually committed, then the offence of conspiracy is merged in the felony ; but if the object of the conspirators be to commit an offence, which, if committed, would only amount to a misdemeanor, the offence of conspiracy would not be merged, though the offence were actually committed, for one misdemeanor cannot be merged in another, being of-

---

(¹) 3 M. & S. 67.
(²) 2 East P. C. 858.
(³) Anderson's Case, 5 Rand. 627 ; Delaval's Case, 3 Burr. 1434 ; 2 Yeates 114.
(⁴) State v. Younger, 1st Devereux 357.
(⁵) 2 Ld. Ray. 1179.
(⁶) 5 Har. & J. 317.
(⁷) Ecles' Case, 1 Leach 274.

(⁸) State v. De Wit, 1 Hill's S. C. R. 282.
(⁹) 1 Leach 45 ; Foster 130.
(¹⁰) 2 Ld. Ray. 1167 ; 2 Mass. Rep. 536.
(¹¹) Rex v. Hollingsburry, 4 B. & C. 329 ; 6 D. & R. 345.
(¹²) Buchanan's Case, 5 Har. & Johnson 317 ; 8 Serg. & Rawle 20 ; 3 Serg. & R. 220.
(¹³) Anderson's Case, 5 Rand. 627.

fences of equal dignity, and both may be charged in the same indictment.(¹)

From the nature of this offence, one person alone cannot be convicted of it, unless he be indicted for conspiring with others unknown, and then the act of conspiracy must be proven, though the other conspirators be unknown ;(²) and if one of two indicted for conspiracy be acquitted, both must be. But where three were indicted for conspiracy and one was acquitted and the other died before trial, it was held that the third could nevertheless be convicted.(³) A person joining a conspiracy after it is formed, is equally guilty with the original conspirators.(⁴)

Prosecutions for conspiracy are unusual in this State, and it is apprehended that the following forms will answer all the purposes of the Virginia Justice.

(No. 1.)

Form of a Warrant of Arrest for a conspiracy to charge a man with felony.

———— County, to wit:

To X. Y., Constable of the said County :

Whereas, A. B. has this day made complaint and oath before me J. T., a Justice of the said County, that C. D., E. F. and G. H. of the said County,(*) intending unlawfully to subject him the said A. B., without just cause, to disgrace and grievous bodily punishment, on the —— day of ———— 18—, at the County aforesaid, did falsely and maliciously conspire, confederate and agree together, to charge and accuse him the said A. B., that he had then lately before feloniously (here describe the offence with which the conspirators charged him, as for instance, "stolen, taken and carried away one horse of the value of one hundred dollars, of the goods and chattels of the said E. F. :") These are, therefore, in the name of the Commonwealth, to command you forthwith to apprehend the said C. D., E. F. and G. H., and bring their bodies before me or some other Justice of the said County, to answer the complaint aforesaid, and to be farther dealt with according to law. Given under my hand and seal, this —— day of ———— 18—.

J. T., J. P. [L. S.]

[NOTE.—The foregoing form may be adapted to any case of conspiracy to charge another with an offence less than felony, by omitting the word *feloniously*, and substituting for it the word *unlawfully*.]

(¹) 7 Serg. & R. 469 ; 4 Wend. 365.
(²) 1 Hawk. c. 72.
(³) R. *v.* Kinnersley, 1 Str. 193 ; R *v.* Nicholls, 2 Str. 1227.
(⁴) 34 E. C. L. 397.

(No. 2.)

Form of a Warrant of Arrest for a conspiracy by persons confined in jail to effect their escape.

Follow form No. 1, to the (*), and proceed thus: "On the —— day of ——, were persons lawfully imprisoned in the common jail of the said County, situated at the Courthouse of the said County, and then and there lawfully detained in the custody of the keeper of the said jail by virtue of legal process against them, and that they the said C. D., E. F. and G. H., unlawfully intending to effect their escape from and out of the said jail and custody, did then and there conspire, confederate and agree among themselves, unlawfully to effect their escape from and out of the said jail and custody: These are, therefore, &c. (conclude as No. 1.)

(No. 3.)

Form of Warrant of Arrest for a conspiracy to engross and monopolize an article of trade.

Follow form No. 1, to the (*), and proceed thus: "On the —— day of —— 18—, now last past, and for a long time before and after, at the said County, being each of them buyers and sellers of a certain necessary article of food for man, called 'clipped herrings,' they the said C. D., E. F. and G. H., did then and there unlawfully conspire, combine, confederate and agree together, for their private gain, to acquire, obtain and engross into their hands and possession, all clipped herrings then brought to R. in the said County, or then afterwards to be brought there, to make a monopoly thereof, and to make and enhance at their will and pleasure the price of such herrings, the same being a necessary article of food: These are, therefore," &c. (conclude as No. 1.)

(No. 1.)

Indictment for a conspiracy among workmen, to raise their wages and lessen the time of labour.

Commence as No. 1, under head of "INDICTMENTS," and proceed thus: that A. B., C. D. and E. F., all of the County of ——, on the —— day of ——, in the County aforesaid, being all journeymen and workmen in the art and manual occupation of a wheelwright, (or whatever occupation they may be,) not being content to work and labour in that art and occupation, by the usual number of hours in each day, and at the usual rates and prices, for which they and other journeymen and workmen in the said art and occupation, were accustomed to work and labour, but falsely and fraudulently conspiring and combining unjustly and oppressively to increase and augment the wages of themselves and other journeymen and workmen in the said art, and unjustly to exact and extort large sums of money for their labour and hire in their said art, mystery and manual occupation, from their employers who employ them therein, on the same day and year aforesaid, in the County aforesaid, together with divers other journeymen and workmen, in the same art and manual occupation, (whose names are unknown,) unlawfully did assemble and meet together, and so being assembled and met, did then and there unlawfully and corruptly conspire, combine, confederate and agree together and among themselves, that none of the said conspirators after the same —— day of ———, would work at any lower or less rate than one dollar for the hewing of every hundred spokes for wheels, and two dollars for making every pair of hinder wheels, for or on account of any person or employer whatsoever in the said art and occupation; and also, that none of the said conspirators would work day work or labour any longer than from the hour of six in the morning till the hour of seven in the evening in each day from thenceforth, against the peace and dignity of the Commonwealth of Virginia.

(No. 2.)

Indictment for a conspiracy to defraud an illiterate person, by falsely reading to him a deed of bargain and sale, as and for a bond of indemnity.

Commence as No. 1, under head of "INDICTMENTS," and proceed thus: that A. B., C. D. and E. F. of the County aforesaid, unlawfully devising and intending one G. H. to injure, deceive and defraud, and him the said G. H. fraudulently to deprive of his property and estate, on the —— day of ————, did unlawfully conspire, combine, confederate and agree among themselves, falsely and fraudulently to obtain from the said G. H. a deed of bargain and sale of a certain lot of land ————; and that, in pursuance of, and according to the conspiracy, combination, confederacy and agreement aforesaid, so as aforesaid had, they the said A. B., C. D. and E. F., did falsely and fraudulently prepare, make out and fabricate a deed of bargain and sale of the said lot of land, to be signed and executed by him the said G. H., and did then and there falsely and fraudulently present the same to him the said G. H., and did then and there falsely and fraudulently, and in pursuance of the conspiracy, combination, confederacy and agreement aforesaid, read the same to him the said G. H. as a bond and obligation for the sum of seventy dollars, to be given by him the said G. H. to one I. J., as a consideration, that he the said G. H. should indemnify the said I. J. against the payment of certain notes of hand, which he the said G. H. had before the day aforesaid, made and given to one K. L.; he the said G. H. being then and there an illiterate person, and by reason thereof, wholly unable to read the deed so as aforesaid falsely and fraudulently made out and presented to him, against the peace and dignity of the Commonwealth of Virginia.

(No. 3.)

Indictment for a conspiracy by persons confined in prison, to effect their own escape and that of others.

Commence as No. 1, under head of "INDICTMENTS," and proceed thus: that A. B., C. D. and E. F., on the —— day of ————, were lawfully confined in the prison and common jail of the County aforesaid, and then and there lawfully detained in the custody of the keeper of said prison, by divers legal processes then and there in force against them the said A. B., C. D. and E. F., (state the cause of detention of each of the defendants;) and that said A. B., C. D. and E. F., unlawfully contriving and intending to effect the escape of themselves and divers other persons, to the said jurors unknown, who were then and there prisoners lawfully confined in the said prison, and in the custody of the keeper thereof, from out of said prison, did then and there conspire, combine, confederate and agree together, unlawfully to effect the escape of themselves, the said A. B., C. D. and E. F., and the said other prisoners then so lawfully confined in said prison, from and out of the same, against the peace and dignity of the Commonwealth of Virginia.

(No. 4.)

An Indictment for a conspiracy to engross and monopolize an article of trade.

—— County, to wit: ⎫ The jurors of the Commonwealth of Virgi-
In the County Court of ⎬ nia, in and for the body of the County of ——,
the said County. ⎭ and now attending the said Court, upon their oath present, that A. B., C. D. and E. F., on the —— day of —— in the year one thousand eight hundred and ——, now last past, and for a long time before and after, at the said County, being each of them buyers and sellers of a certain necessary article of food for man, called "clipped herrings," did then and there falsely and fraudulently conspire, combine, confederate and agree together, for their private gain, to acquire, obtain and engross into their hands and possession, all clipped herrings then brought to R., in the said County, or then afterwards to be brought there, to make a monopoly thereof, and to make and enhance at their will and pleasure, the price of such herrings, the same being a necessary article of food, against the peace and dignity of the Commonwealth of Virginia.

CONSTABLES—See Officers.

CHAPTER XXV.

CONVEYANCES—(*Public.*)

By Sec. 18, Chap. 191. If any driver, conductor or captain of any vehicle or boat for public conveyance, being free, shall, in the management of such vehicle or boat, wilfully or negligently inflict bodily injury on any person, he shall be punished as for a misdemeanor.

(No. 1.)

Form of Warrant of Arrest against the driver of a stage coach for injuring a person by negligent driving.

———— County, to wit:

To all or any one of the Constables of said County:

Whereas, A. B. of said County, has this day made complaint and information on oath before me J. T., a Justice of the said County, that C. D., on the ——— day of ——— 18—, in said County, (he the said C. D. then being the driver of a certain stage coach for public conveyance,) did, by his management of the said stage coach, as driver thereof, negligently inflict bodily injury upon the said A. B., by (here state the injury:) These are, therefore, to command you, in the name of the Commonwealth of Virginia, forthwith to apprehend the said C. D., and bring him before me or some other Justice of the said County, to answer the said complaint, and to be farther dealt with according to law. Given under my hand and seal, this ——— day of ——— 18—.

J. T., J. P. [L. s.]

(No. 2.)

Form of a Warrant of Arrest against the conductor of a railroad car.

———— County, to wit:

To all or any one of the Constables of said County:

Whereas, A. B. of said County, has this day made complaint and information on oath before me J. T., a Justice of the said County, that C. D., on the ——— day of ——— 18—, in said County, (he the said C. D. then being the conductor of a certain railroad car for public conveyance,) in the use of the (state the railroad company to which the car belonged,) did, by his management of the said car, as conductor thereof, negligently inflict bodily injury upon the said A. B., by (state the injury:) These are, therefore, to command you, in the name of the Commonwealth of Virginia, forthwith to apprehend the said C. D., and bring him before me or some other Justice of the said County, to answer the said complaint, and to be farther dealt with according to law. Given under my hand and seal, this ——— day of ——— 18—.

J. T., J. P. [L. s.]

(No. 3.)

Form of Mittimus where a party is committed to answer an Indictment in the County Court for a misdemeanor.

―― County, to wit:

To X. Z., *Constable of said County, and to the Keeper of the Jail of said County:*

These are to command you, the said Constable, in the name of the Commonwealth of Virginia, forthwith to convey and deliver into the custody of the keeper of the said jail, together with this warrant, the body of C. D., charged before me J. T., a Justice of the said County, on the oath of A. B., with a misdemeanor by him committed, in this, that the said C. D., on the ―― day of ―――― in the year 18―, in the said County, (here describe the offence as in the warrant of arrest.) And you, the said keeper of the said jail, are hereby required to receive the said C. D. into your jail and custody, to answer an indictment to be preferred against him for the said offence, in the County Court of said County, and him there safely keep until he shall be discharged by due course of law. Given under my hand and seal, this ―― day of ―――― in the year 18―.

J. T., J. P. [L. S.]

(No. 4.)

Form of Recognizance of Bail.

Turn to head of RECOGNIZANCE, and follow No. 4, and state the offence succinctly, for which the party is recognized.

(No. 5.)

Form of Certificate of the Commitment, or Letting to Bail, to be sent to the Clerk of the County Court.

―― County, to wit:

To the Clerk of the County Court of said County:

I, J. T., a Justice of the said County, do hereby certify, that C. D. was this day committed to the jail of this County by my warrant, (or *was this day admitted to bail by me*, as the case may be,) to answer an indictment to be preferred against him, in the County Court of the said County, for a misdemeanor by him committed, in this, that he did, on the ―― day of ―――― 18―, in said County, (here describe the offence as in the warrant of arrest.) Given under my hand, this ―― day of ―――― 18―.

J. T., J. P.

(No. 6.)

Form of Recognizance of Witness to appear and give evidence to the Grand Jury upon the Indictment.

Follow No. 5, under head of RECOGNIZANCE.

CONVEYANCES—(*Public*)—(*Indictments for.*) 179

(No. 1.)

An Indictment against the driver of a stage coach for injuring a person by negligent driving.

—— County, to wit: } The jurors of the Commonwealth of Virginia, in and for the body of the County of —— , and now attending the said Court, upon their oath present, that A. B., on the —— day of ——, in the year one thousand eight hundred and ——, in the said County, he the said A. B. being then the driver of a certain stage coach for public conveyance, did, by his management of the said stage coach, as driver thereof, wilfully (or *negligently*) inflict an injury upon one C. D., by (here state the wilful act and the kind of injury:)* against the peace and dignity of the Commonwealth of Virginia.

In the County Court of the said County.

———

(No. 2.)

An Indictment against the conductor of a railroad car for injuring a person by negligent management.

—— County, to wit: } The jurors of the Commonwealth of Virginia, in and for the body of the County of ——, and now attending the said Court, upon their oath present, that A. B., on the —— day of —— in the year one thousand eight hundred and ——, in the said County, he the said A. B. being then and there the conductor of a certain railroad car for public conveyance, in the use of the "Richmond, Fredericksburg and Potomac railroad company," (or whatever other company it may be,) did, by his management of the said car, as conductor therof, wilfully (or *negligently*) inflict upon the person of one C. D., an injury, by (here state the injury as directed in the foregoing precedent,) against the peace and dignity of the Commonwealth of Virginia.

In the County Court of the said County.

———

* *Query.*—But is this necessary? It can certainly be no objection to the indictment, and from analogy, would seem the safer course.

CHAPTER XXVI.

CONVICTS—(*Bringing them into the State.*)

BY SEC. 37, CHAP. 198. If a master of a vessel, or other person, knowingly import or bring into this State, any person convicted of felony out of this State, or any slave sold and transported beyond the limits of this State, for crime, he shall be confined in jail for three months, and be fined one hundred dollars.

(No. 1.)

Form of Warrant of Arrest for bringing a person convicted of felony out of this Commonwealth, into this Commonwealth.

——— County, to wit:

To all or any one of the Constables of said County:

Whereas, A. B. of said County, has this day made complaint and information on oath before me J. T., a Justice of the said County, that C. D., on the ——— day of ——— 18—, in said County, did knowingly import and bring into this Commonwealth, one H. L., who had then lately before been convicted of felony in the State of New York, to wit, of feloniously stealing, taking and carrying away the goods and chattels of one E. T., he the said C. D. then well knowing that the said H. L. had been before convicted of said felony in the said State of New York: These are, therefore, to command you, in the name of the Commonwealth of Virginia, forthwith to apprehend the said C. D., and bring him before me or some other Justice of the said County, to answer the said complaint, and to be farther dealt with according to law. Given under my hand and seal, this ——— day of ——— 18—.

J. T., J. P. [L. S.]

(No. 2.)

Form of Warrant of Arrest for bringing back into this Commonwealth a slave sold and transported beyond the limits of the Commonwealth for crime.

——— County, to wit:

To all or any one of the Constables of said County:

Whereas, A. B. of said County, has this day made complaint and information on oath before me J. T., a Justice of the said County, that C. D., on the ——— day of ——— 18—, in said County, did knowingly import and bring into this Commonwealth, and into the said County, Jack, a slave, who had before that time, been sold and transported beyond the limits of this Commonwealth for the crime of (state the crime, as for instance, *burglary* or *arson*,) he the said C. D. then knowing that the said slave had been so sold and transported for the said crime: These are, therefore, to command you, in the name of the Commonwealth of Virginia, forthwith to apprehend the said C. D., and bring him before me or some other Justice of the said County, to answer the said complaint, and to be farther dealt with according to law. Given under my hand and seal, this ——— day of ——— 18—.

J. T., J. P. [L. S.]

(No. 3.)

Form of Mittimus where a party is committed to answer an indictment in the County Court, for bringing into this Commonwealth a person convicted of felony.

—— County, to wit:
    To X. Z., Constable of said County, and to the Keeper of the Jail of said County:

These are to command you, the said Constable, in the name of the Commonwealth of Virginia, forthwith to convey and deliver into the custody of the keeper of the said jail, together with this warrant, the body of C. D., charged before me J. T., a Justice of the said County, on the oath of A. B., with a misdemeanor by him committed, in this, that the said C. D., on the —— day of —— in the year 18—, in the said County, (here describe the offence as in the warrant of arrest.) And you, the said keeper of the said jail, are hereby required to receive the said C. D. into your jail and custody, to answer an indictment to be preferred against him for the said offence, in the County Court of said County, and him there safely keep, until he shall be discharged by due course of law. Given under my hand and seal, this —— day of —— in the year 18—.

                                    J. T., *J. P.* [L. S.]

(No. 4.)

Form of Recognizance of Bail.

Turn to head of RECOGNIZANCE, and follow No. 4, and state the offence succinctly, for which the party is recognized.

(No. 5.)

Form of Certificate of the Commitment or Letting to Bail, to be sent to the Clerk of the County Court.

—— County, to wit:
    To the Clerk of the County Court of the said County:

I, J. T., a Justice of the said County, do hereby certify, that C. D. was this day committed to the jail of this County, by my warrant, (or *was this day admitted to bail by me*, as the case may be,) to answer an indictment to be preferred against him in the County Court of the said County, for a misdemeanor by him committed, in this that he did, on the —— day of —— 18—, in said County, (here describe the offence as in the warrant of arrest.) Given under my hand, this —— day of —— 18—.

                                      J. T., *J. P.*

(No. 6.)

Form of Recognizance of Witness to appear and give evidence to the Grand Jury upon the indictment.

Follow No. 5, under the head of RECOGNIZANCE.

CHAPTER XXVII.

CORONERS.

By Sec. 10, Chap. 49. Whenever, in any county or corporation, there may be no Coroner thereof, the court thereof shall nominate two persons residing therein, one of whom the Governor may appoint to be Coroner of such county or corporation. And, though, in any county or corporation there may be one Coroner therefor, yet if the court thereof shall be of opinion that there ought to be an additional Coroner, it may nominate two other persons residing in the county or corporation, one of whom the Governor may appoint to the office. Every Coroner may hold his office during good behaviour.

By the 15th and 16th Sections of the same Chapter, a Coroner may, with the assent of the court, appoint a deputy, who may be removed from office either by his principal or by the court; and, during his continuance in office, the deputy may discharge any official duty of his principal, except to take an inquest. This, as will be presently seen, is a judicial act, to be performed by the Coroner in person.

The office of Coroner is said to be of such high antiquity, that its commencement is unknown; it certainly existed in the reign of Alfred, for he punished with death a Judge who sentenced a party to suffer death, upon the Coroner's record, without allowing the delinquent liberty to traverse.([1]) To say nothing of the duties it imposes, the continuance of this office from a period so remote, affords pregnant proof of its value. But so important are these duties, that the office itself, in England, is thought not unworthy the Chief Justice of the Court of King's Bench, who is Supreme Coroner over all England.([2]) Yet, in this State, it is sometimes conferred upon those who are ignorant of every duty it imposes. For the use of such persons this short chapter is here introduced, with the hope that it will enable them to act, at least, with some tolerable degree of accuracy, and with more promptness and decision than is now usual.

Coroners may be considered in two points of view: first, as judicial officers in the administration of criminal justice; and, secondly, as ministerial law officers. They have, it is true, other duties conferred by statute, not immediately embraced in either of these divisions, though springing out of the one or the other of them. It would, however, be going

---

([1]) 6 Vin. Abr. 242. ([2]) 4 Rep. 37 b.

beyond the purposes of this work, to notice them farther than as judicial and ministerial law officers strictly.

First, then, as to their judicial functions, Coroners are conservators of the peace at Common Law, by virtue of their office, and have the power to cause felons to be apprehended, as well those who have been found guilty after inquisition, as those suspected of guilt before the inquisition; for, as Lord Hale remarks, many times the inquests are long in their enquiry, and the offender may escape, if the Coroner stay until the inquisition is delivered up.([1])

The Coroner may bind any person to the peace who makes an affray in his presence.([2])

But the most important judicial duty of Coroners, and that which they are most frequently called upon to discharge, is the inquisition of death, *super visum corporis*, (upon view of the body.) This was a high judicial duty at Common Law, and so continues to be under the sanction of the statute, which, for the most part, is merely directory, and in affirmance of the Common Law, and does not excuse the Coroner from any part of his duty not mentioned in it, and which was incident to his office at Common Law.([3])

BY SEC. 1, CHAP. 202. Upon notice of a death, supposed to have been caused by violence and not by casualty, the Coroner of the City of Richmond, if the dead body be in the penitentiary, and in any other case the Coroner of the county or corporation in which the dead body is, shall issue a warrant to the following effect: "―――― county, (or *corporation of* ――――,) to wit: To the Sheriff (or *Sergeant*) or any Constable of ―――― county, (or *the corporation of* ――――:) You are required to summon twelve jurors of the county (or *corporation*) of ――――, to attend before me, a Coroner of said county, (or *corporation*,) at the dwelling house of ――――, (or *at a place called* ――――,) in said county, (or *corporation*,) at the hour of ――――, to enquire upon the view of the body of ――――, (or *a person unknown*,) there lying dead, when, how and by what means he came to his death. Given under my hand, this ―― day of ――――18―.

――――, *Coroner.*"

BY SEC. 2. The Coroner may issue a summons, directed like the warrant, commanding the officer to summon witnesses to attend before him at such time and place as he may direct.

BY SEC. 3. Any such officer to whom the warrant or summons may be delivered, shall forthwith execute it and make return thereof to the Coroner, at the time and place named

―――――――――――――
([1]) 2 Hale P. C. 107; 1 Salk. 347; Jervis on Coroners 21.
([2]) 1 Bac. Abr. 491.
([3]) 2 Hawk. c. 9, § 21; 3 Inst. 52.

therein; if he fail so to execute and return the same, he shall forfeit twenty dollars, and if any person summoned as a juror fail to attend as required, without sufficient excuse, he shall forfeit ten dollars.

By Sec. 4. If twelve jurors do not attend, the Coroner may require the officer or any other person to summon others. When the full number of twelve have appeared, the Coroner, in view of the body, shall administer to them the following oath: "You swear that you will diligently enquire and true presentment make, when, how and by what means the person whose body here lies dead, came to his death, and return a true inquest thereof upon your own knowledge and the evidence before you. So help you God."

By Sec. 5. Witnesses on whom the summons before mentioned is served, may be compelled by the Coroner to attend and give evidence, and shall be liable in like manner as if the summons had been issued by a Justice in a criminal case; they shall be sworn by the Coroner before giving evidence to the inquest, and their evidence shall be reduced to writing by him or under his direction, and subscribed by them respectively.

By Sec. 6. The jury, after hearing the evidence and making all needful enquiries, shall deliver to the Coroner their inquisition, wherein they shall state the name of the deceased, (if it be known,) the material circumstances attending his death, and if they find that he came to his death by unlawful violence, who were guilty thereof, either as principal or accessary. The inquisition may be to the following effect: "———— county, (or *corporation of* ————;) to wit: An inquisition taken at ———— in the county, (or *corporation*) of ———— on the ———— day of ———— in the year ————, before ————, a Coroner of the said county, (or *corporation*,) upon the view of the body of ————, (or *a person unknown*,) there lying dead. The jurors sworn to enquire when, how and by what means the said ———— (or *person*) came to his death, upon their oaths do say: (then insert when, how and by what person, means, weapon or instrument he was killed, and any material circumstances.) In testimony whereof, the said Coroner and jurors hereto set their hands."

By Sec. 7. The Coroner shall return to his county or corporation court the inquisition, written testimony and recognizances by him taken; and if the jury find that murder, manslaughter or assault had been committed on the deceased, shall require such witnesses as he thinks proper to give a recognizance to appear and testify at such court when it sits for the examination or trial of the accused.

By Sec. 8. If a person charged with the offence by the inquest be not in custody, the Coroner may for his apprehension issue process in the same manner as a Justice; it shall be returnable before a Justice, and proceeded on as directed by chapter 204.

By Sec. 9. If the dead person be a stranger, (whether an inquest be taken, or the Coroner called on to view the body thinks it unnecessary to have an inquest,) he shall cause the body to be decently buried. If the Coroner certify that he believes the deceased has not sufficient estate in this State to pay the expenses of the burial, the Coroner's fees, and the expenses of the inquest, if one was taken, they shall, when allowed by the court of the Coroner's county or corporation, be paid out of the treasury. In other cases all such charges shall be paid out of the estate of the deceased, if he be a free person, or if a slave, by his owner; or if the estate of the deceased or his owner be insufficient, by the county or corporation aforesaid, unless the inquest be on the body of a convict in the penitentiary, in which case the same shall be paid out of the treasury after being allowed by the executive.

By Sec. 10. In taking an inquest the Coroner may require one or more physicians to attend and give information and render services incident to his profession useful to the jury; and reasonable compensation therefor shall be allowed as part of the costs of the inquest.

By Sec. 11. If a Coroner fail to perform any duty herein required of him, he shall forfeit one hundred dollars. In case of such failure, or if there be no Coroner authorized to act, a Justice of the court by which the nomination of a Coroner so authorized was or might be made, may act as Coroner, and be entitled to the same fees and be subject to the same penalties.

By Sec. 12. Under this chapter, proceedings may be had for summoning a jury and witnesses, and an inquest may be held, as well on Sunday as on any other day.

By Chap. 211, Sec. 14. The name of any person summoned by an officer, and failing to attend as a juror upon an inquest out of court, shall be returned by such officer to the next term of the court from which the process issued requiring such jury, or if there be no such process, to the next term of the court of such officer's county or corporation. Such court shall fine said person, unless he have a reasonable excuse for his failure, ten dollars.

Though the statute mentions only enquiries of death of persons, supposed to have been caused by violence and not by casualty, yet the Coroner, by virtue of his Common Law powers, may and ought to enquire of the death of all persons whomsoever who die in prison, and it is the duty of the Jailor to send for him in all cases of death, before the body be buried.([1])

The dying suddenly, is not to be understood of a fever, apoplexy or other visitation of God; and Coroners ought not in such cases, nor indeed in any case, to obtrude themselves into private families for the purpose of instituting an enquiry,([2]) but should wait until sent for by the peace officers of the place, to whom it is the duty of those in whose houses violent or unnatural deaths occur, to make immediate communication, whilst the body is fresh, and if possible, whilst it remains in the same situation as when the person died. But under whatever circumstances, this authority must be exercised within the limits of a sound discretion, and unless there be a reasonable ground of suspicion that the party came to his death by violence and unnatural means, there is no occasion, except in the case of a person dying in jail, for the interference of the Coroner. Indeed, they have not only been censured on several occasions by the court for holding unnecessary inquests,([3]) but if a Coroner intrude himself into the enquiry without fair and reasonable ground for suspecting that the death occurred from violence or unnatural cause, he is entitled to no remuneration. As, for instance, if he take an inquisition upon a dead body, manifestly drowned in the high seas and cast upon the shore within his jurisdiction.([4])

In taking an inquisition of death, the view of the body is absolutely necessary to give jurisdiction to the Coroner, and unless the inquest be taken *super visum corporis*, the inquisition will be merely an extrajudicial proceeding and void. This is clearly laid down by all the writers on the subject,([5]) and it should appear on the face of the inquisition itself, that the inquest was held on the view of the body, and where the body lies; for if it lie out of the Coroner's jurisdiction, though the death may have occurred within it, he has no power to take the view, and without this, he has no jurisdiction.([6])

Both the Coroner and jury must view the body at the same time, for the inquisition proceeds upon the body lying dead, and the oath ought regularly to be administered by the Coroner to the jury *super visum corporis*.([7]) So essential is the view to the validity of the inquisition, that if the body is not found, or if from any other cause, the view cannot be had, no inquest should be taken by the Coroner. For the purpose of having the view, the Coroner may order the body to be disinterred

---

([1]) 1 Hawk. c. 9, § 21; Jervis on Cor. 24.
([2]) 11 East 229.
([3]) Jervis on Cor.; 2 East P. C. 382.
([4]) 1 Nolan 141.
([5]) 2 Hale 58; 2 Hawk. c. 9, § 32; 2 R. 32; 3 B. & A. 260; and see Ump. & Jervis on Cors.
([6]) Jervis on Cor. 250-1; 6 B. & C. 247.
([7]) Jervis on Cor. 27.

within a reasonable time after the death of the person, either for the purpose of taking an original inquisition, where none has been taken, or a further inquisition, where the first was insufficient.(¹) Of this right, there can be no question, and it should be exercised whenever it is at all probable, under the circumstances, that a view of the body would throw any light upon the enquiry; but when it has been buried so long that it may reasonably be presumed, that the view of it would afford no information whatever of the cause of death, the Coroner ought not to disinter it.

But notwithstanding the inquest must be on view of the body, it is not necessary that it should be taken at the same place where the body was viewed, for the Coroner may adjourn the jury from time to time, and from one place to another within his jurisdiction, provided the real place at which the inquest was held, (that is, where the view was,) be stated in the inquisition.(²)

The enquiries to be instituted by the Coroner are so clearly and fully indicated by the statute itself, that it is unnecessary to repeat them. But it is proper to remark, that as the Coroner's enquiry is restricted to the cause of the death of the person, upon whose body the inquest is taken—and as accessaries after the fact merely, cannot in any wise be implicated in the cause of the death, his enquiry cannot extend to them. He should however enquire of accessaries before the fact, for such are instrumental to the death.(³)

The Coroner's inquest is to ascertain truly the cause of the party's death, and is rather for information of the truth of the fact than for accusation. On this account, it is the duty of the Coroner to receive evidence on oath, as well on behalf of any party who may be accused, as for the Commonwealth.(⁴)

It is the duty of all persons who are acquainted with the circumstances attending the subject of the Coroner's enquiry, to appear before the inquest as witnesses. Should they neglect or refuse to do so, the Coroner, as incident to his office, has authority to issue a summons to compel their appearance, and to commit them for their contempt, should they refuse to appear, or for refusing to give evidence upon the subject of the enquiry after appearing.(⁵) And if, during the time of investigation, the Coroner be informed of any person who can give evidence material to the enquiry, he may in like manner force the attendance of such person before him, to testify.(⁶) See forms at the end of this chapter.

(¹) 2 Hawk. c. 9, § 23; Jervis on Cor. 29.
(²) Jervis on Cor. 27.
(³) 2 Hawk. P. C. c. 9, § 26, 27.
(⁴) 1 Leach 43; Jervis on Cor. 30.
(⁵) Jervis on Cor. 229-30; 1 Ch. Cr. L. 164; and see 5th section of statute.
(⁶) Jervis on Cor. 30.

In regard to taking down the evidence, the statute does not authorize the Coroner to put down his own conception of the evidence, and not the words of the witnesses, but contemplates that the examination of the witnesses should be taken down with the greatest possible accuracy as to all material points of the enquiry, so that one great benefit of the act, which is to enable the court to which it is returned, to compare the examination with the evidence given before it, may not be defeated. It is not essential that letters, syllables, or even words, should be adhered to, although even these should not be needlessly departed from; but the fair and obvious meaning of the words spoken, and not the result of the evidence, should be reduced to writing, (in the hearing of the accused, if he be present,) and, so far as is consistent with the circumstances, in the exact natural language and peculiar expressions used by the witnesses. Such a course will avoid the difficulty too frequently experienced from witnesses being unable to recollect what they have sworn before the Coroner, and obviate the just complaint of the culpable neglect of the Coroners in this respect. It may be useful to observe, that the most correct mode of taking an examination is to follow the precise expressions of the witness, in the first person.[1]

After the proceeding has been instituted and concluded by one Coroner, the act of any other will be void.[2]

Though the Coroner is not fettered by any stated allegations in pleading, which require particular proof, he is, in taking an inquisition, to be governed by the general rules of evidence applicable alike to all civil and criminal proceedings.[3] He is to judge of the *competency* of the evidence, and leave its weight to the inquest; and upon a question of competency, it is stated as a universal maxim, that a fact must be established by the same rules of evidence, whether it be followed by a criminal or civil consequence.[4] See chapter on EVIDENCE.

The evidence being closed, the Coroner draws up the inquisition according to the finding of the jury, to which both he and the jury must put their hands and seals, and it is then returned, with the evidence, to the office of the Clerk of the county or corporation court.

The proceedings, after the inquisition, are so clearly pointed out by the statute, that farther notice of them is unnecessary, except to give such forms as are not prescribed by the statute.

What has been said relates principally to the judicial acts of a Coroner. In certain contingencies the statute devolves upon him many of the ministerial duties of Sheriff. By sec. 21,

---

[1] See 2 East P. C.
[2] See Jervis on Cor.
[3] Jervis on Cor. 238.
[4] Id.

chap. 49, when, by death, resignation or otherwise, there is no person acting in any county as Sheriff, or Deputy Sheriff thereof, or no person acting in any corporation as Sergeant, or Deputy Sergeant thereof, the Coroner or Coroners of such county or corporation, shall perform all the duties pertaining to the office of Sheriff or Sergeant thereof, except such as relate to the collection of the taxes, levies, militia fines and officers' fees. And when it is unfit for a Sheriff or Sergeant to serve any process, or to summon a jury, by reason of his being interested, or from any other cause, such process shall be directed to and served by, and such jury shall be summoned by, a Coroner of the county or corporation. But, before any Coroner shall have authority to receive any money, or serve any execution under this provision, the 22d section requires the court to take from him a bond in such penalty as it may deem fit.

For Coroners' fees, see COSTS.

(No. 1.)

Warrant to summon inquest.

Follow the form given in the statute just cited.

(No. 2.)

Proclamation to be made by the Constable when the inquest is assembled.

You have been summoned to appear here this day to enquire for the Commonwealth, when, how and by what means C. D. came to his death; answer to your names as you shall be called.

(No. 3.)

Form of foreman's oath.

See form prescribed in the statute.

(No. 4.)

Proclamation for attendance of witnesses.

The inquest being sworn, the Constable makes this proclamation:

If any one can give evidence in behalf of the Commonwealth, when, how and by what means C. D. came to his death, let him come forth, and he shall be heard.

(No. 5.)

Oath to be administered to witnesses.

The evidence which you shall give to this inquest on behalf of the Commonwealth, touching the death of C. D., shall be the truth, the whole truth and nothing but the truth. So help you God.

(No. 6.)

Summons for Witness.

——— County, to wit:

To A. B., *Constable of the said County:*

By virtue of my office, I do, in the name of the Commonwealth, command you, upon sight hereof, to summon X. Y., personally to be and appear before me, at ———, at ——— o'clock in the ——— noon, on the ——— day of ——— 18—, then and there to give evidence and be examined on behalf of the Commonwealth, before me and my inquest, touching the death of C. D., now there lying dead. Herein fail you not. Given under my hand and seal, this ——— day of ——— 18—.

R. T., *Coroner,* [L. S.]

(No. 7.)

Warrant against a witness for contempt, in refusing to obey the summons.

——— County, to wit:

To A. B., *Constable of the said County:*

Whereas, X. Y. hath this day been duly summoned to appear at the time and place in the said summons specified, and give evidence on behalf of the Commonwealth, touching the death of C. D., now lying dead at ———, in the said County, as fully appears to me by the return of A. B., Constable, in writing upon the said summons; and whereas the said X. Y. hath refused and neglected so to do, to the great hindrance and delay of justice: These are, therefore, by virtue of my office, in the name of the Commonwealth, to command you to apprehend and bring before me, now sitting at the place aforesaid, and in the County aforesaid, by virtue of my said office, the body of the said X. Y., that he may be dealt with according to law, and for your so doing, this is your warrant. Given under my hand and seal, this ——— day of ———18—.

R. T., *Coroner,* [L. S.]

(No. 8.)

Form of Arrest Warrant by Coroner.

——— County, to wit:

To all or any one of the Constable of the said County:

Whereas, by an inquisition taken before me, one of the Commonwealth's Coroners for the said County of ———, this ——— day of ——— 18—, at the said County, on view of the body of A. B., then and there lying dead, one C. D. stands charged with the wilful murder of the said A. B. : These are, therefore, by virtue of my office as Coroner, to command you and each of you, in the name of the Commonwealth of Virginia, forthwith to apprehend the said C. D., and without delay to carry him before some one of the Justices of the said County, that he may be dealt with according to law, and for so doing, this is your warrant. Given under my hand and seal, this —— day of ——— 18—.

T. W., *Coroner*, [L. S.]

[NOTE.—If the party be arrested by virtue of this warrant and carried before a Justice, he should proceed with the case in all respects as though the prisoner were brought before him by his own warrant. For which, see title HOMICIDE.]

(No. 9.)

Form of Commitment by Coroner.

——— County, to wit:

To *A. B.* *Constable of the said County, and to the Keeper of the Jail of the said County:*

Whereas, by an inquisition duly taken before me, one of the Commonwealth's Coroners for the said County, on the —— day of ——— 18—, on view of the body of C. D., lying dead in the said County, E. F. who was present at the taking of the said inquisition, stands charged with the wilful murder of the said C. D., (or if the inquisition find it to be a case of manslaughter and not murder, say : "stands charged with feloniously and unlawfully killing the said C. D. :") These are, therefore, by virtue of my office and in the name of the Commonwealth of Virginia, to command you, the said Constable, forthwith to convey the said E. F. to the jail of the said County, and safely to deliver him, together with this warrant, to the keeper of the said jail. And these are, likewise, by virtue of my office, to command you, the keeper of the said jail, to receive the body of the said E. F. into your custody, and him safely to keep in the said jail until he shall thence be discharged by due course of law, and for your so doing, this shall be your warrant. Given under my hand and seal, this —— day of ——— 18—.

J. M., *Coroner*, [L. S.]

(No. 10.)

Form of Recognizance of Witness entered into before a Coroner to appear before a County Court, upon the examination or trial of a party committed by a Coroner.

——— County, to wit:

Be it remembered, that on the —— day of ——— 18—, X. Y. came before me T. W., one of the Coroners in and for the said County, and acknowledged himself to be indebted to the Commonwealth of Virginia, in the sum of ——— dollars, good and lawful money of the United States, to be made and levied of his goods and chattels, lands and tenements, for the use of the Commonwealth of Virginia, if the said X. Y. shall make default in the performance of the underwritten condition.

The condition of the above recognizance is such, that whereas, by an inquisition taken before me, one of the Coroners in and for the County of

―――, this ―― day of ――― 18―, at the said County, on the view of the body of A. B., then and there lying dead, C. D. was found guilty, and now stands charged with the felonious and wilful murder of the said A. B.: Now, if the above bound X. Y. shall personally appear before the County Court of the said County, on the first day of the next term thereof, at the Courthouse in the said County, then and there to give to the said Court such evidence on behalf of the Commonwealth, as he knows against the said C. D., touching the murder and felony aforesaid, and shall not depart thence without the leave of the said Court, then this recognizance shall be void, otherwise to remain in full force and virtue.

Acknowledged before me, the day and year first above written.

T. W., *Coroner*, [L. S.]

CHAPTER XXVIII.

COSTS.

In the prosecution or defence of legal proceedings, either criminal or civil, the parties necessarily incur certain expenses called "costs." It is a maxim of the Common Law, that the government neither pays nor receives costs, but it is otherwise under the statute.

By SECTIONS 35 AND 36 OF CHAP. 176, it is provided, that "a person attending as a witness, under a summons, shall have fifty cents for each day's attendance, and four cents per mile for each mile, beyond ten miles, necessarily travelled to the place of attendance, and the same for returning, besides the tolls at the bridges and ferries which he crosses, or turnpike gates he may pass. A witness, to entitle himself to compensation, should enter his attendance, on oath, such entry to be made when before either house or a committee of the General Assembly, by the clerk of such house or committee, and in other cases, by the clerk of the court in which the cause is, or the person before whom the witness attended. A witness summoned to attend in several cases, may have the entry made against either of the parties by whom he is summoned, but no witness shall be allowed for his attendance in more than one case at the same time. The payment to such witness, shall be on a certificate of the person required to make the entry. Any dispute, before or after the issuing of the certificate, between the witness and the party against whom the claim is made, as to its justice or amount, may, when the case is in a court, or before a Justice, be determined by such court or Justice. In case of attendance before either house, or a committee of the General Assembly, and in any other case

COSTS.   193

in which the attendance is for the Commonwealth, except where it is otherwise specially provided, the sum to which a witness is entitled, shall be paid out of the treasury; in all other cases, it shall be paid by the party for whom the summons issued.

By Sec. 11, Chap. 134, a Sheriff, Sergeant or Crier, is allowed the following fees:

Sheriff, Sergeant or Crier's fees.

For serving on any person a declaration in ejectment, or an order, notice, summons or other process, where the body is not taken, and making return thereof,	$ 0 50
Except that the fee for summoning a witness shall only be,	0 20
For serving on any person an attachment or other process, under which the body is taken,	0 60
For receiving a person in jail, 25 cents, and the like sum for discharging him therefrom.	
For carrying a prisoner to or from jail, for each mile of necessary travel, either in going or returning,	0 5
For taking any bond,	0 60
Where a jury is sworn in court, for summoning and empanneling such jury,	1 00
Where a party is summoned upon a writ of *elegit* or *ad quod damnum*, or any inquest in vacation, for summoning them, $ 1; and for attending at the place of their meeting, $ 1; and if the jury attend there, and an inquisition be found and returned,	2 00
For serving a writ of possession,	1 50
For serving a writ of *distringas* on a judgment or decree for personal property, if the specific thing be taken,	1 50
For keeping and supporting any slave or other person confined in jail, for each day,	0 30

For keeping and supporting any horse or live stock, distrained or levied on, 17 cents per day for each horse, mule or mare, and if the mare have a sucking colt, no more; 5 cents per day for each hog or head of horned cattle, and 3 cents per day for every sheep or goat.

The court of any county or corporation may, at any time, when the acting Justices have been summoned to consider the subject, or a majority thereof is present, fix or alter the rates to be thenceforth paid in such county or corporation for keeping and supporting any person in jail, or any horse or live stock; but the rates as fixed or altered, shall never exceed those hereinbefore mentioned.

The officer shall be repaid any necessary expense incurred by him in keeping property not before mentioned, or in removing any property; and when, after distraining or levying, he neither sells nor receives payment, and either takes no forthcoming bond, or takes one which is not forfeited, he shall, if no default, have (in addition to the 60 cents for a bond, if one was taken,) a fee of three dollars, unless this be more than the half of what his commission would have amounted to, if he had received payment; in which case, he shall (whether a bond was taken or not) have a fee of sixty cents, at the least, and so much more as is necessary to make the said half. The commission to be included in a forthcoming bond, (when one is taken,) shall be five per centum on the first $300 of the money for which the distress or levy is, and two per centum on the residue of said money; but such commission shall not be received, unless the bond be forfeited, or the amount (including the commission) be paid to the plaintiff.

An officer receiving payment in money or selling goods, shall have the like commission of five per centum on the first $300 of the money paid or proceeding from the sale, and two per centum on the residue; except, that when such payment or sale is on an execution on a forthcoming bond, his commission shall be only half what it would be, if the execution were not on such bond.

By Sec. 12, Chap. 184, a Coroner or Constable is allowed the following fees:

Coroner or Constable's fees.

A Coroner shall have, for taking an inquest on a dead body, five dollars, and a Constable, for summoning a Coroner's jury and the witnesses, three dollars. A Constable shall have, for removing a person by virtue of a warrant issued under chapter 51, by a Justice or one of the overseers of the poor, (to be charged to said overseers,) four cents for each mile of necessary travel, either in going or returning.

For whipping a slave, (to be paid by the owner,) - $0 50
For serving a warrant under chapter 150, or taking a bond, or giving a notice therein, - - 0 30
But the fee for summoning a witness, or a garnishee, on an attachment, shall only be, - - 0 20
For other services, not otherwise provided for, a Coroner or Constable shall have the same fees as a Sheriff or Sergeant, for similar services.

BY THE 13TH SECTION OF CHAP. 184, those fees are chargeable to the party at whose instance the services are performed, except, that the fees for entering or certifying the attendance of witnesses, and the proceedings to compel payment for such attendance, shall be charged to the party for whom the witness attended.

THE 17TH AND 18TH SECTIONS are as follows: "§ 17. Every officer to whom the second section applies, [to wit, Sheriffs, Surveyors, Clerks, &c.] shall keep a fee book, wherein shall be entered the fees for every service performed by him, and the fact of such fees being paid, or of a bill being made out therefor, whichever shall happen first. The fee books of a clerk shall be submitted to the inspection of the commissioners appointed to examine the clerk's office. § 18. No person shall be compelled to pay any fees before mentioned, until there be produced to him a fee bill, signed by the officer to whom the fees are due, expressing the particulars for which such fees are charged. And no such fee bill shall be made out for any service not previously performed, unless a person desire to pay before such performance, in which case, there shall be mentioned in such fee bill, the nature of the service and the fact that it is to be performed. Nor shall an officer, for any service, make out a fee bill for more than is allowed therefor. Nor shall he, for the same service, attempt to obtain payment a second time, or even make out a fee bill a second time, unless he endorse the fact and swear that the former bill remains unpaid. For each item, in which an officer shall violate this section, he shall forfeit five dollars to any person prosecuting therefor, and the circuit, county or corporation court of the county or corporation in which an officer resides, may, on motion, after reasonable notice to him, quash any fee bill made out by him contrary to law."

COSTS.

The following fees are chargeable to the Commonwealth, and to be paid out of the treasury:

To the Sheriff or any other officer.

BY SEC. 30, CHAP. 184. For an arrest for felony, one dollar; and for conveying any person charged with or convicted of felony, to jail, or from one jail to another, or to the penitentiary, for each mile in going and returning, ten cents. The officer shall also be allowed, for the support of the prisoner during the removal, and for assistance to make the arrest or effect the removal, such charge as may have been necessarily incurred by him, to be shewn by his own affidavit; and where he has assistance, by the affidavit also of each person employed by him, such charge for assistance not to exceed, where it is in making an arrest, seventy-five cents per day for each person employed to assist him, and not to exceed, where it is in conveying a prisoner, ten cents per mile, going and returning, for each guard.

BY SEC. 31. For executing a writ of *venire facias*, one dollar and fifty cents; for whipping a free person by order of a Court or Justice, fifty cents; and for executing a sentence of death, five dollars, in addition to the expenses actually incurred by the officer in its execution.

To a Constable.

BY SEC. 32, CHAP. 184. For an arrest in any criminal case other than felony, - - $0 50
For summoning a witness in any criminal case, - 0 20
For executing a search warrant, - - - 0 50

IT IS ENACTED BY SECTION 4 OF CHAP. 210, that "the 34th, 35th and 36th sections of chapter 176, shall apply to a person attending as a witness, under a recognizance or summons in a criminal case, as well as to a person attending under a summons in a civil case; except, that in a criminal case, a witness, who travels over fifty miles to the place of attendance, shall have, for each day's attendance, one dollar, instead of fifty cents; and, a person residing out of the State, who attends a court therein as a witness, may be allowed by said court, for attendance and for travel to and from the place of his abode, as if he resided in this State.

BY SEC. 5. "The sum to which a witness is entitled, who attends for the Commonwealth, or any other legal charges incurred, in a case wherein there is a prosecutor, shall be paid by such prosecutor, as if he were plaintiff in the case, unless there be judgment against the defendant, in which case the same shall be taxed in the costs and paid to the persons entitled thereto, by the Sheriff or officer who may receive the same.

By Sec. 6. "Payment shall not be made out of the treasury to a witness attending for the Commonwealth in any prosecution for a misdemeanor, unless it appear that the sum to which the witness is entitled cannot be obtained, if it be a case wherein there is a prosecutor, and the defendant is convicted, by reason of his insolvency, or if it be a case in which there is no prosecutor, by reason of the acquittal or insolvency of the defendant, or other cause.

By Sec. 7. "A Sheriff or other officer, for travelling out of his county or corporation, to execute process in a criminal case and doing any act in the service thereof, for which no other compensation is provided, shall receive therefor, out of the treasury, such compensation as the court, from which the process issued, may certify to be reasonable, and when, in a criminal case, an officer renders any other service, for which no specific compensation is provided, the circuit court of the county or corporation in which such case may be, may allow therefor what it deems reasonable; and such allowance shall be paid out of the treasury. This section shall not prevent any payment under the 13th section of chapter 45, which could have been made, if this section had not been enacted.

By Sec. 8. "The certificate required by the 27th section of chapter 184, shall, when the payment is to be to a Clerk, be from the court whereof he is Clerk; and, when it is to be to a Sheriff or other officer, be from the court in which the prosecution is, or to which a Justice shall certify, as hereinafter mentioned. Any other expense incident to a proceeding, in a criminal case, which is payable out of the treasury, otherwise than under the preceding section, or under the 13th section of chapter 45, shall be certified by such last mentioned court, where it is not otherwise provided. With the certificate of allowance, there shall be transmitted to the first auditor, the vouchers on which it is made.

By Sec. 10. "A Justice, before whom there is any proceeding in a criminal case, shall certify to the Clerk of the court of his county or corporation, and a Judge or Court, before whom there is, in a criminal case, any proceeding preliminary to conviction in another court, upon receiving information of the conviction from the Clerk of the court wherein it is, shall certify to such Clerk, all the expenses incident to such proceeding, which are payable out of the treasury.

By Sec. 11. "In every criminal case, the Clerk of the court in which the accused is convicted, or if the conviction be before a Justice, the Clerk to which the Justice certifies as aforesaid, shall, as soon as may be, make up a statement of all the expenses incident to the prosecution, including such as are certified under the preceding section, and execution for the amount of such expenses shall be issued and proceeded with, and chapter 45 shall apply thereto, in like manner as if, on the day of completing said statement, there was a judgment in such court in favour of the Commonwealth against the accused for the said amount, as a fine.

BY SEC. 12. "If, by reason of the failure of a person to present his claim in due time, a sum be not included in such execution, which would have been included, if so presented, such claim, unless there be good cause for the failure, shall be disallowed."

The costs incurred by the Commonwealth in the arrest and examination of persons charged before a Justice with felony, must be certified to the court; those incurred in prosecutions for fines and other cases cognizable by a Justice, in which he can issue no execution, must be certified to the Clerk of the county or corporation court. In making these certificates, the Justice should adhere strictly to the statute, and restrict all officers and others to their legal fees.

Form of Certificate of Costs to Court in case of felony.

Commonwealth against A. B., charged with (state what, as for instance,) larceny. } Commonwealth's costs incurred before me in this prosecution, and which I hereby certify to the County Court.

To X. Y., Constable, for arresting defendant, - - - $1 00
To same, for summoning A. B., witness, - - - 0 20
To attendance of C. D., for —— days as witness for Commonwealth, 0 00

[NOTE.—If the party be arrested in any criminal proceeding other than felony, the fee for arrest is 50 cents; and in case of a search, a separate fee is allowed therefor, of 50 cents.]

CHAPTER XXIX.

COURTS.

Besides the ordinary jurisdiction of the county and corporation courts, the Justices have cognizance of criminal cases, both as examining courts and courts of oyer and terminer, but act in each with different and distinct powers; the one being a court for the *examination* of free white persons charged with any felony whatever, and free negroes charged with felonious homicide of any degree, or any capital offence, preparatory to a final trial in the circuit court; and the other, a court for the *trial* of free negroes charged with any felony, except those just mentioned, and for the trial of slaves in all cases of felony.

I. *As to examining courts.*

By Sec. 1, Chap. 205. Before a white person charged with a felony, or a free negro charged with felonious homicide, or any offence punishable with death, is tried before a circuit court or the general court, he shall be examined as hereafter provided, unless, by his assent entered of record in such court, such examination be dispensed with.

By Sec. 2. Every such examination shall be had before the court of the county or corporation in which the offence was committed *or may be prosecuted*,* and may be before the said court at a regular term or special session thereof, as the Judge or Justice (who considers that there is sufficient cause for charging with the offence the person accused thereof) may, in his discretion, determine.

By Sec. 3. If a Judge or Justice determine on a special session of such county or corporation court for any such examination, he shall forthwith issue his warrant to the officer of such court, requiring him to summon at least eight of the Justices (if so many there be) of the county or corporation, to meet (for the examination of the fact) at their courthouse on such day as said Judge or Justice shall appoint, not being less than five, nor more than ten days after the date of the warrant.

By Sec. 4. Every such court, whether at its regular term or at such special session, shall consist of at least five of the Justices of the county or corporation. The Justice who com-

---
*See Jurisdiction.

mitted or recognized the accused for examination, shall not, without the consent of the accused entered of record, be of the examining court.

By Sec. 5. The court, at any such special session, may adjourn the examination to the next regular term, quarterly or monthly, or to an earlier day, and at a regular term may continue any examination from term to term, so that such continuance, except on the motion of the accused, shall not be beyond the third regular term after the examination was ordered. But if an examination be commenced at any term, such term may be extended until the examination is concluded.

By Sec. 6. Upon any such examination, if it appear to the court that there is not probable cause for charging the accused with the offence, he shall be discharged.

By Sec. 7. If it appear, on the examination of such negro or person, as is mentioned in the first section, that a felony has been committed, and that there is probable cause to charge the accused therewith, the court shall remand him for trial in the circuit court or general court having cognizance of the case; take the depositions of all material witnesses on such examination, and require of them and such as the accused may desire on his behalf, a recognizance for their attendance at the trial.

By Sec. 8. Should the court be of opinion that the accused is entitled to bail, it shall let him to bail, if he give sufficient bail, or if he do not then give it, shall enter of record, that he is entitled to bail, and in what sum, and he may thereafter be admitted to bail by any Justice.

By Sec. 9. When a Justice admits such person to bail, he shall transmit the recognizance to the Clerk of the said circuit or general court, and issue a warrant for the discharge of the prisoner from jail, upon which he shall be discharged therefrom, if detained for no other cause.

By Sec. 10. When a person is remanded as aforesaid by a county or corporation court, the Clerk thereof shall certify to the Clerk of the court in which he is to be tried, copies of all recognizances taken by the said examining court, and to the attorney prosecuting for the Commonwealth in the court wherein the trial is to be, a copy of the order remanding the accused, and of the depositions taken on the examination, and of any warrant in the case which remains filed in the clerk's office.

By Sec. 11. If the court in which a person is examined as aforesaid, discharge him, he shall not thereafter be questioned or tried for the same offence.

By Sec. 12. If the accused be remanded for trial in a court whose jail is not the jail of the examining court, the latter court, by its order, or if it fail, any two Justices of the county or corporation, by their warrant, shall direct the officer of such court to (and he shall) remove the prisoner to the jail of the court in which he is to be tried, and the jailor thereof shall receive and keep him safely until discharged by law.

BY SEC. 13. If such examining court be of opinion that the accused is guilty of a misdemeanor, for which he ought to be tried in the county or corporation court, he shall, unless let to bail, be committed to jail, to answer an indictment against him in such court, which indictment may be preferred so soon as there may be a grand jury in said court. The court shall recognize, or cause to be summoned in the case, such witnesses, and to such time as may appear to it proper.

BY SEC. 14. The clerk of a county or corporation court, which determines that *a person* ought to be tried in the circuit court or general court, shall, as soon as may be, issue a *venire facias*, directed to the officer of the court in which the trial is to be, requiring him to summon jurors for such trial.

II. *As to courts of oyer and terminer.*

BY SEC. 1, CHAP. 212. A negro who is a slave for a term of years, or for the life of another person, shall be prosecuted, tried and punished for an offence as a slave. A negro detained as a slave, but suing for his freedom, shall be prosecuted and tried for an offence as a free negro.

BY SEC. 2. The county and corporation courts, consisting of five Justices thereof at the least, shall be courts of *oyer* and *terminer*, for the trial of negroes charged with felony, except in the case of free negroes charged with felonious homicide, or an offence punishable with death. Such trial shall be on a charge entered of record, stating the offence, but without a jury, or a presentment, information or indictment. The Justice who committed or recognized the accused, shall not sit on his trial.

BY SEC. 3. No Justice interested in a slave, shall sit on his trial for felony.

BY SEC. 4. The court on a trial of a slave for felony, shall assign him counsel, and allow such counsel a fee not exceeding twenty-five dollars, which shall be paid by the owner of the slave.

BY SEC. 5. No slave shall be condemned to death, nor a free negro to the penitentiary, unless all the Justices sitting on his trial agree in the sentence.

By Sec. 6. When a slave is condemned to death, or a free negro to the penitentiary, the court shall cause the testimony given on his trial, to be committed to writing and filed of record, and the clerk shall forthwith transmit a copy of the whole record to the Executive.

By Sec. 7. The court for good cause, may continue such trial from term to term. But if it be continued until the end of the third regular term after the commitment of the accused, or a recognizance for his appearance for trial, he shall be discharged unless such continuance was on his own application, or because of his insanity or his escape from custody, or failure to appear; or by reason of the witnesses for the Commonwealth being enticed or kept away, or prevented from attending, by sickness or some inevitable accident.

By Sec. 8. On a charge against a negro for felony, in a county or corporation court, the court may adjudge the accused not guilty of the offence charged, but guilty of any offence of which a free white person might be found guilty on an indictment against him for such felony, and ascertain the punishment so far as it is not fixed by law, and give judgment accordingly.

In concluding this chapter, we remark that the statute clearly designates to which of these courts a party charged with felony, should be sent by the committing magistrate, to be farther proceeded against, and that the marked distinction between them must not be lost sight of by the Justice. One is a court with jurisdiction to *try*, and by its judgment finally to *convict* and *punish*, or *acquit;* the other can only *enquire* into an alleged offence and *remand* the offender for final *trial* before the circuit court, or discharge him from farther prosecution. Examining courts are the mere creatures of the statute law, and cannot upon any principle exercise any power or jurisdiction which has not been expressly conferred on them by that law, or which does not result to them as the means necessary to carry the jurisdiction expressly given them into effect.([1]) It is the action of the Justice, upon the *commitment* of a prisoner, that marks the powers of the Justices when convened to exercise criminal jurisdiction in cases of felony, and the Commonwealth *v.* Tyree,([2]) forcibly exemplifies the necessity of observing the distinction between the two jurisdictions in committing an offender in the first instance. In that case, an examining court was convened to enquire into an offence charged upon the prisoner, and he was remanded for final trial before the circuit court as a free man, but before the trial, he was claimed as a slave, and the proof fully sustained

---

([1]) Myers' Case, 1 Va. Cases 243.   ([2]) 2 Va. Cases 262.

the claim. Yet upon *habeas corpus*, obtained at the instance of the master, the circuit court refused to surrender the prisoner, and he was afterwards tried (slave as he was) in the circuit court as a free man and sent to the penitentiary. The court decided, that when a black person is brought before an examining court, it is the duty of that court to enquire whether he be free or a slave, and if a slave, they cannot send the prisoner on for trial to the circuit court, but must remand him to the proper tribunal. See also the more recent case of Ex parte Ball, &c., 2 Gratt. 588, which fully recognizes the authority of the Commonwealth *v.* Tyree.

An examining court being restricted in its enquiry to the examination of the fact,([1]) and having no power to try, cannot pass sentence for any crime; and to send on a slave for any offence whatever, or a free negro charged with any crime less than capital, or a case of felonious homicide, to an examining court, is to convene a tribunal merely to have submitted to it a case over which it can take no cognizance, and to subject the Commonwealth to costs.

An examining court has no power of discriminating between the different degrees of felony growing out of the same facts, so as to determine for what degree of offence the party shall be sent on for farther prosecution in the circuit court; as for instance, in felonious homicide, it cannot acquit of murder and remand the prisoner to be tried for manslaughter.([2]) Its province is to ascertain, in the first place, whether the felonious *fact* charged upon the prisoner has been committed, and in the next, whether there is probable cause to believe him guilty, and if the court determine both of these propositions in the affirmative, the prisoner must be remanded for that fact, and it is for the circuit court and the jury to determine the grade of offence. But in burglary, if the prisoner be also charged in the warrant with larceny, the court may acquit of the burglary and remand for grand larceny.([3]) So, we presume, in any other case of compound felony, where all the ingredients necessary to constitute the specific crime are not proved, and it sufficiently appears that an offence has been committed, though not attended with all the circumstances necessary to make out the offence as charged, the court may acquit of that specific offence and remand for the other. For example, if a prisoner were charged with breaking and entering a dwelling house in the day time, with intent to rob, and with then and there committing robbery, and there was proof of the robbery, but not of the breaking into or entering the house, it would be competent for the court to discharge of the break-

---

([1]) Myers' Case, 1 Va. Cases 234.　　([2]) Id. 188.　　([3]) Id.

ing and remand for the robbery. So, in robbery, where there was no proof of taking by violence or putting in fear, but proof of simple larceny, the prisoner may be discharged of the robbery and remanded for the larceny. For in these cases, as in burglary, the court does not discriminate between the different degrees of an offence arising out of the same felonious fact, but denies the existence of certain facts, which, if affirmed, would establish a felony of a different character.

If in any case before an examining court, it appears that the offence amounts to petit larceny only, the prisoner must be discharged. The power to discharge in such a case, if it be one of discrimination at all, necessarily results from the want of jurisdiction in an examining court to examine into any misdemeanor whatever. As to the course to be pursued in all such cases, see section 13 of the statute quoted.

To give the circuit court jurisdiction in cases of felony, it must appear by the records of the examining court, for what criminal *fact* the prisoner has been remanded, and for this purpose the circuit court will look to the warrant summoning the Magistrates, as it is a part of the record, but will not look to the mittimus, that being no part of it;*([1]) and if it does not appear from the record for what *criminal fact* the prisoner was examined and remanded, but that he was charged before the examining court with *felony* generally, any indictment charging him with any particular offence, founded upon such an examination, will be quashed.([2]) It is essential, therefore, that the warrant to summon the court should state for what criminal *fact* the prisoner is to be examined, and if it do not, the examining court, upon motion, or without motion, should quash it. If, however, the criminal *fact* be distinctly set forth, it is sufficient, for the record of an examining court need not set forth the offence with the precision and certainty of an indictment, and therefore, in an examination for horse stealing, it was held not to be necessary to charge in the warrant that the horse was *feloniously* taken ; *stealing* is sufficient ; and it was further held that it was not necessary to charge the horse to be the property of any person ;([3]) for the offence consists in the larceny of the subject, and the property of the goods is merely an incident, and does not enter into the essence of the

---

([1]) M'Cauly's Case, 1 Va. Cases 300.   ([3]) Halkem's Case, 2 Va. Cases 4.
([2]) Mabry's Case, 2 Va. Cases 396.

*The law authorizes the Justice to commit, for examination, either to a special session or to the regular term of the county or corporation court ; and in the latter case, he is to certify the commitment to the Clerk. This certificate (as the warrant in the first case) is the basis upon which the record of the examining court must stand, and forming necessarily a part of it, would, as we presume, be looked to by the circuit court for any purpose that it would look to a warrant convening a special session.

crime.(¹) And although, in an indictment, it is absolutely necessary to state to whom the property belongs, and to prove it as alleged, it is not necessary in the record of an examining court;(²) so the certificate of the Justice to the Clerk, where the case is certified to the regular term of the county court, should set forth the felonious fact, as it is the foundation (and necessarily a part) of the record.

Where the prisoner was charged in the warrant for summoning an examining court, with feloniously stealing sundry checks, drawn by sundry individuals upon the Exchange Bank at Norfolk, and sundry other checks drawn in like manner upon the Farmers Bank at Norfolk; also treasury notes and other bank notes, amounting to 2324 dollars, of the value of $ 2324, the property of John S. Moody, and the record of the court stated that the prisoner was examined upon a charge of feloniously stealing *divers* goods and chattels, the property of J. S. M., it was held that both the warrant and examination were sufficient, and an indictment for the larceny of divers checks, bank notes and United States treasury notes, the property of J. S. M., was sustained thereby.(³)

No exception is allowed to the opinion of an examining court.(⁴)

When a Justice commits a prisoner for *trial*, he has no discretion, but must certify the case to the clerk of the court, to be *tried* at a *regular term* of the court; but when he commits for *examination*, he may, in his discretion, *certify* the commitment to the *regular term*, or *issue his warrant* to convene a *special session* of the court at any time, not less than five, nor more than ten days from the date of the warrant of commitment. In computing the time, the five days must be either exclusive of both days, or inclusive of one and exclusive of the other, and must not be inclusive of both.

[The form of the certificate to the Clerk, when the case is sent on to a regular term of the Court, will be found under each head of offence. The following forms are proper when the Justices are convened in special session, as an Examining Court.]

(No. 1.)

Form of Warrant to summon an Examining Court, where the prisoner is committed to jail.

——— County, to wit:

To the Sheriff of said County:

Whereas, A. B. has this day been committed to the jail of the said County, by my warrant, for a felony by him committed, in this, that he did, on the ——— day of ——— 18—, in the said County, feloniously (here describe the

(¹) Mabry's Case, 2 Va. Cases 396. (³) Boyd's Case, 1 Rob. 691.
(²) Id. (⁴) Sec. 1, Chap. 219, N. C.

offence as in the warrant of commitment;) and being of opinion that there is sufficient cause for charging the said A. B. with the said offence, I command you, in the name of the Commonwealth of Virginia, to summon at least eight of the Justices of the said County, (if so many there be,) to meet at the Courthouse of the said County, on the —— day of ——— 18—, (the day fixed must not be less than five, nor more than ten days from the date of the warrant,) to hold a Court for the *examination* of the *fact* with which the said A. B. stands charged, and for such other purposes concerning the premises as is by law required; and you are commanded to have then and there this warrant, and return how you have executed the same. Given under my hand and seal, this —— day of ——— 18—.

J. T., J. P. [L. S.]

(No. 2.)

Form of Warrant to summon an Examining Court, where the prisoner is let to bail.

—— County, to wit:

To the Sheriff of the said County:

Whereas, A. B. has this day been recognized by me J. T., a Justice of the said County, to appear before the Justices of the said County, at a Court to be holden by them at the County Courthouse thereof, on the —— day of ——— 18—, for the examination of the said A. B., for a felony by him committed, in this, that he did, on the —— day of ——— 18—, in the said County, feloniously (here describe the offence as in the warrant of arrest:) and being of opinion that there is sufficient cause for charging the said A. B. with the said offence, I command you, in the name of the Commonwealth of Virginia, to summon at least eight of the Justices of the said County, (if so many there be,) to meet at the County Courthouse of the said County, on the —— day of ——— 18—, (the day fixed must not be less than five nor more than ten days from the date of the warrant,) then and there to hold a Court for the examination of the fact with which the said A. B. stands charged, and for such other purposes concerning the premises as is by law required; and you are commanded then and there to have this warrant, and return how you have executed the same. Given under my hand and seal, this —— day of ——— 18—.

J. T., J. P. [L. S.]

(No. 3.)

Recognizance of Bail to appear before a special session of the County Court, sitting as an Examining Court.

—— County, to wit:

Be it remembered, that on this —— day of ——— 18—, A. B. and C. D. of the said County, came before me J. T., a Justice of the said County, and severally acknowledged themselves to owe to the Commonwealth of Virginia, that is to say: The said A. B. the sum of ——— dollars, and the said C. D. the sum of ——— dollars, to be respectively made and levied of their several goods and chattels, lands and tenements, if he the said A. B. shall make default in the performance of the condition underwritten.

The condition of the above recognizance is such, that if the above bound A. B. do and shall personally appear before the Justices of the County of ———, at a special session of the County Court, by them to be held for the examination of the said A. B., at the County Courthouse of the said County, on the —— day of ——— 18—, and shall then and there answer the Commonwealth of Virginia, for and concerning a certain felony by him committed, in feloniously (here describe the offence succintly,) wherewith the said A. B. stands charged, and shall not depart thence without the leave of the said Court, then the above recognizance shall be void, else to remain in full force and virtue.

Taken and acknowledged before me, in the said County, the day and year first above written.
J. T., J. P.

(No. 4.)

Form of Recognizance of a Witness to appear and give evidence before a special session of an Examining Court.

——— County, to wit:

Be it remembered, that on this —— day of ——— 18—, A. B. of the said County, personally came before me J. T., a Justice of the said County, and acknowledged himself to be indebted to the Commonwealth of Virginia, the sum of ——— dollars, to be made and levied of his goods and chattels, lands and tenements, if he the said A. B. shall make default in the performance of the condition underwritten.

The condition of the above recognizance is such, that if the above bound A. B. shall personally appear before the Justices of the County of ———, at a special session of the County Court, by them to be held, (for the examination of C. D.,) at the County Courthouse of the said County, on the —— day of ——— 18—, to give evidence in behalf of the Commonwealth against C. D., who stands charged with felony, in feloniously (state the offence briefly, as for instance, *in murdering J. S.*, or *stealing the goods of J. S.*,) and shall not thence depart without the leave of the said Court, then the above obligation to be void, otherwise to remain in full force and virtue.

Taken and acknowledged before me, the day and year first above written.
J. T., J. P.

(No. 5.)

Form of Record of a Court of Examination, for felony.

At a County Court for H. County, held at the Courthouse, on Friday the —— day of ——— one thousand eight hundred and ——— :

Present, J. E., T. C., &c., Gentlemen Justices.

A. B., who stands charged with a felony by him committed in the County of H., and within the jurisdiction of this Court, in this, (here insert the charge from the certificate of the committing Justice,) was this day set to the bar, in custody of the Sheriff of this County, and the Court having heard the evidence, are of opinion that the said A. B. ought to be tried for the offence of which he stands charged before the Circuit Court of H. County. And the said A. B. is remanded to jail. (If the prisoner be admitted to bail, leave out the last sentence remanding him to jail, and say :) " The said A. B. moved the Court to be allowed to enter into a recognizance, with security for his appearance before the said Circuit Court, which motion the Court entertained, and allowed the said A. B. to enter into such recognizance, himself in the sum of $ ———, with sufficient security in a like sum: And thereupon the said A. B. entered into a recognizance in the sum of $ ———, with R. S. his surety in a like sum, conditioned for the appearance of the said A. B. before the Judge of the Circuit Court of the County of H., on the first day of the next term of that Court, to answer the Commonwealth of and concerning the offence wherewith he stands charged, and not to depart without the leave of the said Court."

The following is a copy of the certificate of the committing Justice (or " of the warrant summoning the Court for the examination of the said A. B.," as the case may be,) by virtue of which this examination was had, viz:

(Here insert the certificate, or *warrant*, as the case may be.)

The following are copies of the depositions of the witnesses for the Commonwealth, taken down in Court and filed, viz:

(Here insert the depositions of the witnesses.)

A transcript of the record.

Teste,

R. P., *Clerk.*

(No. 6.)

Form of Record of a trial of a free negro, for felony, other than homicide, or where punishment is death.

At a County Court for H. County, held at the Courthouse, on Friday the ——— day of ——— one thousand eight hundred and ———:

Present, J. E., T. C., &c., Gentlemen Justices.

D. F., a free man of colour, who stands charged with a felony by him committed in the County of H., and within the jurisdiction of this Court, in this, (here insert the charge from the certificate of the committing Justice,) was this day set to the bar, in custody of the Sheriff of this County, and being arraigned, pleaded not guilty; and the Court having heard the evidence, are unanimously of opinion that the said D. F. is guilty of the offence wherewith he stands charged: Therefore it is considered by the Court, that the said D. F. be imprisoned in the public jail and penitentiary house of this Commonwealth, for the term of ——— years, therein to be kept and treated as the law directs. And it is ordered, that the Sheriff of this County shall, as soon as may be convenient after the adjournment of this Court, remove and securely convey the said D. F. from the jail of this County, to the said public jail and penitentiary house, and there deliver him to the superintendent thereof. And the said D. F. is remanded to jail.

The following is a copy of the certificate of the committing Justice, by virtue of which this trial was had, viz:

(Here insert the certificate.)

The following are copies of the depositions of the witnesses examined, taken down in Court and filed, viz:

(Here insert the depositions of the witnesses.)

A transcript of the record.

Teste,

R. P., *Clerk.*

(No. 7.)

Form of Record of a trial of a slave for felony.

At a County Court for H. County, held at the Courthouse, on Friday the ―― day of ―――― one thousand eight hundred and ―――― :

Present, J. E., T. C., &c., Gentlemen Justices.

G. L., a slave, the property of J. K. of ―――― County, who stands charged with a felony by him committed in the County of H., and within the jurisdiction of this Court, in this, (here insert the charge from the certificate of the committing Justice,) was this day set to the bar, in custody of the Sheriff of this County, and X. Y. being assigned by the Court his counsel, [on the motion of the attorney for the Commonwealth, he was allowed to file an information against the said slave G. L., and thereupon he filed the same in the words and figures, to wit: (here insert the information;)] and the said slave G. L., being thereupon arraigned, pleaded not guilty; and the Court having heard the evidence, are unanimously of opinion that the said slave G. L. is guilty of the offence wherewith he stands charged. And it being demanded of the said slave G. L., if any thing he had, or knew to say, why the Court should not now proceed to pronounce judgment on him, and nothing being offered or alleged in arrest or delay of judgment: It is considered by the Court, that the said slave G. L. be hanged by the neck until he be dead. And it is ordered, that the Sheriff of the County, cause execution of this sentence to be done upon the said slave G. L., on Friday the ―― day of ―――― next, between the hours of ten in the forenoon and four in the afternoon, at the usual place of execution. And the said slave is remanded to jail. And the Court proceeding to value the said slave G. L., as the law directs, each of the Justices present in Court affixed to him such a value as in his opinion the said slave would bring, if sold publicly, under a knowledge of the circumstances of his guilt; whereupon J. E. valued the said slave at $――――, T. C. at $――――, &c., from which the legal value of the said slave is ascertained to be $――――.

The following is a copy of the certificate of the committing Justice, by virtue of which this trial was had, viz:

(Here insert the certificate.)

The following are copies of the depositions of the witnesses examined, taken down in Court and filed, viz:

(Here insert the depositions of the witnesses.)

A transcript of the record.

Teste,

R. P., *Clerk.*

[By the new Code, the attorney for the Commonwealth is not required to file an information in any case against a slave; we presume, however, that he may do it with the leave of the Court. Where none is filed, leave out what is in brackets. The Court should not allow the attorney, in filing an information, to depart from the charge made in the certificate of the committing Justice, so as to charge and prosecute the prisoner for another and distinct offence not sustained by the facts set forth in the certificate.]

(No. 8.)

Form of Warrant by two Justices to transfer a prisoner from the County jail to the jail of the Circuit Court, after his examination.

———— County, to wit:
  To the Sheriff of the said County, and to the Keeper of the Jail of the Circuit Court of the County of ————:

Whereas, at a Court held by the Justices of the said County, at the Courthouse thereof, on the ——— day of ——— 18—, for the examination of A. B., charged with (state the offence according to the record,) it was the opinion of the said Court, that the said A. B., for the said felony, ought to be tried in the Circuit Court for the County of ———; and thereupon the said A. B. was remanded to the jail of the said County, as appears to us of record: We, J. T. and F. W., Justices of the said County, hereby command you, the said Sheriff, in the name of the Commonwealth, forthwith to remove the body of the said A. B. from the jail of said County, and him securely convey to the jail of the Circuit Court of said County of ————, and there deliver him to the keeper of the jail of said Circuit Court, together with this precept. And you, the said keeper of the jail of the said Circuit Court are hereby required, in the name of the said Commonwealth, to receive the said A. B. into your jail and custody, and him there safely keep until he shall thence be discharged by due course of law. Given under our hands and seals, this ——— day of ——— 18—.

[L. S.]
[L. S.]

DEAD BODIES—See BURIAL.

CHAPTER XXX.

DEER.

Killing wild deer prohibited.

BY SEC. 1, CHAP. 101. If any person shall in any year after the first day of January, and before the first day of August, in Mason county, or in any county east of the Alleghany and west of the Blue Ridge of mountains, or after the first day of February and before the first day of September, in any county east of the Blue Ridge, kill a deer, or be in possession of any so killed, (the same not being his own tamed or enclosed in a park,) he shall for every such deer forfeit five dollars.

Shooting tame deer prohibited.

BY SEC. 3, same chapter. If any person shoot or kill a tame deer having a bell or collar on its neck, he shall pay to the owner the value of such deer.

(No. 1.)

Form of Summons for killing wild deer.

Follow No. 16, under head of "FINES," and describe the offence thus: did on the —— day of ——— 18—, kill a deer, the said deer then not being his own, tamed, nor enclosed in a park.

[NOTE.—If the offence be committed in Mason county, or in any county east of the Alleghanies and west of the Blue Ridge, the blank in the above form must be filled with some day after the first day of January, and before the first day of August, and if it be east of the Blue Ridge, with a day between the first of February and the first day of September.]

(No. 2.)

Form of Conviction.

The judgment may be rendered in this form on the back of the summons: "Case heard, and upon the testimony of E. F., defendant found guilty, and adjudged to pay five dollars fine and ——— dollars costs of prosecution."

[No execution can be issued by the Justice unless he believes the party is about to escape. The proceedings should be sent to the Clerk of the County Court. See FINES AND CONVICTIONS.]

CHAPTER XXXI.

DOGS.

BY SEC. 5, CHAP. 102. Any Justice, on proof that any dog is mad, or has been bitten by a mad dog, or has killed or worried any sheep, shall order such dog to be killed.

BY SEC. 6. If the owner of any dog, so ordered to be killed, shall conceal him, or cause him to be concealed, to prevent the order from being executed, he shall forfeit four dollars for every day such dog shall be so concealed.

BY SEC. 7. A fee of one dollar is allowed for each dog killed under the preceding sections, and any officer failing to execute the order of the Justice, forfeits one dollar for each case.

(No. 1.)

Form of Order of a Justice to kill a dog which has been bitten by a mad dog, or has killed sheep.

────── County, to wit:
   To X. Y., Constable of said County:

Whereas, it is proved to me J. T., a Justice of the said County, upon the evidence on oath of A. B., that a dog belonging to C. D. in said County, has been bitten by a mad dog, (or *has killed the sheep of the said A. B.* :) These are, therefore, to command you forthwith to kill the said dog wherever found in your County. Given under my hand and seal, this ──── day of ──── 18──.

J. T., J. P. [L. S.]

(No. 2.)

Form of Summons for concealing a dog to prevent his being killed under the order of a Justice.

────── County, to wit:
   To X. Y., Constable of said County:

Whereas, upon the evidence of A. B., given on oath before me, I, J. T., a Justice of the said County, did, on the ──── day of ──── 18──, order E. F., Constable of the said County, to kill a certain dog belonging to C. D., and which dog, as was then proved before me, by the testimony on oath of A. B., had before that time been bitten by a mad dog, (or *had killed the sheep of the said A. B.*) And whereas the said C. D., to prevent the said order from being executed, has concealed the said dog in said County, for ──── days: These are, therefore, to command you, in the name of the Commonwealth, to summon the said C. D. to appear before me (or such other Justice as may then be there,) at ──── in the said County, on the ──── day of

—— 18—, at — o'clock, in the —— noon of that day, to answer the said complaint, and to be farther dealt with according to law. Given under my hand and seal, this —— day of —— 18—.

J. T., J. P. [L. S.]

[NOTE.—For every dog killed by the order of a Justice, the Constable is entitled to a fee of one dollar, to be paid by the owner, if known and able to pay, and if not, by the county or corporation. And if the Constable fail to execute the order, he forfeits an amount equal to his fees. Sec. 7, chap. 102.]

CHAPTER XXXII.

DRUNKENNESS AND PROFANE SWEARING.

[See NUISANCE.]

BY SEC. 15, CHAP. 197. If a white person, arrived at the age of discretion, profanely curse or swear, or get drunk, he shall be fined by a Justice one dollar for each offence.

Form of Summons against a person for profane swearing and for getting drunk.

—— County, to wit:
To X. Y., *Constable of said County:*

Whereas, complaint on oath has this day been made before me J. T., a Justice of said County, by A. B., that on the —— day of —— 18—, in said County, C. D., a white person, did profanely curse and swear, by uttering with a loud voice, in the presence of divers persons, these profane words, (here state the words uttered:) These are, therefore, to command you, in the name of the Commonwealth, to summon the said C. D. to appear at ——, in said County, on the —— day of —— 18—, at — o'clock in the —— noon, before me or such other Justice of said County as may then be there, to hear the said complaint, to answer the same, and to be farther dealt with according to law. Given under my hand and seal, this —— day of —— 18—.

J. T., J. P. [L. S.]

[If it be for getting drunk, say "did get drunk."]

Form of Judgment.

In either case if defendant be found guilty, endorse judgment on summons, thus: Defendant found guilty, and adjudged to pay $1 fine, and the costs, $——.

See FINES AND CONVICTIONS.

CHAPTER XXXIII.

DUELLING.

Duelling is the fighting of two persons one against the other, at an appointed time and place, upon a precedent quarrel. Where one of the parties is killed, the survivor is guilty of murder.(¹) And the fighting a duel, where there is no fatal result, is itself a misdemeanor.(²) So also a challenge to fight a duel, or even an endeavour to provoke another to send a challenge, is a high misdemeanor at Common Law; and the messenger or bearer of a challenge, is equally culpable with him who sends it.(³)

It is no excuse that the challenge is given under provoking charges, however grievous, against the character and conduct of the party sending it.(⁴) The law has not left the party thus outraged, without redress, for even words spoken, which tend to a breach of the peace, are indictable,(⁵) and the party may also bring his action for damages. The Common Law punishment for sending or bearing a challenge to fight a duel, is fine and imprisonment only. But to suppress this barbarous practice, which often results in murder, the statute provides:

By Sec. 19, Chap. 191. If any free person resident in this State, by previous agreement made within the same, fight a duel without this State, and in so doing inflict a mortal wound, he shall be deemed guilty of murder in this State.

By Sec. 20. If any free person, resident in this State, by like agreement, be the second of either party in such duel as is mentioned in the preceding section, and be present as such when such mortal wound is inflicted, he shall be deemed an accessary before the fact to the crime of murder in this State.

By Sec. 21. An offender, under either of the two preceding sections, may be prosecuted in the county or corporation in which the death occurs, if it occur within this State; and if not, in any county or corporation in which such offender may be found.

By Sec. 22. If any free person fight in a duel, with any deadly weapon, though no death ensue, or send or deliver to another a challenge, or message intended to be a challenge, oral or written, to fight a duel, though no duel ensue, he shall

---

(¹) 1 Russ. 443.
(²) Ros. Cr. Ev. 610.
(³) Hawk. c. 63, § 3.
(⁴) R. v. Rice, 3 East R. 581.
(⁵) 2 Ld. Ray. 1031; 1 Deac. 219.

be confined in jail not more than one year and be fined not exceeding one thousand dollars.

BY SEC. 23. And if any free person accept, or knowingly carry or deliver any such challenge or message, or advise, encourage or promote such duel, he shall be confined in jail not more than six months and fined not exceeding five hundred dollars.

BY SEC. 24. If any free person resident in this State, leave the same for the purpose of eluding the provisions herein contained respecting duelling or challenges to fight, and without the State engage in a duel, (though no death ensue) or challenge another, or send or deliver a message intended to be a challenge to fight such duel, or accept, or knowingly carry or deliver any such challenge or message, or be present at the fighting of such a duel, with deadly weapons, as an aid, second or surgeon, or advise, encourage or promote such duel, he shall be deemed as guilty, and subject to the like punishment as if the offence had been committed in this State.

BY SEC. 25. A person indicted in this State under the 19th, 20th, 21st or 24th section, may plead his conviction or acquittal of the same offence in another State in bar of such indictment.

BY SEC. 26. If any free person post another, or in writing or in print use any reproachful or contemptuous language to or concerning another for not fighting a duel, or for not sending or accepting a challenge, he shall be confined in jail not more than six months or fined not exceeding one hundred dollars.

BY SEC. 27. If any Justice or Judge have good cause to suspect that any persons are about to be engaged in a duel, he may issue his warrant to bring them before him, and if he think proper to take from them a recognizance to keep the peace, he shall insert therein a condition that they will not during the time for which they may be bound, be concerned in a duel directly or indirectly.

The attention of the Justice is particularly directed to that provision of the statute which authorizes any Judge or Justice, when he has *good cause to suspect* that any person or persons are about to be engaged in a duel, to issue his warrant to bring the parties before him.

Duels are arranged in secret, and all positive and direct knowledge that one is to take place, confined to those who are about to disturb the public peace, by engaging in them; and, as experience teaches, that even the high sanctions of the statute are of themselves insufficient to suppress this practice, and that the prompt action of the functionaries of the law is necessary to effect that object, the unusual power of arresting, on *suspicion*, is here conferred upon the Justice, to prevent murder. It is the remark of an eminent author on the duties of Magistrates, " that every Justice of the Peace should be a walking grand jury."* Keeping in view that watchfulness over the public peace, indicated by this remark, with the power given him by the statute, the vigilant and energetic Magistrate may do much to suppress this high crime, by the timely interposition of his authority. Salutary, however, as this power is, it should not be resorted to capriciously, or on mere conjecture; yet, owing to the secrecy with which duels are conducted, positive knowledge can rarely be obtained by a Justice in time to prevent them. To give efficacy, therefore, to the requirements of this law, he must act on such circumstances as would justify the inference in the exercise of a sound legal discretion, that a duel is about to take place; he alone can judge of these circumstances, and when they bring his mind to the conclusion that he ought to interpose his authority, he should do it with promptness and decision, by causing the immediate arrest of the parties.

It is true, as a Common Law principle, that no man can be arrested upon mere general rumour for a felony already committed; but, even in that case, general rumour, attended with circumstances of its probable truth, is sufficient cause of suspicion to arrest;([1]) and, as the object of the statute is *obviously* to *prevent* the secret commission of crime, by arresting parties suspected of an intention to commit murder, and requiring of them sureties of the peace, the Justice should not disregard rumour, when his suspicions are awakened as to the fact that a duel is about to take place, by any circumstance tending to shew the probable truth of such rumour. If he have good cause to suspect it otherwise, he should not wait until some one comes forward to give him the information upon oath. This would be to defeat the object of the power conferred on him to arrest in such case on suspicion; and would, moreover, impute to the Legislature the absurdity of granting a power already possessed, for every Justice not only has the power, but is bound to issue his warrant to arrest any party who is charged, upon the oath of another, with intention to commit murder, or any other act of violence tending to disturb the public peace.

([1]) See ARREST, page 53, and the authorities there cited.
* Mr. Dickinson.

DUELLING. 217

(No. 1.)

Form of Warrant to arrest parties suspected by a Justice of being about to engage in a duel.

—— County, to wit:
 To the Sheriff and all or any one of the Constables of the said County:
 Forasmuch as I, J. T., a Justice of the said County, have good cause to suspect that A. B. and C. D. are about to break the peace, by being engaged in a duel: These are, therefore, in the name of the Commonwealth of Virginia, to command you, and each of you, forthwith to apprehend and bring before me, the bodies of the said A. B. and C. D., to answer in the premises, and to be dealt with as the law directs. Given under my hand and seal, this —— day of —————— 18—.
              J. T., J. P. [L. S.]

(No. 2.)

Form of Warrant to arrest parties about to engage in a duel, upon information.

—— County, to wit:
 To X. Y., Constable of the said County:
 Whereas, A. B. has this day given information on oath to me J. T., a Justice of the said County, that he has good reason to believe that C. D. and E. F. are about to fight a duel, and that he the said A. B. is afraid that they will do each other some grievous bodily harm, if not prevented from meeting in hostile array, I do therefore command you, in the name of the Commonwealth, forthwith to apprehend the said C. D. and E. F., and bring them before me or some other Justice of the said County, to answer in the premises, and to be farther dealt with as the law directs. Given under my hand and seal, this —— day of —————— 18—.
              J. T., J. P. [L. S.]

(No. 3.)

Form of Recognizance to keep the peace and not to be engaged in a duel.

—— County, to wit:
 Be it remembered, that on this —— day of —————— 18—, A. B. and C. D. of the said County, personally came before me J. T., a Justice of the said County, and severally and respectively acknowledged themselves to be indebted to the Commonwealth of Virginia, in the manner following, that is to say: The said A. B. in the sum of —————— dollars, and the said C. D. in the sum of —————— dollars, to be respectively made and levied of their several goods and chattels, lands and tenements, to the use of the Commonwealth of Virginia, if the said A. B. shall make default in the performance of the underwritten condition.
 The condition of the above recognizance is such, that if the above bound A. B. do and shall keep the peace towards all the citizens of this Common-

wealth, and especially towards C. D., for the space of one year from the date hereof, and shall not directly or indirectly be concerned in a duel with the said C. D. (the other person suspected,) or any other person during that period, then the above recognizance shall be void, or otherwise to remain in full force and virtue.

Taken and acknowledged before me, the day and year above written.

J. T., J. P.

(No. 4.)

Form of Commitment of a party for not finding sureties.

——— County, to wit:

To X. Y., *Constable of said County, and to the Keeper of the Jail of the said County:*

Whereas, upon the complaint and information on oath of A. B., taken before me J. T., a Justice of the said County, on the —— day of ——— 18—, that he has good cause to believe that C. D. and E. F. are about to fight a duel; that he is afraid that they will do each other some grievous bodily harm, if not prevented from meeting in hostile array: And whereas the said C. D. was this day brought before me J. T., Justice of the said County, to answer said complaint, and it now appears in evidence before me, on the oath of W. P., a credible witness, that he the said C. D. did, on the —— day of ——— 18—, send to the said E. F. a challenge to fight a duel, the probable issue of which would be the death of one or both of them; whereupon I, the said Justice, required the said C. D. to find sufficient securities, to be bound with him in the sum of ——— dollars, by recognizance, to keep the peace for the term of ——— towards all the citizens of this Commonwealth, and especially towards the said E. F.; and the said C. D. having refused and still refusing to find such securities to be bound as aforesaid: These are, therefore, in the name of the Commonwealth, to command you, the said Constable, forthwith to convey the said C. D. to the jail of the said County, and to deliver him to the keeper thereof, together with this precept. And I do hereby command you, the said keeper of the said jail, to receive the said C. D. into your custody, in the said jail, and him there safely to keep for the term of ——— from the date hereof, unless in the mean time he find such sureties, or be otherwise discharged by due course of law. Given under my hand and seal, this —— day of ——— 18—.

J. T., J. P. [L. S.]

CHAPTER XXXIV.

EMBEZZLEMENT.

Embezzlement is the fraudulently removing and concealing personal property, with which a party has been entrusted for the use of another, and fraudulently retaining and concealing it. The legal distinction between larceny and embezzlement is this, that in the former, the property is taken from the actual or constructive possession of the master or employer, or has been delivered by him to the servant or agent, for a special purpose, with a bare charge, so that the servant or agent has acquired no qualified property in the thing delivered; and in the latter, the property has either never been in the possession of the master or employer, but received by the servant or agent for his master's use, and fraudulently converted to his own, or where it has come in the possession of the servant or agent by delivery by the master or employer, accompanied by a qualified property, and been fraudulently converted by the servant or agent to his own use. This distinction between larceny and embezzlement, arises out of the rule of the Common Law, that where the offender had the qualified property and actual possession of the goods at the time they were embezzled, he could not be guilty of larceny, and was not punishable, except in the case of a public officer, embezzling public money or property committed to his charge as such, and this was a misdemeanor.(¹) By the new Code, embezzlement is made felony, and the offence enlarged by applying its provisions to parties in various situations of trust.

BY SEC. 20, CHAP. 192. If any director or officer of any incorporated bank, or any officer of public trust in this State, or any officer, agent or clerk of any other incorporated company, embezzle or fraudulently convert to his own use, bullion, money, bank notes or other security for money, or any effects or property of another person, which shall have come to his possession or been placed under his care or management by virtue of his office, place or employment, he shall be deemed guilty of larceny thereof.

BY SEC. 21. If any carrier or other person, being free, to whom money or other property, which may be the subject of larceny, may be delivered to be carried for hire, or any other person who may be entrusted with such property, embezzle or fraudulently convert to his own use, or secrete with intent to

---

(¹) See Dickinson's Guide to Quarter Sessions, by Talfourd, 153 and 219.

do so, any such property, either in mass or otherwise, before delivery thereof at the place at which or to the person to whom they were to be delivered, he shall be deemed guilty of larceny thereof.

By Sec. 22. If any officer or clerk of any bank or joint stock company, make, alter, or omit to make any entry in any account kept in such bank or by such company, with intent in so doing to conceal the true state of such account, or to defraud the said bank or company, or to enable or assist any person to obtain money to which he was not entitled, such officer or clerk shall be confined in the penitentiary not less than two, nor more than ten years.

Some of these provisions are new in this State, and, as yet, no case has arisen in our courts, for their construction, but, as similar provisions have existed for some time, in England, and in some of our sister States, the principles decided upon the construction of their statutes, will, in many instances, apply to ours, and be of use to the Justice in acting under it, though our statute does not embrace clerks or agents of private persons or copartnerships. In order to constitute embezzlement under the statute, these circumstances must concur. The party must be an officer, agent or clerk; he must have received the thing in question by virtue of his employment, and he must fraudulently embezzle it.

1. He must be an officer, agent or clerk, in fact, though he need not be so called. Thus it has been held, under similar statutes, that an accountant or treasurer to overseers of the poor,[1] a female servant,[2] and an apprentice, if employed to receive the money which he purloins, may be guilty of this offence.[3]

The manner in which a party is remunerated for his services is immaterial, in determining the question whether or not he is a servant, and thus, where a person engaged to trade for several houses was allowed a per centage on the orders he obtained, he has been held to be the clerk of each, and to be liable to prosecution for embezzlement, though paid by a per centage, and not a salary.[4] And so, where a person was employed to carry out goods in his employer's barge, and sell them, and was to be remunerated by a share of the profits, and fraudulently retained the entire price of a cargo, he was held guilty of embezzlement.[5]

So, also, where a servant manufactured an article for a customer from the materials of his employer, and received the price of it and retained it, having concealed the order for the

---

[1] Russ. & Ry. 349.
[2] Id. 267.
[3] Russ. & Ry. 80.
[4] Russ. & Ry. 198.
[5] Russ. & Ry. 139.

article from his master, though he would have been entitled to a portion of the money for his work, was held indictable for embezzlement.(¹) A person occasionally employed, is sufficiently a servant within the act, to be liable to its penalties.(²) But a party who is neither officer, agent or clerk, nor in any way under the control of the person by whom he is in a single instance only requested to receive money, is not punishable under the statute, for he could not be said to be acting by virtue of his employment, as clerk or servant.(³)

It has been held to be an offence under an analogous statute in a servant or clerk fraudulently to convert to his own use, the money, funds, &c. of any other person, which have come into his possession or under his care, by virtue of his employment, as well as so to convert the money, goods, &c., of his master or employer, the words "another person," in the statute, meaning any person other than he who is guilty of the embezzlement.(⁴) So, also, it has been decided that a barkeeper in an inn, entrusted to carry letters to and from the postoffice, who fraudulently converts to his own use a letter enclosing money given him to carry to the postoffice, is guilty of embezzlement.(⁵) And so, also, a stage driver entrusted by his employers to carry money from one place to another, is a servant within the meaning of the statute.(⁶) The British act, 39 Geo. 3, chap. 85, does not contain the words "or any other person," and is therefore more restricted than our act, and is limited to the embezzlement of the property of the master or employer.

2. He must have *received* the thing by virtue of his employment. And therefore, where goods are *taken* either from the actual or constructive possession of the master or employer, the statute does not apply, but the offender should be prosecuted for larceny ;(⁷) and if there is any doubt whether the case be one of embezzlement or larceny, both should be charged in the proceedings, as both offences may be charged in the same indictment.(⁸)

To bring a case within the words "by virtue of his employment," in the 20th section of the act, it must either appear that the officer, agent or clerk had a special direction to receive the money of his employer, or that his office or employment was of a description from whence such an authority must necessarily be inferred. As for example, it is necessarily inferred, from the nature of the office, that a book-keeper at a

---

(¹) Russ. & Ry. 145.
(²) Russ. & Ry. 299.
(³) Ry. & Moo. C. C. 259.
(⁴) The people v. Hennessey, 15 Wend. 147.
(⁵) Dalton's Case, 15 Wend. 58.
(⁶) 10 Wend. 289.
(⁷) 2 Leach C. C. 1033; 3 Stark. Ev. 842; Headge's Case; Russ. & Ry. 160; Walker's Case, 8 Leigh.
(⁸) 3 M. & S. 549; Rex v. Johnson; and see Ry. & M. 334.

coach or railroad office is authorized to receive money for his principal for freight or passage; but it is not necessarily inferred that a porter belonging to either, has such authority, and therefore to bring him within the statute, such special authority must appear, or at least a practice of receiving by him to an extent so general, that it must necessarily be implied.(¹) And where one receives money contrary to, and in breach of his duty to his employer, he is guilty of larceny, and not of embezzlement; as where a person employs two servants, one of whom has authority to sell, and the other has not, but merely to receive money, if the one who has no authority to sell, introduces himself behind the counter, and sells his employer's goods, and puts the money into his pocket, this is clearly a stealing; for he sells and receives the money contrary to his authority.(²)

Although the thing must be received by virtue of the prisoner's employment, yet if a servant generally employed by his master to receive sums of one description and at one place only, is employed by him in a particular instance to receive a sum of a different description and at a different place, this latter sum being thus received and afterwards embezzled, will be considered as received by virtue of his employment, because he was a servant, and it was as such, that he was directed to receive the money, though out of the line of his ordinary duty.(³)

3. He must embezzle the money or thing, that is, fraudulently retain and conceal it; and the presumptive evidence of the embezzlement is, that the defendant never accounted with his master or employer for the money or thing received by him, or denied his having received it, or falsely accounted for it.(⁴) But, if the party render true accounts, the mere omission to remit or pay money, according to his duty, will not subject him to an indictment for embezzlement;(⁵) for, this offence necessarily implies secrecy and concealment, and if, therefore, instead of denying the appropriation of property, the prisoner, in rendering his account, admits the appropriation, alleging a right in himself, no matter how unfounded, or setting up an excuse, no matter how frivolous, his offence, in taking and keeping, is no embezzlement.(⁶) And it has also been held that one, whose duty it is to receive money for his employer, receiving money and rendering true accounts of all he has received, is not guilty of embezzlement, though he afterwards absconds and does not pay over the money.(⁷) So,

---

(¹) Dickinson's Guide 156; Russ. & Ry. 80.
(²) 38 Com. Law Rep. 22.
(³) Russ. & Ry. 516 and 319.
(⁴) Rosc. Ev. 364; 3 B. & P. 596; 2 Leach 974; Russ. & Ry. 63.
(⁵) Russ. & Ry. 267.
(⁶) 41 Com. Law Rep. 274.
(⁷) 41 Com. Law Rep. 63.

also, where it *appeared by the books* of a clerk, that he had received much more than he had paid away, from which the prosecutors wished it to be inferred that he must have embezzled some particular note or piece of money, it was held that this was not enough, and that it was necessary to prove some distinct act of embezzlement.(¹) But where a servant, immediately on receiving a sum for his master, enters a smaller sum on his master's book, and ultimately accounts to him for the smaller sum, he may be considered as embezzling the difference, at the time he makes the false entry.(²)

If one embezzles *the halves* of bank notes, sent in a letter, he may be indicted for embezzling goods and chattels.(³) Before the passage of this statute, if goods were entrusted to a common carrier, and he embezzled them before they reached their destination and delivery, without breaking the package, he was guilty of no criminal offence. But, by the 21st section of the act, common carriers violating the trust reposed in them, are put on the footing of agents. It is, however, still larceny in a common carrier to break a package and take goods therefrom, and fraudulently convert them to his own use, or to take goods with a felonious intent, whether he break the package or not, after he has deposited them at the place of delivery, though but for a moment, if the delivery has been complete.

It is sufficient to charge, in the proceedings of the Justice or in an indictment, that the embezzlement was done with intent to defraud generally, without stating an intention to defraud any particular person, and the thing embezzled may be laid to be the property of any one having either a general or special property in it. See INTENT.

(No. 1.)

Form of Warrant of Arrest for embezzlement of bank notes and money by an officer of an incorporated bank.

——— County, to wit:

To all or any one of the Constables of said County:

Whereas, A. B. of said County, has this day made complaint and information on oath before me J. T., a Justice of the said County, that C. D., on the —— day of ——— 18—, in said County, he, the said C. D., then and there being an officer of the Bank of Virginia, to wit, the cashier of the said bank, did feloniously embezzle, and fraudulently convert to his own use, ——— dollars, the money* of the Bank of Virginia, the same then being an incorporated bank, and which said money came to the possession of and was then placed under the care and management of the said C. D., by virtue

---

(¹) Roscoe Cr. Ev. 346.
(²) Russ. & Ry. 463.   (³) Com. Law Rep. 514.

* This general description is sufficient. See Sec. 6, Chap. 107, New Code.

of his office as cashier aforesaid: These are, therefore, to command you, in the name of the Commonwealth of Virginia, forthwith to apprehend the said C. D., and bring him before me or some other Justice of the said County, to answer the said complaint, and to be farther dealt with according to law. Given under my hand and seal, this —— day of —— 18—.

J. T., J. P. [L. S.]

(No. 2.)

Form of Warrant of Arrest for embezzlement of property by a clerk or agent of an incorporated company.

—— County, to wit:

To all or any one of the Constables of said County:

Whereas, A. B. of said County, has this day made complaint and information on oath before me J. T., a Justice of the said County, that C. D., on the —— day of ——— 18—, in said County, he the said C. D. then and there being a clerk (or *agent*) of the (for instance, "James River and Kanawha Company,") the same being an incorporated company, did feloniously embezzle and fraudulently convert to his own use, (here state the property,) of the value of ——— dollars, the same then being the property, goods and chattels of the said ("James River and Kanawha Company,") and which said (the thing embezzled,) came to the possession of, and was then placed under the care and management of the said A. B., by virtue of his employment as clerk (or *agent*) aforesaid: These are, therefore, to command you, in the name of the Commonwealth of Virginia, forthwith to apprehend the said C. D., and bring him before me or some other Justice of the said County, to answer the said complaint, and to be farther dealt with according to law. Given under my hand and seal, this —— day of ——— 18—.

J. T., J. P. [L. S.]

(No. 3.)

Form of Warrant of Arrest for embezzlement by a common carrier.

—— County, to wit:

To all or any one of the Constables of said County:

Whereas, A. B. of said County, has this day made complaint and information on oath before me J. T., a Justice of the said County, that he, the said A. B., did, on the —— day of ——— 18—, in said County, deliver to C. D., he the said C. D. then and there being a common carrier for hire, ten sacks of salt, the property of said A. B., of the value of ——— dollars, to be carried by the said C. D., for hire as a common carrier, from ——— to ———, and to be there delivered to one E. F., and that the said C. D. afterwards, to wit, on the —— day of ——— 18—, in the County of ———, did feloniously embezzle, and fraudulently convert to his own use, the said ten sacks of salt before they were delivered at the said place at which they were to be delivered: These are, therefore, to command you, in the name of the Commonwealth of Virginia, forthwith to apprehend the said C. D., and bring him before me or some other Justice of the said County, to answer the said complaint, and to be farther dealt with according to law. Given under my hand and seal, this —— day of ——— 18—.

J. T., J. P. [L. S.]

[NOTE.—If it be for *secreting*, follow to the words "did feloniously," and then insert the words, "secrete, with intent to."]

EMBEZZLEMENT.   225

(No. 4.)

Form of Warrant against a Clerk of a Bank for fraudulent entries in accounts kept by him as Clerk.

———— County, to wit:
To X. Y., *Constable of the said County:*

Whereas, A. B. has this day made complaint and information on oath before me J. T., Justice of said County, that on the ——— day of ——— 18—, C. D. was a clerk of the Bank of Virginia, in said County, and that one B. G. did on that day have an account with the said Bank of Virginia, and which account was kept by the said C. D. as clerk aforesaid, and that the said C. D. did, as clerk aforesaid, then and there feloniously make (or *omit to make*, as the case may be,) an entry in the said account, with intent thereby to defraud the said Bank of Virginia, and to enable the said B. G. to obtain money from the said bank, to which he was not entitled: These are, therefore, to command you, in the name of the Commonwealth, forthwith to apprehend the said C. D., and to bring him before me or some other Justice of the said County, to answer the said complaint, and to be farther dealt with according to law. Given under my hand and seal, this ——— day of ——— 18—.

J. T., *J. P.* [L. S.]

(No. 5.)

Form of Mittimus where a party is committed for examination or trial in the County Court for embezzlement.

———— County, to wit:
To X. Z., *Constable of said County, and to the Keeper of the Jail of said County:*

These are to command you, the said Constable, in the name of the Commonwealth of Virginia, forthwith to convey and deliver into the custody of the keeper of the said jail, together with this warrant, the body of C. D., a white person, (or *free negro*, as the case may be,) charged before me J. T., a Justice of the said County, on the oath of A. B., with a felony by him committed, in this, that the said C. D., on the ——— day of ——— in the year 18—, in the said County, (here describe the offence as in the warrant of arrest.) And you, the said keeper of the said jail, are hereby required to receive the said C. D. into your jail and custody, that he may be examined (or *tried*) for the said offence by the County Court of said County, and him there safely keep, until he shall be discharged by due course of law. Given under my hand and seal, this ——— day of ——— in the year 18—.

J. T., *J. P.* [L. S.]

[NOTE.—If the prisoner be a white person, he must be committed for examination. If a free negro, the prisoner must be committed for trial.]

(No. 6.)

Form of Certificate of Commitment to be sent to the Clerk of the County Court.

—— County, to wit:
To the Clerk of the County Court of said County:

I, J. T., a Justice of the said County, do hereby certify, that I have, by my warrant, this day committed C. D., (if free negro state it) to the jail of this County, that he may be examined (or *tried,* if negro,) before the County Court of the said County, for a felony by him committed, in this, that he did, on the —— day of ——— 18—, in the said County, (here state the offence as in the mittimus.) Given under my hand, this —— day of ——— in the year 18—.

J. T. J. P.

(No. 7.)

Form of Certificate to the Clerk where party is admitted to bail.

Turn to head of ARREST, and follow No. 6.

(No. 8.)

Form of Recognizance of Bail.

Turn to head of RECOGNIZANCE, and follow No. 1.

(No. 9.)

Form of Recognizance of Witness to appear before the County Court to give evidence upon the examination or trial of a party charged with felony.

Turn to head of RECOGNIZANCE, and follow No. 3.

(No. 1.)

An Indictment against a Clerk of an incorporated company for embezzlement.

—— Judicial Circuit. } The jurors of the Commonwealth of Virginia, in and for the body of the County of ——, and now attending the Circuit Court of the said County, upon their oath present, that A. B., late of the County of ———, on the —— day of ——— in the year 18—, in the County aforesaid, being then and there employed as clerk (or *agent*) of the James river and Kanawha company, the same being an incorporated company by the laws of this Commonwealth, did, by virtue of his place and employment as such clerk,

EMBEZZLEMENT—(*Indictments for.*)

then and there, and whilst he was so employed, receive and take into his possession certain money, to wit, the sum of $100, for and in the name and on the account of the said James river and Kanawha company, and the said money, so as aforesaid coming into his possession by virtue of his employment as clerk aforesaid, he the said A. B. then and there, to wit, on the day and year aforesaid, in the County aforesaid, feloniously did embezzle, and feloniously and fraudulently convert to his use. And so the jurors aforesaid, upon their oath aforesaid, do say, that the said A. B. then and there, in manner and form aforesaid, the said money, the property of the said James river and Kanawha company, an incorporated company as aforesaid, from the said James river and Kanawha company, feloniously did steal, take and carry away, against the peace and dignity of the Commonwealth of Virginia.

Second count.

And the jurors aforesaid, on their oath aforesaid, do farther present, that the said A. B. afterwards, and within six calendar months from the time of committing the said offence, in the first count in this indictment charged and stated, to wit, on the ―― day of ―――― in the year aforesaid, in the County aforesaid, he the said A. B. being then employed as clerk of the said James river and Kanawha company, and the said company then being an incorporated company as aforesaid, did, by virtue of his said last mentioned employment, and as clerk last aforesaid, then and there, and whilst he was so employed as last aforesaid, receive and take into his possession as clerk as last aforesaid, certain other money to a large amount, to wit, to the amount of $100, for and in the name and on the account of the said James river and Kanawha company, and the said last mentioned money then and there feloniously did embezzle, and feloniously and fraudulently convert to his own use. And so the jurors aforesaid, &c. (concluding as the first count.) See chapter 207 of the New Code, sec. 6.

[Add count for larceny.]

―――――

(No. 2.)

An Indictment against a public officer for embezzlement.

―――― Judicial Circuit, ―――― County, to wit: In the Circuit Court of the said County. } The jurors of the Commonwealth of Virginia, in and for the body of the County of ――――, now attending the Circuit Court of the said County, on their oath present, that A. B., late of the said County, on the ―――― day of ―――― in the year one thousand eight hundred and ――――, in the County of ―――― aforesaid, and within the jurisdiction of this Court, was an officer of public trust in this Commonwealth, to wit, (state the office, as for instance, *storekeeper and general agent for the penitentiary,*) and being such officer, did then and there feloniously embezzle, and feloniously and fraudulently convert to his own use, a sum of money, to wit, the sum of ―――― dollars, the money and property of the said Commonwealth, then and there placed under his care and management by virtue of his office aforesaid, against the peace and dignity of the Commonwealth of Virginia.

CHAPTER XXXV.

ESCAPES.

An escape is where one, lawfully arrested, gains his liberty before he is entitled to his deliverance by law.(¹) Escapes are of two kinds, civil and criminal. The former is from the Sheriff or other officer having the legal custody of a party in a civil suit, and the latter is from the Sheriff, Constable, Jailor or other officer, whom the law has placed over a prisoner arrested upon criminal process. It may be by the party himself with or without force, or it may be by others, and this, also, either without force by their permission or negligence, or with force by the rescuing of the party from custody. Where the liberation of the party is effected either by himself or others, without force, it is more properly termed an escape; where it is effected by the party himself, with force, it is called prison breaking. And where it is effected with force, and by the aid of others, it is called a rescue.(²)

Any place whatever, wherein a person under a lawful arrest for a supposed crime is restrained of his liberty, whether in the common jail, or the house of a Constable or private person, is properly a prison; for imprisonment is nothing more than a restraint of liberty.(³)

Escape by prisoner.

By Sec. 10, Chap. 194. A free person confined in jail on conviction of a criminal offence, who escapes thence by force or violence, shall be confined in the penitentiary one year, if previously sentenced to confinement therein, or be confined in jail six months, if previously sentenced to confinement in jail; the term of confinement under this section, to commence from the expiration of the former sentence.

There are two classes of cases embraced in this section: felonies and misdemeanors. To constitute a case of felony, the party must be confined in jail upon a *conviction*, and for which he had been sentenced to confinement in the penitentiary. If the conviction under which he is imprisoned, be for an offence less than felony, then the breaking out of jail will be a misdemeanor only. In both cases the escape must be by force and violence. And this implies an *actual breaking*, for the getting over a wall will not amount to a prison breach.(⁴)

(¹) 1 Russ. 367.
(²) Id.
(³) 2 Hawk. c. 18.
(⁴) 3 P. Wms. 483; 2 Inst. 589.

But the throwing down loose bricks from the top of a prison wall, placed there to prevent escape, has been held to be prison breach at Common Law, though they were thrown down by accident.(¹)

By Sec. 11. If a free person, lawfully imprisoned in jail and not sentenced on conviction of a criminal offence, escape from jail by force or violence, he shall be confined in jail not exceeding one year.

This section embraces all cases of prison breach, where the party is not imprisoned upon a conviction for some previous offence. And whenever a person is in lawful custody, however innocent he may be, or however groundless the prosecution against him, he is bound to submit to his imprisonment until discharged by due course of law. And if he make his escape by *force*, he will be guilty of the offence of prison breaking.(²)

Aiding prisoners to escape.

By Sec. 7. Where a person is lawfully detained as a prisoner in any jail, prison or custody, if a free person shall convey any thing into the jail or prison, with intent to facilitate the prisoner's escape therefrom, or shall, in any way, aid such prisoner to escape, or in the attempt to escape from such jail, prison or custody, or shall forcibly rescue or attempt to rescue him therefrom, such free person, if the rescue or escape be effected, shall, if the prisoner was detained on a conviction or charge of felony, be confined in the penitentiary not less than one nor more than five years, and if the same be not effected, or if the prisoner was not detained on such conviction or charge, be confined in jail six months, and fined not exceeding five hundred dollars.

This provision also makes the distinction between a conviction of felony and a misdemeanor, and extends the offence to cases where the party is only *charged* with an offence, as well as to cases of conviction. To constitute felony under this section, the person must be imprisoned either upon a conviction, or *charge* of felony, and the escape must actually be effected. If the imprisonment be not upon a conviction or charge of felony, or if the escape be not effected, then the offence of aiding will be a misdemeanor. This distinction is important in practice, as in the one case, the offender must be committed for examination or trial before the county or corporation court, and in the other, to answer an indictment to be preferred to the grand jury.

Rescue signifies the forcibly setting any one at liberty from a legal arrest or imprisonment.(³) Where the prisoner is res-

---

(¹) Harwell's Case, Russ. & Ry. 458. (³) 2 Deac. Cr. Co. 1103.
(²) 2 Inst. 590.

cued from a private person, it seems that the rescuer should be shewn to have knowledge of the offence for which the party is under arrest,(¹) but when the prisoner is in the custody of a public officer, as a Constable or Sheriff, the rescuer is, at his peril, bound to take notice of the offence of the prisoner.

Of voluntary and negligent escapes.

By Sec. 8. If a Jailor or other officer voluntarily suffer a prisoner convicted of or charged with felony, to escape from his custody, he shall be confined in the penitentiary not less than one nor more than five years.

By Sec. 9. If a Jailor or other officer negligently suffer a prisoner convicted of or charged with felony, or voluntarily or negligently suffer a prisoner convicted of or charged with an offence not a felony, to escape from his custody, or wilfully refuse to receive into his custody any person lawfully committed thereto, he shall be confined in jail not more than six months, or be fined not exceeding five hundred dollars.

Officers permitting an escape, either by negligence or connivance, are guilty of a high offence against public justice, and are in fact much more culpable than the prisoner. To make him liable, there must be an actual arrest. So that, if he never have the party in his custody, he cannot be charged with an escape, and the arrest and imprisonment must be justifiable.(²) But if a warrant of commitment plainly and expressly charge the party with a criminal offence, the Jailor suffering an escape, is punishable; for where commitments are good in substance, the Jailor is as much bound to observe them, as if they were ever so exact.(³) The imprisonment, however, must not only be justifiable, but it must be for some criminal matter, and continuing at the time of the escape, and its continuance must be grounded on that satisfaction which public justice demands for the crime committed, and not for any individual benefit, as a detention for the officer's fees.(⁴)

Whenever an officer, having the custody of a prisoner charged with and guilty of a criminal offence, knowingly gives him his liberty, with the intention to save him either from his trial or execution, such officer is guilty of a voluntary escape,(⁵) and punishable under the statute.

A negligent escape, is where the party arrested or imprisoned, escapes against the will of him that arrests or imprisons him, and is not freshly pursued and taken again before he has lost

---

(¹) 1 Hale 606; and see Rex *v.* Shaw, R. & R. 526.
(²) 1 Russ. 369.
(³) Id.
(⁴) 1 Dea. Cr. Co. 383; 2 Hawk. c. 19, § 3; 1 Hale 592.
(⁵) 1 Russ. 370.

sight of him, for if he is retaken without losing sight of him, it is no escape.(¹)

To allow a prisoner greater liberty than he by law ought to have, may be an escape, and allowing a prisoner to go at large for a time and return, is an escape, though he return again.(²)

If a prisoner charged with a criminal offence, break jail, it is said that this seems to be a negligent escape, because there wanted either the due strength in the jail that should have secured him, or the due vigilance in the Jailor that should have prevented it.(³)

In concluding this subject, it is proper to remark, that although the 10th and 11th sections of the act punish an escape by a prisoner only when he effects his escape by force or violence, yet it is a Common Law misdemeanor in a prisoner to escape from lawful confinement, though no force or artifice be used on his part to effect such purpose. Thus, if a prisoner go out of his prison without any obstruction, the doors being open by the consent or negligence of the Jailor, or if he escape in any other manner, without using any kind of violence, he will be guilty of a misdemeanor, and if his prison be broken by others without his procurement or consent, and he escape through the breach so made, he may be indicted for the escape.(⁴)

The manner of retaking a prisoner.

When an officer voluntarily suffers a prisoner to escape, it is said that he can no more justify the retaking him than if he had never had him in custody before, because, by his own free consent, he has admitted that he has nothing to do with him, but that he can only detain him if he return and put himself again under the custody of the officer.(⁵) Upon this subject, Mr. Deacon properly remarks, that although this position may hold on civil process, yet as the public good requires that all atrocious offenders should be brought to justice, it would hardly be contended in the present day, that if a Jailor (although voluntarily) suffered a prisoner indicted for murder to escape, he would not be permitted in some measure to redeem his offence by retaking his prisoner when he had the opportunity.

When the escape is by the party's own wrong or through the mere negligence of the officer, the officer may retake him wherever he finds him, though he may fly into another county,(⁶) and may break open doors to retake him, on demand

---

(¹) 1 Russ. 371; 2 Hawk. c. 19, § 61.
(²) 2 Hawk. c. 19, § 5.
(³) 1 Russ. 371.
(⁴) 1 Russ. 367.
(⁵) 1 Russ. 372.
(⁶) 2 Hawk. c. 19, § 12.

and refusal of admittance,(¹) but he is not justified in killing the prisoner in pursuing him after an escape, though otherwise unable to retake him.(²)

A Justice of the Peace, upon proper complaint made to him, may issue his warrant to apprehend and retake any prisoner who has escaped from lawful custody, whether confined under criminal or civil process, and such warrant when issued, runs throughout the Commonwealth, and may be executed on Sunday and at all other times and in any place.

The warrant ought regularly to shew on its face, that the person who issues it, is a Justice of the Peace; yet, on a *habeas corpus* sued out by the person arrested under it, if it is proved that he is a Justice, the prisoner ought not to be discharged.(³)

(No. 1.)

Form of Warrant of Arrest against a person convicted of felony for breaking jail and escaping.

———— County, to wit:

To all or any one of the Constables of said County:

Whereas, A. B. of said County, has this day made complaint and information on oath before me J. T., a Justice of the said County, that C. D., on the —— day of ———— 18—, in said County, he the said C. D. being then confined in the jail of the Circuit Court of the said County, and in the custody of the keeper thereof, upon a conviction for felony, in killing J. S., (or whatever felony according to the conviction,) and for which, the said C. D. was then sentenced to imprisonment in the penitentiary, feloniously and by force and violence did escape from the said jail, and from the custody of the keeper thereof, and is now going at large: These are, therefore, to command you, in the name of the Commonwealth of Virginia, forthwith to apprehend the said C. D., and bring him before me or some other Justice of the said County, to answer the said complaint, and to be farther dealt with according to law. Given under my hand and seal, this —— day of ———— 18—.

J. T., J. P. [L. S.]

(No. 2.)

Form of Warrant of Arrest against a person convicted of a misdemeanor for breaking jail.

———— County, to wit:

To all or any one of the Constables of said County:

Whereas, A. B. of said County, has this day made complaint and information on oath before me J. T., a Justice of the said County, that C. D., on the —— day of ———— 18—, in said County, he the said C. D. being then confined in the County jail of the said County, and in the custody of the

---

(¹) 2 Hawk. c. 14, § 9.   (³) 6 Rand. 678.
(²) 2 Hawk. c. 28, § 11 and 12.

ESCAPES.

keeper thereof, upon a conviction for assaulting and beating one J. S., and for which he the said C. D. was then sentenced to imprisonment in the said jail, did, by force and violence, unlawfully escape from the said jail and custody: These are, therefore, to command you, in the name of the Commonwealth of Virginia, forthwith to apprehend the said C. D., and bring him before me or some other Justice of the said County, to answer the said complaint, and to be farther dealt with according to law. Given under my hand and seal, this —— day of ——— 18—.

J. T., J. P. [L. S.]

(No. 3.)

Form of Warrant of Arrest for conveying instruments to a person convicted of or charged with felony, by means whereof he escaped.

—— County, to wit:

To the Sheriff and to all or any one of the Constables of said County:

Whereas, A. B. of the said County, has this day made complaint and information on oath before me J. T., a Justice of the said County, that C. D. on the —— day of ——— 18—, in the said County, feloniously did convey into the County jail of the said County, (or *into the jail of the Circuit Court of the said County*) three pick lock keys, (state the thing conveyed, according to the fact,) being instruments adapted to and useful in aiding prisoners to escape from jail, with intent thereby to facilitate the escape of one E. F., who was then lawfully imprisoned in the said jail, convicted of (or *charged with*) felony, (state the offence, as for instance, *in stealing the goods and chattels of L. M.*,) and who by means of the said instruments, did effect his escape from the said jail, and is now going at large: These are, therefore, to require you forthwith to apprehend the said C. D., &c. (conclude as No. 1.)

(No. 4.)

Form of Warrant of Arrest against a party escaping, and the person aiding him.

—— County, to wit:

To the Sheriff and to all or any one of the Constables of said County:

Whereas, A. B. of said County, has this day made complaint and information on oath before me J. T., a Justice of the said County, that C. D. on the —— day of ——— 18—, in said County, he the said C. D. being then lawfully detained in the jail of the said County, upon conviction of felony, (or *charged with felony*, as the case may be,) feloniously and by force and violence did make his escape from the said jail; and that E. F. did then and there feloniously aid and assist the said C. D. so to escape from the said jail: These are, therefore, to command you, in the name of the Commonwealth of Virginia, forthwith to apprehend the said C. D. and E. F., and bring them before me or some other Justice of the said County, to answer the said complaint, and to be farther dealt with according to law. Given under my hand and seal, this —— day of ——— 18—.

J. T., J. P. [L. S.]

(No. 5.)

Form of Warrant of Arrest against a Jailor for voluntarily permitting a prisoner in custody for felony to escape.

—— County, to wit:
To X. Y., *Constable of the said County*:

Whereas, A. B. of the said County, has this day made complaint and information on oath before me J. T., a Justice of the said County, that, on the —— day of ——— 18—, at the said County, one C. D. was, by virtue of a warrant of commitment, signed and issued by J. M., a Justice of the said County, duly and legally committed to the common jail of the said County, for safe custody, charged with having feloniously stolen and carried away the goods of T. J.; and moreover, that P. L., the lawful keeper of the said jail, did afterwards, and before the said C. D. was by law entitled to his discharge from the said jail, to wit, on the —— day of ——— 18—, in the County aforesaid, feloniously and voluntarily suffer and permit the said C. D. to escape and go at large out of the said jail: These are, therefore, to command you, in the name of the Commonwealth, forthwith to apprehend the said P. L., and to bring him before me or some other Justice of the said County, to be dealt with according to law. Given under my hand and seal, this —— day of ——— 18—.

J. T., *J. P.* [L. S.]

[If the case be felony, and the prisoner be not discharged, follow these forms from No. 6 to 10; but if the offence be a misdemeanor only, follow forms from No. 11 to 14.]

(No. 6.)

Form of Mittimus where a party is committed for examination or trial in the County Court for a felonious escape.

—— County, to wit:
To X. Z., *Constable of said County, and to the Keeper of the Jail of said County*:

These are to command you, the said Constable, in the name of the Commonwealth of Virginia, forthwith to convey and deliver into the custody of the keeper of the said jail, together with this warrant, the body of C. D., a white person (or *free negro*, or *a slave, the property of E. F.*, as the case may be,) charged before me J. T., a Justice of the said County, on the oath of A. B., with a felony by him committed, in this, that the said C. D., on the —— day of ——— in the year 18—, in the said County, (here describe the offence as in the warrant of arrest.) And you, the said keeper of the said jail, are hereby required to receive the said C. D. into your jail and custody, that he may be examined (or *tried*) for the said offence, by the County Court of said County, and him there safely keep until he shall be discharged by due course of law. Given under my hand and seal, this —— day of ——— in the year 18—.

J. T., *J. P.* [L. S.]

[NOTE.—If the prisoner be a white person, or if he be a free negro charged with homicide of any grade, or with any offence punishable with death, he must be committed for examination. For all other felonies by free negroes, and in all cases of felony by slaves, the prisoner must be committed for trial.]

(No. 7.)

Form of Certificate of Commitment for a felonious escape, to be sent to the Clerk of the County Court.

———— County, to wit:

To the Clerk of the County Court of said County:

I, J. T., a Justice of said County, do hereby certify that I have, by my warrant, this day committed C. D. (if free negro or slave, state which,) to the jail of this County, that he may be examined (or *tried*) before the County Court of the said County, for a felony by him committed, in this, that he did, on the ——— day of ——— 18—, in the said County, (here state the offence as in the mittimus.) Given under my hand, this ——— day of ——— in the year 18—.

J. T., J. P.

(No. 8.)

Form of Certificate to the Clerk where party is admitted to bail.

Turn to head of ARREST, and follow No. 6.

(No. 9.)

Form of Recognizance of Bail.

Turn to head of RECOGNIZANCE, and follow No. 1, if person be free; No. 2, if a slave, and state succinctly the offence for which the person is recognized.

(No. 10.)

Form of Recognizance of Witness to appear before the County Court to give evidence upon the examination or trial of a party charged with felonious escape.

Turn to head of RECOGNIZANCE, and follow No. 3.

(No. 11.)

Form of Mittimus where a party is committed to answer an indictment in the County Court, for a misdemeanor.

———— County, to wit:

To X. Z., Constable of said County, and to the Keeper of the Jail of said County:

These are to command you the said Constable, in the name of the Commonwealth of Virginia, forthwith to convey and deliver into the custody of the keeper of the said jail, together with this warrant, the body of C. D., charged before me J. T., a Justice of the said County, on the oath of A. B., with a misdemeanor by him committed, in this, that the said C. D., on the

—— day of ——— in the year 18—, in the said County (here describe the offence as in the warrant of arrest.) And you the said keeper of the said jail are hereby required to receive the said C. D. into your jail and custody, to answer an indictment to be preferred against him for the said offence in the County Court of said County, and him there safely keep, until he shall be discharged by due course of law. Given under my hand and seal, this ——— day of ——— in the year 18—.

J. T., J. P. [L. S.]

(No. 12.)

Form of Recognizance of Bail.

Turn to head of RECOGNIZANCE, and follow No. 4, and state the offence succinctly for which the party is recognized.

(No. 13.)

Form of Certificate of the Commitment, or Letting to Bail, to be sent to the Clerk of the County Court.

——— County, to wit:

To the Clerk of the County Court of the said County:

I, J. T., a Justice of the said County, do hereby certify, that C. D. was this day committed to the jail of this County, by my warrant, (or *was this day admitted to bail by me*, as the case may be,) to answer an indictment to be preferred against him in the County Court of the said County, for a misdemeanor by him committed, in this, that he did, on the ——— day of ——— 18—, in said County, (here describe the offence as in the warrant of arrest.) Given under my hand, this ——— day of ——— 18—.

J. T., J. P.

(No. 14.)

Form of Recognizance of Witness to appear and give evidence to the Grand Jury upon the indictment.

Follow No. 5, under head of RECOGNIZANCE.

(No. 1.)

An Indictment for breaking jail, against a party convicted of felony.

——— Judicial Circuit, ——— County, to wit: In the Circuit Court of the said County. } The jurors of the Commonwealth of Virginia, in and for the body of the County of ———, now attending the Circuit Court of the said County, upon their oath present, that A. B. was, to wit, on the ——— day of ——— 18—, at the said County, tried and convicted in the Circuit Court of the said County, for feloniously (here set forth the offence as stated in the record of conviction:) and that thereupon the said A. B., for the felony aforesaid, was afterwards, to wit, on the day and year aforesaid, by the judgment of the said Circuit Court of the said County, sentenced to imprisonment in the penitentiary for the term of ——— years, as will more fully

ESCAPES—(*Indictments for.*) 237

and at large appear by the records of the said Court, and which said judgment still remains in full force and is in no wise reversed or made void; and that the said A. B., being so convicted of the felony aforesaid, and sentenced as aforesaid, was, to wit, on the day and year aforesaid, at the County aforesaid, by virtue of the conviction and judgment aforesaid, taken and conveyed to the jail of the said Circuit Court of the said County, and was then and there delivered into the said jail, and into the custody of the keeper of the said jail, and was then and there confined in the said jail on the conviction aforesaid. And the jurors aforesaid, upon their oath aforesaid, do farther present, that the said A. B., being so confined in the jail aforesaid, on the conviction aforesaid, afterwards, to wit, on the ——— day of ——— 18—, at the County aforesaid, did feloniously, by force and violence, break the said jail of the said Circuit Court of the said County, by then and there (here state how the jail was broken,) and did then and there in said County, feloniously, and by force and violence, effect his escape from the said jail, and from the custody of the keeper thereof, and from his confinement aforesaid, and go at large, against the peace and dignity of the Commonwealth of Virginia.

(No. 2.)

An Indictment against a party charged with felony for breaking jail.

——— Judicial Circuit, \
——— County, *to wit:* \
In the Circuit Court of the \
said County.

The jurors of the Commonwealth of Virginia, in and for the body of the County of ———, now attending the Circuit Court of the said County, upon their oath present, that on the ——— day of ———, in the year one thousand eight hundred and ———, A. B. was brought before J. T., Justice of the said County, then and there charged before the said J. T., as Justice aforesaid, by one J. L., upon the oath of the said J. L., that he the said A. B. had then and there lately before, feloniously (here state the offence with which the party was charged in the past tense,) and that the said A. B. was then and there examined before the said J. T., Justice as aforesaid, touching the said offence to him charged as aforesaid, whereupon the said J. T., the Justice aforesaid, did then and there make a certain warrant, under his hand and seal, in due form of law, bearing date on the ——— day of ——— in the year ———, directed to the keeper of the jail of the said County, commanding him to receive into the said jail, and into his custody as the keeper thereof, the said A. B., brought before him and charged upon the oath of the said J. L., with the felony aforesaid, and the said J. T., Justice as aforesaid, by the said warrant, did command the said keeper of the said jail, safely to keep the said A. B. in his jail and custody, until he should thence be discharged by due course of law, by virtue of which said warrant afterwards, to wit, on the day and year last aforesaid, at the County aforesaid, the said A. B. was taken and conveyed to the said jail, and then and there delivered to P. J., the keeper of the said jail, and the said P. J., keeper of the said jail, then and there received him he said A. B. into his custody, in the jail aforesaid, and that the said A. B. was then and there, to wit, on the day and year last aforesaid, lawfully imprisoned in the jail aforesaid, upon the charge aforesaid. And the jurors aforesaid, upon their oath aforesaid, do farther present, that the said A. B., being so confined as aforesaid, did afterwards, to wit, on the ——— day of ——— in the year 18—, in the said County, unlawfully and by force and violence, break the said jail, by (describe the manner of breaking,) by means whereof he the said A. B., on the day and year last aforesaid, did unlawfully, by force and violence, effect his escape from the said jail and from his confinement, and go at large, against the peace and dignity of the Commonwealth of Virginia.

(No. 3.)

An Indictment for aiding prisoner convicted of felony to make his escape by conveying to him in jail instruments for that purpose.

—————— Judicial Circuit, \
—————— County, to wit: \
In the Circuit Court of the \
said County.

The jurors of the Commonwealth of Virginia, in and for the body of the County of ——————, now attending the Circuit Court of the said County, upon their oath present, that before and at the time of the committing of the felony hereinafter mentioned, to wit, on the —— day of —————— in the year 18—, at the County aforesaid, one A. B. stood convicted of felony, by the judgment of the Circuit Court of the said County, for feloniously (here set forth the offence as specified in the record of conviction,) and that the said A. B. was, by the said judgment, for the felony aforesaid, sentenced to —— years imprisonment in the penitentiary, as appears by the records of the said Court, and which judgment is still in full force and in no wise reversed. And that the said A. B. afterwards, to wit, on the day and year aforesaid, at the County aforesaid, was under and by virtue of the said conviction and judgment for the felony aforesaid, a prisoner lawfully detained in the jail of the said Circuit Court of the County aforesaid, and in the custody of the keeper thereof. And the jurors aforesaid, upon their oath aforesaid, do farther present, that C. D. afterwards, and whilst the said A. B. was lawfully detained in the jail aforesaid, on the conviction for felony as aforesaid, as such prisoner, to wit, on the day and year last aforesaid, at the said County, feloniously did convey into the jail aforesaid, one steel file and one iron chisel, (the same being instruments adapted to and useful in aiding prisoners to escape from jail,) and then and there feloniously did deliver the said file and chisel, being such instruments as aforesaid, to the said A. B., (he the said A. B. then and there being such prisoner in the jail aforesaid, and in the custody of the keeper thereof, under and by virtue of the conviction and judgment aforesaid, for felony as aforesaid,) with the felonious intent thereby to facilitate the escape of the said A. B., from the jail and custody aforesaid; and by means of which said instruments, the said A. B. did afterwards, to wit, on the —— day of —————— in the year 18—, at the said County, effect his escape from the said jail and custody, and is now going at large, against the peace and dignity of the Commonwealth of Virginia.

CHAPTER XXXVI.

ESCHEATS.

It is not proposed to do more under this head than briefly to notice the duties of an escheator up to the conclusion of an inquisition of escheat, and to give him the forms of discharging them accurately. For his duties after the inquisition, he is referred to the 113th chapter of the new Code.

By Sec. 1, Chap. 113. The court of each county and corporation shall appoint one escheator for the same.

By Sec. 2. Each escheator shall give bond in the penalty of three thousand dollars, and may continue in office until removed by the court, or until a successor is duly appointed and qualified.

By Sec. 3. Whenever there is no escheator in any such town or county, the Sheriff of the county, or Sergeant of the corporation, shall act as the escheator therefor, until an escheator is appointed and qualified. And where any proceedings have been commenced in the name of any escheator, he shall, unless removed as aforesaid, carry on the same and sell the escheated land and account for the proceeds, even though another escheator may have been appointed.

By Sec. 4. Each commissioner of the revenue shall annually, in May, furnish to the escheator of his county or corporation, a list of all lands within his district, of which any person shall have died, seized of an estate of inheritance, intestate and without any known heir, or to which no person is known by him to be entitled, but no land shall be liable to escheat, which, for twenty years, has been in the actual possession of the person claiming the same, or those under whom he holds, and upon which taxes have been paid within that time.

By Sec. 5. On receiving such list, or upon information from any person in writing and under oath, the escheator shall proceed to hold his inquest and determine whether any such land has escheated to the Commonwealth.

By Sec. 6. For his inquest, there shall be summoned and returned by the Sheriff of the county or Sergeant of the corporation, sixteen freeholders, of whom at least twelve shall be impanneled as jurors. They shall meet at the courthouse and sit in public, and may be adjourned by the escheator from day to day. Every person shall be suffered to give evidence openly in the presence of the jurors.

240   ESCHEATS.

By Sec. 7. If any person, summoned or adjourned as a juror, fail to attend according to the summons or adjournment, the escheator shall return the fact to the next circuit court having jurisdiction over the county or corporation in which the land that is the subject of the inquisition may lie; which court may fine such person not exceeding fifty dollars.

By Sec. 8. When the inquest is ended and a verdict concurred in by the jurors impanneled, or twelve of them, it shall be signed by those so concurring and by the escheator; and he shall, within thirty days, return it to the Clerk of the said circuit court, who shall, within thirty days after receiving it, deliver a copy thereof to the Clerk of the court for the county or corporation in which the land may be; and the said last mentioned Clerk shall record the same.

(No. 1.)

Form of Order of Escheator to summon an inquest, when it appears by list furnished by Commissioner of the Revenue, that lands are liable to escheat.

——— County, to wit:
  To the Sheriff of the said County:

Whereas, A. B. a Commissioner of the Revenue of the said County, has furnished to me C. D., Escheator for the said County, a list of lands within his district, of which persons have died, seized of an estate of inheritance, intestate, without any known heir, and to which no person is known by him to be entitled; and it appearing to me by the said list, that E. F. has died, seized of an estate of inheritance, intestate, and without any known heir, and to which no person is known to be entitled, in a tract of land containing ——— acres, lying in the said County: These are, therefore, to command you, in the name of the Commonwealth of Virginia, to summon sixteen freeholders of your County, to appear and be in attendance before me as Escheator as aforesaid, at the Courthouse of the said County, on the ——— day of ——— 18—, when and where I shall hold an inquest to determine whether the said land has escheated to the Commonwealth of Virginia, at which time and place you will attend and make return how you have executed this warrant. Given under my hand and seal, this ——— day of ——— 18—.

                               C. D., *Escheator,* [L. S.]

(No. 2.)

Form of same, upon the written information on oath of another person.

——— County, to wit:
  To the Sheriff of the said County:

Whereas, A. B. has this day given to me C. D., Escheator of the said County, information in writing and under his oath, that E. F. has died, seized of an estate of inheritance in a certain tract of land containing ———

ESCHEATS. 241

acres, lying in the said County, and that the said E. F. died, so seized, intestate, and without any known heir, and to which no person known to him is entitled: These are, therefore, &c. (conclude as No. 1.)

[NOTE.—In this case, the information must be in writing, and may be in this form:]

To C. D., Escheator for the County of ———— :

I, A. B., do on my oath, hereby inform you, as Escheator of the County of ————, that E. F. has died, seized of an estate of inheritance, containing ———— acres of land, lying in the said County, and that he died, so seized, intestate, and without any known heir, and to which no person known to me is entitled.

A. B.

———— day of ———— 18—.

———— County, to wit:

This day, the above named A. B. appeared before me J. T., a Justice of the said County, and made oath, according to law, that the facts set forth in the foregoing statement, signed by him and addressed to C. D., Escheator of the County of ————, are true. Given under my hand, this ———— day of ———— 18—.

J. T., J. P.

(No. 3.)

Form of Subpœna to be issued by Escheator.

———— County, to wit:

To the Sheriff of the said County:

I, C. D., Escheator for the said County, command you, in the name of the Commonwealth of Virginia, to summon H. P. to appear before me, at the Courthouse of ———— County, on the ———— day of ————, as a witness, to give evidence on behalf of the Commonwealth, before an inquest then and there to be held by me, to ascertain whether a certain estate of inheritance in a parcel of land lying in the said County, and of which E. F. died seized, has escheated to the Commonwealth, and that you then and there make return of this process. Given under my hand, this ———— day of ———— 18—.

C. D., *Escheator.*

(No. 4.)

Form of the Oath to be administered by the Escheator to the jurors.

You, as jurors summoned upon the inquest now to be held by me, do solemnly swear, that you will truly and impartially enquire whether E. F. died seized of an estate of inheritance in a certain tract of land lying in the County of ————, containing ———— acres, and if he died so seized, whether he died intestate and without heirs, and whether any person is known to be entitled to the same. So help you God.

(No. 5.)

Form of Inquisition of Escheat.

An inquisition taken at the County Courthouse of ——— County, on this ——— day of ——— 18—, before me A. B., Escheator for the said County, by X. Y., &c., (naming at least twelve, and as many more of the jurors as are present,) freeholders of the said County, duly summoned and impanneled by the Sheriff of the said County, to take this inquisition, and who being by me, as Escheator for the said County, charged and sworn truly and impartially to enquire whether E. F. died seized of an estate of inheritance in a certain tract of land lying in the said County, containing ——— acres, and whether, if he so died seized of the said land, he died intestate and without heirs, and whether any person is known to be entitled to the said land, do, upon their oath aforesaid, say, that the said E. F. did die seized of an estate of inheritance in the said tract of land lying in the said County, containing ——— acres, (the boundaries may be here specified,) and that the said E. F. so died, seized of an estate of inheritance in the said land, intestate and without heirs, and that there is no person known to us, the jurors aforesaid, to be entitled to the said tract of land.

X. Y.
Z. O., &c.

A. B., Escheator.

[NOTE.—The inquisition must be signed by the escheator and all the jurors who concur, and by twelve at least, otherwise it will be no inquisition. These precedents may be easily made to suit a case of inquest upon any number of tracts of land. It may admit of doubt whether an inquest can be held to enquire generally of what lands a person died seized and liable to escheat, and these precedents therefore, commencing with the order to summon the inquest, specify particular tracts of land liable to escheat.]

CHAPTER XXXVII.

ESTRAYS.

By Sec. 1, Chap. 100. Any person may take up an estray found on his land, or a boat or vessel adrift. He shall immediately inform a Justice of his county or corporation thereof, who shall issue his warrant to three freeholders, requiring them under oath to view and appraise such estray, or boat or vessel, and certify the result, with a description of the kind, marks, brand, stature, colour and age of the animal; or kind, burden and build of the boat or vessel.

By Sec. 2. The said freeholders shall return their certificate, with the warrant, to the clerk of the court of said county or corporation, who shall record the same in a book kept for that purpose, and post a copy thereof at the door of his courthouse, on the first day of two terms of said court next after receiving the certificate.

By Sec. 3. If the owner of such property shall not then have appeared, and the valuation thereof be under five dollars, or if such valuation is as much as five dollars, and the owner shall not have appeared after the said certificate has been published as aforesaid, and also three times in some newspaper published nearest to the place where such property was taken up, it shall belong in either case to the owner of the land on which it was so taken, if an estray, or to the person taking it up, in the case of a boat or vessel.

By Sec. 4. The former owner may, at any time after, recover the valuation money, except the amount of the clerk's and printer's fees, and such compensation for keeping the property as shall be certified under oath, by any two freeholders in the county or corporation where the property was valued, to be reasonoble.

By Sec. 5. If such estray die, or any such property be lost to the said owner of the land or person taking it up, without his fault, he shall not be liable for the same or its valuation.

ESTRAYS.

(No. 1.)

Form of a Warrant to three freeholders to view and appraise an estray.

—— County, to wit:
    To *A. B.*, *C. D.* and *E. F.*, *freeholders of the said County:*

Forasmuch as G. H. has this day given information to me J. T., a Justice of the said County, that he did, on the —— day of —— 18—, on his land in the said County, take up an estray, (here state the kind of animal :) You are hereby commanded (after you shall have been sworn for that purpose) well and truly to view and appraise the said ——, and certify under your hands, the value of the said ——, together with a particular description of the kind, marks, brand, stature, colour and age thereof, and make return, together with this warrant, to the Clerk of the County Court of said County, of such your certificate of valuation and description. Given under my hand and seal, this —— day of —— 18—.

    J. T., J. P. [L. S.]

(No. 2.)

Form of the Oath to be taken by the freeholders appointed to view and appraise an estray.

You, and each of you, do solemnly swear, that you will well and truly view and appraise a horse, (or other animal, as the case may be,) which G. H. has taken up on his land as an estray. So help you God.

(No. 3.)

Form of a Certificate of the freeholders of the appraisement and valuation of an estray.

—— County, to wit:
    To the Clerk of the County Court of said County:

We, M. G., G. R. and J. L., three freeholders of the said County, do hereby certify, that by virtue of a warrant to us directed by J. T., a Justice of the said County, we have this day, on our oaths, viewed and appraised a horse, taken up by G. H. on his land as an estray, and assess the value of the said estray at —— dollars. The said horse is (here describe minutely, the kind, mark, brand, stature, colour and age.) Given under our hands, this —— day of —— 18—.

    M. G.
    G. R.
    J. L.

(No. 4.)

Form of a Warrant to two freeholders to assess a reasonable compensation for keeping and supporting an estray.

—— County, to wit:

To *A. B.* and *C. D., freeholders of the said County:*

Forasmuch as G. H., on the —— day of ——— 18—, upon his land in the said County, did take up an estray, (here describe the animal,) whereof X. Y. is the owner, as fully appears to me J. T. a Justice of the said County, upon due proof this day exhibited to me by the said X. Y.: These are, therefore, to require you (after you shall have been sworn for that purpose) to adjudge and say what is a reasonable compensation to be allowed to the said G. H. by the said X. Y. for keeping and supporting the said estray, and that you certify the same under your hands. Given under my hand and seal, this —— day of ——— 18—.

J. T., J. P. [L. S.]

(No. 5.)

Form of Certificate by two freeholders of reasonable compensation for keeping and supporting an estray.

—— County, to wit:

We, G. M. and G. R., two freeholders of the said County, being for that purpose first duly sworn, do certify, that $ ——— would be a reasonable compensation to be paid by A. B. to G. H. for keeping an estray, (state the animal,) the property of the said A. B., and which was taken up as an estray by the said G. H. Given under our hands, this —— day of ——— 18—.

G. M.
G. R.

[These forms may be readily adapted to the case of a boat or vessel taken adrift.]

CHAPTER XXXVIII.

EVIDENCE.

In the incipient stages of every prosecution, all the facts necessary to shew that the party committed the offence charged upon him, must be so far proved, as to raise in the mind of the Justice, at least a probability of the prisoner's guilt; and in all cases, whether civil or criminal, within his jurisdiction to hear and determine, every essential fact in dispute must be strictly proved. Evidence is the means by which this is to be done, and is of two kinds, parol or written.

I. *Of parol evidence, or that given by witnesses.*

1. *Of the general competency of witnesses.*—The general rule is, that all persons who believe in a God as the avenger of falsehood, whether natives of this or any other country, whatever mode of religious belief they may profess, or in whatever form or ceremony they may think an oath most binding upon their consciences, are admissible as witnesses;([1]) for whatever the form, the meaning of the oath is the same; an appeal to heaven, calling upon God to witness what we say, and invoking his vengeance, if what we say is false.([2]) In Virginia, no person is incapacitated from being a witness on account of his religious belief, nor can a witness be questioned on his *voir dire*, touching his religious opinions.([3])

All persons labouring under a total defect of understanding, as *idiots and lunatics*, are incompetent witnesses; but lunatics, though subject to temporary fits of insanity, may yet be witnesses in their lucid intervals, if they have sufficiently recovered their understanding,([4]) and a person, born deaf and dumb, is a competent witness, if he have sufficient understanding.([5]) So, also, children of any age may be examined as witnesses, if they are capable of understanding between good and evil. The rule does not now depend on their age, but understanding; but whatever be the age of the child, it can only be examined upon oath.([6])

By Sec. 19, Chap. 176. A negro or indian shall be a competent witness in a case of the Commonwealth, for or against a negro or indian, or in a civil case to which only negroes or indians are parties, but not in any other case.

([1]) Willis Rep. 549.
([2]) 1 Phil. 25.
([3]) Perry's Case, 3 Gratt. 632.
([4]) Co. Lit. 6 b.
([5]) 1 Leach 455.
([6]) 1 East P. C. 443; 1 Leach 237.

Though a negro cannot be a witness in any civil suit in which a white person is a party interested, yet he may by his affidavit verify a bill for an injunction, or petition for a *habeas corpus*, where he seeks to obtain his freedom.(¹)

Persons having less than one fourth negro blood in their veins, are competent witnesses upon the trial of a white man, and the fact that a witness is of negro descent, though not so near as to render him incompetent as a witness, is not competent evidence to impeach his credibility. (Dean's Case, 4 Grat. 541.)

2. *Of accomplices.*—An accomplice is unquestionably a competent witness against his companion in guilt,(²) and so he is a competent witness for his associates.(³) But it is the general practice not to convict a prisoner upon the uncorroborated testimony of an accomplice,(⁴) for want of credibility, and for the same reason, it would be unsafe in the Justice to discharge a prisoner, upon the uncorroborated testimony of an accomplice against whom a probable case is made out by other evidence.

3. *Of incompetency from interest.*—By Sec. 17, Chap. 176. No person assessed or liable to be assessed with levies for any county or corporation, shall be disabled from giving evidence by reason only of such assessment or liability.

By Sec. 18. No such person, and no officer of a county or corporation, shall be disabled from giving evidence in any case by reason only of his being a party to such case, or of his being liable to costs in respect thereof, when he is only a nominal party thereto, and liable to contribute to such costs only in common with other persons assessed with the levies of such county or corporation.

The general rule is, that the interest to disqualify a witness, must be some certain *legal* and immediate interest in the event of the *suit* or *proceeding*, or such interest that the judgment rendered, may be given in evidence for him in some other proceeding instituted by or against the witness.(⁵) Thus an informer, who is entitled to any part of the penalty to be recovered, cannot be a witness.(⁶)

So an accessary before or after the fact, is in most cases, an incompetent witness for the principal; for the acquittal of the principal would ensure the discharge of the accessary.(⁷)

However it may affect the credibility of a witness, it is no objection to his competency, that he may have wishes or a

---

(¹) Delacy v. Peter and others, 7 Leigh 428; Dempsey v. Lawrence, Gil. R. 333.
(²) Byrd's Case, 2 Va. Cases 490.
(³) 2 Hale 280; Deac. Cr. Co. 392.
(⁴) 1 Leach 478-9.
(⁵) 3 T. R. 27; 7 T. R. 60; 4 Burr. 2325.
(⁶) 2 Ld. Raymond 1545.
(⁷) Star. Ev. P. IV. p. 764.

strong bias on the subject matter of the proceedings, or that he may expect some benefit from the result of the trial,[1] unless as before stated, that benefit be some certain *legal* and immediate benefit in the event of the suit or proceedings.

A party having such an interest as to disqualify him, may become a witness by releasing all interest in the subject.

No tie of relationship, except that of husband and wife, will disqualify any one as a witness; nor is a witness to be rejected because he stands in the same situation as the party for whom he is called to testify, or because he believes himself to be under an honourary obligation to pay the costs, or believes that he is interested in the event of the proceeding.[2]

In criminal prosecutions, it is a general rule at Common Law, that the party injured is a competent witness,[3] and by the statute, no person who is not jointly tried with the defendant, shall be incompetent to testify in support of any prosecution, by reason of any interest in the subject matter thereof.[4] From motives of public policy, the law will not permit husband and wife to be witnesses for or against each other, except in cases of *personal injury* by the one to the other.[5] In these cases, the wife from necessity is admitted as a witness against her husband.[6]

4. *Of incompetency from infamy.*—By Sec. 19, Chap. 199. Except where it is otherwise expressly provided, a person convicted of felony shall not be a witness, unless he has been pardoned or punished therefor; and a person convicted of perjury, shall not be a witness, although pardoned or punished.

The consequences of incompetency from infamy are, that as the party cannot be a witness, so he cannot make an affidavit to support a complaint against others, and even when he is a subscribing witness to any instrument of writing, he cannot be called to give evidence, but his handwriting as an attesting witness, must be proved as if he were dead.[7]

In order to shew the incompetency of the witness, it is not only necessary to prove a conviction, but also a judgment, for the conviction may have been quashed on motion or in arrest of judgment.[8] Even an admission by the witness himself of his having been guilty of felony or perjury, will not make him incompetent, however it may affect his credit.[9] The conviction and judgment must be proved by an exemplification of the record, though it be the record of a foreign court.[10]

---

[1] 1 Phil. 45; 1 T. R. 164.
[2] 1 Phil. 52; Star. Ev. 746.
[3] 4 East 581; Star. Ev. 771.
[4] Chap. 199, sec. 21.
[5] 1 Phil. 84.
[6] Bull. N. P. 287; 2 Russ. 606.
[7] 1 Deac. C. C. 375; 2 Str. 833.
[8] Phil. Ev. 31.
[9] 8 East 78; 11 East 309.
[10] 2 Star. Rep. 184; 14 John. 182.

5. *Incompetency from privileged communications.*—An attorney is not allowed to testify to any fact, or depose to any information which he has acquired from a client, in the character of attorney. This is the privilege of the client and not the attorney, and so strict does the rule hold, that his incompetency continues even after his employment has ceased, by dismissal or otherwise, or after the cause has entirely ended ;(¹) and it makes no difference that the client is not in any shape a party to the proceedings before the Court or Justice.(²)

But in all cases where an attorney acquired the knowledge of a fact before he is retained, or which he might have knowledge, without being trusted as attorney in the cause, or where he has made himself a party in the transaction, he may then be examined like any other witness.(³)

This privilege does not extend to other professional persons. All other professional men, whether clergymen, physicians or surgeons, are bound to disclose the matters confided to them.(⁴)

Besides professional communications to attorneys, there are some other cases in which, for reasons of public policy, a court of justice will not permit a witness to be interrogated as to the information he has acquired, or the means of obtaining it. Thus a witness, who has been employed to collect secret information for the Executive government, or for the service of the police, is not allowed to reveal the name of his employer or informer, or the nature of the connection between them.(⁵)

How to object to competency. The usual mode of objecting to the incompetency of a witness, is to swear him to answer such questions as shall be propounded to him, and then for the party making the objection, to ask the witness such questions as the answers to which will disclose the grounds upon which the objection is found. But though this be not done, and the witness be sworn in chief, yet if he is found to be incompetent at any period of the trial, his evidence will be struck out, and if he venture on the *voir dire* to deny his interest, it may be proved by other evidence.(⁶) Nevertheless, when a party is cognizant of the interest of a witness at the time he is called, he is bound to make his objection in the first instance, otherwise he might take the chance of getting evidence which he liked, and then if he disliked it, might get rid of it.(⁷)

(¹) 1 Phil. 140.
(²) 2 Camp. 578.
(³) Peake 108 ; Bull. N. P. 284.
(⁴) Peake 78 ; 2 Russ. 648 ; 3 Camp. 377.
(⁵) 2 Brod. & B. 162 ; Hardy's Case. 24 St. Tr. 758, 811 ; 2 Stark. Rep. 136, Watson's Case.
(⁶) 1 T. R. 720 ; 2 Camp. 14 ; Deac. 402.
(⁷) 2 Stark. Rep. 158, and Stark. Ev. 756.

Of the examination of the witness. The witness being called and found competent, he is then sworn or affirmed (according to his religious scruples) by the Justice, which is usually done in this form : " You do swear, upon the Holy Bible, (or *solemnly affirm,*) that the evidence you shall give in the matter now pending before me, shall be the truth, the whole truth, and nothing but the truth. So help you God." In the case of a coloured witness, it is necessary in all cases, before administering the oath, to charge him thus : " You are now brought before me to give evidence, and if it be found out hereafter, that you tell a lie and give false testimony, you will have both of your ears nailed to the pillory, and cut off, and receive nine and thirty lashes upon your bare back, at the public whipping post." This charge must be given, otherwise the witness will not be guilty of perjury, if he swears falsely.

The object of evidence, is to ascertain the truth of the fact or point in dispute, called the issue, and the facts proved must be strictly relevant to it,([1]) and all testimony which has no tendency to this, is irrelevant, and should be excluded, for, even upon a cross examination, no testimony wholly irrelevant to the matter in issue, can be received.([2])

The witness is not bound to answer every question that may be put to him, however pertinent to the issue ; he may refuse to answer not only all those questions where the answer would lead to the conclusion of his guilt, but also all such as tend to criminate him.([3])

It is no objection, however, to his answering a question, that the answer may subject him to a debt, and it would seem, by the most modern authorities, that a witness may be compelled to answer a question tending to disgrace him, provided he is not thereby exposed to punishment.([4])

The credit of a witness may be impeached by proof of former statements made or acts done by him, which may be either inconsistent with his evidence, or in other respects throw suspicion upon his testimony. But to lay the foundation of such discreditory evidence, it is first necessary to ask the witness, on cross examination, whether he has made the statement or done the act which it is intended to prove.([5])

To discredit a witness, evidence may also be introduced to prove his *general character* for want of *veracity*, but no particular fact can be proved for this purpose. The proper question, therefore, to ask a witness so called to discredit another,

---

([1]) 2 Leach 708.
([2]) 7 East 108.
([3]) 3 Taunt. 424 ; 3 Camp. 208.
([4]) 4 T. R. 440 ; 1 Archb. Cr. Pl. 102 ; 1 Mood. & M. 108.
([5]) The Queen's Case, 2 Brod. & B. 299.

is, whether he had the means of knowing the witness's general character for veracity, and whether, from such knowledge, he would believe him on oath.

A party cannot discredit his own witness, where he proves a fact contrary to his expectations, but he may shew, that as to the particular fact sworn to, the witness is mistaken.(¹)

Admitting both the competency and credibility of a witness, questions often arise as to the competency of the testimony which he is about to give. Of this character, are:

1. *Dying declarations.*—The evidence of a declaration of a deceased person as to the cause of his death, is peculiar to the case of homicide. And the principle on which this species of evidence is admitted, is, that it is a declaration made *in extremis*, when the party is at the point of death, and every hope in this world is gone; when every motive to falsehood is silenced, and the mind is induced by the most powerful considerations to speak the truth; a situation so solemn and awful, is considered by the law as creating an obligation equal to that imposed by a positive oath administered in a court of justice.

But before dying declarations can be admitted in evidence, it must clearly appear that the deceased himself was conscious of his approaching end, and that he must inevitably soon appear before his Maker to answer for the truth or falsehood of his assertions.(²) Therefore, if he have the slightest hope of recovery, no statement he may make, is admissible as a dying declaration.(³)

It is not necessary, however, that the deceased should actually express any apprehension of danger, for his consciousness of approaching death, may be inferred from the nature of the wound, or his state of illness or other circumstances of the case;(⁴) the true enquiry being as to his consciousness of his approaching end, which may be proved by any circumstance satisfactory to the mind of the court, for it is a question that must be decided by the court before the evidence is received, and not by the jury.(⁵)

It seems to be a general rule, that dying declarations are only admissible, when the death of the deceased is the *subject of the charge*, and the circumstances of the death, the subject of the dying declarations.(⁶) Thus, in a trial for robbery, the dying declarations of the party robbed, are inadmissible against the prisoner. So, too, when a party was indicted for

---

(¹) 3 B. & C. 750, 746.
(²) 1 Leach 502.
(³) 1 East P. C. 358; 2 Va. Cases 111; 3 Leigh 786; Hill's Case, 2 Gratt.; and see 2 Va. Cases 78.
(⁴) 1 East P. C. 158; 1 Leach 500; 2 Leach 561.
(⁵) 1 East P. C. 360; 1 Stark. R. 523.
(⁶) 2 B. & E. 608.

perjury, it was held, that an affidavit of the dying declarations of the prosecutor as to the transaction out of which the perjury arose, could not be read.([1])

The dying declarations of the wife, are admissible against her husband, on a charge of murder.([2])

2. *Confessions and admissions.*—A *free* and *voluntary* confession of guilt, if duly made and satisfactorily proved, is admissible in evidence, as the highest and most satisfactory degree of proof; because it is presumed that no man would make such a confession against himself, unless the facts confessed were true. And such a confession is sufficient alone to warrant a conviction without any corroborating evidence.([3])

But as the effect of a confession is so decisive against the prisoner, it is the more necessary, when it is not made to a person in authority, as to a Magistrate, that the evidence should be received with the greatest caution; for a confession made to a private person, or one of the subordinate officers of justice. is very liable to be obtained by artifice, false hopes, promises of favour, or menaces; it is likewise seldom remembered accurately or reported with precision, and it is incapable in its nature of being disproved by negative evidence.([4])

Any kind of threat or promise will prevent the confession from being received in evidence. Thus, to say to a prisoner, it will be worse for him if he does not confess, or it will be better for him if he does, is sufficient to exclude the confession.([5]) And when a confession has been obtained from the prisoner, by undue means, any statement afterwards made by him under the influence of that confession, cannot be admitted in evidence.([6])

But although a confession improperly obtained, is not admissible, yet any facts which are brought to light in consequence of the confession, such as the finding of stolen property in the possession of the prisoner, or his dealing with it as his own, may be given in evidence against him; because such facts would, unconnected with any confessions, have been clear evidence in support of the prosecution.([7])

3. *Hearsay evidence.*—As all evidence ought to be given under the sanction of an oath, and the person who states any fact affecting another, ought to do so in his presence, in order that his veracity and means of knowledge, may be probed by the party who is affected by his statement, it is therefore a

---

([1]) 2 B. & E. 605.
([2]) 1 Leach 500.
([3]) 2 Leach 554; 1 Leach 311, note; Russ. & Ry. 440; R. *v.* Faulkner, Id. 481.
([4]) 4 Bl. Com. 357; Fost. 243; 1 Leach 263.
([5]) 2 East P. C. 659.
([6]) 2 East P. C. 658; 1 Phil. Ev. 104.
([7]) Rex *v.* Warwickshall, 1 Leach 263; Mosey's Case, Id. 265.

general rule of law, that no hearsay evidence of a fact is admissible, but that the person who knows the fact must be himself called to prove it. But there are certain exceptions to this rule in case of death, or when the hearsay evidence is considered part of the *res gestae.*

Thus, if there has been a former trial in a civil cause between the same parties, and the point in issue was the same, the testimony of a deceased witness (given at the former trial) may be proved by any one who heard him give evidence; but this cannot be done in a criminal prosecution.(¹) There is also one peculiar kind of hearsay evidence, which (as we have before seen) is admitted in trials for homicide, namely, the declarations of the deceased as to the cause and the manner of the infliction of his mortal wound.

Hearsay evidence is also admissible as part of the *res gestae*, when it is not adduced as a medium of proof, to establish a distinct fact; for the entire exclusion of it, to explain a particular transaction, would be frequently to exclude the only evidence of which the nature of the case is capable. As in a prosecution for rape, or an assault with intent to commit one, the prosecutor may prove that the woman made a complaint against the prisoner recently after the injury, though the particulars of the complaint are not admissible.(²)

Declarations or statements of deceased persons, when they appear to be against their own interests, are also good evidence of the facts therein stated.(³)

4. *As to the evidence being confined to the point in issue.*— As has been before stated, it is a general rule, in the law of evidence, that the facts proved must be strictly relevant to the issue joined; and no facts can be admitted in proof against a prisoner, which have reference to his conduct, unconnected with the particular charge against him in the indictment; for it is this charge alone which he is expected to come prepared to answer.(⁴)

So, notwithstanding several felonies are alleged in the same indictment, it is usual to confine the evidence to one particular felony.(⁵)

But to this rule, there are sundry exceptions and modifications; for example, though it is not in general, allowable to enquire into any other stealing of goods, than that specified in the indictment, yet, for the purpose of ascertaining the iden-

---

(¹) Fin's Case, 5 Rand. 701.
(²) 2 Stark. Rep. 242; 1 East P. C. 444; 1 Phil. 222; Hill's Case, 2 Grattan.
(³) 10 East 109; R. & M. 62; 1 Phil. Ev. 250.
(⁴) 2 Leach 108; Fost. 245; Walker's Case, 2 Va. Cases.
(⁵) 3 T. R. 106; 3 Camp. 132; 8 East 41.

tity of the person, it is permitted to shew that other goods (stolen on the same night from an adjoining part of the premises) were afterwards found in the possession of the prisoner; for this is strong evidence of the prisoner having been near the prosecutor's house on the night of the robbery.(¹) And where several felonies are so connected together, that they form part of one entire transaction, then the one is evidence to shew the character of the other. As where the prisoner was seen to go to a till, in the prosecutor's shop, several times in the same day, and take some money every time, it was held that the prosecutor was not confined to the proof of one of these several acts of felony, but might give evidence of all, as forming an entire transaction.(²) So, where the prisoner was indicted for robbing the prosecutor of a coat, and it appeared that the robbery was effected by the prisoner's threatening to charge the prosecutor with an unnatural crime, evidence was held receivable of a second ineffectual attempt by the prisoner to obtain a £1 note from the prosecutor by similar threats.(³)

So, evidence of other offences committed by the prisoner, though not charged in the indictment, is admissible for the purpose of shewing a guilty *knowledge*. Thus, on an indictment for *uttering a forged bank note*, evidence may be given of other forged bank notes of the same manufacture having been uttered by the prisoner, in order to shew his knowledge of the forgery.(⁴) So, the possession of other forged notes may be proved, as evidence of a guilty knowledge.(⁵)

In like manner, the guilty intent with which an act is done, may be proved by other acts not specified in the indictment. Thus, where the prisoner is indicted for maliciously shooting at the prosecutor, and it is doubtful whether the shooting was by accident or design, proof may be given that the prisoner at *another time* intentionally shot at the same person.(⁶) So also, where three persons were indicted for *uttering a forged note*, evidence of other acts done by all of them jointly, or by any one of them separately, shortly before the offence, was held admissible to shew the confederacy and common purpose; although such acts might constitute distinct felonies.(⁷)

Where, also, several persons are proved to have been engaged in the same design, the acts and declarations of one, in furtherance of that design, may be received in evidence against

---

(¹) 1 Phil. Ev. 159.
(²) 6 B. & C. 145.
(³) Russ. & Ry. 375; and see N. R. 94, per Lord Ellenborough.
(⁴) 1 N. R. 92; 2 Leach 983; Russ. & Ry. 132; 1 Camp. 324.
(⁵) Russ. & Ry. 120; Id. 385.
(⁶) Russ. & Ry. 531.
(⁷) 1 Russ. 22.

another, though not present when the act was done or the declaration uttered.(¹)

The prisoner may always call witnesses to speak to his general character, but proof of particular transactions is not admissible; for it is *general* character alone, which can afford any test of general conduct.(²) The prosecutor cannot enquire into the defendant's character, unless the defendant enable him to do so, by calling witnesses in support of it, and even then the prosecutor cannot examine as to particular facts, the character of the defendant not being a direct matter in issue, but only coming in collaterally.(³)

II. *Of written evidence.*

This consists of proof, either of public or private documents. The first is so rarely called for in the exercise of either the civil or criminal jurisdiction of a Justice of the Peace, that this synopsis will be confined to the latter.

It is a strict rule, with respect to private documents, that when the instrument is attested by a *subscribing witness, that witness* must be called to prove its execution, if he can be produced, and is capable of being examined. And the rule applies not only to deeds and bonds, but also to agreements and promissory notes, or even a notice to quit, or a warrant to distrain.(⁴) So strictly, indeed, is the rule observed, that though the obligor of a bond is proved to have admitted its execution, or the party upon whom a notice is served, to have read it, and made no objection, the attendance of the attesting witness is not dispensed with.(⁵)

The exceptions to the above rule are, when the deed is thirty years old, in which case it proves itself;(⁶) when the attesting witness is dead,(⁷) or insane,(⁸) or blind,(⁹) or infamous,(¹⁰) or absent in a foreign country, and not amenable to the process of the court,(¹¹) or where he cannot be found after diligent enquiry,(¹²) or where he has become interested after the execution of the deed or other instrument.(¹³) In any of these cases, evidence of the handwriting of the witness is sufficient, without any further proof of the identity of the parties, than the identity of the name and description,(¹⁴)

(¹) 6 T. R. 528; Russ. & Ry. 305; Id. 343; Id. 446.
(²) 1 Phil. Ev. 166.
(³) B. N. P. 296.
(⁴) 2 M. & S. 62; 2 Stark. Rep. 210.
(⁵) 1 Doug. 216; 4 East 53; 2 M. & S. 62.
(⁶) B. N. P. 255.
(⁷) Anon. 12; Mod. 607.
(⁸) 3 Camp. 283.
(⁹) 1 Ld. R. 734.
(¹⁰) 2 Str. 833.
(¹¹) 2 East 250; 1 Stark. Rep. 190.
(¹²) 2 East 183.
(¹³) 1 Star. 34.
(¹⁴) Mood. & M. 79, 286.

although the party may only sign the instrument by his mark.(¹)

The handwriting of a party may be proved by any one who has seen him write, and though a witness says he has only seen him write once, yet if he thinks the signature is his handwriting, this is evidence to be weighed,(²) but not so where the witness has only seen the party write his name once, and then for the purpose of making the witness competent to give evidence in a controversy then pending.(³) It is sufficient if the witness has seen the party write his surname only.(⁴)

It is not essential to the proof of handwriting, that the witness should have seen the party write, for there are other means by which he may become acquainted with the handwriting. As a witness may testify as to handwriting from having carried on a correspondence with him, or from an acquaintance gained from having seen handwriting acknowledged to be his, or from having received promissory notes which the party has paid.(⁵)

It is an established rule, that the handwriting of a party cannot be proved, by comparing the signature with any other signature acknowledged to be genuine.(⁶)

The contents of a written instrument can only be proved by the instrument itself, unless it be lost, or be in the hands of the opposite party.(⁷) And this rule is so strict, that even the declarations of the party admitting the existence and validity of the instrument, are not receivable in evidence, unless the non-production of it be accounted for.(⁸)

When, however, there is independent parol evidence to prove the same facts contained in written evidence, then the mere existence of the written evidence will, in some cases, not exclude the parol testimony. Thus, where a memorandum of any transaction is made by a party for the purpose of assisting his recollection, this will not prevent the transaction being proved either by himself or any other witness, without the production of the writing.(⁹) So a receipt in writing, does not exclude the evidence of a witness who saw the money paid, or an admission of the party that he received the money.(¹⁰)

It is an established rule, that parol evidence cannot be introduced either to contradict or vary the terms of a contract in writing, though parol evidence may be admitted to explain

---

(¹) Mood. & M. 177.
(²) 4 Esp. 37.
(³) 1 Esp. 14.
(⁴) Mood. & M. 39.
(⁵) 19 John. 134; 6 Rand. 316.
(⁶) 1 Leigh 216; 4 Deac. 440.
(⁷) 8 B. & C. 708.
(⁸) 1 Ry. & M. 187.
(⁹) 3 B. & A. 326; 4 Esp. 163; 1 Stark. Ev. 394.
(¹⁰) 4 Esp. 213; 1 East 460.

a latent ambiguity, but not an ambiguity apparent upon the face of the instrument. (Chitty on Contracts.) Besides the rules of evidence which have been noted, there are others of a general character; some of them applicable alike both to written and parol evidence, which must now be noticed:

III. *Of general rules of evidence.*

1. *The best possible evidence must be produced.*—It is a general rule, that the best evidence must be produced of which the thing is capable. Thus, as we have seen, if there is a subscribing witness to a written instrument, and it be in the power of the party to produce him as a witness, proof of his handwriting is inadmissible, but if he be dead, the instrument is sufficiently proved, by proof of his handwriting.([1]) And upon the same principle, as has been before stated, the contents of a written instrument can only be proved by the instrument itself, unless it be lost, or in the hands of the opposite party. In such cases, proof of the loss or destruction in the one case, or of the fact of possession and notice to produce, in the other, renders secondary evidence admissible. This rule, requiring the production of the best evidence which the nature of the case is capable of, is founded upon the presumption of a fraudulent suppression of the better evidence, and therefore secondary evidence is in all cases admissible, when it is apparent that it is the best which the party, without any default, has in his power to produce. But to establish the loss of any document, it must be proved that diligent search has been made in every quarter where it was likely to be discovered, and the loss of it must be established with reasonable certainty.([2])

Where secondary evidence is sought to be given on the ground that the primary evidence is in the possession of the adverse party, the fact of such possession must be proved in the first instance, and with respect to the notice to produce, it may be given by parol as well as in writing, and if both the parol and written notice have been given, proof of either is sufficient.([3]) But before a party is permitted to give secondary evidence, the instrument itself must be proved to be genuine.([4])

2. *What allegations must be proved, and what is a variance.*—All the necessary allegations in an indictment, which are requisite to shew that the party committed the offence charged against him, must be strictly proved; and any difference in substance, between the statements in the indictment

([1]) 1 Phil. Ev. 209.
([2]) 8 East 273.
([3]) 1 Deac. 448; 1 Camp. 440.
([4]) 1 Atk. 246; and B. N. P. 254.

and the evidence, will be fatal. Thus, where a prisoner was indicted for *stealing sheep*, and upon the evidence, they appeared to be *lambs*, the variance was held fatal. So, upon the same principle, where a prisoner was indicted under Lord Ellenborough's act, for *cutting* J. S., and the evidence was, that the wound was inflicted by *stabbing*, and not by *cutting*, the Judges held, that as the statute used the alternative, "stab or cut," the variance was fatal.(¹)

3. *As to the proof of negative averments.*—It is another general rule of the law of evidence, that the affirmative of the issue alone, is proved; that is, that the party who asserts a fact, is bound to prove it, and that no party is bound to prove a negative.

But there is an exception, in criminal proceedings, to this general rule of the law of evidence, where the omission to do any act constitutes the offence. In this case, as the prosecutor is bound to aver, so he is also bound to prove the negative; for the law (in favour of innocence) universally presumes that a party has complied with its injunctions, until the contrary appears; and this presumption of law, making a *prima facie* case in the affirmative for the defendant, drives the prosecutor of course, to prove the negative.(²)

When the affirmative, however, is peculiarly within the knowledge of the party accused, the presumption of law in favour of innocence, is not then allowed to operate in his defence; but the general rule applies, that the party who asserts the affirmative, is bound to prove it; and this, notwithstanding the prosecutor is obliged to aver the negative. As in the case of a conviction for selling ale, or keeping an ordinary, without an excise license.(³)

Of compulsory means to obtain evidence by a Justice.

This book being principally confined to the duties of a Justice of the Peace out of court, we have only to notice here the means by which, either in the incipient state of criminal prosecutions, that is, on the information given before a Justice, of an offence having been committed, or on the hearing of some civil warrant, or a prosecution for a penalty within his jurisdiction, the Justice may require the attendance of a witness whose testimony he may deem important in the investigation of the matters pending before him.

The means of doing this, at Common Law, was by summons, and there is no doubt but that a Justice may in criminal prosecutions, as soon as complaint is made to him that an

---

(¹) Russ. & Ry. 356.
(²) 10 East 216; 2 B. & A. 386.
(³) 2 Russ. 693.

offence has been committed, summon a party as a witness to appear before him to give evidence touching the subject of complaint. And in all cases cognizable by him, the Justice has power by statute, to issue a summons for a witness residing in any county within the State, and it is the duty of such witness to attend, either in a civil or criminal proceeding. See § 20, chap. 176, and § 2, chap. 170.

The power of a Justice to attach a witness who refuses obedience to a summons, has been denied by an eminent criminal lawyer of England, Mr. Scarlett, afterwards Lord Abbinger, upon a trial before him at the Chester Spring Assizes, 1816, (referred to in the late edition of Burn's Justice,) but, with deference, we think, upon insufficient reasoning, or if sufficient, the power must be denied altogether, as well as the power to commit upon his refusal to testify when before the Justice, for it is upon the ground that no man should be deprived of his liberty for a moment who is not charged with any crime or the suspicion thereof. Every witness who refuses to attend the trial of a cause in court, however trivial, is liable by process of attachment to be thus deprived of his liberty. The crime charged upon him in that case, is his contempt of court, and of the Commonwealth's process of subpœna. Is that a greater crime than a contempt offered to the Commonwealth's process issued by any other competent authority to ensure his attendance to testify either for or against a party charged with felony? Surely not; and it would seem to be in vain to give the Justices power to enquire into crime, and to confer on them the power of convening courts for the further examination or trial of offenders, without the power to force the attendance of witnesses. Why go through all the forms of a summons, if indeed, it be nothing more than a mere request to the witness to attend, with which he may comply or not, at his pleasure? The author holds, with Mr. Chitty, that the Justice has the power to bring before him, all persons who appear upon the oath of the informer, or who may occur to the Magistrate himself, to be material witnesses for the prosecution, (and we add for the prisoner,) and for this purpose may issue his warrant to a Constable requiring him to cause the witness to appear before him and give evidence.[1] But the statute now expressly gives the power.

A witness duly summoned, is privileged from all arrest, (except for felony and actual breach of the peace,) while attending the Justice, and while going to or returning from his court.[2]

---

[1] 1 Chitty Cr. L. 76-7, and the autorities there cited; see also Dea. Guide 1451, where the power is expressly stated.
[2] 4 Call; Tidd's Practice.

EVIDENCE.

(No. 1.)

Form of a Summons for a witness in a criminal prosecution.

—— County, to wit:

To A. B., Constable of the said County:

Whereas, information has been made before me J. T., a Justice of the said County, that (here set forth the offence generally, as in the complaint or warrant of arrest,) and that M. M. is a material witness to be examined concerning the same: These are, therefore, in the name of the Commonwealth, to require you to summon the said M. M. to appear before me, at —— in the said County, on the —— day of ——— at the hour of ———, in the ——— noon of the same day, to testify his knowledge concerning the premises. Given under my hand and seal, this —— day of ——— 18—.

J. T., J. P. [L. S.]

(No. 2.)

Form of a Warrant to bring a witness who has refused to attend in pursuance of a summons.

—— County, to wit:

To all or any one of the Constables of said County:

These are, in the name of the Commonwealth of Virginia, to command you, and each of you, upon sight hereof, to take and bring before me, one of the Justices of the said County of ———, at ——— in the said County, on the —— day of ——— 18—, the body of M. M., then and there to answer all such matters and things, as on behalf of the said Commonwealth, shall be on oath objected against him, by A. B.: for, that he the said M. M., being a material witness to prove a certain felony lately committed, and having been duly summoned to give evidence touching the same, has neglected and refused to appear in pursuance of said summons. Given under my hand and seal, this —— day of ——— 18—.

J. T., J. P. [L. S.]

(No. 3.)

Form of a Commitment of a Witness for refusing to give evidence.

—— County, to wit:

To the Keeper of the Jail of said County:

Receive into your custody the body of M. M., herewith sent you, brought before me a Justice of the said County. For, that he the said M. M., having knowledge that a certain felony and robbery was committed upon the person of one C. D., (or "that a certain felony and larceny was committed in stealing the goods and chattels of one C. D.," or any other offence described in the complaint,) on the —— day of ——— last past, at the said County, touching which, the said M. M. can give material evidence, and has refused to be examined on oath respecting the same: You are, therefore, commanded the said M. M. in your jail and custody safely to keep, until he shall submit to be examined touching the said felony, or shall be discharged by due course of law; and for so doing, this shall be your warrant. Given under my hand and seal, this —— day of ——— 18—.

J. T., J. P. [L. S.]

(No. 4.)

Form of a Summons for a Witness in a civil warrant.

——— County, to wit:

To *A. B.*, *Constable of the said County:*

I, J. T., a Justice of the said County, do command you, that you summon C. D. to appear before me (or such other Justice as may be then and there sitting upon the trial of civil warrants,) on the —— day of ——— 18—, at ——— in the said County, to testify and the truth to say in behalf of E. F., in a certain matter of controversy depending and undetermined between E. F. and G. H., and have then and there this summons. Given under my hand and seal, this —— day of ——— 18—.

J. T., J. P. [L. S.]

(No. 5.)

Form of Commitment of a Witness refusing to recognize with surety to appear and give evidence.

——— County, to wit:

To *X. Y.*, *Constable of the said County, and to the Keeper of the Jail of said County:*

Whereas, A. B. who is a material witness for the Commonwealth against C. D., whom I, J. T., Justice of said County, have this day committed to the jail of said County, for feloniously (describe the offence generally,) that he may be examined (or *tried*, as the case may be,) for the said offence in the County Court of the said County, was this day required by me, as Justice as aforesaid, to enter into a recognizance, himself in the sum of $———, with one good surety in the like sum, to the Commonwealth of Virginia, conditioned for his the said A. B.'s appearance personally before the County Court of the said County, on the first day of the next term thereof, then and there to give evidence on behalf of the Commonwealth against the said C. D., touching the said felony; and he the said A. B. refused to enter into the said recognizance with surety as aforesaid, and being by me now required so to recognize with surety, still refuses so to do: These are, therefore, to command you, the said Constable, in the name of the Commonwealth, forthwith to convey the said A. B. to the jail of the said County, and there deliver him, together with this precept, to the keeper thereof. And you, the keeper of the said jail, are hereby commanded to receive and keep him the said A. B. in your jail and custody, until he shall so recognize, or be thence otherwise discharged by due course of law. Given under my hand and seal, this —— day of ——— 18—.

J. T., J. P. [L. S.]

EXAMINATION OF PRISONER AFTER ARREST.

See ARREST, page 66, and COURTS, page 199.

CHAPTER XXXIX.

EXTORTION—(*By officers.*)

For extortion by abducting children, see ABDUCTION.
For extortion by threats, see THREATS.
See RECORDS.
See BRIBERY AND CORRUPTION.

Extortion is an offence at Common Law against public justice, consisting in the unlawfully taking, by an officer under colour of his office, any money or other thing of value that is not due to him, or more than is due to him, or before any is due.([1]) The punishment for this offence at Common Law, is by fine and imprisonment, and also by removal from the office, in the execution of which it was committed.([2]) But this punishment is altered by the statute.

BY SEC. 17, CHAP. 194. If any officer for performing an official duty for which a fee or compensation is allowed or provided by law, *knowingly* demand and receive a greater fee or compensation than is so allowed or provided, he shall be fined not exceeding fifty dollars.

BY SEC. 18. If any person authorized by law to charge fees for services performed by him and issue bills therefor, fraudulently issue a fee bill for service not performed by him, or for more than he is entitled to, he shall be fined not exceeding five hundred dollars. And for this offence, by section 20 of the same chapter, he forfeits his office upon conviction, and is forever thereafter incapable of holding any post mentioned in the first section. *Chapter* 12.

It is extortion at Common Law, in a Jailor to obtain money from his prisoner by colour of his office, or in a Sheriff or his deputy to obtain his fees by refusing to execute process till they are paid, or to take a bond for them before they are due.([3])

But it is not criminal for an officer to take a reward voluntarily offered to him for the more diligent or expeditious performance of his duty.([4])

In the proceedings, a specific sum must be stated to have been actually received by the offender, for the taking, and not the extorsive agreement, is the offence, though it is not necessary to prove the exact sum.([5])

([1]) 1 Deac. Cr. C. 474; Co. Litt. 36.
([2]) Id.
([3]) 1 Deac. Cr. Co. 475.
([4]) 2 Inst. 210-11.
([5]) 1 Deac. 475; 1 Ld. Ray. 149; 2 Inst. 210-11.

EXTORTION—(*By officers.*) 263

Several persons may be indicted jointly for extortion, if all are concerned, and in an indictment for this offence, it must be alleged that the defendant took so much *extorsively* or by *colour of his office*, for these words are as essential in prosecutions for extortion, as *feloniously*, in an indictment for felony.(¹)

(No. 1.)

Form of Warrant of Arrest against an officer, for demanding a greater fee than is allowed by law.

———— County, to wit:

To all or any one of the Constables of said County:

Whereas, A. B. of said County, has this day made complaint and information on oath before me J. T., a Justice of the said County, that C. D., on the —— day of ———— 18—, in said County, he the said C. D. then being an inspector of flour at ————, in said County, duly appointed, did, as such inspector, inspect one barrel of flour for the said A. B., and did then and there knowingly demand and receive of the said A. B. for inspecting the same ———— cents, and which sum is more than the fee allowed and provided by law for the service aforesaid : These are, therefore, to command you, in the name of the Commonwealth of Virginia, forthwith to apprehend the said C. D., and bring him before me or some other Justice of the said County, to answer the said complaint, and to be farther dealt with according to law. Given under my hand and seal, this —— day of ———— 18—.

J. T., J. P. [L. S.]

(No. 2.)

Form of Warrant of Arrest against a Sheriff for similar offence.

———— County, to wit:

To all or any one of the Constables of said County:

Whereas, A. B. of said County, has this day made complaint and information on oath before me J. T., a Justice of the said County, that C. D., on the —— day of ———— 18—, in said County, he the said C. D., then being a deputy for A. R., Sheriff of said County, did levy a writ of *fieri facias* in behalf of the said A. B. upon the goods and chattels of E. F., and did, for levying the said writ as such deputy Sheriff, knowingly demand and receive of the said A. B. as fee for the said service, one dollar, (or whatever sum was received over the fee allowed by law,) which sum is more than the fee allowed and provided by law for the service aforesaid : These are, therefore, to command you, in the name of the Commonwealth of Virginia, forthwith to apprehend the said C. D., and bring him before me or some other Justice of the said County, to answer the said complaint, and to be farther dealt with according to law. Given under my hand and seal, this —— day of ———— 18—.

J. T., J. P. [L. S.]

───────────

(¹) 1 Deac. 475, citing 2 Salk. 680.

(No. 3.)

Form of Warrant of Arrest against a Clerk, for issuing fee bill for services not performed.

—— County, to wit:

To all or any one of the Constables of said County:

Whereas, A. B. of said County, has this day made complaint and information on oath before me J. T., a Justice of the said County, that C. D., on the —— day of —— 18—, in said County, (he the said C. D. then being the Clerk of the County Court of the said County,) did fraudulently issue a fee bill against him the said A. B., for issuing from his office as Clerk of the said Court, an attachment in the name of the said A. B., against the estate of one E. F., whereas in fact no such attachment was issued from the said office, and no such service was performed by him the said C. D., as Clerk of the said Court: These are, therefore, to command you, in the name of the Commonwealth of Virginia, forthwith to apprehend the said C. D., and bring him before me or some other Justice of the said County, to answer the said complaint, and to be farther dealt with according to law. Given under my hand and seal, this —— day of —— 18—.

J. T., J. P. [L. S.]

(No. 4.)

Form of Warrant of Arrest against Clerk, for issuing fee bill for more than legal fee.

—— County, to wit:

To all or any one of the Constables of said County:

Whereas, A. B. of said County, has this day made complaint and information on oath before me J. T., a Justice of the said County, that C. D., on the —— day of —— 18—, in said County, (he the said C. D. then being the Clerk of the County Court of the said County,) at the instance of the said A. B., did record in his office as Clerk aforesaid, a certain deed conveying real estate from one E. F. to him the said A. B., and that he the said C. D. thereafter, for recording the said deed in his said office, as such Clerk, fraudulently, did issue a fee bill against the said A. B. for one dollar, (or whatever the sum was,) which sum is more than he the said C. D. is authorized by law to charge for the service aforesaid, and to issue a fee bill therefor: These are, therefore, to command you, in the name of the Commonwealth of Virginia, forthwith to apprehend the said C. D., and bring him before me or some other Justice of the said County, to answer the said complaint, and to be farther dealt with according to law. Given under my hand and seal, this —— day of —— 18—.

J. T., J. P. [L. S.]

(No. 5.)

Form of Mittimus to answer an indictment for extortion.

Follow No. 9, under head of ARREST.

EXTORTION—(*By officers*)—(*Indictment for.*) 265

(No. 6.)

Form of Certificate of Commitment for extortion to be sent to the Clerk.

Follow No. 10, under head of ARREST.

(No. 7.)

Form of the same where the party is admitted to bail.

Follow No. 11, under head of ARREST.

(No. 8.)

Form of Recognizance of Bail to answer an indictment for extortion.

Follow No. 4, under head of RECOGNIZANCE.

(No. 9.)

Form of Recognizance of Witness, to appear and give evidence on the indictment.

Follow No. 5, under head of RECOGNIZANCE.

Form of an Indictment against a Constable for extortion.

—— County, to wit: } The jurors of the Commonwealth of Virginia, in and for the body of the County of said County. } ——, and now attending the County Court of the said County, upon their oath present, that A. B. of the said County, on the —— day of —— 18—, he the said A. B. then being one of the Constables of the said County, duly and legally qualified to perform the duties of the said office of Constable in the County aforesaid, not regarding the duties of his said office, but contriving and intending one C. D. to injure and oppress, on the day and year aforesaid, in the County aforesaid, by colour of his said office of Constable as aforesaid, did knowingly and extorsively demand and receive of him the said C. D., a greater fee and compensation than is allowed aforesaid by law, for levying a certain warrant of distress for rent, duly and lawfully issued by J. T., a Justice of the said County, at the instance and on behalf of the said C. D., against the goods of one E. F., to wit, the sum of $ 2 for the said levy, and which said sum of $ 2 for the levy aforesaid, is a greater fee and compensation than the fee and compensation allowed and provided by law for the service aforesaid, against the peace and dignity of the Commonwealth of Virginia.

CHAPTER XL.

FALSE PRETENCES AND FALSE TOKENS.

[For cheats at Common Law, see CHEATS.]

By Sec. 30, Chap. 192. If a free person obtain, by any false pretence or token, from any person, with intent to defraud, money or other property which may be the subject of larceny, he shall be deemed guilty of the larceny thereof; or if he obtain, by any false pretence or token, with such intent, the signature of any person to a writing, the false making whereof would be forgery, he shall be confined in the penitentiary not less than one nor more than five years, or at the discretion of the jury, if the accused be a white person, or of the court, if he be a negro, be confined in jail not more than one year, and be fined not exceeding five hundred dollars.

The offence of personating another, for the purpose of fraud, whether money or other property be thereby received or not, is a misdemeanor at Common Law;(¹) and if money or other property be actually received, the offence will be felony under the statute, being embraced in the term "false pretence." Whether a party expressly represents himself to be another person, or merely tacitly assumes the character of another person, without making any assertion that he is such person, he is equally guilty of this offence.(²)

False token and counterfeit letters.—A false token is some real visible mark or thing, such as a key or ring, &c., presented by the party as coming from a third person, by which the person defrauded is deceived. And a counterfeit letter is a letter in the name of a third person.(³) So that, without the term "false pretence," recently introduced into the statute, if a party practised a cheat, not affecting the public, by his own assertion or representation, however false or fraudulent, without the intervention of the name of a third party, or without the use of some false token, he was guilty of no offence; but more effectually to prevent private cheats, this term "false pretence" was introduced into the statute, and embraces both false tokens and counterfeit letters.

False pretence.—However general these words are, judicial construction has endeavoured to assign them a limit, by

---

(¹) 2 East P. C. 1010. (³) 2 East P. C. 832, 689; 2 Va.
(²) Rex *v.* Story, Russ. & Ry. 81; 3 Cases 67, in note.
T. R. 98.

holding that they extend no farther than to cases where a party has obtained money or property by falsely representing himself to be in a situation in which he is not, or falsely representing any occurrence which has not happened, to which persons of ordinary caution might give credit, and that they do not extend to a case where the pretence is absurd and irrational, or to such as the party injured, had at the time the means of detection at hand,(¹) and that it is the province of the jury to determine, by the circumstances of the case, whether the pretences were calculated to deceive a man of ordinary intelligence and caution, or whether the goods were obtained from the owner by his own imprudence and want of proper caution.(²) This is a salutary statute, and in applying the above rule of construction, the Justice should not require any great degree of caution and prudence in the party injured, for as the gist of the offence consists in obtaining the property of another by practising a fraud, and not in the ingenuity of the device, it would seem that the guilt of the party is not the less, because the victim of his perfidy is more credulous, and therefore more liable to be cheated than others, and that the degree of prudence to be used by the party injured should have little weight in determining the guilt of the offender. This suggestion is sustained by Whichell's case,(³) in which the court said, "that *all cases* where the false pretence creates the credit are within the statute," and Lord Kenyon remarked upon this very general term, (false pretence,) " that when the criminal law happened to be auxiliary to the law of morality, he felt no inclination to explain it away."

As in larceny, so in this offence, the fraudulent intent must exist at the time the property is obtained, for if the original motive were honest, and the fraudulent design to cheat, conceived after the property was obtained, the case will not be an offence under the statute, though it may be embezzlement. The evidence of the fraudulent intent existing at the time, may be inferred as well from the subsequent conduct of the party, as from his acts and declarations at the time of the transaction.(⁴)

It is not necessary that the pretence should be in words; the conduct and acts of the party will be sufficient, without any verbal representation. Thus, if a person fraudulently obtain goods from another, by giving him in payment, his

---

(¹) 2 Penn. L. Journal 243 ; 4 Hill 9 ; 1 Carr. & Marsh. 251 ; Goodall's Case, R. & R. 461.
(²) 1 Wheel. C. C. 465 ; 11 Wend. 557.
(³) 2 East 830.
(⁴) 2 Penn. Law Jour. 241 ; 3 Id. 86 and 219.

check on a bank, in which he has no account, this is a false pretence under the statute.(¹) So, where a man obtained goods and money for a forged note of hand, for £ 10. 6., knowing it to be forged, it was held to be a false pretence within the statute.(²) And so, where a person at Oxford, who was not a member of the University, went to a shop for the purpose of fraud, wearing a commoner's cap and gown, and obtained goods, this appearing in a cap and gown was held a sufficient false pretence to satisfy the statute, though nothing passed in words.(³) Where the defendants falsely pretended that they had made a bet with A. B., that one of them should run ten miles within an hour, prevailed upon J. N. to join them in the bet, and obtained from him twenty guineas as his share in it, the Judges held this to be within the statute, notwithstanding the pretence was probably one against which common prudence might have guarded.(⁴) One obtaining money falsely under the guise of an attorney, is guilty of this offence ; as where an attorney, who had appeared for a person who had been fined £ 2 on a summary conviction, (before two Magistrates,) called on the person's wife and told her that he had been with another person, who was also fined £ 2 for a like offence, to Mr. B. and Mr. L., (the Magistrates,) and that he had prevailed on them to take £ 1 instead of £ 2, and that if she would give him £ 1, he would go and do the same for her, which she did, and afterwards paid him for his trouble, when, in fact, he never applied to either of the Magistrates respecting either of the fines, and both of which were afterwards paid in full, it was held that the attorney was guilty of obtaining money by false pretences.(⁵)

On an indictment which charged the prisoner with falsely pretending that a post-dated check, drawn by himself, was a good and genuine order for £ 25, and of the value of £ 25, by means of which he obtained a watch and chain, the jury found that the prisoner, before the completion of the sale, by the delivery of the goods, represented to the prosecutor, that he then had an account with bankers at Bristol, trading under the firm of Stuckey & Co., and then had a right to draw on them, though he postponed the date of the check, for his own convenience only, to a future day ; that such representation was false, and that the prisoner, at the time of making it, knew it was so, and that he represented to the prosecutor, before the completion of the sale, by the delivery of the goods, that the

---

(¹) Jackson's Case, 3 Camp. 370.
(²) Furth's Case, Russ. & Ry. 127.
(³) Rex v. Barnard, 32 Com. L. R. 736.
(⁴) Young's Case, 3 T. R. 98.
(⁵) Rex v. Asterly, 32 Com. L. R. 490.

check would be paid on presentment, on or after the day of the date, and that he had no reasonable ground to believe it would be paid at the time, or that he would be able to provide funds for it. Upon this verdict the prisoner was convicted of obtaining goods by false pretences.(¹)

And so, where a married man addressed a woman possessed of considerable property, and obtained a promise of marriage from her, which she afterwards refused to ratify, (not then knowing he was married,) threatened her with an action at law, for breach of marriage promise, telling her at the time, that, by means of such proceeding, he could take half her fortune from her, and she believing that he could and would carry his threat into effect, paid him a sum of money to induce him to refrain from doing so, he was found guilty and convicted, upon the ground that the money was obtained by the false pretence that the prisoner was a single man and in a condition to intermarry with the prosecutrix; and one of the Judges (Maule) was of opinion that the false pretence of the prisoner that he was entitled to maintain an action for breach of promise of marriage, was of itself a sufficient false pretence within the statute.(²)

Where one falsely pretended that he was the individual who had performed a certain cure, and thereby induced another person to buy quack medicine from him, it was held obtaining money by false pretence.(³)

Where a carrier, falsely pretending that he had carried certain goods to A. B., demanded and thereupon received from the consignor sixteen shillings for the carriage of the goods, it was holden to be within the statute;(⁴) and where the foreman of a manufactory, who was in the habit of receiving from his master money to pay the workmen, obtained from him, by means of false written accounts of the wages earned by the men, more than the men had earned, or than he had paid them, it was held to be an offence within the statute; and the Judges said in this case, that all cases *where the false pretence creates the credit are within the statute*, and that the defendant would not have obtained the excess above what was really due to the workmen, were it not for the false account he had delivered to his master.(⁵)

So, where the prisoner went to a tradesman's house and said she came from a neighbour, who would be much obliged if he would let her have half a guinea's worth of silver, and

---

(¹) Rex v. Parker, 32 Com. L. R. 755.
(²) The Queen v. Copeland, 41 Com. L. R. 282.
(³) Bloomfield's Case, 41 Com. L. R. 293.
(⁴) 2 East P. C. 672; 2 East R. 30.
(⁵) 2 East P. C. 830.

that she would send the half guinea presently, this was held to be obtaining money by false pretences, and not larceny.(¹)

The pretence must be of some existing fact made for the purpose of inducing the person to part with his property, and therefore, a pretence that a party *will do* an act that he did not mean to do, as to pay for goods on delivery, is not a false pretence within the meaning of the statute, but merely a promise for future conduct.(²)

The obtaining goods by false pretences does not change the property in the goods.(³) To complete the offence, the goods must actually be obtained; the mere attempt to obtain goods, by false pretence, being a misdemeanor only at Common Law,(⁴) but punishable under another branch of the statute. See title ATTEMPTS.

These words "false pretence," have no technical meaning in law; they are as explicit as the use of other words can render them; and we conclude by repeating, that the offence consists in obtaining other men's property by any false pretence whatever of an existing fact, with intent at the time to commit a fraud; and that whenever this is done under such circumstances as do not amount to larceny, the party is guilty of felony under the statute, and should be committed for examination or trial, according to the following forms:

(No. 1.)

Form of Warrant of Arrest for obtaining goods under false pretence.

—— County, to wit:

To X. Y., *Constable of the said County:*

Whereas, complaint and information has this day been made to me J. T., Justice of said County, upon the oath of A. B., that on the —— day of —— 18—, in said County, C. D. did feloniously, by false pretence then and there made by him, that is to say, (here state briefly the false pretence) obtain certain goods, to wit, (state what) the property of the said A. B., of and from the said A. B., with intent to defraud: These are, therefore, in the name of the Commonwealth, to command you forthwith to apprehend the said C. D., and to bring him before me or some other Justice of said County, to answer the said complaint, and to be farther dealt with according to law. Given under my hand and seal, this —— day of —— 18—.

J. T., J. P. [L. S.]

(¹) 2 East P. C. 672; 2 Leach 303, in note.
(²) Goodall's Case, R. & R. 461; Rex *v.* Clifford, Carrington 334.
(³) Noble *v.* Adams, 7 Taunt. 59.
(⁴) 1 Deac. C. Co. 231.

(No. 2.)

Form of Warrant of Arrest against a party for obtaining money by false pretences.

—— County, to wit:

To all or any one of the Constables of said County:

Whereas, A. B. of said County, has this day made complaint and information on oath before me J. T., a Justice of the said County, that C. D., on the —— day of —————— 18—, in said County, did falsely and feloniously pretend and represent to the said A. B., that he the said C. D. was sent and authorized by E. F. to demand and receive from him the said A. B., for the use of the said E. F., the sum of —————— dollars, and did, by means of the said false pretence, feloniously obtain from the said A. B., the sum of —————— dollars, with intent to defraud: These are, therefore, to command you, in the name of the Commonwealth of Virginia, forthwith to apprehend the said C. D., and bring him before me or some other Justice of the said County, to answer the said complaint, and to be farther dealt with according to law. Given under my hand and seal, this —— day of —————— 18—.

J. T., J. P. [L. S.]

(No. 3.)

Form of Warrant of Arrest for obtaining money under false pretences of drawing an order on a person who the offender pretended was indebted to him and would pay his order.

—— County, to wit:

To all or any one of the Constables of said County:

Whereas, A. B. of said County, has this day made complaint and information on oath before me J. T., a Justice of the said County, that C. D., on the —— day of —————— 18—, in said County, did falsely and feloniously pretend and represent to the said A. B., that one E. F., residing at ——————, would accept and pay a certain order in writing, for money then and there drawn by the said C. D. upon the said E. F., and dated the —— day of —————— 18—, and whereby the said C. D. required the said E. F. to pay to him the said A. B., the sum of —————— dollars, and then and there delivered the same to the said A. B., by which false pretence the said C. D. did, on the —— day of —————— 18—, feloniously obtain from the said A. B., the said sum of money, with intent to defraud, and that in truth and in fact he the said C. D. had no right to require the said E. F. to accept and pay the said order; and the said E. F. would not and did not accept and pay the same: These are, therefore, to command you, in the name of the Commonwealth of Virginia, forthwith to apprehend the said C. D., and bring him before me or some other Justice of the said County, to answer the said complaint, and to be farther dealt with according to law. Given under my hand and seal, this —— day of —————— 18—.

J. T., J. P. [L. S.]

(No. 4.)

Form of Warrant of Arrest for obtaining property by false token or by counterfeit letter.

—— County, to wit:
  To all or any one of the Constables of said County:
  Whereas, A. B. of said County, has this day made complaint and information on oath before me J. T., a Justice of the said County, that C. D., on the —— day of ——— 18—, in said County, did feloniously and falsely, by means of a certain false token, (or *counterfeit letter*,) obtain from the said A. B., divers goods and chattels, the property of the said A. B., to wit: (here describe the goods,) of the value of ——— dollars, with intent to defraud: These are, therefore, to command you, in the name of the Commonwealth of Virginia, forthwith to apprehend the said C. D., and bring him before me or some other Justice of the said County, to answer the said complaint, and to be farther dealt with according to law. Given under my hand and seal, this —— day of ——— 18—.

J. T., J. P. [L. S.]

(No. 5.)

Form of Warrant of Arrest for obtaining a signature to a receipt by false pretence.

—— County, to wit:
  To all or any one of the Constables of said County:
  Whereas, A. B. of said County, has this day made complaint and information on oath before me J. T., a Justice of the said County, that C. D., on the —— day of ——— 18—, in said County, did feloniously and falsely pretend that he the said C. D. had paid to one E. F., the agent of the said A. B., the sum of ——— dollars, being the amount of a debt due from the said C. D. to the said A. B., and did thereby feloniously obtain from the said A. B. his signature to a certain written instrument, to wit, a receipt in full of all demands, with intent to defraud: These are, therefore, to command you, in the name of the Commonwealth of Virginia, forthwith to apprehend the said C. D., and bring him before me or some other Justice of the said County, to answer the said complaint, and to be farther dealt with according to law. Given under my hand and seal, this —— day of ——— 18—.

J. T., J. P. [L. S.]

(No. 6.)

Form of Warrant of Arrest for obtaining property by falsely personating another.

—— County, to wit:
  To all or any one of the Constables of said County:
  Whereas, A. B. of said County, has this day made complaint and information on oath before me J. T., a Justice of the said County, that C. D., on the —— day of ——— 18—, in said County, did falsely and feloniously

personate and represent himself to the said A. B. to be one E. F., and in such assumed name and character, did then and there feloniously receive from the said A. B., a certain gold watch, of the value of fifty dollars, intended by the said A. B. to be delivered to the said E. F., with intent to convert the same to his use : These are, therefore, to command you, in the name of the Commonwealth of Virginia, forthwith to apprehend the said C. D., and bring him before me or some other Justice of the said County, to answer the said complaint, and to be farther dealt with according to law. Given under my hand and seal, this ―― day of ―――― 18――.

J. T., J. P. [L. S.]

[NOTE.—The word "property" is of very general import, and includes money and bank notes, as well as any thing else of value, and the foregoing form will answer for any kind of property, by describing it and stating its value, as for instance, ten pieces of silver coin, current in this Commonwealth, of the value of ten dollars; or one bank note, of the value of ten dollars.]

(No. 7.)

Form of Mittimus where a party is committed for examination or trial in the County Court for felony, in obtaining goods by false pretence.

―――― County, to wit :

 To X. Z., *Constable of said County, and to the Keeper of the Jail of said County :*

These are to command you, the said Constable, in the name of the Commonwealth of Virginia, forthwith to convey and deliver into the custody of the keeper of the said jail, together with this warrant, the body of C. D., a white person (or *free negro*, or *a slave, the property of E. F.*, as the case may be,) charged before me J. T., a Justice of the said County, on the oath of A. B., with a felony by him committed, in this that the said C. D., on the ―― day of ―――― in the year 18―, in the said County, (here describe the offence as in the warrant of arrest.) And you, the said keeper of the said jail, are hereby required to receive the said C. D. into your jail and custody, that he may be examined (or *tried*) for the said offence, by the County Court of said County, and him there safely keep, until he shall be discharged by due course of law. Given under my hand and seal, this ―― day of ―――― in the year 18―.

J. T., J. P. [L. S.]

[NOTE.—If the prisoner be a white person, he must be committed for examination. If a negro, he must be committed for trial.]

(No. 8.)

Form of Certificate of Commitment to be sent to the Clerk of the County Court.

―――― County, to wit :

 To the Clerk of the County Court of said County :

I, J. T., a Justice of the said County, do hereby certify, that I have, by my warrant, this day committed C. D. (if free negro or slave, state which) to the jail of this County, that he may be examined (or *tried*) before the County Court of the said County, for a felony by him committed, in this that he did, on the —— day of —————— 18—, in the said County, (here state the offence as in the mittimus.) Given under my hand, this —— day of —————— in the year 18—.

J. T., J. P.

(No. 9.)

Form of Certificate to the Clerk where party is admitted to bail.

Turn to head of ARREST, and follow No. 6.

(No. 10.)

Form of Recognizance of Bail.

Turn to head of RECOGNIZANCE, and follow No. 1, if person be free; No. 2, if a slave, and state succinctly the offence for which the person is recognized.

(No. 11.)

Form of Recognizance of Witness to appear before the County Court to give evidence upon the examination or trial of a party charged with felony, in obtaining goods by false pretence.

Turn to head of RECOGNIZANCE, and follow No. 3.

An Indictment for obtaining property by false pretence.

—————— Judicial Circuit. \
—————— County, to wit: \
In the Circuit Court of the \
said County.

The jurors of the Commonwealth of Virginia, in and for the body of the County of ——————, now attending the Circuit Court of the said County, on their oath present, that A. B. of the said County, intending feloniously to defraud one C. D. of his property, on the —— day of —————— in the year ——————, in the County aforesaid, feloniously did falsely pretend to him the said C. D. that he the said A. B. then was the servant of one E. F. of ——————, tailor, (the said E. F. then and long before being well known to the said C. D., and a customer of the said C. D. in his business and way of trade as a merchant,) and that he the said A. B. was then sent by the said E. F. to the said C. D. for ten yards of certain superfine woollen cloth; by which said false pretence, the said A. B. did then and there, to wit, on the day and year aforesaid, in the County aforesaid, feloniously obtain from the said C. D. ten yards of superfine woollen cloth of the value of fifty dollars, of the goods, chattels and property of the said C. D., with intent to defraud him the said C. D. Whereas, in truth and in fact, the said A. B. was not then the servant of the said E. F., and whereas, he the said A. B. was not then, or ever hath been sent by the said E. F. to the said C. D. for the said cloth, or for any cloth whatever; and so the jurors aforesaid, upon their oath aforesaid, do say, that the said A. B., then and there, in manner and form aforesaid, the said ten yards of superfine woollen cloth, of the goods and chattels of the said C. D., and of the value aforesaid, feloniously did steal, take and carry away, against the peace and dignity of the Commonwealth of Virginia.

[Add count for larceny.]

In drawing an indictment under the statute, take care to state accurately the pretence. A general allegation that the goods were obtained by false pretence will not suffice ; and care must be taken to negative the pretence. By attention to these requisites, with the aid of the foregoing precedent, it will be easy to frame an indictment to meet any case arising under the statute.

If several persons are present at the time of the false pretence and concur in the fraud, though the words are uttered by one only, all may be included in the indictment; for the act of one is the act of all. (Rex v. Young and als., 3 T. R. 98.) Nor is it any objection that the same indictment includes several charges. (Id.) A mere allegation in the words of the statute, that the defendant obtained the goods by a false pretence will not suffice ; the false pretences must be set out, and the truth of them distinctly negatived, and the evidence must sustain the allegation. (Rex v. Parott, 2 M. & S. 379, 386.) It is not necessary, however, that the whole representation set out, should be stated or proved to have been false ; nor that all the allegations either of pretence or falsehood should be proved ; it will suffice if any untrue allegation of pretence and falsehood is sustained, if it appear that such pretence was the efficient cause of the success of the fraud. (Rex v. Hill, Russ. & Ry. 190.)

CHAPTER XLI.

FELONIES—(*Compounding or concealing of.*)

BY SEC. 16, CHAP. 194. If a free person knowing of the commission of an offence, take any money or reward, or an engagement therefor, upon an agreement or understanding, express or implied, to compound or conceal such offence, or not to prosecute therefor, or not to give evidence thereof, he shall, if such offence be felony, be confined in jail not more than one year, and fined not exceeding five hundred dollars; and if such offence be not a felony, *unless it be punishable merely by a forfeiture to him*, he shall be confined in jail not more than six months, and fined not exceeding one hundred dollars.

(No. 1.)

Form of Warrant for compounding and concealing murder.

———— County, to wit:

To X. Y., Constable of the said County:

Whereas, A. B. of said County, has this day made complaint on oath, before me J. T., a Justice of the said County, that C. D., on the ——— day of ——— 18—, in said County, did feloniously kill and murder one E. F., and that afterwards, to wit, on the ——— day of ——— 18—, in the said County, G. H., well knowing that the said felony and murder had been committed by the said C. D., did, for the sake of gain, take upon himself to compound and conceal the said felony and murder, and did then and there take and receive from the said C. D. the sum of ——— dollars, as a reward for compounding and concealing the said felony and murder, (or *to abstain from any prosecution for the said felony*, or *to withhold all evidence of the said felony and murder*:) These are, therefore, to command you, in the name of the Commonwealth, forthwith to apprehend the said G. H., and bring him before me or some other Justice of the said County, to answer the said complaint, and to be farther dealt with according to law. Given under my hand and seal, this ——— day of ——— 18—.

J. T., J. P. [L. S.]

(No. 2.)

Form of Warrant for concealment only.

———— County, to wit:

To X. Y., Constable of the said County:

Whereas, A. B. of said County, has this day made complaint on oath, before me J. T., a Justice of the said County, that C. D., well knowing that a felony and murder had been committed by E. F., in feloniously and of his malice, killing J. S., in the said County, on the ——— day of ——— 18—, did, for reward received by him, conceal his knowledge of the said felony

FELONIES—(*Compounding or concealing of.*)   277

and murder: These are, therefore, in the name of the Commonwealth, to command you to apprehend the said C. D., and bring him before me or some other Justice of the said County, to answer the said complaint, and to be farther dealt with according to law. Given under my hand and seal, this —— day of —— 18—.

J. T., *J. P.* [L. s.]

(No. 3.)

Form of Warrant of Arrest for compounding and concealing larceny.

—— County, to wit:

To X. Y., *Constable of the said County:*

Whereas, A. B. has this day made complaint on oath, before me J. T., a Justice of said County, that C. D. did, on the —— day of —— 18—, in the said County, feloniously steal, take and carry away one bank note of the value of one hundred dollars, of the money and property of E. F., and that the said E. F., knowing the said C. D. to have committed the said felony, did, on the —— day of ——18—, in the said County, take of the said C. D., the sum of —— dollars, as a reward to compound and conceal the said felony, and that the said E. F. did conceal the same: These are, therefore, to command you, in the name of the Commonwealth of Virginia, forthwith to apprehend the said E. F., and to bring him before me or some other Justice of the said County, to answer the said complaint, and to be farther dealt with according to law. Given under my hand and seal, this —— day of —— 18—.

J. T., *J. P.* [L. s.]

(No. 4.)

Form of Mittimus for compounding felony.

Follow No. 9, under head of ARREST.

(No. 5.)

Form of Recognizance of Bail to appear and answer an indictment for compounding felony.

Follow No. 4, under head of RECOGNIZANCE.

(No. 6.)

Form of Certificate of Commitment or letting to bail to be sent to the Clerk.

Follow No. 10 or 11, under head of ARREST, as the case may be.

278 FELONIES—(*Compounding, &c.*)—(*Indictment for.*)

Indictment for compounding a felony.

Commence as No. 1, under the head of "INDICTMENTS," and proceed thus: that A. B., on the ——— day of ———, in the County aforesaid, came before C. D. Esq., then being one of the Justices of the Peace in and for the said County of ———, duly and legally authorized and qualified to execute and perform the duties of that office, and then and there upon his oath did charge, accuse and complain against one E. F., for feloniously stealing (here set forth the complaint;) upon which accusation and complaint, the said C. D. Esq., issued his warrant, under his hand and seal, in due form of law, for the apprehending and taking the said E. F. to answer to, and be examined and dealt with, touching and concerning the felony aforesaid, so as aforesaid charged upon him the said E. F., as to law and justice might appertain. And the jurors aforesaid, upon their oath aforesaid, do farther present, that afterwards, to wit, on the ——— day of ——— in the year aforesaid, in the County aforesaid, the said E. F. was duly arrested and taken by virtue of the said warrant, for the felony aforesaid ; and was then and there carried before the said C. D. Esq,, the Justice aforesaid, and was then and there examined by him the said Justice, of and concerning the felony aforesaid ; and the subject matter of said complaint was examined into and heard by the said Justice. Upon which said examination and hearing, the said C. D. Esq., did then and there make a certain warrant, under his hand and seal, in due form of law, directed to the keeper of the jail of the said County, thereby commanding the aforesaid keeper to receive into his custody the body of the said E. F., so charged with such felony as aforesaid, and him in his custody safely to keep, until he should be discharged by due course of law. And the jurors aforesaid, upon their oath aforesaid, do farther present, that the said A. B. well knowing the premises, but contriving and intending unlawfully and unjustly to pervert the due course of law in this behalf, and to cause and procure the said E. F., for the felony aforesaid, to escape with impunity, afterwards, to wit, on the ——— day of ——— in the County aforesaid, unlawfully, and for the sake of private gain, did take upon himself to compound the said felony, on behalf of the said E. F., and then and there did take and receive of the said E. F., money, to wit, the sum of ——— dollars, for and as a reward for compounding the said felony, and for desisting from all farther prosecution against the said E. F. for the same ; and that the said A. B. did, for the reward aforesaid, received by him as aforesaid, compound the felony aforesaid, and did desist from all farther prosecution against the said E. F. for the same, against the peace and dignity of the Commonwealth of Virginia.

CHAPTER XLII.

FINES AND SUMMARY CONVICTIONS.

The jurisdiction conferred upon Justices out of court, to try and punish negroes for petit larceny and other misdemeanors committed by them, and to enforce fines, limited in amount to twenty dollars, in all cases, devolves upon them many and important duties.

By Sec. 8, Chap. 200. A negro shall be punished with stripes:

First. If he use provoking language or menacing gestures to a white person.

Secondly. If he furnish a slave, without the consent of his master or manager, any pass, permit or token of his being from home with authority.

Thirdly. If he keep or carry fire arms, sword or other weapon, or balls or ammunition, besides forfeiting to the State any such articles in his possession.

Fourthly. If he be guilty of being in a riot, rout, unlawful assembly, or making seditious speeches.

Fifthly. If he sell, or attempt to sell, or prepare or administer any medicine, except a slave administering medicine by his master's order, in his family or the family of another, with the consent of such other; and except a free negro, administering medicine in his own family or the family of another person, with the consent of such other.

These are specified offences created by statute, and for the punishment of all other misdemeanors committed by slaves, it is provided by the 7th section, that if a slave commit an offence, the commission whereof by a free person is punishable as a misdemeanor, he shall be punished by stripes.

By Sec. 13, Chap. 212. A slave shall be tried for a misdemeanor by a Justice of the county or corporation in which the offence is committed.

By Sec. 14. A free negro shall be tried by such Justice, for a misdemeanor punishable by stripes; for any other misdemeanor, he may be tried as other free persons. But a Justice, before whom a free negro is charged with a misdemeanor, punishable by fine and imprisonment or either, may either try him and inflict on him such punishment as he would inflict on a slave for the same offence, or commit or recognize him for trial at the next court of the county or corporation at which a grand jury will be impanneled.

By Sec. 15. In the case of a negro convicted of a misdemeanor by a Justice, there may be an appeal from the decision to the county or corporation court, by the negro, if free, or if he be a slave, by his owner. Such negro shall, unless let to bail, be committed by the Justice to jail until the next term of such court, and the witnesses shall also be recognized to appear then.

By Sec. 16. Every such appeal shall be tried without pleadings in writing, and without a continuance, except for good cause; the court shall hear all the evidence produced on either side, and give such judgment as seems to it proper, and enforce the execution thereof.

By Sec. 9, Chap. 200. Whenever, by statute, punishment with stripes is prescribed, the number of stripes shall be in the discretion of the Court or Justice by whom the offence is tried, so as not to exceed thirty-nine at one time.

As to the imposition of fines, by section 1st, chapter 43, where any statute imposes a fine, unless it be otherwise expressly provided, or would be inconsitent with the manifest intention of the Legislature, it shall be to the Commonwealth, and recoverable by presentment, indictment or information. Where a fine, without corporal punishment, is prescribed, the same may be recovered, if limited to an amount not exceeding twenty dollars, by warrant, and if not so limited, by action of debt or action on the case, or by motion. The proceeding shall be in the name of the Commonwealth. And by the 2d section, such warrant may be either in the county or corporation wherein the offence was committed or wherein the offender resides.

If the fine for any offence be not limited to twenty dollars, a Justice has no authority to try the offender, and therefore, though the minimum fine be even under twenty dollars, if the maximum be over, the case is not within his jurisdiction to try.

This authority to examine and punish offences in a summary manner, by Justices out of court, is an innovation upon the Common Law trial by jury, and the proceedings under it must conform strictly to the requisitions of the statute creating the offence. In the exercise of this jurisdiction, there are certain principles to be observed, in relation, 1st, to the local limits of the jurisdiction of the Justice; 2d, the proceedings preliminary to the conviction; 3d, to the conviction itself; and 4th, to the proceedings subsequent to the conviction; to each of which the attention of the Justice will now be directed.

FINES AND SUMMARY CONVICTIONS. 281

I. *As to the local limits of his jurisdiction to convict in a summary way.*

It is confined, at Common Law, to offences committed within his county, but the statute has extended it to the county in which the offender resides. Though an act expressly directs the offence to be enquired of by Justices residing near the place where it was committed, that does not give jurisdiction to any other than Justices of the county within which the offence was committed,(¹) or under the statute to those of the county in which the offender resides. There are but few exceptions to this general rule, and they relate generally to offences against the rights of particular individuals to whom the penalty is given, and is recoverable in their name by warrant in debt.

The Justices of a county, and the Justices of a city or borough, sitting in that county, have concurrent jurisdiction in summary convictions for fines, unless the jurisdiction of a county Magistrate be taken away by express statute.(²)

All Justices of the county are equal in authority, but as it would be against the public interest, as well as indecent, that there should be a contest between different Justices, the jurisdiction in a particular case, attaches to the first Justice who has possession and cognizance of the fact; so that the acts of any other, except in conjunction with him, are said to be not only void, but such a breach of the law as would subject him to an indictment.(³) As to the time which limits the authority of a Justice to convict, on penal statutes, it will be sufficient to remark, that all prosecutions for penalties, or for any offence within the jurisdiction of a Justice out of court, except against slaves and free negroes for petit larceny, must be commenced within one year after the offence committed, unless the special statute creating the offence, prescribes otherwise; and the computation of this time is by calendar months, of twelve to the year.

II. *As to the proceedings before the Justice, preliminary to conviction.*

It is requisite in all summary proceedings of a penal nature, that there should be an information or complaint, which is the basis of all the subsequent proceedings, and without which it seems that the Justice is not authorized in intermeddling,(⁴) unless in those cases where he is authorized to convict on view.

(¹) R. *v.* Chandler, 14 East 267; 1 Paley on Conv. 6.
(²) 1 Paley on Conv. 8.
(³) 4 T. R. 456.
(⁴) Lord Ray. 500; Loft. 250.

As it is the duty of Justices to enforce those acts, the execution of which is referred to them, it seems that they cannot properly refuse to receive a complaint regularly made; and whenever the complaint is required by statute to be in writing, that form must be observed; but unless so directed, it is not necessary. Nor is it requisite in prosecutions for fines, that the information be upon oath, if not enjoined by the letter of the statute,(¹) but it should be in prosecutions for petit larceny and other misdemeanors, against slaves and free negroes, where the punishment is corporeal.

If the information appears to justify the interference of the Magistrate, the next step is to give the party accused notice of the accusation and an opportunity to answer it, by issuing a summons containing the substance of the charge, where the prosecution is for a pecuniary penalty, and a warrant of arrest where the punishment is corporeal. It is a rule of natural justice, that the accused should have an opportunity of being heard, before he is condemned, and it is therefore indispensably necessary, in all penal proceedings of a summary nature, by Justices of the Peace, that the party should be summoned to answer the charge. So jealous is the law to enforce this rule, that the neglect of it by a Justice, in proceeding without a previous summons, has been treated as a misdemeanor.(²)

The summons in prosecutions for penalties, should be directed to the proper officer of a Justice, and served on the party against whom the charge is made, and should be signed by the Justice himself, by whom it is issued. It should contain the substance of the charge, and fix a day and place certain for his appearance, otherwise the party commits no default for not appearing, and the Magistrate cannot proceed in the defendant's absence, upon a summons defective in these particulars.(³)

By Sec. 3, Chap. 43. Although a law may allow an informer or person prosecuting to have part of a fine, the whole shall go to the Commonwealth, unless the name of the informer or prosecutor be endorsed on the warrant. This requisition should be strictly observed by the Justice.

In proceeding against slaves and free negroes for misdemeanors, the warrant should be issued, executed and returned as any other warrant of arrest. (See title "ARREST.")

It has been made a question, whether the service of the summons must be personal; and it seems, in general, that it should be, unless in cases where it is expressly dispensed with by statute. But the foregoing rule does not apply to those cases

---

(¹) 1 Paley on Convictions 18.
(²) 1 Pal. on Conv. 21.
(³) 1 Pal. on Conv. 22.

where the defendant appears and pleads; for then there is no longer any question upon the sufficiency or regularity of the summons.(¹)

For offences arising merely by a penal statute and not connected with any breach of the peace, the Justice cannot, (in a case within his jurisdiction to hear and determine,) by his personal authority, as necessarily incident to the cognizance of the offence, enforce an appearance by any compulsory means, unless where the power to apprehend, in such cases, is given by statute, but he can proceed to give judgment *ex parte*; and this he is bound to do in the absence of the defendant,(²) though, in such cases, judgment cannot be given against the party, without the examination of the facts upon oath, with the same formality as if he were present and made defence; for the Justice is bound to take care that the case is duly and properly made out.(³)

Upon the defendant's appearance, he either confesses the charge or denies it, and makes defence immediately. If he plead not guilty and require time to produce his evidence, he should be allowed a proper interval for that purpose. If the charge be confessed, nothing more remains for the Magistrate, but to pass judgment and impose the penalty. But if the defendant appear and deny the charge, or neglect to appear in a prosecution for a fine, after being duly summoned, the next step is to substantiate the information by testimony, which must be done by full proof of all the material facts necessary to constitute the offence. Where the punishment on conviction is corporeal, the Justice cannot proceed, unless the party be apprehended and brought before him.

When witnesses in support of the charge have been heard, the defendant should be called upon for his defence, and the Magistrate is bound to hear the evidence tendered by him. Besides the denial of the charge, the accused may defend himself, by proving that he is within some proviso or exception in the statute, which excuses or qualifies the fact charged, or that the prosecution is barred by the statute of limitations.

When the case has been heard on both sides, it remains for the Magistrate to convict the party, or to dismiss the complaint, according to his judgment, upon the circumstances. The degree of credit due to the evidence on either side, is entirely for his consideration. The Justices, upon their summary convictions, are placed in the situation of the jury, and to authorize a conviction, it is sufficient that there is such evidence before the Magistrate as might lead to a conviction of the

---

(¹) 1 Pal. on Conv. 23.
(²) Id. 25.
(³) 1 Pal. on Convictions 26.

party on an indictment. If the Magistrate think fit to dismiss the charge, although there appear a *prima facie* ground for a conviction, his acquittal cannot be questioned, since there is no appeal from his judgment, when that judgment is for the defendant.

III. *As to the conviction itself.*

A conviction is a record of the summary proceedings upon any penal statute before one or more Justices of the Peace, in a case within their jurisdiction, where the offender has been convicted and sentenced. This jurisdiction is in derogation of the Common Law, and deprives the party of trial by jury. Its authority, therefore, must be confined to the strict letter of the respective statutes under which it is exercised. In revising the proceedings of a Justice, the superior courts, upon a case brought before them, by *certiorari* or otherwise, would doubtless require that rules similar to those adopted by the Common Law in criminal prosecutions, and founded on natural justice, should appear in the conviction to have been observed, unless where the statute expressly dispenses with the form of stating them,(¹) and although it has not been the practice in Virginia to draw up a formal record of conviction, yet it is safer to do so; for, as nothing will be presumed in favour of a limited jurisdiction, the proceedings of a Justice, if reviewed in the superior courts, would be reversed, unless it appear in the conviction itself, not only that the jurisdiction existed, but that it was exercised according to the rules of natural justice. Yet these courts will not always be astute in finding objections to these convictions.(²)

The formal parts of a conviction are:

1st. *The information.*—This must always be stated at large, and where the statute directs it to be on oath, it should be so stated in the conviction. The information should contain the day when it was taken, that it may appear to have been given within the time limited by the statute. The place where it was taken, should also be stated, that it may appear that the Justice was acting within the local limits of his jurisdiction. It should state also the name of the informer, that as some of the statutes give a part of the penalty to him, it may appear afterwards that the witness is not the same person; it being settled that the informer cannot be a witness when he is entitled to any part of the penalty. It should also state the time of committing the offence, that it may appear that the prose-

---

(¹) 1 Burr. 613; 4 Burr. 2281; Brown *v.* Com. by Nicholas, J., Hen. Sup. Ct.
(²) 1 Ld. Ray. 581; 2 Term Rep. 8.

cution has been commenced within the time limited by the statute of limitations. It should also specify the place where the offence was committed, that it may appear to be within the jurisdiction of the Magistrate before whom the information is laid, and must also contain an exact description of the offence. This is best done by describing it in the exact words of the statute, though this rule admits of modifications and exceptions.([1])

2d. *Of the summons or warrant.*—The summons follows the information, and it must appear in the conviction, that the party was actually summoned or arrested.([2])

3d. *Of the judgment.*—The judgment is a necessary part of every conviction, and should contain, first, an adjudication that the defendant is convicted, and secondly, an adjudication of the forfeiture or penalty. In awarding the penalty, whether the conviction be formally drawn out or not, it is essential that the penalty, whether pecuniary or corporeal, be certain and determined, and such as is warranted by the statute under which it is imposed; and whatever is made a constituent part of the punishment by the statute, must form a part of the judgment expressed in the conviction.([3])

The appropriation of the penalty is generally directed by the statute itself, and when the entire penalty goes to the Commonwealth, the conviction need not contain any express award to that effect. It is the policy, however, of some of the statutes inflicting pecuniary penalties, to give part of the penalty to the informer, sometimes to the overseers of the poor. In such cases, the judgment should specifically appoint the manner and proportion in which the penalty is to be distributed, and the judgment should not be for the costs generally; but whatever they are, they should be ascertained by the Justice himself, and judgment rendered for the same.([4])

The several requisites of a conviction will be fully illustrated by the proper forms at the end of this chapter.

IV. *As to the proceedings subsequent to conviction.*

The proceedings subsequent to summary conviction, are either on the side of the prosecution in furtherance of the conviction, or on behalf of the party convicted, for reversal by appeal. And here, again, as in every other branch of his jurisdiction, the Justice must be governed by the statutes regulating these proceedings. The proceedings after conviction, necessarily vary so as to conform to the different punish-

---

([1]) 1 Burr. 679; 1 T. R. 222; 1 Ld. Ray. 581.
([2]) 1 Str. 630.
([3]) Pay. on Conv. 221-2.
([4]) Id. 231.

ments prescribed by the statutes; some imposing a pecuniary penalty only, others corporeal, and in some cases, corporeal punishment is directed where the party fails to pay the fine. These several proceedings will be now noticed; and

1st. *Where the conviction is for a pecuniary penalty only.*— By Sec. 6, Chap. 43. Where any fine is imposed by a Justice, which goes to the Commonwealth either wholly or in part, such Justice shall within thirty days thereafter, return to the clerk of his county or corporation court, the original proceedings and judgment whereby such fine was imposed, together with a statement of the costs thereupon. If he fail to make such return within that time, without good cause, he shall forfeit twenty dollars.

By Sec. 7. Such Justice shall issue no execution for said fine, but if he have good reason to believe that the delinquent will depart without paying it, so that an execution could not probably be levied, he may issue a warrant and cause such delinquent to be arrested and committed to jail.

By Sec. 8. The Constable shall in no case receive such fine or costs, but the same may be paid to such Justice at any time before an execution shall have issued therefor.

By Sec. 9. If any fine shall be received by the Justice imposing it, he shall pay the same into the court of his county or corporation at the next term. For a failure to make such payment, without good cause, he shall forfeit twenty dollars, which, together with the money so received, may be recovered by motion.

2d. *Where corporeal punishment is inflicted on failure to pay the fine.*—In some cases, where the punishment in the first instance is a pecuniary penalty, and corporeal punishment is annexed on failure to pay the fine, the statute directs the infliction of the punishment forthwith; and in such cases, the Justice should, at the time of conviction, demand payment, and if it be not then paid, order the punishment. (See form No. 24.) But in others of this character, the statute imposing the penalty, directs corporeal punishment in case of inability to pay the fine, without prescribing the mode by which this inability is to be judicially ascertained. The practice in England, is to issue a distress for the penalty in the first instance, and if the money be not made, upon the return of the warrant of distress shewing the inability, the Justice orders the punishment.([1])

In prosecutions for fines, an appeal lies as a matter of right from the judgment of a single Justice, to any term of the county or corporation court, in all cases where the fine imposed

---

([1]) See Paley on Conv. part 5, c. 1.

exceeds ten dollars, if not otherwise directed by some special provision of the statute; but the appeal must be taken within ten days after the conviction, and security given for the payment of the fine and all costs and damages, if the judgment be affirmed, before it will be valid. The verbal acknowledgment of the security of his liability, before the Justice, endorsed upon the summons, is not only sufficient, but conclusive evidence of his undertaking. And upon the like terms, an appeal lies from his judgment, without reference to the amount, where the case involves the constitutionality or validity of an ordinance or by-law of a corporation. (New Code, page 596-7.)

For the form of awarding an appeal, see form No. 21.

(No. 1.)

Form of a Complaint to a Justice, of an offence which is within his jurisdiction to try, committed by a negro, where the punishment is corporeal.

—— County, to wit:

A. B. upon oath, complains before me J. T., a Justice of said County, that on the —— day of —————— 18—, in the said County, C. D., a free negro, (or *a slave, the property of E. F.*) did unlawfully, (here state the substance of the charge, as for instance, "steal one hog, of the value of five dollars, the property of the said A. B.;") and prays therefore, that the said C. D. may be apprehended and held to answer the said complaint. Dated this —— day of ————— 18—.

A. B.

—— day of —————— 18—. The said A. B. this day made oath to the truth of the foregoing complaint before me.

J. T., J. P.

(No. 2.)

Form of Warrant of Arrest against a slave or free negro for petit larceny.

—— County, to wit:

To all or any one of the Constables of said County:

Whereas, A. B. of said County, has this day made complaint and information on oath before me J. T., a Justice of the said County, that C. D., a free negro, (or *a slave, the property of E. F.*, as the case may be,) on the —— day of —————— 18—, in said County, did take, steal and carry away one watch, of the value of fifteen dollars, (or any other article not above the value of twenty dollars,) of the goods and chattels of the said A. B.: These are, therefore, to command you, in the name of the Commonwealth of Virginia, forthwith to apprehend the said C. D., and bring him before me or some other Justice of the said County, to answer the said complaint, and to be farther dealt with according to law. Given under my hand and seal, this —— day of —————— 18—.

J. T., J. P. [L. S.]

(No. 3.)

Form of Warrant of Arrest against a slave or free negro, for using provoking language to a white person.

———— County, to wit:
  To all or any one of the Constables of said County:

Whereas, A. B. of said County, has this day made complaint and information on oath before me J. T., a Justice of the said County, that C. D. a free negro, (or *a slave, the property of E. F.*, as the case may be,) on the —— day of ———— 18—, in said County, did use provoking language to the said A. B., by then saying in the hearing of the said A. B., (here state the language:) These are, therefore, to command you, in the name of the Commonwealth of Virginia, forthwith to apprehend the said C. D., and bring him before me or some other Justice of the said County, to answer the said complaint, and to be farther dealt with according to law. Given under my hand and seal, this —— day of ———— 18—.

J. T., J. P. [L. S.]

[NOTE.—For menacing gestures, say "did use menacing gestures to the said A. B.," and state the act done.]

(No. 4.)

Form of Warrant of Arrest against a slave for absenting himself from his master's tenement without a pass.

———— County, to wit:
  To all or any one of the Constables of said County:

Whereas, A. B. of said County, has this day made complaint and information on oath before me J. T., a Justice of the said County, that C. D. a slave, on the —— day of ———— 18, in said County, did absent himself from the tenement of E. F., his master, without any pass or token, whereby it appeared that he so absented himself by permission of his said master: These are, therefore, to command you, in the name of the Commonwealth of Virginia, forthwith to apprehend the said C. D., and bring him before me or some other Justice of the said County, to answer the said complaint, and to be farther dealt with according to law. Given under my hand and seal, this —— day of ———— 18—.

J. T., J. P. [L. S.]

(No. 5.)

Form of Warrant of Arrest against a slave or free negro for furnishing a pass to a slave.

———— County, to wit:
  To all or any one of the Constables of said County:

Whereas, A. B. of said County, has this day made complaint and information on oath before me J. T., a Justice of the said County, that C. D. a free negro, (or *a slave, the property of E. F.*, as the case may be,) on the —— day of ———— 18—, in said County, did furnish a pass to Frank, a slave, the property of G. H., to go from —— to ——, (state where,) without the consent of the said G. H.: These are, therefore, to command you, in the name of the Commonwealth of Virginia, forthwith to apprehend the said C. D., and bring him before me or some other Justice of the said County, to answer the said complaint, and to be farther dealt with according to law. Given under my hand and seal, this —— day of —— 18—.

J. T., J. P. [L. S.]

(No. 6.)

Form of Warrant of Arrest against a slave for selling or administering medicine.

—— County, to wit:

To all or any one of the Constables of said County:

Whereas, A. B. of said County, has this day made complaint and information on oath before me J. T., a Justice of the said County, that C. D., a slave, the property of E. F., on the —— day of —— 18—, in said County, did, without the consent of his master, sell (or *administer*) to one G. H., medicine: These are, therefore, to command you, in the name of the Commonwealth of Virginia, forthwith to apprehend the said C. D., and bring him before me or some other Justice of the said County, to answer the said complaint, and to be farther dealt with according to law. Given under my hand and seal, this —— day of —— 18—.

J. T., J. P. [L. S.]

[NOTE.—If the offender be a free negro, leave out the words "without the consent of his master."]

(No. 7.)

Form of Warrant of Arrest for riot by slaves or free negroes.

—— County, to wit:

To all or any one of the Constables of said County:

Whereas, A. B. of said County, has this day made complaint and information on oath before me J. T., a Justice of the said County, that Frank and John, slaves, the property of E. F., (or *free negroes*,) on the —— day of —— 18—, in said County, with divers other persons, did riotously and unlawfully assemble together to disturb the public peace, and being so riotously assembled, did then and there disturb the public peace, by making a great and unusual noise, to the disturbance and alarm of the people of this Commonwealth: These are, therefore, to command you, in the name of the Commonwealth of Virginia, forthwith to apprehend the said Frank and John, and bring them before me or some other Justice of the said County, to answer the said complaint, and to be farther dealt with according to law. Given under my hand and seal, this —— day of —— 18—.

J. T., J. P. [L. S.]

(No. 8.)

Form of Warrant of Arrest against a free negro or slave for keeping fire arms.

—— County, to wit:
 To X. Y., Constable of said County:

Whereas, A. B. has this day made complaint and information on oath before me J. T., a Justice of the said County, that Frank, a free negro, (or *a slave, the property of E. F.*,) now keeps fire arms, to wit, one gun, and that he also keeps gunpowder and bullets in the said County: These are, therefore, to command you, in the name of the Commonwealth, forthwith to apprehend the said Frank, and bring him before me or some other Justice of the said County, to answer the said complaint, and to be farther dealt with according to law; and you are, moreover, commanded to seize any gun or other fire arms, gunpowder, balls or other ammunition which you may find in his possession, and bring them before me, that they also may be disposed of according to law. Given under my hand and seal, this —— day of ——— 18—.

J. T., J. P. [L. S.]

(No. 9.)

Form of Judgment against a slave or free negro, whose punishment is whipping.

When there is no appeal asked, it may be endorsed in this form, on the warrant: "Defendant found guilty, and adjudged to receive —— lashes on his bare back, and X. Y., Constable, is ordered to execute this judgment." But in cases where an appeal is taken, and especially in petit larceny, the judgment should be more formal.

Cases of petit larceny by slaves and free negroes, so frequently occur, that forms adapted to that offence will be found most useful, and they may be easily altered to suit any other misdemeanor, in which appeals are allowed.

(No. 10.)

Form of Conviction of a slave for petit larceny, and of an appeal from the judgment.

—— County, to wit:

Be it remembered, that on the —— day of ——— 18—, Peter, a slave, (the property of A. B.,) who was brought before me J. T., a Justice of said County, charged with stealing, taking and carrying away, in said County, on the —— day of ——— 18—, one hog, of the value of (any sum not exceeding twenty dollars,) of the goods and chattels of A. L., is by me found guilty of said offence, upon the testimony on oath of C. D. And I do hereby adjudge, that the said Peter, for the said offence, do receive —— lashes, on his bare back, at the public whipping post; and I order X. Y., Constable of said County, to execute this judgment. And now, A. B. the owner of said Peter, prays an appeal from the said judgment, to the County Court of ——; and he having entered into a recognizance for the appearance of the said slave, before the said County Court, on the first day of the next term thereof, then and there to answer for the larceny aforesaid, an appeal is granted to him, according to law; and the execution of the judgment aforesaid, is in the mean time suspended, and the said judgment and conviction as well as the said appeal are hereby certified to the said County Court.

In witness whereof, I, the said Justice, have hereunto set my hand and seal, this —— day of ——— 18—.

J. T., J. P. [L. S.]

(No. 11.)

Form of a Recognizance for the appearance of a slave, upon an appeal from the judgment of a single Justice, in petit larceny.

——— County, to wit:

Be it remembered, that on the —— day of ——— 18—, J. M., the owner of a certain slave named Frank, came before me J. T., a Justice of the said County, and acknowledged himself to be indebted to the Commonwealth of Virginia in the sum of ——— dollars, of lawful money of the United States, to be levied of his goods and chattels, lands and tenements, to the use of the said Commonwealth, if he the said J. M. shall make default in the performance of the condition underwritten.

The condition of the above recognizance is such, that whereas the above named slave Frank, the property of the above bound J. M., has this day been tried by me J. T., a Justice of the said County of ———, for petit larceny, in taking, stealing and carrying away, (here state the article stolen,) of the value of ——— dollars, of the goods and chattels of A. B., and has, by my judgment, been found guilty and convicted of the larceny aforesaid, and sentenced to be punished for the said offence, with stripes, according to law; from which said judgment and sentence, the said J. M., the owner of the said slave, has taken an appeal to the County Court of said County: Now, if the said J. M., shall himself produce the said slave Frank in person, or shall cause the said Frank personally to appear before the said County Court on the first day of the next term thereof, then and there to answer the Commonwealth of Virginia, for and concerning the said offence whereof he has been found guilty and convicted by me, so that the said slave shall not depart thence without the leave of the Court, then this recognizance shall be void, otherwise to remain in full force and virtue.

Taken and acknowledged before me.

J. T., J. P.

(No. 12.)

Form of Conviction of a free negro charged with petit larceny, when an appeal is asked for.

——— County, to wit:

Be it remembered, that on the —— day of ——— 18—, John Logan, a free negro, brought before me J. T., Justice of said County, charged with having, on the —— day of ——— 18—, in said County, stolen, taken and carried away one hog, of the value of (any sum not exceeding $20,) of the goods and chattels of A. B., is by me found guilty of said offence, on the testimony on oath of E. F., and I do hereby adjudge, that the said John Logan, for the said offence, do receive on his bare back, at the public whipping post, ——— lashes, and I order X. Y., Constable of said

County, to execute this judgment. But the said John Logan, having prayed an appeal from this judgment to the County Court of ———, and he having entered into a recognizance with K. L. as his surety, for his personal appearance before said Court, on the first day of the next term thereof, then and there to answer for the said offence, an appeal is granted him according to law; and the execution of said judgment is suspended; and the said conviction and appeal are hereby certified to the County Court of said County. Given under my hand and seal, this —— day of —— 18—.

J. T., J. P. [L. s.]

(No. 13.)

Form of a Recognizance of a free negro, to be entered into on an appeal from the judgment of a Justice, in case of petit larceny.

———— County, to wit:

Be it remembered, that on the —— day of —— 18—, A. B., a free negro, and C. D., personally came before me, J. T., Justice of said County, and severally and respectively acknowledged themselves to be indebted to the Commonwealth of Virginia in the sum of —— dollars each, to be respectively levied of their goods and chattels, lands and tenements, to the use of the said Commonwealth, if the said A. B. shall make default in the performance of the condition underwritten.

The condition of the above recognizance is such, that whereas the above named A. B., a free negro, has this day been tried before me J. T., a Justice of the said County, for petit larceny, by him committed in said County, in taking, stealing and carrying away (here state the articles stolen,) of the value of —— dollars, of the goods and chattels of E. F., and has, by my judgment, been found guilty and convicted of the larceny aforesaid, and sentenced to be punished for the said offence, with stripes, according to law; from which judgment and sentence, the said A. B. has taken an appeal to the County Court of the said County. Now, if the above named A. B. shall personally appear before the said County Court, on the first day of the next term thereof, to answer the Commonwealth of Virginia, for and concerning the said offence, whereof he has been found guilty and convicted by me, and shall not thence depart without the leave of the said Court, then this recognizance shall be void, otherwise to remain in full force and virtue.

Taken and acknowledged before me.

J. T., J. P.

(No. 14.)

Form of Recognizance of witnesses to appear and give evidence on an appeal from the judgment of a single Justice.

———— County, to wit:

Be it remembered, that on the —— day of —— 18—, A. B. personally appeared before me J. T., a Justice of the said County, and acknowledged himself to be indebted to the Commonwealth of Virginia, in the sum of —— dollars, to be levied of his goods and chattels, lands and tenements, for the use of the Commonwealth, if he, the said A. B., shall make default in the performance of the condition underwritten.

The condition of the above recognizance is such, that if the above bound A. B. shall personally appear before the County Court of the said County, on the first day of the next term thereof, to give evidence on behalf of the Commonwealth against Peter, a slave, (or *free negro*, as the case may be,) who has been convicted before me, of petit larceny, in stealing the goods of E. F., and has taken an appeal from my said judgment to the County Court of said County, and shall not thence depart without the leave of the said Court, then the above recognizance to be void, otherwise to remain in full force and virtue.

Taken and acknowledged before me, the day and year first above written.

J. T. J. P.

(No. 15.)

Form of Commitment of a free negro or slave, where an appeal is taken from the judgment of a single Justice, upon his trial for a misdemeanor when the offender fails to give bail.

———— County, to wit:

To X. Y., *Constable of said County, and to the Keeper of the Jail of the said County:*

Whereas, Frank, a free negro, (or *a slave, the property of E. F.*,) was this day brought before me J. T., a Justice of the said County, charged upon the oath of C. D., with having, on the —— day of ———— 18—, in the said County. (here state the offence, as for example, " taken, stolen and carried away one watch, of the value of fifteen dollars, of the goods and chattels of the said C. D.,") and was, on hearing, found guilty and convicted of the said offence, and adjudged by me to receive twenty stripes for the said offence: and whereas the said Frank has taken an appeal from said judgment to the next County Court for the said County, and has failed to give bail for his appearance before the said Court, then and there to answer for the said offence: These are, therefore, to command you, the said Constable, in the name of the Commonwealth, forthwith to convey and deliver into the custody of the keeper of the said jail, together with this warrant, the body of the said Frank. And you, the keeper of the said jail, are hereby required to receive the said Frank into your jail and custody, and him there safely keep until he shall be discharged by due course of law. Given under my hand and seal, this —— day of ———— in the year 18—.

J. T., J. P. [L. S.]

[NOTE.—Should the Justice determine not to try a free negro brought before him, charged with a misdemeanor, but to remand him for trial in Court, he will adopt the following forms of mittimus, certificate and recognizances; that is to say, the form of mittimus, No. 9, under head of ARREST; of certificate to clerk, No. 10 or 11, under same head; of recognizance of bail, No. 4, under head of RECOGNIZANCE, and of recognizance of witness, No. 5, under same head.]

(No. 16.)

Form of a Summons against a party to answer a prosecution for a pecuniary penalty before a single Justice.

——— County, to wit:
    To *A. B., Constable of said County:*

Whereas, information and complaint has this day been made before me J. T., Justice of the said County, by A. B., that C. D., on the ——— day of ——— 18—, in the County aforesaid, did (here set forth the offence charged conformably to the act of Assembly, taking care to make it sufficiently specific:) These are, therefore, to command you forthwith to summon the said C. D. to appear before me or some other Justice of the said County, at ———, in the said County, on the ——— day of ——— 18—, at the hour of ———, in the ——— noon of the same day, to answer the said complaint, and to be farther dealt with according to law; and moreover, that you summon R. S. to appear then and there to give evidence in behalf of the Commonwealth against the said C. D., touching the said offence, and be you then there to certify what you shall have done in the premises. Given under my hand and seal, this ——— day of ——— 18—.

J. T., J. P. [L. S.]

(No. 17.)

Form of Judgment on conviction for fines, which may be endorsed on back of warrant.

Where whole fine goes to the Commonwealth, endorse the judgment in this form: "Defendant found guilty on the testimony on oath of A. B., of the offence charged within, and adjudged to pay $ ——— fine, for the use of the Commonwealth, and $ ——— costs."

J. T., J. P.

Where part only of the fine goes to the Commonwealth, endorse: "Defendant found guilty, upon the testimony on oath of E. F., of the offence charged within, and adjudged to pay $ ——— fine, one half for the use of the Commonwealth, and the other to A. B., the informer; also $ ———, cost of prosecution."

When judgment is for the defendant, and there is no informer, dismiss the warrant. If there be an informer, the form of the judgment should be: "Defendant found not guilty, and judgment against C. D., the informer, for defendant's costs, which I ascertain to be $ ———."

[This is a convenient practice, but in cases where appeals are granted, the safer mode would be to adopt the following forms:]

(No. 18.)

Form of Conviction for fine, when the whole goes to the Commonwealth.

——— County, to wit:

Be it remembered, that on the ——— day of ——— in the year 18—, A. B. is convicted before me J. T., Justice of the said County, upon the evidence on oath of E. F., of (here specify the offence, and when and where committed,) contrary to the form of the statute in that case made; and I do hereby adjudge that the said A. B. has forfeited, for the said offence, the sum of $ ——, for the benefit of the Commonwealth; and I do adjudge the said A. B. to pay the costs of this prosecution, which I ascertain to be $ ——. (*) Given under my hand and seal, this —— day of —— 18—.

J. T., J. P. [L. s.]

(No. 19.)

Form of Conviction, where part only or the whole of the fine goes to the informer.

—— County, to wit:

Be it remembered, that on the —— day of —— in the year 18—, A. B. is convicted before me J. T., Justice of the said County, on the oath of C. D., of (here specify the offence, and when and where committed,) contrary to the statute in that case made and provided; and I do hereby adjudge, that the said A. B. has forfeited, for the said offence, the sum of $ ——, [one half thereof to the Commonwealth, and the other half] to the use of P. Q., who gave information of the said offence; and I do adjudge that the said A. B. pay the costs of this prosecution, which I ascertain to be $ ——. (*) Given under my hand and seal, this —— day of —— 18—.

J. T., J. P. [L. s.]

[NOTE.—Where the whole goes to the informer, leave out what is in brackets.]

(No. 20.)

Form of an Appeal from the judgment imposing a fine.

Commonwealth } —— day of —— 18—. From my judgment in this
    v.   } case an appeal is asked by the defendant, which is allow-
A. B.   } ed; and thereupon, C. D. undertook, as his surety, before me, for the payment of the fine imposed by my said judgment, and for all costs and damages, in case said judgment be affirmed.

J. T., J. P.

(No. 21.)

Form of an Execution upon conviction for a penalty, where the fine enures wholly to the informer.†

—— County, to wit:

To X. Y., Constable of the said County:

Whereas, A. B., of the County of ——, is this day duly convicted before me J. T., a Justice of the said County, for that he, the said A. B., on

---

† The Justice will bear in mind that he can only issue execution in cases where the *whole* penalty goes to the informer.

the ──── day of ──────── 18──, in the said County, did (here describe the offence as in the statute,) contrary to the form of the statute in such case made and provided; whereby he has forfeited the sum of ──────── dollars: These are, therefore, to command you, in the name of the Commonwealth of Virginia, that of the goods and chattels of the said A. B., in your district, you cause to be made ──────── dollars, so by him forfeited; and also the sum of ──────── dollars, which were by me adjudged against him for the costs incurred in the prosecution for the offence aforesaid; and out of the money so made, that you do pay the said sum of ──────── dollars to C. D., the person who informed me of the said offence; and that you do, within ──── days (not to exceed sixty) from the date hereof, make due return of this precept, shewing by your said return in what manner you have executed it. Given under my hand, this ──── day of ──────── 18──.

J. T., J. P.

(No. 22.)

Form of Warrant of Commitment, where the Justice has good reason to believe that the delinquent will abscond before the Clerk can issue execution for the fine, where the whole or part thereof enures to the Commonwealth.

──── County, to wit:
To X. Y., *Constable of the said County*:

Whereas, A. B. was, on the ──── day of ──────── 18──, at the said County, duly convicted before me J. T., a Justice of the said County, of having (here describe the offence of which the party was convicted,) in the said County, and within my jurisdiction, and by me adjudged to forfeit and pay the sum of ──────── dollars, [one moiety thereof to X. Y., the informer, and the other moiety thereof to the Commonwealth of Virginia;] and adjudged also to pay the sum of ──────── dollars, the costs of the prosecution; and I, the said J. T., Justice as aforesaid, having good reason to believe that the said A. B. will depart without paying the said fine, so that an execution to be issued therefor by the Clerk of the County Court of ────────, cannot probably be levied: These are, therefore, to command you, in the name of the Commonwealth of Virginia, forthwith to apprehend him the said A. B., and commit his body to the jail of your County, there to remain until he shall have paid the said fine and costs, or be otherwise discharged by law. In witness whereof, I do hereunto set my hand, and affix my seal, this ──── day of ──────── 18──.

J. T., J. P. [L. S.]

[NOTE.—Where the whole of the fine enures to the Commonwealth leave out what is in brackets, and insert " to the use of the Commonwealth."]

(No. 23.)

Form of a Conviction, where the party fails to pay the fine and costs instanter, and corporeal punishment is adjudged.

Follow form No. 18, where the whole fine goes to the Commonwealth, and No. 19, where a part goes to the informer, to the asterisk(*), and in either case, conclude thus, " and payment of the said fine and costs being by me demanded instanter of the said A. B., and he having failed to pay the same, I do adjudge him, the said A. B., to receive ──────── lashes on his bare back, at the public whipping post, to be well laid on ; and do order X. Y., Constable of the said County, to execute this my judgment. In witness whereof, I have, to this conviction, set my hand and seal, this —— day of ———— 18—.

J. T., J. P. [L. S.]

(No. 24.)

Form of Commitment in default of payment of a fine, when no corporeal punishment is thereby incurred.

———— County, to wit:

To X. Y., Constable of the said County, and to the Keeper of the Jail of said County:

Whereas, A. B. was this day convicted before me J. T., a Justice of the said County, for, that he the said A. B. did (here state the offence as in the judgment,) and I, the said J. T., thereupon adjudged that he had forfeited the sum of ———— dollars, for his said offence, to be paid to the Commonwealth; and the said A. B. being so convicted, and being now required by me to pay the said sum, has not paid the same, but wholly failed to do so: These are, in the name of the Commonwealth, to command you, the said Constable, to take the said A. B. and convey him to the jail of the said County, and there to deliver him to the keeper thereof, together with this precept: And I command you, the keeper of the said jail, to receive the said A. B. into the said jail, and there him safely keep for the term of one year, unless the said sum shall be sooner paid, or until he be otherwise discharged by due course of law. Given under my hand and seal, this ———— day of ———— 18—.

J. T., J. P. [L. S.]

(No. 25.)

Form of Commitment in default of payment of a penalty within a limited time.

———— County, to wit:

To X. Y., Constable of the said County, and to the Keeper of the Jail of the said County:

———— was, on the ———— day of ————, last past, convicted before me J. T., Justice of the said County, for, that he the said A. B. (here state the offence according to the judgment,) and I, the said J. T., thereupon adjudged that the said A. B. had forfeited the sum of ———— dollars, to be paid to the Commonwealth; and I, the said J. T., then and there ordered that the said sum should be paid by the said A. B. on or before the ———— day of ————. And whereas the said A. B. did not pay the said sum on or before the said last mentioned day, nor has he yet paid the same, but has wholly made default therein: These are to command you, the said Constable, &c. (conclude as in the last.)

(No. 26.)

Form of a Warrant to bring a party before a Justice, to hear judgment of whipping, when he is unable to pay the fine and where time is allowed to pay it.

Whereas, A. B. was duly summoned to appear before me J. T., a Justice of the said County, at ——— in the said County, on the ——— day of ——— 18—, to answer a charge then preferred against him, for (here describe the offence;) and whereas, upon the examination of the testimony of C. D., a witness, on oath, (or *upon the confession of the said A. B.*, as the case may be,) the said A. B. was then by me adjudged to be guilty of the said offence, and adjudged to forfeit the sum of ——— dollars, for the said offence, to be paid to E. F. the person who informed me thereof, (or *to the Commonwealth*, where there is no informer,) and was also adjudged by me to pay the sum of ——— dollars, the costs of prosecution for the said offence; which said fine and costs were adjudged by me to be paid on or before the ——— day of ——— 18—, and which the said A. B. has failed to pay, and is now therefore liable to punishment by whipping for the said offence, according to the statute in that case made and provided: These are, therefore, to command you, in the name of the Commonwealth, forthwith to apprehend the body of the said A. B., and bring him before me, to be dealt with according to law. Given under my hand and seal, this ——— day of ——— 18—.

J. T., J. P. [L. S.]

(No. 27.)

Form of a Judgment to be rendered upon the foregoing warrant, and which may be endorsed on it.

Commonwealth
    v.
A. B., upon the information of C. D.

} ——— day of ——— 18—. The within named A. B., being now before me, by virtue of the within warrant, and he still failing to pay the within mentioned fine and costs now demanded of him, I do adjudge and order him the said A. B. to receive ——— lashes on his bare back, at the public whipping post, to be well laid on; and do order X. Y., Constable of the said County, forthwith to execute this my judgment.

J. T., J. P.

bare back, at the public whipping post, to be well laid on ; and do order X. Y., Constable of the said County, to execute this my judgment. In witness whereof, I have, to this conviction, set my hand and seal, this —— day of ——— 18—.

J. T., J. P. [L. S.]

(No. 24.)

Form of Commitment in default of payment of a fine, when no corporeal punishment is thereby incurred.

——— County, to wit:

To X. Y., *Constable of the said County, and to the Keeper of the Jail of said County:*

Whereas, A. B. was this day convicted before me J. T., a Justice of the said County, for, that he the said A. B. did (here state the offence as in the judgment,) and I, the said J. T., thereupon adjudged that he had forfeited the sum of ——— dollars, for his said offence, to be paid to the Commonwealth; and the said A. B. being so convicted, and being now required by me to pay the said sum, has not paid the same, but wholly failed to do so: These are, in the name of the Commonwealth, to command you, the said Constable, to take the said A. B. and convey him to the jail of the said County, and there to deliver him to the keeper thereof, together with this precept: And I command you, the keeper of the said jail, to receive the said A. B. into the said jail, and there him safely keep for the term of one year, unless the said sum shall be sooner paid, or until he be otherwise discharged by due course of law. Given under my hand and seal, this ——— day of ——— 18—.

J. T., J. P. [L. S.]

(No. 25.)

Form of Commitment in default of payment of a penalty within a limited time.

——— County, to wit:

To X. Y., *Constable of the said County, and to the Keeper of the Jail of the said County:*

——— was, on the ——— day of ———, last past, convicted before me J. T., Justice of the said County, for, that he the said A. B. (here state the offence according to the judgment,) and I, the said J. T., thereupon adjudged that the said A. B. had forfeited the sum of ——— dollars, to be paid to the Commonwealth; and I, the said J. T., then and there ordered that the said sum should be paid by the said A. B. on or before the ——— day of ———. And whereas the said A. B. did not pay the said sum on or before the said last mentioned day, nor has he yet paid the same, but has wholly made default therein: These are to command you, the said Constable, &c. (conclude as in the last.)

(No. 26.)

Form of a Warrant to bring a party before a Justice, to hear judgment of whipping, when he is unable to pay the fine and where time is allowed to pay it.

Whereas, A. B. was duly summoned to appear before me J. T., a Justice of the said County, at ——— in the said County, on the ——— day of ——— 18—, to answer a charge then preferred against him, for (here describe the offence ;) and whereas, upon the examination of the testimony of C. D., a witness, on oath, (or *upon the confession of the said A. B.*, as the case may be,) the said A. B. was then by me adjudged to be guilty of the said offence, and adjudged to forfeit the sum of ——— dollars, for the said offence, to be paid to E. F. the person who informed me thereof, (or *to the Commonwealth*, where there is no informer,) and was also adjudged by me to pay the sum of ——— dollars, the costs of prosecution for the said offence; which said fine and costs were adjudged by me to be paid on or before the ——— day of ——— 18—, and which the said A. B. has failed to pay, and is now therefore liable to punishment by whipping for the said offence, according to the statute in that case made and provided : These are, therefore, to command you, in the name of the Commonwealth, forthwith to apprehend the body of the said A. B., and bring him before me, to be dealt with according to law. Given under my hand and seal, this ——— day of ——— 18—.

J. T., J. P. [L. s.]

(No. 27.)

Form of a Judgment to be rendered upon the foregoing warrant, and which may be endorsed on it.

Commonwealth } ——— day of ——— 18—. The within named
      v.   } A. B., being now before me, by virtue of the within
A. B., upon the infor- } warrant, and he still failing to pay the within men-
  mation of C. D. } tioned fine and costs now demanded of him, I do
adjudge and order him the said A. B. to receive ——— lashes on his bare back, at the public whipping post, to be well laid on ; and do order X. Y., Constable of the said County, forthwith to execute this my judgment.

J. T., J. P.

CHAPTER XLIII.

FISH.

By Sec. 4, Chap. 101. If any person shall, in any year after the first day of June, and before the first day of September, haul a seine below the mouth of any river in this State, or in the waters of the county of Northampton, or set a weir or seine in the waters of the county of Accomack, after the fifteenth day of May, and before the fifteenth day of September, he shall forfeit fifty dollars. This section shall not apply to a person hauling a seine in the jurisdiction of Elizabeth City county, between Old Point Comfort and Back river, at any time from the fifteenth day of August until the fifteenth day of June in any year.

By Sec. 5. If any person shall fix in the river Potomac, or any of its branches below the head of tide, any gill net, seine or other obstruction, so as to injure the fisheries on said waters, by preventing the passage of fish, he shall forfeit twenty dollars, and be deemed guilty of a nuisance. The judgment for the forfeiture shall require the nuisance to be abated. If the forfeiture be not forthwith paid, the offender shall be committed to jail for thirty days, unless it be sooner paid.

By Sec. 6. If any person shall fish in the Potomac river, or its tributaries, in March, April, May or June, with nets or seines not laid out from, hauled to and landed upon the shores thereof, he shall be fined not less than fifty nor more than five hundred dollars.

By Sec. 7. If any person shall, during the fishing season, anchor or place a vessel, boat or craft, or other obstruction within the limits of any fishery, so as to interrupt or hinder any person in this State, in the exercise of his right of fishery, and shall not immediately remove such obstruction when required, he shall be fined for each hour such obstruction shall be continued, not less than ten nor more than one hundred dollars; one half of which shall be to the informer; but if such obstruction be unavoidably caused by stress of weather, or other absolute necessity, and the same be removed as soon as it can be safely done, such fine shall not be incurred.

By Sec. 8. If any person shall haul, float or drift in any waters of this State, any seine or net, with a rope or line fixed to the bottom, so constructed as to keep such seine or net in an erect position and obstruct the passage of fish, he shall forfeit one hundred dollars. But this section shall not prevent the use of such seines and nets as had been used in the waters of this State, by citizens thereof, prior to the 13th day of February in the year 1844 ; nor shall it apply to any of the waters within either of the counties of Accomack, Northampton, Norfolk or Essex, nor to any of the waters of the Rappahannock or its tributaries.

By Sec. 9. If any person, not a resident of this State, haul or fish with any seine in any of the waters thereof, or fish in the waters of the Rappahannock river, in any other way than by a line held in the hand, or attached to a pole or rod held in the hand, he shall forfeit not less than ten nor more than one hundred dollars, one half whereof shall be to the informer.

By Sec. 10. If any person shall violate the 4th, 5th, 6th, 7th, 8th or 9th section, in or on the Potomac river, the process and jurisdiction to enforce the penalties or recover damages therefor, shall be according to the compact between Virginia and Maryland, so far as therein provided for, and so far as not so provided for, according to the other laws of this State.

By Sec. 11. If any person, who is not a resident of this State, shall take or catch fish by nets or seines from the Ohio river, or any of its tributaries, within the jurisdiction of this State, he shall forfeit not less than one hundred and fifty dollars, one half whereof shall be to the informer.

By Sec. 23. No person shall be deemed a non-resident of this State within the meaning of any section of this chapter, who is *bona fide* the owner or tenant of any fishery in this State, or of any tract of land on any tide water course therein. Nor shall any such section prohibit such owner or tenant from employing non-resident white labourers in seine hauling for him.

By Sec. 24. Any proceeding under any section of this chapter, may be according to the forty-third chapter, or in any county or corporation adjacent to the waters in which the offence was committed. And where the penalty is incurred by reason of the defendant's being a non-resident, the burden of proof as to his residence shall be upon him.

By Sec. 25. Where a proceeding is instituted for any violation of any section of this chapter, (one hundred and one,) on affidavit of such violation, a Justice may issue his warrant for the apprehension of the offender, and it shall not be necessary therein to name the offender or the vessel in his employment.

By Sec. 26. The Justice before whom he may be brought may, on hearing proof, either discharge the accused, or require him to enter into a recognizance to appear at the next term of the circuit court, or at the next quarterly term of the county or corporation court, as the Justice may determine, to answer for the said offence, and to satisfy the judgment which may be rendered against him therefor.

By Sec. 27. Under the warrant for the apprehension of any offender, in pursuance of either of the two preceding sections, the officer executing such warrant shall take possession of any vessel, boat or skiff, (with its tackle and appurtenances,) which the defendant may belong to, or be using or have used in the commission of the offence for which he is prosecuted, and hold the same until the recognizance required be given, or until the defendant be acquitted. But if judgment be given against the defendant, it shall be part of the judgment of the court, that if the penalty and costs be not forthwith paid, all the property so seized be sold, and the proceeds accounted for, as if it were the property of the defendant, seized under an execution for the satisfaction of the judgment. For the seizure and safe keeping of any vessel, with the equipments, under the provisions of this chapter, the officer effecting the same shall receive a fee of twenty dollars, to be taxed in the costs.

By Sec. 28. The informer, if there be one, shall be entitled to a moiety of any fine imposed by this chapter.

(No. 1.)

Form of Warrant of Arrest for hauling a seine below the mouth of a river, or in the waters of Northampton, after the first of June and before the first of September, under the 4th section.

—— County, to wit:
    To all or any one of the Constables of said County:

Whereas, A. B. of said County, has this day made complaint and information on oath before me J. T., a Justice of the said County, that C. D., in said County, did, after the first day of June and before the first day of September, in the year 18—, to wit, on the —— day of —— 18—, haul a seine below the mouth of the Potomac river, in the waters of this Commonwealth, (or *in the waters of Northampton county, to wit, in Occahannock creek:*) These are, therefore, to command you, in the name of the Commonwealth of Virginia, forthwith to apprehend the said C. D., and bring him before me or some other Justice of the said County, to answer the said complaint, and to be farther dealt with according to law. Given under my hand and seal, this —— day of —— 18—.

J. T., J. P. [L. S.]

(No. 2.)

Form of Warrant of Arrest for setting a weir or seine in the waters of Accomack, under the 4th section.

Follow the above form to the word " after," and say, " the fifteenth day of May and before the fifteenth day of September, to wit, on the —— day of —— 18—, set a weir (or *seine*) in the waters of the County of Accomack, to wit, in Pocomoke bay : These are, therefore, &c. (conclude as No. 1.)

(No. 3.)

Form of Warrant of Arrest for fishing with gill nets in the Potomac, so as to injure fisheries thereon, under the 5th section.

——— County, to wit:
To all or any one of the Constables of said County:

Whereas, A. B. of said County, has this day made complaint and information on oath before me J. T., a Justice of the said County, that C. D., on the ——— day of 18—, in said County, did fix in the river Potomac, below the head of tide water, a certain seine (or *gill net*) so as to injure the fisheries on said river, by preventing the passage of fish: These are, &c. (conclude as No. 1.)

(No. 4.)

Form of the Judgment for the fine, &c., under the 5th section.

This offence is within the jurisdiction of a single Justice, and if upon hearing the case, he should find the party guilty, his judgment should be in this form:

——— County, to wit:

Commonwealth } At ——— in said County, ——— day of ——— 18—.
    v.
A. B. } Upon a hearing, defendant found guilty, and adjudged to pay the fine of twenty dollars and the costs of prosecution, which I ascertain to be ——— dollars, and that the nuisance specified in the within summons be abated by X. Y., Constable; and payment of the said fine being forthwith demanded, and the said A. B. having failed to pay the same, he is committed to jail for thirty days, unless in the mean time he pay the said fine.

J. T., J. P.

(No. 5.)

Form of Commitment for failing to pay the foregoing fine.

——— County, to wit:
To X. Y., Constable and to the Keeper of the Jail of the said County:

Whereas, A. B. was this day duly convicted by me J. T., a Justice of the said County, of having, on the ——— day of ——— 18—, fixed in the Potomac river in said County and below the head of tide water, a seine or gill net, and of preventing thereby the passage of fish therein, to the injury of the fishery of E. F., and adjudged to pay for the said offence, the sum of twenty dollars fine, and also to pay ——— dollars, the costs of the prosecution; and payment of the said fine being by me then demanded, and the said A. B. having failed and now failing to pay the same: These are, therefore, to command you, the said Constable, forthwith to convey the said A. B. to the jail of the said County, and there deliver him, together with this warrant, to the keeper of the said jail; and you, the said keeper, are hereby commanded to receive the said A. B. into your jail and custody, and him safely keep for thirty days, unless in the mean time he shall pay the said fine of twenty dollars. Given under my hand and seal, this ——— day of ——— 18—.

J. T., J. P. [L. S.]

(No. 6.)

Form of Warrant of Arrest for fishing with nets or seines in the Potomac river, in March, April, May or June, under 6th section.

———— County, to wit:
 To all or any one of the Constables of said County:

Whereas, A. B. of said County, has this day made complaint and information on oath before me J. T., a Justice of the said County, that C. D., in said County, did, in the month of March, (or *April, May* or *June,*) to wit, on the ———— day of March 18—, fish in the Potomac river with a certain seine (or *net*) not laid out from, hauled to, or landed upon the shores of said river: These are, &c. (conclude as No. 1.)

(No. 7.)

Form of Warrant of Arrest for obstructing right of fishing, under 7th section.

———— County, to wit:
 To all or any one of the Constables of said County:

Whereas, A. B. of said County, has this day made complaint and information on oath before me J. T., a Justice of the said County, that C. D., in said County, did, during fishing season, to wit, on the ———— day of ———— 18—, anchor (or *place*) a vessel (or *boat*, or *craft*, or whatever other obstruction it may be,) within the limits of the fishery of him the said A. B., in the ———— river in said County, so as to interrupt and hinder him the said A. B. a person in this Commonwealth in his right of fishing in his said fishery, and that the said C. D. being afterwards required by the said A. B. immediately to remove the said obstruction, did not immediately remove the same: These are, therefore, &c. (conclude as No. 1.)

(No. 8.)

Form of Warrant of Arrest for hauling, floating or drifting a seine so as to obstruct the passage of fish in the waters of this Commonwealth, under 8th section.

———— County, to wit:
 To X. Y., Constable of said County:

Whereas, A. B. of the said County, has this day made affidavit and complaint on oath before me J. T., a Justice of the said County, that C. D. did, on the ———— day of ———— 18—, in the waters of the Potomac, (or whatever waters they may be within the Commonwealth,*) in said County, haul, float and drift a certain seine (or *net*) with a line fixed to the bottom thereof, so constructed as then and there to keep the said seine (or *net*) in an erect position and obstruct the passage of fish in the said river, and that said seine (or *net*) was not such a seine (or *net*) as had been used in the waters of this Commonwealth by any citizen thereof prior to the 13th day of February 1844: These are, therefore, &c. (conclude as No. 1.)

---

* But this warrant does not apply to the waters of Accomack, Northampton, Norfolk, Essex, or to the waters of the Rappahannock.

(No. 9.)

Form of Warrant of Arrest against a non-resident for fishing with a seine, under the 9th section.

—— County, to wit:
To all or any one of the Constables of said County:

Whereas, A. B. of said County, has this day made complaint and information on oath before me J. T., a Justice of the said County, that C. D., on the —— day of —— 18—, in said County, did fish with a seine in the waters of this Commonwealth, to wit, in the waters of James river, and that the said C. D. was not then a resident of this Commonwealth: These are, therefore, &c. (conclude as No. 1.)

(No. 10.)

Form of Warrant of Arrest for fishing in the Ohio river by a non-resident.

—— County, to wit:
To X. Y., Constable of the said County:

Whereas, A. B. has this day made complaint on oath, before me J. T., a Justice of said County, that C. D. did, on the —— day of —— 18—, in the said County, take and catch fish from the Ohio river, (or *from* —— *river*, or *creek, a tributary of the Ohio river*,) by a net, (or *seine*,) the said C. D. not then being a resident of this Commonwealth: These are, therefore, to command you, in the name of the Commonwealth, forthwith to apprehend the said C. D., and to bring him before me or some other Justice of the said County, to answer the said complaint, and to be farther dealt with according to law. Given under my hand and seal, this —— day of —— 18—.

J. T., J. P. [L. S.]

[NOTE.—By the 11th section, none are prohibited from fishing in the Ohio, but non-residents.]

(No. 11.)

Form of Recognizance of Bail by non-resident, to answer an indictment for unlawfully catching or taking fish, oysters or wild fowl.

—— County, to wit:

Be it remembered, that on the —— day of —— in the year 18—, A. B. and C. D. personally came before me J. T., Justice of the said County, and acknowledged themselves to owe to the Commonwealth of Virginia; the said A. B. the sum of —— dollars, and the said C. D. the sum of —— dollars, to be levied of their goods and chattels, lands and tenements respectively, if the said A. B. shall make default in the condition underwritten.

The condition of the above obligation is such, that if the above bound A. B., who is a non-resident of this Commonwealth, shall make his personal appearance before the County Court of ——, on the first day of the next quarterly term of the said County, to be held at the Courthouse of the said County, then and there to answer the Commonwealth of Virginia, for unlawfully killing wild fowl, (or *for unlawfully taking and catching oysters*, or for whatever other offence the party is charged with,) and shall satisfy the judgment which may be rendered against him therefor by the said Court, and shall not depart thence without the leave of the said Court, then the above recognizance shall be void, otherwise to remain in full force and virtue.

Taken and acknowledged before me, the day and year first above written.

J. T., J. P.

(No. 12.)

Form of Commitment of a non-resident, to answer an indictment for catching fish or taking oysters, &c. contrary to law.

——— County, to wit:

To X. Y., Constable of said County, and to the Keeper of the Jail of said County:

These are to command you, the said Constable, in the name of the Commonwealth of Virginia, forthwith to convey and deliver into the custody of the keeper of the said jail, the body of C. D., a non-resident of this Commonwealth, together with this warrant, charged before me J. T., a Justice of the said County, on the oath of A. B., with having on the ——— day of ——— 18—, in the said County, caught fish in ——— river, (or *taken oysters in* ———, or *killed wild fowl in* ———,) contrary to law; and you, the keeper of the said jail, are hereby required to receive the said C. D. into your custody in the said jail, and him there safely keep until he shall be thence discharged by due course of law. Given under my hand and seal, this ——— day of ——— 18—.

J. T., J. P. [L. S.]

[Unless against a non-resident, the proceedings after the arrest, for violations of the foregoing provisions of the statute, (except under the fifth section,) are the same as in other cases of misdemeanor. In such cases, for recognizance of bail, follow No. 4, under head of RECOGNIZANCE, and for recognizance of witnesses, whether the accused be a citizen or not, follow No. 5, under the same head. For commitment and certificate to the clerk, see Nos. 9, 10 and 11, under the head of ARREST. In the certificate of commitment to the clerk, if the party be a non-resident, add these words after his name occurs first, "a non-resident of this Commonwealth."]

CHAPTER XLIV.

FORESTALLING, INGROSSING AND REGRATING.

These offences, differing mostly in appellation, are of kindred character, having their common origin in cupidity, and perpetuating their existence by speculations upon the necessities of the public. The Common Law, so admirably adapted to the protection of the rights of individuals and the interest of society generally, holds every practice or device whatever, whether by act, conspiracy, word or news, to enhance the price of victuals or other necessaries of life, to be a misdemeanor,([1]) and by it, forestalling anciently comprehended all offences of this description, including those of ingrossing and regrating. There is no doubt that if one buys up the whole, or any considerable part of the produce from whence the supply of a market is derived, with *intent* to resell the same at an *unreasonable* profit, and thus deprive the people of their ordinary subsistence, or else compel them to purchase it at an exorbitant price, whether such practices fall within the definition of forestalling or regrating, he is guilty of a misdemeanor punishable at Common Law. And although the commodity in question, may not formerly have been used or considered as a common victual or necessary of life, yet if it has become such in the present day, or if it is merely used as an ingredient in the making or preservation of any victuals, (as *hops*, for instance,) it is equally criminal to forestall or ingross it for the purpose of enhancing its price.([2])

To spread false rumours among the hop-planters in a particular neighbourhood, with intent to induce them not to bring their hops to market, and thereby to increase the price of them, was held to be indictable.([3])

The gist of these offences at Common Law, is the intent of the party to raise the price of victuals or other necessaries of life, and to profit himself by thus inflicting an injury on the public,([4]) and it is remarked by Mr. Chitty, that at the present day, it would probably be holden no offence, unless there is an intent to raise the price of provisions ; "for," says he, "the mere transfer of a purchase in the market where it is made, the buying articles before they arrive at a public market, or the purchasing of a large quantity of a particular article, can scarcely be regarded as in themselves necessarily in-

---

([1]) 3 Inst. 196 ; Deac. Cr. Co. 498.
([2]) Rex *v.* Waddington, 1 East R. 154 ; 1 Hawk. c. 80, § 13.
([3]) 1 East 154.
([4]) 1 Hawk. c. 80, § 3 ; Deac. Cr. Co. 498.

jurious to the community, and as such, indictable offences, and many cases may occur in which a most laudable motive may exist for buying large quantities of the same commodity."(¹) Nevertheless, if it be manifest by the conduct of the party, that the purchase is made by him of food or other necessaries of life, with intent to resell the same at an *unreasonable* profit, and thus deprive the people of their ordinary subsistence, or else compel them to purchase it at an exorbitant price, he is guilty of a misdemeanor. There is but little difference between such conduct and *extortion*, and the Common Law has wisely made the practice of thus speculating upon the necessities of others, a crime, and it behooves Justices, especially in market towns, to sustain its humane purposes by a just, but rigid application of it to all who offend against its authority.

(No. 1.)

Form of Warrant of Arrest for forestalling.

——— County, to wit:

To all or any one of the Constables of said County:

Whereas, A. B. of said County, has this day made complaint and information on oath before me J. T., a Justice of the said County, that C. D., on the ——— day of ——— 18—, in said County, did unlawfully buy one hundred hogs of one E. F., for the sum of three hundred dollars, as he the said E. F. then and there was coming to a certain market in the City of R., called the Old Market, to sell the said hogs, and before the same were brought into the said market, where the same should be sold: These are, therefore, to command you, in the name of the Commonwealth of Virginia, forthwith to apprehend the said C. D., and bring him before me or some other Justice of the said County, to answer the said complaint, and to be farther dealt with according to law. Given under my hand and seal, this ——— day of ——— 18—.

J. T., J. P. [L. S.]

(No. 2.)

Form of Warrant of Arrest for regrating.

——— County, to wit :

To all or any one of the Constables of said County:

Whereas, A. B. of said County, has this day made complaint and information on oath before me J. T., a Justice of the said County, that C. D., on the ——— day of ——— 18—, in said County, in a certain market called ———, did buy and get into his possession, ten turkeys, fifty chickens, twenty ducks and fifteen pounds of butter, of and from one G. H., for the sum of five dollars, (the said turkeys, chickens, ducks and butter, then being brought to the said market by the said G. H. to be sold,) and that the said C. D. did, afterwards, on that day, in the said market, unlawfully regrate the said turkeys, chickens, ducks and butter, and sell the same again to one

---

(¹) See 2 Ch. Cr. L. 527, 528, in n.; 14 East 406; 15 East 511.

E. F. for ten dollars: These are, therefore, to command you, in the name of the Commonwealth of Virginia, forthwith to apprehend the said C. D., and bring him before me or some other Justice of the said County, to answer the said complaint, and to be farther dealt with according to law. Given under my hand and seal, this —— day of ——— 18—.

J. T., J. P. [L. S.]

[For proceedings after arrest, see for mittimus, No. 9, under head of ARREST, and No. 10, under the same head, for certificate of commitment. For recognizance of bail and of witness, see Nos. 4 and 5, under head of RECOGNIZANCE.]

An Indictment for regrating.

Commence as No. 2, under the head of "INDICTMENTS," and proceed thus: on the —— day of ——— in the year —— in the County aforesaid, in a certain market there, called ———, did buy, obtain and get into his hands and possession, ten geese, thirty turkeys and fifty ducks, of and from one C. D., for the sum of ten dollars, (the said geese, turkeys and ducks then being brought to the said market by the said C. D. to be sold,) and afterwards, to wit, on the day and year aforesaid, he the said A. B., in the County aforesaid, in the said market, there unlawfully did regrate the said geese, turkeys and ducks, and sell the same again to one J. K., for the sum of twenty dollars, against the peace and dignity of the Commonwealth of Virginia.

[NOTE.—Upon an indictment for forestalling, it is necessary to prove the purchase as laid in the indictment, though the quantity is immaterial. It must also be proved that the article was purchased on the way to market, and before it arrived there.]

In prosecutions for regrating, the purchase and resale must be proved as laid in the indictment. A variance between the indictment and evidence, in the number of articles, or the price at which they were bought or resold, does not seem to be material; nor does it appear to be necessary, to constitute the offence, that the defendant should have derived profit from the resale. See Archbold's Cr. Pl. 473.

An indictment for ingrossing "a great quantity" of fish, geese and ducks, was held bad; for the quantity of each ought to be specified. Rex v. Gilbert, 1 East 583.

CHAPTER XLV.

FORGERY.

The metaphorical term forgery, was early introduced into the Common Law to denote the false and fraudulent making of written instruments with an evil intent, and was at first limited in its operation to comparatively but few kinds of writing : so much so, that the earlier writers on criminal law seemed, as remarked by Mr. East, " to have fettered their definition of the nature and principles of the offence, with its application to the particular species of instruments to which the experience and necessity of their own times alone had extended it." It is, however, characteristic of the Common Law, to adapt itself to the experience and necessity of all times, as a shield against fraud ; and as the necessities, and with them, the transactions of mankind multiplied, so written contracts were extended, and as they assumed a variety of forms unknown in the earlier periods of the Common Law, so also, for the protection of all rights growing out of written instruments, from this species of fraud, the Common Law definition of forgery was enlarged until it now embraces the false making, counterfeiting or altering of any instrument of writing with a fraudulent intent, whereby another *may* be defrauded ; for there is no necessity, in order to complete the offence, that any person should be *actually* defrauded. This is the definition of forgery according to the case of Rex *v.* Goate,([1]) and although the statute has raised the crime to a higher class, it is said to be at least doubtful, whether it has added to the variety of subjects embraced in the more modern definition of the offence ; for at Common Law, writings of every description, whether of a public or private nature, whether written or printed, of record, under seal, or by parol, were equally the subjects of forgery, being equally within the mischief and definition of the crime.([2]) This definition is in substance adopted by all subsequent writers on Crown Law. Mr. East defines forgery to be "a false making," (which includes every alteration of or addition to a true instrument, for the purpose of fraud and deceit,) and says : " that this definition results from all the authorities, ancient and modern, taken together."([3]) Blackstone defines it to be " the fraudulent ma-

---

([1]) 1 Ld. Ray. 737.
([2]) Rex *v.* Ward, 2 Ld. Ray. 1461; Strange 747 ; and see Hammond on Forgery.
([3]) East P. C. 852.

king or alteration of *a writing*, to the prejudice of another's right."(¹) And Mr. Justice Gross, in Rex *v.* Taylor,(²) says, that forgery is " the false making a note or *other instrument*, with intent to defraud."

At Common Law, this offence was only a misdemeanor, but upon the institution and great increase and value of paper credit in the transactions of commerce especially, it was found necessary for its protection against frauds by forgery, to raise the crime to a higher class, and it is now made felony by the statute, which in terms adopts Mr. Blackstone's definition of it.

By Sec. 1, Chap. 193. If a free person forge a public record or a certificate, return or attestation of *a clerk of a court, public register, notary public, judge, justice or* any public officer, in relation to any matter wherein such certificate, return or attestation may be received as legal proof, or utter or attempt to employ as true such forged record, certificate, return or attestation, knowing the same to be forged, he shall be confined in the penitentiary not less than two, nor more than ten years.

By Sec. 2. If a free person forge, or keep or conceal any instrument for the purpose of forging, the seal of a court, or of any public office or body politic or corporate in this State, he shall be confined in the penitentiary not less than two, nor more than ten years.

By Sec. 3. If a free person forge any coin, current by law or usage in this State, or any note or bill of a banking company, or fraudulently make any base coin, or a note or bill, purporting to be the note or bill of a banking company, when such company does not exist, or utter or attempt to employ as true such false, forged or base coin, note or bill, knowing it to be so, he shall be confined in the penitentiary not less than two, nor more than ten years.

By Sec. 4. If a free person engrave, stamp or cast, or otherwise make or amend any plate, block, press or other thing adapted and designed for the forging and false making any writing or other thing, the forging or false making whereof is punishable by this act, or if such person have in his possession any such plate, block, press or other thing, with intent to use, or cause or permit it to be used in forging or false making any such writing or other thing, he shall be confined in the penitentiary not less than two, nor more than ten years.

By Sec. 5. If a free person forge any writing other than such as is mentioned in the first and third sections of this chapter, *to the prejudice of another's right*, or utter or attempt to employ as true such forged writing, knowing it to be forged,

---

(¹) 4 Comm. 247.   (²) 1 Leach 214.

he shall be confined in the penitentiary not less than two, nor more than ten years.

BY SEC. 6. If a free person have in his possession forged bank notes, or pieces of forged or base coin, such as are mentioned in the third section of this chapter, knowing the same to be forged or base, with intent to utter or employ the same as true, he shall, if the number of such notes or pieces of coin in his possession, at the same time, be ten or more, be confined in the penitentiary not less than one nor more than five years; and if the number thereof be less than ten, be punished as for a misdemeanor.

Under this section, if the number be ten or more, the party should be committed for examination or trial; if less than ten, the commitment should be to answer an indictment for the misdemeanor in the county or corporation court.

Forgery, then, in view of the statute, consists in the false making or alteration of any one of the instruments specially designated therein, or of *any other writing whatever, to the prejudice of another's right, with intent to injure and defraud;* covering nothing more, as we conceive, than was before protected by the principle involved in the more modern Common Law definition, which was broad enough to embrace any instrument, the false making of which, with an evil intent, might prejudice the rights of others. What written instruments are "to the prejudice of another's right," is a question that has given rise to much investigation in our courts, but has led to no fixed rule of construction. The discussion of it is beyond our province, though we venture to suggest, that in applying the English cases of construction upon their various statutes, it should be remembered that the language of our statute is more comprehensive than the British statutes, which generally enumerate the different subjects of forgery, and that their decisions, therefore, will aid us but little upon this question. We should go to the Common Law and there learn what writing prejudiced another's rights; what false instruments were reached by the ancient Common Law writs of forgery and deceit, before forgery was made a felony. (See Hammond on Forgery.)

Confining this guide to its proper limits, the Justice will observe, that to constitute the crime of forgery, there must be a false making of the instrument, and that with a fraudulent intent to injure, and that to utter it with like intent, is also a felony under the statute. It is proposed, therefore, to consider the subject briefly in the following order: 1st, of the false making and counterfeiting; 2d, of the uttering and publishing; and 3d, of the fraudulent intent.

I. *The false making and counterfeiting, altering or erasing.*

The making of any instrument which is the subject of forgery, with a fraudulent intent and without lawful authority, is of itself a sufficient completion of the offence without publication; for though publication be the medium by which the intent is usually made manifest, it may be satisfactorily proved by other evidence.([1]) Therefore, though a forged note is kept in the possession of a party and never attempted to be uttered by him, yet it is a question for a jury to determine, under all the circumstances of the case, whether the note was made innocently or not.([2]) The uttering and publishing with knowledge of the forgery, is a substantive offence under the statute, and the false making, with intent to defraud, is sufficient to constitute forgery without any uttering. And so distinct are the two offences, that in a case where the prisoner was examined and remanded by the examining court for trial, for feloniously using and employing as true, for his own benefit, a certain counterfeit note, well knowing the same to be a counterfeit, it was held by the general court, that an indictment for forging the note, was not warranted by the examination, and the indictment was quashed.([3]) Making a fraudulent insertion, alteration or erasure in any material part of a true instrument, though merely in a single letter, if the sense is changed and a new operation is thereby given to it, is as much a forgery, as if the whole instrument had been fabricated; for a man's hand and seal are thus falsely made use of, to testify his assent to an instrument, which, after such an alteration, is no more his than a stranger's.([4]) To alter a bank note or bill of exchange from ten to fifty pounds, falls within this principle, and such alterations may be charged as a making, forging and counterfeiting, though the statute might contain the word "alter," as well as the word "forge,"([5]) and any alteration whatever in a negotiable instrument, for the purpose of giving it greater currency, or for any other purpose with intent to defraud, amounted to the crime of forgery.([6]) So, to alter the date of a bill of exchange, (and, it is presumed, any other obligation,) whereby

---

([1]) Rex v. Ward, 2 Ld. Ray. 1469; 2 Deac. C. C. 1392.

([2]) Rex v. Elliott, 1 Leach 173; 2 East P. C. 951; Rex v. Crocker & Collins, Russ. & Ry. 97; and see Spencer's Case, 2 Leigh 751.

([3]) Page v. Comm'th, 9 Leigh 683; and see Mabrey's Case, 11 Leigh 643, where it was held that if a prisoner be examined for FORGING an order, he could not be tried for uttering and publishing.

([4]) Rex v. Ellsworth, 2 East P. C. 980.

([5]) 2 East P. C. 979; Rex v. John Teague, R. & R. 33; and R. & R. 101, Rex v. Post.

([6]) 2 Deac. Cr. L. 1393; Rex v. Treble, 2 Taunt. 328; 2 Leach 1040.

payment is accelerated, would amount to forgery,([1]) and if done with a fraudulent intent, it would be equally forgery to discharge one endorsement on a bill or note and insert another, or to make a special endorsement a general endorsement ;([2]) and so, the expunging an endorsement upon a bank bill, by means of lemon juice, was held to be an erasing under the statute.([3]) Lord Ellenborough held it to be forgery for a party to make a copy of a receipt for a given sum, and add to such copy the words "in full of all demands," which were not in the original, and then offer it in evidence upon a suggestion of the loss of the original.([4]) Wilfully to insert in an indictment the name of a party against whom it was not found, is forgery.([5]) An instrument may be altered before the party, to be bound by it, signs it, and if it be done with a fraudulent intent, and be afterwards executed by him in ignorance of the deceit, the crime of him who makes the alteration will not the less be forgery. As where a man, who is ordered to draw a will for a sick person, inserts legacies in it of his own head. But the bare omission to insert a legacy in a will, which one man is instructed to draw for another, would not be forgery, unless done wilfully and with a fraudulent intent, and then it seems, the person making such omission, would be guilty of forgery.([6]) The fraudulent application of a true signature to a false instrument for which it was not intended, or *vice versa*, will also be forgery ; as where a man finding another's name at the bottom of a letter at a considerable distance from the other writing, causes the letter to be cut off and a general release to be written above the name, and then takes off the seal and affixes it under the release.([7]) So it is as much a forgery to make a mark to a promissory note or any other document in the name of another person, with intent to defraud, as if the party had signed that person's name.([8]) The common idea of forgery is, that it is the writing of another person's name without his authority, with intent to commit a fraud, but this is not the legal acceptation of the term, for a forgery may be committed even by a party making a false deed in his own name ; as if he make a deed of his lands and date it prior to a former deed made by him conveying the same lands, thereby attempting to give the last an operation which in justice it ought not to have, in order to defraud his own first

---

([1]) 2 East P. C. 853.
([2]) Rex *v.* Birkett, R. & R. 251; 2 Dea. C. L. 1393.
([3]) Rex *v.* Bigg, 3 P. Wms. 419.
([4]) 5 Esp. 100.
([5]) Rex *v.* Marsh, 3 Mod. Rep. 66; 2 Deac. Cr. Co. 1393.

([6]) 3 Inst. 170; 1 Hawk. c. 70, § 2-6;
2 East P. C. 856.
([7]) 2 Russ. Cr. & M. 318; 1 Hawk. c. 70, § 2.
([8]) Rex *v.* Dunn, 1 Leach 57 ; 2 East 962 ; 2 Deac. Cr. Co. 1394.

deed.(¹) So a man may be guilty of forgery in signing any instrument in his *own name*, if he represents himself to be some *other person* of the same name, and delivers the document, whether it be a deed or note, as the deed or note of another person, with intent to commit a fraud.(²) But in such a case, there must be both a false making and fraudulent representation; for it is not forgery merely to *pass for* the person whose endorsement is on a bill of exchange, and thereby to obtain credit in the name of another, as there is no false making.(³) But see FALSE PRETENCE.

As a party may be guilty of forgery by fraudulently making an instrument in his own name and assuming to be another person of that name, so he may be guilty of forgery by assuming and using the name of another and representing himself to be that other person. These cases are common in England, and have occurred in this State. They may be divided into two classes: 1. Where the name assumed and used, is that of a real person. 2. Where the name used, is that of a non-existing or fictitious person.

In the first case, it matters not that the offender passes himself off upon the party to whom the forged instrument is uttered, as the person whose name is used, and so receives credit as such person, for the credit in this case is not given to the impostor personally, without any relation to another, but in reality to that other person whom he represents himself to be. Therefore, where a note is made by a party in an assumed name, with intent to defraud, the offence is holden to be forgery, though the note is made and offered as that of the party himself, and not as the note of another in contradistinction to himself.(⁴)

In the second case, the making of any false instrument, with a fraudulent intent, although in the name of a fictitious person, or one who never existed, is as much a forgery as if it had been made in the name of one who was known to exist and to whom credit was due. And this holds as well with one kind of instrument as another; as in the case of a power of attorney, bill of exchange or check, &c.(⁵)

And in the case of an assumed name, it is immaterial, in order to constitute the crime of forgery, whether any additional credit be gained by the assumption of that name more than would have been obtained by the real name of the

---

(¹) 3 Inst. 169; 1 Hale 683; Fost. 117; 1 Hawk. c. 70, § 2.
(²) 4 T. R. 28; 1 Dick. J. P. 673; and see R. *v.* Brown, 2 Leach 775.
(³) Rex *v.* Hevey, 1 Leach 229; Rex *v.* Webb, R. & R. 405.
(⁴) Dunn's Case, 1 Leach 57; 2 East P. C. 962; Hatfield's Case, 6 Evans Col. St. part 5th, p. 579.
(⁵) 2 East P. C. 957-8; Foster 116; Bolland's Case, 1 Leach 83; Locket's Case, 1 Leach 94; and Rex *v.* Anderson, 2 East P. C. 940.

party.(¹) Notwithstanding the doubt on this point, suggested in Aickle's Case, 2 East P. C. 908, it has been well settled by subsequent cases; for in Whiley's Case, R. & R. 90, it was held, that where the name made use of by the prisoner in the forged instrument, was assumed by him with the intention of defrauding the prosecutor, a conviction for felony was held right, though the prisoner's real name would have carried with it as much credit as the assumed name; and the same point was ruled in Rex v. Francis, Russ. & Ry. 209.

Although it is not material that the forged instrument should be so made, as that if it were genuine, it would be a *valid* instrument, yet it is essential to the crime of forgery, that it should carry on its face the *semblance* of that for which it was counterfeited, and that it should not be illegal in its very frame; so that although it is forgery to make a false will of a living man,(²) yet if it be a will attested by but one witness, (the statute of Virginia requiring two attesting witnesses to a will,) it would not be forgery according to the principle in Wall's Case, 2 East P. C. 953; nor is it forgery to make a promissory note without a signature, because such instruments have no semblance of validity in law.(³) Where the charge is for counterfeiting coin, the moneys charged to be counterfeited must resemble the true and lawful coin, but this resemblance is matter of fact to be judged of by the Justice upon the evidence, as by a jury on the final trial. The rule is, that the resemblance need not be perfect, but such as is calculated to deceive a person using ordinary caution, or in other words, such as may in circulation ordinarily impose upon the world.(⁴) If there is such resemblance, though there is neither head nor tail, or any other impression whatever on the coin, it may be a counterfeit: as in the case of counterfeiting shillings of the similitude and resemblance of old worn shillings, where the counterfeit pieces were quite smooth without the smallest vestige of head or tail, and without any resemblance to the shillings in circulation, except their colour, size and shape, the persons were adjudged guilty of counterfeiting.(⁵)

The possession of forged bank notes, together with the plates and other implements used in forging them, is *prima facie* evidence that the person so found in possession, did feloniously forge them, and that the forgery was committed in

---

(¹) Rex v. Taft, 1 Leach 172; 2 East P. C. 959-60; Rex v. Taylor, 1 Leach 214.
(²) Sterling's Case, 1 Leach 99.
(³) Rex v. Pateman, R. & R. 455; Rex v. Butterwick, 1 Moo. & Rob. 196; and see Rex v. Richards, Russ. & Ry. 193; and Rex v. Randall, Id. 195.
(⁴) 1 Hawk. c. 17, § 81; 1 Hale 178, 184, 211; 1 Russ. 80; U. S. v. Morrow, 4 Wash. C. C. R. 733.
(⁵) 1 Leach 285, 364; 1 East P. C. 164.

the place where such possession was first discovered.(¹) And if several persons make distinct parts of a forged note, for instance, some the plate, others the paper, and another fills up the instrument, each is a principal in the forging, though he does not know by whom the other parts are executed, although the forged instrument is finished by one alone in the absence of the others.(²)

II. *The uttering and publishing.*

Any disposal or negotiation of a forged instrument to another, with a fraudulent intent, will fall within the offence of uttering it. As where one knowingly delivers a forged note to an innocent agent for the purpose of being uttered by him, and he utters it accordingly, this is an uttering by the first party,(³) and so where the note was given to an accomplice for the purpose of being uttered, it was held to be an uttering.(⁴)

And delivering a box containing among other things forged instruments, to the party's own servant, that he may carry them to an inn to be forwarded by a carrier to a person in the country, with intent to commit a fraud, is an uttering.(⁵) So, where the prisoner merely delivered a forged bill of exchange, payable to his own order, but not endorsed by him, to another person as a pledge, for the purpose of obtaining credit from that person, the offence of forgery and of uttering was held complete,(⁶) and, indeed, to assert and declare, either directly or indirectly, by word or action, that the counterfeit offered is a good note, is an uttering and publishing, and it is not necessary that it should be passed, in order to complete the offence of uttering.(⁷) It has been held that the reading out a false document, with intent to commit a fraud, although the party refuses to shew it, is a sufficient uttering,(⁸) and by the statute, the mere offering to pass a forged or counterfeit bill of exchange or bank note or coin, is sufficient to constitute the offence of uttering.

The passing a counterfeit note to a slave, is an offence against the statute, and it may be charged with intent to defraud the banks,(⁹) and now by the statute, it may be laid with intent to defraud generally. See INDICTMENT.

(¹) Spencer's Case, 2 Leigh 751; Mason's R. 470.
(²) Rex *v.* Kirkwood and als. R. & M. C. C. 304; Rex *v.* J. Daul and als., Id. 307.
(³) 1 N. R. 96; 2 Leach 978; R. & R. 72.
(⁴) Ry. & Moody 166.
(⁵) Rex *v.* Collicott, 4 Taunt. 300; R. & R. 212.
(⁶) Rex *v.* Birkett, R. & R. 86.
(⁷) Reg. *v.* Cushland, Jebbs C. C. 112; and cases there cited.
(⁸) Reg. *v.* Green, Jebbs C. C. 289.
(⁹) Brown's Case, 2 Leigh 760-61.

It matters not whether the person to whom the forged instrument is disposed of, knows it to be a forgery, the offence of uttering is complete although the person receiving it receives it as and for a forged instrument at his own solicitation, knowing it at the time to be a forgery, and taking it for the very purpose of bringing the offender to justice.(¹)

The offence of uttering is complete, though it may not be for the benefit of the utterer.(²)

A guilty knowledge that the instrument is a forgery, is of the essence of the crime of a felonious uttering and must be proved. From the nature of the thing, this cannot be done by direct proof unless by the confession of the party, and must therefore be gathered from his acts and conduct. Thus, uttering a forged order for the payment of money under *false representations*, for instance, is evidence of the party's knowing it to be forged, the false representation being the act from which the guilty knowledge is inferred ;(³) and it is now well settled, that this knowledge may be established by proving that the prisoner had before passed off other forged notes, or that he had in his possession and attempted to pass other counterfeit notes or coin of the same kind, to other persons,(⁴) and it seems to be immaterial, whether the notes found in the possession of the prisoner, or which had been before passed off by him, were of another bank or not.(⁵)

It has been properly advised, and deserves to be remembered by the Justice, "that whenever a prosecution upon this statute is brought before a Justice, for passing or being possessed with intent to pass any counterfeit bank bill or coin, every step ought to be immediately taken by the Justice to identify all the bills or pieces of coin which are to be the subjects of the complaint and prosecution. In order to do this, the Justice should direct the person in whose possession he finds them, to put his private mark on each bill and piece of coin in his presence, so that the witness can swear to the identity of the bills or pieces of coin at all times afterwards, into whosoever hands they may subsequently pass. The trouble and expense of a number of witnesses may be frequently saved by this precaution. For if the bills or pieces of coin have no private mark upon them, by which they can be identified on the trial, every person into whose hands they may have passed, must be produced in Court to swear to their identity."

(¹) Rex v. Holden and als., R. & R. 154 ; 7 Taunt. 334 ; 2 Leach 1019.
(²) Murray's Case, 5 Leigh 720.
(³) Rex v. Sheppard, 1 Leach 226 ; 2 East P. C. 967.
(⁴) Rex v. Wylie, 2 Leach 983 ; Rex v. Ball, R. & R. 132 ; 2 N. R. 87.
(⁵) Deac. Cr. Co. 1480-81.

III. *Of the fraudulent intent.*

A fraudulent intent to deceive, is essential to the crime of forgery, and, like guilty knowledge, is difficult to make out by direct evidence ; it must be gathered from the conduct of the party as shewn in proof. When the tendency of his acts is direct and manifest, he must always be presumed to have designed the result of such acts when he acted. Although there must be an intent of the party to deceive or defraud some person or persons, at the time of making the false instrument, when made, to constitute the crime of forgery, it is immaterial whether any person be actually defrauded or not ; it is sufficient if he may be thereby prejudiced.([1])

And the intent need not be to defraud any particular person, but a general intent to defraud is sufficient ; for if a man will do an act, the natural consequence of which is to defraud, it will, in contemplation of law, be evidence of a fraudulent intent.

The intent may be proved by the uttering of a forged instrument, although from some defect in the formation of it, or from some other cause, it would not be available, if genuine, in the hands of the person to whom it is uttered, as where a man forged the acceptance of a bill of exchange, payable to his own order and negotiated it without endorsement, by pledging it to obtain credit.([2])

So an intent to defraud the person who would have to pay the forged instrument, if genuine, will be presumed, although from the manner of executing the forgery, or from that person's ordinary caution, it would not be likely to impose upon him ; and although the object was general to defraud whoever might take the instrument, and the intention of defrauding that person in particular never entered into the prisoner's head ;([3]) indeed if a person put off forged notes with a general intent to defraud, it is sufficient, although, from circumstances of which he is ignorant at the time, he could not in fact defraud the individual upon whom the forged instruments are put off, for it is the intent existing in the mind, which is of the essence of this as well as of every other crime.([4])

Where the necessary effect and consequence of the forging is to defraud a particular individual, this is sufficient evidence of the intent to defraud him, notwithstanding that individual may swear that he believed the party had no such intent.([5])

([1]) 2 East P. C. 854.
([2]) Rex *v.* Birkett, R. & R. 86 ; and see Rex *v.* Wick, R. & R. 149.
([3]) Mazagora's Case, R. & R. 291.
([4]) Rex *v.* Holden, R. & R. 154.
([5]) Rex *v.* Sheppard, R. & R. 169.

FORGERY.

At Common Law great strictness is required in describing the instrument forged, and in stating the party intended to be defrauded. To remedy this, section 7, chapter 207, provides, that in a prosecution for forging or altering, or attempting to employ as true, any forged instrument or other thing, it shall be sufficient to describe the instrument or writing in such manner as would be sufficient in an indictment for stealing the same, without farther setting forth any copy or *fac simile* thereof. By section 9, of the same chapter, it will be sufficient, in the offence of forgery, to allege in the proceedings an intent to defraud generally, without specifying any particular party to be defrauded. See head INTENT.

(No. 1.)

Form of Warrant of Arrest for forging and uttering a bank note, knowing it to be forged.

―――― County, to wit:

To all or any one of the Constables of said County:

Whereas, A. B. of said County, has this day made complaint and information on oath before me J. T., a Justice of the said County, that C. D., on the ―― day of ―――― 18―, in said County, did feloniously forge a certain bank note, of the president, directors and company of the Bank of Virginia, (the same being a banking company authorized by law,) for the payment of ―――― dollars, purporting to be dated on the ―― day of ―――― 18―, and the said forged bank note then and there feloniously did utter and attempt to employ as true, he the said C. D. then and there well knowing the same to be forged, with intent to defraud: These are, therefore, to command you, in the name of the Commonwealth of Virginia, forthwith to apprehend the said C. D., and bring him before me or some other Justice of the said County, to answer the said complaint, and to be farther dealt with according to law. Given under my hand and seal, this ―― day of ―――― 18―.

J. T., J. P. [L. S.]

(No. 2.)

Form of Warrant of Arrest for uttering and employing as true a counterfeit bank note, knowing the same to be a counterfeit.

―――― County, to wit:

To all or any one of the Constables of said County:

Whereas, A. B. of said County, has this day made complaint and information on oath before me J. T., a Justice of the said County, that C. D., on the ―― day of ―――― 18―, in said County, did feloniously utter and attempt to employ as true to P. S. a certain false and forged bank note purporting to be a true and genuine bank note, for the payment of ―――― dollars, of the president, directors and company of the ―― Bank of Virginia, (the same being a banking company authorized by law,) with intent to defraud, he the said C. D. then and there knowing the said forged note to be forged: These are, therefore, to command you, in the name of the Commonwealth of Virginia, forthwith to apprehend the said C. D., and bring him before me or some other Justice of the said County, to answer the said complaint, and to be farther dealt with according to law. Given under my hand and seal, this —— day of —— 18—.

J. T., J. P. [L. s.]

(No. 3.)

Form of Warrant of Arrest for forging a check on a bank, and uttering the same as true.

—— County, to wit:

To all or any one of the Constables of said County:

Whereas, A. B. of said County, has this day made complaint and information on oath before me J. T., a Justice of the said County, that C. D., on the —— day of —— 18—, in said County, did feloniously forge a certain order for the payment of money, commonly called a check, purporting to be the order or draft of one J. A., upon the Bank of Virginia, for the payment of —— dollars, and did then and there feloniously utter and attempt to employ the same as a true and genuine check, he the said C. D. knowing the same to be forged, with intent to defraud: These are, therefore, to command you, in the name of the Commonwealth of Virginia, forthwith to apprehend the said C. D., and bring him before me or some other Justice of the said County, to answer the said complaint, and to be farther dealt with according to law. Given under my hand and seal, this —— day of —— 18—.

J. T., J. P. [L. s.]

(No. 4.)

Form of Warrant of Arrest for forging the acceptance of a bill of exchange.

—— County, to wit:

To all or any one of the Constables of said County:

Whereas, A. B. of said County, has this day made complaint and information on oath before me J. T., a Justice of the said County, that C. D. on the —— day of —— 18—, in said County, did feloniously forge the acceptance of a certain bill of exchange, dated on the —— day of —— 18—, for the payment of —— dollars, purporting to be the acceptance of one E. F., with intent to defraud: These are, therefore, to command you, in the name of the Commonwealth of Virginia, forthwith to apprehend the said C. D., and bring him before me or some other Justice of the said County, to answer the said complaint, and to be farther dealt with according to law. Given under my hand and seal, this —— day of —— 18—.

J. T., J. P. [L. s.]

(No. 5.)

Form of Warrant of Arrest for forging a promissory note.

—— County, to wit:

To all or any one of the Constables of said County:

Whereas, A. B. of said County, has this day made complaint and information on oath before me J. T., a Justice of the said County, that C. D., on

FORGERY.

the —— day of ——— 18—, in said County, did feloniously forge a certain note, commonly called a promissory note, for the payment of ——— dollars, purporting to have been signed by the said A. B., and purporting to be dated on the —— day of ——— 18—, with intent to defraud: These are, therefore, to command you, in the name of the Commonwealth of Virginia, forthwith to apprehend the said C. D., and bring him before me or some other Justice of the said County, to answer the said complaint, and to be farther dealt with according to law. Given under my hand and seal, this —— day of ——— 18—.

J. T., J. P. [L. S.]

(No. 6.)

Form of Warrant of Arrest for forging a bond.

——— County, to wit:

To all or any one of the Constables of said County:

Whereas, A. B. of said County, has this day made complaint and information on oath before me J. T., a Justice of the said County, that C. D., on the —— day of ——— 18—, in said County, did feloniously forge a certain bond for the payment of ——— dollars, purporting to have been signed and sealed by the said A. B., and purporting to be dated on the —— day of ——— 18—, with intent to defraud: These are, therefore, to command you, in the name of the Commonwealth of Virginia, forthwith to apprehend the said C. D., and bring him before me or some other Justice of the said County, to answer the said complaint, and to be farther dealt with according to law. Given under my hand and seal, this —— day of ——— 18—.

J. T., J. P. [L. S.]

(No. 7.)

Form of Warrant of Arrest for forging a receipt.

——— County, to wit:

To all or any one of the Constables of said County:

Whereas, A. B. of said County, has this day made complaint and information on oath before me J. T., a Justice of the said County, that C. D., on the —— day of ——— 18—, in said County, did feloniously forge a certain receipt for ——— dollars, purporting to be the receipt of the said A. B., and purporting to be dated on the —— day of ——— 18—, with intent to defraud: These are, therefore, to command you, in the name of the Commonwealth of Virginia, forthwith to apprehend the said C. D., and bring him before me or some other Justice of the said County, to answer the said complaint, and to be farther dealt with according to law. Given under my hand and seal, this —— day of ——— 18—.

J. T., J. P. [L. S.]

(No. 8.)

Form of Warrant of Arrest for forging an order, and for uttering the same as true.

———— County, to wit:
  To all or any one of the Constables of said County:

Whereas, A. B. of said County, has this day made complaint and information on oath before me J. T., a Justice of the said County, that C. D., on the ——— day of ———— 18—, in said County, did feloniously forge, utter and attempt to employ as true, a certain paper, purporting to be an order drawn by one J. T. on P. J., in favour of D. S., for the payment of ———— dollars, purporting to be dated on the ——— day of ———— 18—, he the said C. D., knowing the said forged order to be forged, with intent to defraud: These are, therefore, to command you, in the name of the Commonweath of Virginia, forthwith to apprehend the said C. D., and bring him before me or some other Justice of the said County, to answer the said complaint, and to be farther dealt with according to law. Given under my hand and seal, this ——— day of ———— 18—.

J. T., J. P. [L. s.]

(No. 9.)

Form of Warrant of Arrest for forging a will.

———— County, to wit:
  To all or any one of the Constables of said County:

Whereas, A. B. of said County, has this day made complaint and information on oath before me J. T., a Justice of the said County, that C. D., on the ——— day of ———— 18—, in said County, did feloniously forge a certain will and testament, purporting to be the last will and testament of one E. F. deceased, and purporting to be dated on the ——— day of ———— 18—, with intent to defraud: These are, therefore, to command you, in the name of the Commonwealth of Virginia, forthwith to apprehend the said C. D., and bring him before me or some other Justice of the said County, to answer the said complaint, and to be farther dealt with according to law. Given under my hand and seal, this ——— day of ———— 18—.

J. T., J. P. [L. s.]

(No. 10.)

Form of Warrant of Arrest for forging a certificate of acknowledgment of a deed.

———— County, to wit:
  To all or any one of the Constables of said County:

Whereas, A. B. of said County, has this day made complaint and information on oath before me J. T., a Justice of the said County, that C. D., on the ——— day of ———— 18—, in said County, did feloniously and falsely forge a certain paper writing, purporting to be a certificate of the acknowledgment of a deed of conveyance from the said A. B. to the said C. D., of certain lands, before J. T. and J. M., two of the Justices of the County of

———, which said forged paper writing is of the purport and effect following, (here insert a copy of the forged writing,) and which may be received as legal proof, with intent to defraud: These are, therefore, to command you, in the name of the Commonwealth of Virginia, forthwith to apprehend the said C. D., and bring him before me or some other Justice of the said County, to answer the said complaint, and to be farther dealt with according to law. Given under my hand and seal, this ——— day of ——— 18—.

J. T., J. P. [L. S.]

(No. 11.)

Form of Warrant of Arrest for having ten forged bank notes in possession at the same time.

——— County, to wit:

To all or any one of the Constables of said County:

Whereas, A. B. of said County, has this day made complaint and information on oath before me J. T., a Justice of the said County, that C. D., on the ——— day of ——— 18—, in said County, feloniously had in his possession at the same time, ten certain forged bank notes with intent to utter and employ the same as true, he the said C. D., then and there knowing the said bank notes to be forged: These are, therefore, to command you, in the name of the Commonwealth of Virginia, forthwith to apprehend the said C. D., and bring him before me or some other Justice of the said County, to answer the said complaint, and to be farther dealt with according to law. Given under my hand and seal, this ——— day of ——— 18—.

J. T., J. P. [L. S.]

(No. 12.)

Form of Warrant of Arrest for counterfeiting coin.

——— County, to wit:

To all or any one of the Constables of said County:

Whereas, A. B. of said County, has this day made complaint and information on oath before me J. T., a Justice of the said County, that C. D., on the ——— day of ——— 18—, in said County, did feloniously and falsely forge and counterfeit divers, to wit, twenty pieces of silver coin, current in this Commonwealth, by the laws and usages thereof, called half dollars, with intent to deceive and defraud: These are, therefore, to command you, in the name of the Commonwealth of Virginia, forthwith to apprehend the said C. D., and bring him before me or some other Justice of the said County, to answer the said complaint, and to be farther dealt with according to law. Given under my hand and seal, this ——— day of ——— 18—.

J. T., J. P. [L. S.]

(No. 13.)

Form of Warrant of Arrest for uttering counterfeit coin, knowing it to be counterfeit.

——— County, to wit:
   To all or any one of the Constables of said County:
   Whereas, A. B. of said County, has this day made complaint and information on oath before me J. T., a Justice of the said County, that C. D., on the ——— day of ——— 18—, in said County, did feloniously and fraudulently utter and employ as true, a certain piece of false, forged and base coin, forged and counterfeited to the likeness and similitude of a silver dollar, current in this Commonwealth by the laws and usages thereof, with intent to deceive and defraud, knowing the same to be false and forged: These are, therefore, to command you, in the name of the Commonwealth of Virginia, forthwith to apprehend the said C. D., and bring him before me or some other Justice of the said County, to answer the said complaint, and to be farther dealt with according to law. Given under my hand and seal, this ——— day of ——— 18—.

J. T., J. P. [L. S.]

(No. 14.)

Form of Warrant of Arrest for having ten pieces of base coin in possession at the same time.

——— County, to wit:
   To all or any one of the Constables of said County:
   Whereas, A. B. of said County, has this day made complaint and information on oath before me J. T., a Justice of the said County, that C. D., on the ——— day of ——— 18—, in said County, did feloniously have in his possession at the same time, ten pieces of forged and base coin, of the likeness and similitude of good and legal silver coin, current within this Commonwealth by the laws and usages thereof, called half dollars, with intent to utter and employ the same as true, he the said C. D. knowing the same to be forged and base: These are, therefore, to command you, in the name of the Commonwealth of Virginia, forthwith to apprehend the said C. D., and bring him before me or some other Justice of the said County, to answer the said complaint, and to be farther dealt with according to law. Given under my hand and seal, this ——— day of ——— 18—.

J. T., J. P. [L. S.]

(No. 15.)

Form of Warrant of Arrest for fraudulently making a note purporting to be the note of a bank not in existence.

——— County, to wit:
   To all or any one of the Constables of said County:
   Whereas, A. B. of said County, has this day made complaint and information on oath before me J. T., a Justice of the said County, that C. D., on the ——— day of ——— 18—, in said County, did feloniously and fraudu-

FORGERY. 325

lently make a certain base note, purporting to be the note of (state the bank,) for the payment of ——— dollars, and purporting to be dated on the ——— day of ———— 18—, when in truth and in fact no such bank then existed: These are, therefore, to command you, in the name of the Commonwealth of Virginia, forthwith to apprehend the said C. D., and bring him before me or some other Justice of the said County, to answer the said complaint, and to be farther dealt with according to law. Given under my hand and seal, this ——— day of ———— 18—.

J. T., J. P. [L. S.]

(No. 16.)

Form of Warrant of Arrest for engraving a plate designed for forging bank notes.

——— County, to wit:

To all or any one of the Constables of said County:

Whereas, A. B. of said County, has this day made complaint and information on oath before me J. T., a Justice of the said County, that C. D., on the ——— day of ———— 18—, in said County, did feloniously engrave and make a plate adapted and designed for the forging and false making of forged bank notes, that is to say: adapted and designed for the forging and false making of forged bank notes of the likeness and similitude of the bank notes of the president, directors and company of the Bank of Virginia, of the denomination of ten dollars, (or *whatever bank or denomination the plate was designed for:*) These are, therefore, to command you, in the name of the Commonwealth of Virginia, forthwith to apprehend the said C. D., and bring him before me or some other Justice of the said County, to answer the said complaint, and to be farther dealt with according to law. Given under my hand and seal, this ——— day of ———— 18—.

J. T., J. P. [L. S.]

(No. 17.)

Form of Warrant of Arrest for making a puncheon for the false making of coin.

——— County, to wit:

To all or any one of the Constables of said County:

Whereas, A. B. of said County, has this day made complaint and information on oath before me J. T., a Justice of the said County, that C. D., on the ——— day of ———— 18—, in said County, did feloniously make one puncheon adapted and designed for the false making base coin, of the likeness and similitude of half dollars of the genuine coin of the United States, current in this Commonwealth: These are, therefore, to command you, in the name of the Commonwealth of Virginia, forthwith to apprehend the said C. D., and bring him before me or some other Justice of the said County, to answer the said complaint, and to be farther dealt with according to law. Given under my hand and seal, this ——— day of ———— 18—.

J. T., J. P. [L. S.]

FORGERY.

(No. 18.)

Form of Mittimus where a party is committed for examination or trial in the County Court for forgery.

——— County, to wit:

To X. Z., *Constable of said County, and to the Keeper of the Jail of said County:*

These are to command you, the said Constable, in the name of the Commonwealth of Virginia, forthwith to convey and deliver into the custody of the keeper of the said jail, together with this warrant, the body of C. D., a white person (or *free negro*, or *a slave, the property of E. F.*, as the case may be,) charged before me J. T., a Justice of the said County, on the oath of A. B., with a felony by him committed, in this, that the said C. D., on the ——— day of ——— in the year 18—, in the said County, (here describe the offence as in the warrant of arrest.) And you, the said keeper of the said jail, are hereby required to receive the said C. D. into your jail and custody, that he may be examined (or *tried*) for the said offence, by the County Court of said County, and him there safely keep until he shall be discharged by due course of law. Given under my hand and seal, this ——— day of ——— in the year 18—.

J. T., *J. P.* [L. S.]

[NOTE.—If the prisoner be a white person, commit him for examination; if a negro, commit him for trial.]

(No. 19.)

Form of Certificate of Commitment to be sent to the Clerk of the County Court, in forgery.

——— County, to wit:

To the Clerk of the County Court of said County:

I, J. T., a Justice of said County, do hereby certify that I have, by my warrant, this day committed C. D. (if free negro or slave, state which,) to the jail of this County, that he may be examined (or *tried*) before the County Court of the said County, for a felony by him committed, in this, that he did, on the ——— day of ——— 18—, in the said County, (here state the offence as in the mittimus.) Given under my hand, this ——— day of ——— in the year 18—.

J. T., *J. P.*

(No. 20.)

Form of Certificate to the Clerk where party is admitted to bail.

Turn to head of ARREST, and follow No. 6.

(No. 21.)

Form of Recognizance of Bail.

Turn to head of RECOGNIZANCE, and follow No. 1, if person be free; No. 2, if a slave, and state succinctly the offence for which the person is recognized.

(No. 22.)

Form of Recognizance of Witness to appear before the County Court to give evidence upon the examination or trial of a party charged with felony.

Turn to head of RECOGNIZANCE, and follow No. 3.

(No. 1.)

Indictment for forging a promissory note and endorsement thereon, and for uttering and attempting to employ the same as true.

—— Judicial Circuit, } The jurors of the Commonwealth of Vir-
—— County, *to wit:* } ginia, in and for the body of the County of
In the Circuit Court of the } ——, and now attending the Circuit Court
said County. } of the said County, do on their oath present,
that A. B., on the —— day of —— 18—, at the County of ——, feloniously did forge a certain promissory note, purporting to be signed by J. K., and to be negotiable and payable at the Bank of Virginia, and which said forged note is of the following purport and effect, that is to say, (insert the note,) with intention to defraud, against the peace and dignity of the Commonwealth of Virginia.

2d Count. And the jurors aforesaid, on their oath aforesaid, do farther present, that the said A. B. afterwards, to wit, on the said —— day of —— 18—, at the said County, feloniously did utter and attempt to employ as true, a certain other forged promissory note, negotiable and payable at the Bank of Virginia, which said last mentioned note is of the following purport and effect, to wit, (set out the note,) with intent to defraud, he the said A. B. at the time he so uttered and attempted to employ as true the said last mentioned forged note, to wit, on the day and year last aforesaid, at the County aforesaid, well knowing the same to be forged, against the peace and dignity of the Commonwealth of Virginia.

3d Count. And the jurors aforesaid, upon their oath aforesaid, do farther present, that the said A. B. afterwards, to wit, on the said —— day of —— 18—, at the County aforesaid, having in his possession a certain other promissory note, purporting to be signed by ——, and to be negotiable and payable at the Bank of Virginia, which said last mentioned note is of the purport and effect following, that is to say, (here set out the note,) he the said A. B., on the said —— day of —— 18—, at the said County, feloniously did forge on the back of the said last mentioned note, an endorsement in writing of C. D., of the said last mentioned note, which said forged endorsement is of the purport following, that is to say, (state the name exactly as written,) with intention to defraud, against the peace and dignity of the Commonwealth of Virginia.

FORGERY—(*Indictments for.*)

4th Count. And the jurors aforesaid, on their oath aforesaid, farther present, that the said A. B. afterwards, to wit, on the said —— day of ———— 18—, at the said County, having in his custody and possession a certain other promissory note, negotiable and payable at the Bank of Virginia, which said last mentioned note is as follows, that is to say, (set out the note,) and on the back of which said last mentioned note there was then and there, to wit, on the said —— day of ———— 18—, at said County, written a certain forged endorsement of one C. D., and which said forged endorsement is of the purport and effect following, that is to say, (here set out the endorsement exactly,) he the said A. B. afterwards, to wit, on the said —— day of ———— 18—, at the said County, feloniously did utter and attempt to employ as true the said last mentioned forged endorsement of the said last mentioned promissory note, with intent to defraud, he the said A. B., at the time he so uttered and attempted to employ as true the said last mentioned forged endorsement of the said last mentioned note, to wit, on the said —— day of ———— 18—, at the County aforesaid, well knowing the said last mentioned endorsement to be forged, against the peace and dignity of the Commonwealth of Virginia.

(No. 2.)

Indictment for making instruments adapted to making base coin.

———— Judicial Circuit, ———— County, to wit: In the Circuit Court of the said County. } The jurors of the Commonwealth of Virginia, in and for the body of the County of ————, now attending the Circuit Court of the said County, do upon their oath present, that A. B., on the —— day of ———— in the year one thousand eight hundred and ————, in the County aforesaid, feloniously did make a certain thing, to wit, one puncheon, adapted and designed for the false making of base coin, resembling genuine coin, current in this Commonwealth, commonly called a half dollar, against the peace and dignity of the Commonwealth of Virginia.

And the jurors aforesaid, upon their oath aforesaid, do farther present, that the said A. B., on the day and year aforesaid, in the County aforesaid, one other puncheon, adapted and designed for the false making of base coin, of the likeness and similitude of the coin of the United States, current in this Commonwealth, commonly called a half dollar, feloniously did make, against the peace and dignity of the Commonwealth of Virginia.

And the jurors aforesaid, upon their oath aforesaid, do farther present, that the said A. B., on the day and year last aforesaid, in the County aforesaid, one other puncheon, adapted and designed for the false making of base coin, and in and upon which there was then made and impressed the figure of one of the sides, that is to say, the head side of a piece of the coin of the United States, current in this Commonwealth, commonly called a half dollar, feloniously did make, against the peace and dignity of this Commonwealth.

[Other counts may be added for a stamp, press, die, &c.]

(No. 3.)

An Indictment for forging a promissory note for the payment of money.

Commence as No. 1, under head of "INDICTMENTS," and say: did feloniously forge a certain promissory note for the payment of money purporting to be made and signed by one C. D. for the sum of ———- dollars, which said forged promissory note is of the purpose and effect following, to wit, (*here insert a true copy of the note in the words and figures of it,*) with intent to defraud, and to the prejudice of the right of the said C. D.,* against the peace and dignity of the Commonwealth.

(No. 4.)

An Indictment for forging a certificate of a Justice of the Peace.

Commence as No. 1, under head of "INDICTMENTS," and say: did feloniously forge a certain certificate and attestation of one J. T., one of the Justices in and for the County of ———, which said forged certificate and attestation is of the purport and effect following, to wit, (*here insert a copy of the certificate in words and figures,*) which said forged certificate and attestation, then and there purported to be the certificate and attestation of a Justice of the Peace, in a matter wherein the said certificate and attestation was receivable and taken as legal proof, with intent to injure and defraud, against the peace and dignity of the Commonwealth of Virginia.

(No. 5.)

An Indictment for uttering a forged instrument, knowing it to be forged.

Commence as No. 1, under head of "INDICTMENTS," and say: had in his possession a certain forged promissory note for the payment of money, purporting to be made and signed by one C. D., for the payment of the sum of ——— dollars; which said forged note is of the following purport and effect, to wit, (*here insert a copy of the note in words and figures,*) and that he the said A. B., the said forged promissory note did then and there, in the County aforesaid, utter and attempt to employ as true, with intent to injure and defraud, he the said A. B. then and there well knowing the said note to be forged, against the peace and dignity of the Commonwealth of Virginia.

FORNICATION.

SEE ADULTERY AND FORNICATION.

---

* *Query.* Is this last averment necessary? If the paper itself as set out in the indictment does not shew that it is a paper, the forging of which is to the prejudice of another's right, this averment will not help it, and if the paper does shew it, the averment would seem unnecessary.

CHAPTER XLVI.

FREEDOM—(*Suits for.*)

BY SEC. 1, CHAP. 106. Any person conceiving himself unlawfully detained as a slave, may petition the circuit court or court of the county or corporation in which he may be detained, for leave to sue for his freedom, or he may complain thereof to a Justice.

BY SEC. 2. If the complaint be made to a Justice, he shall, by precept in writing, give the complainant in charge to the Sheriff or other officer, to be produced before the circuit court or court of the county or corporation, as the complainant may elect, at the next term thereof; and in the mean time, to be safely kept, at the expense of the person claiming to be the owner, and shall cause such person to be notified thereof.

BY SEC. 3. If the person claiming to be the owner, or some one for him, will enter into bond, approved by the officer having the complainant in charge, in a penalty equal to double the value of the complainant, supposing him to be a slave, conditioned to have him forthcoming before the said court at the next term thereof, such officer shall deliver to him the complainant.

BY SEC. 4. The court to which such petition may be presented, shall assign the petitioner counsel, who, without reward, shall aid him in the prosecution of his suit; and until the person claiming to be the owner, or some one for him, will enter into bond before the court or its clerk, in such penalty as the court shall direct, conditioned to have the petitioner forthcoming to abide the judgment of the court, and in the mean time to allow him reasonable opportunity to prepare for trial, shall deliver him in charge to the proper officer for safe keeping, at the expense of the person so claiming to be the owner; but the petitioner may in the mean time be hired out, if the court so order, and the hire shall be disposed of as the court shall direct. The petitioner shall have, free of cost, all needful process, services of officers and attendance of witnesses.

BY SEC. 5. It shall be the duty of the counsel to file with the clerk, a statement in writing of the material facts of the case, with his opinion thereon; and unless it appear manifest therefrom, that the suit ought not to be prosecuted, the court shall cause the person claiming to be the owner to be summoned to answer the petition.

BY SEC. 6. The case may be tried without regard to its place on the docket, at the term of the court to which the summons shall be returned executed; and a jury, free from exception, without the formality of pleading, shall be impanneled to try whether the petitioner be free or not.

BY SEC. 7. If the verdict be for the petitioner, the jury may find damages for his detention pending the suit; and the court shall adjudge the petitioner to be free, and award to him the damages and costs.

(No. 1.)

Form of Warrant of a Justice to take charge of a person suing for freedom.

—— County, to wit:
  To the Sheriff of the said County:

Whereas, George Dimond has this day complained before me J. T., a Justice of said County, that he is unlawfully detained as a slave by A. B., and has petitioned me for leave to sue for his freedom, I hereby command you, in the name of the Commonwealth, forthwith to take charge of the said George Dimond, and him safely keep, at the expense of the said A. B., until the first day of the next term of the Circuit (or *County Court,* in whichever the suit is to be,) of the said County, and that you then and there produce him before the said Court. And I command you, also, to give notice to the said A. B., that you have the said George Dimond in your charge, under this precept. Given under my hand, this —— day of —— 18—.

J. T., *J. P.*

(No. 2.)

Form of Bond to be given by the person claiming to be the owner of a slave suing for freedom.

Know all men by these presents, that we, A. B. and C. D., are held and firmly bound unto the Commonwealth of Virginia, in the sum of —— dollars, lawful money of the United States, to be paid to the said Commonwealth; for the payment whereof, we hereby bind ourselves jointly and severally, and our joint and several heirs, executors and administrators. As witness our hands and seals, this —— day of —— 18—.

The condition of the above obligation is such, that whereas, George Dimond, a person conceiving himself illegally detained as a slave by the above bound A. B., was, upon his complaint to J. T., a Justice of the County of ——, given in charge to T. C., Sheriff of said County, by the precept of the said J. T., as Justice aforesaid, to be by the said T. C. produced before the Circuit (or *County*) Court of —— County, on the first day of the next term thereof; and whereas the said T. C., Sheriff as aforesaid, has this day, upon the application of the said A. B., delivered to him the said George Dimond: Now, if the said A. B., his heirs, executors or administrators, shall have the said George Dimond forthcoming before the said Court on the first day of the next term thereof, then the above obligation to be void, otherwise to remain in full force and virtue.

A. B. [L. S.]
C. D. [L. S.]

Taken and acknowledged
  before me.
    T. C., *Sheriff.*

CHAPTER XLVII.

FUGITIVES FROM JUSTICE.

By Sec. 8, Chap. 17. The Governor shall, whenever required by the executive authority of the United States, pursuant to the constitution and laws thereof, deliver over to justice any person found within the State, who shall be charged with having committed any crime *without* the jurisdiction of the United States.

By Sec. 9. The Governor, though not so required, may in his discretion, deliver over to justice, any person found within the State, who shall be charged with having committed, *without* the jurisdiction of the United States, any crime, except treason, which, by the laws of this State, if committed therein, is punishable by death or imprisonment in the penitentiary; such delivery shall only be made on the requisition of the duly authorized officers or agents of the government, within the jurisdiction of which the crime shall be charged to have been committed; and the Governor shall require such evidence of the guilt of the person so charged, as would be necessary to justify his apprehension and commitment for trial, had the crime charged been committed *within* this State. The expense of apprehension and delivery shall be defrayed by those to whom the delivery is made.

By Sec. 10. Any person charged in another State of this Union, with treason, felony or other crime, who shall flee from justice and be found in this State, shall, on demand of the executive authority of the State from which he fled, made in the manner prescribed by the constitution and laws of the United States, be delivered up according to the said constitution and laws, to be removed to the State having jurisdiction of the crime.

By Sec. 11. Whenever any person shall be found within this State, charged with treason, felony or other crime, committed in any other State, any Justice may, upon complaint on oath, or other satisfactory evidence that such person committed the offence, issue a warrant to bring the person so charged before the same or some other Justice within the State; and the officer to whom such warrant may be directed may execute the same in any county or corporation in the State, and bring the party, when arrested, before any Justice of the same or any other county or corporation.

By Sec. 12. If it shall appear to the Justice before whom the person charged may be brought, that there is reasonable cause to believe that the complaint is true, he shall, if he would have been bailable by a Justice, in case the offence had been committed in this State, be required to recognize, with sufficient sureties, in a reasonable sum, to appear before the court of the county or corporation at a future day, allowing a reasonable time to obtain the warrant of the executive, and to abide the order of the court; and if such person shall not so recognize, he shall be committed to prison, and be there detained until such day. The recognizance, if any, shall be returned to the said court without delay; and if the person so recognizing shall fail to appear, according to the condition of his recognizance, he shall be defaulted, and the like proceedings shall be had as in the case of other recognizances entered into before a Justice; but if such person would not have been bailable by a Justice, in case the offence had been committed in this State, he shall be committed to prison, and there detained until the day so appointed for his appearance before the court.

By Sec. 13. The Justice by whom such person may be so recognized or committed, shall immediately, by letter, apprise the Governor of the fact, who shall thereupon communicate the same to the Executive of the State where the crime is charged to have been committed.

By Sec. 14. If the person so recognized or committed, shall appear before the court upon the day ordered, he shall be discharged, unless he shall be demanded by some person authorized by the warrant of the Governor to receive him, or unless the court shall see cause to commit him, or to require him to recognize anew for his appearance at some other day; and if, when ordered, he shall not so recognize, he shall be committed and detained as before; but whether the person so charged shall be recognized, committed or discharged, any person authorized by the warrant of the Governor may, at all times, take him into custody, and the same shall be a discharge of the recognizance, if any, and shall not be deemed an escape.

By Sec. 15. The complainant in such case shall be answerable for all the actual costs and charges, and for the support in prison of any person so committed, to be paid in the same manner as by a creditor for his debtor, committed on execution; and if the charge for his support in prison shall not be so paid, the Jailor may discharge such person in like manner as if he had been committed for debt on an execution.

By Sec. 16. No person under prosecution for any offence, alleged to be committed within this State, shall be delivered up to the executive authority of another State, or of the United States, until such prosecution shall have been determined, and the person prosecuted shall have been punished, if condemned, nor shall any person under recognizance to appear as a witness in any such prosecution, be so delivered up until said prosecution shall be determined. Nor shall any person who was in custody upon any execution, or upon process in any suit, at the time of being apprehended for a crime charged to have been committed *without* the jurisdiction of this State, be so delivered up, without the consent of the plaintiff in such execution or suit, until the amount of such execution shall have been paid, or until such person shall be otherwise discharged from such execution or process.

It is a principle of the law of nations to deliver up offenders charged with felony and other high crimes, fleeing from the country in which the crime was committed, into a foreign and friendly jurisdiction.(¹) The statute applies the principle to the States and Territories of this Union, and when a Justice is called on to act under it, he should recollect the terms *felony* and other *high crimes* as used by the law of nations, and in cases less than felony decline interference, and leave the application to the action of the Executive. The power conferred by the statute may be greatly abused, and even in cases of felony, the Justice should be careful that the application is to serve the high purposes of public justice, and not to advance private interests.*

(No. 1.)

Form of a Warrant to Arrest a fugitive from justice, upon the oath of a complainant.

—— County, to wit:

To the Sheriff and all or any one of the Constables of the said County:

Forasmuch as A. B. has this day on oath complained and charged before me J. T., a Justice of the said County, that C. D., late of the County of ——, in the State (or *District*, or *Territory*,) of ——, did, on the —— day of —— 18—, in the County of ——, in the State (or *District*, or *Territory*,) of ——, feloniously (here state the crime charged upon the party, according to the evidence,) and that the said C. D. is a fugitive from justice, and that he has good reason to believe that the said C. D. is now lurking in your County: These are, therefore, to command you, in the name of the Commonwealth of Virginia, forthwith to apprehend and bring before me or some other Justice of the said County, the body of the said C. D., to answer the said complaint and charge, and to be farther dealt with according to law. Given under my hand and seal, this —— day of —— 18—.

J. T., J. P. [L. S.]

(¹) By Kent, 4 Johns. Ch. Rep. 106.

*Note.—The author has known this statute resorted to as the oppressive means of coercing the payment of private debts, in utter disregard both of public justice and private rights.

(No. 2.)

Form of a Warrant to arrest a fugitive, upon a charge verified by an indictment found in another State.

—— County, to wit:
To the Sheriff and all or any one of the Constables of the said County:
Whereas, A. B. has this day been charged upon the complaint and information of C. D., with a felony by him committed in the State (or *District* or *Territory,*) of ——, in this, that he the said A. B., on the —— day of —— 18—, at the County of ——, in the said State (or *District* or *Territory,*) of ——, did feloniously (here set forth and describe the offence, as it is described in the copy of the indictment,) contrary to the laws of the said State, (*District* or *Territory,*) which said complaint and charge is verified before me by a duly and legally authenticated copy of an indictment for the offence aforesaid, found against the said A. B., in the —— Court of the County of ——, in the State (*District* or *Territory*) of ——: These are, therefore, to command you, in the name of the Commonwealth of Virginia, forthwith to apprehend and bring before me or some other Justice of the said County, the body of the said C. D., to answer unto the said complaint and charge, and to be farther dealt with according to law. Given under my hand and seal, this —— day of —— 18—.

J. T., J. P. [L. S.]

(No. 3.)

Form of a Warrant to commit a fugitive from justice, upon an indictment found in another State.

—— County, to wit:
To X. Y., Constable of the said County, and to the Keeper of the Jail of said County:
Whereas, A. B. of ——, has been apprehended and brought before me this day, charged upon the complaint and information of C. D., with a felony by him committed in the State (or *District* or *Territory*, as the case may be,) of ——, in this, that he the said A. B., on the —— day of —— 18—, at the County of ——, in the said State (*District* or *Territory*) of ——, did feloniously (here set forth and describe the offence as it is described in the copy of the indictment,) contrary to the laws of the said State, (*District* or *Territory;*) and whereas the said C. D. has fully verified and sustained before me, the said complaint and charge against the said A. B., by producing before me and for my inspection, a duly and legally authenticated copy of an indictment for the offence aforesaid, found against the said A. B., in the —— Court in the County of ——, in the State (or *District* or *Territory,*) aforesaid; and being of opinion, upon full examination of the said indictment, that the said A. B. has committed the offence therein charged, and that he ought to be tried therefor in the said State: Therefore you, the said Constable, are hereby commanded in the name of the Commonwealth of Virginia, forthwith safely to convey and deliver the said A. B. into the custody of the keeper of the said jail; and I do hereby command you, the keeper of the said jail, to receive the said A. B. into your jail and custody, and him there safely keep until the first day of the next —— term of the County Court of the said County, or until he be thence otherwise discharged by law. Given under my hand and seal, this —— day of —— 18—.

J. T., J. P. [L. S.]

(No. 4.)

Form of a Warrant to commit a fugitive from justice from another State, upon the oath of a party.

—— County, to wit:

To X. Y., Constable of the said County, and to the Keeper of the Jail of the said County:

Whereas, A. B. of ——, has been apprehended and this day brought before me J. T., a Justice of the said County, charged upon the oath of C. D., with a felony by him committed in the State (or *District* or *Territory*,) of ——, in this, that the said A. B., on the —— day of —— 18—, at the County of ——, in the State (or *District* or *Territory*,) of ——, did feloniously (here set forth and describe the offence according to the charge,) contrary to the laws of the said State: And I, the said J. T., Justice as aforesaid, having probable cause to believe that the said A. B. has committed the offence wherewith he is so charged, upon the oath of the said C. D., and being of opinion, upon full examination, that he the said A. B. ought to be tried therefor in the said State (or *District* or *Territory*:) Therefore you, the said Constable, are hereby commanded, in the name of the Commonwealth of Virginia, forthwith safely to convey and deliver the said A. B. into the custody of the keeper of the said jail; and I do hereby command you, the keeper of the said jail, to receive the said A. B. into your jail and custody, and him there safely keep until the first day of the —— term of the County Court of the said County, or until he be otherwise thence discharged by law. Given under my hand and seal, this —— day of —— 18—.

J. T., J. P. [L. S.]

(No. 5.)

Form of Recognizance to be entered into by fugitive from justice, to appear and abide judgment of County Court.

—— County, to wit:

Be it remembered, that on the —— day of —— 18—, A. B., C. D. and E. F., came before me J. T., a Justice of the said County, and severally acknowledged themselves to owe to the Commonwealth of Virginia, that is to say, the said A. B. the sum of $——, and the said C. D. and E. F. the sum of $—— each, to be made and levied of their lands and tenements, goods and chattels, respectively, if the said A. B. shall make default in the performance of the condition underwritten.

The condition of the above recognizance is such, that whereas the above bound A. B. was this day arrested and brought before me J. T., Justice as aforesaid, upon the complaint on oath of K. L., charged with a felony, alleged to have been committed by him, on the —— day of —— 18—, in the County of ——, in the State of ——, for the murder of J. S., (or *in stealing the goods of J. S.*,) and that he is now, upon said charge, a fugitive from justice from the said State, found in this State, and which said complaint, I, J. T., Justice as aforesaid, upon examination, believe to be true: Now, if the said A. B. shall personally appear before the County Court of ——, on the first day of the next —— term thereof, then and there to abide such order as the said Court shall make, touching and concerning him the said A. B. as a fugitive from justice upon said complaint and charge, and shall not thence depart without the leave of said Court, then the above recognizance to be void, otherwise to remain in full force and virtue.

Taken and acknowledged before me, this —— day of —— 18—.

J. T., J. P.

CHAPTER XLVIII.

GAMING.

[See NUISANCES.]

BY SEC. 1, CHAP. 198. A free person who shall keep or exhibit a gaming table, commonly called A B C, or E O table, or faro bank, or a table of the like kind, under any denomination, whether the game or table be played with cards, dice or otherwise, or who shall be a partner or concerned in interest in the keeping or exhibiting such table or bank, shall be confined in jail not less than two nor more than twelve months, and be fined not less than one hundred nor more than one thousand dollars. Any such table or faro bank, and all money staked, or exhibited to allure persons to bet, at such table, may be seized by order of a Court, or under the warrant of a Justice, and the money so seized, after deducting therefrom one half for the person making the seizure, shall be forfeited, as is provided in the 32d section of chapter 51, in respect to the forfeiture declared by that chapter, and the table or faro bank burnt.

BY SEC. 2. If a free person knowingly permit a gaming table or faro bank, such as is mentioned in the preceding section, to be kept or exhibited on any premises in his occupation, he shall be confined in jail not more than one year, and fined not less than one hundred nor more than one thousand dollars.

BY SEC. 3. If a free person shall act as doorkeeper, guard or watch, or employ another person to act as such, for a keeper or exhibitor of a gaming table or faro bank, or shall *resist*, or by any means or device prevent, hinder or delay the lawful arrest of such keeper or exhibitor, or the seizure of the table or bank, or money exhibited or staked thereat, *or shall unlawfully take the same from the person seizing it*, he shall be confined in jail not more than one year, and fined not exceeding one thousand dollars.

BY SEC. 4. If a free person *bet or play at any such table or bank as is mentioned in the first section, or if* at any ordinary, racefield or other public place, *he* play at any game except bowls, chess, backgammon, draughts, or a licensed game, or bet on the sides of those who play, he shall be fined thirty dollars, and shall, if required by the court, give security for his good behaviour for one year, or in default thereof, may be imprisoned not more than three months.

43

By Sec. 5. If a free person by playing or betting at any game or wager, elsewhere than at a public place, lose or win within twenty-four hours, a greater sum, or any thing of greater value than twenty dollars, he shall be punished as in the preceding section.

By Sec. 6. If a keeper of an ordinary or house of entertainment permit unlawful gaming at his house, or at any outhouse, booth, arbour, or other place appurtenant thereto or held therewith, he shall be fined one hundred dollars and shall forfeit his license, and give security for his good behaviour for one year, or in default of such security, be imprisoned not more than four months.

By Sec. 7. In a prosecution under the preceding section, if the gaming be proved, it shall be presumed it was permitted by the keeper of the house, unless it appear that he did not know of, or suspect such gaming, or that he endeavoured to prevent it, and gave information of it, with the names of the players, to the next court of the county or corporation.

By Sec. 8. If a keeper of an ordinary or house of entertainment, let or hire to another person, any outhouse or other place, which has been, at any time, appurtenant to or held with the house kept by him, with intent that unlawful gaming be permitted thereat, he shall suffer the same punishment and incur the same forfeiture as if such unlawful gaming were permitted at his own principal house; and in a prosecution therefor, if the gaming be proved, it shall be presumed that such outhouse or other place was let or hired with the intent aforesaid, unless the presumption be repelled in the manner mentioned in the preceding section.

By Sec. 9. If a free person playing at any game, or making a wager, or having share in any stake or wager, or betting on the hands or sides of others playing at any game or making a wager, shall cheat, or by fraudulent means win or acquire for himself or another, money or other valuable thing, he shall be confined in jail not more than one year, and fined not less than five times the value of the money or thing won or acquired.

By Sec. 10. If a free person bet or wager money, or other thing over the value of five dollars, on any election or appointment to any office or place, to be made under authority of the constitution and laws of this State or of the United States, he shall be fined not exceeding the value of such money or other thing.

By Sec. 20. All laws for suppressing gaming, lotteries, unchartered banks, and the circulation of bank notes for less than five dollars, shall be construed as remedial.

By this, the Justice is to construe these laws liberally, so as to "advance the remedy and suppress the evil."

In proceeding to recover the penalty of thirty dollars for gaming at a tavern, under the 4th section of the statute, it must be alleged that the house or place where the gaming occurred, was an ordinary or a public place.(¹) And as to what constitutes a public place, under the statute, it has been held, that a barn, two hundred yards distant from the tavern house, on the same plantation, sixty or seventy yards in the rear of another barn, in a separate enclosure from the tavern house, in which spirits were sold by the tavern keeper, in which a party games, on a day when many persons were assembled at the tavern for the purpose of mustering, was a public place.(²)

So, also, it has been held, that a house located on a public square, and which had been used as a jail, but at the time of the gaming, was not so occupied, but was accessible to any citizen, and was sometimes used by persons employed to guard prisoners in the new jail, and though nothing was kept in the house for sale, nor was any public business transacted therein, was a public place within this act.(³)

So, a storehouse, which was opened to the public in the day time, has been held to be a public place, though after the business of the day was at an end and the door closed, it was held *prima facie* not to be a public place.(⁴)

As to what constitutes unlawful gaming, it will be seen from the statute itself, that every kind of gaming is prohibited at ordinaries and other public places, except at bowls, backgammon, chess, draughts, and such other games as are licensed by law; the mere act of playing at cards in a tavern, whether the person so playing bets or not, is gaming within the meaning of the statute.(⁵)

(No. 1.)

Form of a Warrant against exhibitor of Faro Bank, A B C, or E O.

———— County, to wit:
   To X. Y., Constable of the said County:

Whereas, A. B. has this day made complaint on oath before me J. T., a Justice of the said County, that C. D. did, on the —— day of —————— 18—, in said County, keep and exhibit a certain gaming table, called faro bank, (or *A B C*, or *E O:*) These are, therefore, to command you, in the name of the Commonwealth, forthwith to apprehend the said C. D., and to bring him before me or some other Justice of the said County, to answer the said complaint, and to be farther dealt with according to law. Given under my hand and seal, this —— day of —————— 18—.

                          J. T., J. P. [L. S.]

(¹) Hord's Case, 4 Leigh 674.
(²) 8 Leigh 741.
(³) Walker's Case, 2 Va. Cases 515.
(⁴) 4 Leigh 680.
(⁵) Terry's Case, 2 Va. Cases 77.

(No. 2.)

Form of Warrant to seize money exhibited at gaming table, and also to seize and burn the table.

———— County, to wit:

To X. Y., *Constable of the said County:*

Whereas, information on oath has this day been given to me J. T., a Justice of the said County, by A. B., that one C. D. keeps and exhibits a certain gaming table, called faro bank, (or *A B C*, or *E O*,) in a certain house occupied by him in said County, and that he does there exhibit money to allure other persons to bet at the said game of faro, (or *A B C*, or *E O*, or whatever game it may be,) and that persons do there stake and bet their money at the said game: These are, therefore, to command you, in the name of the Commonwealth, forthwith to enter the said house, and there seize the said gaming table and all the money so there exhibited and staked: and the said gaming table so seized, you are hereby commanded publicly to burn and destroy, and the said money so seized, you are required to account for and pay into the County Court of ————, on the first day of the next term thereof; and make return to me how you have executed this my warrant. Given under my hand and seal, this ———— day of ———— 18—.

J. T., J. P. [L. S.]

(No. 3.)

Form of Recognizance to appear and answer a presentment for keeping and exhibiting faro.

———— County, to wit:

Be it remembered, that on this ———— day of ———— 18—, A. B. and C. D. of the said County, came before me J. T., a Justice of the said County, and severally acknowledged themselves to owe to the Commonwealth of Virginia, that is to say: The said A. B. the sum of ———— dollars, and the said C. D. the sum of ———— dollars, to be respectively made and levied of their several goods and chattels, lands and tenements, if he the said A. B. shall make default in performance of the condition underwritten.

The condition of the above recognizance is such, that whereas the above bound A. B. has been arrested and is now in the custody of the Sheriff of the said County, by virtue of a *capias* issued from the (state what Court the process issued from,) commanding him, the said Sheriff, to take him, the said A. B., and him keep so as to have him before the Justices (or *Judge*) of the said Court at the Courthouse of said County, on the (insert the return day of the *capias*,) to answer a certain presentment therein made by the grand jury against him, for keeping and exhibiting a faro bank in the said County, and now pending in the said Court: Now, if the said A. B. shall personally appear before the said Court, on the first day of the next term thereof, (or whatever may be the day specified in the *capias*,) at the Courthouse of the said County, then and there to answer the said presentment, and shall not thence depart without the leave of the said Court, then the above recognizance to be void, otherwise to remain in full force and virtue.

Taken and acknowledged before me this ———— day of ———— 18—.

J. T. J. P.

(No. 4.)
Form of an Order to liberate the prisoner, upon his entering into the foregoing recognizance.

———— County, to wit:
To the Sheriff of said County, and to the Keeper of the Jail of the said County:

Discharge out of your custody A. B., if detained for no other cause than by virtue of a *capias*, which issued from ———— Court, to answer a presentment therein made against him, for keeping and exhibiting a faro bank, he having this day entered into a recognizance before me, with C. D. as his bail, in the sum of ———— dollars, to appear and answer the said presentment.

J. T., J. P.

CHAPTER XLIX.

HARBOUR MASTERS.

BY SEC. 1, CHAP. 95. The court of any county or corporation, except the City of Norfolk and town of Alexandria, and the councils of the said city and town, may at any time appoint one or more harbour masters, and shall take from each person so appointed, a bond to the Commonwealth in the penalty of five hundred dollars.

BY SEC. 2. Every harbour master shall hold his office at the pleasure of the court or council which appointed him. If appointed by a corporation court, he shall act within its jurisdiction; if by a county court, he shall act in that part of the county which is without such jurisdiction.

BY SEC. 3. Each harbour master shall cause every vessel coming within his jurisdiction, to moor as soon as may be, and at such place as he may judge best for the general safety, such place in the ports of Norfolk or Portsmouth, not being within fifty fathoms of any wharf. He shall not permit any vessel to ride at single anchor longer than one tide, and shall require the master of any vessel, as soon as may be after coming to anchor, (not exceeding twenty-four hours,) to rig in his jib-booms, sprit-sail yards, and all fore-and-aft spars, and have his lower and top-sail yards topped, so that the passage of other vessels, and the boats of any ferry, shall not be obstructed. He shall also attend to the unmooring of any vessel; and if any vessel shall, by stress of weather or other accident, be driven from her mooring, he shall attend to the remooring her, and for so unmooring or remooring any vessel, he shall have half the fees allowed for mooring in the first instance.

By Sec. 4. He shall cause to be removed from any wharf, vessels not employed, to make room for those that are employed in receiving or discharging cargo; and also all flats, lighters and other boats, to make room for ferry boats. The master, owner or consignee, shall immediately remove the same or pay the expense of such removal.

By Sec. 5. Any harbour master who shall fail in any duty prescribed herein, or any master of a vessel or boat, who shall fail to obey the lawful directions of a harbour master, shall pay a fine not exceeding fifty dollars.

By Sec. 6. Every harbour master shall keep a register of the denomination, name, burthen and master's name of each vessel coming within his control as such, and the port to which she belongs, and that from which she last came, which register he shall submit to the inspection of any applicant.

By Sec. 7. For every vessel arriving at any port other than Norfolk or Portsmouth, and for every vessel arriving at the port of Norfolk or Portsmouth, above the point at which the flag staff at Fort Norfolk shall bear northeast, the harbour master shall have a fee, if a square rigged vessel, of two dollars; and if fore-and-aft rigged, one dollar and twenty-five cents.

By Sec. 8. But all vessels sailing under a coasting license of less than seventy-five tons burthen, all vessels engaged in the Dismal Swamp canal trade, and all vessels putting into the port of Norfolk or Portsmouth, on their homeward passage from up the bay or any river of this State, and all packet boats and steamboats regularly trading for the accommodation and conveyance of passengers, shall be exempt from harbour masters' fees, except that steamboats or vessels shall pay in the harbour of Richmond, the same fees as other vessels of the same burthen or class.

By Sec. 9. One of the harbour masters shall be designated by the court of Norfolk county to superintend the county dock in the City of Norfolk.

By Sec. 10. He shall regulate the anchoring and mooring of all lighters, boats, and bay and river craft, which come within said dock, or anchor at or are secured to the county wharf, for which service he shall have a fee of twenty-five cents from the master or owner.

By Sec. 11. He shall also regulate the entrance and departure of all lighters, however loaded, and all boats loaded with wood or fuel, which come into said dock, or anchor at or are secured to the wharf, so as to prevent confusion and disorder; for which he shall have a fee of twelve and a half cents from the master or owner.

By Sec. 12. Nothing in this chapter shall prevent any bay or river craft, or other boat, from going to and anchoring at any private wharf, without fee to any harbour master or superintendent.

By Sec. 13. If the said superintendent shall suffer any vessel, lighter or other boat, to lie across the said county dock, or before any wharf, so as to obstruct the passage of any ferry boat, he shall forfeit to the county of Norfolk ten dollars.

By Sec. 14. No harbour master shall have any control over any vessel while entering, remaining in or leaving the Richmond dock, or any channel leading thereto, constructed by the Richmond dock company, or the James river and Kanawha company.

By Sec. 15. The company last mentioned may appoint a dock master or other officer, who shall enforce such regulations respecting the said dock as it may prescribe, consistent with the laws of the State and the police regulations of the City of Richmond.

(No. 1.)

Form of Warrant of Arrest against a master of a vessel, for failing to obey the directions of a harbour master.

City of ———, to wit:
    To all or any one of the Constables of said City:

Whereas, A. B. of said City, has this day made complaint and information on oath before me J. T., a Justice of the said City, that on the ——— day of ——— 18—, in said City, he the said A. B. then being harbour master of the port of ———, did direct C. D., (he the said C. D. then being the master of a certain ship called the ———, lying in the said port, and within the jurisdiction of the said A. B., as such harbour master,) to moor his said ship at ———, in the said port and jurisdiction, and that the said C. D. did not moor the said ship, or cause the said ship so to be moored, as soon as he might and ought to have done, but failed and refused so to do: These are, therefore, to command you, in the name of the Commonwealth of Virginia, forthwith to apprehend the said C. D., and bring him before me or some other Justice of the said City, to answer the said complaint, and to be farther dealt with according to law. Given under my hand and seal, this ——— day of ——— 18—.

                                              J. T., J. P. [L. S.]

(No. 2.)

Form of Warrant of Arrest against a harbour master for failing to do his duty as harbour master.

City of ———, to wit:
 To all or any one of the Constables of said City:
  Whereas, A. B. of ———, has this day made complaint and information on oath before me J. T., a Justice of the said City, that C. D., on the —— day of ——— 18—, in said City, (he the said C. D. then being harbour master for the port of ———,) did permit a certain ship called the ———, to ride at single anchor longer than one tide in the said port, and within the jurisdiction of the said C. D. as such harbour master: These are, therefore, to command you, in the name of the Commonwealth of Virginia, forthwith to apprehend the said C. D., and bring him before me or some other Justice of the said City, to answer the said complaint, and to be farther dealt with according to law. Given under my hand and seal, this —— day of ——— 18—.

J. T., J. P. [L. S.]

[NOTE.—These forms may be easily changed to suit any other violation of the statute. For form of recognizance of bail and of witnesses, see Nos. 4 and 5, under head of RECOGNIZANCE; and for mittimus, No. 9, under head of ARREST; and for certificate to the clerk, see No. 10, under same head.]

CHAPTER L.

HEALTH—(*Public.*)

[See SMALL POX and QUARANTINE.]

Selling corrupt and unwholesome food, whereby the public health is endangered, is both a nuisance and a cheat at Common Law, and is now punishable by statute.

BY SEC. 1, CHAP. 197. If a free person knowingly sell any diseased, corrupted or unwholesome provisions, whether meat or drink, without making the same known to the buyer, he shall be confined in jail not more than six months, and fined not exceeding one hundred dollars.

BY SEC. 2. If a free person fraudulently adulterate, for the purpose of sale, any thing intended for food or drink, or any drug or medicine, with any substance injurious to health, he shall be confined in jail not more than one year, and fined not exceeding five hundred dollars; and the adulterated articles shall be forfeited and destroyed.

HEALTH—(*Public.*)

(No. 1.)

Form of Warrant of Arrest for selling unwholesome provisions.

——— County, to wit:
To all or any one of the Constables of said County:

Whereas, A. B. of said County, has this day made complaint and information on oath before me J. T., a Justice of the said County, that C. D., on the —— day of ———18—, in said County, did unlawfully sell to the said A. B., to be used and eaten by him, a quantity, to wit, ——— pounds of diseased, corrupted and unwholesome beef, (or *five loaves of unwholesome bread,*) as good and suitable to be eaten, without informing the said A. B. that the said beef was corrupted and unwholesome, (or *that the said bread was unwholesome,*) he the said C. D. then well knowing the same to be corrupt and unwholesome: These are, therefore, to command you, in the name of the Commonwealth of Virginia, forthwith to apprehend the said C. D., and bring him before me or some other Justice of the said County, to answer the said complaint, and to be farther dealt with according to law. Given under my hand and seal, this —— day of ——— 18—.

J. T., J. P. [L. S.]

(No. 2.)

Form of Warrant of Arrest for adulterating liquors.

——— County, to wit:
To all or any one of the Constables of said County:

Whereas, A. B. of said County, has this day made complaint and information on oath before me J. T., a Justice of the said County, that C. D., on the —— day of ——— 18—, in said County, did, for the purpose of selling the same, fraudulently adulterate a quantity of (state the article,) by mixing therewith (state what,) which is injurious to health: These are, therefore, to command you, in the name of the Commonwealth of Virginia, forthwith to apprehend the said C. D., and bring him before me or some other Justice of the said County, to answer the said complaint, and to be farther dealt with according to law. Given under my hand and seal, this —— day of ——— 18—.

J. T., J. P. [L. S.]

(No. 3.)

Form of Warrant of Arrest for fraudulent adulteration of medicine.

——— County, to wit:
To all or any one of the Constables of said County:

Whereas, A. B. of said County, has this day made complaint and information on oath before me J. T., a Justice of the said County, that C. D., on the —— day of ——— 18—, in said County, did fraudulently adulterate, for the purpose of selling the same, a certain drug or medicine, called ———, by mixing with the same a certain substance called ———, in such a manner as to render the said drug or medicine injurious to health:

These are, therefore, to command you, in the name of the Commonwealth of Virginia, forthwith to apprehend the said C. D., and bring him before me or some other Justice of the said County, to answer the said complaint, and to be farther dealt with according to law. Given under my hand and seal, this —— day of —— 18—.

J. T., J. P. [L. S.]

(No. 4.)

Form of Mittimus.

Follow form No. 9, under head of ARREST, and describe the offence as in the warrant.

(No. 5.)

Form of Certificate to the Clerk.

Follow form No. 10, under head of ARREST.

(No. 6.)

Form of Recognizance of Bail.

Follow form No. 4, under head of RECOGNIZANCE.

(No. 7.)

Form of Recognizance of Witnesses.

Follow form No. 5, under head of RECOGNIZANCE.

CHAPTER LI.

HOMICIDE.

By Sec. 1, Chap. 190. Murder by poison, lying in wait, imprisonment, starving, or any wilful, deliberate and premeditated killing, or in the commission of, or attempt to commit, arson, rape, robbery or burglary, is murder of the first degree. All other murder is murder of the second degree.

By Sec. 2. Murder of the first degree shall be punished with death.

By Sec. 3. Murder of the second degree by a free person, shall be punished by confinement in the penitentiary not less than five nor more than eighteen years.

By Sec. 4. Voluntary manslaughter by a free person, shall be punished by confinement in the penitentiary not less than one nor more than five years.

By Sec. 5. Involuntary manslaughter, by a free person, shall be a misdemeanor.

By Sec. 6. If a person be stricken or poisoned in, and die by reason thereof, out of this State, the offender shall be as guilty, and be prosecuted and punished, as if the death had occurred in the county or corporation in which the stroke or poison was given or administered.

Homicide, in a legal sense, signifies the killing of a man by a man,[1] and this killing may or may not be felonious. In this chapter we will notice briefly the various grades of homicide, with their appropriate definitions, and conclude with the necessary forms for a single Justice out of court, to commit an offender for farther examination or trial before the county court for murder or manslaughter.

This will be done in the following order:
    I. Murder.
    II. Manslaughter.
    III. Homicide by misadventure.
    IV. Excusable homicide in self defence.
    V. Justifiable homicide.

I. *Murder.*

Murder is the killing of any person with *malice prepense*, or aforethought, either expressed or implied by law.[2] Malice is the chief characteristic by which murder is to be dis-

---
[1] 1 Hawk. c. 26.   [2] 1 East P. C. 254; 1 Russ. 221.

tinguished from any other species of homicide. But when the law makes use of the term "malice aforethought," as descriptive of the crime of murder, it is not to be understood merely in the ordinary sense of a principle of malevolence to any particular individual, but as meaning that the fact has been attended with such circumstances as are the ordinary symptoms of a wicked, depraved and malignant spirit, indicating a "heart regardless of social duty, and deliberately bent on mischief;"(¹) for though no mischief is intended to any particular individual, yet, if there is a general malice or depraved inclination, fall where it may, and the act is in itself unlawful and attended with danger, the killing will amount to murder. Thus, if a man wilfully discharge a gun among a multitude of people, with intent to do mischief and kill any person, he will be guilty of murder ; so, where a man knowing that people are passing along a street, throws a stone over a house or wall, with *intent* to do *hurt* to people, and one passing is thereby killed, this also is murder, for he *intended* hurt, which is evidence of malice, and it is no excuse that he was merely bent on mischief generally, and had no malice against any particular individual.(²) So also, where there is a malicious intent to hurt a particular individual, and the blow, by mistake or accident, falls upon another, the act done will follow the nature of the act intended to be done ; and the motive being malicious, the act, if death ensue, will amount to murder ; as where A. having malice against B., strikes at and misses him, but kills C. ; this is murder in A.(³) And it may be generally stated, that if a person deliberately commit an unlawful act, dangerous in itself, with intention to commit a felony, or with a malicious intent against a particular individual, or a general mischievous intent against all persons indiscriminately, and death ensue from the commission of the act, though contrary to the party's original intention, he will nevertheless be guilty of murder.(⁴)

The distinction made by the first section of the statute between murder of the first and second degrees, does not dispense with the ingredient of malice in the crime of murder. It must exist in both degrees, for where there is no malice either expressed or implied, there can be no murder of any degree.

Malice may be either expressed or implied by law. Express malice is where one person kills another with a deliberate mind and formed design; such formed design being

---

(¹) Foster 256, 262.
(²) 1 Hale 475 ; 1 Hawk. c. 29, § 42, c. 31, § 68 ; 1 East P. C. 231 ; 2 Dea. Cr. Co. 925.
(³) 1 Hale 438 ; 1 East P. C. 230.
(⁴) Foster 261 ; 1 East P. C. 231 ; Dane's Abr. 125.

evidenced by external circumstances, discovering the inward intent; as lying in wait, antecedent menaces, former grudges and concerted schemes to do the party killed some bodily harm;(¹) and malice is implied by law from any deliberate, cruel act, committed by one person against another, however sudden.(²) This doctrine is fully recognized in our own courts, and according to their decisions it is not necessary to constitute murder in the first degree, that the premeditated design to kill should have existed for any particular length of time.(³)

All persons present, aiding and abetting to a murder, are principals in the felony; and to constitute presence, there need not be an actual standing by, within sight or hearing of the fact; for there may be a constructive presence, as where one commits a murder and another keeps watch or guard at some convenient distance.(⁴) He that counsels, commands or directs the killing of any person, and is himself absent at the time of the fact being done, is an accessary to the murder before the fact;(⁵) and an accessary after the fact, in murder, is where a person, knowing a murder to have been committed, receives, relieves, comforts or assists the offender.(⁶) See ACCESSARIES.

From this definition of the crime and description of malice, the Justice will readily perceive what constitutes murder; and we will conclude this brief notice of the subject, by remarking first, that as a general rule, all homicide is presumed to be malicious and amounts to murder, until the contrary appears; and secondly, that in committing for felonious homicide, the Justice should not take upon himself to discriminate between the degrees of the offence, but commit for the felonious killing; for in Myers's Case, 1 Virginia Cases, it was decided, that even an examining court could not discriminate between the degrees of felonious homicide, so as to discharge of murder and remand for manslaughter, but should remand for the felonious fact, for which the prisoner is examined; that the grade of the offence might be determined in the superior court. Malice is not a felonious fact, but a mere incident, which, if attending the fact of killing, will constitute the crime of murder. And though the Justice should commit for manslaughter in the first instance, the prisoner may be sent on to the superior court for the felonious fact, and be there indicted of murder; otherwise the judgment of the committing Magistrate or of an examining court might fix and control the character of a prosecution

---

(¹) 1 Hale 451; 1 Russ. 421-2.
(²) 1 East P. C. 215.
(³) Whiteford's Case, 6 Rand. 721; and see Jones' Case, 1 Leigh 598; and Bennett's Case, 8 Leigh 745.
(⁴) 1 Russ. 431.
(⁵) 1 Russ. 432.
(⁶) Id. 433.

for felonious homicide, however erroneous that judgment might be.

Murder in the first degree is punished with death, and in the second degree, when committed by a free person, by confinement in the penitentiary for not less than five nor more than eighteen years. Since the statute has made this distinction, the presumption where a felonious homicide is proved, is, that it is murder in the second degree, and that if the Commonwealth seeks to elevate it to murder in the first degree, she must establish the characteristics of that crime.([1])

II. Manslaughter.

Malice is the chief ingredient and characteristic of murder. In manslaughter it is wanting, and although this offence is in its degree felonious, yet it is imputed by the benignity of the law to human infirmity,([2]) and is therefore punished with less severity.

Manslaughter is defined to be the unlawful killing of another without malice, either express or implied, and is either voluntary, upon a sudden heat, or involuntary, in the commission of some unlawful design.

1st. *Of voluntary manslaughter.*—Voluntary manslaughter differs from murder, in this, that manslaughter arises from the sudden heat of the passions, and murder from the wickedness of the heart.([3])

The crime of voluntary manslaughter, in many cases, borders so nearly upon murder, that it requires a minute examination to discriminate between the two offences. Such an examination, if not useless here, is unnecessary, as these nice distinctions are not for the Justice out of court to draw; but should be left to those who *try* the case.* To correct, however, a common error which prevails out of the legal profession, it may be as well to state, that words of reproach, however grievous, are not provocation sufficient to free the party killing from the guilt of murder; nor are contemptuous or insulting actions or gestures, without an assault upon the person; nor is any trespass against lands or goods. This rule governs every case where the party killing upon such provocation, made use of a deadly weapon, or otherwise manifested an intention to kill, or to do some great bodily harm. But if one man had given another a box on the ear, or strikes him with a stick or other weapon *not likely to kill*, and unluckily and against his

---

([1]) Hunter Hill's Case, 2 Grat. 594. ([3]) 4 Black. Com. 191; 2 Dea. Cr.
([2]) 1 Russ. 485; Fost. 290.   Co. 850.

* Note—See M'Whirt's Case, 3 Grat. 594, where these distinctions are elaborately and lucidly discussed in the opinion delivered by the Judges.

intention kill him, it is but manslaughter: for no malignant intention can be collected from such acts.(¹)

2d. *Of involuntary manslaughter.*—The crime of involuntary manslaughter may happen either from an unlawful act done heedlessly and incautiously, or in the commission of a lawful act unlawfully and improperly performed. In regard to the first, it is remarked by Mr. Russell, that "there are many acts so heedless and incautious, as necessarily to be deemed unlawful and wanton, though there may not be an express intent to do mischief; and the party committing them, and causing death by such conduct, will be guilty of manslaughter," and this, although there was no actual intention to kill. As if a person breaking an unruly horse, ride him against a crowd of people and death ensues from the viciousness of the animal, and it appears clearly to have been done heedlessly and incautiously only, *and without intent to do mischief*, it would be manslaughter.(²) So if a man, knowing that people are passing along the street, throw a stone from a house or over a wall, and a person be thereby killed, it would be manslaughter, *though he did not intend to hurt any one*;(³) and the like was held, where a gentleman coming to town in a chaise, before he got out of it, fired his pistols in the street, which by accident, killed a woman, for in each of these cases the act was manifestly improper and likely to cause danger.(⁴) In cases of this character, it is not necessary, in order to render the homicide manslaughter, that the act in the performance of which, death is caused, should be a felony or even a misdemeanor. It is sufficient if it be contrary to law; as, if a person in sport, throw stones down a coal pit and thereby kill another, it will be manslaughter.(⁵) And it should be distinctly borne in mind by the Justice, that it is the absence of all intent to kill or to do hurt, that reduces all such cases to manslaughter.

In regard to manslaughter proceeding from the commission of a lawful act, unlawfully or improperly performed, it may be remarked, that there are many lawful acts permitted and required to be done by various persons, which may be so improperly performed as to render the party guilty of manslaughter, if death ensue from the improper performance of the act.

Thus, immoderate correction, inflicted by a parent, master or other person having authority, (growing out of their domestic relations,) from which the party dies, will be either murder or manslaughter, according to the circumstances of

---

(¹) 1 East P. C. 233.
(²) 1 East P. C. 231; 1 Russ. 526.
(³) 1 Hale 475.
(⁴) 1 Ventr. 481; 2 Dea. Cr. Co. 873.
(⁵) Rex *v.* Fenton, Lew. C. C. 179.

the case. If it be done with such an instrument, or to such an extent as is not likely to kill, though the instrument may be in itself improper for the purpose of correction, or the measure of the correction may be unreasonable, yet where the provocation is great, and the act is manifestly accompanied with a good intent, it will reduce the offence to manslaughter,(¹) but if the punishment is done with an instrument, or to an extent likely to kill, it will be murder if death ensue; for malice will be implied from any cruel and barbarous act. And in such cases, it matters not whether the death proceeds from personal violence or from correction inflicted by means of a system of privation and ill-treatment or gross negligence.(²) Indeed malice, the essential ingredient in murder, may be as well implied from a continued course of cruel and barbarous privation, as from outrageous violence; such, for instance, as wilfully depriving an apprentice for a long time of food or clothing sufficient to support life.(³)

In like manner, if a person driving a cart or other carriage, happen to kill another, and it appears that he might have seen the danger, but did not look before him, it will be manslaughter, for want of due caution.(⁴) In a case where a cartman was driving at an *unusually rapid rate,* and the cart ran over a man and killed him, he was held guilty of manslaughter, though *he called* to the deceased to get out of the way, which the deceased might have done had he not been drunk.(⁵)

This case should admonish the drivers of carts and all heavy carriages, especially in cities and on public highways, to be careful not to urge their horses to a swifter pace than what is proper for vehicles of that description, for it is extremely difficult, if not impossible, to stop or pull up on the instant, so as to avoid running over any one who is unable to get out of the way, and the case itself shews that it is no justification to warn the party of his danger.

If death is caused by gross ignorance or culpable neglect in medical men, though lawfully qualified to practise as such, or apothecaries, in the practice of their respective arts or professions, it will be manslaughter.(⁶) But though it is certainly highly rash and presumptuous for unskilful persons to undertake matters of this nature, the offence will not amount to manslaughter, unless the practitioner is guilty of such criminal misconduct as arises from the grossest ignorance or the most unpardonable neglect.(⁷) On this subject it has been

---

(¹) Foster 262; 1 Hale 454; 1 East P. C. 237.
(²) 1 East P. C. 226; 1 Leach 137.
(³) Rex *v.* Squire, 1 Russ. 426.
(⁴) 1 Russ. 535.
(⁵) R. *v.* Walker, 1 C. & P. 320.
(⁶) Ferguson's Case, Id. 169; Rex *v.* Senior, Mar. & Car. 346; The Queen *v.* Spilling, 2 Moo. & Rob. Rep. 107.
(⁷) Rex *v.* Van Butchall, 14 C. L. R. 493; Rex *v.* Williams, Id. 497.

remarked, that "though it is not just that a medical man, when acting for the best, should be liable to the penalties of manslaughter, if he happen to fall into some mistake in his prescription, or some mischance in an operation, from which the most learned and skilful cannot always be exempt, yet it must be admitted that the law cannot well be too strict in these cases, to deter ignorant people from endeavouring to get their livelihood by trifling with the lives of their fellow creatures."[1]

From what has been said on this subject, it is obvious that cases of involuntary manslaughter sometimes occur, which partake rather of homicide by misadventure than of crime, (morally speaking;) yet they rank at Common Law as cases of *felonious* homicide. To mitigate both the severity of the punishment and the degradation in such cases, the statute makes involuntary manslaughter a misdemeanor only, and a party committing the offence, should be committed or recognized to answer an indictment therefor in the county or corporation court. Unless, however, it be a clear case of involuntary manslaughter, the party should, if a free person, be committed for examination for felonious homicide, so that a jury, if they think proper, may find the accused guilty of involuntary manslaughter, or of any other grade of homicide.[2]

There are no accessaries before the fact in manslaughter, because it is presumed to be altogether sudden and without any premeditation, and in order to make an abettor to manslaughter a principal in the felony, he must be *present* aiding and abetting the fact committed. But there may be accessaries after the fact in manslaughter.[3]

III. *Excusable homicide by misadventure.*

The law is so tender of human life, that the term "excusable homicide," when applied by it to homicide by misadventure, or in self defence, imports at Common Law, some fault in the party by whom it has been committed; but of a nature so trivial, that it excuses it from the guilt of felony, though in strictness, it deems it deserving of some punishment, and therefore inflicted on the delinquent the forfeiture of his goods and chattels, or a portion of them.[4] But even in England this forfeiture is now done away with by statute. (See 9th of Geo. 4, c. 31.) And however tender the law of Virginia has always been of human life, it has long regarded

---

[1] 2 Deac. 877.
[2] See ch. 208, § 30, N. C.
[3] 1 Hale 437 to 450; 1 Hawk. c. 29 and 30.
[4] 1 Russ. C. & M. 538.

homicide by misadventure as an accident to be deplored, and not as a crime to be punished, and therefore inflicted no penalty on the party committing it.

Excusable homicide by misadventure, is where one doing a lawful act, without any intention of bodily pain, and using proper precaution to prevent danger, unfortunately happens to kill another.(¹) The act must be lawful, and not done with intention of great bodily harm, for if *the act* be unlawful, it will amount to murder or manslaughter, according to the circumstances, and if it be done with the intention of great bodily harm, then the legality of the act, considered abstractedly, would be no more than a mere cloak or pretence, and would avail nothing. It must also be done in a proper manner, and with due caution to prevent danger.(²)

Accidental death often happens from the ordinary occupations, or the lawful amusements of mankind, as where a man is at work with a hatchet and the head flies off and kills a stander by, or where a man, driving a carriage or other vehicle, happens to drive over another person and kill him, without any imputation of a want of due care on the part of the driver; these and many cases like them to be found in the books, are cases of excusable homicide by misadventure, for the act in all such cases is lawful, done without any intention to hurt, and with proper precaution to prevent danger, and the effect merely accidental.(³)

The degree of caution to be employed in these cases, depends upon the probability of danger, for where there is danger, and there is any want of due and proper caution, and death ensues, it will be manslaughter. But it should be observed, that the caution which the law requires, is not the utmost caution that can be used, it is sufficient that a reasonable precaution be taken, such as is usual and ordinary in similar cases, and such as has been found by long experience in the ordinary course of things, to answer the end. As, however, the degree of caution to be employed depends upon the probable danger, it follows that persons using articles or instruments, in their nature particularly dangerous, (as, for instance, poison or fire arms,) must proceed with such appropriate and reasonable precaution as the particular circumstances may require. Thus, though where one lays poison to kill rats, and another takes it and dies, this is misadventure; yet it must be understood to have been laid in such manner and place as not easily to be mistaken for food, for that would be-

---

(¹) 1 Russ. C. & M. 539. (³) 1 Deac. Cr. Co. 618; 1 Russ. C.
(²) 1 Russ. C. & M. 539; 1 East & M. 539.
P. C. 261.

token great inadvertence, and might in some cases amount to manslaughter.(¹)

IV. *Excusable homicide in self defence.*

Excusable homicide in self defence, is the killing of another in defence of a man's person or property, upon some sudden affray, and considered by the law as in some measure blameable and barely excusable,(²) or as Mr. Justice Foster expresses it, it is "self defence *culpable*, but through the benignity of the law *excusable*,"(³) and therefore, (as in homicide by misadventure,) although the felony was excused, it was at the same time attended with forfeiture. In the old books, it is sometimes called chance medley, and sometimes *chaud* medley, *chaud* being a French word, signifying hot. These terms are pretty much of the same import, the former signifying a *sudden affray;* the latter an affray in the *heat* of blood, which is usually sudden, though the term chance medley is often erroneously applied to homicide by misadventure.(⁴)

As in cases of felonious homicide, there is often but a slight shade of difference between voluntary manslaughter and murder, so, in frequent instances, excusable homicide in self defence, borders so nearly upon voluntary manslaughter, that the boundaries between the two are scarcely perceivable, though in consideration of law, they have been fixed.(⁵) These nice shades of difference often suggest the plea of self defence to those who defend prisoners upon their examination before Justices. In all such cases, the Justice should act with extreme caution in taking upon himself the responsibility of drawing the line, and should never discharge a party charged with felonious homicide upon this plea, unless a clear case of inevitable necessity is made out by him, for it would be a great reproach to the administrators of the law to suffer one to escape, who has voluntarily taken the life of another, without this overruling necessity clearly made out, and then only when he is wholly without fault in bringing that necessity upon himself. Both Mr. East and Mr. Russell, upon the authority of Justice Blackstone, state the true criterion between manslaughter and homicide in self defence to be this: that when both parties are actually combatting at the time the mortal stroke is given, the slayer is guilty of manslaughter; but if the slayer has not begun to fight, or having begun, endeavours to decline any farther struggle, and afterwards, being closely pressed by his antagonist, kills him to avoid his own destruc-

---

(¹) 1 Russ. C. & M. 540.
(²) 1 Russ. C. & M. 543.
(³) Foster 2731.
(⁴) 1 Dea. Cr. Co. 223; 4 Black. Com. 184.
(⁵) 1 Deac. Cr. Co. 622; Fost. 276.

tion, this is homicide excusable by self defence.(¹)* Whatever may be the accuracy of this distinction, it is certain that before this plea can avail any thing, it is incumbent on the party charged with felonious homicide to prove clearly to the satisfaction of the Justice two things: First, that before the mortal stroke was given, he had declined any farther combat, and had retreated as far as he could with safety; and secondly, that he then killed his adversary through *mere necessity*, in order to avoid immediate death or great bodily harm.(²)

A party, however, is not bound in every instance of an assault to flee from his assailant. Whether he can retreat at all with safety of his life, must, from the necessity of the case, depend upon the nature of the assault, for this may be so fierce and violent, as not to allow a man to yield a step, without manifest danger of life or great bodily harm, and then, in defence he may kill his assailant instantly.(³) But where it can be done, without danger of his own life or great bodily harm, the law requires that the person who kills another in his own defence, should retreat as far as he can, to avoid the violence of the assault, before he turns upon his assailant, and that not fictitiously, or in order to watch his opportunity, but from a real tenderness of shedding the blood of a fellow creature; for in no case will a feigned or any such retreat avail. The party assaulted, must therefore flee as far as he safely can, either by reason of some wall or other impediment, or as far as the fierceness of the assault will permit him.(⁴)

As to the necessity, under which the party is, of killing his adversary, he can in no case avail himself of such excuse, if he kill him even after a retreat, unless there were reasonable grounds to apprehend that he would be killed himself,(⁵) or that he would suffer great bodily harm,(⁶) and moreover should be without fault in bringing that necessity upon himself.

Therefore, in Naylor's Case, where the prisoner gave the deceased (his brother) a mortal stab with a pen knife, (a dangerous weapon,) after he had been violently assaulted, and while in fact the deceased was upon him, beating him on the ground, where he had been thrown by the deceased, as it was manifest that the deceased did not intend to kill, but only to correct his brother for improper conduct to their father, it was held by all the Judges to be manslaughter, there not appear-

(¹) 1 Russ. C. & M. 543; 1 East P. C. 280.
(²) 1 East P. C. 280.
(³) 1 Russ. C. & M. 544; 1 Hale 483.
(⁴) 1 Russ. C. & M. 544; 1 Den. Cr. Co. 623; 1 East P. C. 282.
(⁵) 1 East P. C. 285.
(⁶) 1 Russ. 544.

* But *query*. Will it be excusable self defence if the slayer bring upon himself that necessity by his own first assault? Mr. Deacon, combatting Mr. East's proposition upon this subject, and relying on Hawkins, says: it would be manslaughter. (See 1 Deac. Cr. Co. 623; 1 Hawk. c. 29, § 1; 1 Hale 482.)

ing to be any inevitable necessity, so as to excuse the killing in that manner; for it cannot be inferred from the bare act of striking, without any dangerous weapon, that the aggressor intends to kill, and unless there be a plain manifestation of a *felonious intent*, no assault, however violent, will justify killing the assailant under the plea of necessity.(¹) But if it appeared that a party who was engaged in such an affray without *any fault of his own*, had retreated as far as he could, (as in the above case, where he was thrown upon the ground and the deceased was upon him,) or otherwise manifested an intention to decline the controversy, and then being hard pressed, in mere defence of his person, from the continued blows of his adversary, gave a blow with his *hand*, or in any other manner *not likely to kill;* and it may *fairly* be presumed that he had no such intention, but only to make him desist, it rather seems that such act, though death ensue, is excusable in self defence, or attributable to misadventure, although the party's life was not in danger at the time; for no man is required by law to remain defenceless and suffer another to beat him as long as he pleases, without resistance, although it is evident that the other did not aim at his life; but he may lawfully exert as much force as is necessary to compel him to desist.(²) In doing this, however, let him be careful not to use a dangerous weapon or resort to any other means likely to kill, or from which such an intention may be presumed; otherwise, if death ensue from the act, it will not be justifiable.

V. *Justifiable homicide.*

This species of homicide arises in cases, either from the *command of the law* in the advancement of public justice, or by the *permission of law*, for the like purpose, or in the defence of one's person or property from the commission of a *known felony*, and is therefore without censure or blame in either case; as for example, the law commands the execution of a criminal sentenced to death by a court of competent jurisdiction, and therefore it justifies the proper officer of the court, or his deputy, in executing the sentence by putting the party to death in the manner required by the sentence. But wantonly to kill the greatest malefactor, uncompelled and extrajudicially, would be murder, because the law does not require it.(³) Nor can any other person than the proper officer, or his deputy, execute a legal judgment, for no one else is required by law to do it, and it is this requisition alone, that justifies the homicide. If any other person do it, even the

---

(¹) 1 East P. C. 277-286.
(²) 1 East P. C. 286.

(³) 1 Hawk. 497; 1 Deac. 625.

Judge himself, it is held to be murder.(¹) The judgment must also be executed in pursuance of the sentence of the court, for if an officer beheads one who is sentenced to be hung, or *vice versa*, it is murder.(²)

In some cases, for the advancement of public justice, homicide is justified rather by the permission than the absolute command of the law; for in such cases, without this justification, the law itself would never be carried on with proper vigour.

This permissive homicide, for the advancement of public justice, may occur in many instances. As in the case of *resistance* to a lawful arrest, when an officer, in the execution of his office, either in a civil or criminal cause, is *assaulted* and *resisted*, the officer may repel force by force, and if the party who makes the resistance, is unavoidably killed in the struggle, this homicide is justifiable; for the officer in such case, need not give back, but is justified in proceeding to the last extremity. A rule which, as Mr. Justice Foster observes, is founded in reason and public utility; for few men would quietly submit to an arrest, if in case of resistance, the officer were obliged to desist and leave the business undone.(³)

Where a person also is *indicted for a felony*, and will not suffer himself to be arrested by an officer having a warrant for that purpose, or even without a warrant, if the officer is known as such to the party, the officer may lawfully kill him, if he cannot otherwise take him; and although such person may be innocent, or though no felony has been actually committed, the officer will, in this case, be justifiable; for he is enjoined by law to arrest a party, not only where a felony has actually been committed, but also upon probable suspicion of a felony; and an *indictment* is a suspicion founded on the highest authority, that is, the finding of the fact by the grand jury. But a homicide of this description is only justifiable in the case of an arrest by the officer, and will not be justified by a private person acting on his own authority.(⁴)

So, where a felony has been committed, if the felon flies from justice and cannot be overtaken but by being killed in the pursuit, this will also be justifiable homicide, for it is the duty of an officer, and of every other person, to use his best endeavours to prevent the escape of a felon. This rule is not confined merely to those who are present at the felony; for if fresh suit be made, all those who join in aid of the first pursuit, are under the same protection of the law. But if the fe-

---

(¹) 1 Hale 501; 1 Hawk. c. 28. Fost. 270; 4 Black. Com. 179; 1 East
(²) 4 Bl. Com. 179. P. C. 307.
(³) 1 Hale 404; 1 Hawk. c. 28, § 17; (⁴) 1 Hawk. c. 28, § 12; 2 Hale 84;
1 East P. C. 300; 1 Deac. 626.

lon may be taken without being killed, it is at least manslaughter in him who kills him.(¹) In all misdemeanors, short of felony, and in civil cases, it is unlawful to kill the defendant or party accused, though he fly from the arrest and cannot otherwise be overtaken, and though there be a warrrant to apprehend him. Generally speaking, this will be murder, though in some cases, if it appear that death was not intended, it may only amount to manslaughter.(²) This rule, however, as will be seen from what has just been stated, does not apply to the case of *actual resistance;* the law makes this distinction in civil cases and misdemeanors, between *flying from* an arrest and *actually resisting* the officer in making an arrest. It is proper in every case of arrest by an officer, that he should give the party notice both of his authority and of the cause of arrest. (See title ARREST.)

Jailors and their officers are under the same protection as other ministers of justice, and if, in the necessary discharge of their duty, they meet with resistance, whether from the prisoners themselves, either in civil or criminal cases, or from others on behalf of the prisoners, they are not obliged to retreat as far as they can with safety, but may freely and without retreating, repel force by force; and if the party so resisting happen to be killed, this, on the part of the Jailor or his officer, or any person coming in aid of him, will be justifiable homicide.(³)

So, also, in the case of a riot or rebellious assembly, the peace officers and their assistants, endeavouring to disperse the mob, are justifiable at Common Law in proceeding to the last extremity, if the riot cannot otherwise be suppressed.(⁴)

The law also permits, and therefore justifies, one in repelling force by force, in defence of his person, habitation or property against another, who manifestly intends or endeavours, by *violence* or *surprise,* to commit a known felony, such as murder, rape, robbery, arson, burglary, and the like ; and in these cases he is not obliged to retreat, but may pursue his adversary until he has secured himself from all danger, and apprehended the aggressor; and if he kill him in so doing, it is called justifiable self defence. On the other hand, the killing by such felons of any person so lawfully defending himself, will be murder.(⁵) This species of homicide differs from excusable homicide in self defence, in this, that it does not arise out of a sudden affray; that the party need not

---

(¹) 1 Hale 489; 1 Hawk. c. 28, § 11; Fost. 271; 4 Bl. Com. 179; 1 East P. C. 289.
(²) 1 East P. C. 302, 306.
(³) 1 Hale 481; Fost. 321.
(⁴) 1 Hale 481; 1 East P. C. 304; 1 Deac. Cr. Co. 626; and see c. 195, New Code.
(⁵) 1 East 272; 1 Deac. Cr. Co. 627.

retreat, but may pursue the aggressor until he has both secured himself from all danger and has apprehended the person of the offender,(¹) and this is in accordance with the right of every man to defend himself and property from the commission of a *felony*, and the duty of every man to apprehend a known felon.

This permissive, justifiable homicide does not extend to any case, but to prevent the commission of *felony;* for if one comes to beat another, or take his goods, merely as a trespasser, though the owner may justify the beating of him, so far as to make him desist, yet if he kill him in the conflict, without unavoidable necessity, in defence of his own life, it is manslaughter.(²) Nor does the rule apply to any crime unaccompanied by force, such as filching of pockets,(³) and it must be to prevent the commission of a *known felony;* for a bare fear that a felony will be committed, however well founded, will not warrant or justify one man in killing another by way of prevention. There must be actual danger at the time, and the intention to commit such felony must be apparent and not left in doubt.(⁴) But it is sufficient if there is apparent intent, evidenced by an *overt act* to commit *a felony*.(⁵)

Not only may the individual, whose person or property is threatened with the actual attempt to commit a felony, repel force by force, but any other person *present* may interpose to prevent the mischief, and will be equally justified, though death ensue from his interference.(⁶)

Though the party upon whom a felonious attack is made, or any other person present, may repel the attack by force until all danger of the felony is removed; yet if the aggressor is killed after he is properly secured, and there is no longer any apprehension of danger, such killing will be murder. It might, perhaps, if the blood were still hot from the contest or pursuit, be only manslaughter, on account of the high provocation.(⁷) But if one picks another's pocket, and he cannot otherwise be taken than by killing him, this falls under the general rules of arresting felons.(⁸)

Finally, let it be distinctly borne in mind, that in no case can a man justify the killing of another, under the pretence of necessity, unless he were *wholly* without any fault imputable by law, in bringing that necessity upon himself.(⁹)

(¹) 1 Deac. Cr. Co. 627.
(²) 1 P. C. 272; 1 Deac. Cr. Co. 627.
(³) 1 Hale 848; 4 Bl. Com. 180.
(⁴) 1 East P. C. 272; 1 Hale 484; 1 Deac. Cr. Co. 627.
(⁵) 1 Dea. 627; Mawgride's Case, 1 East 243.
(⁶) 1 Hale 481-84; Foster 274; 2 Bos. & P. 265.
(⁷) 1 Hale 485; 4 Black. Com. 185; 1 East P. C. 293.
(⁸) 1 East P. C. 273.
(⁹) 1 East P. C. 259, 277; 1 Hawk. c. 28, § 22.

(No. 1.)

Form of Warrant of Arrest, for murder.

—— County, to wit:

To the Sheriff, or to any one of his Deputies, and to all or any one of the Constables of said County:

Whereas, A. B. of said County, has this day made complaint and information on oath before me J. T., a Justice of the said County, that C. D., on the —— day of ———— 18—, in said County, feloniously and of his malice did kill and murder one E. F.:* These are, therefore, in the name of the Commonwealth, to command you, forthwith to apprehend the said C. D., and bring him before me or some other Justice of the said County, to answer the said complaint, and to be farther dealt with according to law. Given under my hand and seal, this —— day of ———— 18—.

J. T., J. P. [L. S.]

(No. 2.)

Form of Mittimus where a party is committed for examination or trial in the County Court, for murder.

—— County, to wit:

To X. Z., Constable of said County, and to the Keeper of the Jail of said County:

These are to command you, the said Constable, in the name of the Commonwealth of Virginia, forthwith to convey and deliver into the custody of the keeper of the said jail, together with this warrant, the body of C. D., a white person (or *free negro*, or *a slave, the property of E. F.*, as the case may be,) charged before me J. T., a Justice of the said County, on the oath of A. B., with a felony by him committed, in this, that the said C. D., on the —— day of ———— in the year 18—, in the said County, (here describe the offence as in the warrant of arrest.) And you, the said keeper of the said jail, are hereby required to receive the said C. D. into your jail and custody, that he may be examined (or *tried*) for the said offence, by the County Court of said County, and him there safely keep, until he shall be discharged by due course of law. Given under my hand and seal, this —— day of ———— in the year 18—.

J. T., J. P. [L. S.]

[NOTE.—If the prisoner be a white person, or if he be a free negro charged with homicide of any grade, or with any offence punishable with death, he must be committed for examination. For all other felonies by free negroes, and in all cases of felony by slaves, the prisoner must be committed for trial.]

* If it be a case of manslaughter, leave out the words "and of his malice."

(No. 3.)

Form of Certificate of Commitment to be sent to the Clerk of the County Court, for murder.

—— County, to wit:
To the Clerk of the County Court of said County:

I, J. T., a Justice of the said County, do hereby certify, that I have, by my warrant, this day committed C. D. (if free negro or slave, state which) to the jail of this County, that he may be examined (or *tried*) before the County Court of the said County, for a felony by him committed, in this, that he did, on the —— day of ——— 18—, in the said County, (here state the offence as in the mittimus.) Given under my hand, this —— day of —— in the year 18—.

J. T., J. P.

(No. 4.)

Form of Certificate to the Clerk where party is admitted to bail, for murder.

Turn to head of ARREST, and follow No. 6.

(No. 5.)

Form of Recognizance of Bail, for murder.

Turn to head of RECOGNIZANCE, and follow No. 1, if person be free; No. 2, if a slave, and state succinctly the offence for which the person is recognized.

(No. 6.)

Form of Recognizance of Witness to appear before the County Court to give evidence upon the examination or trial of a party charged with felony, for murder.

Turn to head of RECOGNIZANCE, and follow No. 3.

(No. 7.)

Forms of proceeding for involuntary manslaughter, after arrest.

For mittimus, see No. 9, under head of ARREST; for certificate of commitment to Clerk of County Court, see No. 10, under same head, but if party should be let to bail, see No. 11; for form of recognizance of bail and of witnesses, see Nos. 4. and 5, under head of RECOGNIZANCE.

(No. 1.)

Indictment for murder, by shooting with a pistol.

Commence as No. 1, under head of "INDICTMENTS," and say: that A. B., on the —— day of ————, with force and arms, in the County aforesaid, in and upon the body of one C. D., *in the peace of said Commonwealth then and there being,* feloniously, wilfully and of his malice aforethought, did make an assault; and that the said A. B., a certain pistol, *of the value of two dollars,* then and there charged with gunpowder and one leaden bullet, which said pistol, he the said A. B. in his right hand then and there had and held, then and there feloniously, wilfully and of his malice aforethought, did discharge and shoot off, to, against and upon the said C. D.; and that the said A. B., with the leaden bullet aforesaid, out of the pistol by the said A. B. discharged and shot off, as aforesaid, then and there feloniously, wilfully and of his malice aforethought, did strike, penetrate and wound the said C. D., in and upon the right side of the belly of him the said C. D.; giving to him, the said C. D., then and there with the leaden bullet aforesaid, so as aforesaid discharged and shot out of the pistol aforesaid, by the said A. B., in and upon the right side of the belly of him the said C. D., one mortal wound; of which said mortal wound* he the said C. D. then and there instantly died. And so the jurors aforesaid, upon their oath aforesaid, do say, that the said A. B., him the said C. D., in the manner and by the means aforesaid, feloniously, wilfully and of his malice aforethought, did kill and murder, against the peace and dignity of the Commonwealth of Virginia.

(No. 2.)

Indictment for murder, by stabbing with a knife.

Commence as No. 1, under head of "INDICTMENTS," and say: that A. B., on the —— day of ————, in the County aforesaid, in and upon one C. D., feloniously, wilfully and of his malice aforethought, did make an assault; and that the said A. B., with a certain knife, in his hand then and there held, the said C. D., in and upon the left side of the body, between the ribs of him the said C. D., then and there feloniously, wilfully and of his malice aforethought, did strike and thrust; giving to the said C. D. then and there, with the knife aforesaid, in and upon the aforesaid left side of the body, between the ribs of him the said C. D., one mortal wound, of the breadth of three inches and of the depth of six inches; of which said mortal wound,† he the said C. D., then and there instantly died. And so the jurors aforesaid, upon their oath aforesaid, do say, that the said A. B., him the said C. D., in manner and form aforesaid, feloniously, wilfully and of his malice aforethought, did kill and murder, against the peace and dignity of the Commonwealth of Virginia.

---

* If the death was not immediate, the indictment from this point should conclude thus: "he the said C. D., from the said —— day of ————, in the year aforesaid, to the —— day of ————, in the year aforesaid, in the County aforesaid, did languish, and languishing did live; on which said —— day of ————, in the year 18—, the said C. D., in the County aforesaid, of the said mortal wound died; and so the jurors aforesaid, upon their oath aforesaid, do say, that the said A. B., the said C. D., in manner and form aforesaid, feloniously, wilfully and of his malice aforethought, did kill and murder, against the peace and dignity of the Commonwealth of Virginia.

† See above note.

(No. 3.)

Indictment for murder, by secretly conveying poison to the deceased.

Commence as No. 1, under head of "INDICTMENTS," and say: that C. D., feloniously, wilfully and of his malice aforethought, contriving and intending one E. F., with poison, feloniously, wilfully and of his malice aforethought, to kill and murder, on the —— day of ——, with force and arms, in the County aforesaid, feloniously, wilfully and of his malice aforethought, did privately and secretly convey into, and leave a great quantity of white arsenic, being a deadly poison, in the lodging room of him the said E. F., in the dwelling house of him the said E. F., there situate; and that the said C. D., contriving and intending as aforesaid, afterwards, to wit, on the day and year aforesaid, the same white arsenic, with a certain quantity of beer, in the same house then and there being, then and there feloniously, wilfully and of his malice aforethought, did put, mix and mingle, he the said C. D., then and there well knowing the said white arsenic to be a deadly poison; and also that the said beer, with which the said C. D. did so mix and mingle the said arsenic, was then and there prepared for the use of the said E. F.; and that the said E. F. afterwards, to wit, on the same day and year aforesaid, did take, drink and swallow down a great quantity of the said beer, with which the said white arsenic was mixed and mingled by the said C. D. as aforesaid, he the said E. F. not knowing that there was any white arsenic or other poisonous ingredient mixed or mingled with the said beer as aforesaid; by means whereof, he the said E. F. then and there became sick and distempered in his body, and the said E. F. of the poison aforesaid, so by him taken, drunk and swallowed down as aforesaid, and of the sickness occasioned thereby, from the said —— day of ——, in the year aforesaid, until the —— day of said month, in the same year, in the County aforesaid, did languish, and languishing live; on which said —— day of ——, in the year aforesaid, in the County aforesaid, he the said E. F., of the poison aforesaid, and of the sickness and distemper occasioned thereby, died. And so the jurors aforesaid, upon their oath aforesaid, do say, that he the said C. D., in manner and form aforesaid, him the said E. F., feloniously, wilfully and of his malice aforethought, did poison, kill and murder, against the peace and dignity of the Commonwealth of Virginia.

CHAPTER LII.

HORSES.

[For poisoning horses, see POISON.]
[For wilfully injuring horses, see TRESPASS.]

BY SEC. 1, CHAP. 102. *Diseased horses.* Any Justice, on proof that a horse, afflicted with the glanders or farcy, is permitted by the owner or keeper thereof, wilfully or negligently to go out of his enclosed grounds, shall order such horse to be killed, and to be buried (with the hide on) four feet deep; having first given to the owner of such horse, or to his agent, if any there be resident in the county or corporation, reasonable notice of the time and place when and where such order is proposed to be made. And such owner or keeper shall forfeit twenty dollars.

BY SEC. 2. *Stoned horses.* If any person shall wilfully or negligently permit any unaltered horse, of the age of two years, to go at large out of the enclosed grounds of the owner or keeper, after having been admonished to confine such horse, he shall forfeit twenty dollars; and for the second offence, double that sum; one half of which forfeitures, the informer shall have; and if after a second conviction, the said horse be found so going at large, he shall be the property of any person who will take him up.

(No. 1.)

Form of a Summons to recover the penalty of twenty dollars for suffering a horse with glanders or farcy to go at large.

Follow form No. 16, under head of "FINES AND CONVICTIONS," and describe the offence thus: "did wilfully (or *negligently*) suffer a horse, of which he was then and now is the owner, to go at large, and does now wilfully (or *negligently*) suffer the said horse to go at large, the said horse then and there and now being afflicted with farcy."

(No. 2.)

Concise form of a Judgment against the defendant, upon the above summons.

The Commonwealth } —— day of —————— 18—: Case heard and the de-
  v.   } fendant found guilty, and adjudged to pay the fine of
  A. B.   } twenty dollars and the costs of prosecution, which I
                      ascertain to be —— dollars.

J. T., J. P.

[For a more formal conviction, see No. 18, under head of "FINES." The Justice can issue no execution, but must return his proceeding and judgment to the Clerk's office.]

(No. 3.)

Form of a Notice that application will be made to a Justice to have a horse afflicted with farcy, killed.

To *A. B.*:

You will take notice, that I shall on the —— day of —————— 18—, at ——————, in the County of ——————, apply to a Justice of the said County, to order a Constable of said County, or some other person, to kill a horse owned by you and now suffered by you to go at large, afflicted with farcy.

C. D.

(No. 4.)

Form of Order to kill and bury a horse afflicted with farcy.

—————— County, to wit:

To X. Y., *Constable of the said County:*

Whereas, upon the examination of C. D. upon oath, this day before me J. T., a Justice of the Peace, at ——————, in the said County, it sufficiently appears to me, that a horse, the property of A. B., is afflicted with farcy, and that the said horse so diseased, is wilfully (or *negligently*) suffered to go at large out of the enclosed grounds of the said A. B. by him: These are, therefore, in the name of the Commonwealth, to command you forthwith to kill the said horse, and to bury or cause him to be buried, with his hide on, four feet deep; and for so doing, this shall be your warrant. Given under my hand and seal, this —— day of —————— 18—.

J. T., J. P. [L. S.]

HOUSE BREAKING. 367

(No. 5.)

Form of a Summons for wilfully (or negligently) suffering an unaltered horse to go at large.

Follow No. 16, under head of "FINES," and describe the offence thus: "he the said C. D. being then the owner of an unaltered horse more than two years old, did wilfully (or *negligently*) permit the said horse to go at large out of the enclosed grounds of the said C. D., after he had been admonished to confine the said horse."

(No. 6.)

Form of the Judgment or Conviction.

Commonwealth ⎫ —— day of —— 18—: Case heard upon the testimo-
     v.   ⎬ ny of J. L., and defendant found guilty and adjudged to
  C. D. ⎭ pay the fine of twenty dollars, (one moiety to go to A. B. the informer,) and the costs of the prosecution, which I ascertain to be —— dollars.

For more formal judgment, see No. 19, under head of FINES.

[NOTE.—For the second offence the party must be recognized to answer an indictment; see Nos. 4 and 5, under head of RECOGNIZANCE. The Justice can issue no execution, but must return his proceeding and judgment to the Clerk's office.]

CHAPTER LIII.

HOUSE BREAKING.

[For breaking and entering a dwelling house or any outhouse adjoining thereto and occupied therewith, in the night time, see BURGLARY.]

BY SEC. 12, CHAP. 192. If a free person shall in the *night*, enter *without* breaking, or shall in the *day* time, break and enter a dwelling house, or any outhouse adjoining thereto and occupied therwith, or shall in the night time enter, or break and enter, either in the *day time* or *night time*, any office, shop, storehouse, warehouse, banking house or other house not adjoining to or occupied with a dwelling house, or any ship or vessel within the jurisdiction of any county, with intent to commit murder, rape or robbery, he shall be confined in the penitentiary for not less than three nor more than ten years.

HOUSE BREAKING.

By Sec. 13, Chap. 192. If a free person do any of the acts mentioned in the preceding section, with intent to commit larceny, or any felony other than murder, rape or robbery, he shall be confined in the penitentiary not less than one nor more than ten years, or at the discretion of the jury, if the accused be white, or of the court, if he be a negro, be confined in jail not less than one nor more than twelve months, and in the latter case, may also be punished at the discretion of the court with stripes.

These provisions were introduced into the Code, for the first time, at the session of 1847-8. They embrace offences so nearly allied to burglary, that we deem it proper to point out to the Justice the distinction between them. In burglary, there must be a *breaking* as well as *an entry* into a *dwelling house*, or some house attached thereto and occupied therewith, in the night time, with intent to commit felony. Under these provisions of the statute any *entry* in the night without breaking, with a felonious intent, is sufficient to constitute felony. It is not burglary to break and enter a dwelling house in the *day time*, with an intent to commit felony, but the statute makes this felony also. So it is not burglary to break and enter any house, (*except a dwelling house or some house attached thereto and occupied therewith,*) either in the day or night, with intent to commit felony, but the statute makes it felony to *enter* in the *night*, or to *break* and *enter* in the *night* or *day* any other house, with intent to commit felony.

The following offences, then, are contained in these provisions:

I. *In reference to dwelling houses.*

1. The *entering* a dwelling house or any house attached thereto and occupied therewith, in the night, *without breaking*, with intent to commit felony.

2. The *breaking* and *entering* such house in the *day time*, with like intent.

II. *In reference to other houses and to vessels.*

1. The *entering* them in the *night without breaking*, with intent to commit felony.

2. The breaking and entering, either in the day or night, any such house or vessel, with the like intent.

The offence against these provisions of the statute is consummated by the entering, or breaking and entering, with *intent* merely to commit larceny or any felony, though the felony be not committed; if, however, a party enter, or break and enter, without any intention at the time of committing felony, and being in the house or vessel, then form the design to commit felony therein, and do actually commit the felony, it is not an offence against this statute, but a substantive, distinct felony. As, for example, if A. enter a dwelling house in the night time, without intending at the time to commit larceny, and while in the house form the design to steal, and do actually steal therein, it would be no offence against this statute, but simple larceny at Common Law.

It has been decided, in Massachusetts, upon a similar statute, that a count in an indictment, alleging that the defendant broke and entered a shop, with intent to commit larceny, and did there commit the offence, is not bad for duplicity; and that, by analogy to the law of burglary, a party may be acquitted of the statutory offence and found guilty of simple larceny.([1])

As to what constitutes a breaking or an entry, and when it is night, see BURGLARY.

(No. 1.)

Form of Warrant of Arrest for entering a dwelling house in the night without breaking, or for breaking and entering the same in the day, with intent to commit murder.

———— County, to wit :

To all or any one of the Constables of said County:

Whereas, A. B. of said County, has this day made complaint and information on oath before me J. T., a Justice of the said County, that C. D., on the ———— day of ———— 18—, in said County, did feloniously enter in the night (or *break and enter in the day time*) of that day, the dwelling house of the said A. B., with intent in the said dwelling house then and there feloniously to kill and murder the said A. B. : These are, therefore, to command you, in the name of the Commonwealth of Virginia, forthwith to apprehend the said C. D., and bring him before me or some other Justice of the said County, to answer the said complaint, and to be farther dealt with according to law. Given under my hand and seal, this ———— day of ———— 18—.

J. T., J. P. [L. S.]

([1]) Comm'th *v.* Tuck, 20 Pick. Rep. 356 ; see also Hope's Case, 1 Pick. Rep. 22; and Millard's Case, 1 Mass. Reports 6 ; in which last case, on a charge of shopbreaking and larceny, possession of part of the stolen goods, was held *prima facie* evidence both of the larceny of the whole property stolen, *and of the breaking and entering.* But see The People *v.* Fraser & Courtenay, 2 Wheel. C. C. 55 ; where it was held, that burglary cannot be inferred from finding stolen property in the possession of the accused, although larceny may; for the breaking and entry, or either, might be in the *day* time, and then it would not be burglary.

(No. 2.)

Form of Warrant of Arrest for entering a dwelling house in the night without breaking, or for breaking and entering in the day, with intent to commit rape or robbery.

—————— County, to wit:
  To all or any one *of the Constables of said County:*

Whereas, A. B. of said County, has this day made complaint and information on oath before me J. T., a Justice of the said County, that C. D., on the —— day of ———— 18—, in said County, did feloniously enter in the night (or *break and enter in the day time*) of that day, the dwelling house of the said A. B. with intent then and there in the said dwelling house, feloniously to [ravish and carnally know one E. F., by force and against her will:] These are, therefore, to command you, in the name of the Commonwealth of Virginia, forthwith to apprehend the said C. D., and bring him before me or some other Justice of the said County, to answer the said complaint, and to be farther dealt with according to law. Given under my hand and seal, this —— day of ———— 18—.

J. T., J. P. [L. S.]

[NOTE.—If the intent be to commit robbery, leave out what is in the brackets, and say " rob one E. F."]

———

(No. 3.)

Form of Warrant of Arrest for entering a dwelling house in the night with intent to commit larceny, or for breaking and entering the same in the day time, with like intent.

—————— County, to wit:
  To all or any one *of the Constables of said County:*

Whereas, A. B. of said County, has this day made complaint and information on oath before me J. T., a Justice of the said County, that C. D., on the —— day of ———— 18—, in said County, did feloniously enter the dwelling house of the said A. B., in the night (or *break and enter the dwelling house of the said A. B. in the day time,*) of that day, with intent, in the said dwelling house then and there, the goods and chattels of the said A. B. feloniously to steal, take and carry away, [and one coat of the value of fifteen dollars, of the goods and chattels of the said A. B., in the said dwelling house then being, feloniously did steal, take and carry away:] These are, therefore, to command you, in the name of the Commonwealth of Virginia, forthwith to apprehend the said C. D., and bring him before me or some other Justice of the said County, to answer the said complaint, and to be farther dealt with according to law. Given under my hand and seal, this —— day of ———— 18—.

J. T., J. P. [L. S.]

and enter, without any intention at the time of committing felony, and being in the house or vessel, then form the design to commit felony therein, and do actually commit the felony, it is not an offence against this statute, but a substantive, distinct felony. As, for example, if A. enter a dwelling house in the night time, without intending at the time to commit larceny, and while in the house form the design to steal, and do actually steal therein, it would be no offence against this statute, but simple larceny at Common Law.

It has been decided, in Massachusetts, upon a similar statute, that a count in an indictment, alleging that the defendant broke and entered a shop, with intent to commit larceny, and did there commit the offence, is not bad for duplicity; and that, by analogy to the law of burglary, a party may be acquitted of the statutory offence and found guilty of simple larceny.(1)

As to what constitutes a breaking or an entry, and when it is night, see BURGLARY.

(No. 1.)

Form of Warrant of Arrest for entering a dwelling house in the night without breaking, or for breaking and entering the same in the day, with intent to commit murder.

———— County, to wit:

To all or any one of the Constables of said County:

Whereas, A. B. of said County, has this day made complaint and information on oath before me J. T., a Justice of the said County, that C. D., on the ——— day of ——— 18—, in said County, did feloniously enter in the night (or *break and enter in the day time*) of that day, the dwelling house of the said A. B., with intent in the said dwelling house then and there feloniously to kill and murder the said A. B. : These are, therefore, to command you, in the name of the Commonwealth of Virginia, forthwith to apprehend the said C. D., and bring him before me or some other Justice of the said County, to answer the said complaint, and to be farther dealt with according to law. Given under my hand and seal, this ——— day of ——— 18—.

J. T., J. P. [L. S.]

---

(1) Comm'th *v.* Tuck, 20 Pick. Rep. 356 ; see also Hope's Case, 1 Pick. Rep. 22 ; and Millard's Case, 1 Mass. Reports 6 ; in which last case, on a charge of shopbreaking and larceny, possession of part of the stolen goods, was held *prima facie* evidence both of the larceny of the whole property stolen, *and of the breaking and entering.* But see The People *v.* Fraser & Courtenay, 2 Wheel. C. C. 55 ; where it was held, that burglary cannot be inferred from finding stolen property in the possession of the accused, although larceny may ; for the breaking and entry, or either, might be in the *day* time, and then it would not be burglary.

(No. 2.)

Form of Warrant of Arrest for entering a dwelling house in the night without breaking, or for breaking and entering in the day, with intent to commit rape or robbery.

—————— County, to wit:
    To all or any one of the Constables of said County:
Whereas, A. B. of said County, has this day made complaint and information on oath before me J. T., a Justice of the said County, that C. D., on the ——— day of ———— 18—, in said County, did feloniously enter in the night (or *break and enter in the day time*) of that day, the dwelling house of the said A. B. with intent then and there in the said dwelling house, feloniously to [ravish and carnally know one E. F., by force and against her will:] These are, therefore, to command you, in the name of the Commonwealth of Virginia, forthwith to apprehend the said C. D., and bring him before me or some other Justice of the said County, to answer the said complaint, and to be farther dealt with according to law. Given under my hand and seal, this ——— day of ———— 18—.

J. T., J. P. [L. S.]

[NOTE.—If the intent be to commit robbery, leave out what is in the brackets, and say " rob one E. F."]

(No. 3.)

Form of Warrant of Arrest for entering a dwelling house in the night with intent to commit larceny, or for breaking and entering the same in the day time, with like intent.

—————— County, to wit:
    To all or any one of the Constables of said County:
Whereas, A. B. of said County, has this day made complaint and information on oath before me J. T., a Justice of the said County, that C. D., on the ——— day of ———— 18—, in said County, did feloniously enter the dwelling house of the said A. B., in the night (or *break and enter the dwelling house of the said A. B. in the day time,*) of that day, with intent, in the said dwelling house then and there, the goods and chattels of the said A. B. feloniously to steal, take and carry away, [and one coat of the value of fifteen dollars, of the goods and chattels of the said A. B., in the said dwelling house then being, feloniously did steal, take and carry away:] These are, therefore, to command you, in the name of the Commonwealth of Virginia, forthwith to apprehend the said C. D., and bring him before me or some other Justice of the said County, to answer the said complaint, and to be farther dealt with according to law. Given under my hand and seal, this ——— day of ———— 18—.

J. T., J. P. [L. S.]

HOUSE BREAKING.

(No. 4.)

Form of Warrant of Arrest for entering in the night, a storehouse not adjoining a dwelling house, and stealing therefrom.

—— County, to wit:

To all or any one of the Constables of said County:

Whereas, A. B. of said County, has this day made complaint and information on oath before me J. T., a Justice of the said County, that C. D., on the —— day of ——— 18—, in said County, a certain storehouse not adjoining to or occupied with the dwelling house of the said A. B., in the night time, feloniously did enter, with intent to commit larceny therein, [and that the said C. D., one piece of cloth of the value of fifty dollars, of the goods and chattels of the said A. B., then being in the said storehouse, feloniously did steal, take and carry away:] These are, therefore, to command you, in the name of the Commonwealth of Virginia, forthwith to apprehend the said C. D., and bring him before me or some other Justice of the said County, to answer the said complaint, and to be farther dealt with according to law. Given under my hand and seal, this —— day of ——— 18—.

J. T., J. P. [L. S.]

[NOTE.—It will be easy to adapt the foregoing forms to any other case for entering a house in the night, with intent to steal. If the larceny be not actually committed, leave out all in the brackets.]

(No. 5.)

Form of Warrant of Arrest for breaking and entering in the day an outhouse adjoining to and occupied with a dwelling house, and stealing therefrom.

—— County, to wit:

To all or any one of the Constables of said County:

Whereas, A. B. of said County, has this day made complaint and information on oath before me J. T., a Justice of the said County, that C. D., on the —— day of ——— 18—, in said County, did, in the day time, feloniously break and enter a certain outhouse, the property of the said A. B., adjoining to the dwelling house of the said A. B. and occupied therewith, with intent the goods and chattels of the said A. B. in the said outhouse then being, feloniously to steal, take and carry away, and that he the said C. D., one watch of the value of —— dollars, of the goods and chattels of the said A. B., in the said outhouse then and there did feloniously steal, take and carry away: These are, therefore, to command you, in the name of the Commonwealth of Virginia, forthwith to apprehend the said C. D. and bring him before me or some other Justice of the said County, to answer the said complaint, and to be farther dealt with according to law. Given under my hand and seal, this —— day of ——— 18—.

J. T., J. P. [L. S.]

(No. 6.)

Form of Warrant of Arrest for breaking and entering an office, shop, storehouse, &c., not adjoining to or occupied with a dwelling house.

—— County, to wit:
To all or any one of the Constables of said County:

Whereas, A. B. of said County, has this day made complaint and information on oath before me J. T., a Justice of the said County, that C. D. on the —— day of —— 18—, in said County, did feloniously break and enter a certain office, (*shop, storehouse, warehouse,* or *banking house,* as the case may be,) the property of the said A. B., and not adjoining to or occupied with the dwelling house of the said A. B.; with intent the goods and chattels of the said A. B. in the said office then and there to steal, and that he the said C. D., one watch of the value of —— dollars, of the goods and chattels of the said A. B. in the said office, did feloniously steal, take and carry away: These are, therefore, to command you, in the name of the Commonwealth of Virginia, forthwith to apprehend the said C. D., and bring him before me or some other Justice of the said County, to answer the said complaint, and to be farther dealt with according to law. Given under my hand and seal, this —— day of —— 18—.

J. T., J. P. [L. S.]

(No. 7.)

Form of Warrant of Arrest for breaking and entering a meeting house, and stealing therefrom.

—— County, to wit:
To all or any one of the Constables of said County:

Whereas, A. B. of said County, has this day made complaint and information on oath before me J. T., a Justice of the said County, that C. D., on the —— day of —— 18—, in said County, did feloniously break and enter a certain meeting house, dedicated to the public worship of God, called the —— meeting house, with intent to commit larceny, and did, then, in the said meeting house, feloniously steal, take and carry away one Bible of the value of five dollars, of the goods and chattels of one E. F., (it may be laid to be the property of any one having either the actual or constructive possession of it:) These are, therefore, to command you, in the name of the Commonwealth of Virginia, forthwith to apprehend the said C. D., and bring him before me or some other Justice of the said County, to answer the said complaint, and to be farther dealt with according to law. Given under my hand and seal, this —— day of —— 18—.

J. T., J. P. [L. S.]

(No. 8.)

Form of Mittimus where a party is committed for examination or trial in the County Court for feloniously entering, or breaking and entering houses, with intent to commit felony.

—— County, to wit:

To X. Z., Constable of said County, and to the Keeper of the Jail of said County:

These are to command you, the said Constable, in the name of the Commonwealth of Virginia, forthwith to convey and deliver into the custody of the keeper of the said jail, together with this warrant, the body of C. D., a white person, (or *free negro*, or *a slave, the property of E. F.*, as the case may be,) charged before me J. T., a Justice of the said County, on the oath of A. B., with a felony by him committed, in this, that the said C. D., on the —— day of —— in the year 18—, in the said County, (here describe the offence as in the warrant of arrest.) And you, the said keeper of the said jail, are hereby required to receive the said C. D. into your jail and custody, that he may be examined (or *tried*) for the said offence by the County Court of said County, and him there safely keep, until he shall be discharged by due course of law. Given under my hand and seal, this —— day of —— in the year 18—.

J. T., J. P. [L. S.]

[NOTE.—If the prisoner be a white person, commit him for examination; if a negro, commit him for trial.]

(No. 9.)

Form of Certificate of Commitment to be sent to the Clerk of the County Court.

—— County, to wit:

To the Clerk of the County Court of said County:

I, J. T., a Justice of the said County, do hereby certify, that I have, by my warrant, this day committed C. D., (if free negro or slave, state which,) to the jail of this County, that he may be examined (or *tried*) before the County Court of the said County, for a felony by him committed, in this, that he did, on the —— day of —— 18—, in the said County, (here state the offence as in the mittimus.) Given under my hand, this —— day of —— in the year 18—.

J. T., J. P.

(No. 10.)

Form of Certificate to the Clerk where party is admitted to bail.

Turn to head of ARREST, and follow No. 6.

(No. 11.)

Form of Recognizance of Bail.

Turn to head of RECOGNIZANCE, and follow No. 1, if person be free; No. 2, if a slave, and state succinctly the offence for which the person is recognized.

(No. 12.)

Form of Recognizance of Witness to appear before the County Court to give evidence upon the examination or trial of a party charged with felony.

Turn to head of RECOGNIZANCE, and follow No. 3.

(No. 1.)

Form of an Indictment for entering a dwelling house in the night, without breaking, or for breaking and entering in the day time, and stealing therein.

Commence as No. 1, under head of "INDICTMENTS," and say: the dwelling house of one C. D., there situate, in the night time of that day, feloniously did enter, without breaking the same, with intent the goods and chattels of the said A. B., in the said dwelling house then and there being, feloniously to steal, take and carry away, and one coat of the value of fifteen dollars, and one pair of boots of the value of five dollars, of the goods and chattels of the said A. B., in the said dwelling house then and there being found, feloniously did steal, take and carry away, against the peace and dignity of the Commonwealth of Virginia.

And the jurors aforesaid, upon their oath aforesaid, do farther present, that the said A. B., on the —— day of —————— in the year 18—, in the County of ——————, a certain other dwelling house of one A. B. there situate, in the day time of that day did feloniously break and enter, with, &c. (conclude as first count.)

(No. 2.)

An Indictment for breaking and entering, in the day time, an outhouse adjoining the dwelling house, with intent to steal.

Commence as No. 1, under head of "INDICTMENTS," and say: a certain outhouse called a (state what house,) adjoining to and occupied with the dwelling house of one C. D. there situate, in the day time feloniously did break and enter, with intent the goods and chattels of the said A. B., in the said outhouse then and there being, feloniously to steal, take and carry away, and one coat of the value of ten dollars, of the goods and chattels of the said A. B., in the said outhouse then and there being found, then and there feloniously did steal, take and carry away, against the peace and dignity of the Commonwealth of Virginia.

(No. 3.)

An Indictment for entering in the night, without breaking, a storehouse not adjoining a dwelling house.

Commence as No. 1, under head of "INDICTMENTS," and say: a certain storehouse, not adjoining to or occupied with the dwelling house of one C. D., there situate, in the night time feloniously did enter, without breaking, with intent the goods and chattels of the said A. B., in the storehouse then and there being, feloniously to steal, take and carry away, &c. (charge the larceny as in the above precedent.)

CHAPTER LIV.

HUNTING, RANGING AND FISHING ON THE LAND OF ANOTHER.

BY SEC. 2, CHAP. 101. If any person shall shoot, hunt or range, or fish or fowl, within the enclosed bounds of another person, without license from the owner, he shall forfeit three dollars for each offence, to the informer. Where any person is convicted a third time of said offence, the Justice rendering judgment therefor shall require him to give a recognizance, with good security, for his good behaviour for a year; or if he fail to give such security, commit him to jail for one month, unless it be sooner given. Such recognizance shall be forfeited if such person offend as aforesaid, within the time limited in the recognizance.

(No. 1.)

Form of a Summons for hunting, ranging, &c., in the bounds of another.

Follow form No. 16, under the head of FINES, &c. and describe the offence thus: "did hunt and range (or *did range and fish*) within the enclosed bounds of the said A. B., without license from the said A. B."

(No. 2.)

Form of Conviction or Judgment.

It may be endorsed in this form, on the back of the summons: At ―― on the ―― day of ―――― 18―: Case heard, and upon the evidence of E. F., defendant found guilty and fined three dollars, for the use of A. B. the informer, and adjudged to pay the costs of prosecution, which I ascertain to be ―――― dollars.

For a more formal conviction, see No. 19, under head of FINES.

(No. 3.)

Form of Execution.

The Justice may issue execution for the fine and costs; for form follow No. 21, under head of FINES.

(No. 4.)

Form of Recognizance to keep the peace, to be entered into by a party who has been three times convicted of hunting on the land of others.

——— County, to wit:

Be it remembered, that on this ——— day of ——— 18—, C. D. and E. F. of the said County, personally came before me J. T., a Justice of the said County, and severally acknowledged themselves to owe to the Commonwealth of Virginia; that is to say, the said C. D. the sum of ——— dollars, and the said E. F. the sum of ——— dollars, to be respectively made and levied of their several goods and chattels, lands and tenements, if he the said C. D. shall make default in the performance of the condition underwritten.

The condition of the above recognizance is such, that whereas the above named C. D. has heretofore been twice convicted of the offence of hunting and ranging within the enclosed bounds of other persons, without license from the owner in either case to do so; and whereas he the said C. D. was again this day convicted by the said J. T., as Justice aforesaid, of hunting and ranging within the enclosed bounds of A. B. without his license, (and that being the third time he was convicted of the said offence,) was adjudged therefor to pay a fine of three dollars, and was thereupon required by the said J. T., Justice as aforesaid, to enter into a recognizance to be of good behaviour for one year: Now, if the said C. D. shall be of good behaviour towards all the citizens of this Commonwealth for one year next ensuing the date hereof, then the above recognizance to be void, otherwise to remain in full force and virtue.

Taken and acknowledged before me, the day and date first above written.

J. T., *J. P.*

(No. 5.)

Form of Commitment where the party fails to enter into the recognizance.

——— County, to wit:

To X. Y., Constable of the said County, and to the Keeper of the Jail of the said County:

Whereas, C. D. has been heretofore twice convicted of hunting and ranging within the bounds of other persons, without their license in either case; and whereas the said C. D. was this day convicted before me J. T., a Justice of the said County, upon the testimony on oath of R. R., of hunting and ranging within the bounds of J. S., without the license of the said J. S., whereupon the said C. D. was adjudged by me to pay the fine of $3, and upon the third conviction, this day had before me J. T., Justice of said County, required to enter into a recognizance to be of good behaviour for one year from this date, himself in the sum of $———, with one good surety in the like sum; and whereas the said C. D. has refused, and does now refuse, before me to give such recognizance: These are, therefore, in the name of the Commonwealth, to command you, the said Constable, forthwith to convey the said C. D. to the common jail of the said County, and there to deliver him, together with this precept, to the keeper thereof; and I do hereby command you, the said keeper, in the name of the Commonwealth, to receive the said C. D. into your custody in the said jail, and there him safely to keep for the term of one month next following the date hereof, unless in the mean time he shall be otherwise discharged by due course of law. Given under my hand and seal, this ——— day of ——— 18—.

J. T., J. P. [L. S.]

CHAPTER LV.

INDECENCY—(*Public.*)

[See LEWDNESS.]

All gross, public indecency, is a misdemeanor at Common Law, and is punished not only as a nuisance to the rest of the community, but as being injurious to public morals.(¹) Therefore, when a person was indicted for exhibiting himself naked from the Balcony, in Covent Garden, to a multitude of people, and confessed the indictment, he was sentenced to pay a fine of 2000 marks, to be imprisoned a week, and to give security for his good behaviour for three years.(²) So it is an indictable misdemeanor for a man to undress himself on the beach and bathe in the sea, near inhabited houses, from which he might be distinctly seen, though the houses had been recently erected, and before their erection it had been usual for men to bathe in great numbers at the place in question; for whatever place becomes the habitation of civilized men, there the laws of decency must be enforced.(³) It has likewise been held a misdemeanor, publicly to exhibit for money, a human being of unnatural and monstrous shape; and in one case of this description, where a monstrous child had died and was embalmed, to be kept for show, the Lord Chancellor ordered it to be buried.(⁴)

Selling, or exposing to sale, or circulating obscene books, prints, &c., are offences against decency and morality, and may properly be arranged under this head.

(¹) 1 Hawk. c. 5, § 4; 4 Black. Com. 65.
(²) Sir Charles Sedley's Case.
(³) Rex v. Crunden, 2 Camp. 89.
(⁴) 3 Burn's J. 578.

INDECENCY—(*Public*)—(*Indictment for.*)

By Sec. 11, Chap. 196. If a free person import, print, publish, sell or distribute any book, or other thing, containing obscene language, or any print, picture, figure or description, manifestly tending to corrupt the morals of youth, or introduce into any family or place of education, or buy or have in his possession, any such thing for the purpose of sale, exhibition or circulation, or with intent to introduce it into any family or place of education, he shall be confined in jail not more than one year, and fined not exceeding two hundred dollars.

These offences are considered so injurious to public morals, that by section 2, chapter 203, a search warrant may issue to search suspected places for any book or other thing containing obscene language, or any print, picture, figure or description, manifestly tending to corrupt the morals of youth, and intended to be sold, loaned, circulated or distributed, or to be introduced into a family, school or place of education. For form of this warrant, see No. 5, under the head of SEARCH WARRANTS. See also NUISANCE.

Form of Warrant of Arrest for selling obscene books or prints.

———— County, to wit:
To X. Y., *Constable of the said County:*
Whereas, A. B. of said County, has this day made complaint on oath before me J. T., a Justice of the said County, that on the ——— day of ———— 18—, in the said County, C. D. did sell and distribute a certain book, entitled ————, containing obscene language, (or *did sell and distribute certain obscene and indecent prints, representing,* state what,) manifestly tending to corrupt the morals of youth: These are, therefore, to command you, in the name of the Commonwealth of Virginia, forthwith to apprehend the said C. D., and to bring him before me or some other Justice of the said County, to answer the said complaint, and to be farther dealt with according to law. Given under my hand and seal, this ——— day of ———— 18—.

J. T., J. P. [L. S.]

[For forms of proceeding after arrest, see for commitment and certificate thereof to the clerk, Nos. 9 and 10, under head of ARREST, and for recognizance of bail and of witnesses, see Nos. 4 and 5, under head of RECOGNIZANCE.]

Form of Indictment for publishing an obscene print.

Commence as No. 2, under head of " INDICTMENTS," and say: That A. B., being an evil disposed person, and devising and intending the morals, as well of the youth as of other citizens of this Commonwealth to corrupt and debauch, on the ——— day of ————, in the County aforesaid, unlawfully, wantonly and maliciously did utter and publish to one C. D., a citizen of said Commonwealth, a certain lewd, scandalous and obscene print, on paper, representing a man in an indecent and obscene posture with a woman, that is to say, in the act and posture of carnal copulation with each other, which said lewd, scandalous and obscene print was contained and published in a certain printed book, entitled "Memoirs of a Woman of Pleasure," to the manifest corruption and subversion of the morals and manners of the youth of this Commonwealth, and of the citizens thereof, to the evil and pernicious example of all others in like case to offend, and against the peace and dignity of the Commonwealth of Virginia.

CHAPTER LVI.

INDIANS.

By Sec. 1, Chap. 211. In any criminal case against an Indian, or a person of Indian descent, (other than a negro,) the proceedings shall be as against a white person.

CHAPTER LVII.

INDICTMENTS AND INFORMATIONS.

An indictment is a written accusation of one or more persons of a crime preferred to, and presented upon oath, by a grand jury. It lies at Common Law, for all treason, felonies and misdemeanors of a public nature.

A criminal information is a written accusation of one or more persons of an offence committed, filed in court by the attorney for the Commonwealth, without the intervention of a grand jury.

By Sec. 1, Chap. 207. Prosecutions for offences against the Commonwealth, unless otherwise provided, shall be by presentment, indictment or information. The trial of a white person on a charge of felony, or of a free negro for a felonious homicide, or a felony punishable with death, shall always be by indictment.

By Sec. 2. No information shall be filed unless by leave of the court entered of record, nor unless the accused, being summoned for that purpose, fail to shew good cause to the contrary.

By Sec. 3. In a prosecution for a misdemeanor the name of the prosecutor, if there be one, and the county or corporation of his residence, shall be written at the foot of the presentment, indictment or information, when it is made, found or filed; and for good cause the court may require a prosecutor to give security for the costs, and if he fails to do so, dismiss the prosecution at his costs.

BY SEC. 4. If any proceeding for an offence, had or moved at the instance of a prosecutor, be dismissed, or the accused discharged from the accusation, the court or Justice before whom the proceeding is, may give judgment against the prosecutor in favour of the accused for his costs.

BY SEC. 5. In an indictment or accusation of perjury or subornation of perjury, it shall be sufficient to state the substance of the offence charged against the accused, and in what court or by whom the oath was administered, which is charged to have been falsely taken, and to make an averment that such court or person had competent authority to administer the same, together with the proper averments to falsify the matter wherein the perjury is assigned, without setting forth any part of any record or proceeding at law or equity, or the commission or authority of the court or person before whom the perjury was committed; but nothing herein shall be construed to allow, without the consent of the accused, a part only of any record, proceeding or writing, to be given in evidence on the trial of such indictment or accusation.

BY SEC. 6. In a prosecution against a person accused of embezzling or fraudulently converting to his own use, bullion, money, bank notes, or other security for money, it shall be lawful, in the same indictment to charge, and thereon to proceed against the accused for any number of distinct acts of such embezzlement or fraudulent conversion, which may have been committed by him within six months from the first to the last of such acts; and it shall be sufficient to allege the embezzlement or fraudulent conversion to be of money, without specifying any particular money, gold, silver, note or security; and such allegation, so far as it regards the description of the property, shall be sustained, if the accused be proved to have embezzled any bullion, money, bank note, or security for money, although the particular species be not proved.

BY SEC. 7. In a prosecution for forging, or altering or attempting to employ as true, any forged instrument or other thing, it shall not be necessary to set forth any copy or *fac simile* thereof, but it shall be sufficient to describe the same in such manner as would sustain an indictment for stealing such instrument or other thing, supposing it to be the subject of larceny.

By Sec. 8. In a prosecution for an offence committed upon or relating to, or affecting real estate, or for stealing, embezzling, destroying, injuring or fraudulently receiving or concealing any personal estate, it shall be sufficient to prove that when the offence was committed, the actual or constructive possession, or a general or special property, in the whole or any part of such estate, was in the person or community alleged in the indictment or other accusation to be the owner thereof.

By Sec. 9. Where an intent to injure, defraud or cheat is required to constitute an offence, it shall be sufficient, in an indictment or accusation therefor, to allege generally an intent to injure, defraud or cheat, without naming the person intended to be injured, defrauded or cheated, and it shall be sufficient, and not be deemed a variance, if there appear to be an intent to injure, defraud or cheat the United States, or any State, or any county, corporation, officer or person.

By Sec. 10. All allegations unnecessary to be proved may be omitted in any indictment or other accusation.

By Sec. 11. No indictment or other accusation shall be quashed or deemed invalid for omitting to set forth that it is upon the oaths of the jurors, or upon their oaths and affirmation, or for the insertion of the words "upon their oath," instead of "upon their oaths;" or for not in terms alleging that the offence was committed "within the jurisdiction of the court," when the averments shew that the case is one of which the court has jurisdiction; or for the omission or misstatement of the title, occupation, estate or degree of the accused, or of the name or place of his residence; or for omitting the words "with force and arms;" or the statement of any particular kind of force and arms; or for omitting to state, or stating imperfectly, the time at which the offence was committed, when time is not the essence of the offence; or for failing to allege the value of an instrument which caused death, or to allege that it was of no value; or for omitting to charge the offence to be "against the form of the statute," or statutes; or for the omission or insertion of any other words of mere form or surplusage. Nor shall it be abated for any misnomer of the accused; but the court may, in case of a misnomer appearing before or in the course of a trial, forthwith cause the indictment or accusation to be amended according to the fact.

By Sec. 12. Judgment in any criminal case after a verdict, shall not be arrested or reversed, upon any exception to the indictment or other accusation, if the offence be charged therein with sufficient certainty for judgment to be given thereon according to the very right of the case.

Indictments founded upon a statute, must lay the offence in the language of the statute. Departures from this plain and safe rule have sometimes been (seemingly at least,) allowed by the general court, but in a recent case, it was rigidly applied to an indictment for house burning, with the concurrence of all the Judges.(¹) In that case, the second count in the indictment was for *setting fire* to the house, and the offence alleged, was intended to be prosecuted as an offence punishable under the fourth section of the act, 1 Rev. Co. 1819, chapter 160. The offence under that section of the statute is described as *burning* a house, and the court decided unanimously, that the second count in the indictment, describing the offence as setting fire to the house, was a departure from the language of the statute, which upon demurrer before verdict, was fatal to it. See Howell v. The Comm'th, 5 Grattan 664.

By the provisions of the new statute, the structure of indictments is much simplified, and the forms found in this work are carefully adapted to them, and in accordance with the case above referred to.

(No. 1.)

Form of commencement and conclusion of an Indictment in the Circuit Court.

———— Judicial Circuit, ———— County, to wit: In the Circuit Court of the said County. } The jurors of the Commonwealth of Virginia, in and for the body of the County of ————, and now attending the said Court, upon their oath present, that A. B., on the ———— day of ———— in the year one thousand eight hundred and ————, in the said County, &c. &c., against the peace and dignity of the Commonwealth of Virginia.

(No. 2.)

Form of same in County Court.

———— County, to wit: In the County Court of the said County. } The jurors of the Commonwealth of Virginia, in and for the body of the County of ————, and now attending the said Court, upon their oath present, that A. B., &c. (conclude as above.)

(¹) Howell's Case, 5 Grat. 664.

(No. 3.)

Form of commencement of an Information.

(State the style of the Court, as in No. 1.) } Be it remembered, that T. T., Attorney for the Commonwealth, in the —— Court of ——, and who in this behalf prosecutes for the said Commonwealth, in his proper person, comes into the said Court, on this —— day of ——, and here gives the said Court to understand and be informed, that C. D., on the —— day of —— in the year ——, in the said County, did, &c. &c., against the peace and dignity of the Commonwealth of Virginia.

CHAPTER LVIII.

INTENT.

The intent with which an act constituting an offence is done, is an essential ingredient in most cases of crime, perhaps in all, unless in some of omission. The intent of a person, on doing an act, may be inferred or presumed from the nature or tendency of the act itself, upon the principle that every man must be supposed to intend the necessary consequence of his own act. He who does an act wilfully, necessarily intends that which must be the necessary consequence of the act.[1]

As to what is a sufficient allegation of an intent to injure, defraud or cheat, in all prosecutions requiring such allegations, see title INDICTMENTS.

---

[1] Rex *v.* Farrington, R. & R. C. C. 207; Rex *v.* Philips, R. & M. C. C. 263.

CHAPTER LIX.

JURISDICTION.

By Sec. 12, Chap. 199. Prosecutions for offences, committed wholly or in part without, and made punishable within, this State, may be in any county or corporation in which the offender may be found, or to which he may be sent by any Judge, Justice or Court.

By Sec. 13. An offence committed on the boundary of two counties, or within one hundred yards thereof, may be alleged to have been committed, and may be prosecuted and punished in either county.

By Sec. 14. If a mortal wound, or other violence or injury be inflicted, or poison be administered in one county or corporation, and death ensue therefrom in another county or corporation, the offence may be prosecuted in either.

CHAPTER LX.

KIDNAPPING AND SELLING FREE PERSONS AS SLAVES.

The stealing and carrying away, or secreting of any person, (sometimes called kidnapping,) is an offence at Common Law, punishable by fine and imprisonment.[1] When it is done with intent to use or sell him as a slave, it is made felony by statute.

By Sec. 17, Chap. 191. If any free person sell a free person as a slave, or kidnap a free person with intent to use or sell him as a slave, knowing him to be free, he shall be confined in the penitentiary not less than three nor more than ten years.

In this provision, the term "kidnap" is substituted for "stealing," the term employed in the former law upon this subject; but as kidnapping means the same thing as applied to persons, that "stealing and carrying away" do, as applied to property, doubtless the same construction given to the former law is applicable to this.

---

[1] Russ. 582.

The statute embraces two distinct offences: 1. The actual selling a free person as a slave; and 2. The kidnapping a free person, with intent to sell him as a slave. The stealing a free negro, with intent to sell him as a slave, is a felony under the statute, whether the accused know him to be free or not, but if one be lawfully in possession of a free negro and should sell him as a slave, not knowing him to be free at the time of sale, it is not felony.(¹) Nor is the sale of a free negro as a slave, with his own consent, under a collusive agreement between himself and the seller to divide the proceeds of the sale between them, a felony under this statute.(²) But it would now be felony under the statute against false pretences.

(No. 1.)

Form of Warrant of Arrest for selling a free person as a slave.

———— County, to wit:
To all or any one of the Constables of said County:

Whereas, A. B. of said County, has this day made complaint and information on oath before me J. T., a Justice of the said County, that C. D., on the ——— day of ——— 18—, in said County, did feloniously sell one J. H. a free person, as a slave, he the said C. D. knowing at the time he so sold the said J. H. as a slave, that he the said J. H. was a free person: These are, therefore, to command you, in the name of the Commonwealth of Virginia, forthwith to apprehend the said C. D., and bring him before me or some other Justice of the said County, to answer the said complaint, and to be farther dealt with according to law. Given under my hand and seal, this ——— day of ——— 18—.

J. T., *J. P.* [L. S.]

(No. 2.)

Form of Warrant of Arrest for kidnapping a free person, to use or to sell him as a slave.

———— County, to wit:
To all or any one of the Constables of said County:

Whereas, A. B. of said County, has this day made complaint and information on oath before me J. T., a Justice of the said County, that C. D., on the ——— day of ——— 18—, in said County, did feloniously kidnap one J. H. a free person, with intent to use (or *to sell*) the said J. H. as a slave: These are, therefore, to command you, in the name of the Commonwealth of Virginia, forthwith to apprehend the said C. D., and bring him before me or some other Justice of the said County, to answer the said complaint, and to be farther dealt with according to law. Given under my hand and seal, this ——— day of ——— 18—.

J. T., *J. P.* [L. S.]

(¹) Davenport's Case, 5 Leigh 588.   (²) Mercer's Case, 2 Va. Cases 144.

(No. 3.)

Form of Mittimus where a party is committed for examination or trial in the County Court, for kidnapping.

———— County, to wit:

To X. Z., Constable of said County, and to the Keeper of the Jail of said County:

These are to command you, the said Constable, in the name of the Commonwealth of Virginia, forthwith to convey and deliver into the custody of the keeper of the said jail, together with this warrant, the body of C. D., a white person (or *free negro*, or *a slave, the property of E. F.*, as the case may be,) charged before me J. T., a Justice of the said County, on the oath of A. B., with a felony by him committed, in this, that the said C. D., on the —— day of ———— in the year 18—, in the said County, (here describe the offence as in the warrant of arrest.) And you, the said keeper of the said jail, are hereby required to receive the said C. D. into your jail and custody, that he may be examined (or *tried*) for the said offence, by the County Court of said County, and him there safely keep until he shall be discharged by due course of law. Given under my hand and seal, this —— day of ———— in the year 18—.

J. T., J. P. [L. S.]

[NOTE.—If the prisoner be a white person, he must be committed for examination; if a negro, commit him for trial.]

(No. 4.)

Form of Certificate of Commitment to be sent to the Clerk of the County Court.

———— County, to wit:

To the Clerk of the County Court of said County:

I, J. T., a Justice of said County, do hereby certify that I have, by my warrant, this day committed C. D. (if free negro or slave, state which,) to the jail of this County, that he may be examined (or *tried*) before the County Court of the said County, for a felony by him committed, in this, that he did, on the —— day of ———— 18—, in the said County, (here state the offence as in the mittimus.) Given under my hand, this —— day of ———— in the year 18—.

J. T., J. P.

(No. 5.)

Form of Certificate to the Clerk where party is admitted to bail.

Turn to head of ARREST, and follow No. 6.

(No. 6.)

Form of Recognizance of Bail.

Turn to head of RECOGNIZANCE, and follow No. 1, if person be free; No. 2, if a slave, and state succinctly the offence for which the person is recognized.

(No. 7.)

Form of Recognizance of Witness to appear before the County Court to give evidence upon the examination or trial of a party charged with kidnapping.

Turn to head of RECOGNIZANCE, and follow No. 3.

An Indictment for kidnapping a free person, with intent to use or to sell him as a slave, and for selling him as a slave.

—— Judicial Circuit, ⎱ The jurors of the Commonwealth of Virginia, in and for the body of the County of ——, and now attending in the Circuit Court of the said County, do upon their oath present, that A. B. of said County, on the —— day of —— in the year ——, (he the said A. B., then and there intending unlawfully to injure and oppress one J. H., a free person, and to deprive him of his liberty,) did, on the day and year aforesaid, in the County aforesaid, feloniously (*) kidnap the said J. H., he the said J. H. then and there being a free person, with intent then and there feloniously to sell the said J. H. as a slave, against the peace and dignity of the Commonwealth of Virginia.
—— County, to wit:
In the Circuit Court of the said County.

2d Count—laying the intent to use. Follow the above, but substitute the word "use" for "sell."

3d Count—for selling him as a slave. Proceed as above, to the (*) and say, "sell the said J. H., he the said J. H. then and there being a free person, and he the said A. B., then and there, to wit, on the day and year aforesaid, at the County aforesaid, and at the time he sold the said J. H. as a slave, well knowing that the said J. H. was a free person, against the peace and dignity of the Commonwealth of Virginia."

CHAPTER LXI.

LARCENY.

[For stealing records, see title RECORDS.]
[For petit larceny by slaves and free negroes, see FINES AND CONVICTIONS.]

No subject in the Criminal Code is more replete with legal subtleties than larceny, and a treatise upon it in all its branches, would tend rather to perplex than aid the Justice in the discharge of his duty, out of court, and besides, greatly exceed the prescribed limits of this work. Nothing more, therefore, will be found under this head than a definition of the crime, accompanied by such a general description of its leading characteristics, as will enable the Justice to understand upon what complaint a party charged with the offence may be arrested, and the mode of proceeding after the arrest.

Larceny is the fraudulent taking and carrying away by any person of the mere personal goods of another, from any place, with a felonious intent to convert them to his (the taker's) own use, and to make them his own property, without the consent of the owner.([1]) To constitute the offence, according to this definition, there must be a taking, either actual or constructive, of the goods from the possession of the owner;([2]) but the least removal of the thing, with intent to steal it, is sufficient; and although it is held that some removal is necessary, yet if every part of the thing is removed from the particular space that part occupied, though the whole thing is not removed from the whole space which the whole thing occupied, the taking will be sufficient.([3]) The goods must be taken with a felonious intent, existing at the time of the taking;([4]) that is, with the intent existing at the time fraudulently to convert them to his (the taker's) own use, and make them his property, without the consent of the owner. This intent is an essential ingredient in the crime of larceny, and its existence must be proven; but there is such a variety of circumstances tending to shew the intent with which any act is done, that it would be impossible, even if it were proper in such a work as this, to enumerate all that evince a felonious intent. The most ordinary evidence of such intent, is the clandestinely committing the act in the absence of the owner,

---

([1]) 2 East P. C. 553.
([2]) 2 Russ. 95.
([3]) 2 Russ. 95, 96; R. & M. C. C. 14.
([4]) Melbin's Case, Lewin's C. R. 225.

or by some trick, device or fraudulent expedient.(¹) These are, however, by no means, the only *criteria* of guilt, and upon this point our highest criminal court has said, that "the jury" (and so the Justice) "has a right to infer from all the facts and circumstances of the case, a felonious intent in the original taking; and that not in one case in a hundred could it be proved directly that the original taking was felonious."(²) Here much must be left to the sound discretion of the Justice, who will bear in mind that no larceny can be committed without the existence of this felonious intent at the time of the taking.

There may be, and doubtless, often is, a taking of the goods of one man by another, without any felonious intent; as where goods are taken in the presence of the owner, or of other persons; (unless, indeed, such taking shall amount to robbery, and then it is a different and higher offence;) this is evidence that the intent was not felonious.(³) So, also, where goods are taken under *a fair claim of right*, it negatives the presumption of criminal intent.(⁴) But, in such case, great care should be taken that the proof fully establishes that the claim of right was *fair and bona fide;* and not intended as a mere pretext to cover and conceal a felonious purpose. The taking may also be by mistake; in which case, of course, if the proof sustain it, there can be no guilty intent inferred.

Larceny may also be committed, where there is no actual trespass in the taking, but on the contrary, where the goods are actually delivered by the owner to the thief. Thus, where, with intent to steal a horse, a man applies to a livery stable keeper, or other person, to hire or borrow a horse to ride to a certain place, and when he gets possession of him goes to another place or to the same place and there sells him, or does not return him, but converts him to his own use, this is larceny, because, at the time he got possession of the horse, he intended to steal him.(⁵) And here it may be laid down as a well established principle, that where one man obtains possession of another's goods, with the intent at the time possession is had, to steal the goods, and the owner does not then part with his right of property in the goods, it is larceny, by whatever means the possession was actually gained; but if the owner parts with his right of property in the goods, as well as the possession, it is not larceny;(⁶) although the possession was acquired by fraud; it is a cheat only. (See title FALSE PRETENCES.) On the other hand, where the pos-

---

(¹) Roscoe Cr. Ev. 469.
(²) 4 Grat. 525, Booth's Case.
(³) 2 Russ. 97.
(⁴) 2 Russ. 98; Lewin's Rep. 245 and 195; and Spencer's Case, Id. 197.
(⁵) 2 Russ. 106-7.
(⁶) Roscoe Cr. Ev. 469; Stark's Case, 7 Leigh 753.

session of goods has been obtained *bona fide*, without any fraudulent intent in the first instance, although the party who thus acquired possession have the *animus furandi* (fraudulent intent,) afterwards, and then convert them to his own use, he cannot be guilty of felony.(¹) Under this principle it is held that if a common carrier take goods with a *bona fide* intent, at the time, to carry them from one place to another, and should afterwards, and before arriving at the place of destination, or even there, if, before he puts them out of his custody, conceive the fraudulent intent to convert them to his own use, and actually convert the whole package, that is not larceny: but if he *break* the package and convert a part or the whole of the goods, or if, after getting to their place of destination and landing them, he should take the whole with a fraudulent intent, it is larceny.(²) All cases coming under this rule, are breaches of trust only at Common Law, but are now felony, by statute. (See EMBEZZLEMENT.) There is a class of cases very nearly allied to breaches of trust, amounting to larceny, although the party had no intent to steal the goods at the time he acquired the *actual* possession, and although the actual possession was lawfully acquired, the *legal* possession being in the owner, and the *constructive* taking afterwards arising, when such party having the actual possession, fraudulently converts the goods to his own use. As where servants are entrusted with their masters' goods *by their masters*, no legal possession is transferred to the servants, as this is no contract of bailment, (as there is in the case of the common carrier,) but a bare charge, the possession of the servant being the possession of the master, whose presence and superintendence are always presumed in law, so as to prevent any right of possession being gained by the servant. The servant may therefore commit larceny, by a fraudulent conversion to his own use of goods so confided to him.(³) So, if a banker's clerk be sent to the money drawer for a special purpose, and at the same time, he take the opportunity of purloining money for his own use, he is as guilty of larceny, as if he had no allowed access to it whatever.(⁴) And where a shepherd has the care of his master's sheep and embezzles them, it is larceny, or where one who was a carter to the prosecutor, went away with and disposed of his master's cart, it was held to be larceny,(⁵) or in a more recent case, where the servant of a master cartman employed to cart

---

(¹) 2 East P. C. 693; Archb. Cr. Law 186; 2 Russ. 13, and 7 Leigh 758.
(²) Rex *v.* Brazier, R. & R. 337.
(³) R. *v.* Bass, 1 Leach 251, 523, 524; 2 East P. C. 566; 2 Deac. 750.
(⁴) 1 Hawk. c. 33, § 7; 2 East P. C. 683; 1 Leach 344.
(⁵) 2 East 566; see Moody C. C. 368.

goods, by collusion with others suffered the goods to be taken away, it was held larceny in the servant. And so in Walker's Case, 8 Leigh 743, where it was held larceny for a person employed by a mercantile firm as a salesman, and in that capacity had full control over the goods in the store room and the money in the till, for the purpose of his employment, to abstract a part of the goods and money with intent fraudulently to convert the same to his own use. These are cases of constructive taking. Another class of cases in which properly speaking, there is no actual taking amounting to a trespass, is where goods are lost, and found by a person who conceals the fact of finding and fraudulently converts them to his own use. Thus, if a party finding property know the owner of it, or if there be any mark upon it, (or, as we suppose, any other circumstance known to the finder,) by which the owner can be ascertained, and then instead of restoring it he converts it to his own use, such conversion will constitute a felonious taking; for it is the duty of every man who finds the property of another, to use all due diligence to discover the owner, and not to conceal it and appropriate it to his own use, for this is actually stealing.(¹) Upon this principle, it has been held that if a person drop a chattel, and another take it away, with the intention of appropriating it to his own use, and only restore it because a reward is offered for it, he is guilty of larceny; and that the only cases in which a party finding a chattel of another can be justified in appropriating it to his own use, is where the owner cannot be found, or where it may be fairly said, that the owner has abandoned it.(²)

There is such a community of interest between husband and wife, that ordinarily the wife cannot be guilty of stealing the goods of her husband, nor can an indifferent person steal the goods of the husband, where they are delivered to him by the wife, and if the wife deliver the goods of the husband to an indifferent person, and that person convert them to his own use, it is no larceny: but if the person to whom the goods are delivered by the wife, be an adulterer, it is otherwise, and if he convert the goods so delivered, to his own use, it is larceny; for an adulterer can be properly convicted of stealing the husband's goods, though they be delivered to him by the wife. And although no adultery has been actually committed by the parties, but the goods of the husband are removed from the house by the wife and the intended adulterer, with the intent that the wife should elope with him and live in adultery with him, this taking of the goods is in point of law, a larceny, and in such a case, it is as much a larceny to steal

---

(¹) 2 Russ. 102; 2 East P. C. 664. (²) R. v. Peters, 47 C. L. R. 245; and see Mole's Case, Id. 417.

her clothes, as it would be to steal any thing else that was the husband's property. But if the goods were taken merely to get the wife away from her husband, as a friend only, and without any reference to any such connection between the party and the wife, either actual or pretended, it will not be larceny.(¹)

Larceny at Common Law, cannot be committed of any thing which is part of the freehold, *at the time it is taken*, or of any thing which savours of the realty.(²) But by statute, section 17, chapter 192, things which savour of the realty, and are at the time they are taken part of the freehold, whether they be of the substance or produce thereof, or affixed thereto, shall be deemed goods and chattels, of which larceny may be committed, although there be no interval between the severing and taking away.

Without the aid of the statute, if the thing severed is suffered to remain for any time, and is feloniously taken away at another, however short, so that the act of severing and taking away be not a continuous act, it is larceny.(³) Nor are wild fowl or wild animals unreclaimed, subjects of larceny at Common Law. Yet if they are reclaimed from their wild state, and known to be so, as deer in a park, hares, partridges or pheasants in a mew or trap, fish in a tank or net, swans or other wild fowl in a private pond, creek or river; or if any of these be dead, and in the possession of another, then the taking of them, with a felonious intent, is larceny.(⁴)

So it is not larceny, at Common Law, to steal records, deeds, and *choses in action*, that is, bonds, notes, &c. for the payment of money; but by the statute, section 15, chapter 192, if any free person steal any *bank note*, check or other writing, or paper of value, or any book of accounts, for or concerning money or goods due or to be delivered, he shall be deemed guilty of larceny thereof, and receive the same punishment, according to the value of the thing stolen, that is prescribed for the punishment of larceny of goods or chattels. And the 16th section declares, that in a prosecution under the 15th, the money due on or secured by the writing, paper or book, and remaining unsatisfied, or which in any event might be collected thereon, or the value of the property or money affected thereby, shall be deemed to be the value of the article stolen.

Slaves never were subjects of larceny at Common Law.(⁵)

(¹) Regina v. Tollett & Taylor, 1 Carr. & Marsh. 112.
(²) 1 Hale 501; 2 East 587.
(³) 2 Russ. 137; 2 East P. C. 587; 1 Hale 510; 7 Taunt. 191.
(⁴) 1 Deac. Cr. Co. 763; 3 Inst. 109; Russ. 151.
(⁵) Hayes' Case, 1 Va. Cases 122.

By Sec. 18, Chap. 192. If a free person steal a slave, he shall be confined in the penitentiary not less than two, nor more than ten years.

For stealing free negroes, see title KIDNAPPING.

Simple larceny, at Common Law, was divided into grand and petit larceny; the former, signifying a stealing of goods above the value of one shilling; the latter, the stealing of goods under that value.

By Sec. 14, Chap. 192. If a free person commit simple larceny of goods or chattels, he shall, if they be of the value of twenty dollars or more, be deemed guilty of grand larceny, and be confined in the penitentiary not less than one nor more than five years; and if they be of less value, be deemed guilty of petit larceny, and be confined in jail not exceeding one year, and at the discretion of the court may be punished with stripes.

The thing stolen may be charged as the property of any one having either the general or special right of property in it. This is so as well at Common Law, as under the statute. (See head INDICTMENTS.)

Larceny is often committed under aggravated circumstances, as by breaking into houses or shops, and stealing therefrom. It is then technically called compound larceny, as distinguished from the mere simple act of stealing. (See under the heads of HOUSE BREAKING and SHIPS.)

If goods are stolen in one county and carried by the thief into another county, though long after the theft, it will be larceny also in the latter.[1]

Prosecutions for petit larceny, which is now a misdemeanor by statute, must be commenced within five years after the commission of the offence.

The forms of proceeding against slaves and free negroes, charged with petit larceny, will be found under the head of FINES AND SUMMARY CONVICTIONS. If the party be a white person, the proceedings are the same as in any other misdemeanor. For mittimus and certificate to the clerk, see Nos. 9 and 10, under head of ARREST, and for recognizance of bail and of witnesses, Nos. 4 and 5, under head of RECOGNIZANCE.

---

[1] Rex v. Parkin, Ry. & M. 45.

LARCENY.

(No. 1.)

Form of Warrant of Arrest for stealing goods.

———— County, to wit:

To all or any one of the Constables of said County:

Whereas, A. B. of said County, has this day made complaint and information on oath before me J. T., a Justice of the said County, that C. D., on the ———— day of ———— 18—, in said County, ten bushels of wheat, of the value of ———— dollars, and one hundred pounds of tobacco, of the value of twenty dollars, of the goods and chattels of E. F., feloniously did steal, take and carry away: These are, therefore, to command you, in the name of the Commonwealth of Virginia, forthwith to apprehend the said C. D., and bring him before me or some other Justice of the said County, to answer the said complaint, and to be farther dealt with according to law. Given under my hand and seal, this ———— day of ———— 18—.

J. T., J. P. [L. S.]

(No. 2.)

Form of Warrant of Arrest for stealing two or more articles belonging to different persons, at the same time.

———— County, to wit:

To all or any one of the Constables of said County:

Whereas, A. B. of said County, has this day made complaint and information on oath before me J. T., a Justice of the said County, that C. D., on the ———— day of ———— 18—, in said County, one coat, of the value of ———— dollars, of the goods and chattels of E. F., and one pair of boots, of the value of ———— dollars, of the goods and chattels of G. H., feloniously did steal, take and carry away: These are, therefore, to command you, in the name of the Commonweath of Virginia, forthwith to apprehend the said C. D., and bring him before me or some other Justice of the said County, to answer the said complaint, and to be farther dealt with according to law. Given under my hand and seal, this ———— day of ———— 18—.

J. T., J. P. [L. S.]

(No. 3.)

Form of Warrant of Arrest for stealing a bank note.

———— County, to wit:

To all or any one of the Constables of said County:

Whereas, A. B. of said County, has this day made complaint and information on oath before me J. T., a Justice of the said County, that C. D., on the ———— day of ———— 18—, in said County, one bank note for the payment of ———— dollars, and of the value of ———— dollars, then being the bank note and property of E. F., feloniously did steal, take and carry away: These are, therefore, to command you, in the name of the Commonwealth of Virginia, forthwith to apprehend the said C. D., and bring him before me or some other Justice of the said County, to answer the said complaint, and to be farther dealt with according to law. Given under my hand and seal, this —— day of ——— 18—.

               J. T., J. P. [L. s.]

(No. 4.)

Form of Warrant of Arrest for stealing two or more bank notes.

——— County, to wit:
 To all or any one of the Constables of said County:
 Whereas, A. B. of said County, has this day made complaint and information on oath before me J. T., a Justice of the said County, that C. D., on the —— day of ——— 18—, in said County, divers, to wit, (here state the number of notes stolen, according to the evidence,) bank notes, for the payment of divers sums of money, in the whole amounting to the sum of ——— (insert the whole value of all the notes,) dollars, and of the value of ——— dollars, then being the bank notes and property of the said A. B., feloniously did steal, take and carry away : These are, therefore, to command you, in the name of the Commonwealth of Virginia, forthwith to apprehend the said C. D., and bring him before me or some other Justice of the said County, to answer the said complaint, and to be farther dealt with according to law. Given under my hand and seal, this —— day of ——— 18—.

               J. T., J. P. [L. s.]

[NOTE.—This general description of a bank note or bank notes, as given in the preceding forms, is held sufficient, even upon an indictment, both in this Commonwealth and in England. (See Mosby's Case, 2 Virginia Cases 396; Boyd's Case, 1 Rob. 691 ; and 3 Ch. Cr. L. 973-74, in note ; and see also Richards' Case, 1 Mass. 337.]

(No. 5.)

Form of Warrant of Arrest for stealing coin.

——— County, to wit:
 To all or any one of the Constables of said County:
 Whereas, A. B. of said County, has this day made complaint and information on oath before me J. T., a Justice of the said County, that C. D., on the —— day of ——— 18—, in said County, ten (or whatever is the number) pieces of gold coin, current in this Commonwealth, called " Eagles," of the value of ten dollars each, of the moneys and coin of E. F., then and there being found, feloniously did steal, take and carry away : These are, therefore, to command you, in the name of the Commonwealth of Virginia, forthwith to apprehend the said C. D., and bring him before me or some other Justice of the said County, to answer the said complaint, and to be farther dealt with according to law. Given under my hand and seal, this —— day of ——— 18—.

               J. T., J. P. [L. s.]

(No. 6.)

Form of Warrant of Arrest for stealing a bill of exchange.

—— County, to wit:

To all or any one of the Constables of said County:

Whereas, A. B. of said County, has this day made complaint and information on oath before me J. T., a Justice of the said County, that C. D., on the —— day of —— 18—, in said County, one bill of exchange, for the payment of —— dollars, and of the value of —— dollars, the said bill of exchange, at the time of committing the felony aforesaid, being the property of C. D., and the said sum of —— dollars, payable and secured by and upon the said bill of exchange, being due and unsatisfied to the said C. D., the proprietor thereof, feloniously did steal, take and carry away: These are, therefore, to command you, in the name of the Commonwealth of Virginia, forthwith to apprehend the said C. D., and bring him before me or some other Justice of the said County, to answer the said complaint, and to be farther dealt with according to law. Given under my hand and seal, this —— day of —— 18—.

J. T., J. P. [L. S.]

(No. 7.)

Form of Warrant of Arrest for stealing a promissory note, single bill or bond.

Follow No. 6, in all respects, except leaving out the words "bill of exchange," and inserting in the place of them, the words "promissory note, single bill or bond," according to the fact.

(No. 8.)

Form of Warrant of Arrest for horse stealing.

—— County, to wit:

To all or any one of the Constables of said County:

Whereas, A. B. of said County, has this day made complaint and information on oath before me J. T., a Justice of the said County, that C. D., on the —— day of —— 18—, in said County, one gelding, of the price of —— dollars, of the goods and chattels of the said A. B., feloniously did steal, take and carry away: These are, therefore, to command you, in the name of the Commonwealth of Virginia, forthwith to apprehend the said C. D., and bring him before me or some other Justice of the said County, to answer the said complaint, and to be farther dealt with according to law. Given under my hand and seal, this —— day of —— 18—.

J. T., J. P. [L. S.]

LARCENY.

(No. 9.)

Form of Warrant of Arrest for stealing a slave.

—— County, to wit:
  To all or any one of the Constables of said County:

Whereas, A. B. of said County, has this day made complaint and information on oath before me J. T., a Justice of the said County, that C. D., on the —— day of ——— 18—, in said County, one negro slave, called ———, of the value of ——— dollars, the slave and property of A. B., feloniously did steal, take and carry away: These are, therefore, to command you, in the name of the Commonwealth of Virginia, forthwith to apprehend the said C. D., and bring him before me or some other Justice of the said County, to answer the said complaint, and to be farther dealt with according to law. Given under my hand and seal, this —— day of ——— 18—.

J. T., J. P. [L. S.]

(No. 10.)

Form of Warrant of Arrest for stealing things annexed to the freehold.

—— County, to wit:
  To all or any one of the Constables of said County:

Whereas, A. B. of said County, has this day made complaint and information on oath before me J. T., a Justice of the said County, that C. D., on the —— day of ——— 18—, in said County, did feloniously sever from the dwelling house of him the said A. B., a large quantity of lead, the property of the said A. B., of the value of ——— dollars, and then and there did feloniously take, steal and carry away the said lead: These are, therefore, to command you, in the name of the Commonwealth of Virginia, forthwith to apprehend the said C. D., and bring him before me or some other Justice of the said County, to answer the said complaint, and to be farther dealt with according to law. Given under my hand and seal, this —— day of ——— 18—.

J. T., J. P. [L. S.]

(No. 11.)

Form of Mittimus where a party is committed for examination or trial in the County Court for grand larceny.

—— County, to wit:
  To X. Z., Constable of said County, and to the Keeper of the Jail of said County:

These are to command you the said Constable, in the name of the Commonwealth of Virginia, forthwith to convey and deliver into the custody of the keeper of the said jail, together with this warrant, the body of C. D., a white person (or *free negro,* or *a slave, the property of E. F.,* as the case may be,) charged before me J. T., a Justice of the said County, on the oath of A. B., with a felony by him committed, in this, that the said C. D., on the —— day of ——— in the year 18—, in the said County, (here describe the offence as in the warrant of arrest.) And you, the said keeper of the said jail, are hereby required to receive the said C. D. into your jail and custody, that he may be examined (or *tried*) for the said offence by the County Court of said County, and him there safely keep until he shall be discharged by due course of law. Given under my hand and seal, this ―― day of ―――― in the year 18―.

J. T., J. P. [L. S.]

[NOTE.—If the prisoner be a white person, commit him for examination; if a negro, commit him for trial.]

(No. 12.)

Form of Certificate of Commitment to be sent to the Clerk of the County Court for larceny.

―――― County, to wit :

To the Clerk of the County Court of said County :

I, J. T., a Justice of the said County, do hereby certify, that I have, by my warrant, this day committed C. D. (if free negro or slave, state which,) to the jail of this County, that he may be examined (or *tried*) before the County Court of the said County for a felony by him committed, in this, that he did, on the ―― day of ―――― 18―, in the said County, (here state the offence as in the mittimus.) Given under my hand, this ―― day of ―――― in the year 18―.

J. T., J. P.

(No. 13.)

Form of Certificate to the Clerk where party is admitted to bail, for larceny.

Turn to head of ARREST, and follow No. 6.

(No. 14.)

Form of Recognizance of Bail.

Turn to head of RECOGNIZANCE, and follow No. 1, if person be free ; No. 2, if a slave, and state succinctly the offence for which the person is recognized.

(No. 15.)

Form of Recognizance of Witness to appear before the County Court to give evidence upon the examination or trial of a party charged with felony.

Turn to head of RECOGNIZANCE, and follow No. 3.

LARCENY—(*Indictments for.*)

(No. 1.)

An Indictment for stealing goods.

———— Judicial Circuit, \} The jurors of the Commonwealth of Virginia, in and for the body of the County of ————, and now attending the said Court, upon their oath present, that A. B., on the ———— day of ———— in the year one thousand eight hundred and ————, in the said County, ten bushels of wheat of the value of ———— dollars, and one hundred pounds of tobacco, of the value of ———— dollars, of the goods and chattels of one E. F., then and there being found, feloniously did steal, take and carry away, against the peace and dignity of the Commonwealth of Virginia.

(No. 2.)

An Indictment for stealing two or more articles belonging to different persons.

———— Judicial Circuit, \} The jurors of the Commonwealth of Virginia, in and for the body of the County of ————, and now attending the said Court, upon their oath present, that A. B., on the ———— day of ———— in the year one thousand eight hundred and ————, in the said County, one coat, of the value of ———— dollars, of the goods and chattels of E. F., and one pair of boots, of the value of ———— dollars, of the goods and chattels of G. H., then and there being found, feloniously did steal, take and carry away, against the peace and dignity of the Commonwealth of Virginia.

(No. 3.)

An Indictment for stealing a bank note.

———— Judicial Circuit, \} The jurors of the Commonwealth of Virginia, in and for the body of the County of ————, and now attending the said Court, upon their oath present, that A. B., on the ———— day of ———— in the year one thousand eight hundred and ————, in the said County, one bank note, for the payment of ———— dollars, and of the value of ———— dollars, the bank note and property of E. F., then and there being found, the said sum of ———— dollars, secured and payable by and upon the said bank note, being then and there due and unsatisfied to the said E. F., feloniously did steal, take and carry away, against the peace and dignity of the Commonwealth of Virginia.

LARCENY—(*Indictments for.*)

(No. 4.)

An Indictment for stealing two or more bank notes.

———— Judicial Circuit, ———— County, to wit: In the Circuit Court for the said County. } The jurors of the Commonwealth of Virginia, in and for the body of the County of ————, and now attending the said Court, upon their oath present, that A. B., on the ———— day of ————, in the year one thousand eight hundred and ————, in the said County, divers, to wit, (here insert the number of notes stolen, according to the evidence,) bank notes, for the payment of divers sums of money, in the whole amounting to the sum of ———— (insert the whole value of all the notes,) dollars, and of the value of ———— dollars, the property and bank notes of E. F., then and there being found, the said sum of ———— dollars, secured and payable by and upon the said bank notes, being then and there due and unsatisfied to the said E. F., feloniously did steal, take and carry away, against the peace and dignity of the Commonwealth of Virginia.

[NOTE.—See Mosby's Case, 2 Virginia Cases; and 3 Chit. Crim. Law 973-74, in note.]

————

(No. 5.)

An Indictment for stealing coin.

———— Judicial Circuit, ———— County, to wit: In the Circuit Court for the said County. } The jurors of the Commonwealth of Virginia, in and for the body of the County of ————, and now attending the said Court, upon their oath present, that A. B., on the ———— day of ————, in the year one thousand eight hundred and ————, in the said County, ten (or whatever the number) pieces of gold coin, current in this Commonwealth, called "Eagles," of the value of ten dollars each, of the moneys, property and coin of one E. F., then and there being found, feloniously did steal, take and carry away, against the peace and dignity of the Commonwealth of Virginia.

————

(No. 6.)

An Indictment for stealing a promissory note, single bill or bond.

———— Judicial Circuit, ———— County, to wit: In the Circuit Court for the said County. } The jurors of the Commonwealth of Virginia, in and for the body of the County of ————, and now attending the said Court, upon their oath present, that A. B., on the ———— day of ———— in the year one thousand eight hundred and ————, in the said County, one promissory note, (or *single bill,* or *bond,* according to the fact,) for the payment of ———— dollars, and of the value of ———— dollars, signed by one G. H., the maker thereof, the said promissory note, at the time of committing the felony aforesaid, being the property of C. D., and the said sum of ———— dollars, payable and secured by and upon the said promissory note, being due and unsatisfied to the said C. D., the proprietor thereof, feloniously did steal, take and carry away, against the peace and dignity of the Commonwealth of Virginia.

(No. 7.)

An Indictment for stealing a slave.

——— Judicial Circuit, \
——— *County, to wit:* \
In the Circuit Court for the \
said County.

The jurors of the Commonwealth of Virginia, in and for the body of the County of ———, and now attending the said Court, upon their oath present, that A. B., on the ——— day of ——— in the year one thousand eight hundred and ———, in the said County, one negro slave, called ———, of the value of ——— dollars, the slave and property of C. D., then and there being found, feloniously did steal, take and carry away, against the peace and dignity of the Commonwealth of Virginia.

———

(No. 8.)

An Indictment for stealing things annexed to the freehold.

——— Judicial Circuit, \
——— *County, to wit:* \
In the Circuit Court for the \
said County.

The jurors of the Commonwealth of Virginia, in and for the body of the County of ———, and now attending the said Court, upon their oath present, that A. B., on the ——— day of ——— in the year one thousand eight hundred and ———, in the said County, did feloniously sever from the dwelling house of one C. D., a large quantity of lead, the property of the said C. D., of the value of ——— dollars, and then and there did feloniously take, steal and carry away the said lead, so severed as aforesaid, against the peace and dignity of the Commonwealth of Virginia.

———

CHAPTER LXII.

LEVIES (*County*) AND TAXES.

BY SEC. 4, CHAP. 36. If the taxes with which any person or any estate of a decedent is assessed, be not paid before the first day of September, the Sheriff or Collector may distrain.

BY SEC. 5. On affidavit before a Justice, by the Sheriff or Collector, that he has good cause to suspect, and verily believes, that a person assessed with taxes, intends to remove his property out of the county or corporation, and that, in his opinion, it is probable such taxes will be lost, unless he be authorized to distrain therefor, before the first of September, it shall be lawful for the Justice to give such authority.

BY SEC. 6. No distress shall be made for taxes where the Sheriff or Collector has had more than two years to collect the same.

LEVIES (*County*) AND TAXES.

By Sec. 7. Any goods or chattels in the county or corporation, belonging to the person or estate assessed with taxes, may be distrained therefor.

By Sec. 8. The goods and chattels of the tenant or other person in possession, claiming under the party or estate assessed with taxes on land, may be distrained, if found on the premises. But when taxes are assessed wholly to one person on a tract or lot, part of which has become the freehold of another, by a title recorded before the commencement of the year for which such taxes are assessed, the property belonging to the owner of that part, shall not be distrained for more than a due proportion of the said taxes.

By Sec. 9. Where taxes are assessed on a tract of land lying partly in one county and partly in another, the Sheriff of the county in which the taxes are so assessed, may distrain on that part of the land lying in the other county, in the same manner as if such part was in his own county.

By Sec. 10. No deed of trust or mortgage upon goods or chattels shall prevent the same from being distrained and sold for taxes assessed against the grantor in such deed, while such goods and chattels remain in the grantor's possession, nor shall any such deed prevent the goods and chattels conveyed, from being distrained and sold for taxes assessed thereon, no matter in whose possession they may be found.

By Sec. 11. Where the officer cannot find sufficient goods or chattels to distrain for taxes, any person indebted to, or having in his hands estate of, the party assessed with such taxes, may be applied to for payment thereof, out of such debt or estate, and a payment by such person of the said taxes, either in whole or in part, shall entitle him to charge or credit for so much on account of such debt or estate against the party so assessed. If the person applied to, do not pay so much as it may seem to the officer ought to be recovered on account of the debt or estate in his hands, the officer shall, if the sum due for such taxes exceed not twenty dollars, procure from a Justice a summons, directing such person to appear before some Justice at such time and place as may seem reasonable. And if the sum due exceed twenty dollars, shall procure from the Clerk of the court of the county or corporation, a summons, directing such person to appear before the court of the county or corporation on the first day of the next term thereof. And from the time of the service of any such summons, the said taxes shall constitute a lien on the debt so due from such person, or on the said estate in his hands.

By Sec. 12. If such summons be returned executed, and the person so summoned do not appear, judgment shall be entered against him for the sum due for such taxes, and for the fees of the Clerk and of the officer who may execute the summons.

BY SEC. 8, CHAP. 53. Of the 36th chapter, the fourth, fifth, sixth, seventh, eighth, ninth, tenth, eleventh, twelfth, thirteenth, fourteenth, fifteenth and twentieth sections, shall be applicable to county levies as well as State taxes, in like manner as if enacted with the insertion after the word "taxes," wherever it occurs therein, of the words "or county levies," and with the insertion after the words "the tax," in the fourteenth and fifteenth sections, of the words "or levy."

(No. 1.)

Form of Authority from a Justice to distrain for taxes or County levy.

—————— County, to wit:

Whereas, A. B., Deputy for C. D. Sheriff of said County, has this day made oath before me J. T., a Justice of the said County, that E. F. is assessed with —————— dollars taxes, (or *County levies*,) and that the said A. B. has good cause to suspect, and verily believes, that the said E. F. intends to remove his property out of the said County, and that, in his opinion, it is probable that the said taxes, (or *County levies*,) will be lost to the Commonwealth, (or *County*,) unless he be authorized to distrain therefor, before the first day of September next: These are, therefore, in the name of the Commonwealth, to authorize the said A. B., Deputy aforesaid, forthwith to distrain for the said taxes, (or *County levies*.) Given under my hand, this —————— day of —————— 18——.

J. T., J. P.

(No. 2.)

Form of Summons against a garnishee, to collect taxes or County levies due from persons having no visible effects.

—————— County, to wit:

To *A. B., Deputy for C. D., Sheriff of said County:*

Whereas, upon your application and complaint, this day made to me J. T., a Justice of the said County, it appears to me, that E. F. is assessed in the said County, with —————— dollars, public taxes, (or *County levies*,) and that you cannot find sufficient goods or chattels of the said E. F. to distrain for the taxes, (or *County levies*,) and that G. H. is indebted to the said E. F., (or *has in his hands, estate of the said E. F.*,) and has, upon your application for payment of the said taxes, (or *County levies*,) refused to pay the same: These are, therefore, to require you, in the name of the Commonwealth, to summon the said G. H. to appear before me at ——————, in the said County, at —————— o'clock, A. M., on the —————— day of —————— 18——, to answer the said application and complaint. Given under my hand, this —————— day of —————— 18——.

J. T., J. P.

(No. 3.)

Form of Judgment on the foregoing summons.

If the party do not appear, the judgment may be entered on the back of the summons, in this form: —— day of —————— 18—, at ————. The within named G. H., being this day called to answer the within summons, and he not appearing, judgment is granted against him, for the sum of $ ————, to be applied to the payment of the taxes of E. F., and for $ ———— costs.

J. T., J. P.

If the party appear and make defence, judgment may be rendered in this form: —— day of —————— 18—, at ————. The within named G. H. this day appeared to answer the within summons, and having fully heard the matter of his defence, judgment is given against him for the sum of $ ————, to be applied to the payment of the taxes of E. F., and for $ ———— costs.

J. T. J. P.

Or, this more formal judgment may be adopted.

———— County, to wit: Upon an attachment on the summons of A. B., Deputy Sheriff of the said County, v. G. H., to recover of him the sum of ———— dollars, for taxes, (or *County levies*,) with which he is assessed.

—— day of ————18—, at ————. It appearing to me J. T., a Justice of the said County, that E. F. has been duly assessed with ———— dollars, for taxes, (or *County levies*,) for the said County, and that he has no visible estate from which they can be made; and it appearing also to me, that G. H. has been duly summoned by the said A. B., as Deputy Sheriff of the said County, to appear before me this day, to answer and say whether he was not, on the —— day of ———— 18—, (the day the summons was executed,) indebted to the said E. F., and that before he was summoned, payment of the said taxes, (or *County levies*,) was demanded by him, the said A. B., and that payment thereof was refused by him, the said G. H.; and ☞ it further appearing to me, on examination of witnesses, (or *the confession on oath of the said G. H.*,) that he the said G. H. was indebted to the said E. F. at the time of executing the said summons, in the sum of ———— dollars, ⌒ judgment is hereby granted against him the said G. H., for the sum of ———— dollars, to be applied, when made, to the payment of the taxes (or *County levies*) so assessed upon the said E. F., and also for the farther sum of ———— dollars, the costs. Given under my hand and seal, this —— day of ———— 18—.

J. T., J. P. [L. S.]

[NOTE.—If the garnishee fail to appear and answer the summons, the foregoing form should be varied, by leaving out all between the hands, and inserting in lieu of it, this: "the said G. H. having failed to appear to answer the said summons at the time and place therein mentioned."]

(No. 4.)

Form of an Execution upon the foregoing judgment.

—— County, to wit:
To the Sheriff of the said County:
I, J. T., a Justice of the said County, do hereby command you, that of the goods and chattels of G. H. in your County, you do make the sum of —— dollars, and the same, when made, you do apply to the payment of the taxes, (or *County levies,*) with which E. F. stands assessed, and to whom the said G. H. is indebted ; and that you also make of the goods and chattels of the said G. H., the sum of —— dollars costs. Given under my hand and seal, this —— day of —— 18—.

J. T., J. P. [L. S.]

CHAPTER LXIII.

LEWDNESS, LASCIVIOUS COHABITATION, AND HOUSES OF ILL FAME.

Open and gross lewdness, and houses of ill fame, resorted to for the purposes of prostitution or lewdness, are indictable nuisances at Common Law.(¹) As these offences, together with lewd and lascivious cohabitation, are of a kindred nature, and now punishable by statute, they are noticed here together. Upon these subjects, the statute directs:

By Sec. 7, Chap. 196. If any white persons, not married to each other, lewdly and lasciviously associate and cohabit together, or whether married or not, be guilty of open and gross lewdness and lasciviousness, they shall be fined not less than fifty dollars.

By Sec. 10. If a free person keep a house of ill fame, resorted to for the purpose of prostitution or lewdness, he shall be confined in jail not more than one year and fined not exceeding two hundred dollars.

The Justice will mark the difference between lewdly and lasciviously associating and cohabiting together, and open and gross lewdness. Though a party, by one criminal act, may be guilty of fornication or adultery, or if done openly, of open and gross lewdness, yet to convict for lewdly and lasciviously associating together, there must be a dwelling and living together, and a single unlawful interview will not constitute the offence.(²)

(¹) 1 Hawk. c. 5, § 4, and c. 74.　　(²) 10 Mass. Rep. 153.

Whether the facts proved constitute the offence of open and gross lewdness, must be judged of by the Justice, and if he has any doubt on the subject, he should put the party to answer before a jury.

In prosecutions for keeping a house of ill fame, it is not necessary to prove who frequents the house. If any unknown persons are proved to be there behaving in a disorderly manner, it is sufficient to support the charge; and evidence of particular illicit intercourse at the place may be given for that purpose. A wife, as well as a husband, may be indicted for keeping a house of ill fame.([1])

If the party be not discharged when brought before the Justice for examination, he should be recognized or committed to answer an indictment.

(No. 1.)

Form of Warrant of Arrest for open and gross lewdness.

—— County, to wit:

To all or any one of the Constables of said County:

Whereas, A. B. of said County, has this day made complaint and information on oath before me J. T., a Justice of the said County, that C. D., on the —— day of —— 18—, in said County, was guilty of open and gross lewdness and lascivious behaviour with one E. F., by (here state the act of lewdness:) These are, therefore, to command you, in the name of the Commonwealth of Virginia, forthwith to apprehend the said C. D., and bring him before me or some other Justice of the said County, to answer the said complaint, and to be farther dealt with according to law. Given under my hand and seal, this —— day of —— 18—.

J. T., J. P. [L. S.]

(No. 2.)

Form of Warrant of Arrest for keeping a house of ill fame.

—— County, to wit:

To all or any one of the Constables of said County:

Whereas, A. B. of said County, has this day made complaint and information on oath before me J. T., a Justice of the said County, that C. D., on the —— day of —— 18—, and on divers other days and times thereafter, at the said County, unlawfully did keep and maintain, and does now keep and maintain, a certain house of ill fame, resorted to during all that time, and now resorted to, by divers idle and dissolute persons, both men and women, for the purpose of prostitution and lewdness: These are, therefore, to command you, in the name of the Commonwealth of Virginia, forthwith to apprehend the said C. D., and bring him before me or some other Justice of the said County, to answer the said complaint, and to be farther dealt with according to law. Given under my hand and seal, this —— day of —— 18—.

J. T., J. P. [L. S.]

([1]) 1 Salk. 384.

LEWDNESS, LASCIVIOUS COHABITATION, &C. 407

(No. 3.)

Form of Warrant of Arrest for lascivious cohabitation.

—— County, to wit:
To X. Y., *Constable of the said County:*

Whereas, A. B. of said County, has this day made complaint and information on oath before me J. T., a Justice of the said County, that John Doe and Elizabeth Roe, on the —— day of —————— 18—, and from that day to the —— day of —————— 18—, in the said County, the said John Doe and Elizabeth Roe being white persons, and not at any time being married to each other, did, during all that time, lewdly and lasciviously associate and cohabit together: These are, therefore, to require you forthwith to apprehend the said John Doe and Elizabeth Roe, and bring their bodies before me or some other Justice of the said County, to be farther dealt with according to law. Given under my hand and seal, this —— day of —————— 18—.

J. T., J. P. [L. S.]

(No. 4.)

Form of Mittimus where a party is committed to answer an Indictment in the County Court for a misdemeanor.

—— County, to wit:
To X. Y., *Constable of said County, and to the Keeper of the Jail of said County:*

These are to command you, the said Constable, in the name of the Commonwealth of Virginia, forthwith to convey and deliver into the custody of the keeper of the said jail, together with this warrant, the body of C. D., charged before me J. T., a Justice of the said County, on the oath of A. B., with a misdemeanor by him committed, in this, that the said C. D., on the —— day of —————— in the year 18—, in the said County, (here describe the offence as in the warrant of arrest.) And you, the said keeper of the said jail, are hereby required to receive the said C. D. into your jail and custody, to answer an indictment to be preferred against him for the said offence, in the County Court of said County, and him there safely keep until he shall be discharged by due course of law. Given under my hand and seal, this —— day of —————— in the year 18—.

J. T., J. P. [L. S.]

(No. 5.)

Form of Recognizance of Bail.

Turn to head of RECOGNIZANCE, and follow No. 4, and state the offence succinctly, for which the party is recognized.

LEWDNESS, &c.—(*Indictment for.*)

(No. 6.)

Form of Certificate of the Commitment, or Letting to Bail, to be sent to the Clerk of the County Court.

——— County, to wit:
  To the Clerk of the County Court of the said County:
  I, J. T., a Justice of the said County, do hereby certify, that C. D. was this day committed to the jail of this County, by my warrant, (or *was this day admitted to bail by me,* as the case may be,) to answer an indictment to be preferred against him in the County Court of the said County, for a misdemeanor by him committed, in this, that he did, on the ——— day of ——— 18—, in said County, (here describe the offence as in the warrant of arrest.) Given under my hand, this ——— day of ——— 18—.
  J. T., J. P.

(No. 7.)

Form of Recognizance of Witness to appear and give evidence to the Grand Jury upon the indictment.

Follow No. 5, under head of RECOGNIZANCE.

Indictment for lewd and lascivious cohabitation.

  Commence as No. 2, under head of "INDICTMENTS," and say: "that A. B., on the ——— day of ———, and from that day to the ——— day of ——— in the year ———, in the County aforesaid, did lewdly and lasciviously associate and cohabit with one C. D., the said A. B. and C. D. being white persons, and not married to each other, during all the time aforesaid, against the peace and dignity of the Commonwealthealth of Virginia."

CHAPTER LXIV.

LIMITATIONS.

I. *In criminal cases.*

By Sec. 11, Chap. 199. A prosecution for committing or procuring another person to commit perjury, shall be commenced within three years next after the perjury was committed. And a prosecution for a misdemeanor or any pecuniary fine, forfeiture, penalty or amercement, shall be commenced within one year next after there was cause therefor, except that a prosecution for petit larceny may be commenced within five years after the commission of the offence; and except also, that this section shall not extend to a prosecution against a master or skipper of a vessel for carrying a slave out of the State.

II. *In civil suits.*

By Sec. 5, Chap. 149. Every action to recover money, which is founded upon an award, or on any contract, other than a judgment or recognizance, shall be brought within the following number of years next after the right to bring the same shall have first accrued, that is to say: If the case be upon an indemnifying bond taken under any statute, or upon a bond of an executor, administrator, guardian, curator, committee, Sheriff or Sergeant, Deputy Sheriff or Sergeant, Clerk or Deputy Clerk, or any other fiduciary or public officer, within ten years; if it be upon any other contract by writing under seal, within twenty years; if it be upon an award, or be upon a contract by writing, signed by the party to be charged thereby, or by his agent, but not under seal, within five years; and if it be upon any other contract, within five years, unless it be an action for any articles charged in any store account, in which case the action may be brought within two years, or an action by one partner against his co-partner, for a settlement of the partnership accounts, or upon accounts concerning the trade of merchandize between merchant and merchant, their factors or servants, where the action of account would lie, in either of which cases the action may be brought until the expiration of five years from a cessation of the dealings in which they are interested together, but not after.

By SEC. 6. The right of action upon the bond of an executor, administrator, guardian, curator or committee, or of a Sheriff or Sergeant acting as such, shall be deemed to have first accrued as follows: Upon a bond of a guardian or curator of a ward, from the time of the ward's attaining the age of twenty-one years, or from the termination of the guardian's or curator's office, whichever shall happen first; and upon the bond of any personal representative of a decedent, or committee of an insane person, the right of action of a person obtaining execution against such representative or committee, or to whom payment or delivery of estate in the hands of such representative or committee, shall be ordered by a court acting upon his account, shall be deemed to have first accrued from the return day of such execution, or from the time of the right to require payment or delivery upon such order, whichever shall happen first. And as to any suit against such fiduciary himself, or his representative, which could have been maintained if he had given no bond, there shall be no other limitation than would exist if the preceding section was not passed.

By SEC. 7. If any person, against whom the right shall have so accrued on an award, or on any such contract, shall, by writing signed by him or his agent, promise payment of money on such award or contract, the person to whom the right shall have so accrued may maintain an action for the money so promised, within such number of years after the said promise, as it might originally have been maintained within upon the award or contract, and the plaintiff may either sue on such promise, or on the original cause of action, and in the latter case, in answer to a plea under the fifth section, may, by way of replication, state such promise, and that such action was brought within the said number of years thereafter; but no promise, except by writing as aforesaid, shall take any case out of the operation of the said fifth section, or deprive any party of the benefit thereof. An acknowledgment in writing as aforesaid, from which a promise of payment may be implied, shall be deemed to be such promise in the meaning of this section.

By SEC. 8. No acknowledgment or promise, by any personal representative of a decedent, or by one of two or more joint contractors, shall charge the estate of such decedent, or charge any other of such contractors, in any case in which, but for such acknowledgment or promise, the decedent's estate or another contractor could have been protected under the fifth section.

CHAPTER XLV.

LOTTERIES AND LOTTERY TICKETS, &C.

By Sec. 11, Chap. 198. If a free person, without authority of law, set up or promote a lottery, or raffle for money or other thing of value, or be concerned in managing or drawing such lottery or raffle, or in any house, under his control, knowingly permit such lottery or raffle, or the sale of any lottery ticket or share thereof, or any other writing, certificate, bill, token or other device, purporting or intended to entitle any person to any prize, or share of or interest in a prize, to be drawn in such lottery, or in any foreign lottery, or shall knowingly permit money or other property to be raffled for in such house, or to be won therein by throwing or using dice, or by any other game of chance, he shall be fined not exceeding one thousand dollars.

By Sec. 12. If a free person, for himself or another person, without lawful authority, sell or have in his possession for the purpose of sale, or with intent to exchange or negotiate, or aid in selling, exchanging or negotiating, a ticket, or share of a ticket, in a lottery, or any such writing, certificate, bill, token or device, as is mentioned in the preceding section, he shall be fined not exceeding one hundred dollars.

By Sec. 13. If a free person make, sell, exchange or negotiate, or have in his possession, with intent to sell, exchange or negotiate, or assist in making or selling, or in attempting to sell, exchange or negotiate, any false or fictitious lottery ticket, or share thereof, or any writing, certificate, bill, token or device, before mentioned, or any ticket or share thereof, in any false or fictitious lottery, or if he receive any money or other thing of value for such ticket or share, writing, certificate, bill, token or device, *purporting that any person shall be entitled to receive any prize or share thereof, or other thing of value that may be drawn in such lottery*, he knowing the same to be false or fictitious, he shall be confined in jail not more than one year, and fined not exceeding five hundred dollars.

By Sec. 14. In a prosecution under the preceding section, any ticket or share of a ticket, or any other writing or thing which the accused sold, or offered for sale, shall be presumed to be false or fictitious, unless it be proved that the same is true and genuine, and that such lottery was existing and undrawn, and that such ticket or share thereof, or other writing or thing, before mentioned, was issued by lawful authority, and binding upon the persons who used the same.

BY SEC. 15. All money and things of value, drawn or proposed to be drawn by an inhabitant of this State, and all money or things of value received by such person, by reason of his being the owner or holder of a ticket, or share of a ticket, in any lottery or pretended lottery, contrary to this act, shall be forfeited to the Commonwealth.

These provisions are to be construed as remedial and not as penal statutes.

(No. 1.)

Form of Warrant for selling lottery tickets.

——— County, to wit:

To X. Y., *Constable of the said County:*

Whereas, A .B. of the said County, hath this day made complaint and information on oath before me J. T., a Justice of the said County, that C. D. of the said County, on the ——— day of ——— 18—, in the said County, did unlawfully [sell to one E. F., a lottery ticket in a certain lottery, called the ——— lottery, and which lottery was not authorized by the laws of this Commonwealth:] These are, therefore, to command you, in the name of the Commonwealth, forthwith to apprehend the said C. D., and bring him before me or some other Justice of the said County, to answer the said complaint, and to be farther dealt with according to law. Given under my hand and seal, this ——— day of ——— 18—.

J. T., J. P. [L. S.]

[NOTE.—This form may be adapted to all other breaches of the statute, taking care to state substantially each offence, which is best done by using the words of the statute. As for instance, for advertising lottery tickets, " did advertise and cause to be advertised for sale, certain lottery tickets, in a certain lottery called the ——— lottery, which lottery was not authorized by the laws of this Commonwealth ;" or, drawing a lottery, " did draw, and aid and assist in drawing, a certain lottery, called the ———, not authorized by law ;" or, for being concerned in management of a lottery, say : " was concerned in the management and conducting a certain lottery, called the ——— lottery, and which was not authorized by law."]

(No. 2.)

Form of Commitment and certificate to Clerk.

See Nos. 9, and 10, under the head of ARREST, and describe the offence as in the warrant.

LOTTERIES, &C.—(*Indictments for.*) 413

(No. 3.)

Form of Recognizance of Bail.

See No. 4, under the head of RECOGNIZANCE.

(No. 4.)

Form of Recognizance of Witnesses.

See No. 5, under the head of RECOGNIZANCE.

(No. 1.)

Indictment against a person for selling a lottery ticket.

Commence as No. 1, under head of "INDICTMENTS," and say: that A. B., on the —— day of ——, in the County aforesaid, did unlawfully offer for sale, and did unlawfully sell to one C. D., a lottery ticket, in a certain lottery not authorized by the laws of this Commonwealth, called the —— lottery; which said lottery ticket was then and there taken and kept by the said C. D., so that the jurors aforesaid cannot now here set forth the tenor or substance thereof, against the peace and dignity of the Commonwealth of Virginia.

(No. 2.)

Indictment for exhibiting a sign or other emblematical representation of a lottery, &c.

Commence as No. 1, under head of "INDICTMENTS," and say: that A. B., on the —— day of ——, in the County aforesaid, did unlawfully exhibit a sign, symbol and emblematical representation of a lottery, and of the drawing thereof, called the —— lottery, which said lottery was not authorized by the laws of this Commonwealth, by (here describe the manner in which the sign, symbol, &c. was exhibited,) and did thereby indicate where lottery tickets in said lottery might be purchased and received, and did thereby invite and entice the good citizens of this Commonwealth unlawfully to purchase and receive the said tickets in the aforesaid lottery, against the peace and dignity of the Commonwealth of Virginia.

CHAPTER LXVI.

LUNATICS.

By Sec. 12, Chap. 85, of the revised statutes. Any Justice who shall suspect any person in his county or corporation to be a lunatic, shall issue his warrant, ordering such person to be brought before him. He and two other Justices shall enquire whether such person be a lunatic, and for that purpose summon his physician (if any) and any other witnesses. In addition to any other questions, they shall propound so many of the following as may be applicable to the case. 1. What is the patient's age, and where born? 2. Is he married? If so, how many children has he? 3. What are his habits, occupation and reputed property? 4. How long since indications of insanity appeared? 5. What were they? 6. Does the disease appear to increase? 7. Are there periodical exacerbations? Any lucid intervals, and of what duration? 8. Is his derangement evinced on one or on several subjects? What are they? 9. What is the supposed cause of the disease? 10. What change is there in his bodily condition since the attack? 11. Has there been a former attack? When and of what duration? 12. Has he shewn any disposition to commit violence to himself or others? 13. Whether any and what restraint has been imposed on him? 14. If any, what connexions of his have been insane? Were his parents or grand parents blood relations? If so, in what degree? 15. Has he had any bodily disease from suppression or evacuations, eruptions, sores, injuries or the like, and what is its history? 16. What curative means have been pursued, and their effect, and especially, if depleting remedies, and to what extent, have been used?

By Sec. 13. If the said Justices decide that the person is a lunatic, and ought to be confined in an asylum, and ascertain that he is a citizen of this State, then, unless some person (to whom the Justices, in their discretion, may deliver such lunatic,) will give bond, with sufficient security, to be approved by said Justices, payable to the Commonwealth, with condition to restrain and take proper care of such lunatic until the cause of confinement shall cease, or the lunatic is delivered to the Sheriff of the county or Sergeant of the corporation, to be proceeded with according to law, the said Justices shall order him to be removed to the nearest asylum and received, if there be room therein, and if not, to the other.

BY SEC. 14. The interrogatories to the witnesses and the answers thereto shall be in writing, and together with a written statement by the Justices of any matter known to them as to the fact of insanity, shall be transmitted by them with the order.

BY SEC. 15. The Sheriff or other officer to whom such order of the Justices is directed, shall immediately ascertain by written enquiry of the superintendent of the asylum first named therein, whether there is a vacancy in such asylum, and if there be none, he shall make a similar enquiry of the other superintendent. Until it is ascertained that there is a vacancy, the patient shall be kept in the jail of the county or corporation.

BY SEC. 16. Such officer shall, as soon as he is informed that there is a vacancy, carry the lunatic to the proper asylum.

BY SEC. 17. When such patient arrives at the asylum, the board of directors shall be assembled as soon as may be, and if they concur in opinion with the Justices, shall receive and register him as a patient.

BY SEC. 18. If they refuse to receive the lunatic, the officer in whose custody he may be, shall confine him in the jail of the county or corporation in which he was examined, until lawfully discharged or removed therefrom.

BY SEC. 19. If it appear to the Justices that the person examined by them is a lunatic, and a non-resident of the State, he shall be committed to jail, and if any non-resident be received into an asylum under such order or be committed to jail, the board in the one case, and the court to whose jail he may have been committed in the other, shall, as soon as practicable, cause him to be returned to his friends, or to the proper authorities in the State from which he came.

BY SEC. 20. No non-resident lunatic shall be admitted or retained in either asylum under any contract with the board, except when there is a vacancy therein not applied for on behalf of any person residing in the State. When so admitted, the board may at any time discharge him, and require his friends to take charge of him or send him back to his home, and shall do so whenever it may be necessary, in order to make room for a person residing in the State.

BY SEC. 21. No insane slave shall be received or retained in either asylum, so as to exclude any white person residing in this State; and any such slave received in an asylum, shall by the board be sent back to the jail of the county or corporation from which he came, or delivered to his master, whenever it may be necessary, in order to make room for a white person residing in the State.

By Sec. 22. Insane persons of the naval service of the United States, who may be sent to either asylum by the secretary of the navy, under the thirteenth section of the act of Congress, approved August the third, eighteen hundred and forty-eight, may be received in such asylum; but when it shall become necessary, for the purpose of admitting therein insane persons, who are citizens of this State, the board shall cause such insane persons of the naval service or marine corps, or so many as may be necessary, to be removed from the asylum, and restored to the care of the secretary of the navy.

By Sec. 23. If any idiot be sent to or received in any asylum, the board shall order him to be removed to the county or corporation whence he came, and delivered to his committee, if he have one, or if not, to the overseers of the poor or any of them, who shall give a receipt for him. The costs of such removal shall be paid out of his estate, if sufficient, but if not, shall be provided by the said overseers at the charge of their county or corporation.

By Sec. 24. If any person charged with or convicted of crime, be found in the court before which he is so charged or convicted, to be a lunatic, and such court shall order him to be confined in one of the lunatic asylums, he shall be received and confined, if, or so soon as, there is a vacancy therein. The Sheriff or other officer of the court, by which the order is made, shall immediately proceed in the manner directed by the fifteenth section of this chapter, to ascertain whether such vacancy exists, and until it is ascertained that there is a vacancy, such lunatic shall be kept in the jail of such court.

By Sec. 25. Except in the case of a person charged with crime and subject to be tried therefor, or convicted of crime and subject to be punished therefor, when in a condition to be so tried or punished, the board of any asylum, or the court of any county or corporation, may deliver any lunatic confined in such asylum, or the jail of such county or corporation, to any friend who will give bond with security, with the condition mentioned in the thirteenth section of this chapter; and where a lunatic, except as aforesaid, is deemed by the superintendent of an asylum both harmless and incurable, the board may deliver him without such bond to any friend who is willing, and in the opinion of the board, able to take care of him.

By Sec. 26. If the person giving any bond mentioned in the preceding or the thirteenth section of this chapter, or his representative, shall deliver the lunatic therein mentioned to the Sheriff of the county or Sergeant of the corporation, according to the condition of the bond, such Sheriff or Sergeant shall carry the lunatic before a Justice of his county or corporation, and the same proceedings shall be thereupon had as in the case of a person brought before a Justice under his warrant under the 12th section.

BY SEC. 27. If such person or his representative shall desire to carry the lunatic to an asylum, he shall proceed in the manner in which the Sheriff or Sergeant to whom a lunatic is delivered, under the preceding section, is thereby required to proceed, and shall have the same powers, perform the same duties, and receive the same compensation with those of a Sheriff or Sergeant in such case. And the same course shall be pursued, when the lunatic arrives at the asylum, as if he had been carried there by a Sheriff or other officer as aforesaid.

BY SEC. 28. If any lunatic, confined in either asylum, shall escape, the president of the board, or if required by any person to do so, any Justice of the county where such lunatic may be, shall issue his warrant to the Sheriff of such county, to arrest and carry him back to the asylum, which warrant the Sheriff shall forthwith execute, and may execute in any part of the Commonwealth.

BY SEC. 29. When any person confined in an asylum, charged with crime and subject to be tried therefor, or convicted of crime, shall be restored to sanity, the board shall give notice thereof to the Clerk of the court by whose order he was confined, and deliver him in obedience to the proper precept.

BY SEC. 30. When any other person confined in an asylum or jail as a lunatic, shall be restored to sanity, the board or the court, as the case may be, shall discharge him and give him a certificate thereof.

BY SEC. 31. Each patient in any asylum, shall be deemed an inhabitant of the county or corporation in which he had a legal settlement at the time of his removal to the asylum.

BY SEC. 32. If not previously paid by individuals, the expense of removing any lunatic to and from any asylum, and of the maintenance and care of him therein, shall be paid out of the treasury of the asylum, and the expense of the maintenance and care of any lunatic in any jail, shall be paid out of the public treasury. Such expense, in either case, to be refunded in the manner hereinafter provided.

BY SEC. 33. The Justices or Court who shall order a lunatic to be confined in an asylum, shall cause a certificate of his estate, or if the person be a married woman, or infant who is not an orphan, of the estate of the husband or parent, and also of the probable annual profits of such estate, to be sent to the directors of the asylum, and to the next court for the county or corporation of which the lunatic is an inhabitant.

LUNATICS.

BY SEC. 34. When any person shall be confined in any jail as a lunatic, the Jailor shall certify the fact to the court of the county or corporation, at their next ensuing term. The court shall thereupon cause such person to be examined by two disinterested persons, who shall, as soon as may be, report the result thereof. The court shall then make such provision for the maintenance and care of him as his situation may require.

BY SEC. 35. The court in whose jail any lunatic may be confined, shall, when practicable and proper, contract with some fit person for the maintenance and care of such lunatic out of the jail, and make allowance therefor, not exceeding what is authorized for a lunatic confined in jail. The expenses, services and allowances mentioned in this and the two preceding sections, shall be certified to the first auditor for payment.

BY SEC. 36. Each officer shall be allowed eight cents per mile, besides tolls and ferriages, for himself, and the same for each guard, both going to and returning from the asylum, to carry a lunatic, and the same sum for the lunatic, going and also returning, when he is carried from an asylum. But no officer shall be allowed for more than one person as a guard for one lunatic, without a warrant from the examining Justices, authorizing more than one, nor then, for more than two persons.

BY SEC. 37. No officer shall be allowed any thing for carrying a lunatic to or from any asylum, either for himself, his guard, or the lunatic, unless he shall have previously ascertained that there was a vacancy therein.

BY SEC. 38. The allowance to the Jailor, for the maintenance and care of a lunatic, shall be fixed by the court in whose jail he is confined. No more shall be allowed for his clothing than thirty dollars a year. No such allowance shall be audited and paid, unless it appears, in the certificate of it, that the Jailor proved to the court, that immediately after the commitment of the lunatic, and at least once in every two months thereafter, application was made to the board of directors of both asylums for admission, and that such application was refused for want of room, or that such applications were not continued because the admission of the lunatic had been refused for some other cause than want of room.

BY SEC. 39. When the same attendant, nurse or physician is employed to attend the sick in any jail, as well lunatics as others, the court shall apportion the allowance therefor, so as to ascertain how much is to be allowed for each lunatic.

BY SEC. 40. If a person be found to be insane by Justices before whom he may be examined, or in a court in which he may be charged with crime, as aforesaid, the court of the county or corporation of which he is an inhabitant, shall appoint a committee of him.

BY SEC. 41. If a person residing in this State, not so found, be suspected to be insane, the court of the county or corporation of which such person is an inhabitant, shall, on the application of any party interested, proceed to examine into his state of mind, and being satisfied that he is insane, shall appoint a committee of him.

BY SEC. 42. If a person residing out of the State, but having property therein, be suspected to be insane, the court of the county or corporation wherein the said property or greater part of it is, shall upon like application, and being satisfied that he is insane, appoint a committee of him.

BY SEC. 52. Any money for which any person is liable to an asylum, or to the Commonwealth, on account of a lunatic, may be recovered, with interest from the time it ought to have been paid, by warrant, suit or motion, in the name of the asylum or the Commonwealth, as the case may be. When the suit or motion is brought by the asylum, it may be in any court of the county or corporation in which the asylum is, or in which the defendant resides; and in case of a motion, thirty days notice thereof shall be given.

BY SEC. 54. If any director of an asylum, Justice, Clerk of a court, Sheriff or other officer shall fail to perform any duty required of him in this chapter, or shall offend against any prohibition contained herein, he shall forfeit not less than fifty nor more than one hundred dollars.

BY SEC. 55. The word "lunatic," whenever it occurs in this chapter, shall be construed to include every insane person who is not an idiot.

An idiot is one of non-sane memory from his birth, by constant infirmity, without lucid intervals.

(No. 1.)

Form of Warrant to take and bring a lunatic before a Justice.

―――― County, to wit:

To X. Y., Constable of the said County:

Whereas, upon the complaint and information of A. B., this day made to me J. T., a Justice of said County, I have good reason to suspect that C. D. is a lunatic, and ought to be committed to an asylum: These are, therefore, to command you, in the name of the Commonwealth, forthwith to take the body of the said C. D., and bring him before me, at ――――, in the said County, on the ―――― day of ―――― 18—, that he may be examined touching his lunacy, and to be farther proceeded with according to law. And you are hereby required to request two other Justices of the said County to be then there, to enquire with me whether the said C. D. be a lunatic; and farther, to summon Drs. J. C. and E. F. to attend at the same time and place as witnesses, to testify touching the lunacy of the said C. D. Given under my hand and seal, this —— day of ———— 18—.

J. T., J. P. [L. S.]

(No. 2.)

Form for taking the evidence in a case of lunacy, by three Justices.

—————— County, to wit:

Depositions of witnesses taken before us, J. T., J. S. and J. W., Justices of the said County, now sitting upon the examination of C. D., suspected of lunacy:

The deposition of R. C., of the age of ——, and by profession a physician, (or whatever the profession may be,) being by us first duly sworn, in answer to the following interrogatories, under oath, says:

[Here insert the questions in the order in which they occur in section 12, and let the answer to each question, immediately follow it. For example:
"1st Question.—What is the party's age and where born?
"Answer. ————."
(and conclude thus:)

Sworn to before us, this —— day of ———— 18—.

J. T., J. P.
J. S., J. P.
J. W., J. P.]

(No. 3.)

Form of Commitment of a resident lunatic.

—————— County, to wit:

To the Sheriff of the said County, and to the Superintendent of the Lunatic Asylum at Williamsburg:

Whereas, C. D., who is suspected of being a lunatic, was this day brought before us, J. T., J. S. and J. W., three Justices of said County, to enquire whether he be a lunatic; and whereas, upon the testimony of witnesses, it appears to us, that he is a lunatic and citizen of this Commonwealth, and ought to be confined in a lunatic asylum; and no person appearing before us, to give bond, with sufficient security to be approved by us, payable to the Commonwealth, with condition to restrain and take proper care of the said C. D., until restored to sanity: We do, in the name of the Commonwealth, command you, the said Sheriff, to carry the said C. D. to the lunatic asylum at Williamsburg, that being the nearest asylum to us, and there deliver him, together with this warrant, to the superintendent of the said asylum. And you, the said superintendent, are hereby required to receive into the said asylum, and into your care and charge, the said C. D., to be treated and taken care of as a lunatic. And we do, with this warrant, transmit to you (the said superintendent) the interrogatories and answers thereto, taken in writing by us, touching the lunacy of the said C. D. Given under our hands and seals, this —— day of ———— 18—.

J. T. J. P. [L. S.]
J. S., J. P. [L. S.]
J. W., J. P. [L. S.]

LUNATICS. 421

(No. 4.)

Form of Escape Warrant against a lunatic.

—— County, to wit:

To the Sheriff of —— County, (or any County in which the lunatic may be :)

Whereas, A. B., the Superintendent of the lunatic asylum at Williamsburg, has this day made complaint and information before me J. T., a Justice of said County, that C. D., a lunatic heretofore committed to the said asylum, did, on the —— day of ——— 18—, make his escape therefrom, and is now at large in the County of ———: These are, therefore, to command you, in the name of the Commonwealth, forthwith to arrest the said C. D., and carry him back to the said asylum, and there deliver him to the Superintendent thereof. Given under my hand and seal, this —— day of ——— 18—.

J. T., J. P. [L. S.]

(No. 5.)

Form of Escape Warrant on the application of any other person.

—— County, to wit:

To the Sheriff of the said County:

Whereas, it appears to me J. T., a Justice of the said County, upon the information of A. B., that C. D. a lunatic, did, on the —— day of ——— 18—, make his escape from the lunatic asylum of Staunton, wherein he was then confined, and is now in the said County, and being required by the said A. B. to issue my warrant for the arrest and removal of the said C. D.: These are to command you, in the name of the Commonwealth of Virginia, forthwith to arrest the said C. D., and safely to convey him back to the said asylum, and there deliver him to the Superintendent thereof. Given under my hand and seal, this —— day of ——— 18—.

J. T., J. P. [L. S.]

CHAPTER LXVII.

MAIMING.

[For shooting, stabbing, &c., of white persons, by negroes, with intent to kill, see NEGROES.]

This offence was formerly defined to be, the violently depriving another of the use of such of his members as might render him the less able to fight, and by the ancient law of England was considered such an atrocious injury, that he who maimed any man, whereby he lost any part of his body, was sentenced to lose the like part; but this law of retaliation has been long out of use; so that, by the Common Law, as it stood for many years unaltered by statute, mayhem was a misdemeanor punishable by fine and imprisonment, except in the instance of mayhem by castration, which was felony.[1] But though mayhem proper was a misdemeanor only, it was always regarded as the highest offence under felony, not only because of the great injury to the individual disabled, but because of the high offence against the King's peace, and as tending to deprive him of the aid of his subjects. It was, doubtless, this last consideration, which gave rise to those "quaint distinctions formerly recognized by the law between what was, and what was not, mayhem." Thus, the cutting off, or disabling, or weakening a man's hand, or finger or leg, or striking out his eye or foretooth, or depriving him of those parts, the loss of which tends to abate his courage, were held to be mayhem; whereas, the knocking out his jaw teeth, or cutting off his ear, nose or lip, was accounted no maiming at Common Law, as they were considered of no use in fighting; but tended merely to disfigure and not to weaken. The statute, however, not only makes such acts as constituted mayhem proper, at Common Law, felony, but has so far extended its protection over the persons of individuals, as to make many acts of a similar character, felony, though they do not tend to weaken, but to disfigure only.

BY SEC. 9, CHAP. 191. If any free person maliciously shoot, stab, cut or wound any person, or by any means cause him bodily injury, with intent to maim, disfigure, disable, or kill, he shall, except where it is otherwise provided, be punished by confinement in the penitentiary not less than one, nor more than ten years. If such act be done unlawfully, but not maliciously, with the intent aforesaid, the offender shall,

---

[1] 3 Inst. 62, 118.

at the discretion of the jury, if the accused be white, or of the court, if he be a negro, either be confined in the penitentiary not less than one, nor more than five years, or be confined in jail not exceeding twelve months, and fined not exceeding five hundred dollars.

By Sec. 10. If any free person, in the commission of, or attempt to commit, a felony, unlawfully shoot, stab, cut or wound another person, he shall, at the discretion of the jury, if the accused be white, or of the court, if he be a negro, either be confined in the penitentiary not less than one, nor more than five years, or be confined in jail not exceeding one year, and fined not exceeding five hundred dollars.

By Sec. 11. If a free person unlawfully shoot at another person, whether in any street in any town, or in any place of public resort, whether in a town or elsewhere, he shall be confined in jail not less than six months nor more than three years, and be fined not less than one hundred nor exceeding one thousand dollars.

The first point to which the attention of the Justice is directed, is the distinction between malicious and unlawful maiming, under the ninth section of the statute. To constitute the offence of *malicious* maiming, malice must be proved by a *deliberate design* to do a personal injury to another, of the nature described in the statute ; and for this purpose, evidence is admissible, that the prisoner at another time shot intentionally at the prosecutor.([1]) For the legal definition of malice, the Justice is referred to the title of HOMICIDE.

In the offence of malicious maiming, under the first branch of the 9th section just quoted, the malice must be precisely such, as, if death had ensued, the act would have constituted murder ; on the other hand, if there be no malice, and the act be done in a transport of passion, excited by such a degree of provocation, as on an indictment for murder would reduce the homicide to manslaughter, it will amount to unlawful maiming under the last branch of that section.([2]) As in murder, so in this offence, malice need not be directed against any particular individual ; for if it be conceived against all persons who may happen to fall within the perpetrator's design, the particular mischief done to any one, will be connected with the general malignant intent, so as to bring the offender within the statute.([3])

The remaining points to be considered by the Justice, under this statute, are, 1st. What is stabbing, cutting, wounding and

---

([1]) R. *v.* Voke, R. & R. 531. ([3]) Rex *v.* Hunt, 1 Moo. C. C. 93 ;
([2]) Rex *v.* Gastineaux, 1 Leach 417 ; 1 East P. C. 220; Deac. Cr. Co. 836.
1 East P. C. 412.

shooting? and 2nd. What must be the intent with which the act was done?

Stabbing is perpetrated by wounding with a pointed instrument.(¹)

In the proceedings of a Justice, for unlawful or malicious stabbing, it is not necessary to precede the charge of felonious stabbing by any statement of an assault, beating or wounding. This is unnecessary, even in an indictment.(²)

Cutting, under the statute, means a wounding with an instrument having a sharp edge, making thereby an incised wound.(³) But, whether the instrument is intended for cutting or not, or is ordinarily used for some other purpose, an actual cutting, inflicted by it, will support a charge of felonious cutting, under the statute; as in one case, where the instrument was the claw or sharp part of a hammer,(⁴) and in another, where the cutting was with a piece of iron, generally used for the purpose of opening doors.(⁵) It is not, however, every incised wound that amounts to a cutting; for where such a wound was produced by a blow with the handle of a windlass, it was held not to be a cutting, within the statute.(⁶)

Wounding, means a contused or lacerated wound, such as may be inflicted with an iron bar, the scabbard of a sword, the blunt end of a hammer, or the handle of a windlass, or any other blunt instrument;(⁷) but to constitute a wound, the continuity of the skin must be broken so as to divide the external surface of the body.(⁸) Under the old statute, (1 R. C. 1819,) it was not felony to *cut or wound* another, unless the limb or member cut, was permanently disabled;(⁹) but the new statute makes no distinction in this respect between shooting, stabbing, cutting or wounding; and in a case of stabbing, it has been decided, that if a stab be proved, the question is not what is its extent, but with what intent it was done; for, if done with either of the intents mentioned in the statute, the offence is complete, though the stab itself be slight and not in a vital part.(¹⁰) In cases arising under the 10th section, the question is not as to the intent, but whether the act was done in the perpetration of, or in the attempt to perpetrate, a felony.

The distinction between an injury by cutting, and by stabbing or wounding, must be attended to by the Justice; for however unimportant it may seem to him, the offences in law

---

(¹) 1 Russ. 595; M'Dermot's Case, Ry. & R. 356.
(²) Woodson's Case, 9 Leigh 669.
(³) 1 Russ. 595.
(⁴) R. v. Atkinson, Ry. & R. 104.
(⁵) R. v. Haywood, Id. 78.
(⁶) 1 Russ. 597.
(⁷) 2 Dea. Cr. Co. 837.
(⁸) Rex v. Wood, 1 Moo. C. C.; Rex v. Beckett, 1 Moo. & Ro. 526.
(⁹) 1 Moo. C. C. 29; Lester's Case, 2 Va. Cases 196.
(¹⁰) Hunt's Case, Moo. C. C. 93.

are distinct; so much so, that a charge of one will not be sustained by proof of another.(¹)

2. *As to the intent.* To constitute a felony, under the 9th section, there must not only be a personal injury done to another, of the nature described in the statute, but that injury must be done expressly with one or the other of the intents specified in the statute; that is, with intent "to maim, disfigure, disable or kill;" for it is by uniting one or the other of these intents with the act, that the felony is complete, and before the change made by the New Code, on an indictment, where one or more of these intents were averred, but another and different intent was proved, the party would be discharged of that indictment,(²) though, doubtless, he might have been again indicted upon the same facts, with the proper averment of intent; and now, by section 30, chapter 208, on any indictment for maliciously shooting, stabbing, cutting or wounding a person, or by any means causing him bodily injury, with intent to *kill* him, the jury may find the accused not guilty of the offence charged, but guilty of maliciously doing such act, with intent to maim, disfigure or disable, or of unlawfully doing it, with intent to maim, disfigure, disable or kill such person.

But all these intents may be averred conjunctively in the same warrant or indictment, so as to reach the proof upon any one of them, and it will be sufficient to prove one only.(³)

If the intent be to disable, it must be understood as of a permanent disability, and not merely one which may be temporary;(⁴) so that, although in offences under the 9th section, the extent of the injury need not be enquired into, as has been said before, yet, even in these, if the only *intent is to disable*, it must be understood as an intent to produce a permanent disability. For example; if a party be indicted for maliciously or unlawfully shooting, stabbing, cutting or wounding another, with intent to maim, disfigure, disable and kill, and the jury were to find him guilty of shooting, with intent to *disable temporarily,* and not *permanently,* and were to *negative* all the other intents laid in the indictment, we think he should be discharged of the *felony.*

It may be that a party has two motives in inflicting an injury, such as is described in the statute, one of which is not embraced by it, as when his motive is to prevent a lawful arrest, and yet, to effect this purpose, he may, at the same time, also have the intention to maim the officer or other person making the arrest. In such cases, it is immaterial which is

(¹) Rex *v.* M'Dermot, R. & R. 356.
(²) Rex *v.* Ruffin, Russ. & Ry. 365; R. *v.* Boyce, 1 Moo. C. C. 29.
(³) Angel's Case, 2 Va. Cases 231.
(⁴) 1 Russ. 598; 1 Moo. C. C. 29.

the principal or subordinate intent, the party will be equally guilty;(¹) otherwise the crime of murder itself would often go unpunished, for the chief intent of the offender in committing this high crime, is frequently not so much to kill as to prevent detection or to facilitate escape, and the principle upon which the rule of law is founded, that a man is presumed to intend the necessary consequence of his own act, applies as well to cases of maiming as to any other offence. Where a party is actually present, aiding and assisting another to commit an offence against this statute, he is not to be treated as an accessary, but as a principal.(²) But where several are assisting each other in the commission of some other felony, and upon an alarm being given, they run off and one of them maims a pursuer, to avoid being taken, the others are not to be taken as principals in this act.(³) As to who are accessaries, see that title.

Slaves are within the protection of the statute, and to commit any one of the offences therein enumerated upon the person of a slave, is felony.(⁴)

In an indictment under the statute, it is not necessary to precede the charge of felonious stabbing, by any statement of an assault, beating or wounding.(⁵)

(No. 1.)

Form of Warrant of Arrest for unlawful and malicious stabbing, shooting, cutting or wounding.

———— County, to wit:
  To all or any one of the Constables of said County:
Whereas, A. B. of said County, has this day made complaint and information on oath before me J. T., a Justice of the said County, that C. D., on the —— day of ———— 18—, in said County, did unlawfully, maliciously and feloniously stab (or *cut*, or *shoot*, or *wound*, as the case may be,) the said A. B., with intent to maim, disfigure, disable and kill him the said A. B.: These are, therefore, to command you, in the name of the Commonwealth of Virginia, forthwith to apprehend the said C. D., and bring him before me or some other Justice of the said County, to answer the said complaint, and to be farther dealt with according to law. Given under my hand and seal, this —— day of ———— 18—.

J. T., *J. P.* [L. S.]

(¹) Gillow's Case, 1 Moo. C. C. 85.
(²) Rex *v.* Foushee, R. & R. 314; 2 Marsh. 466.
(³) Rex *v.* White, R. & R. 99.
(⁴) Chappell's Case, 1 Va. Cases; and Carver's Case, 5 Rand. 660.
(⁵) Woodson's Case, 9 Leigh 669.

(No. 2.)

Form of Warrant of Arrest for unlawfully and maliciously biting off the ear or nose.

———— County, to wit:
  To all or any one of the Constables of said County:

Whereas, A. B. of said County, has this day made complaint and information on oath before me J. T., a Justice of the said County, that C. D., on the —— day of ————18—, in said County, did unlawfully, maliciously and feloniously wound the said A. B., by biting off the ear (or *nose*,) of him the said A. B., with intent to maim, disfigure, disable and kill him the said A. B.: These are, therefore, to command you, in the name of the Commonwealth of Virginia, forthwith to apprehend the said C. D., and bring him before me or some other Justice of the said County, to answer the said complaint, and to be farther dealt with according to law. Given under my hand and seal, this —— day of ——— 18—.

J. T., J. P. [L. s.]

[NOTE.—This form may be used for cutting the ear, nose or lip, by omitting the words "bite off" and inserting "cut" the nose, lip or ear, as the case may be.]

(No. 3.)

Form of Warrant of Arrest for cutting, shooting, stabbing or wounding, in the commission of a felony.

———— County, to wit:
  To all or any one of the Constables of said County:

Whereas, A. B. of said County, has this day made complaint and information on oath before me J. T., a Justice of the said County, that C. D., on the —— day of ———— 18—, in said County, did commit burglary, in feloniously breaking and entering the dwelling house of the said A. B., in the night time of that day, with intent to commit felony therein, and did then and there, in the commission of the said burglary, feloniously cut (or *shoot, stab* or *wound,*) the said A. B.: These are, therefore, to command you, in the name of the Commonwealth of Virginia, forthwith to apprehend the said C. D., and bring him before me or some other Justice of the said County, to answer the said complaint, and to be farther dealt with according to law. Given under my hand and seal, this —— day of ———— 18—.

J. T., J. P. [L. s.]

[NOTE.—This form may be altered to suit any other case of cutting, &c. in the commission of a felony, by describing the felony which was committed.]

MAIMING.

(No. 4.)

Form of Warrant of Arrest against a person for causing bodily injury to another, otherwise than by cutting, shooting or stabbing.

—— County, to wit:

To X. Y., Constable of the said County:

Whereas, A. B. has this day made complaint and information on oath before me J. T., a Justice of the said County, that C. D., on the —— day of ——— 18—, in the said County, did feloniously and maliciously cause to him the said A. B. great bodily injury, by maliciously and unlawfully (here state the means by which the injury was caused, as for example, "pouring melted lead into the ear of the said A. B.,") with intent to maim, disfigure, disable or kill him the said A. B.: These are, therefore, to command you, in the name of the Commonwealth of Virginia, forthwith to apprehend the said C. D., and bring him before me or some other Justice of the said County, to answer the said complaint, and to be farther dealt with according to law. Given under my hand and seal, this —— day of ——— 18—.

J. T., J. P. [L. S.]

(No. 5.)

Form of Warrant of Arrest for shooting at a person in a street in town.

City of ——, to wit:

To all or any one of the Constables of said City:

Whereas, A. B. has this day made complaint on oath before me J. T., an Alderman in and for the said City, that C. D., on the —— day of ——— in the year ——, did, in the said City, and in one of the streets of the said City, shoot at him the said A. B., with a pistol loaded with gunpowder and leaden ball: These are, therefore, in the name of the Commonwealth of Virginia, to command you, forthwith to apprehend the said C. D., and bring him before me or some other Justice of the said City, to answer the said complaint, and to be farther dealt with according to law. Given under my hand and seal, this —— day of ——— 18—.

J. T., J. P. [L. S.]

(No. 6.)

Form of Warrant of Arrest for shooting at a person in a public place, not a street.

—— County, to wit:

To all or any one of the Constables of said County:

Whereas, A. B. of said County, has this day made complaint and information on oath before me J. T., a Justice of the said County, that C. D., on the —— day of ——— 18—, in said County, did in a certain place, to wit, (state the place,) the same then being a place of public resort in said County, shoot at him the said A. B., with a pistol loaded with gunpowder and leaden balls: These are, therefore, to command you, in the name of the Common-

MAIMING.

wealth of Virginia, forthwith to apprehend the said C. D., and bring him before me or some other Justice of the said County, to answer the said complaint, and to be farther dealt with according to law. Given under my hand and seal, this —— day of —————— 18—.

J. T., J. P. [L. S.]

(No. 7.)

Form of Mittimus where a party is committed for examination or trial in the County Court, for maiming.

———— County, to wit:

To X. Z., *Constable of said County, and to the Keeper of the Jail of said County:*

These are to command you, the said Constable, in the name of the Commonwealth of Virginia, forthwith to convey and deliver into the custody of the keeper of the said jail, together with this warrant, the body of C. D., a white person (or *free negro,* or *a slave, the property of E. F.,* as the case may be,) charged before me J. T., a Justice of the said County, on the oath of A. B., with a felony by him committed, in this, that the said C. D., on the —— day of —————— in the year 18—, in the said County, (here describe the offence as in the warrant of arrest.) And you, the said keeper of the said jail, are hereby required to receive the said C. D. into your jail and custody, that he may be examined (or *tried*) for the said offence, by the County Court of said County, and him there safely keep, until he shall be discharged by due course of law. Given under my hand and seal, this —— day of —————— in the year 18—.

J. T., J. P. [L. S.]

[NOTE.—If the prisoner be a white person, commit for examination; if a negro, commit for trial.]

(No. 8.)

Form of Certificate of Commitment to be sent to the Clerk of the County Court, for maiming.

———— County, to wit:

To the Clerk of the County Court of said County:

I, J. T., a Justice of the said County, do hereby certify, that I have, by my warrant, this day committed C. D. (if free negro or slave, state which) to the jail of this County, that he may be examined (or *tried*) before the County Court of the said County, for a felony by him committed, in this, that he did, on the —— day of —————— 18—, in the said County, (here state the offence as in the mittimus.) Given under my hand, this —— day of —————— in the year 18—.

J. T., J. P.

MAIMING—(*Indictments for.*)

(No. 9.)

Form of Certificate to the Clerk where party is admitted to bail.

Turn to head of ARREST, and follow No. 6.

(No. 10.)

Form of Recognizance of Bail.

Turn to head of RECOGNIZANCE, and follow No. 1, if person be free; No. 2, if a slave, and state succinctly the offence for which the person is recognized.

(No. 11.)

Form of Recognizance of Witness to appear before the County Court to give evidence upon the examination or trial of a party charged with felony.

Turn to head of RECOGNIZANCE, and follow No. 3.

(No. 1.)

Indictment for maliciously shooting, with intent to maim, &c.

Commence as No. 1, under head of "INDICTMENTS," and say: with a certain gun, then and there loaded with gunpowder and leaden shot, feloniously and of his malice aforethought, did shoot one C. D., with intent him the said C. D., then and there to maim, disfigure, disable and kill, against the peace and dignity of the Commonwealth of Virginia.

2. Add count for unlawful stabbing.

(No. 2.)

Indictment for malicious stabbing, cutting or wounding.

Commence as No. 1, under head of "INDICTMENTS," and say: in and upon one C. D. did make an assault, and him the said C. D. feloniously and maliciously did stab, (or *cut*, or *wound*,) with intent him the said C. D. then and there to maim, disfigure, disable and kill, against the peace and dignity of the Commonwealth.

2. Add count for unlawful stabbing.

MAIMING—(*Indictments for.*)

(No. 3.)

Indictment for maliciously causing bodily injury.

Commence as above directed, and say: "and whilst one C. D. was then and there asleep, a certain large quantity of melted lead, then and there feloniously and maliciously did pour into the right ear of him, the said C. D., and that he the said A. B., by means of the melted lead aforesaid, so poured into the right ear of him, the said C. D. as aforesaid, he the said A. B., then and there, in the County aforesaid, feloniously and maliciously did cause the said C. D. great bodily injury, with intent him the said C. D. to maim, disfigure, disable and kill, against the peace and dignity of the Commonwealth of Virginia.

(No. 4.)

An Indictment for cutting, shooting, stabbing or wounding, in the commission of a felony.

―――― Judicial Circuit, ―――― County, *to wit:* In the Circuit Court for the said County. } The jurors of the Commonwealth of Virginia, in and for the body of the County of ――――, and now attending the said Court, upon their oath present, that A. B., on the ―――― day of ―――― in the year one thousand eight hundred and ――――, in the said County, did [about the hour of 12 o'clock in the night of that day, feloniously and burglariously break and enter the dwelling house of one C. D., with intent then and there, feloniously and burglariously to steal the goods and chattels of him the said C. D.,] and did then and there, in the commission of the said felony, unlawfully and feloniously cut (*shoot, stab* or *wound,*) the said C. D., against the peace and dignity of the Commonwealth of Virginia.

[NOTE.—This form may be altered to suit any other case of cutting, &c. in the commission of a felony, by leaving out what is in the brackets, and describing the felony which was committed.]

MANSLAUGHTER.—See HOMICIDE, page 347.

MITTIMUS.

What? See ARREST.
Form of, in felony, see No. 4, under head of ARREST.
Form of, in misdemeanor, see No. 9, under same head.
Form of, where party surrendered by his bail, see No. 15, under the same head.

CHAPTER LXVIII.

MARRIAGES.

There are various provisions of the statute, punishing incest, regulating marriages between white persons, and prohibiting them between white persons and negroes or mulattoes.

By SEC. 3, CHAP. 196. If any white person marry in violation of the 10th or 11th section of chapter 108, he shall be confined in jail not more than six months, or fined not exceeding five hundred dollars, at the discretion of the jury. And if any persons resident in this State, and within the degrees of relationship mentioned in those sections, shall go out of this State for the purpose of being married, and with the intention of returning, and be married out of it, and afterwards return to and reside in it, cohabiting as man and wife, they shall be as guilty, and be punished as if the marriage had been in this State. The fact of their cohabitation here as man and wife, shall be evidence of their marriage.

The tenth and eleventh sections of chapter 108, provide: First, that no man shall marry his mother, *grandmother*, step-mother, sister, daughter, grand-daughter, half-sister, aunt, uncle's wife, son's wife, *brother's wife*, wife's daughter, or her grand-daughter or step-daughter, brother's daughter, sister's daughter, or wife of his brother's or sister's son. Second, that no woman shall marry her father, grandfather, step-father, brother, son, grandson, half-brother, uncle, aunt's husband, daughter's husband, husband's son, or his grandson or step-son, brother's son, sister's son, or husband of her brother's or sister's daughter.

By SEC. 4. If any clerk of a court knowingly issue a marriage license contrary to law, he shall be confined in jail not more than one year, and fined not exceeding five hundred dollars.

By SEC. 5. If any person knowingly perform the ceremony of marriage between white persons without lawful license, or officiate in celebrating the rites of marriage without being authorized by law to do so, he shall be confined in jail not more than one year, and fined not exceeding five hundred dollars.

By SEC. 8. Any white person who shall intermarry with a negro, shall be confined in jail not more than one year, and fined not exceeding one hundred dollars.

By SEC. 9. Any person who shall perform the ceremony of marriage between a white person and a negro, shall forfeit two hundred dollars, of which the informer shall have one half.

(No. 1.)

Form of Warrant of Arrest for incest.

—————— County, to wit:

To all or any one of the Constables of said County:

Whereas, A. B. of said County, has this day made complaint and information on oath before me J. T., a Justice of the said County, that C. D., a white person, on the —— day of ———— 18—, in said County, did unlawfully marry E. F., she the said E. F., being a white person, and the aunt of the said C. D.: These are, therefore, to command you, in the name of the Commonwealth of Virginia, forthwith to apprehend the said C. D., and bring him before me or some other Justice of the said County, to answer the said complaint, and to be farther dealt with according to law. Given under my hand and seal, this —— day of ———— 18—.

J. T., J. P. [L. S.]

(No. 2.)

Form of Warrant of Arrest against a Clerk of a Court, for issuing a marriage license contrary to law.

—————— County, to wit:

To all or any one of the Constables of said County:

Whereas, A. B. of said County, has this day made complaint and information on oath before me J. T., a Justice of the said County, that C. D., on the —— day of ———— 18—, in said County, he the said C. D., then being the Clerk of the County Court of said County, did unlawfully and knowingly issue, as such Clerk, a marriage license, to authorize the marriage ceremony to be performed between one E. F. and G. H., the said G. H. then being [the aunt of the said E. F., and he the said C. D. then well knowing that the said G. H. was the aunt of the said E. F.:] These are, therefore, to command you, in the name of the Commonwealth of Virginia, forthwith to apprehend the said C. D., and bring him before me or some other Justice of the said County, to answer the said complaint, and to be farther dealt with according to law. Given under my hand and seal, this —— day of ———— 18—.

J. T., J. P. [L. S.]

[NOTE.—This form may be easily varied to suit any case for issuing a marriage license contrary to law, by leaving out all in the brackets, and describing the offence according to the proof, for example: " then an infant under the age of twenty-one years, without the consent of J. H., her father, he the said C. D. well knowing that the said G. H. was then an infant."]

434 MARRIAGES.

(No. 3.)

Form of Warrant of Arrest against a white person for intermarrying with a negro.

———— County, to wit:
 To all or any one of the Constables of said County:

Whereas, A. B. of said County, has this day made complaint and information on oath before me J. T., a Justice of the said County, that C. D., a white person, on the ——— day of ——— 18—, in said County, unlawfully did intermarry with one L. M. a free negro: These are, therefore, to command you, in the name of the Commonwealth of Virginia, forthwith to apprehend the said C. D., and bring him before me or some other Justice of the said County, to answer the said complaint, and to be farther dealt with according to law. Given under my hand and seal, this ——— day of ——— 18—.

J. T., J. P. [L. S.]

(No. 4.)

Form of Warrant of Arrest for performing the marriage ceremony between a white person and a negro.

———— County, to wit:
 To all or any one of the Constables of said County:

Whereas, A. B. of said County, has this day made complaint and information on oath before me J. T., a Justice of the said County, that C. D., on the ——— day of ——— 18—, in said County, did unlawfully perform the ceremony of marriage between E. F., a white person, and G. H., a negro woman, he the said C. D., then being a person authorized by law to perform the ceremony of marriage: These are, therefore, to command you, in the name of the Commonwealth of Virginia, forthwith to apprehend the said C. D., and bring him before me or some other Justice of the said County, to answer the said complaint, and to be farther dealt with according to law. Given under my hand and seal, this ——— day of ——— 18—.

J. T., J. P. [L. S.]

(No. 5.)

Form of Mittimus where a party is committed to answer an indictment in the County Court, for a misdemeanor.

———— County, to wit:
 To X. Z., Constable of the said County, and to the Keeper of the Jail of the said County:

These are to command you, the said Constable, in the name of the Commonwealth of Virginia, forthwith to convey and deliver into the custody of the keeper of the said jail, together with this warrant, the body of C. D., charged before me J. T., a Justice of the said County, on the oath of A. B., with a misdemeanor by him committed, in this, that the said C. D., on the ——— day of ——— in the year 18—, in the said County, (here describe the offence as in the warrant of arrest.) And you, the said keeper of the said jail, are hereby required to receive the said C. D. into your jail and custody, to answer an indictment to be preferred against him for the said offence, in the County Court of said County, and him there safely keep, until he shall be discharged by due course of law. Given under my hand and seal, this —— day of —— in the year 18—.

J. T., J. P. [L. S.]

(No. 6.)

Form of Recognizance of Bail.

Turn to head of RECOGNIZANCE, and follow No. 4, and state the offence succinctly, for which the party is recognized.

(No. 7.)

Form of Certificate of the Commitment or Letting to Bail, to be sent to the Clerk of the County Court.

—— County, to wit:

To the Clerk of the County Court of the said County:

I, J. T., a Justice of the said County, do hereby certify, that C. D. was this day committed to the jail of this County, by my warrant, (or *was this day admitted to bail by me*, as the case may be,) to answer an indictment to be preferred against him in the County Court of the said County, for a misdemeanor by him committed, in this, that he did, on the —— day of —— 18—, in said County, (here describe the offence as in the warrant of arrest.) Given under my hand, this —— day of —— 18—.

J. T., J. P.

(No. 8.)

Form of Recognizance of Witness to appear and give evidence to the Grand Jury upon the indictment.

Follow No. 5, under the head of RECOGNIZANCE.

Indictment for solemnizing a marriage between white persons, without lawful authority.

Commence as No. 2, under head of "INDICTMENTS," and say: " did unlawfully and knowingly perform the ceremony of marriage between C. D. and one E. F., then a single woman, the said C. D. and E. F. both being white persons; he the said A. B. not then being authorized by the laws of this Commonwealth to perform the marriage ceremony between white persons, against the peace and dignity of the Commonwealth of Virginia."

CHAPTER LXIX.

MILLER'S TOLL, AND HIS DUTY.

By Sec. 12, Chap. 63, of the revised statutes. At every mill which grinds grain, whether the same be established under an order of court or not, there shall be well and sufficiently ground all grain brought to the mill, for the consumption when ground, of the person bringing or sending it, or his family, and in due turn as the same is brought; and there shall not be taken for the toll more than one eighth part of any grain, of which the remaining part is ground into meal, nor more than one sixteenth part of any grain, of which the remaining part is ground into hominy or malt. If at any mill, there be a violation of this section in any respect, the proprietor thereof shall for every such violation, forfeit to the party injured, five dollars; but with these provisoes, that the proprietor shall not be obliged to run more than one pair of stones to grind grain brought to his mill for the consumption of the persons bringing or sending it, or their families; and that such proprietor may grind grain for the consumption of his family in preference to that of others.

For the mode of recovering any penalty incurred under this section, see No. 5, under head of Warrants.

CHAPTER LXX.

MISPRISION.

[See Felony—(*Compounding of.*)]

It is the duty of every citizen, knowing of treason or felony having been committed, to give information of it to a Magistrate, and the concealment of the offence, is itself an offence, called misprision. It is either misprision of treason or of felony, at Common Law. Misprision of treason is the concealment *merely* of the crime of treason, for if the concealer gives any assistance to the traitor, he becomes a principal in the crime, as there are no accessaries to treason.([1])

([1]) 2 Deac. Cr. Co. 892.

Misprision of felony is a concealment of felony, or the procuring the concealment of it. Thus, to observe the commission of a felony without giving any alarm or using any endeavours to apprehend the offender, is a misprision, for every man is bound to apprehend a felon and disclose the felony to a Magistrate with all possible expedition, and if he in any way assent to the felony, he will then be either principal or accessary.(¹)

CHAPTER LXXI.

NEGROES—(*Free and Slave.*)

[For petit larceny and other misdemeanors committed by slaves, to be tried by a single Justice and punishable with stripes, see FINES AND SUMMARY CONVICTIONS; under which head all pecuniary fines recoverable before him in the name of the Commonwealth by summons are also treated of.]

By Sec. 1, Chap. 103. None shall be slaves in this State, except those who are so when this chapter takes effect, such free negroes as may be sold as slaves pursuant to law, such slaves as may be lawfully brought into this State, and the future descendants of the female slaves.

By Sec. 2. Slaves born within the limits of the United States, may be brought into this State and held therein, if resident in those limits at the time of removal, and not theretofore convicted of and transported for crime.

By Sec. 3. Every person who has one fourth part, or more, of negro blood, shall be deemed a mulatto, and the word "negro" in any other section of this, or any future statute, shall be construed to mean "mulatto" as well as "negro."

Crimes committed by slaves and free negroes, unconnected with the policy of the State, in the preservation and government of slaves as property, are noticed under the various heads of offences contained in the body of this work, and such parts only of the statute as partake of a police character, designed to secure white persons from violence by negroes, to protect the rights of masters in their slaves, and to keep both slaves and free negroes in good order and subjection, will be found here.

We remark, however, that in the various parts of the criminal statute which declare what shall be felony, and pre-

(¹) 1 Hale 374.

scribe the punishment therefor, free negroes are generally embraced in the term "free persons," and in most cases, the punishment is the same, whether the offender be a white person or a free negro; but from policy, if not necessity, there are certain offences against white persons, when committed by negroes, whether free or slaves, punishable with greater severity.

I. *Of such as may be committed by a free negro.*

By Sec. 4, Chap. 190. If a free person advise or conspire with a slave to rebel or make insurrection, or with *any person* to induce a slave to rebel or make insurrection, he shall be punished with death, whether such rebellion or insurrection be made or not.

By Sec. 1, Chap. 200. If a free negro commit any offence mentioned in the 15th or 16th section of chapter 191, or attempt by force or fraud to have carnal knowledge of a white female, he shall be punished, at the discretion of the jury, either with death or confinement in the penitentiary not less than five nor more than twenty years.

To explain fully this provision it is necessary to recite sections 15 and 16 of chapter 191. The 15th section provides: "If any white person carnally know a female of the age of twelve years or more, against her will, by force, or carnally know a female child *under that age*, he shall be confined in the penitentiary not less than ten nor more than twenty years." So that the bare attempt by a negro, free or slave, to have carnal knowledge of a white female, either by force or fraud, may be a capital felony. The 16th section declares that, "if any white person take away or *detain* against her will, a white female, with intent to marry or defile her, or cause her to be married or defiled by another person, or take from any person having lawful charge of her, a female child under twelve years of age, for the purpose of prostitution or concubinage, he shall be confined in the penitentiary not less than three nor more than ten years."

By Sec. 2, Chap. 200. If a free negro plot or conspire the murder of a white person, or maliciously shoot, stab, cut, wound, or by any means cause bodily injury to a white person, with intent to kill, he shall be punished at the discretion of the jury, either with death or by confinement in the penitentiary, not less than three nor more than ten years.

If a free negro commit an offence against any of the preceding sections, he should be committed for examination and not for trial.

II. *Of such offences committed by slaves.*

By Sec. 4, Chap. 200. If a slave plot or conspire to rebel, or make insurrection, or commit an offence for the commission of which a free negro, at the time of committing the same, is punishable with death, or by confinement in the penitentiary for not less than three years, he shall be punished with death. But unless it be an offence for which a free white person, if he had committed it, might have been punished with death, such slave, instead of being punished with death, may, at the discretion of the court, be punished by sale and transportation beyond the limits of the United States.

As to a plot or conspiracy to murder, we apprehend that one person may plot the murder of another, but that to constitute a conspiracy to commit any offence, there must be two or more persons uniting and agreeing in the unlawful act. In conspiracy, it is not necessary that any act should be done in execution of the design, for the offence is complete by the unlawful agreement between the parties to do the act.([1]) A mere plot to commit an offence by one person, must necessarily be accompanied by some act towards its accomplishment, for if it were possible to conceive a plot without some accompanying act, it would be an intent only, which of itself is not punishable.

These provisions of the statute, founded as they are in policy, embrace all the graver offences which that class of population, against whom they are directed, can commit upon the persons of those designed to be protected. But by whatever necessity dictated, they denounce severe penalties, and in favour of human life, should be construed strictly, and the evidence to convict under them, should leave no rational doubt of the guilt of the accused; especially should the prisoner's guilty intent to murder, be clearly made out in prosecutions under the 2d section last cited; for if the conspiracy be formed, or the act done with intent only to maim, disfigure or disable, or to do any other bodily harm, however grievous, short of killing, it is no violation of these sections, though it may amount to maiming under the 9th section of chapter 191, of the New Code. And to make out the offence, there must be also that distinct proof of malice which would constitute murder, had the death of the party ensued from the act. As to what is stabbing, shooting, cutting and wounding, see Maiming, and for malice, see Homicide.

By Sec. 5. If a slave commit an offence, for which a free negro, if he had committed it, might be punished by confine-

---

([1]) See head of Conspiracy.

ment in the penitentiary for a period less than three years, such slave shall be punished by stripes; and if, having been once sentenced for such offence, he afterwards commit an offence, for which a free negro, if he had committed it, might be punished by such confinement, he shall be punished with death, or at the discretion of the court, by sale and transportation as aforesaid.

Of carrying away slaves or advising them to abscond.

By Sec. 24, Chap. 192. Any free person who shall carry, or cause to be carried, out of any county or corporation, any slave, without the consent of his owner, or of the guardian or committee of the owner, with intent to defraud or deprive the owner of such slave, shall be prosecuted therefor in such county or corporation, and confined in the penitentiary not less than two nor more than ten years, and shall moreover (in lieu of damages,) forfeit to the owner double the value of the slave, and pay him all reasonable expenses incurred by him in regaining or attempting to regain such slave.

By Sec. 25. Any master of a vessel, having a slave on board, and going with him beyond the limits of any county, without the consent aforesaid, and any free person travelling by land, who shall aid any slave to escape out of any county or corporation, shall be considered as carrying off such slave within the meaning of the preceding section.

By Sec. 26. If the master or skipper of any vessel, knowingly receive on board any runaway slave, and permit him to remain on board without proper effort to apprehend him, he shall be confined in the penitentiary not less than two nor more than five years; and if such slave be on board such vessel after leaving port, the master or skipper shall be presumed to have knowingly received him.

By Sec. 27. If a free person advise any slave to abscond from his master, or aid such slave to abscond, by procuring for or delivering to him a pass, register or other writing, or furnishing him money, clothes, provisions or other facility, he shall be confined in the penitentiary not less than two nor more than five years.

By Sec. 28. If any owner or keeper of a ferry or bridge across a water course, separating this from another State, knowingly permit a slave to pass at such ferry or bridge, without the consent of his master, he shall pay to the party injured, twenty-five dollars and all damages occasioned thereby; and if the slave by so passing escape, such owner or keeper shall moreover be confined in the penitentiary not less than one nor more than five years.

NEGROES—(*Free and Slave.*) 441

Of seditious speeches and incendiary publications as to slaves.

BY SEC. 22, CHAP. 198. If a free person, by speaking or writing, maintain that owners have not right of property in their slaves, he shall be confined in jail not more than one year, and fined not exceeding five hundred dollars. He may be arrested and carried before a Justice by any white person.

BY SEC. 23. If a free person write, print, or cause to be written or printed, any book or other writing, with intent to advise or incite negroes in this State, to rebel or make insurrection, or inculcating resistance to the right of property of masters in their slaves, or if he shall, with intent to aid the purposes of any such book or writing, knowingly circulate the same, he shall be confined in the penitentiary not less than one nor more than five years.

BY SEC. 24. If a postmaster or deputy postmaster, know that any such book or other writing has been received at his office in the mail, he shall give notice thereof to some Justice, who shall enquire into the circumstances and have such book or writing burned in his presence; if it appear to him that the person to whom it was directed, subscribed therefor, knowing its character, or agreed to receive it for circulation, to aid the purposes of abolitionists, the Justice shall commit such person to jail. If any postmaster or deputy postmaster violate this section, he shall be fined not exceeding two hundred dollars.

BY SEC. 25. Any Judge or Justice before whom any person may be brought for the offence mentioned in the preceding section, shall cause him to enter into a recognizance, with sufficient surety, to appear before the circuit court having jurisdiction of the offence at the next term thereof, and in default of such recognizance, shall commit him to jail.

BY SEC. 3, CHAP. 200. If a free negro, on any pretext, deliver to a slave, a copy of the register of his freedom, he shall be confined in the penitentiary not less than one nor more than five years.

Free negroes illegally remaining or coming into this State.

BY SEC. 1, CHAP. 107. No negro, emancipated since the first day of May 1806, or hereafter, or claiming his right to freedom under a negro so emancipated, shall after being twenty-one years of age, remain in this State more than one year without lawful permission.

BY SEC. 2, same chapter. Any such negro may be permitted by the court of any county or corporation, to remain in this State, and reside in such county or corporation only; but the order granting the permission shall be void, unless it shew that all the acting Justices were summoned, and a majority of them present and voting on the question of permitting said negro to remain in the State; that notice of the application for such permission was posted at the courthouse door for at least two months immediately preceding; that the attorney for the Commonwealth, or in his absence, some other attorney, appointed by the court for the purpose, represented the State as counsel in the case, and that the applicant produced satisfactory proof of his being of good character, sober, peaceable, orderly and industrious. Such permission shall not be granted to any person, who, having removed from this State, shall have returned into it, nor shall any such permission granted to a female negro, be deemed a permission to the issue of such female, whether born before or after it was granted.

By Sec. 26, Chap. 198. Any negro remaining in this State in violation of chapter 107, shall forfeit his freedom, and may be prosecuted as in a case of misdemeanor, in any county or corporation in which he may be found. In such prosecution, it shall be sufficient to charge, in general terms, that the defendant was emancipated since the first day of May 1806, or claims his right to freedom under a negro emancipated since that day, and that such defendant is remaining in the State without lawful permission. Upon the trial, the defendant shall appear in person or by attorney, and an attested copy of his register shall be *prima facie* evidence of the facts therein stated; unless it appear upon the trial that the defendant has such permission, he shall be deemed guilty, and judgment shall be given that he forfeit his freedom and be sold as a slave. The sale shall be made as in the case of slaves levied upon; and the clerk shall make return to the auditor, and the officer account for and pay the proceeds of sale, as in the case of a pecuniary forfeiture.

By Sec. 27. Any free person who shall bring a free negro into this State, shall be confined in jail not more than six months, and fined not exceeding five hundred dollars. This section shall not apply to a person travelling into or through the State, with a free negro as a servant, nor to a master or skipper of a vessel or steamboat, with a free negro on board, who shall depart therewith; but any such free negro, who shall be found away from such vessel or boat, or from the lodgings of his employer, except on the business or with the written permission of such master or employer, shall be punished with stripes.

By Sec. 28. No free negro shall migrate into this State. If a free negro, not authorized by law to do so, come into or remain in this State, any person may, and every Sheriff, Sergeant and Constable is required to apprehend and carry him before some Justice of the county or corporation where he may be, who shall require him to pay one dollar to the person apprehending him, and give bond in a penalty not less than one hundred dollars, with condition that he will leave the State in ten days and not return therein; such bond shall be returned by the Justice to the court of his county or corporation. If the free negro fail to pay the fee aforesaid, or to give such bond, he may, by order of the Justice, be punished with stripes, which may, by subsequent order of a Justice, be repeated from time to time, so long as the negro remains in the State; but this section shall not apply to a free negro driven by shipwreck or other unavoidable necessity into this State, who shall depart therefrom as soon as he can, nor one employed on a vessel or steamboat, or as a servant as mentioned in the preceding section, if he do not remain in the State longer than thirty days.

By Sec. 29. If a free negro migrate from this State, or be sent out of it for the purpose of education, or go for any purpose to a non-slaveholding State and return into this State, he may be proceeded against as in the preceding section. But if he be an infant, instead of being so expelled before his arrival to twenty-one years of age, the overseers of the poor may bind him out as an apprentice until that time.

Of unlawful assemblage of slaves.

By Sec. 30, Chap. 198. If any person knowingly permit a slave, not belonging to him, to remain on his plantation, lot or tenement, above four hours at one time, without leave of the owner or manager of such slave, he shall be fined three dollars; and any person who shall so permit more than five such slaves to be at one time on his plantation, lot or tenement, shall be fined one dollar for each slave above that number, and such assemblage shall be deemed an unlawful assembly.

The object of the first clause of this section is to protect private rights, by preventing persons from knowingly permitting the slaves of others to tarry on their premises, without the owner's leave, for an unreasonable time. The object of the last clause is to guard the public against assemblages which might be dangerous to the peace or injurious to morals in a much shorter time than four hours, and therefore it has been held in a prosecution under this clause, not to be necessary for the Commonwealth to prove that the slaves remained on the premises more than four hours.[1] It was also held

---

[1] 6 Rand. 669.

that if the information charges an unlawful assemblage of *negro slaves*, the Commonwealth must prove they were slaves. The information charged that they were negro slaves, but did not state that they remained upon the premises without the consent of the owner. In Connor's Case,([1]) (which was a prosecution upon a presentment under the same clause, charging the defendant with knowingly permitting fifteen *negroes*, other than his own, to be and remain at one time on his lot or tenement, without the consent of the owners,) the defendant contended that it was incumbent on the Commonwealth to prove that the slaves remained on his premises without the consent of their owners or overseers, but the court held, that where the Commonwealth establishes, by proof, an assemblage of more than five slaves, not belonging to the defendant, on his lot or tenement at any one time, it should be presumed that such assemblage is unlawful, and that in such case, it is incumbent on the defendant, in order to protect himself, to shew that the slaves were on his lot, with the consent of the owners or overseers, thus strongly intimating, that such a defence, if made out, would have availed the defendant. But it has been since decided not to be necessary to charge in the indictment that the defendant permitted them to remain without the consent of the owner.([2])

By Sec. 31. Every assemblage of negroes for the purpose of religious worship, when such worship is conducted by a negro, and every assemblage of negroes for the purpose of instruction in reading or writing, or in the night time for any purpose, shall be an unlawful assembly. Any Justice may issue his warrant to any officer or other person, requiring him to enter any place where such assemblage may be, and seize any negro therein, and he or any other Justice may order such negro to be punished with stripes.

By Sec. 32. If a white person assemble with slaves, for the purpose of instructing them to read or write, or if he associate with them in an unlawful assembly, he shall be confined in jail not exceeding six months, and fined not exceeding one hundred dollars; and any Justice may require him to enter into a recognizance, with sufficient security, to appear before the circuit, county or corporation court of the county or corporation where the offence was committed, at its next term, to answer therefor, and in the mean time to keep the peace and be of good behaviour.

By Sec. 6, Chap. 103. Any person who shall permit an insane, aged or infirm slave, owned by him or under his control, to go at large without adequate provision for his support,

---

([1]) 5 Leigh 718.   ([2]) 5 Grattan 695.

shall be punished by fine not exceeding fifty dollars, and the overseers of the poor of the county or corporation in which such slave may be found, shall provide for his maintenance, and may charge such person, quarterly or annually, with a sufficient sum therefor, and recover it from time to time by motion. If any person shall, by sale, gift or otherwise, dispose of any insane, aged or infirm slave, which is, or is likely to become chargeable, such person, or the donor or vendor, (at the election of the said overseers,) may be proceeded against as the owner of the slave, under this section.

By Sec. 12, Chap. 103. If any person emancipate a slave who is likely to become chargeable to the county or corporation, without making adequate provision for his support, and such slave become so chargeable, the overseers of the poor shall provide for his maintenance, and charge such person or his estate, quarterly or annually, with a sufficient sum therefor, and may recover it from time to time by motion in the court of such county or corporation.

By Sec. 1, Chap. 104. If any person sell wine, ardent spirits, or any mixture thereof, or any other intoxicating liquor, to a slave, without the written consent of his master, he shall forfeit to the master, four times the value of the thing sold, and also pay a fine of twenty dollars.

By Sec. 2. If any person buy, or receive from, or sell to a slave, without his master's consent, any other article or commodity whatever, he shall forfeit to the master, four times the value of such article or commodity, and also pay a fine not exceeding twenty dollars.

By Sec. 3. If the offender against either of the two preceding sections, be a licensed ordinary keeper, merchant, hawker or pedlar, in addition to the other penalties prescribed by the said section, his license shall be revoked.

By Sec. 4. Any offender against the first or second section of this chapter, shall moreover give security for his good behaviour for a year; and on failure, shall be committed to jail till the security be given, or till the county or corporation court, (where the conviction was before a Justice,) or the court where the conviction was, shall, for good cause shewn, discharge him.

By Sec. 5. If any master or other person, give written permission to a slave to obtain any intoxicating liquor, or furnish him with the same, with the intent that he shall sell, barter or trade the same, or any part thereof, such master or other person shall forfeit twenty dollars, and give security for his good behaviour for one year.

By Sec. 6. Any person permitting a slave under his control to go at large, trade as a free man, or hire himself out, for the benefit of any person whatever, shall forfeit not less than ten nor more than thirty dollars. And if the person so permitting, hold the slave as personal representative, guardian, curator or committee, he shall pay the fine out of his own estate, and not out of that held by him as such fiduciary.

By Sec. 7. Any person may, and officers shall, with or without warrant, arrest any slave, as to whom there is a violation of the preceding section, and carry him before a Justice, who, on due proof of the fact, shall commit him to jail, unless his master or some other person, give recognizance, with good security, for his forthcoming, to abide the result of the prosecution. The Justice shall notify the proceeding to the Commonwealth's attorney of the county or corporation court, at or before the next term thereof, when, if it appear to the court, that the master has violated the preceding section, the court may impose on him a fine of not less than ten nor more than thirty dollars, or direct an information to be filed against him. If he be adjudged guilty by the court, or be convicted by a jury, and fail to pay forthwith the fine, jail fees and all other costs, the said slave shall be sold therefor, in the same manner as a slave taken under execution. Execution may issue as in other cases, if the slave be not forthcoming, or be sold and prove insufficient to pay the fine and costs.

By Sec. 8. Any person harbouring or employing a slave, without the consent of his master, shall forfeit to the master not less than one nor more than five dollars for every day of such harbouring or employment.

By Sec. 7, Chap. 107. The Clerk shall deliver to the free negro, an attested copy of his register, with the seal of the court annexed, receiving therefor a fee of twenty-five cents, and no tax for annexing the seal.

By Sec. 8. Before the register of a free negro is renewed, he shall deliver up the copy which he had of his former register, unless the court be satisfied that it has been casually lost or destroyed, nor shall any copy of a register more than five years old, avail for any of the purposes of this chapter.

By Sec. 9. Where a free negro has received a copy of his register, no other copy shall be delivered him, (on pain of twenty dollars fine to be paid by the Clerk,) until he shall have delivered up the former copy to be destroyed, unless by special order of the court, upon being satisfied that the former one has been accidentally lost or destroyed.

By Sec. 10. Any free negro above twelve years of age, residing in this State, not having such attested copy, (of a register of him, made as before directed,) may be committed to jail by a Justice, until such copy be produced, or till the court be satisfied that it has been casually lost or destroyed, or that such negro, though really free, has not been registered within five years preceding his arrest; in either of which cases he shall be discharged on paying the jail fees. But if he be so arrested a second time, and be found to have suffered the copy of his register to be lost or destroyed, or not to have had his registry made within five years, he shall be punished with stripes.

By Sec. 11. If such free negro be unable to pay the jail fees, he shall, by order of the court, be hired out at not less than ten cents a day, till they be discharged; but the Jailor shall have no fees in such case, unless, immediately upon such free negro's commitment, he shall have informed the Commonwealth's attorney of the fact in writing, and also have informed the court thereof, at its then or next sitting. The court's order shall specify the amount of jail fees then due.

By Sec. 14. Any person employing any free negro who has not such attested copy of his register, shall forfeit five dollars to any person who will warrant therefor.

By Sec. 17. The court of any county or corporation, upon satisfactory proof by a white person of the fact, may grant to any free person of mixed blood, resident therein, a certificate that he is not a negro; which certificate shall protect such person against the penalties and disabilities to which free negroes are subject as such.

By Sec. 18. Free negroes desiring to remove into any county or corporation, shall hereafter apply to the court thereof to be registered. Said courts shall make an order granting or refusing the application, as in their discretion shall seem proper.

By Sec. 19. All free negroes going into any county or corporation, and residing or habitually remaining therein more than two months, without making such application, or found therein at any time after ten days shall have elapsed since such application was made and refused, shall be considered and treated as free negroes going at large without a register.

By Sec. 33, Chap. 198. If a free negro sell or barter, or offer to sell or barter, any agricultural products, without having a certificate in writing from one respectable white person of the county or neighbourhood, of his belief that he raised, or otherwise came honestly by the same, such products shall be forfeited and the negro be punished with stripes. And any white person who shall purchase, or receive in trade, agricultural products of a free negro who has not such certificate, shall be deemed guilty of a misdemeanor. Such products shall, by order of the Justice or Court before whom the offender is convicted, be sold by a Constable or the officer of the court, like goods levied on, and the proceeds, after deducting a commission of ten per cent. for the officer, shall be paid to the overseers of the poor for the county or corporation. This section shall not be in force in any county other than *Accomack* or *Richmond*, or in any corporation, until the county or corporation court (the acting Justices thereof being summoned and a majority of them being present,) shall so order.

(No. 1.)

Form of Warrant of Arrest for advising with a slave to rebel, &c. (Sec. 4, chap. 190.)

—— County, to wit:

To all or any one of the Constables of said County:

Whereas, A. B. of said County, has this day made complaint and information on oath before me J. T., a Justice of the said County, that C. D., on the —— day of ——— 18—, in said County, feloniously did advise and conspire with E. F., a slave, to rebel and make insurrection against the laws and government of this Commonwealth, he the said C. D. then being a slave, the property of G. H. of the said County: These are, therefore, to command you, in the name of the Commonwealth of Virginia, forthwith to apprehend the said C. D., and bring him before me or some other Justice of the said County, to answer the said complaint, and to be farther dealt with according to law. Given under my hand and seal, this —— day of ——— 18—.

J. T., J. P. [L. S.]

(No. 2.)

Form of Warrant of Arrest for writing a pamphlet, &c., with intent to incite rebellion.

—— County, to wit:

To all or any one of the Constables of said County:

Whereas, A. B. of said County, has this day made complaint and information on oath before me J. T., a Justice of the said County, that C. D., on the —— day of ——— 18—, in said County, feloniously did write and print, and cause to be written and printed, a certain book, (or *pamphlet*, or whatever else it may be,) with intent to advise and incite negroes within this Commonwealth to rebel and make rebellion: These are, therefore, to command you, in the name of the Commonwealth of Virginia, forthwith to apprehend the said C. D., and bring him before me or some other Justice of the said County, to answer the said complaint, and to be farther dealt with according to law. Given under my hand and seal, this —— day of ——— 18—.

J. T., J. P. [L. S.]

(No. 3.)

Form of Warrant of Arrest against a slave or free negro, for plotting the death of a white person.

—— County, to wit:
To all or any one of the Constables of said County:

Whereas, A. B. of said County, has this day made complaint and information on oath before me J. T., a Justice of the said County, that Frank, a slave, (or *a free negro*,) on the —— day of ——— 18—, in said County, did feloniously plot the murder of him the said A. B., a white person, by administering poison to him the said A. B., (or *by attempting to poison him the said A. B.:*) These are, therefore, to command you, in the name of the Commonwealth of Virginia, forthwith to apprehend the said Frank, and bring him before me or some other Justice of the said County, to answer the said complaint, and to be farther dealt with according to law. Given under my hand and seal, this —— day of ——— 18—.

J. T., J. P. [L. S.]

(No. 4.)

Form of Warrant of Arrest for conspiracy by negroes to murder a white person.

—— County, to wit:
To all or any one of the Constables of said County:

Whereas, A. B. of said County, has this day made complaint and information on oath before me J. T., a Justice of the said County, that on the —— day of ——— 18—, in said County, Frank and John, slaves, did feloniously and maliciously conspire and agree together, feloniously to murder him the said A. B., he the said A. B. being a white person: These are, therefore, to command you, in the name of the Commonwealth of Virginia, forthwith to apprehend the said Frank and John, and bring them before me or some other Justice of the said County, to answer the said complaint, and to be farther dealt with according to law. Given under my hand and seal, this —— day of ——— 18—.

J. T., J. P. [L. S.]

(No. 5.)

Form of Warrant of Arrest against a free negro, for maliciously shooting, stabbing, cutting or wounding a white person, with intent to kill.

—— County, to wit:
To all or any one of the Constables of said County:

Whereas, A. B. of said County, has this day made complaint and information on oath before me J. T., a Justice of the said County, that C. D., a free negro, on the —— day of ——— 18—, in said County, did feloniously and maliciously shoot, (or *stab, cut* or *wound*, as the case may be,) him the said A. B., a white person, with intent to kill him: These are, therefore, to command you, in the name of the Commonwealth of Virginia, forthwith to apprehend the said C. D., and bring him before me or some other Justice of the said County, to answer the said complaint, and to be farther dealt with according to law. Given under my hand and seal, this —— day of ——— 18—.

J. T., J. P. [L. S.]

(No. 6.)

Form of Warrant of Arrest against a free negro or slave, for beating a white person, with intent to kill.

——— County, to wit:

To all or any one of the Constables of said County:

Whereas, A. B. of said County, has this day made complaint and information on oath before me J. T., a Justice of the said County, that on the —— day of ——— 18—, in said County, E. F., a free negro, (or *a slave the property of G. H.*,) feloniously and maliciously did make an assault upon him the said A. B., a white person, and feloniously and maliciously did beat him the said A. B., with intent to kill him the said A. B.: These are, therefore, to command you, in the name of the Commonwealth of Virginia, forthwith to apprehend the said E. F., and bring him before me or some other Justice of the said County, to answer the said complaint, and to be farther dealt with according to law. Given under my hand and seal, this —— day of ——— 18—.

J. T., J. P. [L. S.]

(No. 7.)

Form of Warrant of Arrest for rape, committed by a slave or free negro, upon a white female person.

——— County, to wit:

To all or any one of the Constables of said County:

Whereas, A. B. of said County, has this day made complaint and information on oath before me J. T., a Justice of the said County, that C. D., a slave, the property of ———, (or *a free negro*,) on the —— day of ——— 18—, in said County, in and upon E. F., a female white person, then and there being, violently and feloniously did make an assault, and her the said E. F., then and there, violently and against her will, feloniously did ravish and carnally know, he the said C. D. being a slave, (or *a free negro*, as the case may be:) These are, therefore, to command you, in the name of the Commonwealth of Virginia, forthwith to apprehend the said C. D., and bring him before me or some other Justice of the said County, to answer the said complaint, and to be farther dealt with according to law. Given under my hand and seal, this —— day of ——— 18—.

J. T., J. P. [L. S.]

NEGROES—(*Free and Slave.*)

(No. 8.)

Form of Warrant of Arrest for a felonious assault by a free negro or slave, upon a white female, with intent to ravish her.

———— County, to wit:

To all or any one of the Constables of said County:

Whereas, A. B. of said County, has this day made complaint and information on oath before me J. T., a Justice of the said County, that C. D., on the —— day of ——— 18—, in said County, in and upon one E. F., a white female person, feloniously did make an assault, with intent her the said E. F., violently and against her will, feloniously to ravish and carnally know, he the said C. D. being a slave, (or *free negro,* as the case may be:) These are, therefore, to command you, in the name of the Commonwealth of Virginia, forthwith to apprehend the said C. D., and bring him before me or some other Justice of the said County, to answer the said complaint, and to be farther dealt with according to law. Given under my hand and seal, this —— day of ——— 18—.

J. T., J. P. [L. S.]

(No. 9.)

Form of Warrant of Arrest against a slave or free negro, for an attempt to ravish a white female by fraud.

———— County, to wit:

To all or any one of the Constables of said County:

Whereas, A. B. of said County, has this day made complaint and information on oath before me J. T., a Justice of the said County, that C. D., on the —— day of ——— 18—, in said County, did feloniously and by fraud, attempt to have carnal knowledge of one E. F., a white female, he the said C. D. being a slave, (or *free negro,* as the case may be,) by (state the fraudulent means by which the attempt was made:) These are, therefore, to command you, in the name of the Commonwealth of Virginia, forthwith to apprehend the said C. D., and bring him before me or some other Justice of the said County, to answer the said complaint, and to be farther dealt with according to law. Given under my hand and seal, this —— day of ——— 18—.

J. T., J. P. [L. S.]

(No. 10.)

Form of Warrant of Arrest against a negro, for taking away a white female, with intent to defile her.

———— County, to wit:

To all or any one of the Constables of said County:

Whereas, A. B. of said County, has this day made complaint and information on oath before me J. T., a Justice of the said County, that Frank, a slave, (or *free negro,* as the case may be,) on the —— day of ——— 18—, in said County, did feloniously take away one E. F., against her will, (she the said E. F. being a white female,) with intent to defile her: These are, therefore, to command you, in the name of the Commonwealth of Virginia, forthwith to apprehend the said Frank, and bring him before me or some other Justice of the said County, to answer the said complaint, and to be farther dealt with according to law. Given under my hand and seal, this —— day of ——— 18—.

J. T., J. P. [L. S.]

(No. 11.)

Form of Warrant of Arrest for feloniously taking a slave out of a County to deprive the owner of him.

——— County, to wit:
To all or any one of the Constables of said County:

Whereas, A. B. of said County, has this day made complaint and information on oath before me J. T., a Justice of the said County, that C. D., on the —— day of ——— 18—, in said County, did feloniously carry and cause to be carried out of the County of ———, Frank, a slave, the property of him the said A. B., without his consent, with intent to defraud and deprive him the said A. B., of the said slave: These are, therefore, to command you, in the name of the Commonwealth of Virginia, forthwith to apprehend the said C. D., and bring him before me or some other Justice of the said County, to answer the said complaint, and to be farther dealt with according to law. Given under my hand and seal, this —— day of ——— 18—.

J. T., J. P. [L. S.]

(No. 12.)

Form of Warrant of Arrest against the master of a vessel for sailing beyond the limits of any County with a slave on board, without the consent of his master.

——— County, to wit:
To all or any one of the Constables of said County:

Whereas, A. B. of said County, has this day made complaint and information on oath before me J. T., a Justice of the said County, that C. D., on the —— day of ——— 18—, in said County, he the said C. D. being then the master of a certain vessel, called the ———, lying in the body of the said County, did feloniously have on board of said vessel, Frank, a slave, the property of said A. B., and did feloniously and without the consent of the said A. B., the owner of the said slave, go in the said vessel, beyond the limits of the said County, with the said slave on board of the said vessel: These are, therefore, to command you, in the name of the Commonwealth of Virginia, forthwith to apprehend the said C. D., and bring him before me or some other Justice of the said County, to answer the said complaint, and to be farther dealt with according to law. Given under my hand and seal, this —— day of ——— 18—.

J. T., J. P. [L. S.]

(No. 13.)

Form of Warrant of Arrest against a person travelling by land, for aiding a slave to make his escape.

────── County, to wit:
    To all or any one of the Constables of said County:

    Whereas, A. B. of said County, has this day made complaint and information on oath before me J. T., a Justice of the said County, that C. D., on the ────── day of ────── 18──, in said County, did feloniously, and without the consent of the said A. B., aid Frank, a slave, the property of said A. B., to escape out of the said County, he the said C. D. then travelling by land: These are, therefore, to command you, in the name of the Commonwealth of Virginia, forthwith to apprehend the said C. D., and bring him before me or some other Justice of the said County, to answer the said complaint, and to be farther dealt with according to law. Given under my hand and seal, this ────── day of ────── 18──.

                                                     J. T., *J. P.* [L. S.]

(No. 14.)

Form of Warrant of Arrest against the master of a vessel, for knowingly receiving a slave on board.

────── County, to wit:
    To all or any one of the Constables of said County:

    Whereas, A. B. of said County, has this day made complaint and information on oath before me J. T., a Justice of the said County, that C. D., on the ────── day of ────── 18──, in said County, he the said C. D. being then and there the master of a certain vessel, called the ──────, did knowingly and feloniously receive on board the said vessel, Frank, a runaway slave, owned by the said A. B., and permit the said Frank to remain on board said vessel without using proper efforts to apprehend the said slave: These are, therefore, to command you, in the name of the Commonwealth of Virginia, forthwith to apprehend the said C. D., and bring him before me or some other Justice of the said County, to answer the said complaint, and to be farther dealt with according to law. Given under my hand and seal, this ────── day of ────── 18──.

                                                     J. T., *J. P.* [L. S.]

(No. 15.)

Form of Warrant to search a vessel for a slave, feloniously carried from a County.

────── County, to wit:
    To X. Y., Constable of said County:

    Whereas, A. B. of said County, has this day made complaint on oath before me J. T., a Justice of the said County, that he has just cause to suspect and does believe, that C. D. did, on the ────── day of ────── 18──, take on board a certain vessel, called the ──────, then lying in the body of the said

County, a slave called Frank, owned by the said A. B., and that he the said C. D. did, on the said ―― day of ―――― 18―, feloniously carry or cause to be carried the said slave Frank, so owned by the said A. B., from the said County, without the consent of the said A. B., with intent to defraud and deprive the said A. B. of his said slave; and moreover, that the said slave is now harboured and concealed on board the said vessel: These are, therefore, in the name of the Commonwealth, to command you forthwith to pursue and board the said vessel, and on board the same diligently to search for the said slave Frank, and if he shall be found on such search, that you bring him, and also the body of the said C. D., before me or some other Justice of the said County, to answer the said complaint, and to be farther dealt with according to law. Given under my hand and seal, this ―― day of ―――― 18―.

J. T., J. P. [L. S.]

(No. 16.)

Form of Warrant of Arrest for aiding or advising a slave to abscond.

―――― County, to wit:

To all or any one of the Constables of said County:

Whereas, A. B. of said County, has this day made complaint and information on oath before me J. T., a Justice of the said County, that C. D., on the ―― day of ―――― 18―, in said County, did feloniously aid Frank, a slave, to abscond from the said A. B., his master, by then and there procuring for and delivering to him the said Frank a pass (or *register*, or other writing, or *furnishing to the said slave money, clothes, provisions*, or whatever else was furnished, for the purpose of enabling the said slave to abscond:) These are, therefore, to command you, in the name of the Commonwealth of Virginia, forthwith to apprehend the said C. D., and bring him before me or some other Justice of the said County, to answer the said complaint, and to be farther dealt with according to law. Given under my hand and seal, this ―― day of ―――― 18―.

J. T., J. P. [L. S.]

[If the offence be for advising a slave to abscond, say: "did feloniously advise Frank, a slave, to abscond from the said A. B., his master."

(No. 17.)

Form of Warrant of Arrest against the keeper of a ferry or bridge, for knowingly permitting a slave to pass, whereby he escaped from the service of his master.

―――― County, to wit:

To all or any one of the Constables of said County:

Whereas, A. B. of said County, has this day made complaint and information on oath before me J. T., a Justice of the said County, that C. D., on the ―― day of ―――― 18―, in said County, he the said C. D. being the owner of a ferry (or *bridge* across the Ohio river, a water course which separates this Commonwealth from the State of Ohio,) did knowingly and feloniously permit Frank, a slave, the property of the said A. B., to pass across the said river at the said ferry, (or *bridge*,) without the consent of the said A. B., the master of the said slave, whereby the said slave made his escape from the service of the said A. B. : These are, therefore, to command you, in the name of the Commonwealth of Virginia, forthwith to apprehend the said C. D., and bring him before me or some other Justice of the said County, to answer the said complaint, and to be farther dealt with according to law. Given under my hand and seal, this —— day of ———— 18—.

J. T., J. P. [L. S.]

(No. 18.)

Form of Warrant of Arrest against a free negro, for delivering to a slave a copy of his register.

———— County, to wit:

To all or any one of the Constables of said County :

Whereas, A. B. of said County, has this day made complaint and information on oath before me J. T., a Justice of the said County, that C. D., on the —— day of ———— 18—, in said County, he the said C. D. being a free negro, did feloniously deliver to Frank, a slave, the property of the said A. B., a copy of the register of the freedom of him the said C. D., a free negro: These are, therefore, to command you, in the name of the Commonwealth of Virginia, forthwith to apprehend the said C. D., and bring him before me or some other Justice of the said County, to answer the said complaint, and to be farther dealt with according to law. Given under my hand and seal, this —— day of ———— 18—.

J. T., J. P. [L. S.]

(No. 19.)

Form of Warrant of Arrest for maintaining that owners have not right of property in slaves.

———— County, to wit:

To all or any one of the Constables of said County :

Whereas, A. B. of said County, has this day made complaint and information on oath before me J. T., a Justice of the said County, that C. D., on the —— day of ———— 18—, in said County, unlawfully did maintain, by speaking, (or *by writing,*) that the owners of slaves in this Commonwealth have not the right of property in the said slaves, by declaring and saying to others, (here state the substance of what was said:) These are, therefore, to command you, in the name of the Commonwealth of Virginia, forthwith to apprehend the said C. D., and bring him before me or some other Justice of the said County, to answer the said complaint, and to be farther dealt with according to law. Given under my hand and seal, this —— day of ———— 18—.

J. T., J. P. [L. S.]

(No. 20.)

Form of Warrant of Arrest for knowingly circulating pamphlets, &c. denying the right of the master to property in slaves, with intent to aid the purposes of such pamphlet.

—— County, to wit:
  To all or any one of the Constables of said County:

Whereas, A. B. of said County, has this day made complaint and information on oath before me J. T., a Justice of the said County, that C. D., on the —— day of ——— 18—, in said County, did feloniously knowingly circulate a certain printed book, printed with intent to advise and incite negroes to rebel and make insurrection in this Commonwealth, with intent to aid the purposes of the said book: These are, therefore, to command you, in the name of the Commonwealth of Virginia, forthwith to apprehend the said C. D., and bring him before me or some other Justice of the said County, to answer the said complaint, and to be farther dealt with according to law. Given under my hand and seal, this —— day of ——— 18—.

J. T., J. P. [L. S.]

(No. 21.)

Form of Warrant of Arrest against a subscriber for an incendiary pamphlet, who receives it to aid abolitionists.

—— County, to wit:
  To X. Y., Constable of the said County:

Whereas, A. B., Postmaster at ———, in the said County, has this day given information on oath to me J. T., a Justice of the said County, that on the —— day of ——— 18—, a certain pamphlet, entitled (set out the title,) written and printed with intent to advise and incite negroes in this Commonwealth to rebel and make insurrection, and denying the right of masters to property in their slaves, and inculcating the duty of resistance to such rights, was received through the medium of the mail at his office, as Postmaster in the said County, directed to C. D.: and whereas it appears to me by the evidence of A. B. on oath, that the said C. D. subscribed for the said pamphlet, well knowing its character and tendency, with intention feloniously to circulate the same, and thereby to aid the purposes of abolitionists: These are, therefore, to command you, in the name of the Commonwealth of Virginia, forthwith to apprehend the said C. D., and bring him before me or some other Justice of the said County, to answer for the said offence, and to be farther dealt with according to law. Given under my hand and seal, this —— day of ——— 18—.

J. T., J. P. [L. S.]

(No. 22.)

Form of the Recognizance to appear before the Superior Court to answer for the above offence.

—— County, to wit:

Be it remembered, that on the —— day of ——— 18—, A. B. and C. D. of the said County, came before me J. T., a Justice of the said County, and severally and respectively acknowledged themselves to be indebted to the Commonwealth of Virginia, in manner and form following, that is to say: The said A. B. in the sum of ——— dollars, good and lawful money of the United States, and the said C. D. in the sum of ——— dollars, of like good and lawful money, to be respectively made and levied of their several goods and chattels, lands and tenements, to the use of the Commonwealth of Virginia, if the said A. B. shall make default in the performance of the condition underwritten.

The condition of the above recognizance is such, that whereas the above bound C. D. has this day been brought before me, J. T., a Justice of the said County, charged upon the oath of A. B., with having subscribed for a certain pamphlet, entitled (set out the title,) and which said pamphlet was written and printed with an intent to advise and incite negroes within this Commonwealth, to rebel and make insurrection, and to deny the rights of masters to property in their slaves, and to inculcate the duty of resistance to such rights; and which said pamphlet was received by A. B., postmaster at ———, in the said County, through the medium of the mail, directed to the said C. D., he the said C. D. well knowing the character and tendency of the said pamphlet at the time he subscribed for the same, and intending thereby to aid the purposes of abolitionists: Now, if the said C. D. shall personally appear before the Circuit Court of the said County, at the Courthouse thereof, on the first day of the next term thereof, then and there to answer the Commonwealth, touching and concerning the said offence, and shall not depart thence without the leave of the said Court, then the above recognizance to be void, otherwise to remain in full force and virtue.

Taken and acknowledged before me, the day and date first above written.

J. T., J. P.

[NOTE.—If the party fail to enter into the recognizance, he should be committed to the jail of the Superior Court, to answer an indictment for the offence.]

(No. 23.)

Form of Warrant of Arrest for assembling with slaves to learn them to read and write, or for associating with an unlawful assembly of slaves.

—— County, to wit:

To all or any one of the Constables of the said County:

Whereas, A. B. of the said County, has this day made complaint and information on oath before me J. T., a Justice of the said County, that C. D., a white person, on the —— day of ——— 18—, in said County, did unlawfully assemble with divers slaves, free negroes and mulattoes, for the purpose of instructing them to read and write, (or " did associate with divers slaves, free negroes and mulattoes, in an unlawful assembly thereof, to wit, an assembly of five at least:") These are, therefore, to command you, in the name of the Commonwealth of Virginia, forthwith to apprehend the said C. D., and bring him before me or some other Justice of the said County, to answer the said complaint, and to be farther dealt with according to law. Given under my hand and seal, this —— day of ——— 18—.

J. T., J. P. [L. S.]

(No. 24.)

Form of Recognizance to answer a prosecution for assembling with slaves to instruct them to read and write, or for associating with them in an unlawful assembly.

——— County, to wit:

Be it remembered, that on the —— day of ——— 18—, A. B. and C. D. of the said County, came before me J. T., a Justice of the said County, and severally and respectively acknowledged themselves to be indebted to the Commonwealth of Virginia, in the manner and form following, that is to say: The said A. B. in the sum of ——— dollars, and the said C. D. in the sum of ——— dollars, to be respectively made and levied of their several goods and chattels, lands and tenements, to the use of the Commonwealth of Virginia, if the said A. B. shall make default in performance of the condition underwritten.

The condition of the above recognizance is such, that if the above bound A. B., a white person, who now stands charged before me J. T., Justice of said County, with having, on the —— day of ——— 18—, in the said County, assembled with divers slaves, free negroes and mulattoes, for the purpose of instructing them to read and write, (or "with having, on the —— day of ——— 18—, in said County, associated with divers slaves, free negroes and mulattoes, in an unlawful assembly thereof,") shall make his personal appearance before the Circuit Court for the County of ————, on the first day of the next term thereof, then and there to answer the Commonwealth for the said offence, and not depart thence without the leave of the said Court, and shall in the mean time keep the peace and be of good behaviour towards all the citizens of this Commonwealth, then the above recognizance to be void, otherwise to remain in full force and virtue.

Taken and acknowledged before me, the day and year first above written.

J. T., J. P.

(No. 25.)

Form of Mittimus on failing to enter into the foregoing recognizance.

——— County, to wit:

To the Keeper of the Jail of the said County:

Receive into your jail and custody, A. B., a white person, charged before me J. T., Justice of said County, upon the oath of C. D., with having, on the —— day of ——— 18—, in said County, assembled with divers slaves, free negroes and mulattoes, for the purpose of instructing them to read and write; and him there safely keep until he shall thence be discharged by due course of law. Given under my hand and seal, this —— day of ——— 18—.

J. T., J. P. [L. S.]

(No. 26.)

Form of Warrant to disperse an unlawful assembly of slaves and free negroes assembled at night.

—— County, to wit:
To X. Y., Constable of the said County:

Whereas, A. B. has made complaint and information on oath before me J. T., a Justice of the said County, that divers slaves, the property of C. D., together with divers free negroes, to wit, two or more, are now, in the night time, assembled together in a certain house, (describe what house,) on the plantation or lot of C. D., in the said County: These are, therefore, to command you, in the name of the Commonwealth, forthwith to enter into the said house and disperse the said unlawful assembly, and to apprehend such slaves and free negroes as you may then find in the night time unlawfully assembled there, and bring them before me or some other Justice of the said County, to be farther dealt with according to law. Given under my hand and seal, this —— day of ——— 18—.

J. T., J. P. [L. S.]

(No. 27.)

Form of Summons against a party for suffering more than five slaves to be upon his lot or tenement at the same time.

Follow No. 16, under head of FINES AND CONVICTIONS, and describe the offence thus: "did suffer and permit more than five slaves, to wit, ten slaves, not his own, to be and remain upon his lot and tenement at the same time."

(No. 28.)

Form of Summons against a party for knowingly permitting a slave belonging to another person, to be and remain more than four hours upon his lot and tenement.

Follow No. 16, under head of FINES AND CONVICTIONS, and describe the offence thus: "did knowingly permit Jack, a slave, the property of A. B., to be and remain on his lot and tenement above four hours at one time, without the consent of the said A. B., the owner of the said slave."

(No. 29.)

Form of Warrant to arrest a slave who is going at large by his master's permission.

—— County, to wit:
To X. Y., Constable of the said County:

Forasmuch as A. B. has this day complained on oath before me J. T., Justice of said County, that Frank, a slave, the property of C. D., and under whose control he is, is now going at large, and hiring himself out in said County for his own or his master's benefit, and with the permission of his master: These are to command you forthwith to arrest the said slave, and bring him before me or some other Justice of the said County, to be dealt with according to law. Given under my hand and seal, this —— day of ———— 18——.

J. T., J. P. [L. S.]

[Though the statute permits any private citizen, and enjoins it upon all officers, to arrest slaves going at large, without a warrant, cases may arise in which it would be proper to obtain a warrant, as where the person employing him were to protect him by keeping him shut within doors, the house could not be entered without a warrant. Where the slave is not taken in custody, the proceeding may be by summons against the master.]

(No. 30.)

Form of a Summons against a person for suffering an insane or infirm negro to go at large.

———— County, to wit:
  To X. Y., Constable of said County:

Whereas, complaint on oath has this day been made before me J. T., a Justice of said County, by A. B., that on the —— day of ———— 18—, in said County, C. D. did permit Jack, an insane slave, (or *an aged* or *infirm slave,*) then owned by the said C. D., (or *then under his control,*) to go at large in said County, without adequate provision for the support of the said slave: These are, therefore, to command you, in the name of the Commonwealth, to summon the said C. D., to appear at ———— in said County, on the —— day of ———— 18—, at —— o'clock in the —— noon, before me or such other Justice of said County, as may then be there, to hear the said complaint, to answer the same, and to be farther dealt with according to law. Given under my hand and seal, this —— day of ———— 18—.

J. T., J. P. [L. S.]

[NOTE.—In this case, the Justice should commit or recognize the party to answer an indictment, and the overseers of the poor should take charge of the slave. For the form of the recognizance, see No. 4, under that head. If the party should fail to appear to answer the summons, his appearance may be forced by warrant. See form of warrant, No. 18, under head of ARREST.]

(No. 31.)

Form of Commitment of a slave, for going at large and hiring himself out.

———— County, to wit:
  To the Keeper of the Jail of said County:

I command you to receive into your custody, Frank, a slave, who has been arrested and brought before me J. T., a Justice of said County, charged upon the oath of A. B., with going at large and hiring himself out (or *trading as a free man*) in said County, by the permission of C. D. his master, and who has the control of him, and him safely keep in your custody until he shall be thence discharged by due course of law. Given under my hand and seal, this —— day of ——— 18—.

J. T., J. P. [L. S.]

(No. 32.)

Form of a Recognizance to be entered into by the master of a slave, for his forthcoming, to abide the result of a prosecution for permitting him to go at large as a free man.

—— County, to wit:

Be it remembered, that on the —— day of ——— 18—, A. B. and C. D. personally came before me J. T., Justice of said County, and acknowledged themselves to owe to the Commonwealth of Virginia, that is to say: The said A. B. the sum of ——— dollars, and the said C. D. the sum of ——— dollars, to be respectively made and levied of their several goods and chattels, lands and tenements, to the use of the Commonwealth, if the said A. B. shall fail in performing the condition here underwritten.

The condition of the above recognizance is such, that whereas Frank, a slave, the property of the above bound A. B., and under his control, was [this day arrested and brought before me J. T., Justice as aforesaid, charged with going at large and hiring himself out (or *with going at large and trading as a free man*) in said County, with the permission of A. B. his master:] Now, if the above bound A. B. shall have his said slave Frank, forthcoming before the County Court of ———, on the first day of the next ——— term thereof, to abide the result of a prosecution to be instituted in said Court against the said A. B., for permitting his said slave, while under his control, to go at large and hire himself out (or *to go at large and trade as a free man*) in said County, then the above recognizance to be void, otherwise to remain in full force.

Taken and acknowledged before me, the day and year first above written.

J. T., J. P.

[If the slave has been already committed, change the above recognizance, by leaving out all in the brackets, and inserting this: "on the —— day of ——— 18—, (the date of the mittimus,) committed to the jail of said County, by the warrant of J. T., Justice of said County, charged with going at large and hiring himself out (or *trading as a free man*) in said County, by the permission of the said A. B.; and whereas the said slave has been this day delivered to the said A. B., upon his entering into the above recognizance."]

Form of Notice to Attorney for the Commonwealth, in the County Court of ———.

Sir,

I have this day committed to jail Frank, a slave, the property of A. B., for going at large and hiring himself out, by the permission of his master.

J. T., J. P.

—— day of ——— 18—.

☞ When a recognizance is given, the following notice is proper:

SIR,

I have this day recognized A. B., the master of Frank, a slave, for the forthcoming of said slave on the first day of the next ―――― term of the County Court, to abide the result of a prosecution against him, for permitting said slave to go at large and hire himself out.

J. T., J. P.

―――― day of ―――― 18―.

(No. 33.)

Form of Recognizance to be entered into by the owner of a slave, where the slave has been sentenced to be sold, for going at large as a free man.

―――― County, to wit:

Be it remembered, that on the ―――― day of ―――― in the year 18―, A. B. and C. D. of the said County, personally appeared before me J. T., Sheriff of the said County, and acknowledged themselves to owe to the Commonwealth of Virginia, that is to say: The said A. B. the sum of two hundred dollars, and the said C. D. the sum of two hundred dollars, good and lawful money of the United States, to be made and levied of their goods and chattels, lands and tenements, respectively, to the use of the Commonwealth, upon condition, if the said A. B. shall make default in the condition here underwritten.

The condition of the above recognizance is such, that whereas, at a County Court, held for the said County, on the ―――― day of ―――― 18―, the above named A. B. was, by the judgment of the said Court, convicted of a misdemeanor, in suffering and permitting his slave Frank, to trade as a free man, and to go at large and hire himself out in said County, and for the said offence, the said A. B. was adjudged by the said Court to pay a fine of ―――― dollars; for the payment whereof the said Court moreover adjudged, that the said slave Frank should be sold by the Sheriff of the said County, for the use of the Commonwealth; and whereas the said Sheriff has taken the said slave Frank, into his jail and custody, by virtue of the said judgment, that he may sell the said slave for the use of the Commonwealth; and whereas the said A. B., to prevent the sale of the said slave, has this day paid the said fine so adjudged by him to be paid, and all costs, jail fees and other expenses attending the prosecution, and now requires the said slave Frank to be discharged from the said jail: Now, if the said slave Frank shall not again be permitted by the said A. B. to trade as a free man, go at large, or hire himself out, then the above recognizance to be void, otherwise to remain in full force and virtue.

Taken and acknowledged before me, the day and year first above written.

J. T., *Sheriff.*

(No. 34.)

Form of Warrant of Arrest for bringing a free negro into this Commonwealth.

—— County, to wit:

To all or any one of the Constables of said County:

Whereas, A. B. of said County, has this day made complaint and information on oath before me J. T., a Justice of the said County, that C. D., on the —— day of —————— 18—, in said County, unlawfully did bring into this Commonwealth, a certain free negro, named Frank Cooper, he the said C. D. not then travelling in or through this Commonwealth with the said free negro in his employment as a servant, and he the said C. D. not then having brought the said free negro into this Commonwealth as a person employed on board of any vessel or steamboat, of which the said C. D. was then master: These are, therefore, to command you, in the name of the Commonwealth of Virginia, forthwith to apprehend the said C. D., and bring him before me or some other Justice of the said County, to answer the said complaint, and to be farther dealt with according to law. Given under my hand and seal, this —— day of —————— 18—.

J. T., J. P. [L. S.]

(No. 35.)

Form of Warrant to arrest a free negro, remaining in the Commonwealth contrary to law.

—— County, to wit:

To X. Y., Constable of the said County:

Whereas, A. B. has this day made complaint and information on oath before me J. T., Justice of said County, that Frank, a negro was emancipated since the first day of May 1806, and that he is now upwards of twenty-one years of age, and has remained in this Commonwealth more than one year after he attained the age of twenty-one years, without the permission of any Court authorized to grant the same, and is now in said County: These are, therefore, to command you, in the name of the Commonwealth, forthwith to apprehend the said Frank, and to bring him before me or some other Justice of the said County, to answer the said complaint, and to be farther dealt with according to law. Given under my hand and seal, this —— day of —————— 18—.

J. T., J. P. [L. S.]

[NOTE.—When brought before the Justice, the party should be committed or recognized to answer an indictment in the County or Corporation Court. For form of mittimus, see No. 9, under head of ARREST, and for recognizance, see No. 4, under head of RECOGNIZANCE.]

(No. 36.)

Form of Bond to be given by free negro, not entitled to residence, to leave the Commonwealth.

$ 100.

Know all men by these presents, that we, A. B. and C. D., are held and firmly bound to the Commonwealth of Virginia, in the just and full sum of one hundred dollars, good and lawful money of the United States, to be paid unto the said Commonwealth; to which payment, well and truly to be made, we bind ourselves jointly and severally, and each of our joint and several heirs, executors and administrators, firmly by these presents. Sealed with our seals, and dated this —— day of —— 18—.

The condition of the above obligation is such, that whereas the above bound A. B., a free negro, is not entitled to residence in this Commonwealth, but has come into, and is now remaining in the County of ——, and has been brought before J. T., a Justice of the said County, to be dealt with according to the statute in that case made and provided: Now, if the above bound A. B., do and shall depart from this Commonwealth within ten days from the date hereof, and shall not return within the limits of this Commonwealth, then the above obligation to be void, otherwise to remain in full force and virtue.

A. B. [L. s.]
C. D. [L. s.]

Teste,
    J. T., J. P.

(No. 37.)

Form of Summons for selling ardent spirits to slave, without written consent of his master.

Follow No. 16, under head of FINES AND CONVICTIONS, and describe the offence thus: "sell ardent spirits to Jack, a slave, the property of C. D., without the written consent of the said C. D., his master."

(No. 38.)

Form of Summons for buying or receiving, or selling any article, other than ardent spirits, to a slave, without consent of his master.

Follow No. 16, under head of FINES AND CONVICTIONS, and describe the offence thus: "did buy of, (or *receive from*, or *sell to*, as the case may be,) Jack, a slave, the property of A. B., one bushel of corn, without the consent of the said A. B., his master."

(No. 39.)

Form of Summons against the master of a slave, for giving written permission to buy and sell liquor.

Follow No. 16, under head of FINES AND CONVICTIONS, and describe the offence thus: "give to Jack, a slave, (of whom the said C. D. was then master,) written permission to obtain intoxicating liquors, with intent that the said slave should thereafter sell, barter or trade the same."

(No. 40.)

Form of Recognizance of good behaviour, to be entered into by a person convicted of dealing with a negro.

—— County, to wit:

Be it remembered, that on this —— day of —— 18—, A. B. and C. D. of the said County, personally came before me J. T., a Justice of the said

County, and severally acknowledged themselves to owe to the Commonwealth of Virginia; that is to say, the said A. B. the sum of —— dollars, and the said C. D. the sum of —— dollars, to be respectively made and levied of their several goods and chattels, lands and tenements, if he the said C. D. shall make default in the performance of the condition underwritten.

The condition of the above recognizance is such, that whereas the above bound A. B. was, the day and year first above written, convicted before J. T., Justice of said County, of the offence of (here state the offence, as for instance, "selling ardent spirits to Jack, a slave, the property of E. F., without the written consent of the said E. F. his master," or "of buying of, or receiving from Jack, the property of E. F., one hog, without the consent of the said E. F. his master:") Now, if the above bound A. B., do and shall be of *good behaviour* towards all the citizens of this Commonwealth, for the term of one year now next ensuing, then the above recognizance is to be void, otherwise to remain in full force.

Taken and acknowledged before me, the day and year above written.

J. T., J. P.

[Note.—If the party fail to enter into the recognizance, the Justice should commit him. See form of mittimus, under head of SURETY OF THE PEACE.]

(No. 41.)

Form of Warrant against a party for harbouring or employing a slave, without consent of master.

Follow No. 5, under head of WARRANTS—(*Civil*,) and describe the cause of warrant thus: " for harbouring (or *employing*) Jack, a slave, the property of C. D., for —— days, without the consent of the said C. D. his master."

(No. 42.)

Form of Warrant for employing a free negro, without his register.

Follow No. 5, under head of WARRANTS, and describe the cause of warrant thus: " for employing E. F., a free negro, who at the time he was so employed, had not, according to law, an attested copy of his register, as a free negro."

(No. 43.)

Form of Summons against a person for suffering more than five slaves to be upon his lot or tenement at the same time.

——— County, to wit:

To X. Y., *Constable of the said County:*

Whereas, complaint on oath has this day been made before me J. T., a Justice of said County, by A. B., that on the —— day of —— 18—, in said County, C. D. did suffer and permit more than five slaves, to wit, ten slaves, not his own, to be and remain upon his lot and tenement at the same time: These are, therefore, to command you, in the name of the Commonwealth, to summon the said C. D. to appear at —— in said County, on the —— day of —————— 18—, at —— o'clock in the —————— noon, before me or such other Justice of said County, as may then be there, to hear the said complaint, to answer the same, and to be farther dealt with according to law. Given under my hand and seal, this —— day of —————— 18—.

J. T., J. P. [L. S.]

(No. 44.)

Form of Summons against a person for knowingly permitting a slave, belonging to another person, to be and remain more than four hours upon his lot and tenement.

—————— County, to wit:

To X. Y., *Constable of the said County:*

Whereas, complaint on oath has this day been made before me J. T., a Justice of said County, by A. B., that on the —— day of —————— 18—, in said County, C. D. did knowingly permit Jack, a slave, the property of A. B., to be and remain on his lot and tenement above four hours at one time, without the consent of A. B. the owner of the said slave: These are, therefore, to command you, in the name of the Commonwealth, to summon the said C. D. to appear at —————— in said County, on the —— day of —————— 18—, at —— o'clock in the —————— noon, before me or such other Justice of said County, as may then be there, to hear the said complaint, to answer the same, and to be farther dealt with according to law. Given under my hand and seal, this —— day of —————— 18—.

J. T., J. P. [L. S.]

(No. 45.)

Form of Mittimus, Certificate and Recognizance.

In any case of felony under this chapter, where no special form is given: For form of mittimus, certificate to Clerk, recognizance of bail and of witness, see from No. 4 to No. 8, under head of ARREST, page 74, 75; but if special session of examining Court is had, for recognizance of bail and witness, see Nos. 3 and 4, under head of COURTS: For forms of proceedings after arrest to answer an indictment for a misdemeanor, where no special form is given in this chapter, for form of mittimus, certificate and recognizance, see from No. 9 to No. 13, under head of ARREST. If the prisoner be a white person, or if he be a free negro, charged with homicide of any grade, or with any offence punishable with death, he must be committed for examination. For all other felonies by free negroes, and in all cases of felony by slaves, the prisoner must be committed for trial.

(No. 1.)

Form of an Indictment for advising or aiding a slave to abscond.

—————— Judicial Circuit, —————— County, to wit: In the Circuit Court of the said County. } The grand jurors of the Commonwealth of Virginia, in and for the body of the County of ——————, and now attending the said Court, upon their oath present, that S. A. S., late of the County of ——————, on the —— day of —————— in the year of our Lord one thousand eight hundred and ——————, in the County aforesaid, and within the jurisdiction of the Circuit Court of the said County, unlawfully and feloniously did advise, entice and persuade a certain slave named Alfred, the property of one G. O., to abscond from his master, the said G. O., with intent in so doing, then and there to defraud and deprive the said G. O. of his said slave Alfred, against the peace and dignity of the Commonwealth of Virginia.

2d count. And the jurors aforesaid, upon their oath aforesaid, do farther present, that the said S. A. S. afterwards, to wit, on the said ——— day of ——— in the year one thousand eight hundred and ———, at the County aforesaid, and within the jurisdiction aforesaid, did unlawfully and feloniously aid a certain other slave named Alfred, the property of the said G. O., to abscond from his master the said G. O., by then and there putting and placing, and causing to be put and placed, the said slave named Alfred, into a certain box, and concealing the said slave named Alfred, in the said box, and by then and there carrying, and causing to be carried and transported, the said box, with the said slave therein concealed, to the depot of the Richmond, Fredericksburg and Potomac Railroad Company, in said County, with intent in so doing, then and there, that the said slave named Alfred, then and there therein contained, and so concealed as aforesaid, should be carried and transported from thence, upon the railroad of the said Company, out of the Commonwealth of Virginia, against the peace and dignity of the Commonwealth of Virginia.

[For indictment against free negro for rape upon white person, see RAPE.]

(No. 2.)

Form of Presentment against a free negro, for remaining in the Commonwealth contrary to law.

In the County Court of ——— County:

The jurors of the Commonwealth of Virginia, in and for the body of the said County, upon their oath, present A. B., a free negro, for this, that he the said A. B. was emancipated from slavery since the first day of May, in the year of Christ one thousand eight hundred and six, and that he the said A. B. was, to wit, on the ——— day of ——— in the year of Christ one thousand eight hundred and ———, found in the County of ———, upwards of twenty-one years old, and that he the said A. B. has remained in the Commonwealth of Virginia more than twelve months since his right to freedom accrued, and more than twelve months since he attained the age of twenty-one years, without any permission from the County Court of the said County where he now resides, to remain in the Commonwealth of Virginia, and to reside in the said County, contrary to the statute in that case made and provided, and against the peace and dignity of the Commonwealth of Virginia.

This presentment is made upon the information and evidence of C. D., a witness called on by the Court, sworn in Court, and sent by the Court to the grand jury to give evidence.

A. P., *Foreman.*

(No. 3.)

Form of same, for permitting a slave to go at large.

We present A. B. for this, that he did, on the ——— day of ——— 18—, in said County, permit John, a slave, then under his control, to go at large in the said County, and hire himself out contrary to law, against the peace and dignity of the Commonwealth of Virginia.

This presentment is made, &c. (conclude as No. 2.)

CHAPTER LXXII.

NOTICES AND MOTIONS.

How notices are served.

BY SEC. 1, CHAP. 167. A notice, no particular mode of serving which is prescribed, may be served by delivering a copy thereof in writing to the party or person; or if he be not found at his usual place of abode, by delivering such copy and giving information of its purport to his wife or any white person found there, who is a member of his family, and above the age of sixteen years, or if neither he nor his wife, nor any such white person be found there, by leaving such copy posted at the front door of said place of abode. Any Sheriff or Sergeant thereto required, shall serve a notice within his bailiwick, and make return of the manner and time of service; for a failure so to do, he shall forfeit twenty dollars. Such return, or a similar return by any other person who verifies it by affidavit, shall be evidence of the manner and time of service.

BY SEC. 2. Any such notice to a person not residing in Virginia, may be served by the publication thereof once a week, for four successive weeks, in a newspaper printed in this State.

What notice must be given for judgments.

BY SEC. 3. In any case wherein there may be judgment or decree for money on motion, such motion shall be, after ten days notice, unless some other time be specified in the section giving such motion.

Motions for judgments, upon what and where made.

BY SEC. 4. The court to which, or in or to whose Clerk or office any bond taken by an officer or given by any Sheriff, Sergeant or Constable, is required to be returned, filed or recorded, may, on motion of any person, give judgment for so much money as he is entitled by virtue of such bond to recover by action.

BY SEC. 5. Any person entitled to recover money by action on any contract, may, on motion before any court which would have jurisdiction in an action otherwise than under the second section of the 169th chapter, obtain judgment for such money after sixty days notice, which notice shall be returned to the Clerk's office of such court forty days before the motion is heard. A motion under this section, which is docketed under the first section of chapter 177, shall not be discontinued by reason of no order of continuance being entered in it from one day to another or from term to term.

By Sec. 6. A person entitled to obtain judgment for money, on motion, may, as to any, or the personal representatives of any, person liable for such money, move severally against each, or jointly against all, or jointly against any intermediate number; and when notice of his motion is not served on all of those to whom it is directed, judgment may nevertheless be given against so many of those liable, as shall appear to have been served with the notice. Such motions may be made from time to time, until there is judgment against every person liable, or his personal representative.

By Sec. 7. On a motion when an issue of fact is joined and either party desire it, or when in the opinion of the court it is proper, a jury shall be empanneled, unless the case be one in which the recovery is limited to an amount not greater than twenty dollars, exclusive of interest.

Form of notices for judgments for money due by contract.

This mode of recovering judgments is an innovation upon the long practice of the State, and apprehending that a rigid construction of the statute will be adopted, the following forms are made to embrace all the substantial requisites of a declaration in a suit at law.

(No. 1.)

Form of Notice for judgment on open account, for goods sold.

——— day of ——— 18—.

To A. B.:

Take notice, that on the ——— day of ——— 18—, I shall move the County Court of ———, (or *the Circuit Court of the County of* ———,) which will then be in session, for a judgment against you, for the sum of ——— dollars, [the price and value of goods sold and delivered you by me at your request,] according to the account hereto annexed, and for which you promised to pay me.

C. D.

(No. 2.)

Form of same, for work done and materials found.

Follow No. 1, leaving out what is in the brackets, and inserting this: "for the price and value of work done by me for you, and materials provided by me for doing the same, at your request."

C. D.

(No. 3.)

Form of same, for money lent.

Follow No. 1, leaving out what is in the brackets, and inserting this: "for money lent you by me, at your request."

(No. 4.)

Form of same, for money paid by one person for another.

Follow No. 1, leaving out what is in the brackets, and inserting this: "for money paid C. D. for you by me, and at your request."

(No. 5.)

Form of same, for money received by one person for the use of another.

Follow No. 1, leaving out all after "dollars," and concluding thus: "for money which you received for my use of C. D., according to the annexed account."

[The foregoing forms may be given when the items in the account are all of the same character, but it often occurs, that an account is made up of items of a different character. In such cases, the following form should be adopted:]

(No. 6.)

Form of Notice for judgment on an open account, composed of items differing in character.

To A. B.:

Take notice, that I shall, on the —— day of —— 18—, move the County Court of —— County, (or *the Circuit Court of —— County,*) for judgment against you, for the sum of —— dollars, which you owe me for goods sold and delivered you by me, at your request, and for the farther sum of —— dollars, which you owe me for work done by me for you, and for materials provided by me in doing the same, and at your request; and for the farther sum of —— dollars, for money lent and for money paid for your use and at your request, and for money also had and received by you for my use and benefit. And for the farther sum of —— dollars, found to be due me by you, on an account stated between us. The items of which several sums, are specified in the account hereto annexed; and which several sums you promised to pay me, but have failed to do so.

C. D.

—— day of —— 18—.

(No. 7.)

Form of Notice for judgment on a promissory note, by the payee against the maker.

To *A. B.*:

Whereas you, on the —— day of ——— 18—, at ———, made your note in writing, signed with your name in your handwriting, and delivered the same to me, and thereby promised to pay to me the sum of $ ——— on demand, (or at whatever time the note specifies for the payment,) for value received, and which you have not yet paid, although requested to do so, you will take notice, that I shall, on the —— day of ——— 18—, move the County Court of ———, (or *the Circuit Court of the County of* ———,) for judgment and award of execution against you, for the said sum of $ ———, with interest thereon, according to law.

J. S.

—— day of ——— 18—.

(No. 8.)

Form of Notice by an endorsee against the maker and an endorser of a negotiable note.

To *A. B. and C. D.*:

Take notice, that whereas you, A. B., did, on the —— day of ———, at ———, make your note, bearing date on that day, whereby you promised to pay to the said C. D. or order, —— days after the date of said note, $ ——, for value received, negotiable and payable at the ——— Bank of Virginia, which note is signed by you, the said A. B., in your handwriting; and whereas you, the said C. D. did, thereafter, and before the money mentioned in the said note was due and payable, by your endorsement on the back thereof, made in your own handwriting, transfer and deliver the same to me; and whereas the said note was, on the —— day of ———, presented by me at the said bank for payment, and payment thereof was then demanded at the said bank, and there refused; and whereas the said note was, on the last mentioned day, protested for non-payment, and notice thereof given to you, the said C. D., on that day, the charges of which protest amounted to $ 2 25, and neither of which sums have either of you yet paid, I shall, therefore, on the —— day of ——— 18—, move the County Court of ————, (or *the Circuit Court of the County of* ————,) for judgment against you, for the said sum of $ ———, with interest thereon from the —— day of ——— 18—, (the day of the protest,) and for the said sum of $ 2 50.

J. S.

—— day of ——— 18—.

(No. 9.)

Form of Notice by endorsee against an endorser of a negotiable note.

To *A. B.*:

Take notice, that whereas C. D. did, at ————, on the —— day of ——— 18—, make his note in writing, signed with his name in his handwriting, bearing date on that day, whereby he promised to pay to you the said A. B. or order, $ 100, sixty days after the date of said note, for value received, negotiable and payable at the ———— Bank of Virginia, and which said note you, thereafter, and before the money therein specified was due and payable, by your endorsement on the back thereof, in your handwriting, transferred and by you delivered to me for value by you received; and whereas the said note was, on the ———— day of ———— 18—, (the day of the date of the protest,) presented at the said bank by me for payment, and payment was then and there demanded and refused, whereupon the said note was, on the day last mentioned, protested for non-payment, and you had notice of said protest on that day, the costs of which protest are $ 2 25; and whereas the said sums of $ 100 and $ 2 25, still remain unpaid, I shall, therefore, move the County Court of ————, (or *the Circuit Court of the County of* ————,) on the ———— day of ———— 18—, for judgment against you, for the said sum of $ 100, with interest thereon from the ———— day of ———— 18—, (the date of the protest,) and for the said sum of $ 2 25, charges of protest.

J. S.

———— day of ———— 18—.

(No. 10.)

Form of Notice by an endorsee, who is not the payee, against the maker of a negotiable note.

To *A. B.*:

Take notice, that whereas you did, at ————, on the ———— day of ———— 18—, make your note in writing, signed with your name in your handwriting, bearing date on that day, and did thereby promise to pay, ———— days after the date thereof, to C. D. or order, $ ———— for value received, negotiable and payable at the ———— Bank of Virginia, which said note the said C. D., thereafter, and before the same became due, by his endorsement on the back thereof, made in his handwriting, transferred to me; and whereas the said note was presented at the said bank by me, on the ———— day of ———— 18—, for payment, and payment then and there demanded and refused, and the said note was then protested for non-payment, and notice thereof on that day given to the said C. D., the charges of which protest amount to $ 2 25, neither of which sums have yet been paid to me, I shall, therefore, move the County Court of ————, (or *the Circuit Court of* ———— *County*,) on the ———— day of ———— 18—, for judgment against you, for the said sum of $ ————, with interest thereon from the ———— day of ———— 18—, (the day of the date of the protest,) and the said sum of $ 2 25.

J. S.

———— day of ———— 18—.

(No. 11.)

Form of Notice by assignee of a bond against the assignor.

To *A. B.*:

Take notice, that whereas C. D. did, on the ———— day of ———— 18—, make his certain writing obligatory, signed with his name and sealed with his seal, whereby he promised to pay you the said A. B. $ 100, and which said writing obligatory, you, thereafter and before the money therein specified was paid, did assign and transfer to me; and whereas the said C. D. has failed to pay the sum of money in said writing obligatory mentioned, and is now notoriously insolvent and unable to pay the same, I shall, therefore, move the County Court of ———, (or *the Circuit Court of the County of* ———,) on the ——— day of ——— 18—, for judgment against you, for the said sum of $100, with interest from the ——— day of ——— 18—.

J. S.

(No. 12.)

Form of Notice against the obligor of bond, or other sealed instrument, for money due for the hire of a slave, and for failing to return him clothed at the end of the year.

To A. B.:

Whereas, you did, on the ——— day of ——— 18—, execute to me your writing obligatory, sealed with your seal and bearing date on that day, whereby you covenanted and agreed to pay me, on the first day of January, then next following, the sum of $75, for the hire of a slave named John, for that year; and moreover, by the said writing obligatory, promised and agreed to return the said slave to me at the end of the year, well clothed with a winter suit, and with a hat and blanket; and whereas you have failed either to pay the said sum of money, or to return the said negro so clothed, and with a hat and blanket, you will take notice, that I shall, on the ——— day of ——— 18—, move the County Court of ———, (or *the Circuit Court of the County of* ———,) for judgment against you, for the said sum of $75, with interest according to law, and for the sum of $15, as the price or value of said clothing, hat and blanket, or for such other sum therefor as the said Court shall think proper to allow for the same.

J. S.

(No. 13.)

Form of Notice for payment on a promissory note, by the payee against the executor of the maker.

To A. B., *Executor of the last will and testament of C. D.*:

Whereas, the said C. D. did, in his lifetime, to wit, on the ——— day of ——— 18—, make his certain note in writing, signed with his name in his handwriting, and deliver the same to me, whereby he promised to pay to me the sum of $———, on demand, (or at whatever time the note specifies for the payment,) for value received, and which sum the said C. D. did not in his lifetime pay, nor have you the said A. B., executor as aforesaid, since his death as yet paid, although requested to do so, you will take notice, that I shall, on the ——— day of ——— 18—, move the County Court of ———, (or *the Circuit Court of the County of* ———,) for judgment and award of execution against you, as executor of the said C. D., for the said sum of $———, with interest thereon according to law.

J. S.

(No. 14.)

Form of Notice by the obligee against the obligor of a bond, or other writing under seal, for payment of money.

To *A. B.* :

Whereas, you did, on the —— day of ——— 18—, execute to me your writing obligatory, dated on that day and sealed with your seal, whereby you bound yourself to pay to me, on or before the —— day of ——— 18—, (or —— *months after date*, or *on demand*, as the case may be,) the sum of $ ———, and which you have not done, you will take notice, that I shall, on the —— day of ——— 18—, move the County Court of the County of ———, (or *the Circuit Court of the County of* ———,) for judgment against you, for the said sum of $———, with interest according to law.

J. S.

(No. 15.)

Form of Notice for judgment by the drawer, who is the payee, against the acceptor of an inland bill of exchange.

To *A. B.* :

Whereas, I did, at ———, on the —— day of ——— 18—, draw my bill of exchange, bearing date on that day, directed to you at ———, whereby I requested you to pay to me or my order, —— days after the date thereof, (or —— *days after sight,*) the sum of —— dollars, which bill of exchange you thereafter accepted and promised to pay, by your acceptance thereof, in your proper handwriting; and whereas you have failed and still fail to pay me the said sum of money, although the time of payment has elapsed, you will take notice, that I shall, on the —— day of ——— 18—, move the County Court of ———, (or *the Circuit Court of the County of* ———,) for judgment against you, for the said sum of $———, with interest thereon according to law.

J. S.

The proof of service of notice may be by affidavit, in one or the other of the following forms:

(No. 16.)

Form of Affidavit of personal service.

—— County, to wit:

This day, X. Y. personally appeared before me, and made oath that he did, on the —— day of ——— 18—, deliver to A. B., the person to whom the foregoing notice is directed, a true copy thereof. As witness my hand, this —— day of ——— 18—.

J. T., J. P.

NOTICES AND MOTIONS. 475

(No. 17.)

Form of Affidavit of Service of Notice, when party not at home, and left with some person living with him.

—— County, to wit:

This day, X. Y. personally appeared before me J. T., a Justice of said County, and made oath, that on the —— day of —————— 18—, he went to the dwelling house of A. B., to whom the foregoing notice is addressed, where he then found C. D., a white person over the age of sixteen years, and that by enquiry of him, the said X. Y. ascertained that the said A. B. had gone from home and could not be found at his dwelling house, and that thereupon, the said X. Y. then and there delivered to the said C. D. a copy of the said notice, and explained to him the purport thereof. Given under my hand, this —— day of —————— 18—.

J. T., J. P.

(No. 18.)

Form of Affidavit of Service of Notice, by leaving copy at place of abode, upon finding no person there with whom to leave it.

—— County, to wit:

This day, X. Y. personally appeared before me, and made oath, that on the —— day of —————— 18—, he went to the dwelling house of A. B., to whom the foregoing notice is directed, and there found, upon enquiry, that he was not then at home, and that there was no white member of his family over the age of sixteen years then there, and that he then posted a true copy of the said notice at the front door of the said house. Given under my hand, this —— day of —————— 18—.

J. T., J. P.

CHAPTER LXXIII.

NUISANCES.

A public or common nuisance, is an offence against the public, either in doing a thing which tends to the annoyance of all the citizens of the State, or by neglecting to do a thing which it is the duty of the party to do, and which the public good requires.[1] For this offence, an indictment lies at Common Law, and it seems now to be settled, that any one may abate a common nuisance, though in doing it, only so much of the thing which causes the nuisance ought to be removed.[2] No length of time will legitimate a public nuisance.[3]

Lewdness and houses of ill fame, highways, bridges and rivers, being noticed elsewhere, it is proposed here, only to notice generally what is a public nuisance, and to furnish the necessary forms to guide the Justice in abating it.

The offending *qualities* of a nuisance, are in general, *smell, noise, danger, indecency* and *obstruction ;* and the existence of it as a *public* nuisance, depends upon the *number of persons annoyed by it*, which is a matter of fact to be judged of by a jury.[4] Thus it is, that all trades and manufactories which are set up in a *town*, and occasion either of the above inconveniences to the whole neighbourhood, or which are carried on so near a public highway as to cause the same inconvenience to persons lawfully passing along it, may be indicted as public nuisances; as the making of candles in a town, by boiling stinking stuff, which annoys the whole neighbourhood with stenches,[5] or the steeping skins in water, for tanning or other purposes, near a public highway, and also near several dwelling houses, by which the air thereabouts is corrupted, and is in its nature a nuisance to those who pass along the highway.[6]

To constitute a nuisance proceeding from a noxious trade, it is not necessary that the smell or vapour caused by it should be absolutely pernicious to *health;* it is sufficient if it affect the comfort of the neighbouring inhabitants.[7] But where a party sets up a noxious trade, remote from habitations and public roads, and new houses are afterwards built, and new roads constructed near it, the party is not guilty of a nuisance

---

(1) 1 Hawk. c. 75, § 1.
(2) 3 Burn J. P. 24th Edi. 579; 14 Wend. 250.
(3) 7 East 195; 3 Camp. 227, 398.
(4) 1 Burr. 333; 5 Rand. 691; 6 Rand. 726.
(5) Cro. Car. 510; 1 Hawk. c. 75, § 10.
(6) 1 Stra. 686.
(7) 1 Burr. 333; 2 C. & P. 484, in note.

for continuing his trade, although it be a nuisance to the new inhabitants and to persons passing the newly constructed road.(¹) Yet if the trade afterwards becomes more noxious, either from the manner in which, or the extent to which it is subsequently carried on, he is then liable for the increase of the mischief, and may be indicted for such nuisance.(²)

Making great noises in the night, to the disturbance of the neighbourhood,(³) and the keeping a bowling alley in a city, (⁴) are held to be indictable offences; but it is no offence to keep a billiard room, where no noise is allowed to disturb the neighbourhood.(⁵)

It is also a public nuisance as affecting health, for any common dealer in provisions, to sell unwholesome food, or to mix noxious ingredients in any thing, made and supplied for the food of man.(⁶) Any thing that is productive of *immediate* danger, or which causes reasonable terror to the inhabitants of a neighbourhood or to persons passing a highway, may be considered as a public nuisance, and therefore, although gunpowder be a necessary thing, yet if it be *negligently* kept in such quantity, and in such a place as to render it dangerous to residents of a neighbourhood or to persons passing along a street or highway, it will be a nuisance.(⁷) So, also, to permit a savage bull to go loose about public thoroughfares, or to let a fierce mastiff or bull-dog, that is used to bite people, go about unmuzzled, to the danger and terror of the neighbourhood, is a nuisance for which the owner may be indicted, if he knows the ferocity of the animal.(⁸)

It is a nuisance, *dangerous* to the public, for a person afflicted with an *infectious disorder*, to go about in the highways and other places of public resort, to the endangering the health and lives of others, and accordingly parties have been convicted for carrying children, infected with *small pox*, along the public highway where persons were passing.(⁹)

So, it is a principle of the Common Law, that whatever outrages decency, and is injurious to *public morals*, is a common nuisance and indictable as a misdemeanor;(¹⁰) and hence, the openly carrying on of scandalous and immoral trades, or keeping indecent brothels or houses of ill fame, gaming houses and disorderly places of resort, of any kind, is an indictable nuisance at Common Law,(¹¹) and in the case of houses of ill

---

(¹) Rex v. Cross, 2 C. & P. 483.
(²) R. v. Watts, M. & M. 281.
(³) 1 Str. 764.
(⁴) 5 Hill N. Y. Rep.
(⁵) 8 Wend. 139.
(⁶) R. v. Dixon, 3 M. & S. 117; see also, title HEALTH.
(⁷) 4 Burn J. P. 758; 1 John. R. 78.
(⁸) Deac. Cr. L. 952; 2 Ld. Ray. 1582.
(⁹) 4 M. & S. 73, 272.
(¹⁰) 1 Hawk. c. 5, § 4; 1 East P. C. c. 1, § 1.
(¹¹) Dickinson's Guide, by Talfourd, 283.

fame and gaming houses, the party is punishable under the statute. (See titles LEWDNESS and GAMING.)

It is held to be an indictable offence, as an outrage to decency, for a master to permit his slaves to pass about in public highways in a state of nakedness,(¹) and so, for any one to exhibit scandalous and indecent prints. (See title INDECENCY.)

Mere drunkenness is not an indictable offence at Common Law, but it becomes so by being open and exposed to public view,(²) so that, if a man be frequently and publicly drunk, he may be indicted as a common nuisance.(³)

A common tippling house, where free negroes and slaves are permitted to resort, as well on Sundays as on other days, for the purpose of tippling, is undoubtedly within the principle governing Common Law nuisances, as being against decency, religion and morality, and tending in other respects to public injury. These houses, unfortunately, are not uncommon in this State, and the Justice may do much, by the exercise of his Common Law powers, to suppress them. Upon a proper case made out, he should not only have the party arrested, to answer the offence as a Common Law nuisance before a jury, but require him to give security to be of good behaviour.

A monster, shown for money, is a common nuisance, for which an indictment lies.(⁴)

Independent of any statutory regulation upon the subject of roads, every unauthorized obstruction of a common highway, to the annoyance of the citizens generally, is a nuisance and indictable,(⁵) even though the highway be established by an erroneous judgment of a court.(⁶) If waggoners or the proprietors of stage coaches, suffer their waggons or coaches to stand on the side of a highway or in the public street, for the accommodation of their business or passengers, so as to obstruct for an unreasonable time the free use and passage of the street or highway, they may be indicted for a misdemeanor, although there be room for other carriages to pass on the opposite side of the street or highway.(⁷) (See ROADS.)

A grant will not be presumed, of a part of a public street, from lapse of time, so as to bar a prosecution for a nuisance;(⁸) nor will the ceasing to use a portion of a road, established by law, in consequence of having acquired by user a right to use for highway purposes a portion of the adjoining land, estop the State from asserting its claim to the old road; and such non-

---

(¹) 3 Humph. 203.
(²) Murphy 229.
(³) Id. and 1 Humph. 396.
(⁴) 3 Burn J. P. 57.
(⁵) 3 Camp. 227.

(⁶) 2 B. & B. 547.
(⁷) 3 Camp. 227; 6 East 427; 1 Russ. 319.
(⁸) 1 Whart. 469; Pick. 44.

user will be no defence in a prosecution for a nuisance for obstructing it.(¹)

All *navigable* rivers, as well above the flowing of the sea, as below it, are *public* rivers,(²) and are in the nature of public highways, which the public have a right to pass ;(³) and therefore a nuisance, occasioned to a public river by obstructing its navigation, is indictable.(⁴)

But this general rule is not to prohibit the erection of quays and wharves, even below low water mark in ports, for the loading and unloading of vessels. Such building is only a nuisance where it is a damage to the port and the navigation, and whether it be a nuisance or not, is a question of fact to be determined by the jury upon the evidence, and not a question of law(⁵) but in these cases, the presumption is against the defendant, who must shew that it is no impediment to navigation or detriment to the public,(⁶) and if the effect of such a wharf is to fill up the channel or divert the current, it is a nuisance.(⁷)

So, it is a common nuisance, to divert a part of a navigable stream, whereby the current is weakened and rendered incapable of carrying vessels of the same burthen that it could before.(⁸) But where an obstruction is occasioned in the navigation of a river, not by any default or misconduct of a party, but by accident and misfortune, (as where a vessel is sunk or wrecked in the channel, no indictment lies against the owner, nor can he be indicted for not removing it.(⁹)

Nuisances, like perjury, assume such a variety of forms, that it is difficult to make a selection of precedents for the use of Magistrates. Frequent, however, as these offences are, in one form or other, it rarely happens that a prosecution for a nuisance originates by a complaint to a Justice of the Peace, but by indictment or presentment. We shall therefore conclude this subject by referring the Justice to the titles LEWDNESS and INDECENCY, and by giving a few forms for his guide, as the general form of proceeding is the same in all, and those furnished may, without difficulty, be altered to suit any case likely to come before him.

(¹) 2 Humph. 543.
(²) Hale De Jure Maris, p. 9.
(³) 1 Hawk. c. 67, § 1.
(⁴) 5 Bac. Ab. Nuisance.
(⁵) Hale De Portibus Maris 85.
(⁶) Thacker's Cr. Cas. 211.
(⁷) 5 Pick. 199.
(⁸) 1 Hawk. c. 75, § 11.
(⁹) R. *v.* Watts, 2 Esp. 675.

(No. 1.)

Warrant for obstructing a highway.

——— County, to wit:
To X. Y., *Constable of the said County:*

Whereas, A. B. of the said County, hath this day made complaint and information on oath before me J. T., a Justice of the said County, that C. D., on the ——— day of ——— 18—, and on divers other days and times, before and afterwards, in the said County, unlawfully and injuriously ☞ did put and place, and caused to be put and placed, in and upon the common highway leading from ——— to ———, divers large pieces of timber and other material, and did unlawfully suffer the same there to be and remain from the said ——— day of ——— 18—, to this day, and doth now unlawfully suffer the same there to be and remain, to the great damage and common nuisance of all the citizens of this Commonwealth passing and repassing in, along and upon the said highway : ⌒ These are, therefore, in the name of the Commonwealth, to command you forthwith to apprehend the said C. D., and bring him before me or some other Justice of the said County, to be farther dealt with according to law. Given under my hand and seal, this ——— day of ——— 18—.

J. T., J. P. [L. S.]

(No. 2.)

Warrant for keeping a disorderly house generally.

Follow form No. 1, leaving out all between the hands, and in the place of it, say : " did keep and maintain, a certain common ill governed and disorderly house, and in the said house, for his own lucre and gain, certain persons, as well men as women, then and on the said other days and times, there unlawfully and willingly did cause and procure to come together ; and the said persons at unlawful times, as well in the night as in the day, then and on the said other days and times, there to be and remain, drinking and making a great noise and misbehaving themselves, unlawfully and wilfully did permit, and still doth permit, to the great damage and common nuisance of all the good people of this Commonwealth there residing, inhabiting and passing : These are, therefore," &c. (conclude as No. 1.)

(No. 3.)

Warrant for keeping a common gaming house.

Follow form No. 1, leaving out all between the hands, and in the place of it say : " did keep and maintain, and doth yet keep and maintain, a certain common gaming house, and did, on the said ——— day of ——— 18—, and on said divers other days and times, unlawfully and injuriously permit and suffer, and doth yet permit and suffer, divers idle and ill disposed persons to assemble and gather together in the said common gaming house, for the purpose of gaming, and did suffer and permit the said persons so assembled, unlawfully and injuriously to game in the said common gaming house, to the great damage and common nuisance of all the citizens of this Commonwealth : These are, therefore," &c. (conclude as No. 1.)

NUISANCES.

(No. 4.)

Form of Warrant against the keeper of a common tippling house, where free negroes and slaves assemble to tipple.

Follow form No. 1, leaving out all between the hands, and in the place of it, insert this : " did keep and maintain, and doth yet keep and maintain, a certain ill governed and disorderly house, and at the said house, then, and on the said other days and times, as well on Sunday as on other days, did unlawfully suffer and permit divers free negroes, and divers slaves, not belonging to him, to assemble and gather together, without the consent of the owner of the said slaves, and did permit and suffer the said free negroes and slaves, in the said house, at unlawful times, as well in the night as in the day, on the days and times aforesaid, there to be and remain, drinking, tippling, cursing, swearing, quarrelling, and otherwise misbehaving themselves, to the great damage and common nuisance of all the peaceable citizens of this Commonwealth there residing, inhabiting and passing : These are, therefore," &c. (conclude as No. 1.)

(No. 5.)

Form of Mittimus where a party is committed to answer an Indictment in the County Court for a misdemeanor.

—— County, to wit:

To X. Z., *Constable of said County, and to the Keeper of the Jail of the said County:*

These are to command you, the said Constable, in the name of the Commonwealth of Virginia, forthwith to convey and deliver into the custody of the keeper of the said jail, together with this warrant, the body of C. D., charged before me J. T., a Justice of the said County, on the oath of A. B., with a misdemeanor by him committed, in this, that the said C. D., on the —— day of —— in the year 18—, in the said County, (here describe the offence as in the warrant of arrest.) And you, the said keeper of the said jail, are hereby required to receive the said C. D. into your jail and custody, to answer an indictment to be preferred against him for the said offence, in the County Court of said County, and him there safely keep until he shall be discharged by due course of law. Given under my hand and seal, this —— day of —— in the year 18—.

J. T., *J. P.* [L. S.]

(No. 6.)

Form of Recognizance of Bail.

Turn to head of RECOGNIZANCE, and follow No. 4, and state the offence succinctly, for which the party is recognized.

(No. 7.)

Form of Certificate of the Commitment, or Letting to Bail, to be sent to the Clerk of the County Court.

—— County, to wit:
To the Clerk of the County Court of the said County:

I, J. T., a Justice of the said County, do hereby certify, that C. D. was this day committed to the jail of this County, by my warrant, (or *was this day admitted to bail by me,* as the case may be,) to answer an indictment to be preferred against him in the County Court of the said County, for a misdemeanor by him committed, in this, that he did, on the —— day of —— 18—, in said County, (here describe the offence as in the warrant of arrest.) Given under my hand, this —— day of —— 18—.

J. T., J. P.

(No. 8.)

Form of Recognizance of Witness to appear and give evidence to the Grand Jury upon the indictment.

Follow No. 5, under head of RECOGNIZANCE.

(No. 1.)

An Indictment for obstructing a highway.

—— County, to wit: } The jurors of the Commonwealth of Virginia, in and for the body of the County of ——, In the County Court of the said County. } and now attending the said Court, upon their oath present, that A. B., on the —— day of —— in the year one thousand eight hundred and ——, in the said County, did, unlawfully and injuriously, put and place, and caused to be put and placed, in and upon the common highway, leading from —— to ——, divers large pieces of timber and other material, and did unlawfully suffer the same there to be and remain, from the said —— day of —— 18—, to this day, and doth now unlawfully suffer the same there to be and remain, to the great damage and common nuisance of all the citizens of this Commonwealth, passing and repassing in, along and upon, the said highway, against the peace and dignity of the Commonwealth of Virginia.

(No. 2.)

An Indictment for keeping a disorderly house.

—— County, to wit: } The jurors of the Commonwealth of Virginia, in and for the body of the County of ——, In the County Court of the said County. } and now attending the said Court, upon their oath present that A. B., on the —— day of —— in the year one thousand eight hundred and ——, and on divers other days, in the said County, unlawfully and injuriously did keep and maintain, and doth yet keep and maintain, a certain common, ill governed and disorderly house, and in the said house, for his own lucre and gain, certain persons, as well men as women, then and on the said other days and times, there unlawfully and willingly did cause and procure to come together; and the said persons at unlawful times, as well in the night as in the day, then and on the said other days and times, there to be and remain, drinking and making a great noise, and misbehaving themselves, unlawfully and wilfully did permit, and still doth permit, to the great damage and common nuisance of all the good people of this Commonwealth there residing, inhabiting and passing, against the peace and dignity of the Commonwealth of Virginia.

(No. 3.)

An Indictment against the keeper of a common tippling house, where free negroes and slaves assemble to tipple.

———— County, to wit: In the County Court of the said County. } The jurors of the Commonwealth of Virginia, in and for the body of the County of ————, and now attending the said Court, upon their oath present, that A. B., on the ———— day of ————, in the year one thousand eight hundred and ————, in the said County, did keep and maintain, and yet doth keep and maintain, a certain ill governed and disorderly house, and at the said house, then and on the said other days and times, as well on Sunday as on other days, did unlawfully suffer and permit divers free negroes and divers slaves, not belonging to him, to assemble and gather together, without the consent of the owner of the said slaves, and did permit and suffer the said free negroes and slaves, in the said house, at unlawful times, as well in the night as in the day, on the days and times aforesaid, there to be and remain, drinking, tippling, cursing, swearing, quarrelling, and otherwise misbehaving themselves, to the great damage and common nuisance of all the peaceable citizens of this Commonwealth there residing, inhabiting and passing, against the peace and dignity of the Commonwealth of Virginia.

CHAPTER LXXIV.

OATHS.

By Sec. 7, Chap. 48. Any oath required to be taken, which is not of such a nature that it must be taken in court, may be administered and certified by a Justice of the Peace, unless otherwise provided.

CHAPTER LXXV.

OFFICERS.

By the Common Law, Constables are conservators of the peace, and, therefore, if any man shall make an affray or assault upon another in the presence of a Constable, or shall threaten to kill or hurt another, or do any act that has a tendency to a breach of the peace, a Constable may commit him to safe custody till he can carry him before a Justice, to find sureties for keeping the peace.([1])

Beside what Constables may do of their own authority, they are important agents in the administration of the law, both civil and criminal, and as executive officers, bear the same relation to Justices of the Peace, acting out of court, that Sheriffs do to courts of record. A Constable is bound to execute the warrant of a Justice, and where a statute authorizes a Justice to convict a person of crime and to levy the penalty, without saying more, the Constable is the proper officer to serve his warrant, and is indictable for disobeying it.([2])

As to a Constable's authority and duty generally, in arresting persons charged with crime, with or without warrant, see title ARREST. His jurisdiction in the execution of *criminal* warrants extends over his county. We are aware that a different opinion was entertained by the late learned author of the digest of the laws of Virginia. In a note to his valuable work, he says, "the plain rule, as laid down by writers on criminal law, and recognized by Best, J., and the court, in the case of King *v.* Weir and others, is; that when a warrant is directed to any one by name, he may execute it any where within the jurisdiction of the Magistrate, but where it is directed by the description of an officer, then the officer cannot act beyond the precincts of his office."([3]) This is undoubtedly the law of England, but as we conceive, has no application in this State, unless, indeed, the county, for this purpose, is to be considered as but one precinct. The learned author seems not to have adverted to the difference in the mode of appointing Constables in Virginia and in England. As before remarked, they are the proper officers of Justices of the Peace, and their authority to execute warrants of arrest, is a Common Law power, attaching necessarily upon their appoint-

---

([1]) 2 Hawk. P. C. c. 8.
([2]) 2 Hawk. P. C. c. 10.
([3]) Tate's Digest, note p. 156, citing R. *v.* Weir, 1 Barn. & Cress. 288.

ment to office. In England they are appointed in a variety of modes, sometimes by Justices out of court, sometimes according to the custom of particular places, and at others by the quarter sessions; yet the appointment is always made fo some particular ville, hamlet, wapentake or other similar division or particular district, and in no instance for a county.(¹) So that the appointment itself limits the authority of each to his proper district. In this State, Constables can only be appointed by the county and corporation courts, and are appointed to serve in the county, and when qualified, the Common Law authority to execute warrants of arrest in criminal cases attaches without restriction, and necessarily extends over the whole county. It is true that that branch of the statute, which confers on them the authority to *serve* civil warrants and to *levy* executions, limits their jurisdiction to particular districts, but this obviously applies to civil proceedings only.

In taking an inquisition of death, the Constable is the officer of the Coroner, and bound to execute his process and attend him during the investigation.

As to a Constable's duties in the execution of such civil process as a Justice out of court is authorized to issue, see ATTACHMENTS, RENTS, and WARRANTS FOR SMALL CLAIMS.

Sheriffs were, by the Common Law, chosen by the county, and are, by the Common Law, conservators of the peace, and the principal Sheriff might award process of the peace, and take surety for it.(²)

A Sheriff is bound to execute the criminal warrant of a Justice of the Peace when directed to him.(³)

Of the power of officers to command the aid of others in the execution of criminal process.

BY SEC. 13, CHAP. 194. If any officer wilfully and corruptly refuse to execute any lawful process requiring him to apprehend or confine a person convicted of or charged with an offence, or shall wilfully and corruptly omit, or delay to execute such process, whereby such person shall escape and go at large, such officer shall be confined in jail not more than six months and be fined not exceeding five hundred dollars.

BY SEC. 14. If a free person shall, on being required by any Sheriff or other officer, refuse or neglect to assist him in the execution of his office in a criminal case, or in the preservation of the peace, or the apprehending or securing of any

---

(¹) Wilcox on Constables, p. 1-5.
(²) 5 Burn J. P. 24 Edition by Chitwynd 233.
(³) Id.; 2 Hawk. c. 13, § 29.

person for a breach of the peace, or in any case of escape or rescue, he shall be confined in jail not more than six months and be fined not exceeding one hundred dollars.

BY SEC. 15. If a free person, being required by a Justice on view of a breach of the peace or other offence to bring him the offender, shall refuse or neglect to obey the Justice, he shall be punished as is provided in the preceding section for refusing to assist a Sheriff, and if the Justice declared himself to be such, or if he be known to the offender, ignorance of his office shall not be pleaded as an excuse.

As to what property may be distrained or levied on by a Sheriff or Constable, and the proceedings, after a distress or levy, *the statute provides:*

BY SEC. 33, CHAP. 49. No growing crop of any kind (not severed) shall be liable to distress or levy, except Indian corn, which may be taken at any time after the 15th day of October in any year.

BY SEC. 34. In the case of a husband or parent, there shall be exempt from such distress or levy, the following articles, or so much or so many thereof as the party may have: one cow, one bedstead, with a bed and necessary bedding for the same, six chairs, one table, six knives, six forks, six plates, two dishes, two basins, one pot, one oven, six pieces of wood or earthenware, one loom and its appurtenances, one spinning wheel, one pair of cards and one axe, five barrels of corn, five bushels of wheat or one barrel of flour, two hundred pounds of bacon or pork, and five dollars in value of forage or hay.

BY SEC. 35. Slaves shall not be distrained or levied upon without the debtor's consent, when there are other goods and chattels of such debtor sufficient for the purpose, which are shewn to the officer, and which it is in his power to take; and the officer shall in no case make an unreasonable distress or levy.

BY SEC. 36. For slaves, horses or any live stock distrained or levied upon, the officer shall provide sufficient sustenance while they remain in his possession. Nothing distrained or levied upon, shall be removed by him out of his county or corporation, unless where it is otherwise specially provided.

BY SEC. 37. In any case of goods or chattels, which an officer shall distrain or levy upon, otherwise than under an attachment, or which he may be directed to sell by an order of a Court, Judge or Justice, (unless such order prescribe a different course,) he shall fix upon a time and place for the sale thereof, and publish notice of the same at least ten days before the day of sale, at the door of the courthouse of his county or corporation, on a court day, and at some place near the residence of the owner, if he reside in the county or corporation. The officer shall, at the time and place so appointed, sell to the highest bidder, for cash, the said goods and chattels, or so much thereof as may be necessary.

By Sec. 38. If such goods and chattels be slaves, mules, work oxen or horses, they shall be sold at the courthouse of the county or corporation, between the hours of ten in the morning and four in the afternoon. The sale shall be on the first day of the term of the court thereof, next succeeding that at which they may be advertised, except where the parties shall, at or before the time for advertising the same, in writing authorize the officer to dispense with the provisions of this section, in which case the sale shall be according to the preceding section, and except also that sales of property taken within the town of *Lynchburg*, shall be in front of the market house in the said town.

By Sec. 39. When there is not time on the day appointed for any such sale, to complete the same, the sale may be adjourned from day to day, until it shall be completed.

For forthcoming, indemnifying and suspending bonds, where property is distrained or levied on, see title Bonds.

CHAPTER LXXVI.

OYSTERS AND TERRAPINS.

By Sec. 12, Chap. 101. If any person other than a citizen of this State, shall take oysters or terrapins in the waters thereof, or in the rivers Pocomoke and Potomac, he shall forfeit two hundred dollars. But this section shall not extend to a citizen of Maryland taking oysters or terrapins in the said mentioned rivers.

By Sec. 13. If any person shall take oysters with any other instrument than common oyster tongs with a bar or head not exceeding twenty-three inches in length, he shall forfeit one hundred dollars.

By Sec. 14. If any person shall export oysters not pickled or planted from the waters of this State, or shall take, catch, buy, sell, receive or deliver the same on board of a vessel for the purpose of exportation, after the first day of May, and before the first day of September in any year, he shall forfeit two hundred dollars for each offence.

By Sec. 15. If any person after the first day of May, and before the first day of October, in any year, shall catch, take, buy or sell oysters, from their natural beds or shoals, in quantities greater than fifty bushels in any one day, he shall forfeit twenty dollars for each offence.

By Sec. 16. If any person after the first day of May, and before the fifteenth day of October in any year, shall take terrapins, or take or disturb terrapin eggs, he shall forfeit one hundred dollars.

By Sec. 17. If any person shall take oysters for the purpose of converting into lime, he shall forfeit five hundred dollars. But this section shall not prevent the citizens of this State from taking oysters for such purpose from the broad water on the sea side.

By Sec. 18. If any person who is not an actual resident of this State, shall catch clams in the waters of York river or its tributaries, or on Egg Island Flats, he shall forfeit twenty dollars, and give a recognizance in a penalty not exceeding fifty dollars, that he will not catch clams contrary to law for one year, and he shall be committed to jail for fifteen days unless the judgment and recognizance be sooner paid and given.

As to the powers of a Justice in issuing warrants for violations of these provisions, (that is, in any provision of chapter 101, except as to clams,) and of the officer in executing them, see sections 23, 24, 25 and 26 of the same chapter, cited under the head of Fish. These sections apply equally to oysters. It will be there seen also that when the offender is alleged to be a non-resident, it is incumbent on him to prove his residence.

By Sec. 23, Chap. 192. If any person take or sell the planted oysters of another, otherwise than from the natural beds or shoals in the channel of a river or creek, he shall be fined not less than fifty nor more than one hundred dollars, and may at the discretion of the court, be confined in the jail not less than one nor more than six months.

(No. 1.)

Form of Warrant of Arrest against a non-resident of the Commonwealth for taking oysters in its waters.

—— County, to wit:

To all or any one of the Constables of said County:

Whereas, A. B. of said County, has this day made complaint and information on oath before me J. T., a Justice of the said County, that C. D., on the —— day of —————— 18—, in said County, did unlawfully take oysters, (or *terrapins*,) in the waters of this Commonwealth, to wit, in York river, he the said C. D. not then being a resident of this Commonwealth: These are, therefore, to command you, in the name of the Commonwealth of Virginia, forthwith to apprehend the said C. D., and bring him before me or some other Justice of the said County, to answer the said complaint, and to be farther dealt with according to law. Given under my hand and seal, this —— day of —————— 18—.

J. T., J. P. [L. S.]

(No. 2.)

Form of Warrant of Arrest for catching oysters with a drag or any other instrument other than oyster tongs.

——— County, to wit:
 To all or any one of the Constables of said County:
 Whereas, A. B. of said County, has this day made complaint and information on oath before me J. T., a Justice of the said County, that C. D., on the —— day of ———18—, in said County, did catch oysters within this Commonwealth, with oyster tongs with a bar or head exceeding twenty-three inches in length, (or *with a drag*, or whatever other instrument was used:) These are, therefore, to command you, in the name of the Commonwealth of Virginia, forthwith to apprehend the said C. D., and bring him before me or some other Justice of the said County, to answer the said complaint, and to be farther dealt with according to law. Given under my hand and seal, this —— day of ——— 18—.

J. T., J. P. [L. S.]

(No. 3.)

Form of Warrant of Arrest for exporting oysters, not pickled or planted, between first of May and September, without license.

——— County, to wit:
 To all or any one of the Constables of said County:
 Whereas, A. B. of said County, has this day made complaint and information on oath before me J. T., a Justice of the said County, that C. D., after the first day of May and before the first day of September 18—, to wit, on the —— day of ——— 18—, in said County, did unlawfully export oysters, not pickled or planted, from the waters of this Commonwealth, to wit, from the waters of (state from what waters,) in said County: These are, therefore, to command you, in the name of the Commonwealth of Virginia, forthwith to apprehend the said C. D., and bring him before me or some other Justice of the said County, to answer the said complaint, and to be farther dealt with according to law. Given under my hand and seal, this —— day of ——— 18—.

J. T., J. P. [L. S.]

(No. 4.)

Form of Warrant of Arrest for taking or catching oysters, for the purpose of exportation after the first day of May and before the first day of September.

——— County, to wit:
 To all or any one of the Constables of said County:
 Whereas, A. B. of said County, has this day made complaint and information on oath before me J. T., a Justice of the said County, that C. D., on the —— day of ——— 18—, in said County, did, after the first day of May and before the first day of September 18—, to wit, on the —— day of ——— 18—, in said County, unlawfully take, (or *catch*,) for the purpose of exportation, oysters not pickled or planted, from the waters of this Commonwealth, to wit, in the waters of (state what waters:) These are, therefore, to com-

mand you, in the name of the Commonwealth of Virginia, forthwith to apprehend the said C. D., and bring him before me or some other Justice of the said County, to answer the said complaint, and to be farther dealt with according to law. Given under my hand and seal, this —— day of ———— 18—.

J. T., J. P. [L. s.]

(No. 5.)

Form of Warrant of Arrest for buying or selling, receiving on board of a vessel, or delivering on board of a vessel, oysters not pickled or planted, for the purpose of exportation, after the first day of May and before the first day of September.

—— County, to wit:

To all or any one of the Constables of said County:

Whereas, A. B. of said County, has this day made complaint and information on oath before me J. T., a Justice of the said County, that C. D., on the —— day of ——— 18—, in said County, did, after the first day of May and before the first day of September 18—, to wit, on the —— day of ——— 18—, in said County, unlawfully buy, (or *sell*, or *receive on board of a vessel*, or *deliver on board of a vessel*,) for the purpose of exportation, oysters not pickled or planted, and which had been taken in the waters of this Commonwealth, to wit, in the waters of (state what waters:) These are, therefore, to command you, in the name of the Commonwealth of Virginia, forthwith to apprehend the said C. D., and bring him before me or some other Justice of the said County, to answer the said complaint, and to be farther dealt with according to law. Given under my hand and seal, this —— day of ——— 18—.

J. T., J. P. [L. s.]

(No. 6.)

Form of Warrant against non-resident persons, whose names are unknown, for taking or buying and receiving oysters on board of a vessel, for exportation.

—— County, to wit:

To X. Y., Constable of said County:

Whereas, A. B. has this day appeared before me J. T., a Justice of the said County, and made affidavit and complaint on oath, that certain persons, to wit, two (or any number,) men on board of a certain vessel now lying in the waters of —— river, in said County, and whose names are unknown to him, but who, he has good reason to suspect, and does believe, are non-residents of this Commonwealth, did, on this day, take oysters, not pickled or planted, from the waters of this Commonwealth, and in said County, (or *did on this day buy and receive on board of the said vessel in said County*,) for the purpose of exportation: These are, therefore, to command you, in the name of the Commonwealth of Virginia, forthwith to apprehend the said persons, whose names are not known, but who are on board the said vessel, and bring them before me or some other Justice of the said County, to answer the said complaint, and to be farther dealt with according to law. Given under my hand and seal, this —— day of ——— 18—.

J. T., J. P. [L. s.]

(No. 7.)

Form of Warrant of Arrest for catching, taking, buying or selling oysters from their natural beds and shoals, over fifty bushels in one day.

———— County, to wit:
 To all or any one of the Constables of said County:

Whereas, A. B. of the said County, has this day made complaint and information on oath before me J. T., a Justice of the said County, that C. D. did, after the first day of May and before the first day of October, to wit, on the —— day of ———— 18—, unlawfully catch, (or *take,* or *buy,* or *sell,*) in one day, oysters from their natural beds and shoals, in quantity greater than fifty bushels, to wit, ———— bushels: These are, therefore, to command you, in the name of the Commonwealth of Virginia, forthwith to apprehend the said C. D., and bring him before me or some other Justice of the said County, to answer the said complaint, and to be farther dealt with according to law. Given under my hand and seal, this —— day of ———— 18—.

J. T., J. P. [L. S.]

(No. 8.)

Form of Warrant of Arrest for taking terrapins, or taking or disturbing terrapin eggs, after the 1st of May and before the 15th day of October.

———— County, to wit:
 To all or any one of the Constables of said County:

Whereas, A. B. of said County, has this day made complaint and information on oath before me J. T., a Justice of the said County, that C. D., on the —— day of ———— 18—, in said County, did, after the first day of May and before the fifteenth day of October, to wit, on the —— day of ———— 18—, unlawfully take terrapins (or *take* or *disturb terrapin eggs:*) These are, therefore, to command you, in the name of the Commonwealth of Virginia, forthwith to apprehend the said C. D., and bring him before me or some other Justice of said County, to answer the said complaint, and to be farther dealt with according to law. Given under my hand and seal, this —— day of ———— 18—.

J. T., J. P. [L. S.]

(No. 9.)

Form of Warrant of Arrest for taking oysters for the purpose of converting into lime.

———— County, to wit:
 To all or any one of the Constables of said County:

Whereas, A. B. of said County, has this day made complaint and information on oath before me J. T., a Justice of the said County, that C. D., on the —— day of ———— 18—, in said County, did take oysters for the purpose of converting into lime, from the waters of ————, not of the broadwater on the seaside: These are, therefore, to command you, in the name of the Commonwealth of Virginia, forthwith to apprehend the said C. D., and bring him before me or some other Justice of the said County, to answer the said complaint, and to be farther dealt with according to law. Given under my hand and seal, this —— day of ———— 18—.

J. T., J. P. [L. S.]

(No. 10.)

Form of Warrant of Arrest for catching clams on York river, or on Egg Island Flats.

——— County, to wit:

To X. Y., *Constable of the said County:*

Whereas, A. B. has this day made affidavit and complaint on oath before me J. T., Justice of said County, that C. D. did, on the ——— day of ——— 18—, in said County, catch clams in the waters of York river, (or *in the waters of ———, a tributary of York river,* or *upon Egg Island Flats,*) he the said C. D. not then being an actual resident of this Commonwealth: These are, therefore, to command you, in the name of the Commonwealth, forthwith to apprehend the said C. D., and to bring him before me or some other Justice of the said County, to answer the said complaint, and to be farther dealt with according to law. Given under my hand and seal, this ——— day of ——— 18—.

J. T., J. P. [L. S.]

[NOTE.—The fine in this case being twenty dollars, the Justice must try it. For the mode of proceeding after the arrest, see FINES AND CONVICTIONS.]

(No. 11.)

Form of Warrant of Arrest for taking or selling planted oysters, under 23d section, chapter 192.

——— County, to wit:

To X. Y., *Constable of the said County:*

Whereas, A. B. has this day complained on oath before me J. T., Justice of said County, that C. D., on the ——— day of ——— 18—, in said County, did unlawfully take (or *sell*) the planted oysters of the said A. B., otherwise than from the natural shoals or beds of any river or creek: These are, therefore, to command you, in the name of the Commonwealth of Virginia, forthwith to apprehend the said C. D., and to bring him before me or some other Justice of the said County, to answer the said complaint, and to be farther dealt with according to law. Given under my hand and seal, this ——— day of ——— 18—.

J. T., J. P. [L. S.]

[NOTE.—This warrant is to be issued and executed as in any other case of misdemeanor, and not according to the provision of chapter 101, just referred to; but it is a principle of the Common Law, that if the name of an offender be unknown, he may be apprehended as a person whose name is unknown, and designating him by the best description that can be given of him under the circumstances. See ARREST.]

After the arrest, the form of proceeding, under the foregoing provisions, against resident citizens, is the same as in other cases of misdemeanor, and for form of commitment, see No. 9, under head of ARREST; for recognizance of bail and of witnesses, Nos. 4 and 5, under head of RECOGNIZANCE, and for certificate to the clerk, No. 10, under ARREST.

(No. 12.)

Form of Recognizance to answer an indictment for taking oysters by a non-resident.

Turn to the head of FISH, and follow No. 11.

[That form may be easily altered to suit any violations of the foregoing provisions, (except in relation to clams,) by describing the offence substantially according to the offence charged.]

(No. 13.)

Form of Commitment of non-resident, if he fail to give bail.

Follow No. 12, under head of FISH, and describe the offence as in the warrant of arrest, or according to the facts as proved.

(No. 14.)

Form of Recognizance of a non-resident, who has been convicted of catching clams in York river.

———— County, to wit:

Be it remembered, that on the ——— day of ——— in the year 18—, A. B. and C. D. personally came before me J. T., Justice of said County, and acknowledged themselves to owe to the Commonwealth of Virginia; the said A. B. the sum of ——— dollars, and the said C. D. the sum of ——— dollars, to be levied of their goods and chattels, lands and tenements, respectively, if the said A. B. shall make default of the condition underwritten.

The condition of the above recognizance is such, that whereas the above bound A. B. has been this day convicted before me J. T., Justice as aforesaid, of catching clams in the waters of York river, (or *on Egg Island Flats*,) contrary to law: Now, if the above bound A. B. shall not again, for one year next following the date hereof, catch clams contrary to law, then the above recognizance to be void, otherwise to remain in full force and virtue.

Taken and acknowledged before me,
the day and year first above written.

J. T., J. P.

CHAPTER LXXVII.

PATROLS.

By Sec. 1, Chap. 98. The county court of each county may, when necessary, appoint for a term not exceeding three months, one or more patrols, consisting of an officer, either commissioned or non-commissioned, who shall be captain of the patrol, and so many privates as it may think requisite to patrol and visit within such bounds as the court may prescribe, as often as they shall require, all negro quarters and other places suspected of having therein unlawful assemblies, or such slaves as may stroll from one plantation to another without permission.

By Sec. 2. Patrols to perform the same duty in any town having a corporation court, may be appointed by such court, which for that purpose may, from time to time, divide the militia of said town into wards or districts, and appoint one or more officers in each ward, to be denominated captains of patrol. The militia of such towns shall be exempt from patrol duty out of the jurisdictions of the towns.

By Sec. 3. Each captain of patrol and his squad, when on duty in such town, shall visit all parts of his ward or district, and shall patrol once every week, or oftener, if required by the court.

By Sec. 4. Such patrols shall take any persons found in an unlawful assembly, or any slaves found strolling as aforesaid, before the Justice nearest the place of capture, to be dealt with according to law; and said patrols, when in search of fire arms or other weapons, under warrant from a Justice, may force open the doors of free negroes or of slaves, in the absence of their masters, if access be denied.

By Sec. 5. Every captain or private of such patrol who shall, without sufficient excuse, fail in any duty so required, shall forfeit five dollars; such forfeitures shall be to the county or town to which such patrol may belong.

By Sec. 6. For every twelve hours service, each captain of a patrol shall be entitled to one dollar, and every other man of the patrol to seventy-five cents, which shall be chargeable on the county or town to which such patrol may belong.

By Sec. 7. Any Justice may order out patrols in his county or corporation, and appoint a captain for each patrol so ordered out by him, which may continue until the next term of the county or corporation court.

The Justice, as well as the court, should appoint an officer captain of patrol.

Form of ordering out a patrol by a Justice.

———— County, to wit:

To *A. B., C. D., E. F., G. H.* and *J. L.*:

I, J. T., a Justice of the said County, do in the name of the Commonwealth, command you the said A. B., C. D., E. F., G. H. and J. L., to patrol until the first day of the next County Court of said County, and visit within the bounds of the said County, at least once a week, all negro quarters and other places suspected of having therein unlawful assemblies, or such slaves as may stroll from one plantation to another, and to take any persons found in an unlawful assembly, or any slaves so found strolling, before some Justice near the place of capture, to be dealt with according to law. And I appoint you the said A. B., captain of the said patrol. Given under my hand, this ——— day of ——— 18—.

J. T., J. P.

[NOTE.—If the Justice thinks proper, he may in his order, limit the bounds of the patrol to any particular portion of his County.]

CHAPTER LXXVIII.

PEACE—(*Justices of.*)

[For breaches of, see SURETY OF; AFFRAY, ASSAULT, and RIOT.]

I. *Their origin.*

Justices of the Peace were unknown to the Common Law. It was not until the 34th year of the reign of Edward III. that those who were assigned to keep the peace acquired the appellation of Justices. The power of trying felonies was then conferred upon them, and from that circumstance they received the title of Justices. Until then they had no other powers than conservators of the peace, who were peculiar officers appointed by the Common Law for the maintenance of the public peace within the counties wherein they resided.[1] They were chosen by the freeholders in full county court before the Sheriff, and were called *custodes et conservatores pacis*, (keepers and conservators of the peace,) because they held the office merely by itself, unconnected with any other.[2] The Common Law also appointed other

---

[1] 1 Blac. Com.   [2] 1 Deac. Cr. Co. 710; 1 Blac. Com.

officers to keep the peace, but as they were known already by their distinct name of office, they retained their appellation and exercised the Common Law powers of conservators of the peace by virtue of their office, as they still do. Coroners, Sheriffs and Constables, within their counties and jurisdictions still are conservators of the peace *virtute officii*. This Common Law method of appointing conservators of the peace by election by the freeholders, was abolished in the first year of the reign of Edward III., and power given to the crown to assign "good men and lawful, which were no maintainers of evil or barrators in the county, to keep the peace.([1]) In the same reign, they acquired the appellation of Justices of the Peace from the circumstance above mentioned.

Though Justices of the Peace were unknown to us in our early colonial history, there were always in the colony from its earliest settlement, certain persons designated to exercise partially the jurisdiction of Justices of the Peace. They were first called "masters of the plantations," subsequently "commissioners of monthly courts," and then "commissioners," the latter being appointed by the Governor to do and execute whatever a Justice of the Peace or two or more Justices of the Peace might do according to the laws of England. (See 10 Hen. Stat. at large.) The power thus conferred upon these commissioners gave them some claim to the title of Justices, till by degrees and without any express law declaring it, they had acquired the appellation of Justices of the Peace before the revolution. As such they were recognized in our colonial legislation and by the constitution of the Commonwealth when originally formed, and now are in terms, commissioned Justices of the Peace by the executive upon the recommendation of the county courts. From this brief view of their origin we may doubtless trace the present mode of appointing them to the statute of Edward III., which took their election from the people, and conferred on the crown the power of assigning certain persons to be conservators of the peace within their respective counties. Independent of the power conferred on them by their commissions, they have in Virginia by statute all the Common Law powers of conservators of the peace.

By Sec. 4, Chap. 48. If any person, appointed Justice of any county, shall fail to take the oaths prescribed by law, within six months after the date of his commission, it shall be void.

With this summary of the origin of Justices of the Peace, we proceed to notice as briefly some of their powers and duties.

([1]) 1 Blac. Com. 350; 1 Dea. 710.

II. *Their powers and duties out of court.*

The power and duties of a Justice of the Peace depend upon his commission and on the several statutes which have created objects of his jurisdiction. His commission, and the various provisions of the statute, empower him to conserve the peace, and thereby give him all the power of the ancient conservators of the peace at Common Law in suppressing riots and affrays, in taking sureties for the peace and in apprehending and committing for felony and other inferior crimes.

Such is the great variety and extent of duties with which Justices are now charged by the statute and Common Law, that a full notice of them would exceed the limits prescribed for this work, and be in many respects inconsistent with its object. What is designed is merely to furnish some general rules for their guide out of court in execution of powers conferred on them. Their more particular jurisdiction and authority as guardians and conservators of the public peace, will be found under the heads of ARREST and SURETY OF THE PEACE.

The general duties of conservators of the peace by the Common Law, is to employ their own and to command the help of others to arrest and pacify all who in their presence and within their jurisdiction and limits, by word or deed, shall go about to break the peace; and if, being required to see the peace kept, he shall be negligent therein, he may be indicted and fined.(¹)

No man should be a judge in his own cause, and therefore a Justice should not execute his office in any case in which he has a private interest; but to this rule, from the necessity of the case, there are exceptions, as where a Justice shall be assaulted, or shall be abused to his face, (especially whilst in the discharge of the duties of his office,) and no other Justice is present with him, then he may commit such offender until he shall find sureties for the peace or good behaviour.(²)

Where a statute requires an act of a judicial nature to be done by two Justices, whether the act to be done be within their civil or criminal jurisdiction, it will be void unless two are *present* to concur and join in it.(³) Taking the privy examination of a married woman is a judicial act.

But though a statute appoints two Justices to hear and determine any misdemeanor or breach of the peace, so that both must be present at the hearing, yet upon complaint made to any one Justice, he may, of his own authority, grant a war-

---

(¹) Dalt. c. 1; 3 Burn J. P. 129.
(²) See statute under head of PEACE; 3 Dick. J. P. 337.
(³) 3 T. R. 38; Rex *v.* Hamstall, 3 T. R. 380; 2 East 244; 2 Dick. J. P. 377; 1 Dea. Cr. Co. 714.

rant to apprehend the offender, in order that he may be brought before himself and some other Justice, for the purpose of hearing and determining the complaint.(¹)

The Congress of the United States cannot give jurisdiction to or require the services of any officer of the State government as such, but may authorize any citizen of the United States to perform any act which the Constitution of the United States does not require to be performed in a different manner.(²) It is not, therefore, the *ex officio* duty of a Justice of the Peace to do any act required by Congress, but he may exercise the authority thus conferred on him or not, at his discretion.

Where a special authority is given to Justices to act out of sessions, (that is out of court,) it ought to appear in their orders (proceedings) that the authority has been exactly pursued,(³) and in all cases where Justices may hear and determine any matter out of court, either on their own view, or confession of the party, or on the oath of witnesses, they should make a record in writing under their hands, of all the matters and proof, which record, if no place is directed by law for its deposite, may be kept by them.(⁴) This salutary injunction, ordained by law as well for the protection of Justices as of the party and the Commonwealth, is too often neglected in practice.

It is settled, and not now to be disputed, that a Justice of the Peace may, at Common Law, issue his warrant for an offence against a penal statute or other misdemeanor cognizable before the county or corporation courts, and cause the offender to be apprehended, and bind him over to answer the offence.(⁵) This has been the long constant and universal practice of Justices, both here and in England, founded in the necessity of the thing, to prevent the escape of offenders, and is now confirmed by the statute.

In cases, however, of summary convictions on penal statutes by Justices out of court, a Magistrate, unless otherwise directed by statute, should, in the first instance, issue a summons against the party and not a warrant,(⁶) and if the party then disobeys the summons, the Justice may properly issue his warrant against him,(⁷) if the offence be such as for any cause the presence of the party becomes necessary. But he may issue a warrant in the first instance, even in these cases, if he have good rea-

(¹) Dalt. c. 6.
(²) Ex parte Pool and others, 2 Va. Cases 276.
(³) 2 Salk. 475; 5 Burr. 2686; 2 Dick. J. P. 338.
(⁴) Dalt. c. 115; 2 Dick. J. P. 379.
(⁵) 2 Hawk. c. 13; 1 Hale 579; 2 Dick. J. P. 379.
(⁶) Rex v. Martin, 13 East 55.
(⁷) 12 Rep. 131 b.; 2 Hawk. c. 13, § 15; Reg. v. Simpson, 10 Mod. 248; Bone v. Bethuen, 2 Bing. 63.

son to believe the party would otherwise escape, and in all cases of felony and in high misdemeanors, where the offender, on conviction, is to suffer corporal punishment, a warrant is the proper process.([1])

If upon a murder or other untimely death by violence, there be no Coroner within the county or corporation where the death shall happen, or if from sickness or other just cause, the Coroner cannot be had to hold an inquest upon the body of the deceased, it is lawful for any one of the Justices in such case, upon notice, to do and perform all the duties appertaining to the office of Coroner.([2])

As to the general power of a Justice officially to commit for trial, or to detain a party charged before him with felony, where there is reasonable cause why the Justice cannot then take or finish the examination, see *Examination*, under head of ARREST.

With respect to his authority to administer an oath to a party who is brought before him to be examined as a witness upon a matter within his jurisdiction, whether it be a proceeding under his Common Law powers, or in the performance of any judicial act required by statute, he has not only the authority, but it is his duty to examine such witness according to the mode prescribed by the Common Law.([3])

Where the penalty incurred by the breach of any penal law, does not exceed twenty dollars, Justices of the Peace have authority to hear and determine the matter thereof,([4]) but from any conviction by a Justice of the Peace on a penal statute, when the judgment shall be for more than ten dollars, an appeal from his judgment lies as a matter of right to the county or corporation court ;([5]) and in all cases of convictions, if any part of the fine enures to the Commonwealth, the judgment of conviction should be returned to the Clerk's office of the county or corporation court. Justices have also the power to try, in a summary manner, slaves and free negroes charged with misdemeanors. See title FINES AND SUMMARY CONVICTIONS.

If a statute gives to a Justice jurisdiction over an offence, it impliedly gives him power to make out a warrant and bring before him any person charged with such offence.([6])

At Common Law it is in the discretion of a Magistrate, when he takes the examination of a person charged before him with felony, whether he will allow the presence of an attor-

---

([1]) 2 Dick. J. P. 379.
([2]) See CORONER.
([3]) 1 Lamb. 213 ; 1 Hale 586 ; Deac. Cr. Co. 719 ; See title OATH.
([4]) See FINES AND CONVICTIONS.
([5]) See FINES, &c.
([6]) 2 Hawk. c. 13, § 15 ; 12 Rep. 131, b.; Q. v. Simpson, 10 Mod. 248 ; Bone v. Bethuen, 2 Bing. 63. See title ARREST.

ney or other legal adviser, either for the prisoner or the prosecutor, for such examination is only a preliminary enquiry, whether there be sufficient grounds to commit the prisoner for trial. But in the case of a trial or summary conviction before a Magistrate, there is a difference; for there, it is reasonable that a party should have professional assistance before he is finally condemned to pay a penalty or suffer a term of imprisonment.(1) And by our statute he is now allowed counsel to aid him in the examination of witnesses, on his examination for felony before the Justice.

A Magistrate may commit a party for a contempt, who makes use of scandalous and insulting language to him whilst in the execution of his office, but as such commitment is by way of punishment, it must be made by warrant in writing, and not by word of mouth only,(2) and must not be "till the party is discharged by due course of law, but for a time certain."(3) The Common Law power to attach for contempt is confirmed by the statute. (See chap. 195, sec. 23.) Unless, however, in cases of great outrage, the proper course for Magistrates to adopt, in cases of contempt, is to require the offender to find sureties for his good behaviour, for such time as he shall think proper, not exceeding twelve months, and in default of his doing so, to commit him for that period, unless he sooner find such sureties;(4) and as such a contempt is an indictable misdemeanor at Common Law, the party should also be recognized to appear before the next quarterly sessions of the county or corporation court, to answer a bill of indictment to be preferred against him for the offence.

The following is a proper form of a commitment for insulting a Justice of the Peace in the execution of his office, and with but slight alteration, may suit any case of contempt offered to him while in the discharge of his official duty.

———— County, to wit:

To A. B., Constable of the said County, and to the Keeper of the Common Jail of the said County:

Whereas, C. D. being personally present this day at ————, in the said County, before me J. T., one of the Commonwealth's Justices of the said County, to answer and make his defence to a certain information exhibited before me, hath this day been guilty of divers gross insults and contemptuous behaviour to me the said Justice, then being in the actual execution of my office as such Justice, by accusing me of partiality and injustice in the execution of my office, (or *by using abusive and opprobrious language to me,* or *making violent and threatening gestures, &c. to me,* according to the fact:)

---

(1) Cox *v.* Coleridge, 1 B. & C. 37; R. *v.* Bonon, 3 B. & A. 432; R. *v.* Justices of Staffordshire, 1 Ch. Rep. 217.

(2) Mayhew *v.* Loche, 7 Taunt. 63; 2 Marsh. 377; R. *v.* Rival, 13 St. Tr. 420; 2 Hawk. c. 1, § 3; 2 Hale 122.

(3) R. *v.* James, 5 B. & A. 292.

(4) Rex *v.* Langley, 2 Ld. R. 1030.

and whereas the said C. D., in consequence of such, his insolent and contemptuous behaviour, is now here, by me the said Justice, required to find sureties for his good behaviour; that is to say, one sufficient surety, to become bound with him in a recognizance in the sum of ——— dollars, conditioned for the personal appearance of the said C. D. at the next ——— term of the County Court of the County of ———, to answer the said offence, and that in the mean time, he should keep the peace and be of good behaviour for one year from this day; but the said C. D. hath refused to find sureties and to become bound in such recognizance as aforesaid: These are, therefore, to command you, the said Constable, to convey and deliver the said C. D. into the custody of the keeper of the common jail of the said County, together with this my warrant; and I hereby command you, the said keeper, to receive the said C. D. into your custody in the said common jail, and him there safely to keep for one year from this day, unless he, in the mean time, find such sureties and enter into such recognizance as aforesaid. Given under my hand and seal, this ——— day of ——— in the year 18—.

J. T., J. P. [L. S.]

CHAPTER LXXIX.

PERJURY.

By the Common Law, perjury was limited to false oaths taken in judicial proceedings,([1]) but by a general provision of the statute, the offence is extended to other oaths, and the punishment made much more penal.

BY SEC. 1, CHAP. 194. If a person to whom an oath is lawfully administered on any occasion, shall on such occasion wilfully swear falsely, touching any material matter or thing, he shall be guilty of perjury.

BY SEC. 2. A free person who commits or procures another person to commit perjury, shall, if the perjury be on a trial for felony, be confined in the penitentiary not less than one nor more than ten years; and if it be on any other occasion, be confined in jail one year, and be fined not exceeding one thousand dollars.

BY SEC. 3. He shall moreover, on conviction thereof, be adjudged forever incapable of holding any post mentioned in the first section of chapter 12, or of serving as a juror or giving evidence as a witness.

At Common Law, as well as under the statute, four things are necessary to constitute this offence: 1. The oath must be wilful. 2. It must be false. 3. It must be taken before competent authority. 4. The thing sworn to must be material.

([1]) Hawk. c. 69, § 1.

1. *Wilfully.* To constitute the crime of perjury, the false oath must be taken wilfully, that is, deliberately and advisedly, for if it be occasioned by surprise or inadvertence, or a mistake of the true meaning of the question, it will not amount to voluntary and corrupt perjury.(¹)

The idea formerly entertained, that a party could not be guilty of perjury, unless he swore *absolutely and directly*,(²) is exploded, and it is now agreed that the crime of perjury does not consist so much in a positive and absolute affirmance or denial of a fact, as upon the deceitful intention of the witness, so that if a man swears that he *believes* a fact to be true, which he must know to be false, there is no doubt he may be indicted for perjury.(³)

2. *Falsely.* The oath must be false, but it would seem to be immaterial whether the fact, which is sworn to, be in itself true or false, for however true the thing sworn to may happen to prove, yet if it were not known to be so at the time by him who swears to it, his offence is altogether as great as if it had been false; and if a witness wilfully swears that he knows a thing to be true, which, at the time, he knows nothing of, he impudently endeavours to induce those before whom he swears, to proceed upon the credit of a statement, which any stranger might make as well as he.(⁴)

3. *The oath must be taken before competent authority.* It must be taken before some court or person legally authorized to administer it; and the court or person before whom it is taken, must be acting under the authority of law upon the subject matter to which the false oath relates.(⁵) For no oath whatever, which is taken before persons acting merely in a private capacity, or before those who presume to administer oaths of a public nature without authority, or before those who are legally authorized to administer some kinds of oaths, but not the particular oath in question which is taken before them, or before those who act under a colourable authority, can ever amount to perjury in the eye of the law.(⁶) For example, a false oath taken before a Clerk of the court, that A. had murdered B., for the purpose of issuing an arrest warrant against A., would not be perjury. So, on the other hand, a false oath to naturalize an alien, taken before a Justice of the Peace, would not be perjury, because in neither case, has the party administering the oath, any lawful authority to do it.

(¹) 1 Hawk. c. 69, § 2; Deac. Cr. Co. 999.
(²) 3 Inst. 166.
(³) Pedley's Case, 1 Leach 327; 3 Wils. 427; Deac. Cr. Co. 1000.
(⁴) 1 Hawk. c. 69, § 6; 6 T. R. 637; 2 Russ. 518, note 2; Deac. Cr. Co. 1000.
(⁵) 1 Hawk. c. 69, § 4.
(⁶) Id.

4. *It must be material.* The thing sworn to must be material to the point in question; for if it be wholly foreign from the purpose, or altogether immaterial, not tending to aggravate or extenuate damages, nor likely to induce a jury (or others who are to act on the subject matter of the oath) to give readier credit to the substantial part of the evidence or thing sworn to, it cannot amount to perjury, because it is in such a case, merely idle and insignificant.(¹) But this position as to the oath's being material to the point in issue, must be taken with the qualification suggested by the terms, to give readier credit to the substantial part of the evidence, for if the object of a question put to a witness, is to sift him as to his knowledge of the transaction which he comes to speak to, by examining him strictly as to all the circumstances, and he gives a particular and distinct account of those circumstances, which afterwards appear to be false, he may be guilty of perjury, though none of the circumstances are directly material to the point in issue. For nothing can be more apt to mislead a jury and incline them to give credit to the whole of a man's evidence, than his thus appearing to have an exact and particular knowledge of all the circumstances relating to the transaction about which enquiry is made. Therefore, when in an action of trespass, a witness swore that he saw thirty or forty sheep in the plaintiff's close, and that he was sure they were the defendant's, because they were marked with such a mark, which he knew to be the defendant's mark, whereas in truth the defendant never used such a mark, it was held that this was a case upon which a prosecution for perjury might well be maintained, for the witness, in giving such a special reason for his remembrance, could not but make his testimony more credible than it would have been without it; and though it signify nothing to the merits of the cause, whether the sheep had any mark or not, yet inasmuch as this circumstance had a direct tendency to corroborate the evidence in other material parts, it was equally prejudicial to the party against whom the witness gave his evidence, and equally tending to abuse the administration of justice.(²)

If the false oath has *any tendency*, however slight, to prove or disprove the matter in issue, however uncircumstantially, it will amount to perjury; as where the party wilfully misrepresents the colour of a man's coat, or speaks falsely to the credit of another witness.(³)

(¹) 1 Hawk. c. 69, § 8; and see the statute before cited.
(²) 1 Hawk. c. 69, § 8; 2 Deac. Cr. Law 1003.
(³) Grieb's Case, 12 Mod. 142; Muscot's Case, 10 Mod. 195.

But the materiality or immateriality of any statement made by a witness, will depend on the whole circumstances connected with the examination, for if, without any intention to deceive, he states some trivial fact incorrectly, when his attention is not particularly called to it, then the inaccuracy of the witness will not render him liable to the penalties of perjury; but if, after being cautioned to weigh well the question before he answers it, he answers positively to a circumstance directly contrary to the truth, *with intent to deceive*, then the answer, though not directly material to the merits of the cause, may be considered indirectly so, by confirming or invalidating the other portions of the testimony, and it may, therefore, now be safely inferred, that the evidence given by the witness need not be so far material as to prove directly the point in question, but that it is sufficient, if it is circumstantially material and conduces to the proof of the point in issue.(¹)

The evidence must not only be material, but if it is in answer to a question propounded to a witness, the question must be a *lawful* one in order to found a prosecution for perjury; for where the alleged perjury was in answer to the question, whether the witness had not been guilty of bribery, the court refused a criminal information against him, as it was a question he was not bound to answer.(²)

It is not essential that the false oath be credited, or that any one is aggrieved by it, to constitute this offence, inasmuch as a prosecution for perjury is not founded on damage to a party, but on the abuse of public justice.(³)

Subornation of perjury, is the offence of procuring another to take such false oath as constitutes perjury in the principal, and is punished as perjury is punished.(⁴)

If a person incited to take a false oath, do not actually take it, the person by whom he was incited, is not guilty of subornation of perjury, but he is nevertheless liable to be punished as for a gross misdemeanor (at Common Law) in attempting to pervert the course of justice.(⁵) (See ATTEMPTS.)

And so, an incitement to give particular evidence, where the incitee does not know whether it is true or false, is also a high misdemeanor at Common Law.(⁶)

In like manner, the dissuading or attempting to dissuade a witness from giving evidence against a person indicted, is an offence at Common Law, punishable by fine and imprisonment.(⁷)

(¹) R. v. Gripe, 1 Ld. Ray. 258; R. v. Rhodes, 2 Ld. Ray. 887.
(²) R. v. Dummer, 1 Salk. 374.
(³) 1 Hawk. c. 69, § 9.
(⁴) Deac. Cr. Co. 998, and the statute.
(⁵) 1 Hawk. c. 69, § 10.
(⁶) 2 Russ. 518; Dea. Cr. Co. 1005.
(⁷) 1 Hawk. c. 21, § 15; Deac. Cr. Co. 1005.

In prosecutions for perjury, in order to convict, the evidence must be stronger than that which was given by the defendant, and which was alleged to be false; and therefore, the evidence of one witness alone, is insufficient to convict, because it would only be oath against oath. Some other independent ("corroborating") evidence ought to be adduced.(¹) But it is not absolutely requisite for two witnesses to disprove every fact sworn to by the defendant; for if any material circumstance be proved by other witnesses, in confirmation of the witness who proves the perjury, this may be sufficient evidence to warrant a conviction.(²)

Nor does the rule as to two witnesses apply where the defendant has sworn to two different statements wholly contradictory. The mere proof of a contradictory statement made by the defendant himself, unless explained by circumstances, seems to be sufficient to convict him.(³)

It is no objection now, that the witness, to prove the perjury, is a party injured by the offence,(⁴) though formerly the contrary was held.

In proceeding against a party charged with perjury, it is not necessary, even in an indictment, to set forth more than the substance of the offence, with the circumstances necessary to render the proceedings intelligible, and to inform the defendant of the allegations against him.(⁵) But the court or tribunal by which the oath is administered, must be correctly stated.(⁶) And where the time of committing the perjury is material, it should be laid in the proceedings with precision.(⁷) *Quere*, unless under the law of 1844-5? See Lodge's Case, 2 Gratt. 579.

In practice, it is important that the Justice should bear in mind, that perjury, when committed on the trial of a party on indictment or information for felony, is itself a felony, and in all other cases a misdemeanor only; for in the one case, the offender is to be committed for examination or trial before the county court, and in the other, to be committed or recognized to answer an indictment by the grand jury in the county court.

Perjury may be committed under such a variety of circumstances, that it would be impossible to give a form for every case, but the forms here given, may be modified to suit any case likely to occur. In describing the offence, the Justice

(¹) 2 Str. 1228; 10 Mod. 193; Ros. Cr. Ev. 769-70.
(²) R. v. Lee, 1 Phil. Ev. 143; 2 Russ. 545.
(³) R. v. Knill, 5 B. & A. 929, in note; Id. 939, note.
(⁴) R. v. Broughton, 2 Str. 1230; Abraham v. Bunn, 4 Burr. 2255; R. v. Boston, 4 East 581.
(⁵) 5 Wend. 271.
(⁶) Rex v. Lincon, Russ. & Ry. 421.
(⁷) 1 T. R. 69; 1 Stark. R. 524.

should state plainly and distinctly what the party swore to, and then negative that statement.

(No. 1.)

Form of Warrant of Arrest for perjury, upon the trial of an indictment for felony.

──── County, to wit:
To X. Y., Constable of the said County:

Whereas, A. B. has this day made complaint and information on oath, before me J. T., a Justice of said County, (*) that C. D., on the ──── day of ──── 18──, in said County, did feloniously commit wilful and corrupt perjury, in the testimony which he gave on oath as a witness upon the trial of one E. F. in the Circuit Court for the said County, for feloniously killing J. S., (or *stabbing J. S.*, or *stealing the goods of J. S.*, or whatever other offence the party was tried for,) and which testimony was material upon the said trial: These are, therefore, to command you, in the name of the Commonwealth, forthwith to apprehend the said C. D., and to bring him before me or some other Justice of the said County, to answer the said complaint, and to be farther dealt with according to law. Given under my hand and seal, this ──── day of ──── 18──.

J. T., *J. P.* [L. S.]

(No. 2.)

Form of Warrant to arrest a party indicted for perjury.

──── County, to wit:
To X. Y., Constable of said County:

Forasmuch as a true bill of indictment in the Circuit Court of ──── County, was, on the ──── day of ──── 18──, found against A. B., for wilful and corrupt perjury, in the testimony which he gave upon oath, &c. (follow the above precedent to the conclusion.)

[NOTE.—If the party be presented, instead of indicted for perjury, say: " Forasmuch as a true presentment was made on the ──── day of ──── 18──, against A. B., in the ──── Court of said County, for wilful," &c.]

(No. 3.)

Form of Warrant of Arrest for subornation of perjury on trial of an indictment for felony.

──── County, to wit:
To X. Y., Constable of said County:

Forasmuch as A. B. has this day made information and complaint on oath before me J. T., a Justice of said County, that C. D., on the ──── day of ──── 18──, in said County, did corruptly and feloniously suborn, and procure E. F. feloniously to commit wilful and corrupt perjury, in the testimony which he said E. F. gave upon oath as a witness upon the trial of one G. H., upon an indictment in the Circuit Court for the County of ────, for feloniously, (here state the felony for which G. H. was tried,) and which testimony was material upon the said trial: These are, therefore, to command you, in the name of the Commonwealth of Virginia, forthwith to apprehend the said C. D., and to bring him before me or some other Justice of the said County, to answer the said complaint, and to be farther dealt with according to law. Given under my hand and seal, this —— day of ——— 18—.

J. T., *J. P.* [L. s.]

(No. 4.)

Form of Mittimus for felonious perjury.

—————— County, to wit:

To X. Y., Constable of the said County, and to the Keeper of the Jail of said County:

These are to command you, the said Constable, in the name of the Commonwealth of Virginia, forthwith to carry and deliver into the custody of the keeper of the jail of the said County, the body of C. D., brought before me J. T., a Justice of the said County, on the —— day of ——— 18—, charged on the oath of G. H. with felony, for this, that he did feloniously commit wilful and corrupt perjury, in the testimony which he gave on oath as a witness upon the trial of one E. F., upon an indictment in the Circuit Court of said County for felony, and which testimony was material upon the said trial; and you, the keeper of the said jail, are hereby commanded to receive the said C. D. into your jail and custody, that he may be examined (or *tried*) by the County Court of the said County, for the felonious perjury aforesaid, and him there safely keep, until he shall be thence discharged by due course of law. Given under my hand and seal, this —— day of ——— 18—.

J. T., *J. P.* [L. s.]

(No. 5.)

Form of Certificate of Commitment to the Clerk, for felonious perjury.

Follow No. 1, under head of ARREST.

(No. 6.)

Form of Recognizance of Bail, for felonious perjury.

If the prisoner be admitted to bail, turn to head of RECOGNIZANCE, and follow form No. 1, and describe the offence thus: "for falsely, wilfully, corruptly and feloniously committing perjury upon the trial of C. D., indicted for felony."

(No. 7.)

Form of Recognizance of Witnesses in a case of felonious perjury.

Turn to head of RECOGNIZANCE, and follow form No. 3.

[NOTE.—The foregoing forms apply only in cases of felonious perjury, where the punishment is confinement in the penitentiary. The following are applicable to misdemeanors only :]

(No. 8.)

Form of Warrant of Arrest for perjury committed on the trial of a civil suit.

Follow form No. 1, to the (*), and proceed thus : " that on the —— day of ——— 18—, at the Courthouse of the said County, a certain cause in which C. D. was plaintiff and K. L., was defendant, was tried before the County Court of the said County, then and there sitting, and that upon the trial of the said cause, A. B. appeared as a witness for and on behalf of the said C. D., and was then and there duly sworn by the said Court, that the evidence he should give relating to the matter in difference between the said parties, should be the truth, the whole truth, and nothing but the truth, (the said Court then and there having authority to administer the said oath,) and that upon the trial of the said cause, it then and there became material to enquire whether (here state what it was material to enquire into,) and that thereupon the said A. B., being so sworn as a witness as aforesaid, did then and there, in said County, on the trial of the said cause, falsely, wilfully and corruptly depose, swear and testify, among other things, that (here state substantially what the witness swore to,) whereas in truth and in fact, (here assign the perjury by negativing the statement made by the witness,) whereby the said A. B. did then and there wilfully and corruptly swear falsely, and commit wilful and corrupt perjury : These are, therefore," &c. (conclude as No. 1.)

(No. 9.)

Form of Mittimus.

Follow No. 9, under head of ARREST.

(No. 10.)

Form of Recognizance of Bail and of Witnesses.

Follow Nos. 4 and 5, under head of RECOGNIZANCE.

(No. 11.)

Form of Certificate of commitment to the Clerk.

Follow No. 10 or 11, under head of ARREST.

(No. 1.)

An Indictment for felonious perjury.

———— Judicial Circuit, } The jurors of the Commonwealth of Vir-
———— County, to wit: } ginia, in and for the body of the County of
In the Circuit Court for the } ————, and now attending the said Court,
said County. } upon their oath present, that on the ———— day
of ————, in the year one thousand eight
hundred and ————, in the said County, and at the Circuit Court held for
the said County, on the ———— day of ———— 18—, at the Courthouse thereof,
by J. S., Judge of the said Court, one C. D. was tried on an indictment for
feloniously (here state the felony for which C. D. was tried,) as more fully
appears by the records of the said Court, and that upon the trial of the said
C. D. for the felony aforesaid, A. B. appeared in said Court as a witness for
and on behalf of the said C. D., and was then and there in said County and
in the Court aforesaid, duly sworn by the said J. S., then and there sitting
as Judge of the said Court, upon the trial aforesaid, that the evidence he
should give upon the said trial, should be the truth, the whole truth, and
nothing but the truth, the said J. S. then and there having authority by
law to administer the said oath: and that upon the trial of the said C. D.
for the felony aforesaid, it then and there became material to enquire whether (here state what the enquiry was,) and that thereupon the said A. B.
being so sworn as a witness, did, on the said trial, in the County aforesaid,
feloniously, wilfully and corruptly depose, swear and testify, among other
things, that (here state substantially what the witness swore to); whereas,
in truth and in fact (here negative what the witness swore to,) whereby the
said A. B. did then and there, upon the said trial in the County aforesaid,
feloniously, wilfully and corruptly swear falsely, and feloniously commit
wilful perjury, against the peace and dignity of the Commonwealth of Virginia.

———

(No. 2.)

*An Indictment for subornation of perjury, in procuring a person to commit
perjury upon the trial of one indicted of felony.*

———— Judicial Circuit, } The jurors of the Commonwealth of Vir-
———— County, to wit: } ginia, in and for the body of the County of
In the Circuit Court for the } ————, and now attending the said Court,
said County. } upon their oath present, that on the ———— day
of ———— in the year one thousand eight
hundred and ————, in the said County, and at the Circuit Court held for
the said County, at the Courthouse thereof, on the ———— day of ———— 18—,
by J. S., Judge of the said Court, one C. D. was tried on an indictment for
felony, and that upon the trial of the said C. D. for the felony aforesaid, A.
B. appeared as a witness for and on behalf of the said C. D., and was then
and there duly sworn by the said J. S., then and there sitting as Judge of
the said Court upon the trial aforesaid, that the evidence he should give
upon the said trial should be the truth, the whole truth, and nothing but the
truth, (the said J. S. then and there having authority by law to administer
the said oath,) and that upon the trial of the said C. D. for felony aforesaid,
it then and there became material to enquire whether (here state the enquiry,) and that thereupon the said C. D. did, in the said County, unlawfully, corruptly and feloniously, by sinister and unlawful means and per-

suasion, suborn and procure the said A. B. to falsely, wilfully and corruptly swear, depose and testify, among other things, that (here state the substance of what was sworn to,) and that he the said A. B. did then and there so depose, swear and testify before the said Court upon the said trial; whereas in truth and in fact, (here negative what the witness swore to,) whereby the said C. D. did then and there wilfully, corruptly and feloniously commit subornation of perjury, by procuring the said A. B. to commit wilful and corrupt perjury, in and by his oath aforesaid, against the peace and dignity of the Commonwealth of Virginia.

(No. 3.)

An Indictment for perjury, committed on the trial of a civil suit.

———— Judicial Circuit, \} The jurors of the Commonwealth of Virginia, in and for the body of the County of ————, and now attending the said Court, upon their oath present, that on the ——— day of ——— in the year one thousand eight hundred and ———, at the Courthouse of the said County, a certain cause in which C. D. was plaintiff and K. L. was defendant, was tried before the County Court of the said County, then and there sitting, and that upon the trial of the said cause, A. B. appeared as a witness for and on behalf of the said C. D., and was then and there duly sworn by the said Court, that the evidence he should give relating to the matter in difference between the said parties, should be the truth, the whole truth, and nothing but the truth, (the said Court having then and there authority to administer the said oath,) and that upon the trial of the said cause, it then and there became material to enquire whether (here state what it was material to enquire into,) and that thereupon the said A. B., being so sworn as a witness as aforesaid, did, in said County, then and there, on the trial of the said cause, falsely, wilfully and corruptly depose, swear and testify, among other things, that (here state substantially what the witness swore to;) whereas in truth and in fact (here assign the perjury by negativing the statement made by the witness,) whereby the said A. B. did then and there wilfully and corruptly swear falsely, and commit wilful and corrupt perjury, against the peace and dignity of the Commonwealth of Virginia.

CHAPTER LXXX.

PLEAS—(*In abatement.*)

(No. 1.)

Form of Plea to the jurisdiction of the Court.

And the said C. D. in his proper person comes into Court here, and having heard the said indictment read, says that the Court here ought not to take cognizance of the offence in the said indictment above specified, because protesting that he is not guilty of the same; nevertheless the said C. D. says, (proceed here to state the matter of the plea;) and this the said C. D. is ready to verify: wherefore he prays judgment if the Court here will or ought to take cognizance of the indictment aforesaid; and that he may be discharged and permitted to go without day.

(No. 2.)

Form of Replication to the above plea.

And hereupon the said attorney for the Commonwealth, on behalf of the said Commonwealth, says that notwithstanding any thing by the said C. D. above in pleading alleged, this Court ought not to be precluded from taking cognizance of the indictment aforesaid, because he says, (here state the matter of the replication, concluding to the country, or with a verification, as the replication may require:) wherefore he prays judgment that the said C. D. may be held to answer to said indictment.

(No. 3.)

Form of Plea in abatement, that grand juror was not a freeholder.

And the said A. B. comes into Court here, and having heard the said presentment read to him, says that he ought not to be compelled to answer the said presentment, because he says that J. D. was one of the persons summoned and sworn as a grand juror, and acted as one of the grand jurors in the said Court when the said presentment was made in the said Court, and by whom it was made. And that the said J. D. was not at the time he was so sworn and acted as a grand juror, and when the said presentment was made, a freeholder of the said County of ———; and this he the said A. B. is ready to verify: wherefore he prays judgment of the said presentment, and that the same may be quashed.

(No. 4.)

Form of Replication to the above plea.

And hereupon R. D., attorney for the Commonwealth, in the said Court, on behalf of the said Commonwealth, says that the said presentment, by reason of any thing by the said A. B. in his plea above alleged, ought not to be quashed, because he says that the said J. D. was, at the time he was sworn in the said Court as a grand juror, and when he acted as such grand juror, and at the time the said presentment was made, a freeholder of the said County of ———; and this the said attorney for the Commonwealth prays may be enquired of by the country.

(No. 5.)

Form of Plea in abatement, for a misnomer.

And now James Long, who in this indictment is called and indicted by the name of George Long, in his proper person, comes into Court here, and having heard the indictment read, says that his name is James, and that by the christian name of James has always hitherto been known and called; without this, that he the said James Long now is, or hitherto has been called or known by the said name of George, as by the said indictment is supposed; and this the said James Long is ready to verify: wherefore he prays judgment of said indictment, and that the same may be quashed.

(No. 6.)

Form of Replication to the plea of misnomer.

And hereupon the said attorney for the Commonwealth, on behalf of said Commonwealth, says that the said indictment, by reason of any thing by the said James Long in his plea above alleged, ought not to be quashed, because he says that the said James Long was, long before and at the time of the preferring of said indictment, and still is known as well by the name of George Long as by the name of James Long; and this the said attorney for the Commonwealth prays may be enquired of by the country.

PLEAS—(*In bar.*)

(No. 1.)

Form of Plea of auterfois acquit.

And the said A. B., in his proper person, comes into Court here, and having heard the said indictment read, says, that the Commonwealth ought not farther to prosecute the said indictment against him, the said A. B., because he says that heretofore, to wit, at the (state the Court) holden at, &c., (here recite the record of the former judgment and acquittal, *verbatim*, from the beginning to the conclusion of it; then proceed thus,) as by the record thereof more fully and at large appears: which said judgment still remains in full force and effect. And the said A. B. avers, and in fact says, that he, the said A. B., and the said A. B. so indicted and acquitted as aforesaid, are one and the same person, and not other and different persons: and that the (felony) of which the said A. B. was indicted and acquitted as aforesaid, and the (felony) of which the said A. B. is now indicted, are one and the same, and not different (felonies,) and this the said A. B. is ready to verify; wherefore he prays judgment, and that he may be dismissed and discharged by the Court here, from the premises in the present indictment specified.

(No. 2.)

Form of Plea of auterfois convict.

And the said A. B. in his proper person comes into Court here, and having heard the indictment read to him, says, that the Commonwealth ought not farther to prosecute the said indictment against him the said A. B., because he says, that heretofore, to wit, at the (state the Court,) holden, &c., (here recite the record of the former judgment and conviction, *verbatim:* then proceed as follows ;) as by the record thereof more fully and at large appears ; which said judgment still remains in full force and effect. And the said A. B. avers, that he the said A. B., and the said A. B. so indicted and convicted, as last aforesaid, are one and the same person, and not other or different persons ; and that the (felony) of which he the said A. B. was so indicted and convicted as aforesaid, and the (felony) of which he is now indicted, are one and the same, and not different (felonies,) and this the said A. B. is ready to verify : wherefore, he prays judgment, and that he may be discharged and dismissed by the Court here, from the premises in the present indictment specified.

(No. 3.)

Form of Demurrer to an indictment.

And the said A. B., in his own proper person comes into Court here, and having heard the said indictment read, says, that the said indictment, and the matters and things therein contained, in manner and form as the same are therein stated and set forth, are not sufficient in law ; and that he, the said A. B., is not bound by the laws of the land to make answer to the same ; and this he is ready to verify : wherefore, for want of a sufficient indictment in this behalf, the said A. B. prays judgment, and that he may, by the Court here, be dismissed and discharged from the premises in the said indictment specified.

(No. 4.)

Form of Joinder in demurrer.

And C. D., attorney for the Commonwealth, who prosecutes in this case for the Commonwealth, says that the said indictment, and the matters and things therein contained, in manner and form as therein stated and set forth, are sufficient in law to compel the said A. B. to answer the same ; and this the said C. D. who prosecutes as aforesaid, is ready to verify and prove as the Court here shall direct and award : wherefore, inasmuch, as the said A. B. has not answered to the said indictment, nor in any manner denied the same, the said C. D., for the said Commonwealth, prays judgment ; and that the said A. B. may be convicted of the premises in the said indictment specified.

PLOTTING AND CONSPIRING.

For plotting and conspiring the murder of a white person by a negro, see title NEGROES.

CHAPTER LXXXI.

POISON.

Murder is a crime so atrocious, that the bare attempt to commit it in any form, is a high misdemeanor at Common Law. Of all the means by which it is effected, that by poison is the most detestable, because it can, the least of all, be guarded against, and moreover, implies that cool and deliberate malice, which no provocation can justify. The bare attempt to kill by such means indicates "a heart" so "void of social duty and deliberately bent on mischief," that the statute law not only declares it felony to administer poison to persons, with intent to kill, but makes the *attempt* even to administer it either to man or *beast*, with that intent, felony.

By Sec. 7, Chap. 191. If any free person administer, or attempt to administer, any poison or destructive thing in food, drink, medicine or otherwise, or poison any spring, well or reservoir of water, with intent to kill or injure another person, he shall be confined in the penitentiary not less than three, nor more than five years.

By one section of the English statute, upon this subject, it is felony, punishable with *death*, to *administer* poison, with intent to murder; and by another, it is felony to attempt to administer it, with the like intent, punishable by *transportation*. Upon this statute it has been there decided, that to constitute the offence of *administering* poison, some portion of it must be *taken* by, or *applied* to the person to whom it is administered, and that merely giving it, if no part was taken or applied, was not sufficient,(¹) but that it is not necessary that the poison should be delivered by the hand of the prisoner; as where a servant put poison into a coffee pot, and when her mistress came down to breakfast, told her that she had put the coffee pot there for her, and the mistress drank it; this was held causing the poison to be administered, under the statute.(²) And so, where A. sent poison, intending it for B., with intent to kill B., and it came into the possession of C., who took it, but did not die, this was held to be a case of administering within the statute.(³) Our statute makes no distinction in the punishment between administering poison and an attempt to administer it, for the gist of the crime consists in the cool and deliberate intent to kill, indicated by such

---

(¹) Camden's Case, 1 Moody's C. C. 114. (²) Harley's Case, 4 Carr & Payne 369.
(³) 6 C. & P. 161.

means accompanied by some act towards the execution of the design, and not in the degree of its proximity to success. Yet, in indicting under the statute, it is proper to count both for *administering* and *attempting* to administer poison, as upon the authority just cited, a count for administering only, would not be sustained by proof of an attempt to administer it.

The Justice should be satisfied that the drug or substance mingled with the food, or put in the well, was a poison or some *destructive* thing, and that it was so mingled or put, with intent to kill or injure; but if he should mistake one kind of poison for another, it will not vitiate the proceedings against the offender, for even upon indictment it will be sufficient to prove that a similar kind was used.(¹)

By Sec. 32, Chap. 192. If a free person maliciously administer poison to, or expose it, with intent that it should be taken by any horse, cattle or other beast of another person, he shall be confined in the penitentiary not less than one, nor more than five years.

Though the maiming of cattle is held in England to be no offence at Common Law, (see title Cattle,) yet it is a misdemeanor at Common Law maliciously to administer poison to horses and other cattle,(²) and the offence by this provision of the statute is very properly ranked among felonies. On an indictment for the offence, it is not necessary to prove that the person was actuated by malice against the owner of the cattle.(³)

(No. 1.)

Form of Warrant of Arrest for administering or attempting to administer poison, with intent to kill an individual.

—— County, to wit:

To all or any one of the Constables of said County:

Whereas, A. B. of said County, has this day made complaint and information on oath before me J. T., a Justice of the said County, that C. D., on the —— day of —— 18—, in said County, did feloniously administer (or *attempt to administer*) unto one J. S. a certain poison, called arsenic, with intent to kill the said J. S.: These are, therefore, to command you, in the name of the Commonwealth of Virginia, forthwith to apprehend the said C. D., and bring him before me or some other Justice of said County, to answer the said complaint, and to be farther dealt with according to law. Given under my hand and seal, this —— day of —— 18—.

J. T., J. P. [L. S.]

[Note.—It is felony to administer or attempt to administer poison with intent merely to injure. In such a case, leave out the word "kill," and insert "injure," or both may be inserted, thus "with intent to injure and kill."]

(¹) Archb. C. 316; 1 Russ. 554. (³) The Queen *v.* Tivey, 1 Car. &
(²) 6 Carr & Payne 364; 1 Mass. R. Kirw. 704.

(No. 2.)

Form of Warrant of Arrest for mingling poison with food, drink or medicine, with intent to injure or kill.

—— County, to wit:
 To all or any one of the Constables of said County:

 Whereas, A. B. of said County, has this day made complaint and information on oath before me J. T., a Justice of the said County, that C. D., on the —— day of —————— 18—, in said County, did feloniously mingle a certain poison, called arsenic, with certain food (or *drink*, or *medicine*, as the case may be,) in order that the same might be taken by one J. S. and other persons, with intent to kill (or *with intent to injure*) the said J. S. and other persons: These are, therefore, to command you, in the name of the Commonwealth of Virginia, forthwith to apprehend the said C. D., and bring him before me or some other Justice of the said County, to answer the said complaint, and to be farther dealt with according to law. Given under my hand and seal, this —— day of —————— 18—.

          J. T., J. P. [L. S.]

(No. 3.)

Form of Warrant of Arrest for poisoning a spring with intent to kill persons.

—— County, to wit:
 To all or any one of the Constables of said County:

 Whereas, A. B. of the said County, has this day made complaint and information on oath before me J. T., a Justice of the said County, that C. D., on the —— day of —————— 18—, in said County, did feloniously poison a certain spring (or *well*, or *reservoir*,) of water, by putting therein a certain poison, called arsenic, (or whatever the thing may be,) in order that the water there so poisoned, might be drunk by J. S. and other persons, with intent to injure and kill the said J. S. and other persons: These are, therefore, to command you, in the name of the Commonwealth of Virginia, forthwith to apprehend the said C. D., and bring him before me or some other Justice of the said County, to answer the said complaint, and to be farther dealt with according to law. Given under my hand and seal, this —— day of —————— 18—.

          J. T., J. P. [L. S.]

(No. 4.)

Form of Warrant of Arrest for maliciously administering poison to horses or cattle.

—— County, to wit:
 To all or any one of the Constables of said County:

 Whereas, A. B. of said County, has this day made complaint and information on oath before me J. T., a Justice of the said County, that C. D., on

the ——— day of ——— 18—, in said County, did feloniously and maliciously administer a certain poison, called arsenic, (or other thing, according to the fact,) to certain horses, (or *cattle*,) the property of one J. S., by mixing the same with the food of the said horses, (or *cattle*,) and with intent that the said poison should be taken and swallowed by them: These are, therefore, to command you, in the name of the Commonwealth of Virginia, forthwith to apprehend the said C. D., and bring him before me or some other Justice of the said County, to answer the said complaint, and to be farther dealt with according to law. Given under my hand and seal, this ——— day of ——— 18—.

J. T., J. P. [L. S.]

(No. 5.)

Form of Warrant of Arrest for maliciously exposing poison, with intent that it should be swallowed by horses, &c.

——— County, to wit:

To all or any one of the Constables of said County:

Whereas, A. B. of said County, has this day made complaint and information on oath before me J. T., a Justice of the said County, that C. D., on the ——— day of ——— 18—, in said County, did feloniously and maliciously put and expose upon the premises of J. S. a certain poisonous substance, that is to say, (state the kind of poison, if known,) so that the same might be taken and swallowed by the horses and cattle of the said J. S., with intent that the said poisonous substance should be taken and swallowed by the horses and cattle of the said J. S.: These are, therefore, to command you, in the name of the Commonwealth of Virginia, forthwith to apprehend the said C. D., and bring him before me or some other Justice of the said County, to answer the said complaint, and to be farther dealt with according to law. Given under my hand and seal, this ——— day of ——— 18—.

J. T., J. P. [L. S.]

(No. 6.)

Form of Mittimus where a party is committed for examination or trial in the County Court, for felonious poisoning.

——— County, to wit:

To X. Z., Constable of said County, and to the Keeper of the Jail of said County:

These are to command you, the said Constable, in the name of the Commonwealth of Virginia, forthwith to convey and deliver into the custody of the keeper of the said jail, together with this warrant, the body of C. D., a white person (or *free negro*, or *a slave, the property of E. F.*, as the case may be,) charged before me J. T., a Justice of the said County, on the oath of A. B., with a felony by him committed, in this, that the said C. D., on the ——— day of ——— in the year 18—, in the said County, (here describe the offence as in the warrant of arrest.) And you, the said keeper of the said jail, are hereby required to receive the said C. D. into your jail and custody, that he may be examined (or *tried*) for the said offence, by the

County Court of said County, and him there safely keep, until he shall be discharged by due course of law. Given under my hand and seal, this —— day of —— in the year 18—.

J. T., J. P. [L. S.]

[NOTE.—If the prisoner be a white person, or if he be a free negro charged with homicide of any grade, or with any offence punishable with death, he must be committed for examination. For all other felonies by free negroes, and in all cases of felony by slaves, the prisoner must be committed for trial.]

(No. 7.)

Form of Certificate of Commitment to be sent to the Clerk of the County Court.

—— County, to wit:

To the Clerk of the County Court of said County:

I, J. T., a Justice of the said County, do hereby certify, that I have, by my warrant, this day committed C. D. (if free negro or slave, state which) to the jail of this County, that he may be examined (or *tried*) before the County Court of the said County, for a felony by him committed, in this, that he did, on the —— day of —— 18—, in the said County, (here state the offence as in the mittimus.) Given under my hand, this —— day of —— in the year 18—.

J. T., J. P.

(No. 8.)

Form of Certificate to the Clerk where party is admitted to bail.

Turn to head of ARREST, and follow No. 6.

(No. 9.)

Form of Recognizance of Bail.

Turn to head of RECOGNIZANCE, and follow No. 1, if person be free; No. 2, if a slave, and state succinctly the offence for which the person is recognized.

(No. 10.)

Form of Recognizance of Witness to appear before the County Court to give evidence upon the examination or trial of a party charged with felony.

Turn to head of RECOGNIZANCE, and follow No. 3.

(No. 1.)

An Indictment for administering poison to an individual, with intent to kill.

—— Judicial Circuit, \
—— County, to wit: \
In the Circuit Court for the \
said County. } The jurors of the Commonwealth of Virginia, in and for the body of the County of ——, and now attending the said Court, upon their oath present, that A. B., on the —— day of ——, in the year one thousand eight hundred and ——, in the said County, did feloniously and maliciously administer to one J. S. a large quantity of a certain deadly poison, called arsenic, to wit, two drachms of the said arsenic, with intent then and there, thereby feloniously and maliciously to injure and kill him the said J. S., against the peace and dignity of the Commonwealth of Virginia.

[Add count for attempting to administer poison.]

(No. 2.)

An Indictment for mingling poison with food, with intent to kill.

—— Judicial Circuit, \
—— County, to wit: \
In the Circuit Court for the \
said County. } The jurors of the Commonwealth of Virginia, in and for the body of the County of ——, and now attending the said Court, upon their oath present, that A. B., on the —— day of —— in the year one thousand eight hundred and ——, in the said County, did feloniously and maliciously attempt to administer to one J. S. a quantity of a certain poison, called arsenic, by then and there mingling the said poison, called arsenic, with certain food, (or *drink*, or *medicine*, as the case may be,) in order that the same might be then and there taken by J. S., and divers other persons, with intent thereby feloniously and maliciously to injure and kill the said J. S., and the said other persons, against the peace and dignity of the Commonwealth of Virginia.

(No. 3.)

An Indictment for maliciously exposing poison, with intent that it should be swallowed by horses, &c.

—— Judicial Circuit, \
—— County, to wit: \
In the Circuit Court for the \
said County. } The jurors of the Commonwealth of Virginia, in and for the body of the County of ——, and now attending the said Court, upon their oath present, that A. B., on the —— day of —— in the year one thousand eight hundred and ——, in the said County, did feloniously and maliciously expose upon the premises of one C. D., deadly poison, to wit, (here state the poison,) with intent that the same should be taken by the horses and cattle of the said C. D., against the peace and dignity of the Commonwealth of Virginia.

CHAPTER LXXXII.

POOR.

A wholesome system of poor laws, well executed, constitutes an important item in the police of the State, for besides the humane purpose of administering to the necessary wants of the indigent, by proper restraint and employment, many strolling paupers may be arrested in that course of vicious indolence, which must end in crime. It behooves the agents of the poor laws to attend faithfully to their execution, by supplying comforts to all entitled to their aid, affording employment and compelling healthy paupers to labour; and by restricting strolling paupers to their places of legal settlement. These are the leading objects which the statute upon the subject has in view.

By Sec. 1, Chap. 51. In any town the council thereof may prescribe the number of overseers of such town, their term of office and compensation, and the time and manner of appointing them.

By Sec. 2. The court of each county shall lay off into districts so much of the county as is without the limits of a town that provides for its poor, and may alter such districts, and prescribe for each one or more overseers.

By Sec. 3. An order for the election of overseers shall be made by the court of every county, within the last three months of the term for which the overseers thereof may have been last elected or appointed, or as soon as may be after the end of that term. The court shall, in such order, fix the day for the election, and a place within each district, for holding the same; and shall also appoint, for each place, a person to superintend the election. The Clerk shall immediately post a copy of such order at the front door of the courthouse, and within ten days deliver another copy thereof to the Sheriff for every such superintendent. The Sheriff shall, within ten days after receiving the same, deliver to each superintendent the copy for him. And the copy so received by any superintendent shall be posted at the place of election in his district.

By Sec. 4. At an election for any such district, every person may vote who is a freeholder or housekeeper therein; and any person shall be eligible who resides and has a freehold therein, unless he is, or within six months preceding the election has been, a collector of county levies.

By Sec. 5. If not so many as ten votes be given in a district, no election shall be considered as made for such district, and the superintendent shall report the fact to the court at the next term; if an election be made, the superintendent shall return the names of the persons elected to the Clerk of the county court, who shall thereupon issue a writ to the Sheriff, commanding him immediately to inform every person so elected of the fact of such election. The Sheriff shall, within ten days after receiving such writ, execute the same and return it to the court at the succeeding term. The term of office of every person so elected shall be three years from the first day of April in the year wherein the order may have been made for such election.

By Sec. 6. The county court shall appoint, for the same term, as many of the overseers prescribed for a district as shall not have been so elected. And when a vacancy happens, in the office of overseer, the county court shall fill such vacancy.

By Sec. 7. Any person appointed a superintendent of any such election, who shall fail to serve, and any superintendent, Clerk or Sheriff, who shall fail to perform any duty prescribed by any preceding section, shall, unless a reasonable excuse be shewn therefor, forfeit thirty dollars.

By Sec. 8. Any person elected or appointed overseer, who shall fail to serve, shall forfeit one hundred dollars, unless he be a person who, in the course of the next preceding nine years, shall have served three, or paid the amount of such forfeiture, or unless he be unable to serve from age or infirmity.

By Sec. 9. If any person so elected or appointed overseer, shall not take the oaths of office within one month after he is informed of such election or appointment, the vacancy may be filled under the sixth section, and a proceeding may be had for the forfeiture prescribed by the preceding section.

By Sec. 10. The court of the county and the council of the town, shall, from time to time, fix upon a day and place for an annual meeting of the overseers. The said overseers shall meet at the said day and place, and may meet at such other times and places as they may fix upon.

By Sec. 11. If, at the time fixed for any meeting, a majority fail to attend, those present may adjourn to another day. The overseers shall appoint a president and clerk. A meeting of the board may be called at any time by the president or one third of the overseers, upon giving to the others reasonable notice of the time for such meeting. If at any meeting, the president of the board be absent, a president *pro tempore* may be appointed.

By Sec. 12. All the proceedings and accounts of the overseers shall be entered in a book, and the said proceedings shall be signed by the person presiding at the meeting at which they may have taken place. If the clerk or any overseer shall, without sufficient excuse, fail to attend any meeting of the board, he shall forfeit two dollars.

By Sec. 13. On application by or on behalf of any person unable to maintain himself, or by or on behalf of the family of a person, when he is unable to maintain it, and the family is unable to maintain itself, such person or family shall be provided for or assisted, if he or they have a legal settlement in a town which has overseers, by one of the said overseers; and if he or they have a legal settlement not within such town, by a majority of the overseers of the district wherein such settlement may be. But a person shall not be deemed to have a legal settlement in such town, until he shall have resided therein for one year, nor in a county, until he shall have resided therein, and without such town, for one year, and shall not be deemed to have a legal settlement in either, if he has migrated into this State within three years, unless at the time of so migrating he was able to maintain himself.

By Sec. 14. When on such application an overseer refuses either provision or assistance, the court of the county or corporation may direct the same.

By Sec. 15. On the complaint of an overseer for any county or town, before a Justice thereof, that any person is come into such county or town, who is likely to be chargeable thereto, such Justice may by warrant cause such person to be removed to the county or town wherein he was last legally settled, unless he be so sick or disabled that he cannot be removed without danger of life, in which case he shall be provided for at the charge, in the first instance, of the county or town wherein he is, and after his recovery shall be removed.

By Sec. 16. The overseers of the county or town wherein such person was last legally settled, shall, upon his being so removed thereto, provide for him and repay all the charges incurred for his maintenance, care and removal. If he die before removal, they shall repay the charges for his burial, and those incurred during his sickness. In case of their failure to comply with this section, complaint may be made before the circuit court of the county or corporation in which they reside, and a summons may be awarded against them; upon the return of which executed on them, or one of them, the circuit court may order them to provide for him, and order repayment of the charges aforesaid, and compel obedience to any such order by attachment or otherwise.

By Sec. 17. The overseers of each county shall be a corporation by the name of "the overseers of the poor," of such county; and with the assent of the court thereof may purchase lands for the use of the poor, and sell and convey lands. They may provide on any of their lands stock and instruments of husbandry, and use such lands as a place of general reception for the poor.

BY SEC. 18. The council of a town or overseers of a county may provide a poorhouse, workhouse and other buildings and improvements, employ managers, physicians, nurses and servants, and prescribe regulations for the government of the several overseers, and discipline for the said houses and the persons therein.

BY SEC. 19. Every overseer shall exert himself to prevent any person from going about begging, or staying in any street or other place to beg. Every such person shall immediately be taken up and conveyed to the place of general reception for the poor of the county or town in which he may be found, or if he has a legal settlement in another county or town of this State, he may be proceeded against according to the fifteenth section, or where he has migrated from another State, and has no legal settlement in this, the board of overseers may cause him to be removed to such other State. To carry into effect this section, an overseer may issue a warrant to a Constable.

BY SEC. 20. Any person to be provided for or assisted by an overseer or overseers, may either be kept at a place of general reception, or be supported or assisted elsewhere, as he or they may deem best; conforming always to such regulations as may, under the eighteenth section, be prescribed. All persons kept at the place of general reception, who are able to work, shall be made to do so.

BY SEC. 21. The overseers of any county may appoint an agent, who, before acting as such, shall execute a bond to the said overseers in such penalty and with such sureties as the board may deem sufficient, conditioned for the faithful performance of his agency.

BY SEC. 22. Such agent shall keep for the board, such money and property as it may authorize him to receive, or have the care of, and dispose of the same as it may direct. He shall in the corporate name of the overseers, recover money or property for them, and defend proceedings against them, the board allowing the expenses of such prosecution or defence.

BY SEC. 23. Annually in April, and more frequently, if required, every agent and overseer shall render to the board a correct account of his transactions, with proper vouchers, and pay, according to its order, such balance as may be in his hands. Any agent or overseer failing so to do shall forfeit not less than thirty nor more than one hundred dollars.

By Sec. 24. The overseers of any county, or the council of any town, may move for and obtain judgment in the court thereof, or in the circuit court of such county or town, or of the county wherein such town may be, against any overseer or his representatives, or against any agent or other person, and his sureties, and his and their personal representatives, for such balance as may be in the hands of, or be owing from such overseer, agent or other person, with lawful interest thereon, and for damages in addition thereto, not exceeding fifteen per centum.

By Sec. 25. Every officer or other person appointed or employed by the board of overseers, shall hold his office or employment at its pleasure, and receive for his services such compensation as the court of the county or council of the town may deem reasonable. Each overseer shall receive one dollar for every day's attendance at the board.

By Sec. 26. A report from the overseers of every county and town for the year ending on the thirty-first day of March, shall be made by those in office on that day. The report shall set forth the number provided for in that year, shewing how many were white and how many coloured; for what length of time, and where each was provided for or assisted; the name of each; the amount received by the overseers for the year, shewing how much from the annual levy and how much otherwise; the amount expended by them for the year, shewing how much was expended at the place of general reception, and how much for those supported or assisted elsewhere; the balance remaining in the hands or under the control of the overseers; what amount in addition they will require to pay arrears of the past, and meet expenditures for the ensuing year; and what will be the nature of the said expenditures. It shall state whether any, and if any, which were kept at work at the place of general reception, for what length of time and in what manner, whether in the workhouse or in tilling the land or otherwise, and may contain such remarks upon the operation of the poor laws as the overseers may deem pertinent.

By Sec. 27. The Second Auditor may prescribe the form for such report. It shall be made in that form, if one be so prescribed; otherwise, in such form as the board may deem best. The president shall attend particularly to the preparation of the report, which shall be delivered to the court of the county on the first day of its May term, and to the council of the town at its first meeting after the first of May. Within sixty days thereafter a copy shall be transmitted by the Clerk of the court or council to the Second Auditor.

BY SEC. 28. In case such report be not so delivered, the president of the board shall forfeit fifty dollars, and in case such report be not so transmitted, the Clerk shall forfeit thirty dollars. The Second Auditor shall immediately give information of such failure to the proper attorney for the Commonwealth, that he may proceed either against the Clerk or against the president.

BY SEC. 29. From the copies so delivered to the Second Auditor, he shall make a report to the General Assembly, which, with so much of the matter contained in the reports of the overseers, as may seem to him advisable, shall be printed under his supervision. A sufficient number of copies shall be printed to furnish one to each member of the General Assembly, the president and each director of the Literary fund, to every overseer, to the general library, the University and each college within the State; and the Governor shall cause the copies so printed to be distributed accordingly.

BY SEC. 30. In every county, the amount which, according to their report, the overseers thereof will require, shall be chargeable on such county, and the county court, when it orders the annual levy, shall provide for the said amount. It shall be payable out of the proceeds of the said levy, to the overseers of the county, and shall be paid thereout to such persons and in such sums as the board of overseers may direct. In every town which has overseers, the expense of the poor shall be provided for by the town council.

BY SEC. 31. This chapter shall not apply to the county of Gloucester, which shall be governed by the act of the twenty-fifth of January eighteen hundred and fourteen. Neither shall it prevent the overseers for the county of James City from continuing the poorhouse and school established under the act of the third of February eighteen hundred and seventeen, for the education as well as the maintenance of the poor in that county. Nor shall it repeal or alter the act passed the twelfth of December seventeen hundred and ninety-one, concerning the poor of the parish of Suffolk, in the county of Nansemond; or the act passed the third of February eighteen hundred and nineteen, to authorize the overseers of the county of Essex to receive a certain legacy; or the act passed the sixteenth of February eighteen hundred and twenty-seven, concerning the overseers of the upper parish of Nansemond county; except in this respect, that the money which, by the three last mentioned acts, is authorized to be levied for by the overseers therein mentioned, shall, upon a report from the said overseers, be levied for by the court of their county.

BY SEC. 32. Every forfeiture declared by this chapter, shall, when incurred in a town, whereof there are overseers, be to such town, and when incurred without such town, be to the overseers of the county.

By Sec. 33. In this chapter, the word "overseer," or the word "overseers," shall be construed as if followed immediately by the words "of the poor."

(No. 1.)

Form of a Warrant to apprehend a pauper strolling from one County to another.

―――― County, to wit:
To X. Y., *Constable of the said County:*

Whereas, A. B. an Overseer of the Poor of the County of ――――, has this day made complaint and information to me J. T., a Justice of the said County, that C. D., a poor person, has come into the said County to reside, and is likely to become chargeable to the said County, and that moreover the said C. D. has gained no legal settlement therein, but was last legally settled in the County of ――――: These are, therefore, to command you, in the name of the Commonwealth of Virginia, to bring the said C. D. before me or some other Justice of the said County of ――――, to answer the said complaint, and to be farther dealt with according to law. Given under my hand and seal, this ―― day of ―――― 18—.

J. T., *J. P.* [L. S.]

(No. 2.)

Form of a Warrant to remove a pauper to the County where he was last legally settled.

―――― County, to wit:
To X. Y., *Constable of the said County, and to the Overseers of the Poor of the County of H.*

Whereas, A. B., one of the Overseers of the Poor of the County of ――――, has this day made complaint and information before me J. T., a Justice of the County of ――――, that C. D., a poor person, has left the County of H., where he was last legally settled, and has come into the said County of ――――, and is going about in said County begging, and likely to become chargeable thereto; and whereas, upon examination had before me, on due proof, it appears to me that the said complaint is true, I do adjudge that the said C. D. is likely to become chargeable to the said County of ――――, if permitted to remain in the same, and that his last place of legal settlement is the said County of H., and that the said C. D. ought to be removed to the said County of H. where he belongs, and there delivered to the Overseers of the County last mentioned: These are, therefore, in the name of the Commonwealth, to command you forthwith to carry the said C. D. to the said County of H., and there to deliver him to one of the Overseers of said County, there to be provided for. Given under my hand and seal, this ―― day of ―――― 18—.

J. T., *J. P.* [L. S.]

(No. 3.)

Form of Warrant of Overseer to remove a pauper who has migrated into this State from another.

——— County, to wit:
 To X. Y., *Constable of the said County:*
 Whereas, at a meeting of the board of Overseers of said County, convened on the ——— day of ——— 18—, it was made to appear to them that one A. B. migrated into this Commonwealth within three years last past, from the State of New York, and was not at the time he so emigrated, able to maintain himself; and that he then was in the said County going about begging therein, without any legal settlement in this Commonwealth, and the said board then ordered the said A. B. to be removed from this Commonwealth to the State of New York: Now, therefore, I, J. T., one of the Overseers of said County, in execution of the said order, do, in the name of the Commonwealth of Virginia, hereby command you forthwith to arrest the said A. B., and to carry him back to the State of New York. Given under my hand and seal, this ——— day of ——— 18—.

J. T., *Overseer,* [L. S.]

POSSE COMITATUS—See Officers and Riots.

CHAPTER LXXXIII.

QUARANTINE.

[See Small Pox.]

By Sec. 12, Chap. 86. The council of any town may establish a quarantine ground for such town, and the councils of any two or more towns, may establish a quarantine ground for their common use; but if the place fixed on for such quarantine ground, be without the limits of a town, the assent of the court of the county to its use must first be obtained.

By Sec. 13. The council of any such town may, from time to time, prescribe the quarantine to be performed by all vessels arriving within the harbour or vicinity of such town, and regulations therefor, not contrary to law.

By Sec. 14. Such regulations may extend to all persons, goods and effects arriving in such vessels, and to all persons who may go on board of the same. If any person violate such regulations, after notice thereof shall have been given, by publishing the same in some newspaper printed in the town, or where there is none such, by posting it up in some public place therein, he shall forfeit not less than five nor more than five hundred dollars.

By Sec. 15. The health officer in such town, may cause any vessel arriving in its port or vicinity, if the vessel or its cargo be, in his opinion, so foul or infected as to endanger the public health, to be removed to the quarantine ground or other proper place, and to be purified; and cause all persons arriving in, or going on board of such vessel, or handling such cargo, to be removed to a hospital.

By Sec. 16. If any master, seaman or passenger belonging to a vessel supposed to have any infection on board, or from a port where any dangerous, infectious disease prevails, shall refuse to answer on oath such enquiries as may be made by any health officer or other authorized person, relating to such infection or disease, he shall forfeit not less than one hundred nor more than five hundred dollars.

By Sec. 17. The master of a vessel ordered to perform quarantine, shall deliver to the officer appointed to see it performed, his bills of health and manifests, and his log book and journal. If he fail to do so, or to repair in proper time, after notice, to the quarantine ground, or shall depart thence without authority to do so, he shall forfeit not more than five hundred dollars.

By Sec. 18. If any person ordered to perform quarantine shall escape, a Justice, on complaint thereof, made under oath, may issue his warrant to a Sheriff, Sergeant or Constable, commanding him to arrest such fugitive and deliver him to the custody of the officers of quarantine. Any such person attempting to escape, may be forcibly detained at the place of quarantine by such officers.

By Sec. 19. Any person coming into any town by land, from a place infected with a dangerous, infectious disease, may be compelled to perform quarantine by the health officer, and restrained from travelling until discharged. Any such person who shall, before he is discharged, travel in this State, unless it be to return, by the most direct route, to the State from which he came, shall forfeit one hundred dollars.

By Sec. 20. All expenses and costs incurred by any town, on account of any person, vessel or goods, under quarantine regulations, shall be paid or reimbursed to it by such person, or the owner of such vessel or goods, respectively, and the said town may detain any such vessel or goods until such expenses and costs are paid.

By Sec. 21. The word "town," wherever it occurs in this chapter, shall include a city, and the word "council" shall include any body authorized to make ordinances for a town.

(No. 1.)

Form of a Warrant to apprehend the master of a vessel, for refusing to answer enquiries by a health officer, relating to infectious diseases on board of his vessel.

———— County, to wit:
To X. Y., *Constable of the said County:*

Whereas, A. B., a health officer of the town of ————, has this day complained on oath before me J. T., a Justice of the said County, that he did, on the ———— day of ———— 18—, (or *on this day,*) in the County of ————, enquire of C. D., the master of a vessel, called the ————, now lying in the port of ————, (state the enquiry,) and that he the said C. D. then refused to answer the said enquiry, the said A. B. then supposing there was an infectious disease, to wit, the cholera, on board the said vessel, (or " then believing that the said vessel came from N. O. a port where the cholera, a dangerous infectious disease, prevails:") These are, therefore, to command you, in the name of the Commonwealth of Virginia, forthwith to apprehend the said C. D., and to bring him before me or some other Justice of the said County, to answer the said complaint, and to be farther dealt with according to law. Given under my hand and seal, this ———— day of ———— 18—.

J. T., J. P. [L. S.]

(No. 2.)

Form of a Warrant against the master of a vessel ordered to perform quarantine, for failing to deliver his bills of health, &c. to the officer appointed to see quarantine performed.

———— County, to wit:
To X. Y., *Constable of the said County:*

Whereas, A. B. has this day made complaint on oath before me J. T., a Justice of the said County, that on the ———— day of ———— 18—, in said County, C. D., then the health officer for the town of ————, ordered E. F. the master of a certain vessel, called the ————, then lying in the port of ————, (or *then in* ———— *river, and coming to the port of* ————,) to perform quarantine with his said vessel within the quarantine ground of the said town, and that he the said [A. B., an officer appointed to see that the said vessel and her crew performed quarantine according to the said order, on the ———— day of ———— 18—, in the said County, required the said E. F., as master of the said vessel, to deliver to him the said A. B., his bills of health and manifests, and his log book and journal, and that he the said E. F., as master as aforesaid, failed and refused to do so :] These are, therefore, in the name of the Commonwealth of Virginia, to command you forthwith to apprehend the said E. F., and to bring him before me or some other Justice of the said County, to answer the said complaint, and to be farther dealt with according to law. Given under my hand and seal, this ———— day of ———— 18—.

J. T., J. P. [L. S.]

[NOTE.—If the complaint be for not repairing to the quarantine ground, leave out all in the brackets, and say: "E. F. did not, after the said order and notice thereof given him, repair in proper time to the said quarantine ground."]

(No. 3.)

Form of a Warrant to apprehend a person escaping from a vessel ordered to perform quarantine.

—— County, to wit:
 To X. Y., Constable of said County:

Whereas, A. B. has this day complained on oath, before me J. T., a Justice of the said County, that E. F., a person on board of a vessel, called the ———, lying in the port of ———, was, to wit, on the —— day of —— 18—, in the said County, ordered by C. D. the health officer of the town of ———, to perform quarantine within the quarantine ground of the said town, and that he did, after the said order, to wit, on the —— day of —— 18—, escape from the said vessel, and that he is now going at large in the said County, and without the bounds of the said quarantine ground: These are, therefore, in the name of the Commonwealth of Virginia, to command you forthwith to apprehend the said E. F., and to convey and deliver him into the custody of the quarantine officers of the said town. Given under my hand and seal, this —— day of —— 18—.

J. T., J. P. [L. S.]

[NOTE.—A party incurring any penalty under the foregoing provisions of the statute, is to be prosecuted by indictment as in other cases of misdemeanor.]

(No. 4.)

Form of Mittimus where a party is committed to answer an Indictment in the County Court for violating quarantine.

—— County, to wit:
 To X. Z., Constable of said County, and to the Keeper of the Jail of the said County:

These are to command you, the said Constable, in the name of the Commonwealth of Virginia, forthwith to convey and deliver into the custody of the keeper of the said jail, together with this warrant, the body of C. D., charged before me J. T., a Justice of the said County, on the oath of A. B., with a misdemeanor by him committed, in this, that the said C. D., on the —— day of —— in the year 18—, in the said County, (here describe the offence as in the warrant of arrest.) And you, the said keeper of the said jail, are hereby required to receive the said C. D. into your jail and custody, to answer an indictment to be preferred against him for the said offence, in the County Court of said County, and him there safely keep until he shall be discharged by due course of law. Given under my hand and seal, this —— day of —— in the year 18—.

J. T., J. P. [L. S.]

(No. 5.)

Form of Recognizance of Bail.

Turn to head of RECOGNIZANCE, and follow No. 4, and state the offence succinctly, for which the party is recognized.

(No. 6.)

Form of Certificate of the Commitment, or Letting to Bail, to be sent to the Clerk of the County Court.

—— County, to wit:
To the Clerk of the County Court of the said County:
I, J. T., a Justice of the said County, do hereby certify, that C. D. was this day committed to the jail of this County, by my warrant, (or *was this day admitted to bail by me*, as the case may be,) to answer an indictment to be preferred against him in the County Court of the said County, for a misdemeanor by him committed, in this, that he did, on the —— day of —— 18—, in said County, (here describe the offence as in the warrant of arrest.) Given under my hand, this —— day of —— 18—.

J. T., J. P.

(No. 7.)

Form of Recognizance of Witness to appear and give evidence to the Grand Jury upon the indictment.

Follow No. 5, under head of RECOGNIZANCE.

CHAPTER LXXXIV.

RAILROADS AND CANALS.

Injuries to, where life is perilled.

BY SEC. 33, CHAP. 192. If a free person maliciously obstruct, remove or injure any part of a canal or railroad, or any bridge or fixture thereof, or obstruct any machinery, work or engine thereof, whereby the life of any traveller on such canal or road is put in peril, he shall be confined in the penitentiary not less than three nor more than five years.

[For injuries to railroad bridges, by burning, where no life is put in peril, see BURNING; and for other malicious injuries to railroads and canals, see TRESPASSES.]

(No. 1.)

Form of Warrant of Arrest for maliciously injuring or removing a railroad, whereby the lives of passengers are put in peril.

———— County, to wit:
 To all or any one of the Constables of said County:
 Whereas, A. B. of said County, has this day made complaint and information on oath before me J. T., a Justice of the said County, that C. D., on the —— day of ———— 18—, in said County, did feloniously and maliciously break, injure and remove a part of a certain railroad there situate, to wit, the Richmond and Petersburg railroad, (or any other railroad, as the case may be,) whereby the life of A. B. and divers other persons travelling on the said railroad was put in peril: These are, therefore, to command you, in the name of the Commonwealth of Virginia, forthwith to apprehend the said C. D., and bring him before me or some other Justice of the said County, to answer the said complaint, and to be farther dealt with according to law. Given under my hand and seal, this —— day of ———— 18—.

J. T., J. P. [L. S.]

(No. 2.)

Form of Warrant of Arrest for maliciously obstructing a railroad, and thereby putting the lives of persons in peril.

———— County, to wit:
 To all or any one of the Constables of said County:
 Whereas, A. B. of said County, has this day made complaint and information on oath before me J. T., a Justice of the said County, that C. D., on the —— day of ———— 18—, in said County, did feloniously and maliciously place and put upon a certain railroad there situate, to wit, the Richmond and Petersburg railroad, (or whatever other railroad it may be,) a large piece of wood, (or "a stone,") and thereby obstruct the passage of the cars upon the said railroad, whereby the life of A. B. and divers other persons travelling on the said railroad was put in peril: These are, therefore, to command you, in the name of the Commonwealth of Virginia, forthwith to apprehend the said C. D., and bring him before me or some other Justice of the said County, to answer the said complaint, and to be farther dealt with according to law. Given under my hand and seal, this —— day of ———— 18—.

J. T., J. P. [L. S.]

(No. 3.)

Form of Warrant of Arrest for obstructing machinery of railroad.

———— County, to wit:
 To all or any one of the Constables of said County:
 Whereas, A. B. of said County, has this day made complaint and information on oath before me J. T., a Justice of the said County, that C. D., on the —— day of ———— 18—, in said County, did feloniously and maliciously

obstruct the machinery, to wit, an engine of the Richmond, Fredericksburg and Potomac railroad, by (state by what the machine was obstructed,) whereby the life of the said A. B., who was then travelling upon the said railroad, was put in peril: These are, therefore, to command you, in the name of the Commonwealth of Virginia, forthwith to apprehend the said C. D., and bring him before me or some other Justice of the said County, to answer the said complaint, and to be farther dealt with according to law. Given under my hand and seal, this ―― day of ――― 18―.

J. T., J. P. [L. S.]

(No. 4.)

Form of Mittimus.

Follow form No. 4, under the head of ARREST, and describe the offence as in the warrant of arrest.

(No. 5.)

Form of Recognizance of Bail.

Follow No. 1 or 2, under head of RECOGNIZANCE.

(No. 6.)

Form of Recognizance of Witnesses.

Turn to the head of RECOGNIZANCE and follow form No. 3.

An Indictment for maliciously obstructing a railroad, whereby the lives of travellers were put in peril.

Commence as No. 1, under head of "INDICTMENTS," and say: "a certain part of a certain railroad, called the Richmond and Petersburg railroad, passing along and through the said County, feloniously and maliciously did obstruct, (state how the obstruction was effected,) whereby the lives of divers persons, to wit, twenty persons, then and there travelling upon the said railroad, were by the obstruction aforesaid, feloniously and maliciously put in great peril, against the peace and dignity of the Commonwealth of Virginia.

CHAPTER LXXXV.

RAPE.

[For rape by negro on white person, see NEGROES.]

This crime, so detestable in itself and injurious in its consequences to society, is upon every principle of justice and sound policy severely punished.

By SEC. 15, CHAP. 191. If any white person carnally know a female of the age of twelve years or more, against her will by force, or carnally know a female child under that age, he shall be confined in the penitentiary not less than ten nor more than twenty years.

This provision embraces substantially the Common Law definition of rape, which is the having unlawful and carnal knowledge of a woman by force, and against her will.(¹) The offence, when committed by a free negro or slave upon a white person, is punishable with death.

From the terms by which the offence is defined, there can be no rape where the woman previously consents, for the act must be done against her will. But though she first yield her assent, yet if she be afterwards forced against her consent, it will be rape. So the offence may be committed, though the woman at last yields to the violence, if such her consent was forced by fear of death or duress; and it will be no excuse that she consented after the fact.(²) If, by the use of intoxicating liquors or narcotics, a woman is rendered insensible and deprived of her free will, and the act be committed while she is in a state of insensibility, it will be rape; for in such condition, she can no more be said to yield her consent than when actual force is resorted to.(³)

But mere fraud, practised upon a woman possessed of her reason, by means of which she submits to sexual intercourse, will not be construed to mean force at Common Law. As where a man had carnal knowledge of a married woman, under circumstances which induced her to believe it was her husband, it was held not to be rape.(⁴)*

To support the charge of rape, there must be proof of penetration; for without it, the crime is not complete. But the

---

(¹) 1 Hawk. P. C. c. 41, § 2; 1 Russ. C. & M. 556.
(²) 1 Russ. C. & M. 557.
(³) 47 Com. L. R. 746, by 15 Judges.
(⁴) Rex v. Jackson, Russ. & Ry. 487; Bartow's Case, 1 Wheel. C. C. 378; and Field's Case, 4 Leigh 648; see, also, 2 Wheel. C. C. 152, and 47 Com. L. R. 414.

*But by statute, it is felony in a negro to have carnal knowledge of a white female by fraud. See NEGROES.

least degree of penetration, no matter how little, is sufficient, though it may not be attended with the deprivation of the marks of virginity.(¹) The principle is now fully settled, notwithstanding the difficulty suggested by Mr. Beck in his medical jurisprudence, (page 53,) of making out the charge where the hymen is entire. It is nevertheless possible, and although in one case, it was said by a single Judge, that if the hymen is not ruptured, there is not a sufficient penetration to constitute the offence,(²) yet in another more recent, the Judge, who tried the prisoner, with the concurrence of two other Judges, said "it is not necessary in order to complete the offence, that the hymen should be ruptured, provided it be clearly proved that there was penetration."(³) And in a still more recent case, the court left it to the jury to say, whether at any time any part of the *virile* member of the prisoner was within the *labia* of the *pudendum* of the prosecutrix; for if it was, he remarks, no matter how little, that will be sufficient to constitute penetration.(⁴)

The disgusting enquiry of *emissio seminis*, was put an end to in this Commonwealth in 1812, by the decision in Thomas' Case, 1 Va. Cases 309. It is not necessary to complete the crime of rape, that there should be emission; and so now is the law of England, by statute (9 George 4, c. 31, § 18,) passed to settle a variety of conflicting decisions on the point in their courts.(⁵)

A boy under the age of fourteen years, is presumed by law to be incapable of committing rape, and therefore he can neither be convicted of this offence, nor of an assault with intent to commit it; for though, in other felonies, malice supplies age, yet as to this offence, the law supposes an imbecility of both body and mind;(⁶) so much so, that in one case, the Judge said, that in his opinion, if the boy was under fourteen years, no evidence was admissible to shew that in point of fact, he could not commit the offence of rape.(⁷) But as this doctrine is founded upon imbecility, rather than the want of discretion, a boy under fourteen, who (being present,) *aids* and assists another person in the commission of the offence, is not the less a principal in the second degree, if it appear, under all circumstances, that he had a mischievous discretion.(⁸) The husband cannot, himself, be guilty of actual rape upon his wife, but he likewise may be guilty as a prin-

(¹) 1 Russ. C. & M. 558.
(²) Gammon's Case, 5 C. & P. 321.
(³) By Bosanquet. Present, Coleridge and Coltman, M'Kue's Case, 8 C. & P. 562.
(⁴) Line's Case, 47 Com. L. R. 393.
(⁵) See 1 Russ. C. & M. 558 to 560.
(⁶) Deac. Cr. Co. 1081; Elder Shaw's Case, 3 C. & P. 396; Groombridge's Case, 7 C. & P. 502.
(⁷) By Patteson, J., in Phillips' Case, 8 C. & P. 736; but query, see 2 Dick. J. P. 380.
(⁸) 1 Hale 630.

cipal, in the second degree, by being present, assisting another person to commit a rape upon her.(¹)

The law affords its protection to all women against this violent and atrocious outrage, and it is no excuse to the party committing the offence, that she was a common strumpet, for even she is under its protection, and may not be forced. Neither is it any justification that she was a concubine to the ravisher himself; for as a woman may reform her unlawful course of life, the law will not presume her incapable of amendment.(²)

The material difference between rape proper and the carnal knowledge of a girl, under the age of twelve years, consists in this, that in the latter, it is equally a felony, whether the infant consent or not, but in the former, it is not rape.(³) And therefore, in prosecutions under this clause of the statute, it is not necessary to allege in any part of the proceedings of the Justice, that the act was done against the consent of the infant.(⁴)

Evidence.

It has been truly said that rape is an accusation easily made, and though hard to be proven, it is still harder to be defended by the party accused, innocent as he may be, and Lord Hale recommends great caution upon trials for this offence, least, from its heinousness, courts and juries be so far transported with indignation against the prisoner, as to be induced overhastily to convict him, on the confident testimony of false and malicious witnesses.

Since emission is no longer necessary to constitute the crime, the only points to be proved, are want of consent on the part of the woman, and penetration, and of this, there must be decisive proof.

The party grieved, (as in all other criminal cases,) may of course be admitted as a witness; the great difficulty, however, exists in duly weighing the credibility of her testimony. For this reason, where she is a common prostitute or a concubine, it is very material to hear that matter in favour of the party accused, where the woman's testimony is not corroborated.(⁵)

General evidence of the prosecutrix's bad character may be given in evidence, but she cannot be asked whether she had connection with any particular person,(⁶) unless it be with the prisoner, and this she may be asked.(⁷)

(¹) 6 St. Tr. 387; Lord Audley's Case, sometimes cited as Lord Castlehaven's Case. Lord Audley was also Earl of Castlehaven in Ireland.
(²) 1 Russ. 557.
(³) Bennett's Case, 2 Va. Cases 235.
(⁴) Id.
(⁵) 1 Hawk. c. 41, § 7; East P. C. 445; Deac. 1082.
(⁶) Hudson's Case, Russ. & Ry. 218.
(⁷) 2 Stark. Ev. 216, and Martin's Case, 6 C. & P. 562; see also Barker's Case, 3 C. & P. 589.

The old absurdity that conception was evidence of consent on the part of the woman, is now exploded.(¹)

With respect to the evidence to prove the rape or carnal knowledge of a child under twelve years of age, the Justice must remember, that consent in this case neither excuses nor mitigates the crime. Therefore, the only proofs required for the prosecution, are: first, the penetration; and secondly, that the child is only twelve years of age.

To prove the offence, the child herself may be examined, however young, if capable of distinguishing right from wrong, but like other witnesses, she must in all cases be examined upon oath,(²) for her declarations are inadmissible,(³) though the fact itself that the child speedily complained of the injury, is of course, as in every case of rape, not only admissible, but strong confirmatory evidence of the crime.(⁴)

When the child is uninformed as to the nature and obligations of an oath, it is the practice in England to postpone the trial, that she may be taught these obligations.(⁵)

The age of the child must be proven,(⁶) except in the case of rape by a slave or free negro on a white child. In these cases, it is unnecessary, as the statute makes no distinction between infants and adults.

The Justice in his proceedings, should treat all persons present, aiding and abetting, as principals.

(No. 1.)

Form of Warrant of Arrest for rape on a woman.

———— County, to wit:

To all or any one of the Constables of said County:

Whereas, A. B. a white person, of said County, has this day made complaint and information on oath before me J. T., a Justice of the said County, that C. D., a white person, on the —— day of —————— 18—, in said County, violently and against her will, by force, feloniously did ravish and carnally know her, the said A. B., she the said A. B. then being twelve years old and more, to wit, of the age of —— years: These are, therefore, to command you, in the name of the Commonwealth of Virginia, forthwith to apprehend the said C. D., and bring him before me or some other Justice of the said County, to answer the said complaint, and to be farther dealt with according to law. Given under my hand and seal, this —— day of ———— 18—.

J. T., J. P. [L. S.]

(¹) 1 Russ. 557.
(²) Brazier's Case, 1 Leach 199; Powell's Case, Id. 110.
(³) Tucker's Case, 1 Phil. Ev. 21.
(⁴) Brazier's Case, just cited.
(⁵) White's Case, 1 Leach 430; but query as to the propriety of this practice?
(⁶) Rosc. Cr. Ev. 810.

(No. 2.)

Form of Warrant of Arrest for carnal knowledge and abuse of a girl under the age of twelve years.

—— County, to wit:
To all or any one of the Constables of said County:

Whereas, A. B. of said County, has this day made complaint and information on oath before me J. T., a Justice of the said County, that C. D., a white person, on the —— day of —— 18—, in said County, feloniously and unlawfully did carnally know and abuse A. B., an infant under the age of twelve years, to wit, of the age of ten years: These are, therefore, to command you, in the name of the Commonwealth of Virginia, forthwith to apprehend the said C. D., and bring him before me or some other Justice of the said County, to answer the said complaint, and to be farther dealt with according to law. Given under my hand and seal, this —— day of —— 18—.

J. T., J. P. [L. s.]

(No. 3.)

Form of Warrant of Arrest against a negro for a rape committed on a negro.

—— County, to wit:
To all or any one of the Constables of said County:

Whereas, A. B. of said County, has this day made complaint and information on oath before me J. T., a Justice of the said County, that C. D., a negro, on the —— day of —— 18—, in said County, in and upon one E. F., a negro, then and there being, violently and feloniously did make an assault, and her the said E. F. then and there violently and against her will, by force, feloniously did ravish and carnally know: These are, therefore, to command you, in the name of the Commonweath of Virginia, forthwith to apprehend the said C. D., and bring him before me or some other Justice of the said County, to answer the said complaint, and to be farther dealt with according to law. Given under my hand and seal, this —— day of —— 18—.

J. T., J. P. [L. s.]

(No. 4.)

Form of Warrant of Arrest against a negro for carnally knowing and abusing a negro girl, under the age of twelve years.

—— County, to wit:
To all or any one of the Constables of said County:

Whereas, A. B. of said County, has this day made complaint and information on oath before me J. T., a Justice of the said County, that C. D., a negro slave, the property of ——, (or *a free negro,*) on the —— day of —— 18—, in said County, in and upon one E. F., a coloured infant under the age of twelve years, feloniously and unlawfully did make an assault, and her

RAPE.

the said E. F., then and there did feloniously carnally know and abuse: These are, therefore, to command you, in the name of the Commonwealth of Virginia, forthwith to apprehend the said C. D., and bring him before me or some other Justice of the said County, to answer the said complaint, and to be farther dealt with according to law. Given under my hand and seal, this —— day of ——— 18—.

J. T., J. P. [L. s.]

(No. 5.)

Form of Mittimus where a party is committed for examination or trial in the County Court, for rape.

———— County, to wit:

To X. Z., Constable of said County, and to the Keeper of the Jail of said County:

These are to command you the said Constable, in the name of the Commonwealth of Virginia, forthwith to convey and deliver into the custody of the keeper of the said jail, together with this warrant, the body of C. D., a white person (or *free negro*, or *a slave, the property of E. F.*, as the case may be,) charged before me J. T., a Justice of the said County, on the oath of A. B., with a felony by him committed, in this, that the said C. D., on the —— day of ——— in the year 18—, in the said County, (here describe the offence as in the warrant of arrest.) And you, the said keeper of the said jail, are hereby required to receive the said C. D. into your jail and custody, that he may be examined (or *tried*) for the said offence by the County Court of said County, and him there safely keep until he shall be discharged by due course of law. Given under my hand and seal, this —— day of ——— in the year 18—.

J. T., J. P. [L. s.]

[NOTE.—If the prisoner be a white person, or if he be a free negro, charged with homicide of any grade, or with any offence punishable with death, he must be committed for examination. For all other felonies by free negroes, and in all cases of felony by slaves, the prisoner must be committed for trial.]

(No. 6.)

Form of Certificate of Commitment to be sent to the Clerk of the County Court, for rape.

———— County, to wit:

To the Clerk of the County Court of said County:

I, J. T., a Justice of the said County, do hereby certify, that I have, by my warrant, this day committed C. D., a white person, (or if free negro or slave, state which,) to the jail of this County, that he may be examined (or *tried*) before the County Court of the said County for a felony by him committed, in this, that he did, on the —— day of ——— 18—, in the said County, (here state the offence as in the mittimus.) Given under my hand, this —— day of ——— in the year 18—.

J. T., J. P.

540   RAPE—(*Indictments for.*)

(No. 7.)

Form of Certificate to the Clerk where party is admitted to bail.

Turn to head of ARREST, and follow No. 6.

(No. 8.)

Form of Recognizance of Bail.

Turn to head of RECOGNIZANCE, and follow No. 1, if person be free; No. 2, if a slave, and state succinctly the offence for which the person is recognized.

(No. 9.)

Form of Recognizance of Witness to appear before the County Court to give evidence upon the examination or trial of a party charged with felony.

Turn to head of RECOGNIZANCE, and follow No. 3.

(No. 1.)

Indictment for a rape.

Commence as No. 1, under the head of "INDICTMENTS," and say: that A. B., a white person, on the ―― day of ――――, at the County aforesaid, with force and arms, in and upon one C. D., the said C. D. then being over the age of twelve years, to wit, of the age of twenty years, violently and feloniously did make an assault; and her the said C. D. then and there, to wit, on the day and year aforesaid, at the County aforesaid, feloniously did ravish and carnally know, against her will and by force, against the peace and dignity of the Commonwealth of Virginia.

(No. 2.)

Indictment for carnally knowing and abusing a female child, under the age of twelve years.

Commence as No. 1, under head of "INDICTMENTS," and say: that A. B., a white person, on the ―― day of ――――, with force and arms, in the County aforesaid, in and upon one C. D., a female child, under the age of twelve years, to wit, of the age of ten years, feloniously did make an assault; and her the said C. D., then and there, to wit, on the day and year aforesaid, at the County aforesaid, unlawfully and feloniously did carnally know and abuse, against the peace and dignity of the Commonwealth of Virginia.

RAPE—(*Indictments for.*)

(No. 3.)

Form of an Indictment against a free negro, for rape on a white woman.

Commence as No. 1, under head of "INDICTMENTS," and say: in and upon one E. F., a white female over the age of twelve years, to wit, of the age of twenty years, violently and feloniously an assault did make, and her the said E. F., then and there, to wit, on the day and year aforesaid, at the County aforesaid, feloniously and against the will of the said E. F., and by force did ravish and carnally know, he the said A. B., then and there being a free negro, against the peace and dignity of the Commonwealth of Virginia.

(No. 4.)

Form of an Indictment against a free negro for an assault upon a white female, with intent to ravish her.

Commence as No. 1, under head of "INDICTMENTS," and say: in and upon one E. F., a white female, an assault feloniously did make, with intent her the said E. F., then and there, to wit, on the day and year aforesaid, in the County aforesaid, feloniously and against her will, and by force carnally to know, he the said A. B. then and there being a free negro, against the peace and dignity of the Commonwealth of Virginia.

REBELLION—See NEGROES.

CHAPTER LXXXVI.

RECEIVING STOLEN GOODS.

BY SEC. 19, CHAP. 192. If any free person buy or receive from another person, or aid in concealing any stolen goods or other thing, knowing the same to have been stolen, he shall be deemed guilty of larceny thereof, and may be proceeded against although the principal offender be not convicted.

In prosecutions for this offence, nice distinctions are often made as to what shall be construed an act of stealing, so as to make the case one of larceny, and what an act of receiving, so as to constitute a felonious receiving under the statute, and it is difficult sometimes to draw the line where the act of stealing ends and that of receiving begins. The true distinction seems to be this: that where the goods are wholly taken away by one person from the possession of the owner, or from their place of lawful deposit, and carried to another place, that here the larceny is complete, and if they are afterwards removed from this place by an accomplice, he will be guilty of a felonious receiving; as where two men, in the absence of the prisoner, broke into a warehouse and stole therefrom several firkins of butter and some cheese, and carried them to a distance of thirty yards in another street and left them there, and then went for the prisoner and brought him to the place where they had left the goods, and upon their informing him what they had done, he assisted them in carrying the goods away, in a cart which they had provided for that purpose, the prisoner was held guilty of receiving.([1]) But where the original taking and carrying away is not fully completed, but requires some additional act to be done to consummate the original felonious intent, then all those present aiding in the subsequent act, are principal felons, and are guilty of larceny. Thus, where the master of a boat was employed to bring some barilla on shore, and some of his servants, without his privity, removed it to another part of the boat, with intent to steal it, and concealed it under some rope, and the master afterwards assisted them in removing it from the boat for the purpose of carrying it off, he was held guilty of larceny; for though the first removal was sufficient to convict the servants of larceny, the court held this to be but a continuous transaction to effect the original felonious purpose, and could not

---

([1]) R. v. King, Ry. & Russ. 332 and 333, note b., and Kelley's Case, Ry. & R. 421.

be said to be completed till the removal of the barilla from out of the boat.(¹) These and similar cases which frequently occur in practice, make it difficult sometimes to determine whether the case is one of larceny or receiving. The two offences may be joined in the same indictment,(²) and there is no reason why they should not be in the same warrant of commitment. The Justice may unite in the same warrant, a charge against the principal for larceny, and a charge of felonious receiving against the receiver.

Although it is not known by whom the goods are actually stolen, a party may nevertheless be proceeded against for receiving them; for one of the objects of the statute, is to punish the receiver when the thief cannot be discovered,(³) and by the terms of the statute, the receiver may be proceeded against, notwithstanding the principal be not convicted.

It is stated, upon the authority of Walke's Case,(⁴) that where the principal is known, the fact should be stated according to the truth. Although there can be no objection to this practice, yet it is apprehended to be unnecessary. The statute makes it felony to receive stolen goods, knowing them to be stolen, without regard to the person from whom received, and it is sufficient to charge the offence in the language of the statute ;(⁵) and this position is sustained by the learned author of a recent valuable digest of the criminal code of England, in commenting upon the case of R. v. Messingham.(⁶)

Upon a joint charge against husband and wife, of receiving stolen goods, if the husband be convicted, the wife cannot be found guilty, unless she receive the goods in the absence of her husband,(⁷) and if two persons are charged as joint receivers, a joint act of receiving must be proved; for proof that one received in the absence of the other, and afterwards delivered the goods to him, will not suffice. Successive receivers, however, are all punishable, if proceeded against separately.(⁸)

The guilty knowledge is the very gist of the offence, and it must be proved that the prisoner received the goods in question, *knowing them to have been stolen*. In this, as in other cases, it is sufficient, if circumstances are proved, which, to persons of ordinary understanding, and situated as the prisoner was, must have led to the conclusion that the goods were ille-

---

(¹) Dyer's Case, 2 East P. C. 767; and Owen's Case, R. & M. 96.
(²) Galloway's Case, Ry. & M. 234.
(³) 2 East P. C. 781; Bush's Case, Ry. & R. 372.
(⁴) 3 Camp. 264.
(⁵) Deac. C. C. 1092; R. v. Jervis, 6 C. & P. 330.
(⁶) 1 Deac. Cr. Co., title RECEIVING; and Ry. & M. 257.
(⁷) Rex v. Archer, R. & M. 143.
(⁸) Rex v. Messingham, R. & M. 257.

gally acquired. Thus, if it be proved that the prisoner received watches, jewelry, large quantities of money, bundles of clothes of various kinds, or moveables of any sort, to a considerable value, from boys or other persons destitute of property, and without any means of acquiring them, (and this remark is strikingly applicable to slaves,) and under circumstances of evident concealment, it is impossible to arrive at any other conclusion, but that they were received in the full understanding of the guilty mode of their acquisition.([1])

If the goods were bought by the receiver much below their value, it is presumptive proof of a guilty knowledge; and for the purpose of proving guilty knowledge, it is competent to give in evidence, that the person pledged or otherwise disposed of other articles of stolen property besides those for the receiving of which he is charged.([2]) And so, where the receiving of another article has been made the subject of another and distinct charge, it is admissible to give that in evidence to prove guilty knowledge.([3])

If the party charged knew at the time he received the goods, that they were stolen, it matters not whether he received them for profit or advantage or not, or merely to conceal them, or to assist the thief, he is guilty of this offence just as much as if he had purchased them.([4])

(No. 1.)

Form of Warrant of Arrest for feloniously receiving stolen goods.

—— County, to wit:

To all or any one of the Constables of said County:

Whereas, A. B. of said County, has this day made complaint and information on oath before me J. T., a Justice of the said County, that C. D., on the —— day of —— 18—, in said County, did feloniously buy and receive one coat, of the value of ten dollars, one vest of the value of five dollars, (or any other article, as the case may be,) of the goods and chattels of the said A. B., which said goods and chattels were lately before feloniously taken, stolen and carried away from the said A. B., he the said C. D. then well knowing the said goods and chattels to have been feloniously taken, stolen and carried away: These are, therefore, to command you, in the name of the Commonwealth of Virginia, forthwith to apprehend the said C. D., and bring him before me or some other Justice of the said County, to answer the said complaint, and to be farther dealt with according to law. Given under my hand and seal, this —— day of —— 18—.

J. T., J. P. [L. s.]

NOTE.—This form may be easily adapted to any kind of property. Where the case is for receiving any article usually valued by measure, it may be described thus: "ten bushels of wheat, of the value of —— dollars;" and where the article is usually valued by weight, state it thus: "one hundred pounds of tobacco, of the value of," &c.

([1]) Allison's Pr. Cr. L. 330.
([2]) Dunn's Case, Moo. C. C. 150.
([3]) Rex v. Davis, 6 C. & P. 342.
([4]) Rex v. Davis and another, 6 C. & P. 341.

(No. 2.)

Form of Warrant of Arrest for feloniously receiving a stolen bank note.

——— County, to wit:
    To all or any one of the Constables of said County:

Whereas, A. B. of said County, has this day made complaint and information on oath before me J. T., a Justice of the said County, that C. D., on the ——— day of ——— 18—, in said County, did feloniously buy and receive one bank note, for the payment of ——— dollars, and of the value of ——— dollars, the property and bank note of R. M., which said bank note was lately before feloniously taken, stolen and carried away from the said R. M., he the said C. D. then well knowing the said bank note to have been feloniously taken, stolen and carried away from the said R. M.: These are, therefore, to command you, in the name of the Commonwealth of Virginia, forthwith to apprehend the said C. D., and bring him before me or some other Justice of the said County, to answer the said complaint, and to be farther dealt with according to law. Given under my hand and seal, this ——— day of ——— 18—.

                                                  J. T., *J. P.* [L. S.]

(No. 3.)

Form of Warrant of Arrest for feloniously receiving coin.

——— County, to wit:
    To all or any one of the Constables of said County:

Whereas, A. B. of said County, has this day made complaint and information on oath before me J. T., a Justice of the said County, that C. D., on the ——— day of ——— 18—, in said County, did feloniously receive and have five pieces of silver coin, current in this Commonwealth, called half dollars, and of the value of fifty cents each, of the moneys and coin of A. B., which said pieces of silver coin were lately before feloniously taken, stolen and carried away from the said A. B., he the said C. D. then well knowing the said pieces of silver coin to have been feloniously taken, stolen and carried away: These are, therefore, to command you, in the name of the Commonwealth of Virginia, forthwith to apprehend the said C. D., and bring him before me or some other Justice of the said County, to answer the said complaint, and to be farther dealt with according to law. Given under my hand and seal, this ——— day of ——— 18—.

                                                  J. T., *J. P.* [L. S.]

(No. 4.)

Form of Warrant of Arrest for aiding in concealing stolen goods.

——— County, to wit:
    To all or any one of the Constables of said County:

Whereas, A. B. of said County, has this day made complaint and information on oath before me J. T., a Justice of the said County, that C. D., on the ——— day of ——— 18—, in said County, did feloniously aid one E. F. in concealing one watch, (or *one bank note*,) the property of the said A. B., and of the value of ——— dollars, which he, the said E. F. had before feloniously taken, stolen and carried away from the said A. B., he the said C. D. knowing at the time he so aided the said E. F., that the said watch (or *bank note*) had been stolen, taken and carried away from the said A. B.: These are, therefore, to command you, in the name of the Commonwealth of Virginia, forthwith to apprehend the said C. D., and bring him before me or some other Justice of the said County, to answer the said complaint, and to be farther dealt with according to law. Given under my hand and seal, this —— day of —— 18—.

J. T., J. P. [L. s.]

(No. 5.)

Form of Mittimus where a party is committed for examination or trial in the County Court, for receiving stolen goods.

—— County, to wit:

To X. Z., *Constable of said County, and to the Keeper of the Jail of said County:*

These are to command you, the said Constable, in the name of the Commonwealth of Virginia, forthwith to convey and deliver into the custody of the keeper of the said jail, together with this warrant, the body of C. D., a white person (or *free negro*, or *a slave, the property of E. F.*, as the case may be,) charged before me J. T., a Justice of the said County, on the oath of A. B., with a felony by him committed, in this, that the said C. D., on the —— day of —— in the year 18—, in the said County, (here describe the offence as in the warrant of arrest.) And you, the said keeper of the said jail, are hereby required to receive the said C. D. into your jail and custody, that he may be examined (or *tried*) for the said offence, by the County Court of said County, and him there safely keep until he shall be discharged by due course of law. Given under my hand and seal, this —— day of —— in the year 18—.

J. T., J. P. [L. s.]

[NOTE.—If the prisoner be a white person, or if he be a free negro charged with homicide of any grade, or with any offence, punishable with death, he must be committed for examination. For all other felonies by free negroes, and in all cases of felony by slaves, the prisoner must be committed for trial.]

(No. 6.)

Form of Certificate of Commitment for receiving stolen goods, to be sent to the Clerk of the County Court.

—— County, to wit:

To the Clerk of the County Court of said County:

I, J. T., a Justice of said County, do hereby certify that I have, by my warrant, this day committed C. D. (if free negro or slave, state which,) to the jail of this County, that he may be examined (or *tried*) before the County Court of the said County, for a felony by him committed, in this, that he did, on the —— day of —— 18—, in the said County, (here state the offence as in the mittimus.) Given under my hand, this —— day of —— in the year 18—.

J. T., J. P.

(No. 7.)

Form of Certificate to the Clerk where party is admitted to bail.

Turn to head of ARREST, and follow No. 6.

(No. 8.)

Form of Recognizance of Bail.

Turn to head of RECOGNIZANCE, and follow No. 1, if person be free; No. 2, if a slave, and state succinctly the offence for which the person is recognized.

(No. 9.)

Form of Recognizance of Witness to appear before the County Court to give evidence upon the examination or trial of a party charged with receiving stolen goods.

Turn to head of RECOGNIZANCE, and follow No. 3.

(No. 1.)

An Indictment for receiving stolen goods, knowing them to be stolen.

—— Judicial Circuit, —— County, to wit: In the Circuit Court of the said County. } The jurors of the Commonwealth of Virginia, in and for the body of the County of ——, upon their oath present, that A. B., of the said County, on the —— day of —— in the year 18—, in the County aforesaid, one silver watch of the value of fifty dollars, of the goods and chattels of one C. D., then lately before feloniously stolen, taken and carried away, feloniously did buy and receive, he the said A. B. then and there well knowing the said goods and chattels to have been feloniously stolen, taken and carried away, against the peace and dignity of the Commonwealth of Virginia.

2d Count. And the jurors aforesaid, upon their oath aforesaid, do farther present, that the said A. B., to wit, on the day and year aforesaid, in the County aforesaid, one other silver watch of the value of fifty dollars, of the goods and chattels of the said C. D., by one J. G., then lately before feloniously stolen, taken and carried away, of him, the said J. G., then and there feloniously did buy and receive, he, the said A. B., then and there well knowing the said last mentioned goods and chattels to have been feloniously stolen, taken and carried away, against the peace and dignity of the Commonwealth of Virginia.

3d Count. And the jurors aforesaid, upon their oath aforesaid, do farther present, that the said A. B., to wit, on the day and year last aforesaid, in the County aforesaid, one other silver watch of the value of fifty dollars, of the goods and chattels of one C. D., then lately before feloniously stolen, taken and carried away, by some evil disposed person to the jurors unknown, of the said evil disposed person feloniously did buy and receive, he, the said

A. B. then and there, to wit, on the day and year last aforesaid, in the County aforesaid, well knowing the said last mentioned goods and chattels to have been feloniously stolen, taken and carried away, against the peace and dignity of the Commonwealth of Virginia.

[Add count for simple larceny.]

(No. 2.)

An Indictment for feloniously receiving a stolen bank note.

—— Judicial Circuit, —— County, to wit: In the Circuit Court for the said County. } The jurors of the Commonwealth of Virginia, in and for the body of the County of ——, and now attending the said Court, upon their oath present, that A. B., on the —— day of —— in the year one thousand eight hundred and ——, in the said County, did feloniously buy and receive one bank note, for the payment of —— dollars, and of the value of —— dollars, the property and bank note of R. M., which said bank note was lately before feloniously taken, stolen and carried away from the said R. M., he the said A. B. then and there well knowing the said bank note to have been feloniously taken, stolen and carried away from the said R. M., against the peace and dignity of the Commonwealth of Virginia.

CHAPTER LXXXVII.

RECOGNIZANCE.

In the discharge of his official duty, it is often necessary for a Justice of the Peace to take the obligation of a prisoner, with sureties, to appear and answer a criminal prosecution, and of witnesses to appear and give evidence against him on behalf of the Commonwealth, or it may be necessary to take it of a party to do some other act required by law to be done. This obligation is called a recognizance, and is a bond or obligation of record, which a man enters into before some Court of record, Judge, Justice of the Peace, or other public functionary duly authorized to take it, whereby he acknowledges himself to owe to the Commonwealth a certain sum, with a condition to do some certain act, as to appear at court, to keep the peace, or be of good behaviour, or the like, and upon the performance of the condition, the debt becomes discharged.([1]) And in general, when a Justice has the authority to order a man to do some particular thing, it seems that he has the implied power at Common Law to bind him by recognizance to

---

([1]) 2 Deac. Cr. L. 1093.

do it, and upon his refusal to be so bound, to commit him for contempt.(¹)

BY SEC. 4, CHAP. 211, TITLE 55. Recognizances in criminal cases, shall be payable to the Commonwealth of Virginia. Every recognizance under any chapter of this title, shall be in such sum as the court or officer requiring it may direct, and unless it be of a witness, shall be with surety deemed sufficient by the court or officer taking it. The condition, when it is taken of a person charged with a criminal offence, shall be, that he appear before the Court, Judge or Justice before whom the proceeding on such charge will be, at such time as may be prescribed by the court or officer taking it, to answer for the offence with which such person is charged; and when it is taken of a witness, in a case against any such person, shall be, that he so appear to give evidence on such charge; and in either case, shall be, that the person or witness shall not depart thence without the leave of said Court, Judge or Justice. When taken for any other purpose than to appear so to answer or give evidence, it shall be with condition that the person of whom it is taken, shall keep the peace and be of good behaviour for such time, not exceeding one year, as the court or officer requiring it may direct; and if such court or officer direct, it may, when taken of a person so charged, be with condition for so keeping the peace and being of good behaviour, in addition to the other condition of his recognizance.

This provision confers no new powers upon the Justice, but is merely declaratory of the Common Law. Its design is to condense and bring the subjects of recognizance embraced in the 55th title, under one general provision, without repeating in each case for what the party is bound. For instance, by the 4th section, chapter 201, of the same title, for the *prevention* of crime, by requiring surety of the peace, it is said, he (meaning the Justice) "may require a recognizance," without stating for what. This provision declares for what, that is, to keep the peace and be of good behaviour. So in chapter 204, providing for the arrest and examination of persons who have *committed* crime, it is said in the 7th section, "upon taking a recognizance for his (that is, a person under arrest for an offence already committed,) appearance before the court having cognizance of the case," but does not say for what he is to appear. The same provision states for what, that is, to appear and answer the charge preferred against him.

The object of all criminal proceedings being either to *prevent* or to *punish* violations of law, in the doing of which it

---

(¹) Cromp. 125; 2 Deac. 1093; 3 M. & S. 1.

is necessary to bring the party accused, and the witnesses against him, before some tribunal competent to take cognizance of the matter, it is obvious that recognizances generally are taken either to appear and answer some charge, or to keep the peace and be of good behaviour, or to appear and testify. But under some special provisions of the statute, parties are required to enter into recognizances for other purposes.

These are noticed in this work under their proper heads, and the form given for each case according to the special provision. Under the head of SURETY OF THE PEACE, will be found all forms of recognizances for the *prevention* of crime; all general forms to appear and answer for crimes committed, or to testify, are inserted at the end of this title, and the manner of describing the offence in each, as far as necessary, is given under each separate head of offence.

There are other matters in relation to recognizances, whether taken under authority derived from the statute or from the Common Law, of which the Justice should be informed.

Every recognizance should of necessity contain the names of the parties, and the sum in which they are bound,([1]) and ought properly to specify the abode of the parties, so that if forfeited, process may more readily be served on them; though this is not necessary to its validity.

A Justice can take no recognizance of any other matter than what concerns his duty as a Magistrate, and a recognizance entered into before him in a cause, or touching a matter over which he has no jurisdiction, is void;([2]) and therefore, (inasmuch as nothing will be presumed in favour of an inferior jurisdiction,) every recognizance taken by a Justice ought to recite so much of the complaint or cause of taking it, as to shew that he has authority to take it.([3]) It is sufficient, however, if the offence charged, or cause of taking it, be substantially though not technically set forth.([4])

It should not only shew, upon its face, that it is taken in reference to a subject matter, over which the Justice has jurisdiction, but it ought not to be generally for a prisoner to appear and answer whatever matter or thing may be alleged against him, and in the mean time to keep the peace, but the particular kind of offence for which the party is to answer, should be designated and substantially described in the condition of the recognizance. General forms of recognizance may be found in the older books, but the principle here stated

---

([1]) 3 Dick. J. P. 66.
([2]) Cromp. 125; 2 Deac. 1093; 3 M. & S. 1.
([3]) D. Davis J. P. 947; 7 Mass.
Rep. 340; and see the precedents in Dick. J. P., Burn. J. P. and Chitty's Cr. L.
([4]) 17 Wend. 252.

is sustained by the Supreme Court of Massachusetts, and the most approved precedents of modern works.(¹) The propriety of rejecting the general form, is manifest in the supposed case (not unlikely to occur,) of a party being recognized, with separate sureties in different amounts, to appear at the same time and place, to answer two or more felonies generally, and if he should fail to appear, so that each recognizance becomes forfeited, by what means would the Commonwealth fix the several responsibilities of each surety? The recognizance being a matter of record, ought to be certain in its terms, and put beyond the reach of any state of circumstances that might render a call for explanation necessary, and the circumspect Justice will never subject it to the hazardous result of such explanation, by evidence not appearing in the recognizance itself.

So, also, a recognizance taken by a Justice of the Peace, unless by virtue of some statute authorizing it, is void, if taken to appear before any other tribunal than before himself or some other Justice of his county, or before a court of which he is a member, and in a case which that court can try or enquire into ;(²) as for example, he has no authority to recognize a party to appear before a superior court, for an assault, and in the mean time to keep the peace.(³)

A recognizance need not be signed by the parties to make it valid,(⁴) for it derives its force not from their signatures, but from their acknowledgment before the Justice, and his attestation of that acknowledgment.

When drawn out in form, it must be certified by the Justice, which is usually done at the foot of it in these words: "taken and acknowledged before me J. T., J. P.;" but it becomes a debt of record as soon as it is entered into, and before it is formally drawn up.(⁵) The Justice, however, as soon as practicable, should reduce the acknowledgment to form, and transmit it at once to the proper court or depository, and after it has been once taken, he should never vary its terms. (See Bias v. Floyd, Gov., 7 Leigh 640.)

It is the duty of the Justice to bind, by recognizance, all material witnesses in behalf of the Commonwealth, to appear at the court in which the prisoner is to be examined or tried, to give evidence; and in doing so, all the witnesses may be bound in one recognizance. The practice of taking a sepa-

---

(¹) Comw'th v. Downey, 9 Mass. Rep. 520; Comw'th v. Dagget, 16 Mass. Rep. 447; and see case of Bias v. Floyd, Gov., 7 Leigh 640; 1 Dick. J. P. 185-6; 1 Burn's J. P. 264-65, 24 Lond. Edition by Chetwynd; Chitty C. L. vol. 4; Toones' Manual 55.
(²) 5 Dane's Abr. 280.
(³) 1 Leigh 586.
(⁴) 1 Dick. J. P. 66.
(⁵) 3 Dick. J. P. 66, 67.

rate recognizance for each witness, is not only unnecessary, but in some respects inconvenient. If the accused require it, his witnesses should also be recognized.

By Sec. 5, Chap. 211. A recognizance, which would be taken of a person, but for his or her being insane, or a married woman, minor or slave, may be taken of another person, and without further surety, if such other person be deemed sufficient.

By Sec. 6. A person not giving, and for whom no other person gives, a recognizance required, shall be committed to jail. He shall be discharged therefrom when such recognizance is given before the court or a conservator of the peace; or if it be to appear and give evidence, when such evidence is given; or if it be to keep the peace and be of good behaviour, when the period for which it was required has elapsed; or in any case, when the discharge of such person is directed by the court in whose jail he is.

By Sec. 7. A person taking a recognizance out of court, shall forthwith transmit it to the Clerk of the court, for appearance before which it is taken, or if it be not for appearance before a court, to the Clerk of the county or corporation in which it is taken; and it shall remain filed in the Clerk's office.

By Sec. 12. A surety in a recognizance may at any time take his principal and surrender him to the Court or Judge before whom the recognizance was taken, or if it was taken by a court which is not in session, or by a Justice, to a Judge or Justice of such court, or a Justice of the county or corporation in which it was taken; whereupon said surety shall be discharged from liability for any act of the principal subsequent thereto.

By Sec. 13. If the surrender be before a Judge or Justice, he shall give the surety a certificate thereof, and the accused may be let to bail anew for the residue of the term, or to appear as before required, and on failure so to recognize, shall be committed to jail as in other cases of failure to give bail. If the surrender be to the court, it shall take such order as it deems proper.

As to what recognizances may be discharged by a Justice, and the manner of doing it, see head of Supersedeas.

[For form to appear before a special session of examining Court, see No. 3, under head of COURTS.]

(No. 1.)

Form of Recognizance of Bail to appear before the County Court, to answer a charge of felony.

―――― County, to wit :

Be it remembered, that on the ―― day of ―――― 18―, A. B. and C. D. of the said County, came before me J. T., a Justice of the said County, and severally and respectively acknowledged themselves to be indebted to the Commonwealth of Virginia, in manner and form following, that is to say : The said A. B. in the sum of ―――― dollars, good and lawful money of the United States, and the said D. C. in the sum of ―――― dollars, of like good and lawful money, to be respectively made and levied of their several goods and chattels, lands and tenements, to the use of the Commonwealth of Virginia, if the said A. B. shall make default in performance of the condition underwritten.

The condition of the above recognizance is such, that if the above bound A. B. do and shall personally appear before the County Court of ―――― on the first day of the next term thereof, then and there to answer the Commonwealth for and concerning a certain felony by him committed, in feloniously (here state succinctly the offence, as for instance, *in killing J. S.,* or *burglariously breaking into the dwelling house of J. S.,* or *stealing the goods of J. S.,*) wherewith the said A. B. stands charged, and shall not depart thence without the leave of the said Court, then the above recognizance shall be void, else to remain in full force and virtue.

Taken and acknowledged before me,
in the said County, the day and year
first above written.

J. T., J. P.

――――

(No. 2.)

Form of Recognizance of the owner of a slave, for his appearance before the County Court, to answer a charge of felony.

―――― County, to wit :

Be it remembered, that on the ―― day of ―――― 18―, J. M. of the said County, (the owner of a certain slave named Jack,) came before me J. T., a Justice of the said County, and acknowledged himself to be indebted to the Commonwealth of Virginia, in the sum of ―――― dollars, good and lawful money of the United States, to be made and levied of his goods and chattels, lands and tenements, to the use of the said Commonwealth, if default shall be made in the performance of the condition underwritten.

The condition of the above recognizance is such, that if the above mentioned Jack, the slave of the above bound J. M., do and shall personally appear before the County Court of ――――, on the first day of the next term thereof, and shall then and there answer the said Commonwealth, for a certain felony by him committed, in feloniously (here state succinctly the offence,) wherewith he the said Jack stands charged, and shall not depart thence without the leave of the said court. then the above recognizance shall be void, otherwise to remain in full force and virtue.

Taken and acknowledged before me,
in the said County, the day and year
first above written.
J. T., J. P.

(No. 3.)

Form of Recognizance of Witnesses to appear before the County Court of ———, for the examination or trial of a person charged with felony.

——— County, to wit :

Be it remembered, that on the ——— day of ——— 18—, A. B. and C. D. of the said County, personally appeared before me J. T., a Justice of the said County, at the said County, and each of them separately and individually, and by and for himself, acknowledged himself separately and individually to be indebted to the Commonwealth of Virginia, in the sum of ——— dollars, lawful money of the United States, to be levied of each of their goods and chattels, lands and tenements, to the use of the Commonwealth, if the said A. B. or C. D. shall make default in the performance of the condition underwritten.

The condition of this recognizance is such, that if the above bound A. B. and C. D., and every of them, shall personally appear before the County Court of said County, on the ——— day of the next term thereof, to give evidence in behalf of the Commonwealth against E. F., who stands charged with felony, (state the kind of offence, as *in stealing the goods of J. S.*, or *for killing J. S.*,) and do not depart thence without the leave of said Court, then this recognizance to be void, otherwise to remain in full force and virtue.

Taken and acknowledged before me,
in the said County, the day and year
first above written.
J. T., J. P.

[NOTE.—For form of recognizance to appear before a special session of examining court, see No. 4, under head of COURTS.]

(No. 4.)

Form of Recognizance of Bail to appear and answer a bill of indictment, to be preferred to the grand jury for a misdemeanor.

——— County, to wit :

Be it remembered, that on this ——— day of ——— 18—, A. B. and C. D. of the said County, personally came before me J. T., a Justice of the said County, and severally and respectively acknowledged themselves to be indebted to the Commonwealth of Virginia, in the manner and form following, that is to say : The said A. B. in the sum of ——— dollars, good and lawful money of the United States, and the said C. D. in the sum of ——— dollars, of like good and lawful money, to be respectively made and levied of their several goods and chattels, lands and tenements, to the use of the Commonwealth of Virginia, if the said A. B. shall make default in the performance of the underwritten condition.

The condition of the above recognizance is such, that if the above bound A. B. do and shall personally appear on the —— day of ———* 18—, before the County Court of the said County, at the Courthouse thereof, and then and there answer a bill of indictment, to be preferred to the grand jury in and for the said County, against him the said A. B., for a misdemeanor by him committed, for unlawfully (here describe succinctly the offence, for instance, *in assaulting and beating one C. D.*,) whereof the said A. B. stands charged, and shall not thence depart without the leave of said Court, then the above recognizance shall be void and of no effect, otherwise to remain in full force and virtue.

Taken and acknowledged before me, the day and year first above written.

J. T., *J. P.*

(No. 5.)

Form of Recognizance for a witness to appear and give evidence to a grand jury, upon an indictment for a misdemeanor.

—— County, to wit:

Be it remembered, that on the —— day of ——— 18—, A. B. of the said County, personally appeared before me J. T., a Justice of the said County, and acknowledged himself to be indebted to the Commonwealth of Virginia, in the sum of —— dollars, lawful money of the United States, to be levied of his goods and chattels, lands and tenements, to the use of the said Commonwealth, if the said A. B. shall make default in the performance of the condition underwritten.

The condition of this recognizance is such, that if the above bound A. B. shall personally appear before the Justices of the said County, on the —— day of ——— 18—, at a Court by them to be holden in and for the said County, at the Courthouse of the said County, then and there to give evidence on a bill of indictment to be preferred to the grand jury of the Commonwealth, in and for the said County, against H. L., for a misdemeanor by him committed, (here describe the offence briefly,) and do not thence depart without leave of said Court, then this recognizance to be void, otherwise to remain in full force and virtue.

Taken and acknowledged before me, in said County, the day and year first above written.

J. T., *J. P.*

(Where there are two or more witnesses, the following is the proper form:)

—— County, to wit:

Be it remembered, that on the —— day of ——— 18—, A. B., C. D. and E. F. of the said County, personally appeared before me J. T., a Justice of the said County, and each of them separately and individually acknowledged himself separately and individually to be indebted to the Commonwealth of Virginia in the sum of three hundred dollars, lawful money of the United

---

* This day must be the first day of the Court on which the grand jury is to appear.

States, to be levied of their goods and chattels, lands and tenements, respectively, to the use of the Commonwealth, if the said A. B. and C. D. shall make default in the condition underwritten.

The condition of the above recognizance is such, that if the above bound A. B., C. D. and E. F., and every of them, shall personally appear before the Justices of the said County, on the —— day of ———— 18—, at a Court by them to be holden for the said County, at the Courthouse of the said County, then and there to give evidence on a bill of indictment to be preferred to the grand jury of the Commonwealth, in and for the said County, against H. L. for a misdemeanor, to wit, (here describe the offence briefly, as for example, *for an assault and battery by him committed on P. J.*,) and do not depart without leave of said Court, then this recognizance to be void, otherwise to remain in full force and virtue.

Taken and acknowledged before me, in the said County, and within the day and year first above written.

J. T., J. P.

(No. 6.)

Form of Recognizance for the appearance of the prisoner before a Justice during the examination, and for recording his default upon failing to appear.

—————— County, to wit:

Be it remembered, that on this —— day of ———— 18—, W. S. and B. F., of the said County, personally came before me J. T., a Justice of the said County, and each acknowledged himself to be indebted to the Commonwealth of Virginia, in the manner and form following, to wit: The said W. S. in the sum of —— dollars, good and lawful money of the United States, and the said B. F. in the sum of —— dollars, like good and lawful money, to be respectively made and levied of their several goods and chattels, lands and tenements, to the use of the Commonwealth of Virginia, if the said W. S. shall make default in the performance of the underwritten condition.

The condition of the above recognizance is such, that if the above bound W. S. do and shall personally appear on the —— day of ———— 18—, at the hour of —— of the clock, A. M., at (here specify with certainty the place of appearance,) in the said County, there to answer before J. T., Justice as aforesaid, or some other Justice of the said County, the charge of having, on the —— day of ———— 18—, within the said County, (here describe the offence with sufficient certainty to shew what the offence is, though it need not be technically done,*) on which charge the said W. S. has been duly arrested, and is now in custody before the said J. T., Justice as aforesaid, upon examination for the said offence, and the farther examination thereof, for good cause continued till the said —— day of ———— 18—, then the above obligation to be void, otherwise to remain in full force and virtue.

Taken and acknowledged before me, the day and year first above written.

J. T., J. P.

---

* This recognizance can only be taken in a case of misdemeanor. See ARREST.

If the person fail to appear upon being called, his default should be immediately recorded, which may be done according to the following form, upon the back of the recognizance:

——— County, to wit:
At ———, in the said County:
——— day of ——— 18—, — A. M., (or *P. M.*)
The within named W. S., who stands bound by the within recognizance, acknowledged before J. T., a Justice of the said County, with B. F. his surety, to appear here this day, to answer the charge set forth in the within condition, was by my order, this day solemnly called to answer the said charge, but came not; all of which is certified.
J. T., *J. P.*

(No. 7.)

Form of Recognizance of Bail to be taken by a single Justice, where the Court upon examination have certified in their proceedings that the prisoner may be bailed.

——— County to wit:
Be it remembered, that on this ——— day of ——— 18—, A. B. and C. D. of the said County, personally appeared before me, J. T., a Justice of the said County, and severally and respectively acknowledged themselves to be indebted to the Commonwealth of Virginia, in the manner and form following, that is to say: The said A. B., in the sum of ——— dollars, lawful money of the United States, and the said C. D. in the sum of ——— dollars, like good and lawful money, to be respectively made and levied of their several goods and chattels, lands and tenements, to the use of the Commonwealth of Virginia, if the said A. B. shall make default in the performance of the underwritten condition.

The condition of the above recognizance is such, that whereas, at a County Court, holden on the ——— day of ——— 18—, at the County Courthouse of the said County, consisting of at least five of the Justices of the said County, the above bound A. B. was by the said Court examined, for a felony by him committed, in feloniously (here describe the offence as it is set forth in the record of the examination,) and the said Court were of opinion, that the said A. B. ought to be tried for the felony aforesaid, in the Circuit Court for the said County, and remanded the said A. B. to jail for trial; and the said Court being of opinion, that the said A. B. should be admitted to give bail to answer the felony aforesaid; and having entered this their opinion, in the proceedings of the said Court, and also the sums of money in which the said A. B. and his bail ought to be bound, to wit, the said A. B. in the sum of ——— dollars, and his bail in the sum of ——— dollars, and the said J. T., Justice as aforesaid, having accepted the above bound C. D. as bail for the said A. B., according to the said opinion and proceedings of the said Court: Now, if the said A. B. do and shall personally appear before the Judge of the Circuit Court for the said County of ———, in open Court, on the first day of the next term of the said Circuit Court to be holden for the said County, then and there to answer for the offence aforesaid, wherewith the said A. B. stands charged, and shall not depart thence without the leave of the said Court, then the above recognizance shall be void, otherwise to remain in full force and virtue.

Acknowledged before me, in the said County, the day and year first above written.
J. T., *J. P.*

(No. 8.)

Form of Warrant for the deliverance of a prisoner who has been remanded upon his examination in Court, and who has given bail before a single Justice.

—— County, to wit:

Whereas, at a County Court, holden on the —— day of —— 18—, at the Courthouse of the said County, by five of the Justices thereof, for the examination of A. B., who was then and there charged before the said County Court, with a felony by him committed in the said County, in feloniously (here state succinctly the offence as charged in the record of the examining Court,) the said Court remanded the said A. B. to jail for farther trial, and certified upon the record of their proceedings, that the said A. B. should be admitted to give bail, himself in the sum of —— dollars, and his bail in the sum of —— dollars, to answer the Commonwealth for the felony aforesaid. And the said A. B. having this day entered into a recognizance before me, a Justice of the said County, with sufficient bail in the sums aforesaid, to answer according to law the felony aforesaid: You are hereby commanded, in the name of the Commonwealth, to deliver out of your jail and custody, the said A. B., and set him at liberty, if detained therein for no other cause. Given under my hand and seal, this —— day of —— 18—.

J. T., J. P. [L. S.]

[NOTE.—If the prisoner has not been transferred to the jail of the Superior Court, this warrant should be directed thus: "to the Jailor of the County of ——." If he has been transferred by the warrant of two Justices, to the Superior Court, then the warrant should be directed to the Jailor of that Court.]

(No. 9.)

Form of Recognizance of Bail to appear and hear judgment after verdict, in a prosecution for misdemeanor.

—— County, to wit:

Be it remembered, that on this —— day of —— 18—, A. B. and C. D. of the said County, came before me J. T., Sheriff of the said County, and severally acknowledged themselves to be indebted to the Commonwealth of Virginia, in the manner and form following, that is to say: The said A. B. in the sum of —— dollars, lawful money of the United States, and the said C. D. in the sum of —— dollars, of like lawful money, to be respectively made and levied of their several goods and chattels, lands and tenements, to the use of the Commonwealth of Virginia, if the said A. B. shall fail in performing the condition underwritten.

The condition of the above recognizance is such, that whereas the above bound A. B. has been arrested by J. T., Sheriff of the County of ——, by virtue of a *capias* issued from the (state here what Court,) to him directed, commanding him, the said Sheriff, to take the body of the above bound A. B., and him safely keep, so as to have his body before the Justices (or *Judge*) of the said Court, at the Courthouse thereof, on the (the return day of the *capias*,) (*) to hear judgment pronounced by the said Court, in a certain prosecution therein pending against him the said A. B., upon an indictment for (state the offence set out in the *capias*,) whereof the said A.

B. is convicted by the verdict of a jury rendered against him in the said Court, upon the indictment aforesaid: Now, if the above bound A. B. shall personally appear in Court before the Justices of the County Court of ———, (or *before the Judge of,* stating what Court,) at the Courthouse thereof, on the first day of the next term of the said Court, then and there to hear the judgment of the said Court, upon the said verdict, whereby the said A. B. stands convicted, and shall not thence depart without the leave of the said Court, then the above recognizance shall be void, otherwise to remain in full force and virtue.

Taken and acknowledged before me, the day and year first above written, in the County of ———.

J. T., *Sheriff.*

(No. 10.)

Form of Recognizance of Bail to appear and answer an indictment or presentment for a misdemeanor, where the party is arrested upon a capias to answer.

Follow above form No. 9, to the mark (*) and then proceed as follows: " to answer a certain indictment therein found against him by the grand jury (or *to answer a certain presentment therein made against him by the grand jury*) and now pending in the said Court, for (state the offence as set forth in the *capias* :) Now, if the above bound A. B. shall personally appear in Court, before the Justices of the County Court of ———, (or *before the Judge of,* stating the Court,) at the Courthouse thereof, on the first day of the next ——— term of the said Court, to answer for the offence aforesaid, and shall not thence depart without the leave of the said Court, then the above recognizance shall be void, otherwise to remain in full force and virtue.

Taken and acknowledged before me, the day and year first above written, in the County of ———.

J. T., *Sheriff.*

(No. 11.)

Form of new Recognizance of Bail, where a party has been surrendered by his former bail.

Follow form No. 1, to the condition, and conclude with this condition :

The condition of the above recognizance is such, that whereas E. F., who stood bound as the bail of the above bound A. B., for his appearance before the (here insert the Court before whom the prisoner is to appear,) on the first day of the next term thereof, to answer the Commonwealth for a felony by him committed, in feloniously (here state the offence as in the first recognizance,) has this day taken the body of the said A. B. and surrendered him before me J. T., a Justice of the said County, in discharge of his said recognizance; and whereas the above bound C. D. has undertaken before me, as Justice aforesaid, as surety of the said A. B., for his appearance at the Court aforesaid, on the first day of the next term thereof, to answer the

Commonwealth for the felony aforesaid, and that he the said A. B. will not then depart from the said Court, without the leave of the said Court: Now, if the said A. B. do and shall personally appear before the (state the Court) on the first day of the next term thereof, to answer the Commonwealth for the felony aforesaid, wherewith he stands charged, and shall not thence depart without leave of the said Court, then the above recognizance to be void, otherwise to remain in full force and virtue.

Taken and acknowledged before me, in the said County, on the day and year first above written.

J. T., J. P.

CHAPTER LXXXVIII.

RECORDS.

BY SEC. 19, CHAP. 194. If a Clerk of a Court, or other public officer, fraudulently make a false entry, or erase, alter, secrete, or destroy any record in his keeping, and belonging to his office, he shall be confined in jail not more than one year, and fined not exceeding one thousand dollars.

BY SEC. 20. Every person convicted under the preceding section, shall, moreover, forfeit his office, and be forever incapable of holding any post mentioned in the first section of chapter twelve.

BY SEC. 21. If a free person steal, or fraudulently secrete or destroy a public record, or part thereof, he shall, if the offence be not embraced by the 19th section, be confined in jail not more than one year, and fined not exceeding one thousand dollars.

(No. 1.)

Form of Warrant of Arrest against the Clerk of a Court for making a false entry in a record.

———— County, to wit:

To all or any one of the Constables of said County:

Whereas, A. B. of said County, has this day made complaint and information on oath before me J. T., a Justice of the said County, that C. D., on the —— day of ———— 18—, in said County, he the said C. D. then being the Clerk of the (state what Court he was Clerk of) did fraudulently make a false entry in a certain record then in his keeping, and belonging to his office as such Clerk, to wit, the record of a suit pending in said Court between E. F. plaintiff, and G. H. defendant, by (state the false entry, and how made:) These are, therefore, to command you, in the name of the Commonwealth of Virginia, forthwith to apprehend the said C. D., and bring him before me or some other Justice of the said County, to answer the said complaint, and to be farther dealt with according to law. Given under my hand and seal, this ―― day of ――― 18―.

J. T., J. P. [L. S.]

(No. 2.)

Form of Warrant of Arrest against same for erasing and altering a record.

――― County, to wit:

To all or any one of the Constables of said County:

Whereas, A. B. of said County, has this day made complaint and information on oath before me J. T., a Justice of the said County, that C. D., on the ―― day of ――― 18―, in said County, he the said C. D. then being the Clerk of the (state what Court) did fraudulently erase and alter a certain record then in his keeping, and belonging to his office as such Clerk, to wit, an order of the said Court, entered and recorded in the minutes and proceeding of the said Court, granting to John, a free negro, permission to remain in this Commonwealth and to reside in the said County, by erasing the name of John from the said order, and inserting in the place thereof, the name of Frank: These are, therefore, to command you, in the name of the Commonwealth of Virginia, forthwith to apprehend the said C. D., and bring him before me or some other Justice of the said County, to answer the said complaint, and to be farther dealt with according to law. Given under my hand and seal, this ―― day of ――― 18―.

J. T., J. P. [L. S.]

(No. 3.)

Form of Warrant of Arrest for stealing, secreting or destroying a public record.

――― County, to wit:

To all or any one of the Constables of said County:

Whereas, A. B. of said County, has this day made complaint and information on oath before me J. T., a Justice of the said County, that C. D., on the ―― day of ――― 18―, in said County, did steal (or *secrete*, or *destroy*) a public record, to wit, the public record of (state what record, as for example, " the orders and judgments of the Circuit Court of the said County,") entered in the order book of the said Court: These are, therefore, to command you, in the name of the Commonwealth of Virginia, forthwith to apprehend the said C. D., and bring him before me or some other Justice of the said County, to answer the said complaint, and to be farther dealt with according to law. Given under my hand and seal, this ―― day of ――― 18―.

J. T., J. P. [L. S.]

[The section of the statute upon which this warrant is drawn does not apply to the stealing of bonds or other securities filed in suits or elsewhere; for the stealing of such securities, is as much a larceny, as if they were stolen from the private desk of the owner.]

For form of mittimus, see No. 9, under head of ARREST, and for certificate of commitment to the clerk, see Nos. 10 and 11, under same head. For recognizance of bail, see Nos. 4 and 5, under head of RECOGNIZANCE.

CHAPTER LXXXIX.

RENT.

By Sec. 1, Chap. 138. A grantee or assignee of any land let to lease, or of the reversion thereof, and his personal representative or assigns, shall enjoy against the lessee, his heirs, personal representative or assigns, the like advantage by action or entry, for any forfeiture, or by action upon any covenant or promise in the lease, which the grantor, assignor or lessor, or his heirs, might have enjoyed.

By Sec. 2. A lessee, his personal representative or assigns, may have against a grantee or alienee, of the reversion or of any part thereof, his heirs or assigns, the like benefit of any condition, covenant or promise in the lease, as he could have had against the lessors themselves, and their heirs and assigns; except the benefit of any warranty in deed or law.

By Sec. 3. In conveyances or devises of rents, in fee, with powers of distress and re-entry, or either of them, such powers shall pass to the grantee or devisee without express words; a grant or devise of rent, or of a reversion or remainder, shall be good and effectual without attornment of the tenant; but no tenant, who before notice of the grant or devise, shall have paid the rent to the grantor, shall suffer any damage thereby.

By Sec. 4. The attornment of a tenant to any stranger, shall be void, unless it be with the consent of the landlord of such tenant, or pursuant to, or in consequence of, the judgment, order or decree of a court.

By Sec. 5. A tenancy from year to year, may be terminated by either party giving notice in writing, prior to the end of any year, for three months, if it be of land within, and for six months, if it be of land without a town, of his intention to terminate the same. When such notice is to the tenant, it may be served upon him, or upon any one holding under him the leased premises or any part thereof. When it is by the tenant, it may be served upon any one, who at the time owns the premises in whole or in part, or the agent of such owner, or according to the common law. This section shall not apply, where by special agreement, no notice is to be given. Nor shall notice be necessary from or to a tenant, whose term is to end at a certain time.

By Sec. 6. If any tenant from whom rent is in arrear, and unpaid, shall desert the demised premises, and leave the same uncultivated or unoccupied, without goods thereon subject to distress, sufficient to satisfy the said rent, the lessor or his agent may post a notice in writing, upon a conspicuous part of the premises, requiring the tenant to pay the said rent within one month. If the same be not paid within that time, the lessor shall be entitled to possession of the premises, and may enter thereon; and the right of such tenant thereto, shall thenceforth be at an end. But the landlord may recover the rent up to that time.

BY SEC. 7. Rent of every kind may be recovered by distress or action. A landlord may also, by action, recover (when the agreement is not by deed,) a reasonable satisfaction for the use and occupation of lands; on the trial of which action, if any parol demise, or any agreement, (not being by deed,) whereon a certain rent was reserved, shall appear in evidence, the plaintiff shall not therefore be nonsuited, but may use the same as evidence of the amount of his debt or damages. In any action for rent, or for such use and occupation, interest shall be allowed as on other contracts.

BY SEC. 8. He to whom rent or compensation is due, whether he have the reversion or not, his personal representative or assignee, may recover it, as provided in the preceding section, whatever be the estate of the person owning it, or though his estate or interest in the land be ended. And when the owner of real estate in fee, or holder of a term yielding him rent, dies, the rent thereafter due, shall be recoverable by such owner's heirs or devisee, or such term-holder's personal representative. And if the owner or holder, alien or assign his estate or term, or the rent thereafter to fall due thereon, his alienee or assignee may recover such rent.

BY SEC. 9. Rent may be recovered from the lessee or other person owing it, or his assignee, or the personal representative of either. But no assignee is to be liable for rent which became due before his interest began. Nothing herein shall impair or change the liability of heirs or devisees for rent, as for other debts of their ancestor or devisor.

BY SEC. 10. Rent may be distrained for within five years from the time it becomes due, and not afterwards, whether the lease be ended or not. The distress shall be made by a Constable, Sheriff, or other officer of the county or corporation wherein the premises yielding the rent, or some part thereof, may be, or the goods liable to distress may be found, under warrant from a Justice, founded upon an affidavit of the person claiming the rent, or his agent, that the amount of money or other thing to be distrained for, (to be specified in the affidavit,) as he verily believes, is justly due to the claimant for rent reserved upon contract, from the person of whom it is claimed.

By Sec. 11. The distress may be levied on any goods of the lessee, or his assignee or undertenant, found on the premises, or which may have been removed therefrom not more than thirty days. If the goods of such lessee, assignee or undertenant, when carried on the premises, are subject to a lien, which is valid against his creditors, his interest only in such goods shall be liable to such distress. If any lien be created thereon while they are upon the leased premises, they shall be liable to distress, but for not more than one year's rent, whether it shall have accrued before or after the creation of the lien. No other goods shall be liable to distress than such as are declared to be so liable in this section.

By Sec. 12. If, after the commencement of any tenancy, a lien be obtained or created by deed of trust, mortgage or otherwise, upon the interest or property in goods on premises leased or rented, of any person liable for the rent, the party having such lien may remove said goods from the premises, on the following terms, and not otherwise: that is to say, on the terms of paying to the person entitled to the rent so much as is in arrear, and securing to him so much as is to become due; what is so paid or secured not being more, altogether, than a year's rent in any case. If the goods be taken under legal process, the officer executing it shall, out of the proceeds of the goods, make such payment of what is in arrear, and as to what is to become due, he shall sell a sufficient portion of the goods, on a credit till then, taking from the purchasers bonds, with good security, payable to the person so entitled, and delivering such bonds to him. If the goods be not taken under legal process, such payment and security shall be made and given before their removal. Neither this, nor the preceding section, shall affect any lien for taxes, levies or militia fines.

By Sec. 13. The officer having such distress warrant, if there be need for it, may, in the day time, break open and enter into any house or close in which there may be goods liable to the distress, and may, either in the day or night, break open and enter into any house or close wherein there may be any goods so liable, which have been fraudulently or clandestinely removed from the demised premises.

By Sec. 14. Where distress shall be made for rent justly due, and any irregularity or unlawful act shall be afterwards done by the party distraining, or his agent, the distress itself shall not be deemed to be unlawful, nor the party making it, be therefore deemed a trespasser *ab initio*; but the party aggrieved by such irregularity or unlawful act, may, by action, recover full satisfaction for the special damage he shall have sustained thereby.

By Sec. 15. Where goods are distrained or attached for rent, reserved in a share of the crop, or in any thing other than money, the claimant of the rent having given the tenant ten days notice, or if he be out of the county, having set up the notice in some conspicuous place on the premises, may apply to the court to which the attachment is returnable, or the court of the county or corporation in which the distress is made. The court having ascertained the value, either by its own judgment, or if either party require it, by the verdict of a jury, impanneled without the formality of pleading, shall order the goods distrained or attached, to be sold to pay the amount so ascertained.

By Sec. 16. Any person who shall have a right to re-enter into lands, by reason of any rent issuing thereout being in arrear, or by reason of the breach of any covenant or condition, may serve a declaration in ejectment on the tenant in possession, where there shall be such tenant, or, if the possession be vacant, by affixing the declaration upon the chief door of any messuage, or at any other notorious place on the premises; which service shall be in lieu of a demand and re-entry, and upon proof to the court by affidavit, in case of judgment by default, or upon proof on the trial, that the rent claimed was due, and no sufficient distress was upon the premises, or that the covenant or condition was broken before the service of the declaration, and that the plaintiff had power thereupon to re-enter, he shall recover judgment, and have execution for such lands.

By Sec. 17. Should the defendant, or other person for him, not pay the rent in arrear, with interest and costs, nor file a bill in equity for relief against such forfeiture, within twelve calendar months after execution executed, he shall be barred of all right in law or equity, to be restored to such lands.

By Sec. 18. Any mortgagee or trustee of such lands, not in possession thereof, may within twelve calendar months after execution executed, pay the rent and all arrears, with interest and costs, or file a bill in equity, for relief against such forfeiture; and thereupon may be relieved against it, on the same terms and conditions as the owner of such lands would be entitled to.

By Sec. 19. If the owner of such lands, or any person having right or claim thereto, shall, within the time aforesaid, file his bill for relief in any court of equity, he shall not have or continue any injunction against the proceedings at law, on the ejectment, unless he shall, within thirty days next after a full and perfect answer filed by the plaintiff in ejectment, bring into court, or deposit in some bank within the State, to the credit of the cause, such money as the plaintiff in ejectment shall in his answer, swear to be due and in arrear, over and above all just allowances, and also the costs taxed in the suit, there to remain, till the hearing of the cause, or to be paid out to the plaintiff on good security, subject to the decree of the court. And in case the bill shall be filed within the time aforesaid, and after execution executed, the plaintiff shall be accountable for no more than he shall really and *bona fide*, without fraud, deceit or wilful neglect, make of the premises, from the time of his entering into the actual possession thereof; and if it should be less than the rent payable, then the possession shall not be restored until the plaintiff be paid the sum which the money so made shall fall short of the rent, for the time he so held the lands.

By Sec. 20. If any party having right or claim to such lands, shall at any time before the trial in such ejectment, pay or tender to the party entitled to such rent, or to his attorney in the cause, or pay into court, all the rent and arrears, with interest and costs, all further proceedings in the ejectment shall cease. If the person claiming the land shall, upon bill filed as aforesaid, be relieved in equity, he shall hold the lands as before the proceedings began, without a new lease or conveyance.

By Sec. 21. In case the time for re-entering, be specified in the instrument creating the rent, covenant or condition, the proceedings in ejectment shall not be begun until such time shall have elapsed.

By Sec. 22. Where actual re-entry shall be made, the party by or for whom the same shall be made, shall return a written act of re-entry, sworn to by the Sheriff or other officer acting therein, to the Clerk of the county or corporation wherein the lands shall be, who shall record the same in the deed book, and shall deliver to the party making the re-entry, a certificate, setting forth the substance of such written act, and that the same had been left in his office to be recorded; which certificate shall be published at least once a week for two months successively in some newspaper published in or nearest to such county or corporation; which publication shall be proved by affidavit, to the satisfaction of the said Clerk, who shall note the fact in the margin of the record book, against the record of the act of re-entry, in the words "publication made and proved according to law, A. B. Clerk," and shall return the original act of re-entry, to the party entitled thereto. Said written act of re-entry, when recorded, and the record thereof, or a duly certified copy from such record, shall be evidence in all cases of the facts therein set forth.

By Sec. 23. The Clerk shall be paid for recording, granting certificate, and noting publication as aforesaid, one dollar and fifty cents, and shall collect and account for the same tax upon every such act of re-entry offered for record, as shall then be levied by law upon deeds of conveyance.

By Sec. 24. Should the person entitled to such lands at the time of re-entry made, or having claim thereto, not pay or tender the rent and all arrears thereof, with interest and all reasonable expenses incurred about such re-entry, within one year from the first day of publication, as aforesaid, he shall be forever barred from all right in law or equity, to the said lands. In case any party having right, shall pay or tender the said rent and arrears, with interest and expenses as aforesaid, to the party making re-entry, within the time aforementioned therefor, he shall be reinstated in his possession, to hold as if the re-entry had not been made.

By Sec. 25. No person who, or those under whom he claims, shall have been possessed of lands by virtue of a re-entry, for the term of two years, after the commencement of this act, shall be disturbed therein, by suit or otherwise, for any defect of proceedings in such entry.

By Sec. 4, Chap. 151. On complaint by any lessor or his agent to a Justice, that any person liable to him for rent, intends to remove or is removing, or has within thirty days removed, his effects from the leased premises, if such lessor or his agent make oath to the truth of such complaint, to the best of his belief, and to the rent which is reserved, (whether in money or other thing,) and will be payable within one year, and the time or times when it will be so payable; and also make oath, either that there is not, or he believes, unless an attachment issues, there will not be left on such premises, property liable to distress sufficient to satisfy the rent so to become payable, such Justice shall issue an attachment for the said rent against such goods as might be distrained for the same, if it had become payable, and against any other estate of the person so liable therefor.

By Sec. 1, Chap. 189. Forthcoming bonds may be given upon warrants of distress for rent, as upon writs of *fieri facias;* and by chapter 152, the officer levying a distress warrant may require an indemnifying bond, and when that is given, any person claiming the property levied on, may suspend the sale and assert his right to the property by giving a suspending bond. The statute abolishes the action of replevin, and supplies by the provisions contained in the chapters referred to, more simple and speedy remedies for all cases of illegal distress for rent.

See title Bonds.

(No. 1.)

Form of an Affidavit for warrant of distress.

—— County, to wit:

This day, A. B. made oath before me J. T., a Justice of the said County, that he verily believes that C. D., his tenant, is justly indebted to him in the sum of —— dollars, for rent reserved upon contract, for a certain messuage and tenement situated in the said County. Given under my hand, this —— day of —— 18—.

J. T., J. P.

(No. 2.)

Form of Warrant of distress.

—— County, to wit:

To X. Y., *Constable of the said County*:

Whereas, A. B. hath this day made oath before me J. T., a Justice of the said County, that he verily believes that C. D. his tenant, is justly indebted to him in the sum of —— dollars, for rent reserved upon contract, for a certain messuage and tenement situated in the said County: These are, therefore, in the name of the Commonwealth, to require you forthwith to distrain so much of the goods and chattels of the said C. D., in and upon the said messuage and tenement, as shall be sufficient to satisfy the rent due and in arrear as aforesaid, and the costs of distress; and for your so doing, this shall be your authority. Given under my hand and seal, this —— day of —— 18—.

J. T., J. P. [L. S.]

(No. 3.)

Form of an Attachment for rent, where the landlord believes his tenant will remove or is removing his effects from the leased premises.

—— County, to wit:

To X. Y., *Constable of the said County*:

Whereas, A. B. has this day made complaint on oath before me J. T., a Justice of the said County, that C. D., his tenant, is liable to pay him the said A. B., for rent of a certain messuage and tenement situated and being in the said County, the sum of —— dollars, which will be due and payable within one year from this date, and at the times and in the manner following, to wit, the sum of (here specify the times when each portion of the rent will fall due) of which he has received no part, and has moreover made oath before me that he verily believes that the said C. D. intends to remove (or *is removing*) his effects from the leased tenement aforesaid before the times of the payment of the rent aforesaid, and that unless an attachment issues, there will not be left on the said leased premises property liable to distress sufficient to satisfy the said rent so to become payable: These are, therefore, in the name of the Commonwealth, to require you to attach such goods of the said C. D. as might be distrained for it the said rent, if it had become payable, and any other estate of the said C. D., or so much thereof as will be sufficient to satisfy the said A. B. the rent aforesaid, and that you secure the said goods and estate so attached in your hands, or so provide that the same may be liable to farther proceedings thereon to be had [at the next County (or *Circuit*) Court of the said County,] when and where you are to make return how you have executed this warrant. Given under my hand and seal, this —— day of ———— 18—, at said County.

J. T., J. P. [L. S.]

(No. 4.)

Form of Attachment for rent, where the tenant has actually removed his effects from the leased premises, to prevent a distress.

———— County, to wit:
To X. Y., *Constable of the said County:*

Whereas, A. B. has this day made complaint on oath before me J. T., a Justice of the said County, that C. D. his tenant, is liable to pay him the said A. B. for the rent of a certain messuage and tenement situated in the said County, the sum of ———— dollars, payable within one year, and which will be due at the times and in the manner following, to wit: (here specify the time when each portion of the rent will become due,) of which he has received no part, and moreover made oath, that he verily believes that the said C. D. has actually removed his effects, within thirty days last past, from the said leased tenement, before the said rent reserved thereon, has become due, so that there is not left on the said tenement, property liable to distress sufficient to satisfy the said rent so to become payable: These are, therefore, in the name of the Commonwealth, to require you to attach such goods of the said A. B. as might be distrained for the said rent, if the same were now payable, and any other estate of the said C. D., or so much thereof as will be sufficient to satisfy the said sum of ———— dollars, the rent aforesaid, and that you so secure the said goods and estate so attached, in your hands, or so provide that the same may be liable to farther proceedings thereon to be had [at the next term of the County (or *Circuit*) Court of the said County at the Courthouse thereof,] when and where you are to make return how you have executed this warrant. Given under my hand and seal, this —— day of ———— 18—.

J. T., J. P. [L. S.]

[NOTE.—If the sum be under twenty dollars, the attachment should be returnable before a Justice. In that case, leave out what is in brackets in the two preceding forms, and in lieu of it, say: " before me or some other Justice of the said County, at ———— in said County, on the —— day of ———— 18—."]

(No. 5.)

Bond given by Landlord on an attachment for rent.

Know all men by these presents, that we A. B. and L. M., both of the County of H., are held and firmly bound unto C. D., of the same County, in the just and full sum of ———— dollars, lawful money of the United States, to be paid to the said C. D., his executors or administrators; to which payment, well and truly to be made, we bind ourselves and our heirs, executors and administrators, jointly and severally, firmly by these presents. Sealed with our seals, and dated this —— day of ———— 18—.

The condition of the above obligation is such, that whereas the said A. B. did, on the —— day of ———— 18—, upon his complaint on oath made in due form of law, before J. T., a Justice of said County, obtain from the said J. T. an attachment against the goods and estate of the said C. D., for the sum of —— dollars, for rent to become payable by the said C. D., to the said A. B., within one year from the —— day of ——— 18—, in the manner following, that is to say, (state the time of payment as in the attachment,) which said attachment is directed to the Sheriff, or any Constable of the said County of H., and is made returnable to the Circuit (or *County*) Court of the said County, (or if the sum be under twenty dollars, "at ——, in the said County, on the —— day of ——— 18—, before the said J. T., or some other Justice of the said County:") Now, therefore, if the said A. B. shall pay all costs and damages which may be awarded against him, or sustained by any person by reason of his suing out the said attachment, then the above obligation to be void, otherwise to remain in full force.

A. B. [L. s.]
C. D. [L. s.]

[NOTE.—When the bond is given, the Justice should make this endorsement on the attachment: "Bond taken of A. B., plaintiff in the within attachment, with C. D. his surety, in the sum of —— dollars, conditioned according to law." The penalty of the bond should be double the amount of rent claimed.]

(No. 6.)

Form of Replevy Bond taken by the officer levying the attachment.

Follow No. 5, to the condition, and insert this condition:

The condition of the above obligation is such, that whereas, the above named C. D. did, on the —— day of ——— 18—, upon his complaint on oath made in due form of law, before J. T., a Justice of said County, obtain from the said J. T. an attachment against the goods and estate of the said C. D., for the sum of —— dollars, for rent then to become payble in one year, as specified in the said attachment, that is to say, (state the times at which the rent will be payable,) which said attachment is directed to the Sheriff or any Constable of the said County of ———, and is made returnable to the Circuit (or *County*) Court of the said County, (or "at —— in the said County, on the —— day of ——— 18—, before the said J. T., or some other Justice of the said County;") and whereas the said attachment having come to the hands of J. K., Sheriff (or *Constable*, or *of J. M., deputy for J. K. Sheriff*,) of the said County, to be served, the following property of the said C. D. has been attached by virtue of the same, to wit, (here specify the property levied on,) and the said C. D. being desirous to release from the said attachment the property and estate so attached, has tendered the above bound E. F. as his surety in such a bond as the law requires for that purpose: Now, therefore, if the said C. D. shall perform the judgment of the said Court or Justice, in case the said attachment be sustained, then the above obligation to be void, otherwise to remain in full force.

C. D. [L. s.]
E. F. [L. s.]

RESCUE—See ESCAPES.

CHAPTER XC.

RIOTS, ROUTS AND UNLAWFUL ASSEMBLIES.

[For unlawful assembly by negroes, see NEGROES.]

BY SEC. 1, CHAP. 195. All Judges and Justices may suppress riots, routs and unlawful assemblies within their jurisdiction. And it shall be the duty of each of them to go among, or as near as may be, with safety, to persons riotously, tumultuously or unlawfully assembled, and in the name of the law, command them to disperse, and if they shall not, thereupon, immediately and peaceably disperse, such Judge or Justice giving the command, and any other present, shall command the assistance of all persons present, and of the Sheriff or Sergeant of the county or corporation, with his *posse*, if need be, in arresting and securing those so assembled. If any white person present, on being required to give his assistance or depart, fail to obey, he shall be deemed a rioter.

BY SEC. 2. If a white person be arrested for a riot, rout or unlawful assembly, the Judge or Justice ordering the arrest, or any other Justice, shall commit him to jail, unless he shall enter into recognizance, with sufficient security, to appear before the circuit court having jurisdiction of the offence, at its then next term, to answer therefor, and in the mean time to be of good behaviour and keep the peace.

BY SEC. 3. If any Judge or Justice have notice of a riotous, tumultuous or unlawful assembly in the county or corporation in which he resides, and fail to proceed immediately to the place of such assembly, or as near as he may safely, or fail to exercise his authority for suppressing it and arresting the offenders, he shall be fined not exceeding one hundred dollars.

BY SEC. 4. If any person, engaged in such assembly, being commanded as aforesaid to disperse, fail to do so without delay, any such Judge or Justice may require the aid of a sufficient number of persons in arms or otherwise, and proceed in such manner as he may deem expedient to disperse and suppress such assembly, and arrest and secure those engaged in it.

BY SEC. 5. If by any means taken under authority of this act to disperse any such assembly, or arrest and secure those engaged in it, any person present as a spectator or otherwise, be killed or wounded, any Judge or Justice exercising such authority, and every one acting under his order, shall be held guiltless; and if the Judge or Justice, or any person acting under the order of either of them, be killed or wounded in taking such means, or by the rioters, all persons engaged in such assembly shall be deemed guilty of such killing or wounding.

By Sec. 6. If any rioter, being free, pull down or destroy, in whole or in part, any dwelling house, or assist therein, he shall be confined in the penitentiary not less than one nor more than five years; and though no such house be so injured, every rioter and every person unlawfully or tumultuously assembled, if free, shall be confined in jail not more than one year, and fined not exceeding one hundred dollars.

This act does not, in any of its provisions, declare what shall constitute a riot, and resort must therefore be had to the Common Law, to ascertain in what the offence consists.

I. *Then what is a riot, rout and unlawful assembly.*

The distinction between these offences appears to be, that a *riot* is a tumultuous meeting of persons upon some purpose, which they *actually* execute with violence; a *rout* is a similar meeting, upon a purpose which, if executed, would make them rioters, and which they actually make *a motion to execute;* and an unlawful *assembly* is a mere assembly of persons upon a purpose which, if executed, would make them rioters, but which they do not execute, nor *make any motion* to execute.([1])

1. A riot is a tumultuous meeting of three or more persons, who actually do an unlawful act with violence, or even a lawful act in a violent and tumultuous manner, which is calculated to excite public terror.([2]) But the riotous assembly must be for a private, and not a public purpose; for the proceedings of a riotous assembly, for the purpose of resisting the government and the execution of its laws, may amount to overt acts of treason;([3]) but if the injury or grievance complained of, and intended to be revenged or remedied by a riotous assembly, relate to some *private* quarrel only, as to take possession of another's house, or has relation merely to the interest or disputes of *particular persons*, whatever the subject matter thereof may be, and in no way concerns the public, it is a riot,([4]) and punishable under the statute.

([1]) 1 Hawk. P. C. c. 65, § 1, 8, 9; 3 Inst. 176; 4 Blac. Com. 146; 1 Russ. C. & M. 24.

([2]) 1 Hale 463; 2 Camp. 370; 1 Russ. C. & M. 24.

([3]) 4 Blac. Com. 14; 1 Hawk. P. C. c. 65, § 6; 1 Russ. C. & M. 248.

([4]) 1 Russ. C. & M. 248; 2 Dea. Cr. Co. 1113; 1 Hawk. P. C. c. 65, § 12.

To constitute a riot, there must also be some circumstances of actual force or violence, or at least of an apparent tendency thereto, which are calculated to strike *terror among the people*, such as the show of offensive weapons, threatening speeches or turbulent gestures. But it is not necessary that personal violence should have been actually committed.(¹) This principle of terror to the people, is essentially necessary to constitute a riot, so that there may be an assemblage of three or more persons to do even an unlawful act without constituting a riot, although the act be done; as where a man assembles a number of persons to carry away any piece of property to which he claims a right, and which cannot be carried away without a number of persons, that will not be of itself a riot, if the number of persons are not more than necessary for the purpose, and if there be no threatening words used or other disturbance of the peace, although another man has better right to the thing carried away, and the act is therefore unlawful;(²) much more then, may any person, in a *peaceable manner*, assemble a fit number of persons to do any lawful thing, as to remove a common nuisance, or a nuisance to his own house or land; and he may do this before any prejudice is received from the nuisance, and for that purpose enter upon another man's ground.(³)

But the legality or illegality of the act intended to be done, is not material if there be force and violence used; for the law will not suffer persons to redress their private grievances by such dangerous disturbances of the public peace, and therefore if one goes to assert his rights by force and violence, he may be guilty of a riot, as where three or more persons assist a man to make a forcible entry into lands to which one of them has a right of entry, or if the like number, in a violent and tumultuous manner, join together in removing a nuisance or other thing which may lawfully be done in a peaceable manner, they are as properly rioters as if the act intended to be done by them were ever so unlawful.(⁴)

This violence and tumult must, in some degree, be premeditated, in order strictly to constitute the offence a riot. For, if a number of persons being met together on any lawful occasion, on a sudden, quarrel and fall together by the ears, this is not a riot, but only a sudden affray, of which none are guilty but those who actually engage in it.(⁵) But if parties

---

(¹) 1 Hawk. P. C. c. 65, § 5; Clifford v. Brandon, 2 Camp. 369; 1 Russ. C. & M. 248.
(²) 1 Hawk. c. 65, § 5; Burn J. P. Riot; 1 Russ. C. & M. 248-49.
(³) Dalt. c. 137; 1 Russ. C. & M. 249; R. v. Loley, 11 Mod. 117.
(⁴) 1 Hawk. c. 65, § 7; 2 Mod. 648; 1 Russ. C. & M. 249.
(⁵) 1 Hawk. c. 65, § 3; 2 Dea. Cr. Co. 1114.

met together on a lawful occasion, should afterwards, upon a dispute happening to arise among them, form themselves into parties, with promises of mutual assistance, and then make an affray, they are guilty of a riot; because, upon their confederating together with an intent to break the peace, they may be deemed to have assembled together for that purpose from the time of such confederacy. So, although parties may assemble for an innocent purpose in the first instance, yet if a sudden proposal should be started of going together in a body to commit any act of violence, to the disturbance of the public peace, and such proposal is accordingly executed, all persons concerned are clearly guilty of a riot; for the associating themselves together for such a new purpose, is in no wise extenuated by their having met first upon another.(¹) And if there be any predetermined purpose to act with violence and tumult, even though no personal violence is offered to any individual, the conduct of the parties may be deemed riotous. As where a number of persons, in a public theatre, go to it for the purpose of interrupting the performance, and making a great noise and disturbance, so as to render the actors inaudible, for though the audience have a right to express their feelings excited at the moment of the performance, and in so doing to applaud or hiss any piece which is represented, or any performer who exhibits himself on the stage, yet they have no right to assemble with a concerted plan to make such a tumult and uproar, as to render the actors entirely inaudible, and endanger the public peace, (though no personal violence be offered to any individual, or any injury done to the house,) if they do, they are guilty of a riot.(²)

There are no accessaries in a riot; all concerned in it are principals. When a person, on seeing others actually engaged in a riot, joins himself to them and assists them, he is as much a rioter as if he had first assembled with them for that purpose,(³) and whoever encourages or procures, or takes part in a riot, whether by words, signs or gestures, or by wearing the badge or ensign of the rioters, is himself to be considered a rioter; for in this offence, all are principals,(⁴) and even to incite persons to assemble in a riotous way, seems to be an indictable offence.(⁵)

Women are punishable as rioters, but infants, under the age of discretion, are not.(⁶) It is proper here to remark, that in

(¹) 1 Hawk. c. 65, § 3; 2 Dea. Cr. Co. 1114.
(²) 2 Camp. 358; 2 Dea. Cr. Co. 1114; 1 Russ. 249-50.
(³) 1 Hawk. c. 65, § 3.
(⁴) 2 Camp. 370; 4 Burr. 2073; 1 Hale 463; Deac. Cr. Co. 1115.
(⁵) Cro. Cir. Comp. 420; 2 Chit. Cr. L. 506; and see the 3d section of the statute as to who are farther to be considered rioters.
(⁶) 1 Hawk. c. 65, § 14; Dea. Cr. Co. 1115.

the criminal law, fourteen years is the age at which infants attain to legal discretion,(¹) and that at that age, he is as liable to suffer for this offence as a person of the full age of twenty-one.(²)

2. A rout is a disturbance of the peace by persons assembling together with intention to do a thing which, if executed, will make them rioters, and actually making a *motion* towards the execution of the purpose. In fact, it agrees generally in all the particulars of a riot, except that it may be a complete offence without the execution of the intended enterprise. It is a mere move by three or more persons to do that which, if done, would constitute a riot.(³)

3. An unlawful assembly at Common Law, is a disturbance of the peace by three or more persons barely assembling themselves together, with an intent to do a thing which, were it executed, would make them rioters, but neither executing it nor making a motion towards its execution ;(⁴) and all persons who join an unlawful assembly, disregarding its probable effects and the alarm and consternation likely to ensue, and all who gave countenance and support to it, are criminal parties to it. (See 1 Russ. 254, and cases there cited.)

II. *How a riot may be suppressed.*

The high character of this offence is manifest, not only from the punishment which the law prescribes for it, but from the extraordinary powers it confers upon the Magistrates to suppress it, and the penalties it imposes upon them for refusing or neglecting to exercise those powers.

Independent, however, of the statute by the Common Law, the Sheriff, Constable, and other peace officers may and ought to do all that in them lies towards suppressing a riot, and may command others to assist them,(⁵) who, if they refuse to assist, are indictable. And by the Common Law a private person may lawfully endeavour to suppress a riot, by staying those whom he shall see engaged therein, from executing their purpose, and may also stop others whom he shall see coming to join them. It is said that a private person, in the suppression of a riot, may arm himself and make use of arms if there be a necessity, either in defence of his own life and property, or to protect the lives and property of others,(⁶) and this upon the ground, that it is lawful for a private person to do any act

(¹) 1 Hale P. C. 25.
(²) 1 Hale 25 ; 1 Russ. C. & M. 2.
(³) 1 Russ. 253-4 ; 2 Deac. Cr. Co. 1115.
(⁴) 1 Russ. C. & M. 254 ; 2 Deac. Cr. Co. 1115.
(⁵) 1 Hawk. c. 65 ; 2 Dick. J. P. 333.
(⁶) 1 Hawk. c. 64, § 11 ; 2 Deac. Cr. Co. 1118 ; and 2 Bos. & P. 265.

to prevent a felony. But the necessity must be manifest to justify homicide under such circumstances. Indeed, in any case, the most cautious discretion must be used in regulating the conduct of a private person in preventing a mere breach of the peace.

(No. 1.)

Form of Warrant of Arrest for riotously destroying a house, under the 6th section of the statute.

—— County, to wit:
To X. Y., *Constable of the said County:*

Whereas, A. B. of the said County, hath this day made complaint and information on oath before me J. T., a Justice of the said County, that C. D. and E. F., with divers other persons, on the —— day of —— 18—, in the said County, did riotously, tumultuously and unlawfully assemble together, to disturb the public peace, and being so riotously, tumultuously and unlawfully assembled together, did [feloniously pull down and destroy (or *in part pull down and destroy,*) the dwelling house of A. B.] there situate: These are, therefore, to command you, in the name of the Commonwealth, forthwith to apprehend and bring before me or some other Justice of the said County, the said C. D. and E. F., to answer the said complaint, and to be farther dealt with according to law. Given under my hand and seal, this —— day of —— in the year 18—.

J. T., *J. P.* [L. S.]

(No. 2.)

Form of same for riotously assembling and committing an assault.

Follow form No. 1, and omit all in the brackets, and in the place of it, say: "unlawfully and riotously assault and beat the said A. B., to the great disturbance and terror of the people of this Commonwealth."

[NOTE.—The foregoing are proper when the Justice is not present at the riot, as he cannot arrest any one for a misdemeanor committed out of his view, but must issue his warrant. If he be present, as it is his duty whenever he is informed of a riot, he should openly and with a loud voice, order the persons riotously assembled, immediately to depart. It may be done in these words: "In the name of the law, I charge and command all persons here assembled, immediately to disperse themselves, and peaceably to depart to their habitations, or to their lawful pursuits, upon the pains of the act made for preventing riots and unlawful assemblies."

If, proclamation being made, the rioters do not disperse, the Justice, with the aid furnished him by the statute, is to cause them to be seized and secured in custody for trial. This is to be done, where no dwelling house is demolished or partly demolished, by the parties giving bail at once, to answer the offence in the Superior Court, or committing them, on their failure to do so. But if any dwelling house is pulled down or destroyed, or partly pulled down or destroyed, the party, if a white person, is to be committed for examination by the County Court; and for trial, if a slave or free negro, for the felony. The forms of proceeding will now be continued.

(No. 3.)

Form of a Recognizance to answer an indictment for a riot in the Superior Court, where the case is not felony.

———— County, to wit:

Be it remembered, that on the ——— day of ——— 18—, A. B. and C. D. of the said County, came before me J. T., a Justice of the said County, and severally acknowledged themselves to owe to the Commonwealth of Virginia, that is to say: The said A. B. the sum of ——— dollars, and the said C. D. the sum of ——— dollars, to be respectively made and levied of their several goods and chattels, lands and tenements, if he the said A. B. shall make default in performance of the condition underwritten.

The condition of the above recognizance is such, that whereas the above bound A. B. stands charged before me J. T., a Justice of the said County, with having, on the ——— day of ——— 18—, in the said County, together with E. F., and divers other persons, unlawfully and riotously assembled together to disturb the peace, and with having then and there assaulted and beat one L. M., to the great disturbance and terror of the people of this Commonwealth: Now, if the above bound A. B. do and shall personally appear before the Circuit Court, on the first day of the next term thereof, to be holden for the County of ———, there to answer for the said offence, and shall not thence depart without the leave of the said Court, and shall in the mean time keep the peace and be of good behaviour to all the people of this Commonwealth, then the above recognizance shall be void, otherwise to remain in full force and virtue.

Taken and acknowledged before me, this ——— day of ——— 18—.

J. T., J. P.

[NOTE.—The recognizance is the same whether the party be arrested in the presence of the Justice or by his warrant.]

(No. 4.)

Form of Commitment for want of bail, to appear before the Superior Court to answer an indictment for riot, under the 2d section of the statute.

———— County, to wit:

To X. Z., Constable of the said County, and to the Keeper of the Jail of the Circuit Court for the said County:

Whereas, A. B. was this day arrested and brought before me J. T., a Justice of the said County, by my order, for a misdemeanor by him, together with E. F. and divers other persons, committed in my view and presence, in this, that he the said A. B., with the said E. F. and divers other evil disposed persons, did, on this ——— day of ——— 18—, at the said County, unlawfully and riotously assemble together to disturb the peace, and did then and there riotously and unlawfully assault and beat one K. L., to the terror and disturbance of the people of this Commonwealth, and did refuse to depart from the place of the said riot, being first by me commanded so to do: and whereas the said A. B. stands now charged before me with the said offence, and hath been required by me to find sufficient sureties, as well for his appearance at the next term of the Circuit Court to be holden for the said County, to answer for the said offence, as also in the mean time to keep the peace and be of good behaviour towards all the people of this Commonwealth, but the said C. D. hath refused and neglected, and still refuses and neglects, to find such sureties, I do hereby command you, the said Constable, forthwith to convey the said C. D. to the jail of the said Circuit Court for the said County, and to deliver him to the keeper thereof, together with this warrant; and I command you, the said keeper, to receive the said C. D. into your custody, and him there safely keep until he shall be thence discharged by due course of law. Given under my hand and seal, this ⸺ day of ⸺ 18—.

J. T., J. P. [L. S.]

(No. 5.)

Form of Commitment for feloniously and riotously demolishing a dwelling house.

⸺ County, to wit:

To X. Y., *Constable of the said County, and to the Keeper of the Jail of the said County:*

These are to command you, the said Constable, in the name of the Commonwealth of Virginia, forthwith to convey and deliver into the custody of the keeper of the said jail, together with this warrant, the body of C. D., charged before me J. T., a Justice of the said County, on the oath of A. B., with a felony by him committed, in this, that he, with one E. F., on the ⸺ day of ⸺ 18—, in the said County, and divers other persons, did unlawfully and riotously assemble together, to the disturbance of the public peace, and being so assembled, did then and there feloniously demolish, pull down and destroy (or *partly pull down and destroy*) the dwelling house of the said A. B., and for which said offence, he is remanded by me for examination (if a free negro or slave, say *for trial*) before the County Court of the said County; and you, the keeper of the said jail, are hereby commanded to receive the said C. D. into your jail and custody, together with this warrant, and him there safely keep until he shall be thence discharged by due course of law. Given under my hand and seal, this ⸺ day of ⸺ 18—.

J. T., J. P. [L. S.]

(No. 6.)

Form of Certificate to the Clerk of the County Court.

Follow form No. 6, under the head of ARREST, and describe the offence as in the mittimus; if case be misdemeanor only, follow No. 10, under same head.

(No. 7.)

Form of Recognizance of Bail and Witnesses.

Follow forms Nos. 4 and 5, under head of RECOGNIZANCE, if offence be a misdemeanor, but if it be felony, follow Nos. 1 and 2, under same head.

(No. 1.)

Indictment for a Riot only.

Commence as No. 1, under head of "INDICTMENTS," and say: Upon their oaths present, that A. B., C. D. and E. F., together with divers others, to the number of ten, whose names are to the jurors aforesaid, as yet unknown, on ——— at ——— aforesaid, in the County aforesaid, and within the jurisdiction of this Court, with force and arms, did unlawfully, riotously and routously assemble and gather themselves together, to disturb the peace of the said Commonwealth, and then and there being so assembled and gathered together, did then and there make a great riot, noise, tumult and disturbance, and then and there unlawfully, riotously, routously and tumultuously are mained and continued together, making such noises, riot, tumult and disturbance, for the space of six hours then next following, to the great terror and disturbance of all the citizens of the said Commonwealth, there passing and repassing in and along the public streets and common highways there, and against the peace and dignity of the Commonwealth of Virginia.

(No. 2.)

Indictment for Riot and Assault.

Commence as No. 1, under head of "INDICTMENTS," and say: Upon their oaths present, that A. B., C. D. and E. F., all of, &c., together with divers others, evil disposed persons, to the jurors aforesaid unknown, on the ——— day of ———, with force and arms, in the County aforesaid, and within the jurisdiction of this Court, did unlawfully, riotously and routously assemble and gather themselves together to disturb the peace of the Commonwealth, and being then and there so assembled and gathered together, in and upon one G. H., unlawfully, riotously and routously did make an assault, and him, the said G. H. then and there, to wit, on the day and year aforesaid, at the County aforesaid, unlawfully, riotously and routously did beat, wound and ill treat, and other wrongs to him the said G. H. then and there unlawfully, riotously and routously did and committed, to the great damage of him, the said G. H., to the great terror of the people, and against the peace and dignity of the Commonwealth of Virginia.

(No. 3.)

Indictment for a Riot and pulling down a dwelling house.

Commence as No. 1, under head of "INDICTMENTS," and say: Upon their oaths present, that A. B., C. D. and E. F., together with other evil disposed and riotous persons, to the said jurors unknown, on ———, in the said County, and within the jurisdiction of this Court, with force and arms, did feloniously, unlawfully, riotously and routously assemble and gather together to disturb the peace of the said Commonwealth, and being so assembled and gathered together, the dwelling house of one J. K., then and there, to wit, on the day and year aforesaid, at the County aforesaid, unlawfully, riotously, routously and feloniously did pull down and destroy, (or *in part pull down and in part destroy*,) to the great disturbance and terror of the people there residing and being, against the statute in that case made and provided, and against the peace and dignity of the Commonwealth of Virginia.

CHAPTER XCI.

ROADS.

I. *As to the width and manner of keeping roads in repair.*

By Sec. 5, Chap. 52. Every road shall be thirty feet wide, unless the county court order it to be less. When a majority of the acting Justices is present, the county court may order a road adjoining a town or a village, to be made therefrom wider for a distance not exceeding eight hundred and fifty yards. In such case, the width shall not exceed sixty feet.

By Sec. 22. The owner or occupier of every dam shall, so far as a road passes over the same, keep such dam in good order, at least twelve feet wide at the top, and also keep in good order a bridge of like width over the pier head flood gates, or any waste cut through or round the dam, and shall erect and keep in good order a strong railing on both sides of such bridge or dam, unless such railing be dispensed with by the county court. If he fail to comply with this section, he shall pay a fine for every twenty-four hours failure, of two dollars. But the fine shall not, in any one prosecution, exceed fifty dollars. And where a mill dam is carried away or destroyed, the owner or occupier thereof shall not be thenceforth subject to such fine until one month after the mill shall have been put into operation.

By Sec. 23. The court of each county shall divide into precincts all the county roads not kept in order under any contract, and as often as it pleases may appoint a surveyor for each precinct, who shall hold his office until another be appointed in his stead. The Clerk of the court shall, upon such an appointment, issue a writ to the Sheriff, commanding him to give information thereof to the person so appointed, which writ the Sheriff shall execute and return to the court at the succeeding term. The Clerk shall, moreover, annually, at his March court, publish at the door of the courthouse, a list of the precincts and of the names of the surveyors. Any Clerk or Sheriff failing in such duty, shall forfeit therefor five dollars.

By Sec. 24. Any person, after being surveyor for two years, may give up his office if his road be in good order, and shall not within two years thereafter, be appointed surveyor without his consent.

BY SEC. 25. Every such surveyor shall superintend the roads in his precinct. He shall cause the same to be kept cleared, smoothed of rocks and obstructions, of necessary width, well drained and otherwise in good order, and secure from the falling of dead timber therein. He shall cause to be placed and kept at the fork or crossing of every road, a sign board, on which shall be stated in plain letters, the most noted place to which each road leads, and across every stream, where it is necessary and practicable, a sufficient bridge, bench or log, for the accommodation of foot passengers. When any more important bridge or causeway is necessary, and it is practicable for him to have it made, he shall cause it to be made twelve feet broad at the least, and safe and convenient. Every bridge or causeway in his precinct shall be kept by him in as good order as the means in his power will permit.

BY SEC. 26. All male persons in each county shall be appointed by the court thereof, and compelled to work on some public road therein, with the following exceptions, viz: persons under sixteen and above sixty years of age; persons who reside in a town that provides for its poor and keeps it streets in order; the officers of the penitentiary or any lunatic or other State asylum; the servants or slaves employed therein; the persons necessarily employed at any ferry; those employed on any State road, or any turpike, canal or railroad; and the officers of any literary institution, and ministers of the gospel. A list or designation of the persons appointed to work on any road, shall be endorsed on the writ issued under the 23d section, and a copy thereof shall be delivered by the Sheriff to the surveyor.

BY SEC. 27. When the court of any county deems it proper, for the purpose of opening a new road, or repairing great damages casually occurring to an existing one, it may appoint to work thereon persons appointed to work on other roads, provided not more than ten days of extra labour within one year be required of any person under this section.

BY SEC. 28. Every person appointed under either of the two preceding sections shall, either in person or by a sufficient substitute, when required by the proper surveyor, attend with proper tools, and work the road on such days as the surveyor may direct. For every day on which there may be a failure, seventy-five cents shall be paid to the surveyor, within twenty days thereafter, by the person in default, if a person of full age; or if he be an infant, by his parent or guardian; or if he be a servant or slave, by his overseer, if he be under one; otherwise, by his master. If the money be not paid, it shall be recoverable by the surveyor, with costs, before a Justice. Any money received by a surveyor under this section, after the payment of costs, shall be applied to the improvement of the road of which he is surveyor.

By Sec. 29. The court of any county may authorize the surveyor of any road therein, to hire so many labourers, as with those allotted to work thereon, will suffice to keep it in good order; to purchase gunpowder for the removal of obstructions therein, and to purchase tools or implements, which shall be preserved and transferred from one surveyor to another, as the court may direct. The surveyor shall return to the court, a particular account on oath of the expenses so incurred, and also the expenses of placing and keeping up sign boards as before mentioned, and the court shall allow the same, or so much thereof as may be justly due, in the next county levy.

By Sec. 30. The surveyor shall keep an exact account of all money received by him by virtue of his office, and of the manner of expending it. Annually, at the May or June term of the county court, he shall render to the court such an account verified on oath. If any part of the money so received shall then remain unexpended, he shall thereafter apply the same to the use of roads or bridges in the county, as the court may direct.

By Sec. 31. Whenever it may be necessary to have the assistance of wheel carriages or ploughs for making or repairing any road or bridge, or causeway therein, the surveyor of such road may obtain by consent of the owner, or if he cannot so obtain, may by warrant of a Justice impress such necessary carriages, ploughs, draft horses or oxen, with their gear and driver, belonging to any persons appointed to work on the road, and shall appoint two honest housekeepers, who upon oath shall value by the day the use of such carriages and other property. The valuation so made, with a certificate from the surveyor, of the number of days the said property was used on the road, shall entitle the owner to an allowance for the same in the next county levy.

By Sec. 32. The surveyor of any road may take from any convenient lands, so much wood, stone, gravel or earth as may be necessary to be used in constructing or repairing such road, or any bridge or causeway therein; and may for the purpose of draining the road, cause a ditch to be cut through any lands adjoining the same, provided such wood and other articles be not taken from, and such ditch be not cut through, any lot in a town, without the consent of the owner.

By Sec. 33. If the owner or tenant of any such lands shall think himself injured thereby, a Justice, upon application to him, shall issue a warrant to three freeholders, requiring them to view the said lands, and ascertain what is a just compensation to such owner or tenant, for the damage to him by reason of any thing done under the preceding section. The said freeholders after being sworn, shall accordingly ascertain such compensation, and report the same to the county court, and an allowance shall be made therefor in the next county levy.

By Sec. 34. Every surveyor of a road shall be entitled to compensation, at the discretion of the county court, to be paid out of the county levy, not exceeding one dollar and fifty cents per day, for the time actually employed in superintending the work on the road, which time shall be stated in writing and sworn to. Any surveyor of a road who shall fail to perform any duty required of him in this chapter, shall pay a fine of not less than five nor more than thirty dollars.

II. *As to obstruction to roads and hindrance to travellers.*

By Sec. 1, Chap. 97. Any person who shall kill a tree and leave it standing within the distance of fifty feet from the road, or shall knowingly and wilfully, without lawful authority, break down, destroy or injure any bridge, bench or log, placed across a stream for the accommodation, or any sign board, mile stone or post for the direction of travellers, or obstruct any road or any ditch made for the purpose of draining any such road, shall be punished by fine, at the discretion of a jury.

By Sec. 2. Any driver of a vehicle meeting any other vehicle on a road or bridge, shall seasonably drive to the right hand, so that each may pass the other without interference. And when a vehicle is overtaken by any other vehicle, the driver of the former shall bear to the right, and the driver of the latter shall bear to the left, until the latter shall have passed. Any driver failing so to do, shall forfeit two dollars.

By Sec. 3. Any person who shall drive or ride over a bridge faster than a walk, shall forfeit five dollars.

By Sec. 4. If any horse race be run on any road, bridge or landing, the rider of any horse in such race, the owner, if he assent thereto, and every person who shall bet on the race, shall pay a fine not exceeding ten dollars.

By Sec. 5. In this chapter, the construction of the word "road" shall be, that it embraces any turnpike, State road or county road, or the Cumberland road; of the word "bridge," that it embraces any bridge of the State or a county, or any toll bridge; and the word "landing," that it means a county landing.

By Sec. 6. Any fine or forfeiture incurred, under the first or third section of this chapter, shall, in the case of a county road, bridge or landing, be to the county; and in the case of a turnpike or bridge owned by a company or person, shall be to such company or person; and in the case of the Cumberland road or any State work, shall be to the Board of public works.

[NOTE.—The mode of recovering these fines, is by warrant in the name of the county, person or company to whom they go. See No. 5, under the head of WARRANTS.]

(No. 1.)

Form of Warrant by a Justice to impress wagons, &c., for the use of the surveyor of a road.

―――― County, to wit:

Whereas, A. B., surveyor of the public road leading through the said County, in precinct No. ―, has this day informed me J. T., a Justice of the said County, that it is necessary for the repairing of said road, that he, as surveyor thereof, should have the assistance of wheel carriages and ploughs, and that he cannot obtain them by consent of the owner: These are, therefore, in the name of the Commonwealth, to authorize the said A. B., as surveyor of said road, to impress such carriages, ploughs, draft horses or oxen, with their gear and driver, belonging to any person appointed to work on the said road, within the precinct aforesaid, as he shall deem necessary to repair the same. Given under my hand and seal, this ―― day of ―― 18―.

J. T., J. P. [L. S.]

(No. 2.)

Form of Warrant by a Justice to value articles obtained by the surveyor of a road.

―――― County, to wit:

To J. K. and Q. R., Housekeepers of the said County:

You are hereby commanded, after you shall have been sworn for that purpose, well and truly to estimate the value by the day, of (here state the articles,) which A. B., surveyor of the public road leading through said County, in precinct No. ―, has obtained of C. D. to keep the said road in repair, and return to the County Court of said County a certificate of your valuation thereof. Given under my hand and seal, this ―― day of ―― 18―.

J. T., J. P. [L. S.]

(No. 3.)

Form of the Oath to be administered to the housekeepers.

You, J. K. and Q. R., do swear on the Holy Bible, that you will, according to the best of your judgment, value by the day, the use of (here state the articles,) and which A. B., the surveyor of the public road leading through the said County, and in precinct No. ―, has obtained of C. D., to keep the said road in repair.

(No. 4.)

Form of Certificate of two housekeepers.

We, J. K. and Q. R., two housekeepers of the County of ———, being first duly sworn for that purpose, have, in pursuance of a warrant to us directed, issued by J. T., a Justice of the said County, this day viewed a plough and two horses, (or *a cart and four oxen,* as the case may be,) belonging to O. P., and impressed by A. B., as surveyor of the public road leading through the said County, in precinct No. —, to assist in repairing the said road, and do value the use of the said plough and horses, (or *the said cart and oxen, and the driver thereof,*) at ——— dollars, by the day.

                  J. K.
                  Q. R.

(No. 5.)

Form of Warrant of Justice directed to three freeholders to assess damages to the owners of lands, for cutting a ditch through the same, or taking stone, &c. from same by surveyor of road.

——— County, to wit:
 To E. F., G. H. and G. L., *Freeholders of said County:*

Forasmuch as A. B., as surveyor of the public road leading from ——— to ———, in the said County, hath, for the purpose of draining the said road, cut a ditch through the land of C. D., adjoining the said road, (or *has for the purpose of repairing the said road, taken stone and gravel from the land of the said C. D.,*) whereby the said C. D., as he alleges, has been injured: Now, therefore, I, J. T., a Justice of the said County, on the application of the said C. D., do hereby require you, the said E. F., G. H. and G. L., three freeholders of the said County, (after you shall have been sworn for that purpose,) to view the said land and ditch, (or *stone* or *gravel,* as the case may be,) and ascertain the damages which the said C. D. has sustained by the cutting of the said ditch, (or *taking the said stone and gravel,*) and report your assessment thereof to the next County Court of your County. Given under my hand and seal, this ——— day of ——— 18—.

              J. T., J. P. [L. S.]

(No. 6.)

Form of Certificate to be made in obedience to the foregoing warrant, and which may be made on the back of it.

We, the undersigned freeholders, mentioned in the within warrant, having been first duly sworn by J. T., a Justice of the Peace, to view the land mentioned in the said warrant, and ascertain the damages which C. D. has sustained by the cutting of the said ditch, (or *taking said stone,*) have viewed the said land, and ascertain and assess the damage which the said C. D. has sustained by reason of the cutting said ditch (or *taking said stone,*) to be ——— dollars, which we hereby certify.

                 E. F.
                 G. H.
                 G. L.

(No. 7.)

Form of Summons against a party for failing to work on a road when required by the surveyor.

—— County, to wit:
 To X. Y., *Constable of the said County:*

I command you, in the name of the Commonwealth of Virginia, to summon A. B., if he be found in your district, to appear at ——, in the said County, on the —— day of ——. 18—, before me or such other Justice of the said County as shall then be there, to try this warrant, to answer the complaint of C. D., the surveyor of the public road, in precinct No. —, in said County, in debt for —— dollars, the penalty incurred by him, the said A. B., for failing to attend with proper tools and work on the said road for —— days, when required to do so by the said C. D., as such surveyor, contrary to law. And have then there this warrant.

J. T., J. P.

(No. 8.)

Form of Judgment for plaintiff upon the above summons.

C. D., surveyor, &c. ⎱ —— day of —— 18—, at ——, case heard,
 v.   ⎰ and judgment for —— dollars fine against the de-
A. B.   ⎱ fendant, and for plaintiff's costs, which I ascertain to
               ⎰ be —— dollars.

J. T., J. P.

(No. 9.)

Form of Warrant for not keeping a road passing over a dam in good order.

—— County, to wit:
 To X. Y., *Constable of said County:*

I command you, in the name of the Commonwealth of Virginia, to summon A. B., if he be found in your district, to appear at ——, in the said County, on the —— day of —— 18—, before me or such other Justice of said County as shall then be there to try this warrant, to answer the complaint of C. D. the surveyor of the public road in precinct No. —— in said County, in debt for —— dollars, the penalty incurred by him the said A. B., for failing for —— hours to keep in good order, and at least twelve feet wide, the said road as it passes over a dam of which the said A. B. is owner in said precinct. Given under my hand, this —— day of —— 18—.

J. T., J. P.

[Form of judgment as in No. 8.]

(No. 10.)

Form of Summons against a person for riding a horse race in public road.

―――― County, to wit:
To X. Y., *Constable of said County:*

Whereas, complaint on oath has this day been made before me J. T., a Justice of said County, by A. B., that on the ―― day of ―――― 18―, in said County, C. D. did ride a horse race in the public County road leading from ―――― to ――――, in said County: These are, therefore, to command you, in the name of the Commonwealth, to summon the said C. D. to appear at ――――, in said County, on the ―― day of ―――― 18―, at ―――― o'clock in the ―――― noon, before me or such other Justice of said County, as may then be there, to hear the said complaint, to answer the same, and to be farther dealt with according to law. Given under my hand and seal, this ―― day of ―――― 18―.

J. T., J. P. [L. S.]

(No. 11.)

Form of Summons against a person for suffering his horse to run a race in public road.

―――― County, to wit:
To X. Y., *Constable of said County:*

Whereas, complaint on oath has this day been made before me J. T., a Justice of said County, by A. B., that on the ―― day of ―――― 18―, in said County, a horse race was ran in the public County road, leading from ―――― to ――――, in said County, and that a certain horse then owned by C. D., did run in the said race, with the knowledge and assent of the said C. D.: These are, therefore, to command you, in the name of the Commonwealth, to summon the said C. D. to appear at ――――, in said County, on the ―― day of ―――― 18―, at ―――― o'clock in the ―――― noon, before me or such other Justice of said County, as may then be there, to hear the said complaint, to answer the same, and to be farther dealt with according to law. Given under my hand and seal, this ―― day of ―――― 18―.

J. T., J. P. [L. S.]

(No. 12.)

Form of Summons against a person for breaking down, destroying or injuring bridge, bench or log across a creek.

―――― County, to wit:
To X. Y., *Constable of said County:*

Whereas, complaint on oath has this day been made before me J. T., a Justice of said County, by A. B., that on the ―― day of ―――― 18―, in said County, C. D. did knowingly and wilfully, without lawful authority, break down (or *destroy*, or *injure*) a certain bridge (or *bench*, or *log*) placed across ―――― creek for the accommodation of travellers: These are, therefore, to command you, in the name of the Commonwealth, to summon the said C. D. to appear at ———, in said County, on the —— day of ——— 18—, at —— o'clock in the ——— noon, before me or such other Justice of said County as may then be there, to hear the said complaint, to answer the same, and to be farther dealt with according to law. Given under my hand and seal, this —— day of ——— 18—.

J. T., J. P. [L. S.]

(No. 13.)

Form of Summons against a person for breaking down sign board or mile stone.

——— County, to wit:
 To X. Y., *Constable of said County:*

Whereas, complaint on oath has this day been made before me J. T., a Justice of said County, by A. B., that on the —— day of ——— 18—, in said County, C. D. did, knowingly and wilfully, without lawful authority, break down a certain sign board (or *mile stone*) placed for the accommodation of travellers on the —— road in said County : These are, therefore, to command you, in the name of the Commonwealth, to summon the said C. D. to appear at ———, in said County, on the —— day of ——— 18—, at —— o'clock in the ——— noon, before me or such other Justice of said County as may then be there, to hear the said complaint, to answer the same, and to be farther dealt with according to law. Given under my hand and seal, this —— day of ——— 18—.

J. T., J. P. [L. S.]

(No. 1.)

Form of Presentment against surveyor of a road for failing to keep the same in good order.

The grand jurors summoned to attend the County Court of ——— County, at the —— term thereof, in the year 18—, upon their oaths present, (*) that A. B., on the —— day of ——— 18—, at the said County, (he the said A. B. then and there being the surveyor of that part of a certain road, leading from ———— in the said County to ———— in said County, and in precinct No. —,) did not as such surveyor on that day cause that part of the said road to be kept cleared, smoothed of rocks and obstructions, of the necessary width, well drained, and otherwise in good order, and secure from the falling of dead timber therein, but did, on that day and on divers other days between that day and the day of making this presentment, and whilst he was surveyor as aforesaid, suffer that part of the said road to be and remain for a long space of time obstructed and in bad order and insecure from the falling of dead timber therein.

This presentment is made upon the testimony of C. D., a witness called on by the Court, sworn in Court and sent to the grand jury to give evidence. (Or " This presentment is made on the information and knowledge of C. D. and E. F. two of our own body.")

J. T., *Foreman.*

(No. 2.)

Form of Presentment against the owner of a dam over which a road passes, for not keeping the same in order.

Follow No. 1, to the star, and say: "A. B. for this, that he the said A. B. was, on the —— day of ——— 18—, and now is, the owner of a certain dam in the said County, over which a certain public road then passed and now passes, and that the said A. B. as owner of the said dam, did not on the day and year aforesaid, keep the said dam as far as the said road then passed and now passes over the same, at least twelve feet wide at the top thereof, with a strong railing on both sides of the said dam, (the said railing not having been dispensed with by the County Court of the said County,) but that he the said A. B. did, on that and on divers other days and times between that day and the day of making this presentment, to wit, for the space of ten days, fail to keep the said dam, so far as the said road then passed and now passes over the same, in good order, at least twelve feet wide at the top, with a strong railing on both sides of the said dam.

This presentment, &c. (conclude as No. 1.)

CHAPTER XCI.

ROBBERY.

BY SEC. 12, CHAP. 191. If any free person commit robbery, being armed with a dangerous weapon, he shall be confined in the penitentiary not less than five nor more than ten years; if not so armed, he shall be confined therein not less than three nor more than ten years.

By this provision, the punishment is greater where the offender is, at the time of committing the offence, armed with a dangerous weapon, and in prosecutions under it, the question as to what is a dangerous weapon may arise. Any weapon, the use of which is calculated to cause death or great bodily harm, is a dangerous weapon. In Nailor's Case, which was a prosecution for murder, a pen knife was said by the court to be a dangerous weapon.[1]

Robbery is defined by Mr. East to be "a felonious taking of money or goods to any value, from the person of another or in his presence, against his will by violence or putting in fear."[2] This definition differs somewhat from that given by writers who preceded him; it is, however, drawn with exact conformity to the current of adjudged cases, and is followed by the most approved authors who have succeeded him.[3]

According to this definition, there must be, 1. The taking of money or goods of some value; 2. The taking must be from the person of another or in his presence and against his will; and 3. It must be by violence or putting in fear. These requisites will be noticed in their order.

I. *Of the felonious taking and value of the property.*

The gist of this offence being in the force and terror used by the offender, the value of the property stolen is quite immaterial; for a penny, as well as a pound, forcibly taken or extorted by fear, constitutes in law robbery.[4] But *something* of value, however small that value may be, must be taken from the person, either actually or constructively, and the taking must in all cases be accompanied with a felonious intent.[5] This intent must of course be collected from the circumstances of each case. In this offence, as in simple

---

[1] 1 East P. C. 277.
[2] 2 East P. C. 707.
[3] 1 Leach 139, 193, 280; Russ. & Ry. C. C. 146, 375; 2 Deac. Cr. Co.
[4] 3 Inst. 69; 1 Hawk. c. 34, § 16; 2 Russ. on C. & M. 62.
[5] R. v. Phepoe, 2 Leach 673; 1 Hale 532; 2 Russ. 64.

larceny, if the felonious intent be wanting, then though the goods be taken by such force or putting in fear, as would otherwise be sufficient to constitute robbery, it will only amount to trespass. As if one person, acting under a *bona fide* impression that the property is his own, obtains possession of it by force or putting in fear, it will not constitute robbery.([1])

The taking must also be such as to give the offender *possession* of the property stolen, though that possession need only be for one moment. As where a man had his purse fastened to his girdle, and a thief intending to rob him of it, cut the girdle, and thereby the purse fell to the ground, but was not taken up by the thief, this was held not to be robbery, because the thief never had possession of the purse;([2]) but where a thief, intending to rob a lady, snatched from her ear a diamond ear-ring, by tearing the ear through as she was stepping into her carriage, and the ear-ring dropped from his fingers into the curls of her hair, at the moment he had seized it, it was held to be a sufficient taking, as he had it for a moment in his actual possession, and it was taken by *violence* from her possession.([3])

There may be a taking, however, in law as well as in fact; as when there is not actual violence offered to the person, but the property is delivered up under the *influence of fear*. Thus, where thieves, finding no property on a man, force him by menaces of death, to fetch them money, which he delivers to them while the fear of the menace still continues upon him and they receive it, this is a sufficient taking in law; for the thief may, in all such cases, as correctly be said to take the property from the owner, as if he had actually taken it out of his pocket.([4])

But the taking is not sufficient to constitute robbery, if it precede the violence or putting in fear; to make it robbery, the taking must in all cases, be *by means* of the violence or putting in fear.([5])

II. *The taking from the person or presence.*

The taking need not be immediately from the person of the owner, it is enough if it *be in his presence*, so that in taking it from his immediate personal care and protection, there be violence to his person, or putting him in fear. As

---

([1]) R. v. Hale, 3 C. & P. 409; 2 Deac. Cr. Co. 1129.
([2]) 3 Inst. 69.
([3]) 1 Leach 320; 2 Deac. Cr. Co. 1127.
([4]) 1 Hale 533; 3 Inst. 68; 2 East P. C. 711, 714.
([5]) 1 Hale 534; 1 Hawk. c. 34, § 7; 2 East P. C. 726.

when a thief, having assaulted a man, takes away his horse standing by him, or takes up his hat, which has fallen, (while he is endeavouring to make his escape,) and carries it away; or when a thief, having put a man in fear, drives his cattle openly and before his face out of his pasture, such taking, or such driving away of the cattle, being done in the presence of the owner, will amount to robbing.([1])

A taking by violence or putting in fear, implies, of course, a taking against the will of the owner. See Fost. 121, 128; and 2 Deac. 1129; and

III. *By violence or putting in fear.*

The words violence or fear, in the definition of this offence, *are in the alternative,* and if the property be taken by either of these means, against the will of the owner, such taking will be sufficient to constitute robbery.([2]) The principle of robbery, indeed, is violence, but it has been often holden, that actual violence is not the only means by which a robbery may be effected, but that it may also be effected by fear, which the law considers as constructive violence.([3])

It is not every degree of actual violence, where there is no putting in fear, that will constitute this offence. There must be something more than a sudden taking or snatching from the person unawares; for unless some greater force is used by the thief to overpower or prevent resistance, or there is some actual struggle on the part of the owner to retain his property, it will not amount to a robbery.([4]) But if any injury be done, or there be any struggle on the part of the owner to retain his property, then the violence will be sufficient to make the offence robbery; as in Lappier's Case, where the ear-ring was so violently pulled from the ear, that it was torn through and made to bleed, it was held to be robbery.([5]) In this case, although the ear-ring was suddenly snatched, yet there was injury to the person. And so in the King against Mason, R. & Ry. 419, where the prisoner jerked a gentleman's watch from his fob, and by two jerks broke a steel chain which fastened it to his neck, in order to get the watch, it was held to be robbery; for although there was no actual injury to the person, yet the prisoner had to overcome the resistance made by the chain, and used actual force for that purpose. See, also,

---

([1]) 1 Hawk. c. 34, § 6; 2 Deac. 1128; 2 Str. 1015; 2 Russ. 65.
([2]) 2 East P. C. 127; Foster 128; 2 Russ. 67.
([3]) 1 Leach 196-7; 2 East P. C. 727; 2 Russ. 67.
([4]) Macauley's Case, 1 Leach 287; R. v. Baker, Id. 290; 2 East P. C. 702-3; R. v. Grosil, 1 C. & P. 304.
([5]) 1 Leach 320.

2 East P. C. 709; R. v. Davies, and R. v. Moore, 1 Leach 339.

There may be a constructive, as well as an actual force; fear will supply the place of force,([1]) for when such terror is impressed on the mind as not to leave the party a free agent, and in order to get rid of that terror, he delivers his money to the thief, this is a sufficient force in law.([2]) And where actual violence is used, there need not be actual fear; for the law, *in odium spoliatoris* will presume it.([3]) As where a man is knocked down, without previous warning, and stripped of his property while he is senseless, though he cannot be said to be *put in fear* while his property is being taken from him, yet this is undoubtedly robbery.([4])

When a robbery consists by putting in fear without actual violence, this does not necessarily imply any great degree of terror or affright in the party robbed, but only such force or threatening by word or gesture as may create a reasonable apprehension of danger, or induce a man to part with his property against his will, and the law *in odium spoliatoris*, presumes fear whenever the reasonable apprehension of danger exists.([5])

Where violence is made use of to obtain property or money with a felonious intent, it will not the less amount to robbery on account of the thief's having recourse to some colourable or specious pretence, in order the better to effect his object; thus where a man was carrying his cheese along the highway and was stopped by the prisoner, who insisted on seizing them for want of a permit, which was a mere pretence, as no permit was necessary, this was held to be robbery.([6]) And so where a bailiff handcuffed a woman under pretext of carrying her to prison with greater safety, and by violence extorted money from her when so handcuffed, it was held to be robbery.([7]) In all such cases, the existence of the felonious intent must be determined by the evidence, and it will not be difficult for the Justice to decide whether it is a trespass only or a felony, and whenever the taking is by violence or putting in fear, and against the will of the owner, with intent at the time fraudulently to convert the goods to the use of the taker, it amounts to robbery, however specious the means resorted *to* in accomplishing the design.

([1]) 2 Deac. 1130; 2 East P. C. 727.
([2]) 2 Russ. C. & M. 67; 1 Leach 193, Donnally's Case; Rean's Case, 2 Leach 616.
([3]) 2 East P. C. 711; Foster 128.
([4]) 4 Blac. Com. 224.
([5]) 2 Deac. Cr. Co. 1131-2.
([6]) 2 Russ. 68; 2 East P. C. 709.
([7]) Gascoigne's Case, 1 Leach 280.

It is not the apprehension of every injury, that constitutes robbery. The fear of injury to the person, is that which is most commonly excited in this offence, and this principle is extended to a man's wife or child, so that if money is extorted from him by fear of violence to the person of either, it is sufficient to constitute the offence of robbery.([1])

In a modern work of high authority in England, it is stated, as a general proposition, that a fear of immediate injury to property, as to a horse, will be sufficient to constitute this offence, but the proposition is broader than the cases on which it is founded will justify. They are all cases of apprehended injury to the dwelling house, and in which the terror excited was of the probable outrages of a mob.([2]) In all the cases, there was more than one person concerned in the robbery, and most of them were attended by mobs threatening the *destruction* of the *dwelling*, and under circumstances calculated to induce the fear of personal violence. Mr. East, in his work on the Pleas of the Crown, has collected these cases, and from a note appended to them, seems to think that this doctrine is founded on the principle, that the threat of burning down a man's dwelling house by a mob, conveys in itself a threat of personal danger. Although the cases may not have been determined on this principle alone, but may embrace the case of fear produced by threats to destroy the dwelling house, unconnected with any fear of personal violence, we think the rule should be restricted to the fear of the destruction of the dwelling house, and not extended to the destruction of personal property.

The fear of injury to one's character, has been held sufficient to constitute this offence, and here again the cases of robbery, in which property has been obtained by means of fear being excited of injury to the character of the party robbed, appear to be all of one description, that is, of threats to destroy the character of the party pillaged, by accusing him or threatening to accuse him of unnatural crime or unnatural propensities.([3])

([1]) 2 Russ. 72; 2 Deac. Cr. Co. 1172.   ([3]) 2 Russ. 75; 2 Deac. Cr. Co. 1136.
([2]) 2 East P. C. 729, 30, 31.

ROBBERY.

(No. 1.)

Form of Warrant of Arrest.

—— County, to wit:

To all or any one of the Constables of said County:

Forasmuch as A. B. of the said County, has this day made complaint on oath before me J. T., a Justice of the said County, that C. D. of the said County, on the —— day of ——— 18—, in the said County, he the said C. D. [being then armed with a dangerous weapon, to wit, with a loaded gun,] on him the said A. B. feloniously did make an assault, and him the said A. B., in bodily fear, did feloniously put, and one gold watch of the value of fifty dollars, and one bank note of the value of five dollars, of the goods and chattels, bank note and property of the said A. B., from the person and against the will of the said A. B., feloniously and violently did steal, take and carry away: These are, therefore, in the name of the Commonwealth, to command you forthwith to apprehend and bring before me or some other Justice of the said County, the said C. D., to answer the said complaint, and to be farther dealt with according to law. Given under my hand and seal, this —— day of ——— 18—.

J. T., J. P. [L. S.]

[NOTE.—This form will answer when no dangerous weapon is used, by leaving out what is in the brackets.]

———

(No. 2.)

Form of Mittimus where a party is committed for examination or trial in the County Court, for robbery.

—— County, to wit:

To X. Z., Constable of said County, and to the Keeper of the Jail of said County:

These are to command you, the said Constable, in the name of the Commonwealth of Virginia, forthwith to convey and deliver into the custody of the keeper of the said jail, together with this warrant, the body of C. D., a white person (or *free negro*, or *a slave, the property of E. F.*, as the case may be,) charged before me J. T., a Justice of the said County, on the oath of A. B., with a felony by him committed, in this, that the said C. D., on the —— day of ——— in the year 18—, in the said County, (here describe the offence as in the warrant of arrest.) And you, the said keeper of the said jail, are hereby required to receive the said C. D. into your jail and custody, that he may be examined (or *tried*) for the said offence, by the County Court of said County, and him there safely keep, until he shall be discharged by due course of law. Given under my hand and seal, this —— day of ——— in the year 18—.

J. T., J. P. [L. S.]

[NOTE.—If the prisoner be a white person, commit him for examination; if a negro, commit him for trial.]

(No. 3.)

Form of Certificate of Commitment to be sent to the Clerk of the County Court, for robbery.

—— County, to wit:

To the Clerk of the County Court of said County:

I, J. T., a Justice of the said County, do hereby certify, that I have, by my warrant, this day committed C. D., a white person, (or if free negro or slave, state which,) to the jail of this County, that he may be examined (or *tried*) before the County Court of the said County for a felony by him committed, in this, that he did, on the —— day of ——— 18—, in the said County, (here state the offence as in the mittimus.) Given under my hand, this —— day of ——— in the year 18—.

J. T., J. P.

(No. 4.)

Form of Certificate to the Clerk where party is admitted to bail.

Turn to head of ARREST, and follow No. 6.

(No. 5.)

Form of Recognizance of Bail.

Turn to head of RECOGNIZANCE, and follow No. 1, if person be free; No. 2, if a slave, and state succinctly the offence for which the person is recognized.

(No. 6.)

Form of Recognizance of Witness to appear before the County Court to give evidence upon the examination or trial of a party charged with felony.

Turn to head of RECOGNIZANCE, and follow No. 3.

An Indictment for robbery.

—— Judicial Circuit, } The jurors of the Commonwealth of Vir-
—— County, to wit: } ginia, in and for the body of the County of
In the Circuit Court for the } ——, and now attending the said Court,
said County. } upon their oath present, that A. B., on the
—— day of ———, in the year one thousand eight hundred and ———, in the said County, [he the said A. B. being then armed with a dangerous weapon, to wit, with a loaded gun,] on one C. D. feloniously did make an assault, and him the said C. D. in bodily fear did

feloniously put, and one gold watch of the value of fifty dollars, and one bank note of the value of five dollars, of the goods and chattels, bank note and property of the said C. D., from the person and against the will of the said C. D., then and there, to wit, on the day and year aforesaid, in the County aforesaid, feloniously and violently did steal, take and carry away, against the peace and dignity of the Commonwealth of Virginia.

[NOTE.—This form will answer when no dangerous weapon is used, by leaving out what is in the brackets.]

CHAPTER XCII.

RUNAWAY SLAVES.

BY SEC. 1, CHAP. 105. Every slave arrested as a runaway, shall be taken before a Justice, and if there be reasonable cause to suspect that such slave is a runaway, the Justice shall give a certificate thereof, stating therein, as near as may be, if the same be known, the distance of the place of arrest from that from which the slave may be supposed to have fled, and the sum of money demandable therefor by the person making the arrest, including mileage. If the arrest be made without the State, the slave shall be taken before a Justice of the county or corporation into which he may be first brought, and such Justice shall give the proper certificate.

BY SEC. 2. The Justice giving the certificate, by his precept endorsed thereon, shall command the person applying for the same forthwith to deliver the slave, for safe keeping, (together with the said certificate,) to the Jailor of his county or corporation, who shall give his receipt therefor, or if the owner of the slave or his agent be known, the precept may command the delivery to be made to such owner or agent, upon the payment of the sum of money demandable for the arrest and mileage, and upon default of such payment, to the Jailor of the county or corporation in which such default is made.

BY SEC. 4. Every person who may arrest a runaway slave, and deliver him to the owner or his agent, or to some Jailor at his jail, with the certificate of a Justice, in the manner herein provided, shall be entitled to demand of such owner a reward therefor, that is to say: If such slave be arrested in this State, and within fifty miles of his residence, a reward of five dollars, or if more than fifty miles, ten dollars. If in any other slaveholding State, and within fifty miles of his residence, ten dollars, or if more than fifty miles, twenty dollars. If in any non-slaveholding State, and within fifty miles of his residence, fifty dollars, or if more than fifty miles, one hundred dollars. If on board a vessel departing or about to depart from any point in this State, a reward of forty dollars. And in every case the person making the arrest and delivery, shall be allowed mileage, at the rate of ten cents a mile, for necessary travel from the place of arrest. The hirer of a slave shall not be liable for the payment of any reward allowed by this section, unless such running away was caused by the bad treatment of the hirer, or otherwise by his act or procurement, and in that event the hirer shall pay to the owner the whole of such reward and expense of apprehending such slave.

By Sec. 5. If any private reward be offered for the arrest of a runaway slave, the person making the arrest may, at his option, demand such reward, or the reward and mileage allowed by law.

By Sec. 6. The reward and mileage allowed or offered as aforesaid, shall be a lien on the slave from the time of his apprehension till the same be paid, or till he be delivered to the owner or discharged by the court, and on the proceeds of sale, if sold as hereinafter provided.

By Sec. 7. The court of the county or corporation in which a runaway slave may be confined, or any Justice thereof, may order such slave to be delivered to the owner or his agent, upon payment to the Jailor of all lawful charges incident upon his arrest.

By Sec. 8. The Jailor having so delivered such slave, he and his sureties shall be liable to the person making the arrest for his reward and mileage. The liability shall be only for the reward and mileage prescribed by law, if the Jailor had no notice that a larger reward was offered, and the owner or his agent before the delivery made oath that no larger reward had been offered by the owner, or any person authorized by him.

By Sec. 9. When a runaway slave is committed to jail, the Jailor shall forthwith set up an advertisement, describing the slave and his apparel, at the door of the courthouse of his county or corporation. If no owner claim him within one month, the Jailor shall cause a like advertisement to be published for six weeks in some newspaper in the City of Richmond, and also (where the jail is not in that City,) in some newspaper circulating near the jail. He shall also endeavour to ascertain the owner's name and residence, and upon obtaining any information thereof, shall send the supposed owner by mail, post paid, an unsealed letter, directed to the postoffice supposed to be nearest to his residence, describing the runaway, and stating any other facts deemed material. If the Jailor omit any of the duties prescribed by this section, his fees for receiving and keeping the slave shall be reduced to such extent as the court of his county or corporation may think proper.

By Sec. 10. If such runaway be not claimed by the owner within four months after the advertisement aforesaid is ended, the county or corporation court, upon the Jailor's report and proof of such advertisement, shall order its officer to sell the slave. The sale shall be made at the same time and place, and after such notice at the courthouse door, as in the case of slaves levied on.

By Sec. 11. The said officer, after deducting from the proceeds, a commission of five per centum, the Jailor's lawful fees, and other charges, and the apprehender's dues, (all of which are to be paid by the said officer,) shall pay the residue into the public treasury, at the same time, and under the same penalties for failure as in the case of taxes.

By Sec. 12. If such officer fail to make a report of the sale as prescribed by the forty-ninth chapter, he shall forfeit one hundred dollars to the Commonwealth, unless before a proceeding therefor, the owner of the slave appear and prove his ownership, in which case the forfeiture shall be to such owner.

By Sec. 13. When a runaway is so ordered to be sold, the clerk of the court shall, as soon as may be, transmit to the first auditor a copy of the order, and also of the officer's report of the sale, for each of which copies, the clerk shall have a fee of fifty cents, to be paid from the proceeds of sale. A clerk failing to transmit a copy of the order or report within twenty days after the former is made or the latter is returned, shall forfeit fifty dollars.

By Sec. 14. The court, by whose order the sale was made, may at any time thereafter, order the nett proceeds thereof, to be paid to the owner, by the officer making the sale, if the money be still in his hands, or out of the treasury if it be therein.

By Sec. 15. When an imprisoned runaway is not sufficiently clothed, the Jailor shall furnish him with proper negro clothing, the cost of which shall be adjudged by the county or corporation court, or two Justices.

By Sec. 16. If such slave die in jail, the Jailor's fees and other lawful charges shall be paid by the owner; if he be not known or unable to pay, then out of the treasury, on being allowed and certified by the court.

(No. 1.)

Form of Certificate to be given by Justice to the person arresting a runaway slave.

———— County, to wit:

I, J. T., Justice of said County, do certify that A. B. has arrested and this day brought before me, Frank a slave, the property of C. D. of the County of ————, as a runaway, and having upon the examination of said A. B., reasonable cause to suspect that said Frank is a runaway slave, I do farther certify that said slave was apprehended in ———— County, in this State, (or *in the State of* ————,) and that the distance from the place of his arrest to the residence of said C. D., from whence he is supposed by me to have fled, is ———— miles, and that said A. B. is entitled to demand of said C. D. ———— dollars for arresting said slave, including mileage at the rate of ten cents a mile for necessary travel from the place of his arrest. Given under my hand, this ———— day of ———— 18—.

J. T., J. P.

When the slave is ordered to jail, this endorsement should be made on the precept:

To the within named A. B.:

I command you forthwith to deliver the within mentioned slave to the Jailor of the County of ————, for safe keeping, together with this precept, and I hereby require the said Jailor to receive said slave into his jail, and to give you his receipt for him.

J. T., J. P.

But the Justice may order the slave to be delivered to the owner, and in that case, the endorsement should end in this form:

To the within named A. B.:

I command you, that without delay, you carry to C. D., his owner, the within named slave, and that upon the payment to you of the within sum of $ ————,* you deliver him the said slave. But if he make default in the payment thereof, then you are commanded to deliver the said slave, with this precept, to the Jailor of the County of ————, (the County in which payment was refused,) who is hereby required to receive him, and give to you his receipt for the said slave. Given under my hand, this ———— day of ———— 18—.

J. T., J. P.

(No. 2.)

Form of a Justice's order to a Jailor to deliver a runaway to his owner.

———— County, to wit:

To the Keeper of the Jail of said County:

I command you, upon payment to you of all lawful charges incident upon the arrest of Frank, a runaway slave, now in your jail, that you deliver him to C. D., who is the owner of said slave, (or *to E. F. the agent of C. D.*) Given under my hand, this ———— day of ———— 18—.

J. T., J. P.

---

* This blank will be filled according to the distance travelled, and the reward allowed by the 4th section of the statute.

CHAPTER XCIII.

SABBATH DAY—(*Breach of.*)

Besides the religious duty of obeying the commands of God, and the scandalous indecency of an open disregard of this duty, by a profanation of the Sabbath, "the keeping one day in seven holy, as a time of relaxation and refreshment, as well as of public worship, is of admirable service in a State, considered merely as a civil institution. It humanizes, by the help of conversation and society, the manners of the people, which would otherwise degenerate into a sordid ferocity and savage selfishness of spirit. It enables the industrious workman to pursue his occupation in the ensuing week with health and cheerfulness; it imprints, on the minds of the people, that sense of their duty to God, so necessary to make them good citizens, but which would be worn out and defaced by an unremitted continuance of labour, without any stated times of recalling them to the worship of their maker."

By SEC. 15, CHAP. 196. If a white person, arrived at the age of discretion, profanely curse or swear, or get drunk, he shall be fined by a Justice one dollar for each offence.

By SEC. 16. If a free person, on a Sabbath day, be found labouring at any trade or calling, or employ his apprentices, servants or slaves, in labour or other business, except in household or other work of necessity or charity, he shall forfeit two dollars for each offence ; every day any servant, apprentice or slave is so employed constituting a distinct offence.

By SEC. 17. No forfeiture shall be incurred under the preceding section for the transportation on Sunday of the mail, or of passengers and their baggage. And the said forfeiture shall not be incurred by any person who conscientiously believes that the seventh day of the week ought to be observed as a Sabbath, and actually refrains from all secular business and labour on that day, provided he does not compel a slave, apprentice or servant, not of his belief, to do secular work or business on Sunday, and does not, on that day, disturb any other person.

By SEC. 18. If a free person wilfully interrupt or disturb any assembly met for the worship of God, he shall be confined in jail not more than six months and fined not exceeding one hundred dollars, and a Justice may put him under restraint during religious worship, and bind him for not more than one year to be of good behaviour.

A person convicted of exercising his calling on a Sabbath, can only be charged with one penalty under the statute, although he works for different persons or sells to different customers; for there is no idea conveyed, by the statute, that these are so many distinct offences, but one entire offence of exercising his ordinary trade on the Lord's day, which, whether longer or shorter in point of duration, or whether the profanation of it consists of a number of particular acts, makes no manner of difference, it is still one offence, compounded of different acts. The offence consists in carrying on trade on the Sabbath, and if the trade be the selling of goods, one sale is sufficient to constitute it, and a dozen to different individuals will do no more.(¹) But, under our statute, every apprentice, servant or slave so employed, constitutes a distinct offence, and subjects the master to a separate fine for each.

(No. 1.)

Form of Warrant against a person for disturbing a religious meeting.

———— County, to wit:

To X. Y., *Constable of the said County:*

Whereas, A. B. of said County, has this day complained on oath before me J. T., a Justice of the said County, that C. D. did, on the ———— day of ———— 18—, in said County, wilfully interrupt and disturb an assembly of people, then and there met for the public worship of God, in a certain house there situated, called the Presbyterian church, (or whatever other place it may be,) by rude and indecent behaviour, (or "by the use of profane language," or "by making a loud noise in said church," or "by making a noise so near the said church, as to disturb the order and solemnity of the meeting:") These are, therefore, to command you, in the name of the Commonwealth, forthwith to apprehend the said C. D., and bring him before me or some other Justice, to be farther dealt with according to law. Given under my hand and seal, this ———— day of ———— 18—.

J. T., J. P. [L. S.]

[NOTE.—This is a misdemeanor, and upon being brought before the Justice, the party is to be committed or recognized to answer an indictment.]

(No. 2.)

Form of Recognizance to be of good behaviour by a person disturbing religious assemblies in the presence of a Justice.

———— County, to wit:

Be it remembered, that on the ———— day of ———— 18—, A. B. and C. D. of the said County, came before me J. T., a Justice of the said County, and severally acknowledged themselves to owe to the Commonwealth of Vir-

(¹) Cripps *v.* Durde, Cowp. 640.

ginia, that is to say: The said A. B. the sum of ——— dollars, and the said C. D. the sum of ——— dollars, to be respectively made and levied of their several goods and chattels, lands and tenements, if he the said A. B. shall make default in performance of the condition underwritten.

The condition of the above recognizance is such, that whereas the above named A. B. did this day, in my presence, wilfully interrupt and disturb an assembly of people met for the worship of God, at a certain house situated in the said County, called the (here designate the church or meeting house,) and was by me as Justice aforesaid, put under restraint therefor, and required to give security to be of good behaviour: Now, if the said A. B. shall be of good behaviour for the term of twelve months next ensuing the date hereof, towards all the people of this Commonwealth, then the above recognizance to be void, otherwise to remain in full force and virtue.

Taken and acknowledged before me, the day and date first above written.

J. T., J. P.

[If the party refuse to enter into the recognizance, he may be committed as in other cases of a breach of the peace. For the form of commitment, see No. 6, under head of SURETY OF THE PEACE.]

The offence of working on the Sabbath day, is within the jurisdiction of a single Justice to try, and should be proceeded against by summons.

(No. 3.)

Form of Summons against a person for working on the Sabbath.

——— County, to wit:

To X. Y., Constable of the said County:

Whereas, complaint on oath has this day been made before me J. T., a Justice of said County, by A. B., that on a Sabbath day, to wit, on the ——— day of ——— 18—, in said County, C. D. was found labouring at his trade and calling, and did then, on the said Sabbath, labour at his said trade and calling, by (here state what labour or business C. D. was engaged in,) and which was neither a work of necessity or charity: These are, therefore, to command you, in the name of the Commonwealth, to summon the said C. D. to appear at ———, in said County, on the ——— day of ——— 18—, at ——— o'clock in the ——— noon, before me or such other Justice of said County as may then be there, to hear the said complaint, to answer the same, and to be farther dealt with according to law. Given under my hand and seal, this ——— day of ——— 18—.

J. T., J. P. [L. S.]

If defendant be found guilty, endorse judgment on summons. It may be done thus: "Defendant found guilty, and judgment against him for two dollars fine and the costs, which I ascertain to be $ ———."

J. T., J. P.

Execution.

If judgment be rendered against the defendant, the Justice can issue no execution; but if in his favour, he should issue execution for costs. See for form under head of FINES.

(No. 1.)

Indictment for interrupting and disturbing public worship.

Commence as No. 2, under head of "INDICTMENTS," and say: that A. B. being a person regardless of the duties and solemnities of the public worship of God, and of the due observance of the Lord's day, on the —— day of ——, at —— church, in the County aforesaid, did wilfully interrupt and disturb a certain assembly of people, there met for the public worship of God, within the place of their assembling, by making divers loud and indecent noises and tumults during the performance of divine service in said church, to the great insult and injury of the orderly people then and there assembled in the said church, for the purposes aforesaid, against good morals and good manners, and against the peace and dignity of the Commonwealth of Virginia.

(No. 2.)

Indictment for keeping an open shop on the Lord's day.

Commence as No. 2, under head of "INDICTMENTS," and say: that A. B., on the —— day of ——, at the County aforesaid, and continually afterwards, until the day of the taking of this inquisition, on the —— day of ——, in the County aforesaid, was and yet is a common Sabbath breaker and profaner of the Sabbath day; and that the said A. B., on the —— day of ——, being a Sabbath day, and at divers other days and times, being a Sabbath day, during the times aforesaid, did keep open his the said A. B.'s shop, he the said A. B. being then a merchant, and did keep an open and common public shop; and in the said shop did then and there, and on the said other days and times, being Sabbath days, open and publicly carry on his business as merchant, and did sell and expose to sale, goods, wares and merchandize, to divers persons, to the great injury and common nuisance of all the citizens of said Commonwealth, and against the peace and dignity of the Commonwealth of Virginia.

CHAPTER XCIV.

SEAMEN.

Desertion of.

BY SEC. 1, CHAP. 94. If any seaman or mariner, who is under a contract in writing, to serve on board of any *merchant* vessel, or any apprentice, who is lawfully bound to the master or owner of any such vessel, for the purpose of being taught to be a seaman or mariner, shall desert or absent himself, without lawful permission, from such vessel, any Justice, upon complaint thereof being made by any officer of such vessel, shall issue his warrant to apprehend such seaman, mariner or apprentice, and bring him before the same or some other Justice.

BY SEC. 2. The Justice before whom the complaint is tried, shall, if it be proved, commit such seaman, mariner or apprentice to the jail of his county or corporation, there to remain until he shall be delivered to the master or commander of such vessel, or until she shall sail upon her voyage.

BY SEC. 3. But if it appear that any such seaman, mariner or apprentice, has been cruelly treated while on board such vessel by the master thereof, or that there is good ground to apprehend danger to *his life, or to limb or health*, from the master, should he be compelled to go on board such vessel, the said Justice may discharge him from custody. The officer making the complaint, shall, in either case, pay the costs of the arrest and imprisonment.

Landing sick seamen.

BY SEC. 13, CHAP. 93. If a commander of any vessel shall discharge or cause to be put on shore in this State, any sick or disabled seaman, whose term of service has not expired, without making provision for his maintenance, and for proper medical attendance on him, he shall forfeit sixty dollars. And if he shall land from on board his vessel, any passenger, who has not the means of procuring his maintenance for a month, he shall forfeit fifty dollars.

Burial of seamen.

BY SEC. 12. When any person shall die on board of any vessel in this State, the master thereof, shall cause the body to be buried above high water mark, and at least four feet deep. If he fail to do so, he shall forfeit one hundred and fifty dollars.

(No. 1.)

Form of Warrant to arrest a seaman who has deserted his vessel.

———— County, to wit:
To X. Y., *Constable of the said County:*

Whereas, A. B. has this day made complaint and information on oath before me J. T., a Justice of the said County, that he is the master of a certain merchant vessel, called the ————, now lying in the said County, and that R. S., who is a seaman now under contract in writing, duly signed by him, to serve as such on board the said vessel, did, on the ———— day of ———— 18—, in said County, desert and absent himself from the said vessel, and that the said R. S. is now absent from the said vessel without lawful permission, and without the consent of the said A. B., and in violation of his said contract in writing: These are, therefore, to command you, in the name of the Commonwealth, forthwith to apprehend the said R. S., and bring him before me or some other Justice of the said County, to answer the said complaint, and to be farther dealt with according to law. Given under my hand, this ———— day of ———— 18—.

J. T., J. P.

(No. 2.)

Form of Commitment of a deserting seaman.

———— County, to wit:
To X. Y., *Constable of the said County:*

Whereas, R. S. was this day brought before me J. T., a Justice of the said County, charged upon the oath of A. B., the master of a certain merchant vessel, called the ————, with having deserted and absented himself from on board the said vessel, without lawful authority, he the said R. S. then being a seaman under contract in writing duly signed by him to serve on board the said vessel, and which said contract was then in full force; and it appearing to me by the oath of credible witnesses, upon hearing the said complaint, that the said R. S., was so bound to serve on board the said vessel, and that he is now bound by the said contract so to serve, and that he has without just or lawful cause, deserted and absented himself from the said vessel without lawful authority: These are, therefore, in the name of the Commonwealth of Virginia, to command you, the said Constable, forthwith to convey the said R. S. to the jail of the said County, and to deliver him, together with this warrant, to the keeper of the said jail; and you, the said keeper, are hereby required to receive into your jail and custody, the said R. S., and there him safely keep until he shall be delivered to the said A. B., to serve as a seaman on board the said vessel, or until he shall be otherwise discharged by due course of law. Given under my hand and seal, this ———— day of ———— 18—.

J. T., J. P. [L. S.]

[NOTE.—These forms may be adapted to the case of an apprentice, by describing him as such, and saying that he was bound to the master by indentures of apprenticeship for the purpose of being taught to be a seaman. If the complaint be dismissed, the Justice may verbally order his discharge.]

(No. 3.)

Form of Warrant against master of a vessel for putting on shore a disabled seaman.

——— County, to wit:

To X. Y., Constable of the said County:

Whereas, A. B. of said County, has this day made complaint and information on oath before me J. T., a Justice of the said County, that C. D., on the ——— day of ——— 18—, in said County, he the said C. D. being then the commander of a certain vessel, called the ———, lying in said County, did discharge and caused to be put on shore from the said vessel, in said County, R. S., a seaman, whose term of service on board the said vessel had not then expired, without making provision for his maintenance and for proper medical attendance on him, he the said R. S. then being a sick and disabled seaman: These are, therefore, to command you, in the name of the Commonwealth, to apprehend the said C. D., and bring him before me or some other Justice of the said County, to answer the said complaint, and to be farther dealt with according to law. Given under my hand and seal, this ——— day of ——— 18—.

J. T., J. P. [L. S.]

(No. 4.)

Form of Warrant for failing to bury a person who has died on board of a vessel.

——— County, to wit:

To X. Y., Constable of the said County:

Whereas, A. B. of the said County, has this day made complaint and information on oath before me J. T., a Justice of the said County, that on the ——— day of ——— 18—, one E. F., a seaman, died on board of a certain vessel called the ———, then lying within the body of the said County, and that C. D. then was the commander of the said vessel, and that he the said C. D. did not cause the body of the said E. F. to be buried above high water mark, at least four feet deep, but failed so to do: These are, therefore, in the name of the Commonwealth, to command you to apprehend the said C. D., and to bring him forthwith before me or some other Justice of the said County, to answer the said complaint, and to be farther dealt with according to law. Given under my hand and seal, this ——— day of ——— 18—.

J. T., J. P. [L. S.]

CHAPTER XCV.

SEARCH WARRANTS.

For the purpose of consolidating the laws upon the subject of Search Warrants, CHAPTER 203 provides:

BY SEC. 1. If there be complaint on oath, that personal property has been stolen, embezzled or obtained by false pretences, and that it is believed to be concealed in a particular house, or other place, the Justice or Justices to whom such complaint is made, if satisfied that there is reasonable cause for such belief, shall issue a warrant to search such place for the property.

BY SEC. 2. On like complaint, on oath, according to the nature of the case, the Justice or Justices to whom it is made, if satisfied that there is reasonable cause therefor, shall issue a warrant to search specified places for the following things:

First. Counterfeit or spurious coin, forged bank notes, and other instruments or writings, or any tools, machines or materials for making them.

Secondly. Any book or other thing containing obscene language, or any print, picture, figure, or description, manifestly tending to corrupt the morals of youth, and intended to be sold, loaned, circulated or distributed, or to be introduced into a family, school, or place of education.

Thirdly. Lottery tickets, or materials unlawfully made, provided or procured for drawing a lottery.

Fourthly. Any gaming apparatus or implements used, or kept and provided to be used, in unlawful gaming, or in any place resorted to for unlawful gaming.

Fifthly. Any fire arms, sword, or other weapon or ammunition in possession of a negro.

Sixthly. Any harboured runaway slave.

BY SEC. 3. Every search warrant shall be directed to the Sheriff, Sergeant, or a Constable of the county or corporation in which the place to be searched may be, and shall command *him, if it be issued by one Justice,* to search in the day time the place designated, *and if it be issued by two Justices, to search the said place either in the day or night,* and, *in either case,* to seize such stolen property or other things, and bring the same and the persons in whose possession they may be found, before a Justice or Court having cognizance of the case.

BY SEC. 4. If any such search warrant be executed by the seizure of any such runaway slave, he shall be returned to

SEARCH WARRANTS. 609

the owner or committed to jail as a runaway by the Justice before whom he is brought; and if it be executed by the seizure of other property, or of any other of the things aforesaid, the same shall be safely kept by the direction of such Justice or Court, to be used in evidence; and as soon as may be afterwards, such stolen or embezzled property shall be restored to its owner, and the other things specified aforesaid burnt or otherwise destroyed under such direction.

In issuing search warrants, the Justice should carefully adhere to the terms of the statute, and confine the search to the particular places which the party swears he has reason to suspect contains the property; for a general warrant to search all suspected houses is illegal on its face.([1]) The warrant must be directed to an officer, and not to a private person.

It is not necessary for the Magistrate's justification in issuing the warrant, that the party applying for it should swear *positively* that the offence, which is the ground of the application, has been actually committed; as for instance, in larceny, it is sufficient if he swears that he has reason to suspect that the property has been stolen.([2]) The party who makes the charge, if he has no reasonable ground of suspicion, is alone responsible to the party aggrieved.

In the execution of the warrant, the officer to whom it is directed, must strictly observe its instructions; for a warrant directing a search in a particular house only, will not justify a search in another; nor will a warrant to seize one kind of goods, justify him in seizing another.([3]) But if other articles found by the officer would be likely to furnish evidence of the identity of the articles actually stolen and mentioned in the warrant, then the officer would have reasonable ground for seizing them; for he is not necessarily a trespasser for seizing articles not mentioned in the warrant.([4]) If the door of the house, in which the officer is authorized to make the search, be shut, and those within refuse to open it, after demand made by the officer for that purpose, he may break it open to make the search, whether the stolen goods are found in the house or not, though if they are not found, the party at whose instance the search was made, is answerable.([5])

Upon the return of a warrant to search for stolen goods, if it appear that the goods seized by the officer were stolen, they should not be delivered to the owner, but be deposited in some legal custody, by the authority of the Magistrate, to be

---

([1]) See Bill of Rights; 2 Hawk. c. 13, § 10, 17.
([2]) Else *v.* Smith, 1 Dow. & R. 97.
([3]) Price *v.* Messenger, 2 B. & P. 158.
([4]) Crozier *v.* Cundey, 6 B. & C. 232.
([5]) 2 Hale 117, 152.

used as evidence; for the party to whom they belong, can only have restitution, by indicting and convicting the offender.(¹) If the party in whose possession the stolen goods were found was ignorant of the theft, he should be discharged, but the Justice should recognize him to give evidence against him who stole them. If, however, it appear that he knew they were stolen, and that he was not himself the thief, the Justice should either commit him or bind him over to answer for the felony in receiving stolen goods, knowing them to have been stolen.

A search warrant to be executed, in the night time, can only be awarded by two Justices, and it would seem to be an act which required the presence and concurrence of both.

It is proper, in all cases, that the complainant should accompany the officer in the search, to identify the thing to be searched for.

(No. 1.)

Form of Warrant to search for stolen goods in the day time.

—————— County, to wit:

To the Sheriff and all or any one of the Constables of the said County:

Whereas, A. B. of the said County, hath this day made complaint and information on oath before me J. T., a Justice of the said County, that on the —— day of ——— 18—, (or *within* ——— *days last past,*) in the said County, [twelve table spoons, one coat, and one gold watch, (or whatever else was stolen, taking care to describe the article accurately,) of the goods and chattels of him the said A. B., were feloniously taken, stolen and carried away from him by one C. D., (or if the thief be unknown, say *by some person unknown,*)] and that he hath just cause to suspect, and doth suspect, that the said goods are concealed in the dwelling house (or *barn,* or *kitchen,* according to the fact,) of the said C. D., in the said County: These are, therefore, to authorize and require you, in the name of the Commonwealth of Virginia, with necessary aid, to enter in the day time, the said dwelling house (or *barn,* or *kitchen,* as the case may be,) of the said C. D., and there diligently search for the said goods. And if the same or any part thereof shall be found upon such search, that you bring the said goods, and also the body of the said C. D., before me or some other Justice of the said County, to be disposed of and dealt with according to law. Given under my hand and seal, this —— day of ——— 18—.

J. T., J. P. [L. S.]

[NOTE.—This form may be adapted to a case of embezzlement or obtaining goods by false pretences, by leaving out all between the brackets, and stating the offence thus: " did feloniously embezzle one gold watch, and one bank note for the payment of ten dollars, of the goods and property of the said A. B." Or, in the case of obtaining goods by false pretences, say: " did feloniously and fraudulently obtain by false pretences one gold watch," &c.]

(¹) 2 Hale 117, 152.

(No. 2.)

Form of Search Warrant for a harboured runaway slave.

—— County, to wit:

To the Sheriff and all or any one of the Constables of the said County:

Whereas, it appears to me J. T., a Justice of the said County, by the information on oath of A. B. of the said County, that there is reason to suspect and believe, that Frank* a runaway slave, the property of the said A. B., is concealed and harboured in the dwelling house (or *kitchen*, or *barn*, stating the particular house,) of one C. D., in the said County: These are, therefore, in the name of the Commonwealth of Virginia, to authorize and require you, with the necessary and proper assistance, to enter in the day time, into the said dwelling house (or *kitchen*, or *barn*,) and there diligently to search for the said slave; and if the said slave shall be found upon such search, that you seize him and bring him before me or some other Justice of the said County, that he may be disposed of and dealt with according to law. Given under my hand and seal, this —— day of ——— 18—.

J. T., J. P. [L. S.]

(No. 3.)

Form of Search Warrant for fire arms, &c. in possession of free negroes.

Follow form No. 2, to the star, and proceed thus: " a free negro, has in his possession and in his dwelling house, in said County, fire arms, to wit, one gun and gunpowder and balls: These are, therefore, in the name of the Commonwealth of Virginia, to authorize and require you, with the necessary and proper aid, to enter into the said dwelling house in the day time, and there diligently search for the said fire arms, balls and gunpowder; and if any such articles be there found upon such search, that you seize the same and make known to me or to some other Justice of the said County, what you have done herein, that any such fire arms, balls and gunpowder may be disposed of and dealt with according to law. Given under my hand and seal, this —— day of ——— 18—.

J. T., J. P. [L. S.]

[For the form of a warrant to search a vessel for a slave, see NEGROES.]

(No. 4.)

Form of Search Warrant for indecent books, prints, &c.

—— County, to wit:

To X. Y., Constable of the said County:

Whereas, A. B. of said County, has this day made complaint and information on oath before me J. T., a Justice of the said County, that he has good cause to believe and does believe, that C. D. has in his possession, in

---

*From the general terms of the law which allows this warrant, it may be issued to search for a runaway slave, though his name and that of his owner also, may be unknown. In such cases, follow the above warrant, leaving out the words " Frank, a runaway slave, the property of," and insert instead of them, these: "a runaway slave, whose owner is unknown to the said A. B."

said County, certain books containing obscene language, and entitled (state the title,) (or "certain obscene and indecent prints, figures, pictures and descriptions, representing," state what the pictures represent,) manifestly tending to corrupt the morals of youth, and which are intended to be sold, loaned, circulated and distributed by him, and that the said A. B. has good cause to believe and does believe, that the said books (or *pictures*) are in the dwelling house (or *store*) of the said C. D., in said County, and being satisfied that there is reasonable cause for such belief: These are, therefore, in the name of the Commonwealth of Virginia, to command you, with the necessary and proper assistance, to enter in the day time, the dwelling house (or *store*, as the case may be, taking care to specify the house,) and there diligently to search for the said books, (or *pictures*,) and if the same or any portion thereof shall be found upon such search, that you bring the same, and also the body of the said C. D., before me or some other Justice of the said County, to be disposed of and dealt with according to law. Given under my hand and seal, this —— day of —— 18—.

J. T., J. P. [L. s.]

(No. 5.)

Form of Warrant to search for counterfeit coin or forged bank notes.

——— County, to wit:

To X. Y., *Constable of said County*:

Whereas, A. B. of said County, has this day made complaint and information on oath before me, J. T. Justice of said County, that he has good cause to suspect, and does believe, that C. D. has in his possession certain pieces of counterfeit and spurious coin, of the similitude of the legal coin, current in this Commonwealth, called half dollars, (or whatever coin it may be,) and that he, the said A. B. has also good cause to suspect, and does believe, that the said pieces of counterfeit and spurious coin, are concealed in the dwelling house, (or wherever else it may be) of the said C. D., in the said County: These are, therefore, to command you, with necessary and proper assistance, to enter in the day time, into the dwelling house of the said C. D., (or whatever place it may be,) in the said County, and there diligently search for the said counterfeit and spurious coin; and if the same or any part thereof shall be found upon such search, that you bring the same, and also the body of the said C. D., before me or some other Justice of the said County, to be disposed of and dealt with according to law. Given under my hand and seal, this —— day of —— 18—.

J. T., J. P. [L. s.]

[NOTE.—It is not necessary to specify the particular denomination of the coin, but it is better to do so if it can be done, as it will call the attention of the officer more directly to the thing searched for.]

CHAPTER XCVI.

SHIPS.

By SEC. 7, CHAP. 192. If a free person maliciously burn any ship, boat or other vessel, of the value of one hundred dollars or more, he shall be punished by confinement in the penitentiary not less than three nor more than ten years, and if the value be less than one hundred dollars, he shall be confined in jail not exceeding one year, and be fined not exceeding two hundred dollars.

Under this provision, if the vessel burnt, be of the value of one hundred dollars or more, it is felony, and the party must be committed for examination, if a free white person, and for trial, if a slave or free negro; if of less value than one hundred dollars, the offence is a misdemeanor only, and if the offender be a white person, he should be recognized to answer an indictment; if a slave, the Justice must try him; if a free negro, it is discretionary with the Justice whether to try him as a slave, or as in the case of a white person, to commit or recognize him to answer an indictment. See FINES AND CONVICTIONS.

By SEC. 12, CHAP. 192, it is provided, that if a free person shall, in the night time enter, without breaking, or shall break and enter, either in the day time or night time, any ship or vessel within the jurisdiction of any county, with intent to commit murder, rape or robbery, he shall be confined in the penitentiary not less than three nor more than ten years; and by the 13th section of the same chapter, it is provided, that if any free person do any of the acts mentioned in the preceding section, with intent to commit larceny or any felony other than murder, rape or robbery, he shall be confined in the penitentiary not less than one nor more than ten years, or at the discretion of the jury, if the accused be white, or of the court, if he be a negro, be confined in jail not less than one nor more than twelve months, and in the latter case, may also be punished at the discretion of the court, with stripes.

White offenders, under 12th and 13th sections of the statute, must be committed or recognized for examination; slaves and free negroes, for trial.

By SEC. 31, CHAP. 192. If a free person wilfully cast away or otherwise destroy a ship or vessel within any county, with intent to injure or defraud any owner thereof, or of any property on board the same, or any insurer of the ship, vessel or property, or any part thereof, he shall be confined in the penitentiary not less than one nor more than five years.

As to what constitutes night time, or a breaking and entering, under the 12th and 13th sections of the statute, see BURGLARY.

A ship or vessel is within the body of a county when it lies in the water which flows within the county and not on the high seas.(¹)

(No. 1.)

Form of Warrant of Arrest for maliciously burning a vessel of the value of one hundred dollars and upwards.

—— County, to wit:
   To all or any one of the Constables of said County:

Whereas, A. B. of said County, has this day made complaint and information on oath before me J. T., a Justice of the said County, that C. D., on —— day of ——— 18—, in said County, did feloniously and maliciously burn a certain vessel, called (state the name,) of the value of —— dollars, (state the value, which must be at least $ 100 :) These are, therefore, to command you, in the name of the Commonwealth of Virginia, forthwith to apprehend the said C. D., and bring him before me or some other Justice of the said County, to answer the said complaint, and to be farther dealt with according to law. Given under my hand and seal, this —— day of ——— 18—.

                                      J. T., J. P. [L. S.]

(No. 2.)

Form of Warrant of Arrest for maliciously burning a vessel of less value than one hundred dollars.

—— County, to wit:
   To all or any one of the Constables of said County:

Whereas, A. B. of said County, has this day made complaint and information on oath before me J. T., a Justice of the said County, that C. D., on the —— day of ——— 18—, in said County, did unlawfully and maliciously burn a certain vessel, called the ———, of the value of ——— dollars, (state the value, which must be less than $ 100 :) These are, therefore, to command you, in the name of the Commonwealth of Virginia, forthwith to apprehend the said C. D., and bring him before me or some other Justice of the said County, to answer the said complaint, and to be farther dealt with according to law. Given under my hand and seal, this —— day of ——— 18—.

                                      J. T., J. P. [L. S.]

(¹) Thacker's C. C. 240.

SHIPS.   615

(No. 3.)

Form of Warrant of Arrest for wilfully destroying a vessel with intent to injure the owner thereof, or the insurers.

—— County, to wit:
  To all or any one of the Constables of said County:

Whereas, A. B. of said County, has this day made complaint and information on oath before me J. T., a Justice of said County, that C. D., on the —— day of ——— 18—, in said County, did feloniously and wilfully destroy a certain vessel called the ———, with intent to injure and defraud E. F., the owner thereof (or *with intent to injure the* ——— *insurance company*, the *insurers of said vessel:*) These are, therefore, to command you, in the name of the Commonwealth of Virginia, forthwith to apprehend the said C. D., and bring him before me or some other Justice of the said County, to answer the said complaint, and to be farther dealt with according to law. Given under my hand and seal, this —— day of ——— 18—.

J. T., J. P. [L. S.]

(No. 4.)

Form of Warrant of Arrest for wilfully destroying a vessel with intent to injure property on board thereof.

—— County, to wit:
  To all or any one of the Constables of said County:

Whereas, A. B. of said County, has this day made complaint and information on oath before me J. T., a Justice of said County, that C. D., on the —— day of ——— 18—, in said County, did feloniously and wilfully destroy a certain vessel called the ———, with intent to injure certain property then being on board of the said vessel, and being the property of E. & F.: These are, therefore, to command you, in the name of the Commonwealth of Virginia, forthwith to apprehend the said C. D., and bring him before me or some other Justice of the said County, to answer the said complaint, and to be farther dealt with according to law. Given under my hand and seal, this —— day of ——— 18—.

J. T., J. P. [L. S.]

(No. 5.)

Form of Warrant of Arrest for entering a vessel in the night time without breaking, with intent to commit murder, rape or robbery.

—— County, to wit:
  To all or any one of the Constables of said County:

Whereas, A. B. of said County, has this day made complaint and information on oath before me J. T., a Justice of the said County, that C. D., on the —— day of ——— 18—, in said County, did feloniously in the night time, enter without breaking, a certain vessel, called the ———, then lying in the body of the said County, with intent to murder one E. F. (or *with intent to rob one E. F.*, or *with intent to ravish one E. F.*) therein: These are therefore, to command you, in the name of the Commonwealth of Virginia, forthwith to apprehend the said C. D., and bring him before me or some other Justice of the said County, to answer the said complaint, and to be farther dealt with according to law. Given under my hand and seal, this —— day of ——— 18—.

J. T., J. P. [L. s.]

(No. 6.)

Form of Warrant of Arrest for breaking and entering a vessel with intent to commit murder, rape or robbery.

—— County, to wit :
    To all or any one of the Constables of said County :

Whereas, A. B. of said County, has this day made complaint and information on oath before me J. T., a Justice of the said County, that C. D., on the —— day of ——— 18—, in said County, did feloniously break and enter a certain vessel, called the ———, then lying in the body of the said County, with intent to murder one E. F. (or *to rob one E. F.*, or *to ravish one E. F.*) therein : These are, therefore, to command you, in the name of the Commonwealth of Virginia, forthwith to apprehend the said C. D., and bring him before me or some other Justice of the said County, to answer the said complaint, and to be farther dealt with according to law. Given under my hand and seal, this —— day of ——— 18—.

J. T., J. P. [L. s.]

(No. 7.)

Form of Warrant of Arrest for entering a vessel in the night, or for breaking and entering it either in the day or night, with intent to steal, and stealing therefrom.

—— County, to wit:
    To all or any one of the Constables of said County :

Whereas, A. B. of said County, has this day made complaint and information on oath before me J. T., a Justice of the said County, that C. D., on the —— day of ——— 18—, in said County, did feloniously enter in the night time without breaking (or *did feloniously break and enter*) a certain vessel called the ———, lying in the body of the said County, with intent to steal, [and did in the said vessel then feloniously take, steal and carry away one watch of the value of twenty dollars, of the goods and chattels of the said A. B. :] These are, therefore, to command you, in the name of the Commonwealth of Virginia, forthwith to apprehend the said C. D., and bring him before me or some other Justice of the said County, to answer the said complaint, and to be farther dealt with according to law. Given under my hand and seal, this —— day of ——— 18—.

J. T., J. P. [L. s.]

[NOTE.—If the party failed in accomplishing his intent, and did not actually steal, leave out all in the brackets.]

If the case be felony follow these forms:

(No. 8.)

Form of Mittimus where a party is committed for examination or trial in the County Court.

—— County, to wit:

To X. Z., *Constable of said County, and to the Keeper of the Jail of said County:*

These are to command you the said Constable, in the name of the Commonwealth of Virginia, forthwith to convey and deliver into the custody of the keeper of the said jail, together with this warrant, the body of C. D., a white person (or *free negro*, or *a slave, the property of E. F.*, as the case may be,) charged before me J. T., a Justice of the said County, on the oath of A. B., with a felony by him committed, in this, that the said C. D., on the —— day of —— in the year 18—, in the said County, (here describe the offence as in the warrant of arrest.) And you, the said keeper of the said jail, are hereby required to receive the said C. D. into your jail and custody, that he may be examined (or *tried*) for the said offence by the County Court of said County, and him there safely keep until he shall be discharged by due course of law. Given under my hand and seal, this —— day of —— in the year 18—.

J. T., J. P. [L. S.]

[NOTE.—If the prisoner be a white person, he must be committed for examination; if a negro, commit him for trial.]

(No. 9.)

Form of Certificate of Commitment to be sent to the Clerk of the County Court.

—— County, to wit:

To the Clerk of the County Court of said County:

I, J. T., a Justice of the said County, do hereby certify, that I have, by my warrant, this day committed C. D. (if free negro or slave, state which) to the jail of this County, that he may be examined (or *tried*) before the County Court of the said County, for a felony by him committed, in this, that he did, on the —— day of —— 18—, in the said County, (here state the offence as in the mittimus.) Given under my hand, this —— day of —— in the year 18—.

J. T., J. P.

(No. 10.)

Form of Certificate to the Clerk where party is admitted to bail.

Turn to head of ARREST, and follow No. 6.

SHIPS—(*Indictment for, &c.*)

(No. 11.)

Form of Recognizance of Bail.

Turn to head of RECOGNIZANCE, and follow No. 1, if person be free; No. 2, if a slave, and state succinctly the offence for which the person is recognized.

(No. 12.)

Form of Recognizance of Witness to appear before the County Court to give evidence upon the examination or trial of a party charged with felony.

Turn to head of RECOGNIZANCE, and follow No. 3.

If the case be not felony, for mittimus and certificate, follow Nos. 9 and 10, under head of ARREST; and for recognizance of bail and witnesses, follow Nos. 4 and 5, under head of RECOGNIZANCE.

Indictment for maliciously burning a vessel lying within the body of the County.

Commence as No. 1, under head of "INDICTMENTS," and say: Upon their oath present, that A. B., late of the County of ———, labourer, on the ——— day of ——— 18—, in the County aforesaid, a certain vessel called ———, and of the value of one hundred dollars, being the property of one C. D., then and there lying and being within the body of the said County of ———, did feloniously and maliciously burn, against the peace and dignity of the Commonwealth of Virginia.

CHAPTER XCVII.

SMALL POX AND OTHER DANGEROUS DISEASES.

[See QUARANTINE.]

BY SEC. 1, CHAP. 86. The council of any town or the court of any county, may establish in such county, or in or near such town, hospitals, which shall be subject to regulations not contrary to law, made by such council or court.

BY SEC. 2. The cost of establishing and maintaining such hospitals, shall be chargeable to the town or county, as the case may be.

BY SEC. 3. Any person who shall inoculate himself, or another, or suffer himself to be inoculated for the small pox, unless at a hospital established by law, shall forfeit, for every such offence, not exceeding three hundred dollars. And if any person shall bring into this State, the small pox or any variolous matter thereof, with the intent of propagating such disease, he shall forfeit one thousand dollars.

BY SEC. 4. The council or health officer of a town, or any two Justices of a county, may cause any person in said town or county, infected with any infectious disease, dangerous to the public health, to be removed to a hospital or other place of reception for the infected, unless such person be sick in his own place of residence, or cannot be removed without danger to his life.

BY SEC. 5. If a person who has not had the small pox or cow pox, shall go into a house in which any one is infected with the small pox, and return thence, a Justice may cause such person to be carried to the nearest hospital where the disease is, and remain there until discharged on the certificate of the physician of the hospital, that he may depart without danger of spreading the contagion.

BY SEC. 6. If any person who knows himself to be infected with a dangerous infectious disease, or who has recently had such disease, and has not had his person and clothes so cleansed as to be free from the infection, go into the company of any one who is liable to take the infection, or fail to retire from a public road or street on the approach of a passenger, without warning such passenger of his being so infected, he shall forfeit ten dollars for each offence. Such penalty shall be paid, if the offender be a married woman, by her husband; if an infant, by his parent or guardian; and if a slave, by his master.

By Sec. 7. When the health officer of any town, shall make complaint under oath, that there is good cause of suspicion or belief, that there is on any lot, or in any house in such town, or in any vessel arriving at the port thereof, any nuisance, source of filth or cause of sickness proper to be destroyed or removed, or one or more persons (not in his own place of residence,) infected with contagious disease, and that he has been refused admittance into such lot, building or vessel, any Justice of the corporation or of the county in which such town is, may issue his warrant to the Sheriff of the county, Sergeant of the corporation, or any Constable of either, requiring him to enter such lot, house or vessel, and under the direction of such health officer, to remove such infected person, or remove or destroy any such nuisance, source of filth or cause of sickness.

By Sec. 8. All expenses incurred for the removal of any person infected with a dangerous disease, and for maintaining, nursing and curing him, or incurred in entering any lot, house or vessel suspected of having persons or things infected with a dangerous infectious disease therein, and of removing them to a hospital or other place of reception therefor, shall be paid by such infected person, or by the owner of such lot, house or vessel, as the case may be, or if such person or owner be a married woman, by her husband; if an infant, by his parent or guardian; and if a slave, by his owner. But if they be not so paid, they shall be chargeable to the town or county in which they were incurred.

(No. 1.)

Form of Warrant against a party for bringing small pox into the Commonwealth, with intent to propagate it.

———— County, to wit:

To X. Y., Constable of said County:

Whereas, A. B. has this day made information and complaint on oath before me J. T., a Justice of the said County, that C. D. has, within ———— days last past, brought into this Commonwealth and into the said County, small pox and variolous matter thereof, with intent to propagate the small pox: These are, therefore, to command you, in the name of the Commonwealth, forthwith to apprehend the said C. D., and bring him before me or some other Justice of said County, to answer the said complaint, and to be farther dealt with according to law. Given under my hand and seal, this ———— day of ———— 18—.

J. T., J. P. [L. S.]

[NOTE.—This offence is to be proceeded in by recognizing the party to answer an indictment for it. For recognizance of bail and witnesses, see Nos. 4 and 5, under RECOGNIZANCE, and for mittimus and certificate, see Nos. 9 and 10, under head of ARREST.]

(No. 2.)

Form of Warrant to remove an infected person to a hospital.

—— County, to wit:
  To X. Y., *Constable of said County:*
  Whereas, it appears to us, J. T. and J. S., two Justices of the said County, upon the information of A. B., (or *upon our own knowledge*,) that C. D., now in the said County, but not at his own residence, is infected with the small pox, a disease dangerous to public health, and that he may be removed without danger to his life: These are, therefore, to command you, in the name of the Commonwealth, to remove the body of the said C. D. to the hospital of the said County, or to such other place as has been provided by said County, for the reception of persons infected with small pox; and for so doing, this shall be your warrant. Given under our hands and seals, this —— day of ——— 18—.

J. T., *J. P.* [L. S.]
J. S., *J. P.* [L. S.]

(No. 3.)

Form of Warrant to carry a person, who has been into and returned from a house in which some one is infected with small pox, to a hospital.

—— County, to wit:
  To X. Y., *Constable of said County:*
  Whereas, A. B. has this day made complaint and information on oath before me J. T., a Justice of the said County, that C. D. did within ——— days last past, go into the house of E. F. in said County, wherein one G. H. was then infected with small pox, and did return from the said house, he the said C. D. not then having had the small pox or cow pox: These are, therefore, to command you, in the name of the Commonwealth, forthwith to take the said C. D., and carry him to the hospital in said County, where the said disease is, there to remain until he shall be discharged on the certificate of the physician of the said hospital, that he may depart without danger of spreading the said disease. Given under my hand and seal, this —— day of ——— 18—.

J. T., *J. P.* [L. S.]

(No. 4.)

Form of an Order to remove a nuisance, upon the application of a health officer.

Corporation of ———, to wit:
  To the *Sergeant or High Constable of the said Corporation:*
  Whereas, A. B., health officer, appointed by the Council of the said Corporation, has this day made complaint and information on oath before me J. T., a Justice of the said Corporation, that he has good cause to suspect, and does verily believe, that there now is (*) on the lot, (or *in the house*) of C. D., in the said Corporation, a nuisance and source of filth, consisting of (state what) and which is a cause of sickness, proper to be removed from

the said lot, and that he the said C. D., has refused to permit him, the said A. B., to enter upon the said lot (or *into the said house,*) to remove the said nuisance and filth: These are, therefore, to command you, or any one of you, to enter upon the said lot, (or *into the said house,*) and to remove therefrom, and under the direction of the said A. B., any nuisance and source of filth and cause of sickness, that you may there find. Given under my hand, this —— day of ——— 18—.

J. T., J. P.

(No. 5.)

Form of Warrant to enter a house to remove a person infected with small pox.

Follow the above form to the star, and proceed thus: "in the house of C. D. in said Corporation, one or more persons infected with small pox, and whom it is proper to remove therefrom, and that he has been refused admittance into the said house, for that purpose: These are, therefore, to command you, or any one of you, in the name of the Commonwealth, to enter into the said house, and to remove therefrom, under the direction of the said A. B., all persons found therein infected with small pox, to such place as you shall be directed by the said A. B. Given under my hand and seal, this —— day of ——— 18—.

J. T., J. P. [L. S.]

[NOTE.—These forms can be easily adapted to any other infectious disease; and to the entering into a vessel.]

CHAPTER XCVIII.

SODOMY AND BESTIALITY.

This violation of the law of nature and the express ordinance of God, is sometimes alluded to in the law books as the offence not even to be named among christians. There is but one instance of it to be found on our records, and with that exception, the crime is only known in Virginia, through the judicial history of other nations. Yet, in a work professing to give the forms of proceeding in all cases of felony, it is proper to do so in this instance, however revolting the crime.

By SEC. 12, CHAP. 196. If any free person shall commit the crime of buggery, either with mankind or with any brute animal, he shall be confined in the penitentiary not less than one nor more than five years.

SODOMY AND BESTIALITY.

(No. 1.)

Form of Warrant of Arrest for sodomy and bestiality with a beast.

——— County, to wit:

To all or any one of the Constables of said County:

Whereas, A. B. of said County, has this day made complaint and information on oath before me J. T., a Justice of the said County, that C. D., on the ——— day of ——— 18—, in said County, feloniously did commit the detestable and abominable crime against nature, by having carnal intercourse and copulation with a beast, to wit, with a mare: These are, therefore, to command you, in the name of the Commonwealth of Virginia, forthwith to apprehend the said C. D., and bring him before me or some other Justice of the said County, to answer the said complaint, and to be farther dealt with according to law. Given under my hand and seal, this ——— day of ——— 18—.

J. T., J. P. [L. S.]

(No. 2.)

Form of Warrant of Arrest for sodomy committed with a boy.

——— County, to wit:

To all or any one of the Constables of said County:

Whereas, A. B. of said County, has this day made complaint and information on oath before me J. T., a Justice of the said County, that C. D., on the ——— day of ——— 18—, in said County, did feloniously make an assault upon one E. F., a male child about the age of sixteen years, and then and there feloniously did commit the detestable and abominable crime against nature, by then and there having carnal knowledge of the body of the said E. F., against the order of nature: These are, therefore, to command you, in the name of the Commonwealth of Virginia, forthwith to apprehend the said C. D., and bring him before me or some other Justice of the said County, to answer the said complaint, and to be farther dealt with according to law. Given under my hand and seal, this ——— day of ——— 18—.

J. T., J. P. [L. S.]

(No. 3.)

Form of Mittimus where a party is committed for examination or trial in the County Court, for sodomy.

——— County, to wit:

To X. Z., Constable of said County, and to the Keeper of the Jail of said County:

These are to command you, the said Constable, in the name of the Commonwealth of Virginia, forthwith to convey and deliver into the custody of the keeper of the said jail, together with this warrant, the body of C. D., a white person (or *free negro*, or *a slave, the property of E. F.*, as the case may be,) charged before me J. T., a Justice of the said County, on the oath of A. B., with a felony by him committed, in this, that the said C. D., on the ——— day of ——— in the year 18—, in the said County, (here describe the offence as in the warrant of arrest.) And you, the said keeper of the said jail, are hereby required to receive the said C. D. into your jail and custody, that he may be examined (or *tried*) for the said offence, by the County Court of said County, and him there safely keep until he shall be discharged by due course of law. Given under my hand and seal, this ——— day of ——— in the year 18—.

J. T., J. P. [L. S.]

[NOTE.—If the prisoner be a white person, commit him for examination; if a negro, commit him for trial.]

(No. 4.)

Form of Certificate of Commitment for sodomy, to be sent to the Clerk of the County Court.

——— County, to wit:

To the Clerk of the County Court of said County:

I, J. T., a Justice of the said County, do hereby certify, that I have, by my warrant, this day committed C. D. (if free negro or slave, state which,) to the jail of this County, that he may be examined (or *tried*) before the County Court of the said County, for a felony by him committed, in this, that he did, on the ——— day of ——— 18—, in the said County, (here state the offence as in the mittimus.) Given under my hand, this ——— day of ——— in the year 18—.

J. T., J. P.

(No. 5.)

Form of Certificate to the Clerk where party is admitted to bail.

Turn to head of ARREST, and follow No. 6.

(No. 6.)

Form of Recognizance of Bail.

Turn to head of RECOGNIZANCE, and follow No. 1, if person be free; No. 2, if a slave, and state succinctly the offence for which the person is recognized.

(No. 7.)

Form of Recognizance of Witness to appear before the County Court to give evidence upon the examination or trial of a party charged with sodomy.

Turn to head of RECOGNIZANCE, and follow No. 3.

(No. 1.)

An Indictment for sodomy and bestiality with a beast.

———— Judicial Circuit, } The jurors of the Commonwealth of Virginia, in and for the body of the County of ————, and now attending the said Court, upon their oath present, that A. B., on the ———— day of ———— in the year one thousand eight hundred and ————, in the said County, feloniously did commit the detestable and abominable crime against nature, by then and there, to wit, on the day and year aforesaid, in the County aforesaid, feloniously having carnal intercourse and copulation with a beast, to wit, with (state what,) against the peace and dignity of the Commonwealth of Virginia.

(No. 2.)

An Indictment for sodomy committed with a boy.

———— Judicial Circuit, } The jurors of the Commonwealth of Virginia, in and for the body of the County of ————, and now attending the said Court, upon their oath present, that A. B., on the ———— day of ———— in the year one thousand eight hundred and ————, in the said County, did feloniously make an assault upon one C. D., a male child about the age of sixteen years, and then and there feloniously did commit the detestable and abominable crime against nature, by then and there, to wit, on the day and year aforesaid, in the County aforesaid, feloniously having carnal knowledge of the body of the said C. D., against the order of nature, against the peace and dignity of the Commonwealth of Virginia.

CHAPTER XCIX.

SUPERSEDEAS—(*Commitment.*)

By Sec. 30, Chap. 15. When any person shall be committed to prison, or be under recognizance to answer to any charge of assault and battery or other misdemeanor, for which the party injured may have a remedy by civil action, except when the offence was committed by or upon any Sheriff or other officer of justice ; or riotously, or with intent to commit a felony, if the party injured shall appear before the Magistrate who made the commitment or took the recognizance, and acknowledge in writing that he has received satisfaction for the injury, the Magistrate may, in his discretion, on payment of the costs that have accrued, discharge the recognizance or supersede the commitment, by an order under his hand.

By Sec. 31. Every such order of the Magistrate discharging the recognizance of the party or witnesses, shall be filed in the office of the clerk, before the sitting of the court, at which they are bound to appear ; and every order superseding the commitment of the party charged, or of any witness, shall be delivered to the keeper of the jail in which he is confined, who shall forthwith discharge him ; and every such order, if so filed and delivered, and not otherwise, shall forever bar all remedy by civil action for such injury.

The Justice will perceive that this provision does not apply to cases of felony, or to any offence committed *by* a Sheriff or any officer of justice, or to offences committed *upon* any Sheriff or other officer of justice, or to any offence committed riotously or with intent to commit felony.

No other Justice than he who commits or takes the recognizance, can act under these provisions ; he may do it or not, according to his discretion, and in the exercise of it, should never discharge a party in a case seriously affecting public interest.

SUPERSEDEAS—(*Commitment.*)

(No. 1.)

Form of supersedeas to Warrant of Commitment for an assault and battery.

——— County, to wit:

To the Keeper of the Jail of the said County:

Whereas, A. B. was committed to the jail of the said County, by my warrant, dated on the ——— day of ——— 18—, to answer an indictment for an assault and battery, committed by him on C. D., and for that cause is now in your jail and custody; and whereas the said C. D. has this day appeared personally before me and acknowledged in writing that he has received from the said A. B. satisfaction for the said assault and battery, and has petitioned me to supersede the said commitment: I, therefore, command you, in the name of the Commonwealth, that if the said A. B. be detained in your jail for no other cause than what is mentioned in my said warrant, and do pay all the costs that have accrued in the prosecution against him for the said offence, that you forbear to detain him longer, but that you deliver him thence and suffer him to go at large. Given under my hand and seal, this ——— day of ——— 18—.

J. T., *J. P.* [L. S.]

(No. 2.)

Form of an Order of a Justice discharging a recognizance of bail.

——— County, to wit:

Whereas, I, J. T., a Justice of the said County, on the ——— day of ——— 18—, took the recognizance of A. B., himself, in the sum of ——— dollars, with C. D., his surety, in the like sum, conditioned for the personal appearance of the said A. B. before the County Court of the said County, on the first day of the ——— term thereof, to answer the Commonwealth for an assault and battery, committed by him on C. D.; and whereas the said C. D. personally appeared before me this day, and acknowledged in writing that he has received satisfaction for the said assault and battery, and all injury he has sustained thereby, and the said A. B. having paid all the costs that have accrued upon the said prosecution, I do hereby discharge the said recognizance. Given under my hand and seal, this ——— day of ——— 18—.

J. T., *J. P.* [L. S.]

[NOTE.—These forms may be adapted to any case coming within the statute, by describing the offence as in the mittimus or recognizance.]

CHAPTER C.

SURETY OF THE PEACE.

By Sec. 1, Chap. 201. Every Judge throughout the State, and every Justice and commissioner in chancery, within his county or corporation, shall be a conservator of the peace, and may require from persons not of good fame, security for their good behaviour, for a term not exceeding one year.

By Sec. 2. If complaint be made to any such conservator, that there is good cause to fear that a person intends to commit an offence against the person or property of another, he shall examine on oath the complainant, and any witnesses who may be produced, reduce the complaint to writing, and cause it to be signed by the complainant.

By Sec. 3. If it appear proper, such conservator shall issue a warrant reciting the complaint, and requiring the person complained of forthwith to be apprehended and brought before him or some other conservator.

By Sec. 4. When such person appears, if the conservator, on hearing the parties, consider that there is not good cause for the complaint, he shall discharge the said person, and may give judgment in his favour against the complainant for his costs. If he consider that there is good cause therefor, he may require a recognizance of the person against whom it is, and give judgment against him for the costs of the prosecution, or any part thereof; and unless such recognizance be given, he shall commit him to jail by a warrant, stating the sum and time in and for which the recognizance is directed. The person giving judgment, under this section, for costs, may issue a writ of *fieri facias* thereon, if an appeal be not allowed; and proceedings thereupon may be according to the 9th and 11th sections of chapter 150.*

By Sec. 5. A person from whom such recognizance is required, may, on giving it, appeal to the court of the county or corporation; in such case, the officer from whose judgment the appeal is taken, shall recognize such of the witnesses as he thinks proper.

By Sec. 6. The court may dismiss the complaint or affirm the judgment, and make what order it sees fit as to the costs.

---

*This section merely provides that a recognizance may be required of the party complained of, without stating the nature of the recognizance. This is done under a general provision in relation to all recognizances taken under any chapter of title 55, which embraces this chapter. See title Recognizance, where this subject is more fully explained.

If it award costs against the appellant, the recognizance which he may have given shall stand as a security therefor. When there is a failure to prosecute the appeal, such recognizance shall remain in force, although there be no order of affirmance. On any appeal, the court may require of the appellant a new recognizance if it see fit.

By Sec. 7. Any person committed to jail under this chapter may be discharged by the county or corporation court on such terms as it may deem reasonable.

By Sec. 8. If a white person go armed with a deadly or dangerous weapon, without reasonable cause to fear violence to his person, family or property, he may be required to give a recognizance, with the right of appeal, as before provided, and like proceedings shall be had on such appeal.

By Sec. 9. If a person, in the presence of a court or a conservator of the peace, make an affray, or threaten to kill or beat another, or to commit violence against his person or property, or contend with angry words, to the disturbance of the peace, he may, without process or further proof, if he be a white person, be required to give a recognizance, and if he be a negro, be punished with stripes.

The first section of this statute confers no new power upon Justices, who were before conservators of the peace by virtue of their office, with authority to require recognizance of the peace of all those who threatened *personal violence to another* or who *threatened to burn the house of another.*

The affinity between surety for the peace and good behaviour, renders it both convenient and proper to notice them in connection. In common parlance, they are generally understood to mean the same thing, but in law they are different; for although every breach of the peace includes a breach of good behaviour, a breach of good behaviour does not by any means necessarily include a breach of the peace,[1] and this distinction will be observed in the arrangement of the subject.

I. *Of surety for the peace.*

What is it? Surety of the peace consists in being bound with one or more sureties, in a recognizance to the Commonwealth of Virginia, taken before some court, or by a Judge of the court of appeals or general court, Justice of the Peace or commissioner in chancery, whereby the parties acknowledge themselves to be indebted to the Commonwealth in the sum required, with a condition to be void and of no effect, if the

---

[1] 1 Deac. C. C. 1270.

party complained of, shall, during a period therein specified, keep the peace, either generally towards all the people of the Commonwealth, or particularly, also, towards the person who complains and asks the security. When required by a Justice out of court, it is intended merely for prevention, and not the punishment of crime, and is called for by a probable suspicion, that some crime or misdemeanor is intended.(¹) It can only be granted where there is fear of present or future danger, and not for any breach of the peace that is passed.(²) The party wronged, or the Justice of his own motion, should he think the public interest demands it, may cause the offender to be prosecuted for the act passed, and to that end may bind him over to appear at the quarterly session of the county court to answer an indictment for the offence.

By the Common Law, surety of the peace could only be required to prevent bodily injury or the firing of houses,(³) but in this respect, the statute has so enlarged the power of the Justice, that if, in his opinion, there be good cause to fear that the person complained of intends to do any act, which, if done, would amount to any offence whatever, either against the person, or property of any kind of another, he may require of him surety of the peace and good behaviour.

Surety of the peace may also be demanded of all persons, who having before been bound to the peace, have broken it and forfeited their recognizance.(⁴)

As a general rule, it should be granted in all cases, if he who demands it makes oath that he is actually under fear of death or bodily harm, or any other injury either to his person or property, which, if done, would amount to an offence, and that he does not require such surety from malice. But notwithstanding the oath, if the Justice believes that surety is applied for merely of malice or for vexation, without any just cause of fear, or because the complainant is at variance with another, he should deny it.(⁵)

Upon just and reasonable grounds of suspicion, a Justice may, in his discretion, demand it from any person whatever, whether he be of age or not.(⁶)

At whose request and against whom. All free persons, being of sane memory, whether citizens or aliens, have a right to demand surety of the peace.

A parent may claim surety of the peace for his child under the age of discretion, and the Justice may grant it on the oath of the parent; and so may a husband demand it for the pro-

---

(¹) 1 Deac. C. C. 1271.
(²) 2 Dick. J. P. 398.
(³) 5 Burn, 24 edition, 298.
(⁴) 2 Deac. Cr. Co. 1271.
(⁵) 5 Burn J. P. 298; Dick. Guide 477.
(⁶) 2 Dick. J. P. 399.

tection of his wife,(¹) upon his oath; and a wife may demand it against her husband; and the husband may have it against his wife,(²) but infants and married women must find sureties by their friends and cannot bind themselves.

How granted. If the offending party be present at the time of making the complaint, he may be required at once to enter into the requisite recognizance, but if he be absent and there be just cause of fear, the Justice should issue his warrant, requiring the officer to whom it may be directed, forthwith to apprehend the party complained of, shewing the cause for which it was granted and upon whose complaint.(³) This warrant may be executed by breaking doors, and in the same manner, in all respects, that any other criminal process may be executed.(⁴)

If the warrant direct specially that the party be brought before the Justice who issued it, the Constable should carry him before that Justice, but if it be as it usually is, to bring the party before that Justice or some other Justice of the county, he should be taken to the most convenient Magistrate, whose duty it is then to proceed in the matter, in all respects, as the warrant requires.(⁵)

If a Constable or other officer arrest a party upon an alleged breach of the peace, and do not, in a reasonable time, carry him before a Justice to find sureties, he is not only liable to prosecution by indictment for such neglect, but the party may have his action against him for false imprisonment, and his warrant will afford him no justification.(⁶) But the officer is justified in keeping the party in confinement for a reasonable time, upon his own authority, to enable him to find sureties before he takes him to the Justice; for a person solemnly charged on oath with an intention to break the peace, is, at all events, to be prevented from accomplishing his purpose, while, at the same time, he should have the earliest opportunity of obtaining his liberty by finding sureties to keep the peace.

Proceedings after arrest. In taking surety of the peace, the Justice must be regulated by his sound discretion, both as to the number and sufficiency of the sureties, the amount of the sum and the period for which the party shall be bound, provided the time does not exceed twelve months.

Applications for surety of the peace, are often malicious, frivolous and unfounded; in such cases, the Justice, in the exercise of that discretion with which the statute has invested

---

(¹) 2 Dick. J. P. 398; Robinson's Guide 339.
(²) Id.
(³) 5 Rep. and the statute, 3d section.
(⁴) 2 Dick. J. P. 400; and see *ante*, title ARREST.
(⁵) 2 Dick. J. P. 411.
(⁶) Dalt. c. 1, 118.

him, should dismiss the complaint, with judgment against the complainant for the costs of prosecution.

The recognizances are all to be transmitted by the Magistrate to the court of the county or corporation on or before the first day of the next court after they are taken, and there filed on record by the clerk.

Recognizance, how forfeited and discharged. It is forfeited by an actual violence to the person of another, or the commission of any offence against the life or property of another, whether done by the party himself, or by others through his procurement, by attending any unlawful assembly to the terror of the people, and even by words, tending to a breach of the peace, as by challenging another to fight, or in his presence threatening to beat him. But mere words of reproach, as calling a man a liar or a knave, will not forfeit the recognizance, for they are regarded as the effect merely of unmeaning heat and passion, unless indeed they amount to a challenge to fight.[1] The recognizance is discharged by the death of the principal party who is bound by it, if it was not before forfeited, but the sureties are not discharged by their death, their executors continuing to be bound as their testators were.[2]

II. *Surety for good behaviour.*

Surety for good behaviour includes something more than surety to keep the peace; for one bound for good behaviour is also necessarily bound to keep the peace, and a man may forfeit his recognizance for good behaviour, although he committed no actual breach of the peace.

In the cases of the breach of the peace, embraced by the second section of the statute, the recognizance must be both for keeping the peace and being of good behaviour, (see title RECOGNIZANCE,) but there are cases, both at Common Law and under the statute, where a party may be required to find sureties for good behaviour without apprehension of danger either to the person or property of another, as of persons of ill fame, mentioned in the first section; so that the combined effect of the statute requiring a recognizance to do both in cases of breach of the peace, and the Common Law principle, that a recognizance to be of good behaviour, includes a breach of the peace, results in practice to a recognizance to keep the peace and be of good behaviour in every instance. Yet as the law makes the distinction in terms, and particularly when it is made by statute, it should be observed.

---

[1] 4 Inst. 101; 1 Hawk. c. 60, § 20.   [2] 1 Hawk. c. 60, § 17.

The term "not of good fame," is so comprehensive and uncertain in its meaning, as to leave much to the discretion of the Justice. In the exercise of a power so indefinite, he should act with great caution, (falling short of, rather than exceeding his authority,) and not bind a party to his good behaviour merely for evil rumour in general;(¹) for, as Doctor Burns properly remarks, to bind a man to his good behaviour for evil fame in general, may not always be done with safety, because the veracity of fame is proverbially not the most to be relied on, and many a good man is often evilly spoken of. According to some writers, these words include within their meaning, persons suspected to be quarrelsome; those who sleep in the day and go abroad in the night; suspected persons, who live idly and fare well and are well appareled; having nothing whereon to live.(²) But in these days a Magistrate would have enough to do, especially in cities, were he obliged to require all such persons to be bound for their good behaviour. Such a practice may enrich jailors, at the expense of the State, without advancing its moral condition. It is admitted, that under the general words of the statute, a man may be bound to his good behaviour for causes of scandal, *contra mores*, as well as against the peace; such as, for haunting bawdy houses with women of bad fame, or keeping such women in his own house, or for words in abuse of the officers of justice, especially when in the execution of their office. A Justice may also require this security from eavesdroppers, such as keep suspicious company or are reported to be pilferers or robbers; common drunkards, gamesters, libellers, hawkers of obscene books or pictures; persons who endeavour to deter witnesses and prosecutors from giving evidence; cheats and idle vagabonds. At last, it must rest in the sound discretion of the Justice, from what persons to require this surety, and recollecting that legal discretion does not authorize him to act according to his will and private affections, but according to reason, law and justice, it would be prudent before he requires a party to find sureties for his good behaviour, where no actual breach of the peace has been committed or is apprehended, that he should be satisfied by *evidence on oath*, not only that the individual is not of good fame or reputation, but that his *conduct* and *actions* have been so scandalous as to justify his interference. If the party is committed for want of sureties, the Justice should take care to shew the cause with sufficient certainty.

Recognizance how forfeited. A recognizance for good behaviour, may be forfeited, not only by an actual breach of the

---

(¹) 2 Deac. Cr. Co. 1275.   (²) 1 Hawk. c. 61, § 4.

peace, but for conduct which leads to a breach of the peace, and for such actual misbehaviour as was intended to be prevented by the recognizance; but not for giving cause barely of suspicion of what may never happen.(¹)

(No. 1.)

Form of Complaint to be made on oath by a party applying for a peace Warrant.

—— County, to wit:

A. B. of the said County, came personally before me J. T., a Justice of the said County, on this —— day of —————— 18—, and made complaint on oath that C. D. did, on the —— day of —————— 18—, in the said County, declare and threaten that he would (here state the threats,) by reason whereof, he this complainant, is afraid and has good cause to fear that the said C. D. will do him some grievous bodily injury, (or *will burn his house*,) and therefore prays he may be required to give surety to keep the peace towards him. And the said A. B. also says on oath, that he does not make the complaint against the said C. D., nor require such surety, from any hatred, malice or ill will, but merely for the preservation of his person (or *of his property*) from injury.

A. B.

Sworn to before me.
J. T.

[NOTE.—The form of this complaint is easily adapted to any case. The Justice has only to state the threat and the fear, according to the facts as stated by the complainant.]

(No. 2.)

Form of Warrant of the peace.

—— County, to wit:

To X. Y., *Constable of the said County:*

Forasmuch, as A. B. has this day complained on oath before me J. T., a Justice of the said County, that C. D. of the said County, did, on the —— day of —————— 18—, threaten to (state the threat, according to the fact, as *to beat him*, or *to do bodily injury to his slave Jack*, or *to poison his horse*, or *to burn his house*,) and has required surety of the peace of the said C. D.: I command you, in the name of the Commonwealth of Virginia, forthwith to apprehend the said C. D., and to bring him before me or some other Justice of the said County, to answer the said complaint. Given under my hand and seal, this —— day of —————— 18—.

J. T., J. P. [L. S.]

(¹) 1 Hawk. c. 61, § 6.

SURETY OF THE PEACE. 635

(No. 3.)

Form of Judgment requiring the party to give sureties.

Complaint heard, and the defendant required to recognize, himself in the sum of ——— dollars, with one surety in the like sum, to keep the peace and be of good behaviour for ——— months from this day, and to pay ——— dollars, the costs of this complaint; and he having found the surety required and paid the costs, is discharged, or ("not having found the surety required of him and paid the costs, is committed.")

J. T., J. P.

(No. 4.)

Form of Judgment dismissing the complaint.

Complaint heard and dismissed, and judgment against A. B. complainant, for ——— dollars, costs.

In cases of appeal, should the Justice prefer it, he can adopt the following more formal judgment:

Commonwealth against C. D. upon the complaint of A. B., for breach of the peace. } ——— day of ——— 18—. Case heard, and defendant C. D. ordered to recognize, himself in the sum of $———, with one surety in the like sum, (or where more than one surety is required, say *with two sureties, in the sum of* $——— *each*,) to keep the peace and be of good behaviour towards all the citizens of this Commonwealth, and especially towards him the said A. B., for the term of ——— months. And I do adjudge that the said C. D. pay the costs of this prosecution, which I now ascertain and settle to be $———, and in default of immediate payment thereof, that the said C. D. be committed to jail until he pay the same.

J. T., J. P.

Costs taxed and ascertained:

Constable's costs:
  For service of warrant, $0 50
  To summoning witness, 20
Attendance of witness:
  To E. F. one day, 50

Commonwealth against C. D., on complaint of A. B., for breach of the peace. } Case heard and complaint dismissed, and judgment is given against A. B. for the costs of the prosecution, which I do now ascertain and adjudge to be $———.

J. T., J. P.

(No. 5.)

Form of Recognizance for the peace or good behaviour.

——— County, to wit:

Be it remembered, that on this ——— day of ——— 18—, C. D. and E. F., of the said County, personally came before me, J. T., a Justice of the said County, and severally acknowledged themselves to owe to the Commonwealth of Virginia, that is to say, the said C. D. the sum of ——— dollars, and the said E. F. the sum of ——— dollars, to be respectively made and levied of their several goods and chattels, lands and tenements, if he the said C. D. shall make default in the performance of the condition underwritten.

The condition of the above recognizance is such, that if the above bound C. D. shall keep the peace and be of good behaviour towards all the citizens of this Commonwealth, and especially towards A. B., for and during the term of one year, (or for such other time as the Justice shall require, not exceeding one year,) from the date hereof, then this recognizance shall be void, otherwise to remain in full force and virtue.

Taken and acknowledged before me, in the said County, the day and year first above written.

J. T., J. P.

(No. 6.)

Form of Commitment for want of sureties to keep the peace.

——— County, to wit :

To X. Y., Constable of the said County, and to the Keeper of the Jail of said County:

Whereas, C. D. is now brought before me, J. T,, a Justice of the said County, upon the complaint on oath of A. B., and required to find sufficient sureties to be bound with him in the sum of ——— dollars, by a recognizance to keep the peace for the term of one year from this day, towards all the citizens of this Commonwealth, and especially towards the said A. B. ; and whereas the said C. D. has refused, and does now refuse before me, to find such sureties : These are, therefore, in the name of the Commonwealth of Virginia, to command you, the said Constable, forthwith to convey the said C. D. to the jail of the said County, and to deliver him to the keeper thereof, together with this precept ; and I command you, the said keeper, to receive the said C. D. into your custody in the said jail, and him safely keep for the term of one year from the date hereof, unless in the mean time he shall find such sureties, or be otherwise discharged by due course of law. Given under my hand and seal, this ——— day of ——— 18—.

J. T., J. P. [L. S.]

(No. 7.)

Form of Commitment for refusing to pay the costs.

——— County, to wit:

To X. Y., Constable of said County, and to the Keeper of the Jail of the said County :

Whereas, C. D. of the said County, was this day brought before me J. T., a Justice of the said County, to answer the complaint of A. B., for a breach of the peace ; and I, the said Justice, upon hearing the said complaint, adjudged and ordered that the said C. D. should enter into a recognizance to keep the peace and be of good behaviour for the term of ——— months, and pay the costs of the prosecution, which I ascertained to be ——— dollars, and that unless immediate payment thereof be made, that he should be committed to jail until he pay the same ; and whereas the said

C. D. has refused, and still refuses to pay the said sum of ——— dollars, the costs of the said prosecution: These are, therefore, to command you, the said Constable, in the name of the Commonwealth of Virginia, to convey and deliver the said C. D., together with this warrant, to the keeper of the said jail; and to command you, the said keeper, to receive into your jail and custody the said C. D., and him there safely keep until he pay the costs aforesaid, or until he shall be otherwise discharged by due course of law. Given under my hand and seal, this —— day of ——— 18—.

J. T., J. P. [L. S.]

(No. 8.)

Form of Recognizance where a party has been committed for failing to give the surety in the first instance and afterwards gives it.

Follow form No. 5, to the condition, and conclude thus: The condition of the above recognizance is such, that whereas the above bound C. D. was, upon the complaint on oath of A. B., by the warrant of J. T., a Justice of the said County, committed to the jail of the said County, on the —— day of ——— 18—, for not finding sureties to keep the peace for one year, in the sum of ———dollars, with surety in the like sum, and the above named E. F. hath undertaken before me J. M., a Justice of the said County, this day, for the said C. D., that he will keep the peace towards all the good people of this Commonwealth, and especially towards the said A. B., for one year: Now, if the said C. D. shall keep the peace towards all the people of this Commonwealth, and especially towards the said A. B., for one year from this day, then the above recognizance shall be void, otherwise to remain in full force and virtue.

Taken and acknowledged before me,
the day and year first above written.

J. M., J. P.

(No. 9.)

Form of Order of a Justice to discharge one committed for want of sureties of the peace.

——— County, to wit:

To the Keeper of the Jail of the said County:

Discharge out of your custody the body of C. D., imprisoned in the jail of the said County, on the complaint of A. B., for want of sufficient sureties for his keeping the peace for the term of twelve months, towards all the citizens of this Commonwealth, and especially towards the said A. B., if detained for no other cause, he, the said C. D., having this day entered into a recognizance before me J. T., a Justice of the said County, in the sum of ——— dollars himself, with E. F., his surety, in the sum of ——— dollars, to keep the peace and be of good behaviour towards all the citizens of this Commonwealth, and especially towards the said A. B., for the term of twelve months now next ensuing. Given under my hand and seal, this —— day of ——— 18—.

J. T., J. P. [L. S.]

CHAPTER CI.

TAVERNS AND HOUSES OF ENTERTAINMENT.

By Sec. 4, Chap. 38. No person shall, without license, keep either an ordinary, house of private entertainment, or bowling saloon or alley.

By Sec. 9, Chap. 38. Any person who shall, in any way, keep an ordinary, without obtaining a license to do so, shall pay a fine of not less than thirty nor more than one hundred dollars; and any person who shall keep a house of private entertainment, without license, shall pay a fine not exceeding fifty dollars.

By Sec. 1, Chap. 96. Any person who shall, for compensation, furnish lodging or diet to a person boarding in his house, or provender for a horse, feeding in his stable or on his land, (except a drove of live stock and persons attending it,) and sell by retail, wine or ardent spirits, or a mixture thereof, to be drunk in or at the place of sale, shall be deemed to keep an ordinary or house of public entertainment.

By Sec. 2, Chap. 96. Any person who shall, for a time not exceeding one month, if within, or not exceeding one week, if without, a city or town, furnish, for compensation, lodging or diet to one boarding in his house, or provender for a horse, feeding in his stable or on his land, except as aforesaid, shall, if he be not the keeper of an ordinary according to the preceding section, be deemed to keep a house of private entertainment; unless the place of furnishing the same, when without a city or town, be more than eight hundred yards from a public road or highway.

By Sec. 3, Chap. 96. For a license to keep a house of entertainment, the application shall be, when the house is in a town having a corporation court, to such court, and when it is not in any such town, to the court of the county wherein it is. If the court be of opinion that the applicant is sober and of good character, and will probably keep a house orderly, useful, and such as the law requires, it may grant such license; and if the house be in a town, the court, when it grants the same, may, if the applicant desire it, dispense with the necessity of his providing for horses. If any such application be refused, the refusal shall be entered of record, and a license shall not be granted to the applicant before the next May term, unless by a court composed of the Justices to whom the first application was made, or a majority of the acting Justices of the county or corporation.

By Sec. 4, Chap. 96. Every person licensed to keep an ordinary or house of public entertainment, shall constantly provide the same with lodging and diet for travellers and their servants, and unless it be dispensed with as aforesaid, with stableage and provender, or pasturage and provender, (as the season may require,) for their horses. Any such person may, at the place of a muster or public sale, distant a mile or more from another ordinary, with the consent of the proprietor of such place, vend meat or drink as at his ordinary.

By Sec. 5, Chap. 96. Upon the motion of the Commonwealth's attorney for the county or corporation, or of any other person, after ten days notice to any person so licensed, the court which granted such license may revoke it. It shall always revoke the same, when it is satisfied that the object of obtaining the license is not to provide lodging or diet for travellers, but to use it merely as a facility for selling wine or ardent spirits, or a mixture thereof, to be drunk in or at the place of sale.

By Sec. 6, Chap. 96. A license to keep a bowling saloon or alley, in a town having a corporation court, may be granted by such court, and when it is to be kept not in such town, by the court of the county wherein it is to be kept. Such license may be revoked like any other license granted under this chapter.

By Sec. 14, Chap. 38. It is provided that if a merchant shall desire his license to include permission to sell by retail, wine, ardent spirits, or a mixture thereof, he shall pay the additional tax prescribed for this privilege, and obtain from the court of the county or corporation in which his store or place of sale is situated, a certificate that he is a person of good character, and that the court sees no objection to such permission being granted.

This section applies to the sale of ardent spirits by retail, without paying the additional tax for that privilege and obtaining a certificate of good character; and to constitute an offence under it, it is not necessary that the liquor should be sold to be drunk at the place where sold.

By Sec. 18, Chap. 38. If any person shall, without paying the tax, and obtaining the certificate prescribed by the fourteenth section, sell by retail, wine, ardent spirits, or a mixture thereof, he shall forfeit thirty dollars. And if any person sell, by retail, wine, ardent spirits, or a mixture thereof, to be drunk in or at the store or other place of sale, he shall, unless he be licensed to keep an ordinary at such store or place, forfeit thirty dollars.

By Sec. 19, Chap. 38. Upon the motion of any inhabitant of the county or corporation, after ten days notice to any merchant who has obtained such certificate, the court which granted it, if it see cause to do so, may revoke the same. And if, after such revocation, such merchant shall sell by retail, wine, ardent spirits, or any mixture thereof, he shall, for every such offence, forfeit fifty dollars.

By Sec. 20, Chap. 38. The two preceding sections shall not be construed to prohibit any person from selling by retail, liquors actually made from the produce of his estate, or distilled by him or those in his employment, when such liquors are not drunk in or at the place of sale.

By Sec. 10, Chap. 201. If any Justice suspect any free person of selling by retail, wine or ardent spirits, or a mixture thereof, contrary to law, he shall summon the person and such witnesses as he may think proper, to appear before him; and upon the person's appearing, or failing to appear, if the Justice, on examining the witnesses on oath, find sufficient cause, he shall direct the Commonwealth's attorney for the court of his county or corporation, to institute a prosecution against such person, and shall recognize the material witnesses, or cause them to be summoned to appear at the next term of the said court at which a grand jury may be impanneled. Such Justice may also require the person suspected to enter into a recognizance to keep the peace and be of good behaviour for a time not exceeding one year. If such recognizance be given, the condition thereof shall be deemed to be broken, if during the period for which it was given, such person shall sell by retail, wine or ardent spirits, or a mixture thereof, contrary to law.

Taverns are places for the lodging and entertainment of *travellers*, and from the facilities they offer to indulge in intemperance, gaming and other evil practices, are regarded at best as nuisances, and tolerated alone from public necessity. The statute has placed them under the control of the county and corporation courts, and a judicious exercise of their authority in rejecting all applications for ordinary license, even when made by persons of good character, unless the place be *useful* for *travellers*, would go far to suppress those evils which have given to taverns the character of necessary nuisances. Unfortunately, however, licenses are easily obtained, and when granted, often used as the means of legalizing prolific sources of crime, (especially of felonious homicide,) as is proved by the judicial records of every country where tippling houses are suffered to exist under the guise of taverns.

Inn keepers have no right to select their guests, or to say to one, you may come into my inn, and to another, you shall not; as every one, coming and conducting himself in a proper manner, has a right to be received. For this purpose, inn keepers are a sort of public servants, and have in return the privilege of entertaining travellers and supplying them with what they want; and an indictment lies at Common Law against an inn keeper for refusing to receive a guest, who applies peaceably for admittance, if at the time he has room in his house to accommodate him, and the guest tenders him the price of entertainment, or such circumstances occur as will dispense with that tender.(¹)

All disorderly inns or taverns, are common nuisances, for which the keepers may be indicted, and to protect them from such a consequence, as well as to ensure comfort and rest to travellers, an inn keeper may, if a person conducts himself in a disorderly manner in his tavern, request him to depart, and if he refuse to do so, the landlord is justified in laying hands on him to put him out. If under such circumstances, the person lay hands on the landlord to resist him, it is an assault, for which he may be taken into custody by a peace officer, if done in his view. And so, if a person without committing an assault, make such a noise and disturbance in a tavern as would create alarm, or disquiet the neighbourhood and the persons passing along the adjacent street, this would be such a breach of the peace, as not only to justify the landlord in putting the person out of the house, but would justify him also in giving him immediately into the custody of any peace officer in whose presence this disturbance occurred.

An inn keeper is not only bound to admit all persons who apply peaceably for admittance as guests, but he must also guard their goods brought in, with proper care, and though he is liable only for such goods as are brought within the inn, yet if brought in, a delivery of them into his actual custody, is not necessary in order to make him responsible, for he is bound to pay for them, if they are stolen or carried away from his tavern, though he may not know any thing of such goods.(²) He is responsible for the acts both of his other guests, and for the acts of his domestics and servants, if the goods are stolen or lost, and in these respects, there is no difference between money and goods; the principle of liability being to compel him to take care that no improper person be admitted into his house, and to prevent collusion between the inn keeper and such persons.(³) If he receive the guest, the custody of the goods may be considered as incidental to the principal contract, and the price paid for the apartments as ex-

(¹) Rex v. Evans, 32 Com. L. R. 493; and Hawthorn v. Hammond, 47 Id. 404.
(²) 8 Co. 32; 14 John. R. 175; Hay. N. C. R. 4.
(³) 2 Barn. & Adol. 803; 1 Adol. & Ellis 522; 22 Com. L. R. 186.

tending to the care of the goods, and furnishing a sufficient consideration to support the contract of bailment.(¹)

The degree of care that an inn keeper is bound to take of goods brought by *travellers* to his inn, is uncommon care, and he will be bound even for slight negligence,(²) but he will be excused whenever the loss has occurred by the fault of the guest ;(³) and he is not responsible for the loss of articles deposited merely in his house for the purpose of being forwarded by a carrier.(⁴)

As the law compels a tavern keeper to receive all orderly *travellers*, and holds him to such strict accountability for goods brought by them to his inn, it gives him a lien upon their goods to obtain his compensation.(⁵) But he is not compelled to receive *boarders* or to take a horse on *livery*, and therefore he has no lien on the goods of a boarder, nor a horse at livery.(⁶)

Prosecutions for selling by retail ardent spirits, to be drunk at the place where sold, may be tried upon presentment. In such cases, it is necessary to allege and prove that the liquors were sold, to be drunk at the place where sold, without a license, for the intent with which they are sold, is an essential ingredient in the offence.(⁷)

The retailing to two distinct persons at the same time and place, constitutes separate and distinct offences, and not one offence only ;(⁸) and it is not necessary, in the indictment, presentment or other proceedings, to name the persons to whom the liquors were sold.(⁹)

(No. 1.)

Form of Summons against a person suspected of retailing ardent spirits contrary to law, under section 10, *chapter* 292.

———— County, to wit :

To X. Y., *Constable of said County :*

Forasmuch, as I, J. T., a Justice of said County, do suspect C. D. to be guilty of selling by retail, [at his house in said County, wine and ardent spirits, and a mixture thereof, to be drunk at his said house, the place where sold, without a license to keep an ordinary at his said house :] These are, therefore, to command you, in the name of the Commonwealth of Vir-

---

(¹) Jones on Bailment 94 ; Story on Bailment, § 470 ; 2 Kent's Com. 458 to 463.
(²) 8 Co. 32.
(³) Story's Bailment, § 483 ; 4 M. & S. 306.
(⁴) 32 Com. L. R. 353.
(⁵) 3 Barn. & Ald. 287 ; 4 M. & S. 305-325.
(⁶) 8 Mod. 172.
(⁷) Coe's Case, 9 Leigh 620 ; Phillips' Case, 6 East 474.
(⁸) Dove's Case, 2 Va. Cases 26.
(⁹) Adams' Case, 17 Wend. ; Halstead's Case, 5 Leigh 724 ; Tiffit's Case, 8 Leigh 721.

ginia, to summon the said C. D. to appear before me at ———, in the said County, on the —— day of ——— 18—, at —— o'clock in the ——— noon of that day, to answer the Commonwealth touching the said offence; and you are moreover commanded to summon E. F. and G. H. to appear before me, at the time and place aforesaid, as witnesses, to give evidence in behalf of the Commonwealth against the said C. D. for the said offence. Given under my hand, this —— day of ——— 18—.

J. T., J. P.

[NOTE.—If it be for retailing spirits, without the certificate of good character, under section 14, chapter 38, leave out what is in the brackets, and in place of it, say: "at his store in the said County, wine and ardent spirits, and a mixture thereof, without having paid the additional tax prescribed by law for the privilege so to do, and without having first obtained from the County Court of the said County, a certificate that he is a person of good character."]

(No. 2.)

Form of Recognizance for good behaviour, under the above section.

——— County, to wit:

Be it remembered, that on this —— day of ——— 18—, C. D. and A. B. personally appeared before me J. T., a Justice of the said County, and severally acknowledged themselves to owe to the Commonwealth of Virginia, the said C. D. the sum of ——— dollars, and the said A. B. the sum of ——— dollars, to be levied of their goods and chattels, lands and tenements, respectively, upon condition that the said C. D. shall make default in the condition underwritten.

The condition of the above recognizance is such, that whereas the above bound C. D. has been summoned to appear before the above named J. T., Justice as aforesaid, upon a charge of retailing wine and ardent spirits, to be drunk at his house, the place where sold in said County, without a license to keep an ordinary at his said house; and upon the examination of G. H., a witness on oath, is required by the said J. T., as such Justice, to enter into a recognizance to keep the peace and be of good behaviour for one year: Now, if the said C. D. shall keep the peace and be of good behaviour for the term of one year next ensuing the date hereof, then the above recognizance shall be void, otherwise to remain in full force and virtue.

Taken and acknowledged before me, the day and year first above written.

J. T., J. P.

(No. 3.)

Form of Order to Attorney for the Commonwealth, to institute a prosecution for retailing liquors without license.

———— County, to wit:
 To R. D., *Attorney for the Commonwealth in County Court:*
SIR,
  Upon the examination of C. D. on oath this day, I found sufficient cause to direct you, as I now do, to institute a prosecution against E. F. for selling, by retail, ardent spirits, to be drunk at his house, the place where sold, without a license to keep a tavern in his said house.

           J. T., J. P.
        —— day of ———— 18—.

(No. 4.)

Form of Presentment for retailing spirits, to be drunk at the place where sold, without an ordinary license.

———— County, to wit:
 In the County Court of said County:
  We present A. B. for this, that he the said A. B., on the —— day of ———— 18—, at his house, in the said County, did sell by retail, wine, rum, brandy, whiskey, and other ardent spirits, and a mixture thereof, to be drunk at his said house, the place where sold in the said County, without having first obtained a license, according to law, to keep an ordinary at his said house.
  This presentment is made on the testimony of E. F., a witness called on by the Court, sworn in Court, and sent to the grand jury to give evidence.

(No. 5.)

Form of same for retailing ardent spirits, without paying the tax required by law.

  We present A. B. for this, that he the said A. B., did, on the —— day of ———— 18—, at his store in the County of ————, sell by retail, wine and ardent spirits, and a mixture thereof, without having paid the additional tax prescribed by law for the privilege so to do, and without first having obtained from the County Court of the said County, a certificate that he is a person of good character, (conclude as above.)

CHAPTER CII.

THREATS AND THREATENING LETTERS.

If one man *threaten* another, in order to deter him from doing some lawful act, or to compel him to do an unlawful one, or with intent to extort money from him, or to obtain any other benefit to the person who makes use of the threat, this has always been considered a misdemeanor at Common Law.(¹) With respect to threats of personal violence, or other threats made in the presence of the party, by which he is put in fear, and by means of which, money or other property is actually extorted from him, the Justice is referred to the head of ROBBERY.

The bare attempt to extort money or property by threats, is a misdemeanor, and is to be proceeded in by apprehending the offender and committing him or recognizing him to answer an indictment; but the threats which it is our purpose to notice here, are those recently made felony.

BY SEC. 13, CHAP. 191. If any free person threaten injury to the character, person or property of another person, or to accuse him of any offence, and thereby extort money or pecuniary benefit, he shall be confined in the penitentiary not less than one nor more than five years.

To constitute the offence, under the statute, the threat need not be malicious, nor made by letter, but the money or other pecuniary advantage must be actually extorted, as a mere attempt to extort by such means, would only be a misdemeanor. It has been held, that proof of a prisoner's delivering a threatening letter sealed up, to a person to carry it to the post office, is evidence of his knowledge of its contents, to be submitted to a jury.(²)

If the threat be by letter, it must be sent or delivered to the person threatened; but it seems that sending a letter to A. in order that he may deliver it to B., is a sending it to B., if the letter be delivered by A. to B.;(³) and it has been held, that dropping a letter in a man's way, in order that he may pick it up, is a sending to him.(⁴)

(¹) Deac. Cr. Co. 1292.
(²) 1 Leach 142.
(³) Russ. & Ry. 484.

(⁴) Russ. & Ry. 498; and 47 Com. Law Rep. 592.

(No. 1.)

Form of Warrant of Arrest for threatening to accuse another person of crime, and thereby extorting money.

―――― County, to wit:
To all or any one of the Constables of said County:

Whereas, A. B. of said County, has this day made complaint and information on oath before me J. T., a Justice of the said County, that C. D., on the ―― day of ―――― 18―, in said County, did feloniously threaten to accuse him the said A. B. of having committed the crime of murder, by maliciously killing one J. S. (or *of the crime of arson, by maliciously burning the dwelling house of J. S.*) and did thereby feloniously extort money from him the said A. B., to wit, the sum of ―――― dollars: These are, therefore, to command you, in the name of the Commonwealth of Virginia, forthwith to apprehend the said C. D., and bring him before me or some other Justice of the said County, to answer the said complaint, and to be farther dealt with according to law. Given under my hand and seal, this ―― day of ―――― 18―.

J. T., J. P. [L. S.]

[NOTE.—If the threat be of personal violence, and the person threatened be present and part with his money from fear of such violence, it will be robbery.]

(No. 2.)

Form of Warrant of Arrest for obtaining money by threatening to injure the character of another.

―――― County, to wit:
To all or any one of the Constables of said County:

Whereas, A. B. of said County, has this day made complaint and information on oath before me J. T., a Justice of the said County, that C. D., on the ―― day of ―――― 18―, in said County, did feloniously threaten to injure the character of the said A. B., by then and there feloniously threatening to accuse him the said A. B. of the crime of (state the crime) and did then and there, by means of the said threat, feloniously extort money, to wit, the sum of $100, from him the said A. B.: These are, therefore, to command you, in the name of the Commonwealth of Virginia, forthwith to apprehend the said C. D., and bring him before me or some other Justice of the said County, to answer the said complaint, and to be farther dealt with according to law. Given under my hand and seal, this ―― day of ―――― 18―.

J. T., J. P. [L. S.]

(No. 3.)

Form of Mittimus where a party is committed for examination or trial in the County Court for obtaining money by threats.

——— County, to wit:

To X. Z., *Constable of said County, and to the Keeper of the Jail of said County:*

These are to command you, the said Constable, in the name of the Commonwealth of Virginia, forthwith to convey and deliver into the custody of the keeper of the said jail, together with this warrant, the body of C. D., a white person, (or *free negro*, or *a slave, the property of E. F.*, as the case may be,) charged before me J. T., a Justice of the said County, on the oath of A. B., with a felony by him committed, in this, that the said C. D., on the —— day of —— in the year 18—, in the said County, (here describe the offence as in the warrant of arrest.) And you, the said keeper of the said jail, are hereby required to receive the said C. D. into your jail and custody, that he may be examined (or *tried*) for the said offence by the County Court of said County, and him there safely keep, until he shall be discharged by due course of law. Given under my hand and seal, this —— day of —— in the year 18—.

J. T., J. P. [L. s.]

[NOTE.—If the prisoner be a white person, he must be committed for examination; if a negro, commit him for trial.]

(No. 4.)

Form of Certificate of Commitment to be sent to the Clerk of the County Court.

——— County, to wit:

To the Clerk of the County Court of said County:

I, J. T., a Justice of the said County, do hereby certify, that I have, by my warrant, this day committed C. D., (if free negro or slave, state which,) to the jail of this County, that he may be examined (or *tried*) before the County Court of the said County, for a felony by him committed, in this, that he did, on the —— day of —— 18—, in the said County, (here state the offence as in the mittimus.) Given under my hand, this —— day of —— in the year 18—.

J. T., J. P.

(No. 5.)

Form of Certificate to the Clerk where party is admitted to bail.

Turn to head of ARREST, and follow No. 6.

(No. 6.)

Form of Recognizance of Bail.

Turn to head of RECOGNIZANCE, and follow No. 1, if person be free; No. 2, if a slave, and state succinctly the offence for which the person is recognized.

(No. 7.)

Form of Recognizance of Witness to appear before the County Court to give evidence upon the examination or trial of a party charged with felony.

Turn to head of RECOGNIZANCE, and follow No. 3.

CHAPTER CIII.

TOBACCO.

BY SEC. 35, CHAP. 198. If an inspector of tobacco issue or cause to be issued his receipt or note for any tobacco not received into the warehouse of which he is inspector, or more than one receipt or note for the same tobacco, except when authorized by law to do so, or re-issue or pass away a tobacco receipt or note, after the delivery of the tobacco for which it was given, he shall be confined in the penitentiary not less than one nor more than five years.

(No. 1.)

Form of Warrant against inspector, for issuing receipt for tobacco not received into warehouse.

———— County, to wit:

To X. Y., *Constable of said County:*

Whereas, A. B. of said County, has this day made complaint on oath before me J. T., a Justice of the said County, that C. D., on the ——— day of ———— 18—, in said County, he the said C. D. being then an inspector of tobacco at ———— warehouse in said County, did, as such inspector, feloniously deliver and issue, and did feloniously cause to be issued and delivered, his receipt for one certain hogshead of tobacco, purporting to be for a hogshead of tobacco which had then been received into the said warehouse, belonging to one S. H., when in fact no such hogshead of tobacco had been actually received into the said warehouse, and when he was not authorized by law to do so: These are, therefore, in the name of the Commonwealth, to command you, forthwith to apprehend the said C. D., and to bring him before me or some other Justice of the said County, to answer the said complaint, and to be farther dealt with according to law. Given under my hand and seal, this —— day of ——— 18—.

J. T., J. P. [L. S.]

(No. 2.)

Form of Warrant against Inspector for issuing two receipts for the same tobacco.

Follow No. 1, leaving out all in the brackets, and insert in the place of it, this: " issue, when he was not authorized by law, two receipts for the same hogshead of tobacco, to wit, for a hogshead of tobacco weighing ——— pounds, and for which he had before issued a receipt to one G. H., dated on the —— day of ——— 18—."

(No. 3.)

Form of Warrant against Inspector for re-issuing tobacco receipt.

Follow No. 1, leaving out what is in brackets, and in place of it, describe the offence thus: " re-issue and pass away a tobacco receipt, dated on the —— day of ——— 18—, for a certain hogshead of tobacco weighing ——— pounds, deposited in the said warehouse by G. H., after the delivery of the said hogshead of tobacco for which the said receipt was given."

(No. 4.)

Form of Commitment of an Inspector for examination in the County Court.

——— County, to wit:

To X. Z., Constable of said County, and to the Keeper of the Jail of said County:

These are to command you, the said Constable, in the name of the Commonwealth of Virginia, forthwith to convey and deliver into the custody of the keeper of the said jail, together with this warrant, the body of C. D., charged before me J. T., a Justice of the said County, on the oath of A. B., with a felony by him committed, in this, that the said C. D., he being an inspector of tobacco at ——— warehouse, on the —— day of ——— in the year 18—, in the said County, (here describe the offence as in the warrant of arrest.) And you, the said keeper of the said jail, are hereby required to receive the said C. D. into your jail and custody, that he may be examined for the said offence, by the County Court of said County, and him there safely keep until he shall be discharged by due course of law. Given under my hand and seal, this —— day of ——— in the year 18—.

J. T., J. P. [L. S.]

(No. 5.)

Form of Certificate of Commitment to be sent to the Clerk of the County Court.

—— County, to wit :
 To the Clerk of the County Court of said County :
 I, J. T., a Justice of the said County, do hereby certify, that I have, by my warrant, this day committed C. D., (if free negro or slave, state which,) to the jail of this County, that he may be examined (or *tried*) before the County Court of the said County, for a felony by him committed, in this, that he did, on the —— day of —— 18—, in the said County, (here state the offence as in the mittimus.) Given under my hand, this —— day of —— in the year 18—.

J. T., J. P.

(No. 6.)

Form of Certificate to the Clerk where party is admitted to bail.

Turn to head of ARREST, and follow No. 6.

(No. 7.)

Form of Recognizance of Bail.

Turn to head of RECOGNIZANCE, and follow No. 1, and state succinctly the offence for which the person is recognized.

(No. 8.)

Form of Recognizance of Witness to appear before the County Court to give evidence upon the examination or trial of a party charged with felony.

Turn to head of RECOGNIZANCE, and follow No. 3.

CHAPTER CIV.

TREASON.

By Sec. 1, Chap. 190. Treason shall consist only in levying war against the State, or adhering to its enemies, giving them aid and comfort, or establishing, without authority of the Legislature, any government within its limits, separate from the existing government, or holding or executing in such usurped government, any office, or professing allegiance or fidelity to it, or resisting the execution of the laws, under colour of its authority; and such treason, if proved by the testimony of two witnesses, to the same overt act, or by confession in court, shall be punished with death.

By Sec. 2. If a free person, knowing of any such treason, shall not as soon as may be, give information thereof to the governor, or some conservator of the peace, he shall be punished by fine not exceeding one thousand dollars, or by confinement in the penitentiary not less than three nor more than five years.

By Sec. 3. If a free person attempt to establish any such usurped government, and commit an overt act therefor, or by writing or speaking, endeavour to instigate others to establish such government, he shall be confined in jail not exceeding twelve months, and fined not exceeding one thousand dollars.

By Sec. 4. If a free person advise or conspire with a slave to rebel or make insurrection, or with any person to induce a slave to rebel or make insurrection, he shall be punished with death, whether such rebellion or insurrection be made or not.

(No. 1.)

Form of Warrant for Treason, in levying war.

—— County, to wit:

To the Sheriff of the said County, and to all the Constables of the said County:

Whereas, A. B. of the said County, has this day made complaint and information on oath before me J. T., a Justice of the said County, that C. D., on the —— day of —————— 18—, in the said County, together with other false traitors, to me unknown, armed in a warlike manner, did traitorously levy and make war against this Commonwealth: These are, therefore, in the name of the Commonwealth of Virginia, to command you forthwith to apprehend the said C. D., and to bring him before me or some other Justice of the said County, to answer the said complaint, and to be farther dealt with according to law. Given under my hand and seal, this —— day of —————— 18—.

J. T., J. P. [L. S.]

(No. 2.)

Form of Warrant of Arrest for instigation of treason.

—— County, to wit:

To the Sheriff, and each and all the Constables of the said County:

Whereas, A. B. of the said County, has this day made complaint and information on oath before me J. T., a Justice of the said County, that C. D., on the —— day of —————— 18—, in the said County, did traitorously, by advised speaking, attempt to instigate E. F. and others to establish a government within the limits of this Commonwealth, separate from the existing government thereof, and did then and there, in execution of the said attempt, maliciously and advisedly speak and say to the said E. F. and others, that (set out what the party said:) These are, therefore, in the name of the Commonwealth of Virginia, to command you forthwith to apprehend the said C. D., and bring him before me or some other Justice of the said County, to answer the said complaint, and to be farther dealt with according to law. Given under my hand and seal, this —— day of —————— 18—.

J. T., J. P. [L. S.]

(No. 3.)

Form of same for conspiring with slaves to rebel.

—— County, to wit:

To the Sheriff, and each and all of the Constables of the said County:

Whereas, A. B. of the said County, has this day made complaint and information on oath before me J. T., a Justice of the said County, that C. D., on the —— day of —————— 18—, in the said County, he the said C. D. being a free person, did feloniously conspire with Jack, a slave, and divers other persons to me unknown, to rebel and make insurrection against the government and laws of this Commonwealth: These are, therefore, in the name of the Commonwealth of Virginia, to command you, forthwith to apprehend the said C. D., and bring him before me or some other Justice of the said County, to answer the said complaint, and to be farther dealt with according to law. Given under my hand and seal, this —— day of —————— 18—.

J. T., J. P. [L. S.]

For form of mittimus, see No. 4, under head of ARREST; and for certificate of commitment to the Clerk, see Nos. 5 and 6, under same head. For recognizance of bail, see No. 1, under head of RECOGNIZANCE; and for recognizance of witness, see No. 3, under same head.

CHAPTER CV.

TRESPASS—(*Wilful.*)

At Common Law, a mere trespass committed by one person upon the property of another, unaccompanied by any circumstances constituting a breach of the peace, is not indictable.([1])

By Sec. 34, Chap. 192. If a free person unlawfully, but not feloniously, take and carry away, or destroy, deface or injure any property, real or personal, not his own, or break down, destroy, deface, injure or remove any monument, erected for the purpose of designating the boundaries of any town, tract, or lot of land, or any tree marked for that purpose, he shall be deemed guilty of a misdemeanor.

The Justice will remark, that to constitute an offence under this statute, the act must be done knowingly and wilfully, that is, with a wicked intention to do an injury ;([2]) it is not, however, confined to an intention to injure any particular individual, but imports an evil and wicked design to injure,([3]) whether that design result in the injury of property belonging to the particular person intended to be injured by the act, or to another; for, as in homicide, if A., with an evil and wicked design to kill B., should happen to kill C., against whom he had no malice, will be guilty of murder; so if a man, with an evil and corrupt design to injure the property of A., were to injure that of B., he would be guilty of a malicious trespass, under the statute; and accordingly, in a prosecution for maliciously wounding cattle, it is held not to be necessary to prove that the prisoner was actuated by malice against the owner.([4]) And it is a general rule, that when a man commits an act, unaccompanied by any circumstance justifying it, the law presumes the act to have been done advisedly, and with a design to produce the consequences of the act.([5])

Under the guise of a criminal prosecution, this statute is sometimes resorted to as the means of redressing private injury. Such perversion of the authority of the Commonwealth, should be discountenanced. To constitute an offence under it, the act must be done wilfully and without lawful authority; and as in the law of larceny, if a party take property under a fair and *bona fide* claim of right, he will not be guilty of stealing, so under this statute, if one take the goods of ano-

---

([1]) 1 Russ. 5.
([2]) 4 Mason R. 115; 1 Salk. R. 524.
([3]) 1 Dea. Cr. C. 898.
([4]) Tyny's Case, 1 Car. & K. 704.
([5]) Russ. & Ry. 307; 1 Moody C. C. 263; and title Homicide.

ther, or cut down a tree standing upon the land of another, under a fair and *bona fide* claim of right, and not knowingly and wilfully to injure another, he will not be guilty of a wilful trespass.([1])

In stating the injury to property in the proceeding, the manner of injury should be stated, especially if it be an injury to a horse or other beast, so as to shew that it was not done by administering poison, for then it would be felony. See POISON.

(No. 1.)

Form of Warrant of Arrest for injuring or disfiguring a horse or other animal.

―――― County, to wit:

To all or any one of the Constables of said County:

Whereas, A. B. of said County, has this day made complaint and information on oath before me J. T., a Justice of the said County, that C. D., on the ―― day of ―――― 18―, in said County, did unlawfully, but not feloniously, injure, maim and disfigure a certain horse, (or other animal, as the case may be,) the property of the said A. B., by (here state wherein the injury and disfiguration consists, as by cutting off the ears:) These are, therefore, to command you, in the name of the Commonwealth of Virginia, forthwith to apprehend the said C. D., and bring him before me or some other Justice of the said County, to answer the said complaint, and to be farther dealt with according to law. Given under my hand and seal, this ―― day of ―――― 18―.

J. T., *J. P.* [L. S.]

[NOTE.—This form may be altered to suit the injury of any kind of personal property, taking care to specify what the property is, and in what the injury consists.]

(No. 2.)

Form of Warrant of Arrest for injuring a dam, reservoir or canal.

―――― County, to wit:

To all or any one of the Constables of said County:

Whereas, A. B. of said County, has this day made complaint and information on oath before me J. T., a Justice of the said County, that C. D., on the ―― day of ―――― 18―, in said County, did unlawfully, but not feloniously, injure a certain dam, (or *reservoir*, or *canal*, as the case may be,) belonging to the said A. B., by (here state in what the injury consists:) These are, therefore, to command you, in the name of the Commonwealth of Virginia, forthwith to apprehend the said C. D., and bring him before me or some other Justice of the said County, to answer the said complaint, and to be farther dealt with according to law. Given under my hand and seal, this ―― day of ―――― 18―.

J. T., *J. P.* [L. S.]

([1]) Campbell *v.* The Com'th, 2 Gratt. 791; Ratcliff *v.* The Com'th, 3 Gratt.

(No. 3.)

Form of Warrant of Arrest for injury to the machinery of a water mill.

———— County, to wit:
    To all or any one of the Constables of said County:

Whereas, A. B. of said County, has this day made complaint and information on oath before me J. T., a Justice of said County, that C. D., on the ——— day of ——— 18—, in said County, did unlawfully, but not feloniously, injure the machinery of a certain water mill, the property of the said A. B., by (here describe the injury, as for instance, *by breaking the wheels of the said mill:*) These are, therefore, to command you, in the name of the Commonwealth of Virginia, forthwith to apprehend the said C. D., and bring him before me or some other Justice of the said County, to answer the said complaint, and to be farther dealt with according to law. Given under my hand and seal, this ——— day of ——— 18—.

                                    J. T., J. P. [L. S.]

(No. 4.)

Form of Warrant of Arrest for defacing a church.

———— County, to wit:
    To all or any one of the Constables of said County:

Whereas, A. B. of said County, has this day made complaint and information on oath before me J. T., a Justice of the said County, that C. D., on the ——— day of ——— 18—, in said County, did unlawfully, but not feloniously, deface and injure a certain building, erected for the purpose of religious worship, called the ——— church, (not his own,) by (state the injury:) These are, therefore, to command you, in the name of the Commonwealth of Virginia, forthwith to apprehend the said C. D., and bring him before me or some other Justice of the said County, to answer the said complaint, and to be farther dealt with according to law. Given under my hand and seal, this ——— day of ——— 18—.

                                    J. T., J. P. [L. S.]

(No. 5.)

Form of Warrant of Arrest for injury to telegraph fixtures.

———— County, to wit:
    To all or any one of the Constables of said County:

Whereas, A. B. of said County, has this day made complaint and information on oath before me J. T., a Justice of the said County, that C. D., on the ——— day of ——— 18—, in said County, did unlawfully, but not feloniously, injure a certain post, (or *wire*, or whatever else was injured,) the said post (or *wire*) then and there being a fixture for the communication of intelligence by telegraph, and appertaining to the line of the telegraph from

——— to ———, the property of (here state the owners of the telegraph :) These are, therefore, to command you, in the name of the Commonwealth of Virginia, forthwith to apprehend the said C. D., and bring him before me or some other Justice of the said County, to answer the said complaint, and to be farther dealt with according to law. Given under my hand and seal, this ——— day of ——— 18—.

J. T., J. P. [L. S.]

(No. 6.)

Form of Warrant of Arrest for wilfully and unlawfully cutting forest trees.

——— County, to wit:

To all or any one of the Constables of said County:

Whereas, A. B. of said County, has this day made complaint and information on oath before me J. T., a Justice of the said County, that C. D., on the ——— day of ——— 18—, in said County, did unlawfully, but not feloniously, injure and destroy ten forest trees, standing and growing upon a certain piece of land belonging to the said A. B., and which said ten trees were the property of the said A. B.: These are, therefore, to command you, in the name of the Commonwealth of Virginia, forthwith to apprehend the said C. D., and bring him before me or some other Justice of the said County, to answer the said complaint, and to be farther dealt with according to law. Given under my hand and seal, this ——— day of ——— 18—.

J. T., J. P. [L. S.]

(No. 7.)

Form of Warrant of Arrest for carrying away wood and timber already cut.

——— County, to wit:

To all or any one of the Constables of said County:

Whereas, A. B. of said County, has this day made complaint and information on oath before me J. T., a Justice of the said County, that C. D., on the ——— day of ——— 18—, in said County, did unlawfully, but not feloniously, carry away a quantity of wood and timber, then cut down and lying upon the land of the said A. B., and belonging to the said A. B.: These are, therefore, to command you, in the name of the Commonwealth of Virginia, forthwith to apprehend the said C. D., and bring him before me or some other Justice of the said County, to answer the said complaint, and to be farther dealt with according to law. Given under my hand and seal, this ——— day of ——— 18—.

J. T., J. P. [L. S.]

(No. 8.)

Form of Warrant of Arrest for cutting down trees growing for ornament.

—————— County, to wit:
    To all or any one of the Constables of said County:

    Whereas, A. B. of said County, has this day made complaint and information on oath before me J. T., a Justice of the said County, that C. D., on the —— day of ———— 18—, in said County, did unlawfully, but not feloniously, cut down and destroy one poplar tree, upon the land of the said A. B., then and there planted, placed and growing for use, shade and ornament, the said tree then and there not being the tree of him the said C. D., but the property of the said A. B.: These are, therefore, to command you, in the name of the Commonwealth of Virginia, forthwith to apprehend the said C. D., and bring him before me or some other Justice of the said County, to answer the said complaint, and to be farther dealt with according to law. Given under my hand and seal, this —— day of ———— 18—.

                                            J. T., *J. P.* [L. S.]

(No. 9.)

Form of Warrant of Arrest for injuring fruit trees.

—————— County, to wit:
    To all or any one of the Constables of said County:

    Whereas, A. B. of said County, has this day made complaint and information on oath before me J. T., a Justice of the said County, that C. D., on the —— day of ———— 18—, in said County, did unlawfully, but not feloniously, injure a number of fruit trees, to wit, ten apple trees of the said A. B., standing and growing upon the land of the said A. B.: These are, therefore, to command you, in the name of the Commonwealth of Virginia, forthwith to apprehend the said C. D., and bring him before me or some other Justice of the said County, to answer the said complaint, and to be farther dealt with according to law. Given under my hand and seal, this —— day of ———— 18—.

                                            J. T., *J. P.* [L. S.]

(No. 10.)

Form of Warrant of Arrest for breaking down and injuring a fence.

—————— County, to wit:
    To all or any one of the Constables of said County:

    Whereas, A. B. of said County, has this day made complaint and information on oath before me J. T., a Justice of the said County, that C. D., on the —— day of ———— 18—, in said County, did unlawfully, but not feloniously, break down and injure, and carry away a certain fence, then and there enclosing a certain piece of land there, the said fence and land then and there being the fence and land of him the said A. B., and not belonging to the said C. D.: These are, therefore, to command you, in the name of the Commonwealth of Virginia, forthwith to apprehend the said C. D., and bring him before me or some other Justice of the said County, to answer the said complaint, and to be farther dealt with according to law. Given under my hand and seal, this —— day of ——— 18—.

J. T., J. P. [L. S.]

(No. 11.)

Form of Warrant of Arrest for cutting down and destroying a line tree.

——— County, to wit :

To all or any one of the Constables of said County :

Whereas, A. B. of said County, has this day made complaint and information on oath before me J. T., a Justice of the said County, that C. D., on the —— day of ——— 18—, in said County, did unlawfully, but not feloniously, cut down and destroy a certain tree, marked for the purpose of designating the boundaries of a tract of land in the said County, belonging to the said A. B. and one E. F., and which tree was not then owned by the said C. D.: These are, therefore, to command you, in the name of the Commonwealth of Virginia, forthwith to apprehend the said C. D., and bring him before me or some other Justice of said County, to answer the said complaint, and to be farther dealt with according to law. Given under my hand and seal, this —— day of ——— 18—.

J. T., J. P. [L. S.]

(No. 12.)

Form of Warrant of Arrest for digging up and carrying away stone, &c. from the land of another.

——— County, to wit :

To all or any one of the Constables of said County :

Whereas, A. B. of said County, has this day made complaint and information on oath before me J. T., a Justice of the said County, that C. D., on the —— day of ——— 18—, in said County, did unlawfully, but not feloniously, dig up and carry away from the land of him the said A. B., a quantity of stone, (or *ore*, say what kind of ore,) he the said C. D. not being the owner of the said stone : These are, therefore, to command you, in the name of the Commonwealth of Virginia, forthwith to apprehend the said C. D., and bring him before me or some other Justice of the said County, to answer the said complaint, and to be farther dealt with according to law. Given under my hand and seal, this —— day of ——— 18—.

J. T., J. P. [L. S.]

(No. 13.)

Form of Warrant of Arrest for breaking a window, and severing it from the freehold.

—— County, to wit:
  To all or any one of the Constables of said County:

Whereas, A. B. of said County, has this day made complaint and information on oath before me J. T., a Justice of the said County, that C. D., on the —— day of —— 18—, in said County, did unlawfully, but not feloniously, injure and destroy twenty panes of window glass, in a certain building there situate, not his own, but which said building was then and there the property of the said A. B., and which said twenty panes of window glass were attached to the freehold of the said A. B., and by the breaking aforesaid, were then and there severed from the said freehold: These are, therefore, to command you, in the name of the Commonwealth of Virginia, forthwith to apprehend the said C. D., and bring him before me or some other Justice of the said County, to answer the said complaint, and to be farther dealt with according to law. Given under my hand and seal, this —— day of —— 18—.

J. T., J. P. [L. S.]

(No. 14.)

Form of Warrant of Arrest for breaking and defacing a mile stone or sign post.

—— County, to wit:
  To all or any one of the Constables of said County:

Whereas, A. B. of said County, has this day made complaint and information on oath before me J. T., a Justice of the said County, that C. D., on the —— day of —— 18—, in said County, did unlawfully, but not feloniously, break, deface and destroy a certain mile stone, (or *sign post,*) placed and put up upon a public road in the said County, for public convenience: These are, therefore, to command you, in the name of the Commonwealth of Virginia, forthwith to apprehend the said C. D., and bring him before me or some other Justice of the said County, to answer the said complaint, and to be farther dealt with according to law. Given under my hand and seal, this —— day of —— 18—.

J. T., J. P. [L. S.]

These various offences are all misdemeanors, for which the party charged, if a free white person, should be recognized to answer an indictment, if in the opinion of the Justice the case ought to be prosecuted. If a free negro, he may either be recognized to answer the offence, or be tried by the Justice. If a slave, he must be tried by the Justice. And as to the mode of proceeding before a single Justice, to try either a slave or free negro for misdemeanors, see head of FINES AND SUMMARY CONVICTIONS.

TRESPASS—(*Wilful.*)

(No. 15.)

Form of Mittimus where a party is committed to answer an indictment in the County Court, for a wilful trespass.

——— County, to wit:
  To X. Z., *Constable of the said County, and to the Keeper of the Jail of the said County:*

These are to command you, the said Constable, in the name of the Commonwealth of Virginia, forthwith to convey and deliver into the custody of the keeper of the said jail, together with this warrant, the body of C. D., charged before me J. T., a Justice of the said County, on the oath of A. B., with a misdemeanor by him committed, in this, that the said C. D., on the ——— day of ——— in the year 18—, in the said County, (here describe the offence as in the warrant of arrest.) And you, the said keeper of the said jail, are hereby required to receive the said C. D. into your jail and custody, to answer an indictment to be preferred against him for the said offence, in the County Court of said County, and him there safely keep, until he shall be discharged by due course of law. Given under my hand and seal, this ——— day of ——— in the year 18—.

J. T., J. P. [L. S.]

(No. 16.)

Form of Recognizance of Bail.

Turn to head of RECOGNIZANCE, and follow No. 4, and state the offence succinctly, for which the party is recognized.

(No. 17.)

Form of Certificate of the Commitment or Letting to Bail, to be sent to the Clerk of the County Court.

——— County, to wit:
  To the Clerk of the County Court of the said County:

I, J. T., a Justice of the said County, do hereby certify, that C. D. was this day committed to the jail of this County, by my warrant, (or *was this day admitted to bail by me*, as the case may be,) to answer an indictment to be preferred against him in the County Court of the said County, for a misdemeanor by him committed, in this, that he did, on the ——— day of ——— 18—, in said County, (here describe the offence as in the warrant of arrest.) Given under my hand, this ——— day of ——— 18—.

J. T., J. P.

(No. 18.)

Form of Recognizance of Witness to appear and give evidence to the Grand Jury upon the indictment.

Follow No. 5, under head of RECOGNIZANCE.

TRESPASS—(*Wilful*)—(*Indictments for.*)

(No. 1.)

Indictment for cutting down trees, growing for ornament.

Commence as No. 2, under head of "INDICTMENTS," and say : that A. B., on the —— day of ——— 18—, at the County aforesaid, did unlawfully, but not feloniously, cut down and destroy two elm trees, in a certain avenue to the dwelling house of one C. D., there planted, placed and growing for use, shade and ornament, on land not his own, or belonging to him the said A. B., to wit, on the land of the said C. D., and of which he the said C. D. was the lawful owner, he the said A. B. then and there not having the consent therefor, from the said C. D. the owner of said land, against the peace and dignity of this Commonwealth.

[NOTE.—*Quere.* If it be for forest trees, is it necessary to state the kind of forest trees ? We think not, but if the kind be stated, it must be proved as laid, for proof of cutting black oak, will not sustain a charge of cutting white oak trees. Commonwealth *v.* Belcher, 4 Grat. 544.]

(No. 2.)

Indictment for wilfully defacing and breaking a mile stone.

Commence as No. 2, under head of "INDICTMENTS," and say : that A. B., on the —— day of ——— 18—, at the County aforesaid, a certain mile stone, placed and put up in a public road in said County, for public convenience and for the information of travellers, did unlawfully and wilfully break, deface and destroy, he the said A. B. not being then and there legally authorized so to do, against the peace and dignity of this Commonwealth.

UNLAWFUL ASSEMBLY.

See RIOTS, and SLAVES AND FREE NEGROES.

WARRANT—(CRIMINAL.)

What. See ARREST.

General form of, see No. 2, under head of ARREST.

Form of, to transfer a prisoner from one County to another, see No. 14, under head of ARREST.

Form of, where a party fails to appear and answer a summons, see No. 21, under head of ARREST.

For special forms of warrants of arrest, see under each separate head of offence.

CHAPTER CVI.

WARRANTS—(*Civil.*)

How issued and proceeded on to judgment.

BY SEC. 1, CHAP. 150. Any claim to property or to any debt, fine or other money, which would be recoverable by action at law or suit in equity, if of greater value or amount than thirty dollars, (exclusive of interest,) shall, when the claim is to a fine, if it be limited to an amount not exceeding twenty dollars, and in other cases, if the claim be not of greater value or amount than thirty dollars, (exclusive of interest,) be cognizable by a Justice; and even if the claim be for or against the town or county in which such Justice resides. But in every case where the sum or thing in controversy exceeds the amount or value of twenty dollars, the Justice shall, upon the application of the defendant, at any time before trial, remove the cause to the court of the county or corporation wherein the same shall be brought, and the Clerk of the said court shall docket the same, and it shall be proceeded in as if it were a motion in said court, under the fifth section of chapter one hundred and sixty-seven, of which the notice was docketed at the time such case is so docketed.

BY SEC. 2. A Justice, when applied to by any person, shall issue a warrant to a Constable, requiring him to summon the person against whom the claim is made, to appear before him or some other Justice, on a certain day, not exceeding thirty days from the date thereof, to answer such claim. It shall be made returnable to some place within the Constable's district in which the defendant resides, unless the Justice, for good cause shewn on oath, direct it to be returned to some other place within his county or corporation.

BY SEC. 3. Subpœnas for witnesses may be issued by a Justice, directed to a Constable of any county or corporation. Any person, summoned to attend as a witness before a Justice, who shall fail so to attend, shall, unless he shew a reasonable excuse therefor, within ten days, after being summoned to state such excuse, be fined by the Justice before whom the failure occurred, a sum not exceeding five dollars, for the use of the party on whose behalf he was summoned.

BY SEC. 4. The Justice shall try such warrant according to the principles of law and equity, and give judgment for the sum due to either party, with interest, or for the property to which the plaintiff is entitled, (or its value,) with damages.

Costs shall be awarded or refused to either party, on the like principles.

BY SEC. 5. The Justice rendering any such judgment, shall, in a book kept for such purpose, enter the date thereof, the name of the person for, and of the person against, whom it is, and its amount; also, the date of any execution issued thereon, and to whom delivered. If he fail to do so, he shall forfeit twenty dollars. The cost of such book shall be chargeable on the county or corporation. The Justice shall also write on the face of the paper or writing on which the warrant issued, or on any writing allowed as a set-off, the date and amount of the judgment and costs, and affix his name thereto.

BY SEC. 6. After thirty days from any such judgment, no new trial shall be granted in the case; nor shall it be granted within the thirty days, unless the opposite party be present at the time of the application, or unless after five days notice to him (if in the county or corporation) of the time and place of the application for such new trial. The Justice, who rendered the judgment, shall alone have power to grant such new trial, while he is in office; if he die, resign, be absent from the county, or be removed, it may be granted by another Justice.

BY SEC. 7. If a judgment of a Justice be for a sum exceeding ten dollars and not exceeding twenty, exclusive of interest and costs, the Justice rendering it may stay execution on it forty days from its date, and if said judgment exceed twenty dollars, he may stay execution on it sixty days from its date, on such security being given, in either case, for its payment, as he may deem sufficient. From any such judgment, the Justice rendering it may, within ten days, on such security being given as he approves for the payment of the same and all costs and damages, (if it be affirmed,) allow an appeal where the case involves the constitutionality or validity of an ordinance, or by-law of a corporation, or where the matter in controversy, exclusive of interest, is of greater amount or value than ten dollars. The verbal acknowledgment of any surety, taken under this section, shall be sufficient, and the endorsement by the Justice of the name of such surety upon the warrant on which the judgment is rendered, shall be conclusive evidence of such acknowledgment. The court in which the appeal is cognizable, may, on motion, for good cause shewn, require the appellant to give new or additional security, reasonable notice of such motion having been given to said appellant; and if he fail to give such security, the appeal shall be dismissed with costs, and the court shall award execution on the judgment rendered by the Justice, with costs, against the appellant and his surety.

How execution is issued, directed and returnable.

BY SEC. 8. The Justice rendering any judgment, may issue a writ of *fieri facias* thereon immediately, if there be not a new trial granted, nor an appeal allowed, nor a stay of execution. And where there is such stay of execution, if the judgment be not paid within the forty or sixty days, as the case may be, a writ of *fieri facias* shall thereupon be issued by a Justice against the party and his surety jointly, on which no security shall be taken.

BY SEC. 9. A writ of *fieri facias*, issued by a Justice, shall be directed to a Constable. It may be directed to and executed by a Constable of any county or corporation which the plaintiff may designate, and shall be returnable within sixty days. If not wholly satisfied, it may, within one year from the judgment, be returned to and renewed by a Justice, notwithstanding the provisions of chapter forty-nine. But every execution issued by a Justice, which is not so returned and renewed, shall be returned by the Constable to the Clerk's office of the court by which he was appointed.

BY SEC. 10. The Clerk shall file, alphabetically, in a bundle, all executions returned by a Constable within any year which shall, and in a separate bundle such as shall not, appear to be satisfied. Such farther executions may be issued for the recovery of the amount due on any execution so returned, as if the judgment on which it issued had been rendered in court. The same may, at the option of the plaintiff, be directed to and executed either by a Constable or by a Sheriff or Sergeant; and the same proceedings shall be had upon executions issued under this section, as upon executions issued upon judgments of courts.

Motions against Constables.

BY SEC. 11. A copy from the entry in the Justice's book, of the date of any execution issued by him, and to whom delivered, shall be evidence in any proceeding against the officer to whom it is entered as delivered, for failing to make due return thereof, or for failing to pay over money received thereon. If a Justice, upon being applied to for a copy of any entry, shall refuse it, and afterwards, upon being summoned to produce the book in which such entry is or ought to have been made, shall fail to produce such entry, he shall forfeit twenty dollars to the person on whose behalf he is summoned.

BY SEC. 12. If an officer fail to make due return of any execution issued by a Justice, he may, after ten days notice, be fined from time to time by a Justice, on the motion of the

WARRANTS—(*Civil.*)

plaintiff in such execution, in like manner as a court may fine an officer who fails to make due return of an execution issued from such court. And if an officer shall make such return upon an execution issued by a Justice, as would, on a motion against the officer, authorize judgment to be entered against him for the amount of such execution, or any part thereof, if the execution had issued from a court, the creditor on whose behalf such execution issued, or his personal representative, may, on a motion before a Justice, after like notice, obtain such judgment against the officer, his sureties and others, as could be given by a court, if the execution had issued from a court. This section shall not prevent a motion in court under chapter forty-nine, or under the fourth section of chapter one hundred and sixty-seven.

By Sec. 13. If a Constable collect money mentioned in an execution after the return day thereof, he and his sureties shall be liable for the money so collected, in like manner as if the collection had been before the return day. And if a Constable receive money on account of any claim entrusted to him to warrant for, and recoverable by warrant, he and his sureties shall be liable for the money so received, as for money collected under execution; and after six months from the date of any receipt for such claim, signed in his official character, such receipt shall be *prima facie* evidence of the receipt of the money.

Where distress or levy on property not exceeding value of twenty dollars; and title disputed.

By Sec. 14. When an execution on a judgment of a Justice, or a warrant of distress, is levied upon property not of greater value than twenty dollars, which is claimed by any person other than the party against whom it issued, such person may apply to a Justice of the county or corporation in which the levy is, for a warrant to a Constable, requiring him to summon both the creditor and debtor, to shew cause why the property should not be discharged from the levy. The Justice shall issue such warrant, returnable in not less than five days: and if an earlier day shall have been fixed for the sale of the property, he shall make an order on the warrant, requiring the postponement of the sale until after the return day. Upon hearing the parties, or such of them as may attend after being summoned, he shall order the officer to deliver the property to the claimant, or the person from whom it was taken, or shall dismiss the summons, as may seem most proper, and may give such judgment for costs as he may deem just. If the property be of the value of ten dollars, the Justice shall, within five days, allow an appeal from such order and judgment, on security being given, as in the appeals before mentioned in this chapter.

When appeal from judgment of Justice.

By SEC. 15. The Justice, from whose judgment an appeal is allowed, shall immediately deliver to the Clerk of the court, which has cognizance of the appeal, the original warrant, with the judgment and the name of the surety endorsed thereon, and the Clerk shall docket the same.

By SEC. 16. When an appeal is allowed from any order or judgment of a Justice, it shall be cognizable by the court to which such Justice belongs, unless it be in a case involving the constitutionality or validity of an ordinance, or by-law of a corporation, in which case it shall be cognizable by the circuit court having jurisdiction over the county or corporation in which the judgment is rendered.

By SEC. 17. Every such appeal shall be tried in a summary way, without pleadings in writing. The court trying it shall hear all the evidence produced by either party, whether the same were produced before the Justice, from whose decision the appeal is taken or not, and determine it according to the principles of law and equity. If the decision be affirmed, execution shall issue against the principal and his surety, jointly, or separately, for the amount of the original judgment, including interest and costs, with damages on the aggregate, at the rate of ten per centum per annum, from the date of that judgment till payment, and for the costs of the appeal; and the execution shall be endorsed "*no security to be taken.*" If the decision be reversed, the appellant shall recover his costs; and such order or judgment shall be made or given, as ought to have been made or given by the Justice. Where the appeal is from an order or judgment under the fourteenth section, the court shall give such judgment, respecting the property, the expense of keeping it, and any injury done to it, as may be equitable among the parties.

By SEC. 18. Either party to an appeal, may give ten days notice to the other party, that a motion will be made to try the appeal, and the court shall, on the day named in the notice, whether at a quarterly or monthly term, try the appeal, without regard to its place on the docket, unless good cause be shewn by the adverse party for a continuance, and, if so continued, shall try it as soon as may be thereafter.

Exception as to the City of Richmond.

By Sec. 19. Nothing contained in this chapter, in conflict with the act entitled "*an act concerning the jurisdiction of the Mayor's court of the City of Richmond,*" passed the twenty-seventh day of February, one thousand eight hundred and forty-nine, shall be construed to repeal the same.

There can be no demand for money not of greater amount than thirty dollars (exclusive of interest) arising out of *contract*, or any claim to *personal* property of any kind not exceeding thirty dollars in value, that may not be asserted before a single Justice by virtue of the preceding chapter of the statute, whether the demand or claim be founded upon principles of law or of equity, and the statute directs the mode by which this may be done.

Although in proceedings under the statute, the Justice should discourage, if not entirely disregard, technical objections, it would seem that the purposes of justice require that the nature of the claim should be so stated in the summons as to inform the defendant distinctly what it is he is called to answer, and that a summons to answer generally a claim for money not exceeding thirty dollars, exclusive of interest, or for property of the value of thirty dollars, without describing it, would be insufficient.

In regard to claims for money, it is not to be presumed that the Legislature meant to perplex the Justice with the distinctions between the various actions at law to recover it, as for instance, between debt and assumpsit. The well settled practice under the former law, so long acquiesced in, is against such a presumption. According to that practice, a warrant in debt was the remedy for asserting before a single Justice, any claim for money arising upon contract, whether the sum was certain and due by express agreement between the parties, or upon an implied contract for an uncertain sum to be ascertained and fixed by him upon the hearing of the case; and any innovation now, requiring Justices on the trial of warrants, to draw the often nice distinctions between the actions of debt and assumpsit, would often subvert justice and defeat the object which the law has in view, by conferring this summary jurisdiction upon them out of sessions. For uniformity of practice, therefore, as well as for convenience, the Justice is advised in all such cases (except in breaches of covenant) to issue the summons in the language of the statute, to answer a claim for money, with sufficient description of the claim to notify the defendant of its true character.

A Justice can take cognizance of no case for damages arising out of wrongs, unless on a claim of property by detinue or trover. He cannot try a case in trespass, as for assault and battery; nor in trespass on the case, as in slander; for however small the damages in such cases may be, they must be ascertained by the verdict of a jury.

His jurisdiction is limited to thirty dollars, and if a party has a demand on another for a greater amount due in the same right, and for the recovery of which, one action at law would lie, he cannot split up the entire demand into sums of thirty dollars or less, so as to bring the cases within the jurisdiction of a single Justice. In such a case, the party must be put to his action at law to recover the entire sum,[1] though where the plaintiff's claim exceeds thirty dollars, he may abate the excess, and warrant for that sum.

By the statute, both Common Law and equity jurisdiction are conferred upon the Justice, and it is the practice of courts of equity, where the plaintiff is found to be indebted to the defendant, to decree against the plaintiff for the sum ascertained to be due; so in a warrant for money, if the Justice, upon hearing the parties, finds that the plaintiff is indebted to the defendant, he should give judgment against the plaintiff for whatever sum he ascertains to be due to the defendant, if that sum be under thirty dollars, exclusive of interest.

The mode of recovering fines which enure, either in whole or in part, to the Commonwealth, has already been noticed under the head of FINES AND SUMMARY CONVICTIONS, and are to be proceeded for in the name of the Commonwealth.

To recover property or its value, the warrant should be either in detinue or trover. Detinue is the proper remedy for the recovery of any specific chattel or thing, (as for a cow,) or for the alternate value of it,[2] where that value does not exceed thirty dollars. To sustain a warrant in detinue, the plaintiff must have an absolute or special property in the thing for which it is brought, and a right to the immediate possession of it at the time the warrant is issued,[3] but it is not necessary that the thing should have been previously in the actual possession of the plaintiff.[4]

If one detains the goods of a married woman, which came to his possession before her marriage, the husband alone must bring the warrant, because the right of property is in him alone at the time the warrant is brought.[5] The gist of the suit is the wrongful detention of the property, and though it has been said that detinue cannot be maintained where the

---

[1] Hutson v. Laury, 2 Va. Cases.
[2] Leigh's N. P. 781.
[3] Id.
[4] Id.
[5] Id.

defendant has taken the goods wrongfully, the law is now settled to be otherwise.(¹)

The judgment in detinue is, that the plaintiff recover against the defendant the goods, or the value thereof if he cannot have the goods themselves, together with damages for their detention,(²) and from courts of record, a distringas may issue to compel the production of the goods, but under the statute, a *fieri facias* is the only execution that a Justice can award, and therefore the peculiar value of a warrant in detinue, is lost to the plaintiff, and is but little else in its result than a warrant in trover.

To support a warrant in trover, the plaintiff must shew, first, that he had absolute or special property in the goods which are the subject of the warrant, at the time they came into the possession of the defendant who converted them; secondly, that the plaintiff had the right of possession in the thing, for without the right of possession he cannot recover, though he may have the right of property; as where A. hires a horse to B. for a given time, he cannot maintain trover against B. for the value of the horse, until the expiration of the time of hiring; for though A. has the right of property in the horse, the right of possession remains in B. during the time of hiring; and so in detinue; thirdly, that personal goods constitute the subject of the warrant; and fourthly, that the defendant has been guilty of a wrongful conversion.(³)

Under the very comprehensive language of the first section of the statute, the Justice has jurisdiction in breaches of covenant, where the damages sought to be recovered do not exceed thirty dollars. Covenant lies in all cases for the recovery of damages for breach of an agreement *under seal*, to do or not to do a particular thing, and any words amounting to an agreement to do or not to do any particular thing, will constitute a covenant.(⁴)

A covenant is to be construed according to the obvious meaning of the parties to it, as collected from the whole context of the instrument, and according to the reasonable sense of its words. If there be any ambiguity in it, such construction should be made as is most strong against the covenantor.(⁵)

In the exercise of the power of awarding new trials, the Justice is to act, not according to his arbitrary will, but according to sound legal discretion, so as to promote the ends of substantial justice, and although in the nature of things, there can be no fixed rule upon this subject, applicable to all cases,

---

(¹) 2 Leigh N. P. 782.
(²) 2 Leigh 283.
(³) 2 Leigh N. P. 516.
(⁴) Cowan's J. P. 23.
(⁵) 1 Selwyn's N. P. 376.

670   WARRANTS—(*Civil.*)

as each must depend upon its peculiar circumstances, there are certain general rules having the same object in view, which prevail in courts of record, and which are equally applicable to motions for new trials in civil warrants.

1st. It is a general rule, that all disingenuous attempts to stifle or suppress evidence, to thwart the proceedings, or to obtain an unconscionable advantage, or to mislead the Justice, will be defeated by awarding a new trial.([1])

2d. The absence of the party may, under peculiar circumstances, be the ground of a new trial, as where there is a meritorious defence, and the party is absent from necessity or misapprehension, and the cause is undefended.([2]) But if the absence be occasioned by neglect, or not satisfactorily accounted for, a new trial ought not to be granted.([3])

3d. Where a party is taken by surprise, whether by fraud or accident, on a *material point* or circumstance which could not reasonably have been anticipated, and when want of skill or attention cannot be justly imputed, and injustice has been done, a new trial should be granted. But to entitle the party to relief, there must be merits, and the surprise must be such as care and prudence could not provide against. The slightest negligence will defeat the application.([4])

4th. A party will not be relieved from the consequences of mere ignorance, inadvertence or neglect, by granting a new trial.([5]) To grant it for such causes, would encourage great negligence in preparing for trial in the first instance.

The regular time for objecting to the competency of witnesses, is at the trial, and a new trial should not be granted to furnish an opportunity to impeach a witness, upon a subsequent discovery of his interest or turpitude, or general bad character.([6])

The Justice may sometimes, on the trial of warrants, err in rejecting legal evidence, or in receiving illegal evidence on the merits; in either case, if upon farther consideration, he be satisfied that he erred, and that the justice of the case requires it, he should award a new trial.([7]) So, also, if after judgment, he be satisfied that he mistook any question of law material to the issue, and that thereby injustice has been done, he should award a new trial ;([8]) but if no injustice has been

---

([1]) Graham on New Trials 56, and authorities there cited.
([2]) Id. 162.
([3]) Id. 106.
([4]) Id. 174.
([5]) Id. 187.
([6]) Id. 228 ; and the case of Turner *v.* Pearte, 1 Term. Rep. 717, where Buller, J. said: "There has been no instance of this court's (K. B.) granting a new trial on an allegation that some of the witnesses examined were interested, and I should be very sorry to make the first precedent."
([7]) Graham N. T. 237, 252.
([8]) Id. 262.

done, and a new trial in his opinion would produce the same result, he should refuse it.(¹)

A new trial should never be granted against the justice of the case, for any technical objection to the proceedings. This is a fixed rule in courts of record, and should be rigidly adhered to by Justices out of court.

Applications for new trials are frequently made upon the ground of newly discovered evidence, and in such cases, the Justice has the power to award new trials. But the exercise of it is liable to such abuses, that nothing but a clear case of injustice, occasioned by means beyond the control of the party, and the strong probability, if not certainty, of correcting it by those means since brought to light and placed within the reach of the applicant, will answer the purpose. "Motions of this kind are to be received with great caution, because there are few cases of contest tried, in which something new may not be hunted up; and because it tends very much to the introduction of perjury, to admit new evidence after the party who has lost his case, has had an opportunity of discovering both his adversary's strength and his own weakness." It is, therefore, incumbent on him, who asks for a new trial on the ground of newly discovered evidence, to satisfy the Justice, 1. That the evidence has come to his knowledge since the trial; 2. That it was not owing to want of due diligence that it did not come sooner; 3. That it would probably produce a different judgment if a new trial was granted;(²) and great strictness is required in making his vigilance apparent, for if it is left even doubtful that he knew of the evidence, or that he might, but for negligence, have known and produced it, he will not succeed in his application.(³)

It is a settled rule, that a new trial will not be allowed upon the ground of newly discovered evidence, if the evidence is merely in corroboration of testimony given at the former trial,(⁴) nor will it be allowed, upon this ground, if the alleged newly discovered evidence is to discredit witnesses who testified at the former trial.(⁵)

(¹) Graham N. T. 262, 301.
(²) Graham N. T. 464, citing 5 Sergt. & Rawle 41.
(³) Id. 473.
(⁴) Id. 485, citing 2 Tidd 938.
(⁵) Id. 496.

(No. 1.)

Form for removing a Warrant to the County Court, upon the application of the defendant, where the subject in controversy exceeds the value of $20, and which may be endorsed on the warrant.

―――― County, to wit, ―――― day of ―――― 18――:

The subject in controversy upon this warrant exceeding the amount (if it be for money, or *the value,* if it be for property,) of twenty dollars, I do, upon the application of the defendant before trial, remove the case to the Courty Court of ――――.

J. T., J. P.

(No. 2.)

Form of Warrant for money due on note or other written acknowledgment.

―――― County, to wit :

To X. Y., *Constable of the said County:*

I hereby command you to summon A. B., if to be found in your district, to appear at ――――, in the said County, on the ―――― day of ―――― 18――, before me or such other Justice of the said County as may then be there to try this warrant, to answer the complaint of C. D. upon a claim for money not exceeding thirty dollars, exclusive of interest, to wit, for the sum of $ ――――, due by note, (or *bond,* or whatever the written acknowledgment may be,) and then and there make return of this warrant. Given under my hand, this ―――― day of ―――― 18――.

J. T., J. P.

(No. 3.)

Form of Warrant for money due by open account.

―――― County, to wit:

To X. Y., *Constable of said County:*

I hereby command you to summon A. B., if to be found in your district, to appear at ――――, in the said County, on the ―――― day of ―――― 18――, before me or such other Justice of the said County, as may then be there to try this warrant, to answer the complaint of C. D., upon a claim for money, not exceeding thirty dollars, exclusive of interest, to wit, for the sum of $ ――――, due for goods sold and delivered, (or if for any thing else, state what ;) and then and there make return of this warrant. Given under my hand, this ―――― day of ―――― 18――.

J. T., J. P.

(No. 4.)

Form of Summons against a husband for a debt contracted by the wife before marriage.

—— County, to wit:

To X. Y., *Constable of the said County:*

I command you to summon A. B., to appear at ——, in the said County, on the —— day of —— 18—, before me or such other Justice of the said County as may then be there to try this warrant, to answer the complaint of C. D., upon a claim for money, not exceeding thirty dollars, exclusive of interest, to wit, for the sum of $——, due by note made by F. B., the present wife of the said A. B., while she was a single woman. Given under my hand and seal, this —— day of —— 18—.

J. T., J. P. [L. S.]

(No. 5.)

Form of Warrant in debt for a penalty.

—— County, to wit:

To X. Y., *Constable of the said County:*

I command you, in the name of the Commonwealth of Virginia, to summon J. F., if to be found in your district, to appear at ——, in the said County, on the —— day of —— 18—, before me or such other Justice of the said County as shall then be there to try this warrant, to answer the complaint of P. A., in debt, for $——, the fine incurred by him the said J. F., for (here state how the penalty was incurred,) contrary to law: and have then and there this warrant. Given under my hand, this —— day of —— 18—.

J. T., J. P.

(No. 6.)

Form of Summons in the name of the husband for debt due to his wife before marriage.

—— County, to wit:

To X. Y., *Constable of the said County:*

I hereby command you to summon A. B., to appear before me or such other Justice of the said County as may then be there to try this warrant, at ——, in the said County, on the —— day of —— 18—, to answer the complaint of C. D. upon a claim for money, not exceeding thirty dollars, exclusive of interest, due by a note (or *bond*) made by the said A. B. to F. D., the present wife of the said C. D., when a single woman. Given under my hand, this —— day of —— 18—.

J. T., J. P.

(No. 7.)

Form of Warrant in trover.

—— County, to wit:
   To X. Y., *Constable of the said County:*

I command you, in the name of the Commonwealth, to summon A. B., if he be found in your district, to appear at ——, in the said County, on the —— day of —— 18—, before me or such other Justice of the said County, as may then be there to try this warrant, to answer the claim of C. D. in trover, for (here describe the property, as for instance, *for one horse,*) not exceeding the value of $30, which the said C. D. claims to be his property, and which, as he alleges, the said A. B. has converted to his own use; and then and there make return of this warrant. Given under my hand, this —— day of —— 18—.

J. T., J. P.

(No. 8.)

Form of Warrant in detinue.

Follow the above to the word "trover," and conclude thus: in detinue, for (here describe the property claimed, accurately,) not exceeding the value of $30, which the said C. D. claims to be his property, and which as he alleges, the said A. B. unjustly detains from him; and have then and there this warrant. Given under my hand, this —— day of —— 18—.

J. T., J. P.

(No. 9.)

Form of Subpœna for a witness.

—— County, to wit:
   To X. Y., *Constable of the said County:*

I command you, in the name of the Commonwealth of Virginia, to summon E. F. to appear, on the —— day of —— 18—, at ——, in the said County, before me or such other Justice of the said County as may then be there, to give evidence in behalf of A. B., in a warrant then and there to be tried between the said A. B. plaintiff, and C. D. defendant. Given under my hand, this —— day of —— 18—.

J. T., J. P.

(No. 10.)

Form of Summons against a witness, to shew cause why he should not be fined for not attending.

—— County, to wit:
   To X. Y., *Constable of the said County:*

I, J. T., a Justice of the said County, do hereby command you, in the name of the Commonwealth of Virginia, that you summon E. F. to appear

WARRANTS—(*Civil.*) 675

at ———, in the said County, on the ——— day of ——— 18—, before me or such other Justice of the said County, as shall then be there, to shew cause, if any he can, why he should not be fined for his contempt in not attending before me on this day, as witness for A. B. in a certain matter of controversy pending before me, by warrant, wherein the said A. B. is plaintiff, and C. D. is defendant, he the said E. F. having been duly summoned for that purpose, and not appearing when solemnly called; and have then there this process. Given under my hand, this ——— day of ——— 18—.

J. T., J. P.

(No. 11.)

Form of Judgment in debt for money.

C. D. ⎱ In debt.
v. ⎰ ——— day of ——— 18—, at ———:
A. B. ⎱ Judgment that the plaintiff recover of the defendant $ ———, with interest from the ——— day of ——— 18—, till paid, and $ ——— for his costs.

J. T., J. P.

(No. 12.)

Form of Judgment in detinue.

C. D. ⎱ In detinue.
v. ⎰ ——— day of ——— 18—, at ———:
A. B. ⎱ Judgment that the plaintiff recover of the defendant the cow in the warrant mentioned, of the value of $ ———, and also the sum of $ ——— for damages sustained by him for the wrongful detention of said cow, and also his costs, which I ascertain to be $ ———.

J. T., J. P.

(No. 13.)

Form of Judgment in trover.

C. D. ⎱ In trover.
v. ⎰ ——— day of ——— 18—, at ———:
A. B. ⎱ Judgment that the plaintiff recover of the defendant $ ———, for the damages sustained by him for the conversion and disposing of the (horse or whatever property) in the warrant mentioned by the defendant, and for $ ———, his costs.

J. T., J. P.

(No. 14.)

Form of Judgment on warrant for a penalty.

C. D. ⎱ Warrant in debt for a penalty.
v. ⎰ ——— day of ——— 18—, at ———:
A. B. ⎱ Judgment that the plaintiff recover against the defendant $ ———, the fine imposed by law, for (state how the penalty was incurred,) and for $ ——— his costs.

J. T., J. P.

(No. 15.)

Form of entering an Appeal to the County Court from the judgment of a single Justice.

A. B. ⎫ —— day of ——— 18—:
  v. ⎬   The said C. D. (or *A. B.*, according to which of the parties asks
C. D. ⎭ for an appeal,) having prayed an appeal from my judgment in this cause, and tendered E. F. as his surety, who thereupon undertook, as his surety, for the payment of the said judgment, and all costs and damages, in case the same shall be affirmed, an appeal from the said judgment is granted the said C. D. (or *A. B.*, as the case may be,) to the next term of the County Court.

J. T., J. P.

(No. 16.)

Form for suspending Execution for forty or sixty days.

A. B. ⎫ —— day of ——— 18—:
  v. ⎬   Judgment having been rendered in this case for ——— dollars,
C. D. ⎭ exclusive of interest and costs, and the defendant having requested stay of execution upon the said judgment, whereupon E. F. undertook as the surety of the said C. D. for the payment of the said judgment, execution is stayed thereon for ——* days from the date.

J. T., J. P.

(No. 17.)

Form of an Execution upon a judgment in debt before a single Justice.

———— County, to wit:

    To *X. Y.*, *Constable of the said County:*

    I command you, in the name of the Commonwealth of Virginia, that of the goods and chattels of A. B., in your district, you cause to be made the sum of ——— dollars, with interest thereon from the —— day of ——— 18—, till paid, which C. D. has recovered before me, (or *E. F.*, if judgment be rendered by another Justice,) in a warrant in debt, and also the sum of ——— dollars, which were adjudged to the said C. D. for costs in prosecuting his said warrant. Given under my hand, this —— day of ——— 18—.

J. T., J. P.

---

* When the judgment is over ten and not exceeding twenty dollars, exclusive of interest and costs, fill this blank with the word "forty," and if the judgment exceed twenty dollars, fill it with the word "sixty."

(No. 18.)

Form of Execution in trover.

——— County, to wit:

To X. Y., *Constable of said County:*

I command you, in the name of the Commonwealth of Virginia, that of the goods and chattels of A. B., in your district, you cause to be made the sum of ——— dolars, which C. D. has recovered before me, (*or before E. F.*, if the judgment was rendered by another Justice,) in a warrant in trover, for his damages, which he sustained by the occasion of converting and disposing of certain goods and chattels of the said C. D. by the said A. B., and also ——— dollars, which were adjudged to the said C. D. for his costs in prosecuting his said warrant. Given under my hand, this ——— day of ——— 18—.

J. T., J. P.

(No. 19.)

Form of Execution in detinue.

——— County, to wit:

To X. Y., *Constable of said County:*

I command you, in the name of the Commonwealth of Virginia, that of the goods and chattels of A. B., in your district, you cause to be made the sum of ——— dollars, which C. D. has recovered before me, (or *E. F.*, if the judgment was rendered by another Justice,) in a warrant in detinue, for the value of a certain cow, and also $ ———, for his damages, which he sustained by occasion of the detention of the said cow by the said A. B., and ——— dollars, which were adjudged to the said C. D. for his costs in prosecuting his said warrant. Given under my hand, this ——— day of ——— 18—.

J. T., J. P.

(No. 20.)

Form of Execution against an executor or administrator.

——— County, to wit:

To X. Y., *Constable of said County:*

I command you, in the name of the Commonwealth of Virginia, that of the goods and chattels of J. R. deceased, in the hands of B. R., executor (or *administrator*, as the case may be,) of the said J. R. deceased, to be administered, you cause to be made in your district, the sum of ——— dollars, with interest thereon from the ——— day of ——— 18—, till paid, which A. B. recovered before me, by a warrant against the said B. R. as executor (or *administrator*) of the said J. R. deceased, and also ——— dollars, which were adjudged to the said A. B. for his costs in prosecuting his said warrant. Given under my hand, this ——— day of ——— 18—.

J. T., J. P.

(No. 21.)

Form of Application to a Justice for a summons against the debtor and creditor, in an execution which has been levied on the property claimed by another.

To J. T., a Justice for the County of ———— :

The petition of G. H. of the said County, represents, that an execution awarded by you (or if by another Justice, say *by J. K., another Justice of the said County*,) upon a judgment rendered by you (or *by him*, as the case may be,) upon a warrant in favour of A. B. against C. D., for the sum of ———— dollars, has been levied on (here describe the property) by X. Y., a Constable of the said County, who has advertised the same to be sold on the ———— day of ———— 18—, to satisfy the said execution ; that the said (here mention the property,) is the property of your petitioner, and is now claimed by him, and not of greater value than twenty dollars, and ought not to be sold to satisfy the said execution : Your petitioner therefore asks you to award him a summons against both the said A. B. and C. D., returnable in not less than five days from the date thereof, to shew cause why the said property should not be discharged from the said levy.

X. Y.

(No. 22.)

Form of Summons to be awarded by the Justice, upon the above application.

———— County, to wit :

To P. Q., Constable of the said County :

Whereas, it appears to me J. T., a Justice of the said County, upon the application of G. H., that an execution awarded by me (or if by another Justice, say *J. K., a Justice of the said County*,) upon a judgment rendered by me (or *by him*, as the case may be,) on a warrant in favour of A. B. plaintiff, against C. D. defendant, has been levied on (here describe the property) by X. Y., a Constable of the said County, and that the said property is now advertised to be sold by the said Constable, on the ———— day of ———— 18—, to satisfy the said execution ; and whereas the said G. H. claims the said (here insert the property levied on) as his property, and avers that the same is not liable to said execution, and it appearing to me that the said property is not of greater value than twenty dollars : I hereby command you, in the name of the Commonwealth, to summon the said A. B. and C. D., both to appear before me at ————, in the said County, on the ———— day of ———— 18—, (the day fixed must not be less than five, exclusive either of the day when the summons is dated, or the day of its return,) to shew cause why the said (here insert the property) should not be discharged from the said levy. Given under my hand and seal, this ———— day of ———— 18—.

J. T., J. P. [L. S.]

[NOTE.—If the day fixed for the sale, comes earlier than the return day of the summons, the Justice will make this order on the back of the summons :]

I do require and order, that the sale of the within mentioned property, taken to satisfy the within mentioned execution, be postponed until after the ———— day of ———— 18—, (fill these blanks with the return day of the summons.)

J. T., J. P.

(No. 23.)

Form of the Judgment of the Justice in favour of the claimant, upon the above summons.

G. H., plaintiff,
against
A. B. and C. D., defendants.

Upon a summons to shew cause why (state the property) claimed by the said G. H., and which had been levied on to satisfy an execution upon a warrant in favour of the said A. B., against the said C. D., should not be restored to him.

⎱ —— day of —————— 18—:
⎰ The summons in this case being duly executed, as appears by the return of the Constable, upon hearing the parties and the examination of the testimony adduced, I do adjudge that the (describe the property) mentioned in the within summons, is ☞ not liable to the within mentioned execution levied on the same, and I do therefore order and direct the said X. Y. Constable, to restore the said property to the said G. H.; and I do moreover adjudge that the said A. B. pay to the said G. H., the sum of —————— dollars, for his costs by him expended in the prosecution of this summons. Given under my hand, this —— day of —————— 18—.

J. T., J. P.

[NOTE.—If the judgment is against the party claiming the property, follow the above form to the hand, and conclude thus: "is liable to the within mentioned execution, and I do therefore dismiss the complaint and summons of the said G. H.; and do moreover adjudge him to pay to the said A. B. —————— dollars, for his costs expended by him in defending the said summons. Given under my hand, this —— day of —————— 18—.

J. T., J. P.

(No. 24.)

Form of entering an Appeal from the above judgment.

Follow form No. 15.

The appeal must be taken in five days. The Justice must remember, that the presumption of the law is in favour of the levy, and that the burthen of proof is on the party claiming the property, as he holds the affirmative.

For the forms of forthcoming, indemnifying and suspending bonds, to be taken by a Constable, see title BONDS.

(No. 25.)

FORM OF RECORD BOOK OF A JUSTICE.

Record of Judgment rendered by J. T., Justice of —————— County, upon trial of Warrants, and of Executions issued thereon.

PARTIES.	JUDGMENT.				EXECUTION.		
	Date of Judgment.	Am't of Judgment, exclusive of costs.	Interest from.	Costs.	Execution, date of.	Execution, to whom delivered.	Execution, when returnable.
A. B.., *Plff.* v. C. D., *Deft.* Judgment against defendant.	1 Mar. 1849.	15 20	2 Mar. 1848.	$ Cts.	1 Mar. 1849.	T. C., Cons'ble.	20 Apr. 1849.

J. T., J. P., 1st March 1849.

CHAPTER CVII.

WILD FOWL.

By Sec. 19, Chap. 101. If any person, who is not an actual resident of this State, shall shoot at, catch or kill any wild fowl in any waters or on any marshes, islands or beaches within the jurisdiction of the State, below the head of tidewater, he shall forfeit one hundred dollars, one half whereof shall be to the informer.

By Sec. 20. If any person, except from the land, shall shoot at or kill wild fowl during the night, within this State, or if any person shall, from a skiff, or with the aid thereof, within the jurisdiction of the counties of Accomack, Fairfax or Prince William, whether in the night or day time, shoot at or kill wild fowl, he may be convicted thereof before a Justice, and on conviction, shall surrender his gun and any such skiff, and the same shall be forfeited to the Commonwealth. If he fail to surrender them, he shall be committed to jail for thirty days, unless the surrender be sooner made. And if any person offending against this section be not an actual resident of this State, he shall moreover forfeit two hundred dollars.

By Sec. 21. The preceding section shall not apply to any person shooting or using a skiff while hunting wild fowl in a marsh owned by him, nor to any person residing on or near the Potomac, in the county of Westmoreland, or any county below the same, on the Potomac, shooting wild fowl not for sale, but for his own use.

By Sec. 22. If any person shall, at any time, either in the night or day time, shoot at wild fowl in any county bordering on the Potomac, or on the waters of the same, with any gun which cannot be easily discharged from the shoulder at arms length without a rest, a Justice of any such county shall require such gun to be surrendered, and shall order it to be destroyed. If the offender fail to surrender the same, he shall be committed to jail, to remain until discharged by the court of such county.

For the special authority of the Justice to issue warrants against non-residents, and the powers given to the officer executing them, see sections 23, 24, 25, 26 and 27, recited under the head of FISH. The leading object of the law upon the subject of fish, oysters and wild fowl, is to protect our waters from depredation by caterers for foreign markets, and to effect it, the Justice may issue his warrant to apprehend a non-resident person engaged in violating the statute, without mentioning his name, and the officer executing the warrant, may take both the person and the vessel in which he may be employed.

(No. 1.)

Form of Warrant of Arrest againt a non-resident of the Commonwealth, whose name is unknown, for shooting at, catching or killing wild fowl.

———— County, to wit :

To all or any one of the Constables of said County :

Whereas, A. B. of said County, has this day made complaint and affidavit on oath before me J. T., a Justice of the said County, that on the ——— day of ——— 18—, in said County, divers persons then on board of a certain vessel lying in the Potomac river, below the head of the tide water of the said river, and whose names and the name of the said vessel are unknown to the said A. B., but who are now employed on board of the said vessel, and not actual residents of this Commonwealth, did in said river, and below the head of tide water thereof, shoot at, catch and kill certain wild fowl, to wit, wild ducks : These are, therefore, to command you, in the name of the Commonwealth of Virginia, forthwith to go on board of the said vessel, and to apprehend all persons found thereon belonging to and employed on board thereof, and to bring them before me or some other Justice of the said County, to answer the said complaint, and to be farther dealt with according to law ; and I do moreover command you, to take possession of the said vessel, her tackle and appurtenances, and keep the same in your custody until it shall be discharged therefrom by due course of law. Given under my hand and seal, this ——— day of ——— 18—.

J. T., J. P. [L. S.]

(No. 2.)

Form of Warrant of Arrest for shooting wild fowl by a non-resident, whose name is known.

—— County, to wit:
 To X. Y., *Constable of said County:*

Whereas, A. B. of said County, has this day made complaint on oath before me J. T., a Justice of the said County, that C. D., on the —— day of ——— 18—, [in said County, and below the head of tidewater in the Potomac river, (or such other water as may be,) did shoot at (or *catch,* or *kill*) certain wild fowl, to wit, wild ducks, he the said C. D. not then being an actual resident of this Commonwealth:] These are, therefore, in the name of the Commonwealth, to command you forthwith to apprehend the said C. D., and bring him before me or some other Justice of the said County, to answer the said complaint, and to be farther dealt with according to law. Given under my hand and seal, this —— day of ——— 18—.

J. T., *J. P.* [L. S.]

[NOTE.—Upon being arrested, the party, unless discharged by the Justice, should be recognized or committed to answer an indictment for the offence.]

(No. 3.)

Form of Warrant of Arrest for shooting at or killing wild fowl in the night.

—— County, to wit:
 To all or any one of the *Constables of said County:*

Whereas, A. B. of said County, has this day made complaint and information on oath before me J. T., a Justice of the said County, that C. D., on the —— day of ——— 18—, in said County, did, during the night, and not from the land, shoot at (or *kill*) wild fowl, that is to say, wild ducks: These are, therefore, to command you, in the name of the Commonwealth of Virginia, forthwith to apprehend the said C. D., and bring him before me or some other Justice of the said County, to answer the said complaint, and to be farther dealt with according to law. Given under my hand and seal, this —— day of ——— 18—.

J. T., *J. P.* [L. S.]

(No. 4.)

Form of Warrant for shooting wild fowl from a skiff.

[This warrant is only applicable to the counties of Accomack, Fairfax and Prince William.]

—— County, to wit:
 To X. Y., *Constable of said County:*

Whereas, A. B. of said County, has this day made complaint and information on oath before me, J. T., a Justice of the said County, that C. D., on the —— day of ——— 18—, in the said County, [and within the jurisdiction of the said County, did, from a skiff, shoot at, (or *kill*) with a gun, certain wild fowl, to wit, wild ducks:] These are, therefore, in the name of the Commonwealth, to command you, forthwith to apprehend the said C. D., and bring him before me or some other Justice of the said County, to answer the said complaint, and to be farther dealt with according to law. Given under my hand and seal, this —— day of ———— 18—.

J. T., J. P. [L. S.]

Judgment.

In either of the two last cases, the judgment may be in this form : ———— day of ———— 18—, cause heard, and defendant found guilty of shooting at wild fowl, with a gun from a skiff: and I adjudge the said gun (or *gun and skiff*,) to be forfeited to the Commonwealth, and that the defendant pay the costs of prosecution, which I ascertain to be ———— dollars, and order the said C. D. to surrender said gun, (or *gun and skiff*,) and the said C. D. failing to surrender the same, is committed to jail for thirty days.

J. T., J. P.

(No. 5.)

Form of Warrant of Arrest for shooting wild fowl with a gun which cannot conveniently be discharged from the shoulder.

———— County, to wit :

To all or any one of the Constables of said County :

Whereas, A. B. of said County, has this day made complaint and information on oath before me J. T., a Justice of the said County, that C. D., on the —— day of ———— 18—, in said County, did shoot at wild fowl, to wit, wild ducks, with a gun which could not then be conveniently discharged from the shoulder at arms length without a rest : These are, therefore, to command you, in the name of the Commonwealth of Virginia, forthwith to apprehend the said C. D., and bring him before me or some other Justice of the said County, to answer the said complaint, and to be farther dealt with according to law. Given under my hand and seal, this —— day of ———— 18—.

J. T., J. P. [L. S.]

[This warrant only applies to Counties bordering on the Potomac or its waters.]

(No. 6.)

Form of Mittimus for failing to surrender the gun, &c.

———— County, to wit :

To X. Y., Constable of said County, and to the Keeper of the Jail of the said County :

Whereas, C. D. was, upon the testimony of A. B. on oath, this day committed by me J. T., a Justice of the said County, for shooting at wild fowl in said County, [in the night, and was ordered by me to surrender the said gun, which he failed to do :] These are, therefore, in the name of the Commonwealth, to command you, the said Constable, to convey the said C. D. to the jail of the said County, and there deliver him, with this warrant, to the keeper of the said jail. And you, the keeper of the said jail, are hereby commanded to receive into your jail and custody the said C. D., and him safely keep for thirty days from the date hereof, unless in the mean time he surrender the said gun. Given under my hand and seal, this —— day of ———— 18—.

J. T., J. P. [L. S.]

If the offence be for shooting from a skiff, leave out all in brackets, and insert this: "with a gun, from a skiff, in the jurisdiction of Accomack, (or *Fairfax*, or *Prince William*,) and was ordered by me to surrender the said gun and skiff, which he failed to do: These" &c.

WEAPONS—(CONCEALED.)

For carrying of, see SURETY OF THE PEACE.

CHAPTER CVIII.

WILLS.

BY SEC. 29, CHAP. 192. If a free person fraudulently destroy or conceal any will or codicil, with intent to prevent the probat thereof, he shall be confined in the penitentiary not less than two nor more than five years.

(No. 1.)

Form of Warrant of Arrest for concealing or destroying a will to prevent the probat thereof.

———— County, to wit:

To all or any one of the Constables of said County:

Whereas, A. B. of said County, has this day made complaint and information on oath before me J. T., a Justice of the said County, that C. D., on the —— day of ———— 18—, in said County, did feloniously and fraudulently destroy (or *conceal*) the will of T. T., deceased, with intent to prevent the probat thereof: These are, therefore, to command you, in the name of the Commonwealth of Virginia, forthwith to apprehend the said C. D., and bring him before me or some other Justice of the said County, to answer the said complaint, and to be farther dealt with according to law. Given under my hand and seal, this —— day of ———— 18—.

J. T., J. P. [L. S.]

(No. 2.)

Form of Mittimus where a party is committed for examination or trial in the County Court, for concealing or destroying a will.

——— County, to wit:

To X. Z., Constable of said County, and to the Keeper of the Jail of said County:

These are to command you the said Constable, in the name of the Commonwealth of Virginia, forthwith to convey and deliver into the custody of the keeper of the said jail, together with this warrant, the body of C. D., a white person (or *free negro*, or *a slave, the property of E. F.*, as the case may be,) charged before me J. T., a Justice of the said County, on the oath of A. B., with a felony by him committed, in this, that the said C. D., on the ——— day of ——— in the year 18—, in the said County, (here describe the offence as in the warrant of arrest.) And you, the said keeper of the said jail, are hereby required to receive the said C. D. into your jail and custody, that he may be examined (or *tried*) for the said offence by the County Court of said County, and him there safely keep until he shall be discharged by due course of law. Given under my hand and seal, this ——— day of ——— in the year 18—.

J. T., J. P. [L. S.]

[NOTE.—If the prisoner be a white person, he must be committed for examination; if he be a negro, commit him for trial.]

———

(No. 3.)

Form of Certificate of Commitment to be sent to the Clerk of the County Court.

——— County, to wit:

To the Clerk of the County Court of said County:

I, J. T., a Justice of the said County, do hereby certify, that I have, by my warrant, this day committed C. D. (if free negro or slave, state which) to the jail of this County, that he may be examined (or *tried*) before the County Court of the said County, for a felony by him committed, in this, that he did, on the ——— day of ——— 18—, in the said County, (here state the offence as in the mittimus.) Given under my hand, this ——— day of ——— in the year 18—.

J. T., J. P.

———

(No. 4.)

Form of Certificate to the Clerk where party is admitted to bail.

Turn to head of ARREST, and follow No. 6.

(No. 5.)

Form of Recognizance of Bail.

Turn to head of RECOGNIZANCE, and follow No. 1, if person be free; No. 2, if a slave, and state succinctly the offence for which the person is recognized.

(No. 6.)

Form of Recognizance of Witness to appear before the County Court to give evidence upon the examination or trial of a party charged with felony.

Turn to head of RECOGNIZANCE, and follow No. 3.

WITNESSES.

For subpœnas for, see EVIDENCE and WARRANTS.

INDEX.

ABDUCTION.
Abduction of females and children for purpose of marriage or defilement, statutory provision concerning, 17; of infants with view to extort money, &c., a felony by statute, 19. See *Arrest Warrants*.

ABORTION.
Infant in its mother's womb not subject of murder, 23; statutory provision concerning abortion, 23; in what offence consists, 23. See *Arrest Warrants*.

ACCESSARIES.
Who are accessaries, 27; accessary before the fact, 27; how punishable, 26; accessary after the fact, 27; how punishable, 26; who *not* accessary after the fact, 26; accessary amenable, whether principal be convicted or not, 26; may be indicted either with principal or separately, 26; warrants of arrest against accessary before the fact, 28, 29; same against accessary after the fact, 29; forms of mittimus, certificate and indictment against accessaries before and after the fact, 29, 30, 31, 32.

ADULTERY.
Adultery defined, 33; distinguished from *fornication*, 33; penalty for, 33. See *Arrest Warrants*.

AIDERS AND ABETTORS.
See *Accessaries*.

ANIMALS.
Cruelty to, 39. See *Arrest Warrants*.

APPEALS.
See *Fines and Convictions*, and *Warrants—(Civil.)*

APPRENTICES.
How bound, 40; to what age, 40; reciprocal duties of master and apprentice, 41, 42; indenture by overseers of the poor, 44; indenture by father, when apprentice under age of fourteen years, 45; indenture when apprentice is fourteen, 46; written consent of apprentice, 46; bond by master for payment of money to guardian, &c., 45.

ARREST.
Arrest defined, 55; who may issue warrant of arrest, 47; mode of proceeding in granting warrant, 47-50; when officer may pursue offender from one county into another, 47; his course of proceeding, 47; how offender let to bail, 47, 48; adjournment of examination from day to day, 48; justice's duty on party failing to appear, 47; commitment of offender, 48; justice's duty, when offender brought before him, 48; when justice shall discharge, 49; when commit or bail, 49; when commit for examination, 49; when for trial, 49; duty of justice to certify commitment, 49; may associate one or more justices on examination, 49; when prisoner, for assault, &c., may be discharged, 49; how complaint for arrest should be framed, 50; should be reduced to writing, 51; may generally be preferred by any person, 50; not by persons disqualified as witnesses, 50; what proof should be furnished, 50, 51; error of justice not to render him liable, 51; who liable to arrest for crime, 55; arrest before indictment in cases of treason, felony, &c., 56; where arrest to be made, 56; manner of making arrest, 56; what authorizes arrest, 56; if by warrant to officer, what his duty and what his power, 56, 57; what warrant should shew on its face, 57; private individual should shew warrant, if demanded, 57; and so with officers where not commonly known, 57; safest course, 57; generally officers not bound to part with warrant, 57; exceptions to this rule, 57; where party is already in prison on civil or criminal suit, 58; after arrest, officer's duty to bring party before justice, 58; prisoner permitted to go at large after arrest, 58, 59; party returning into custody, 59; when justice may arrest without warrant, 59; when he must issue warrant, 59; sheriff's power to arrest for felony, without warrant, 59; in capital offences may arrest on suspicion, 59; his authority when assaulted, 59; duty of magistrate having personal knowledge of offence, 59, 60; private individual's duty when offence committed in his presence, 60; after indictment found, private individual may arrest, 61. See *Breaking Doors, Coroner* and *Constable.*

ARREST WARRANTS AND INDICTMENTS—(*Forms of.*)
General form of arrest warrant, 73; commencement and conclusion of indictments, 382.
Forms of arrest warrants and indictments for following offences, viz:
ABDUCTION. Warrant for taking away female over age of 12 years, with intent to marry or defile her, 19; indictment for same, 22; warrant for taking away white female over 12, with intent to cause her to be married or defiled, 19; warrant for taking child under 12, for purpose of prostitution, &c., 20; indictment for same, 22; warrant for taking away another's child, for purpose of extorting money, 20; indictment for same, 22.
ABORTION. Arrest warrant for, 23; indictment, 25.
ACCESSARIES. See *Accessaries*, p. 1, of this index.
ADULTERY AND FORNICATION. Arrest warrant, 33.
AFFRAYERS. Arrest warrant, 37.
ANIMALS. Arrest warrant for cruelly beating and torturing a horse, 39.
ASSAULT. Arrest warrant for, 85; indictment, 86; indictment for assault upon a constable in execution of his office, 87; indictment for assault with intent to kill, 87; same for an assault to commit rape or to rob, 87.
BANKS. Warrant against member or agent of an unchartered bank for carrying on banking, 115; same for unlawfully issuing note with intent to create a circulating medium, 116; same for bringing into this state a bank note of lower denomination than five dollars, with intent to put it in circulation, 116; same for passing a note of less denomination than five dollars issued by bank of another state, 117.
BASTARDY. Warrant against putative father of bastard child, 121; proceedings after arrest, 121, 122.
BIGAMY. Warrant for bigamy, 123; indictment, 125.
BRIBERY AND CORRUPTION. Warrant for offering to bribe a judge, 136; indictment for endeavouring to bribe constable, 137.
BURGLARY. Warrant for burglary, upon positive charge, 144; warrant for burglary, upon belief, 145; indictment, 146.
BURIAL OF DEAD. Warrant for disinterring dead body, 147; of a slave, 148; of a free person, 148.
BURNING. Warrant for burning dwelling house in night time, 154; indictment for same, 162; warrant for burning dwelling house in day time, 155; same for setting fire to outbuilding in night time whereby dwelling house is burnt in night time, 155; indictment for same, 162; warrant for setting fire to outbuilding in day time whereby dwelling house is burnt in day time, 155; same for burning a prison or jail in night, 155; indictment for same, 162; warrant for burning a meeting house, 156; indictment for same, 162; warrant for burning a banking house, &c., of value of 1000 dollars, 156; same for setting fire to any thing whereby a storehouse with property therein contained of value of 1000 dollars, is burnt, 157; indictment for same, 163; warrant for burning a barn, &c., of value of 100 dollars, 157; same against party for burning his own house to defraud insurers, 158; indictment for same, 163; warrant for burning bridge, &c., of value of 100 dollars, 158; same for unlawfully setting fire to woods, &c., 158.
CATTLE. Warrant for driving distempered cattle through the state, 165.
CHEATS. Warrant for selling by false weights, 168; indictment for same 161.
COLLEGES. Warrant for trading with a student of an incorporated college, 170; indictment for same, 170.
CONSPIRACY. Warrant for a conspiracy to charge a man with felony, 173; same by persons confined in jail to make their escape, 174; indictment for same, 175; warrant for a conspiracy to engross article of trade, 174; indictment for same, 176; same for conspiracy among workmen to raise wages, and lessen time of labour, 174; same for conspiracy to defraud an illiterate person by falsely reading to him a deed of bargain and sale as and for a bond of indemnity, 175.
CONVEYANCES—(*Public.*) Warrant against driver of stage coach for injuring person by negligently driving, 177; indictment for same, 179; warrant against conductor of railroad car for injuring a person by negligent management, 177; indictment for same, 179.
DUELLING. Warrant against parties suspected by justice of being about to engage in a duel, 217; same against same, upon information, 217.
EMBEZZLEMENT. Warrant for embezzlement of bank notes and money by officer of incorporated bank, 223; same for embezzlement of property

by clerk or agent of incorporated company, 224; indictment for same, 226; warrant for embezzlement by common carrier, 224; same against clerk of bank for fraudulent entries in accounts kept by him as clerk, 225; indictment against public officer for embezzlement, 227.

ESCAPES. Warrant against person convicted of felony for breaking jail and escaping, 232; indictment for same, 236; same against party charged with felony for breaking jail, 237; warrant against person convicted of misdemeanor for breaking jail, 232; same for conveying instruments to person convicted of or charged with felony, 233; indictment for same, 238; warrant against party escaping and the person aiding him, 233; same against jailor for voluntary escape, 234.

EXTORTION. Warrant against officer for demanding a greater fee than is allowed by law, 263; same against sheriff for same, 263; same against a clerk for issuing fee bill for services not performed, 264; same against clerk for issuing fee bill for more than legal fee, 264; indictment against constable for extortion, 265.

FALSE PRETENCES, &c. Warrant of arrest for obtaining goods under, 270; indictment for, 274; warrant of arrest for obtaining money by, 271; same for obtaining money under false pretences of drawing an order, 271; same for obtaining property by false token, 272; same for obtaining a signature to a receipt by, 272; same for obtaining property by false personation, 272.

FELONIES, (*Compounding or Concealing of.*) Warrant for compounding and concealing murder, 276; same for concealment only, 276; same for compounding and concealing larceny, 277; indictment for compounding felony, 278.

FINES AND SUMMARY CONVICTIONS. See below *Slaves, &c.*

FISH. Warrant for hauling a seine below the mouth of a river or in the waters of Northampton after 1st June and before 1st September, 301; same for setting a weir in the waters of Accomack, 301; same for fishing with gill nets in the Potomac, 302; same for fishing with nets or seines in the Potomac river, 303; same for obstructing right of fishing, 303; same for hauling, &c. seine so as to obstruct passage of fish in waters of this state, 303; same against a non-resident for fishing, under 9th, 304; same for fishing in Ohio river by non-residents, 304.

FORESTALLING, &c. Warrant of arrest for, 307; same for regrating, 307; indictment for regrating, 309.

FORGERY. Warrant for forging and uttering a bank note, 319; same for uttering and employing as true a counterfeit bank note, 319; same for forging and uttering a check, 320; same for forging acceptance of bill of exchange, 320; same for forging promissory note, 320; indictment for, 321; warrant for forging a bond, 321; same for forging a receipt, 321; same for forging an order and for uttering it as true, 322; same for forging a will, 322; same for forging a certificate of acknowledgment of a deed, 322; same for having ten forged bank notes in possession at the same time, 323; same for counterfeiting coin, 323; same for uttering counterfeit coin, 324; same for having ten pieces of base coin in possession at same time, 324; same for fraudulently making a note purporting to be the note of a bank not in existence, 324; same for engraving a plate for forging bank notes, 325; same for making a puncheon for the false making of coin, 325; indictment for forging a promissory note and endorsement thereon, and for uttering and attempting to employ the same as true, 327; same for making instruments adapted to making base coin, 328; same for forging a certificate of a justice of the peace, 329; same for uttering a forged instrument, 329.

FUGITIVES FROM JUSTICE. Warrant to arrest fugitive from justice on the oath of a complainant, 334; same upon an indictment found, 335.

GAMING. Warrant against exhibitors of faro bank, A B C or E O tables, 339; warrant to seize money exhibited at gaming table and to seize and burn the table, 340.

HARBOUR MASTERS. Warrant of arrest against master of a vessel, for failing to obey directions of harbour master, 343; same against harbour master for failing to do his duty as such, 344.

HEALTH—(*Public.*) Warrant for selling unwholesome provisions, 345; same for adulterating liquors, 345; same for fraudulent adulteration of medicine, 345.

HOMICIDE. Warrant for murder, 361; indictment for murder by shooting, 363; indictment for murder by stabbing, 363; indictment for murder by poison, 364.

HOUSEBREAKING. Warrant of arrest for entering a dwelling house in night without breaking, or for breaking and entering same in day, with intent to commit murder, 369; warrant of arrest for entering a dwelling house in night without breaking, or for breaking and entering in day, with intent to commit rape or robbery, 370; warrant of arrest for entering dwelling house in night with intent to commit larceny, or for breaking and entering same in day time, with like intent, 370; warrant of arrest for entering in night a storehouse adjoining a dwelling house, and stealing therefrom, 371; warrant of arrest for breaking and entering in day an outhouse adjoining to and occupied with dwelling house, and stealing therefrom, 371; warrant of arrest for breaking and entering an office, shop, storehouse, &c., not adjoining to or occupied with dwelling house, 372; warrant of arrest for breaking and entering meeting house, and stealing therefrom, 372; indictment for entering dwelling house in night without breaking, or for breaking and entering in day time and stealing therein, 374; same for breaking and entering in day time an outhouse adjoining dwelling house, with intent to steal, 374; same for entering in night without breaking a storehouse not adjoining dwelling house, 374.

INCEST. See *Marriage*.

INDECENCY—(*Public*.) Warrant for selling obscene books or prints, 378; indictment for publishing obscene print, 378.

KIDNAPPING, &c. Warrant for selling free person as slave, 385; same for kidnapping free person, 385; indictment for kidnapping free person, with intent to use or sell him as slave, and for selling him as slave, 387.

LARCENY. Warrant for stealing goods, 394; indictment for same, 399; warrant for stealing two or more articles belonging to different persons, at the same time, 394; indictment for same, 399; warrant for stealing two or more bank notes, 395; indictment for same, 400; warrant for stealing coin, 395; indictment for same, 400; warrant for stealing a bill of exchange, 396; same for stealing a promissory note, single bill or bond, 396; indictment for same, 400; warrant for horse stealing, 396; same for stealing a slave, 397; indictment for same, 401; warrant for stealing things annexed to freehold, 397; indictment for same, 401.

LEWDNESS. Warrant for open and gross lewdness, 406; warrant for keeping house of ill fame, 406; same for lascivious cohabitation, 407; indictment for lewd and lascivious cohabitation, 408.

LOTTERIES. Warrant for selling lottery tickets, 412; indictment for selling lottery ticket, 413; same for exhibiting sign or other emblematical representation of lottery, 413.

MAIMING. Warrant for unlawfully biting off ear or nose, 427; same for, by cutting, shooting, stabbing or wounding, or in the commission of felony, 427; indictment for same, 431; warrant for causing bodily injury by cutting, &c., 428; indictment for same, 431; warrant for shooting at person in street in town, 428; same for shooting at person in any other public place, 428.

MARRIAGE. Warrant for incest, 433; same against clerk for issuing license contrary to law, 433; same against white person for intermarrying with negro, 434; same for performing marriage ceremony between white person and negro, 434; indictment for solemnizing marriage between white persons without lawful authority, 435.

NEGROES. See title *Negroes*.

NUISANCES. Warrant for obstructing highway, 480; indictment for same, 482; warrant for keeping disorderly house generally, 480; indictment for, 482; warrant for keeping common gaming house, 480; warrant against keeper of common tippling house, where free negroes and slaves assemble to tipple, 481; indictment for, 483.

OYSTERS AND TERRAPINS. Warrant against non-resident for taking oysters in waters of the state, 488; same for catching oysters with drag and other instrument than oyster tongs, 489; same for exporting oysters not pickled or planted, between 1st of May and 1st of September, without license, 489; same for taking or catching oysters, for purpose of exportation, after 1st of May and before 1st of September, 489; same for buying or selling, receiving on board of a vessel, &c., oysters not pickled or planted, &c., after 1st of May and before 1st of September, 490; warrant against non-resident, whose name is unknown, for taking or buying, &c., oysters on board of vessel, for exportation, 490; warrant for catching, &c., from their natural beds and shoals, over fifty bushels in one day, 491; warrant for taking terrapins or taking terrapin eggs, 491; warrant for taking oysters for purpose of converting into lime, 491;

warrant for catching clams on York river or on Egg island flats, 492; same for taking or selling planted oysters, 492.

PERJURY. Warrant for perjury upon trial of an indictment for felony, 506; warrant for perjury, 506; indictment for felonious perjury, 509; same for subornation of perjury, on trial of one indicted for felony, 509; same for perjury, committed on trial of civil suit, 510.

QUARANTINE. Warrant against master of vessel for refusing to answer enquiries of health officer, 529; same against master of vessel ordered to perform quarantine, for failing to deliver his bills of health, &c., to officer, 529.

RAPE. Warrant for rape on a woman, 537; indictment for same, 540; warrant for carnal knowledge and abuse of a girl under age of 12 years, 538; indictment for, 540; warrant against negro for rape committed on negro, 538; same against negro for carnally knowing and abusing negro girl under age of 12 years, 538; indictment for carnally knowing and abusing female child under age of 12 years, 540; same against free negro for rape on white woman, 541; same against free negro for assault on white female, with intent to ravish her, 541.

REBELLION. See title *Negroes.*

RECEIVING STOLEN GOODS. Warrant for feloniously receiving stolen goods, 544; indictment for, 547; warrant for feloniously receiving stolen bank note, 545; indictment for, 548; warrant for feloniously receiving coin, 545; same for aiding in concealing stolen goods, 545.

RECORDS. Warrant against clerk for making false entry in, 560; same for erasing or altering record, 561; same for stealing, secreting or destroying public record, 561.

RELIGIOUS ASSEMBLIES. See *Sabbath Day.*

RIOTS, &c. Warrant for riotously destroying house, 576; same for riotously assembling and committing assault, 576; indictment for a riot, 579; same for riot and assault, 579; same for riot and pulling down a dwelling house, 579.

ROBBERY. Warrant for robbery, 595.

SABBATH DAY. Warrant for disturbing religious meeting, 602; indictment for interrupting and disturbing public worship, 604; same for keeping an open shop on Lord's day, 604.

SEAMAN. Warrant to arrest seaman for deserting vessel, 606; same against master of vessel for putting on shore disabled seaman, 607; same for failing to bury person who has died on board of vessel, 607.

SHIPS. Warrant for maliciously burning vessel of value of 100 dollars, 614; same where vessel of less value than 100 dollars, 614; same for wilfully destroying vessel, with intent to injure owner thereof or the insurers, 615; same for same, with intent to injure property on board thereof, 615; same for entering vessel in night without breaking, with intent to commit murder, &c., 615; same for breaking and entering vessel with same intent, 616; same for entering vessel in night or for breaking and entering it either in day or night, with intent to steal and stealing therefrom, 616; indictment for maliciously burning vessel, 618.

SMALL POX, &c. Warrant against party bringing small pox into the state, 620. See title *Small Pox.*

SODOMY AND BESTIALITY. Warrant for, 623; indictment for same, 625; warrant for sodomy committed with a boy, 623; indictment for same, 625.

THREATS, &c. Warrant for threatening to accuse another of crime and thereby extorting money, 646; same for obtaining money by threatening to injure character, 646.

TOBACCO. Warrant against inspector for issuing receipt for tobacco not received into warehouse, 648; same against, for issuing two receipts for same tobacco, 649; same against, for reissuing tobacco note, 649.

TREASON. Warrant for, in levying war, 651; same for instigation of, 652; same for conspiring with slaves to rebel, 652.

TRESPASS—(*Wilful.*) Warrant for injuring or disfiguring a horse, 654; same for injuring a dam, 654; same for injuring machinery of water mill, 655; same for defacing a church, 655; same for injuring telegraph fixtures, 655; same for cutting forest trees, 656; same for carrying away wood and timber already cut, 656; same for cutting down trees growing for ornament, 657; same for injuring fruit trees, 657; same for breaking down and injuring fence, 657; same for cutting and destroying line tree, 658; same for digging up and carrying away stone, &c., from land of another, 658; same for breaking a window and severing it from freehold, 659; same for breaking and defacing mile stone or sign post, 659; indictment for cutting down trees, growing for

ornament, 661; same for defacing and breaking mile stone, 661.
UNLAWFUL ASSEMBLY. See *Riots.*
WILD FOWL. Warrant against non-resident whose name is unknown, for shooting at wild fowl, &c., 681; same where name is known, 682; same for shooting at or killing wild fowl in night, 682; same for shooting wild fowl from skiff, 682; same for shooting wild fowl with a gun not conveniently discharged from shoulder, 683.
WEAPONS—(*Concealed.*) See title *Surety of Peace.*
WILLS. Warrant for concealing or destroying will to prevent probat, 684.
For warrant by coroner, see 190.

ASSAULT AND BATTERY.
What constitutes assault and battery, 82, 83; when justifiable, 84, 85; See *Arrest Warrants.*

ATTACHMENTS
Against non-residents, statute, 88; when defendant is removing his effects out of state before judgment can be obtained, 88, 89; when debtor is removing or intends to remove his effects, 89; against vessels, &c., in certain waters, 89; to whom directed and how returnable, 89, 90; how executed, 90; in equity, when granted and how proceeded in, 91; effect of levy of, 91; how property levied on may be replevied, 91, 92; how property disposed of after levy, 92, 93; garnishees how proceeded with, 90, 93; order of publication in, 93; defence to, when and how made, 94; how claim to or lien on property attached, to be made, and proceedings in relation thereto, 94, 95; priority of lien, 95; how debtor may appear and open case, 95; for debts under $20, 96; forms of attachments for debts under twenty dollars, 97-99; attachment bond may be given by one not a party, 96; forms of attachments by justices, 97-100; forthcoming bond taken in, 101; forms of attachments by clerks, 101-105; attachment bonds by clerk, 106; forms of bonds taken by justice, 107, 108; form of replevy bond, 108; forms of judgments, 108, 109; attachment for rent when, by whom, and how issued, 567; form of, where tenant will or is removing effects, 568; form of, where tenant is removing effects, 568; bond by landlord on attachment for rent, 569; replevy bond by tenant on levy of attachment for rent, 570.

ATTEMPT TO COMMIT CRIME.
When felony and when misdemeanor, and how punished, 110; when justice to commit for examination or trial, and when to recognize to answer indictment for, 110. See *Arrest Warrants.*

BAIL.
What it is, 70; when allowed, 70. See *Arrest.*

BANKS.
Who not to trade as a bank, 115; penalty for issuing or passing note without authority of law, 115; who not to pass note issued in another state of less denomination than five dollars, 115. See *Arrest Warrants.*

BARRATRY.
Barratry, maintenance and champerty defined, 118, 119.

BASTARDY.
How accusation made and by whom, 119; justice's duty, 119; recognizance to be taken, 119; woman a competent witness, 120; party accused may be examined, 120; if accused found guilty to pay for maintenance of child, bond required, 120; failing to give bond for payment, may be committed to jail, 120; motion upon bond, 120; warrant to arrest father of bastard child, 121; recognizance to overseer of poor, 121; mittimus, 122.

BIGAMY.
Defined, 122; punishment for, 122; when person may marry second time, 122; what evidence on charge of bigamy, 123. See *Arrest Warrants.*

BOAT.
See *Estrays.*

BONDS.
Statutory provisions in relation to, 126-129; sheriff, &c., levying fieri facias or distress warrant may take forthcoming bond, 126; bond to be returned to clerk of court, 126; clerk to endorse date of return, 126; for what obligors in forfeited bond liable, 126; defence on motion on bond under distress warrant, 126; remedy of obligee against debtor not lost, if bond quashed, 126; when forthcoming bond not to be taken, 126, 127; when clerk's duty to endorse, "no security to be taken," 127; trial of title to property under execution or distress warrant, 127; same when property of more value than twenty dollars taken under warrant of distress or execution issued by justice, 127, 128; officer requiring indemnifying bond to give notice, 128; if indemnifying bond not given, officer may refuse to levy, 128; where indemnifying bond given when no levy, or after levy made, bond to be re-

INDEX.   693

turned to clerk's office, 128; liability of officer on taking bond, 128; form of forthcoming bond on distress for rent, 129; indemnifying bond taken on distress, 129; forthcoming bond under fi. fa., 130; indemnifying bond under levy of fi. fa., 131; forthcoming bond under fi. fa. by a justice, 131; indemnifying bond under same, 132; bond for suspending sale, upon levy of fi. fa. issued by justice, 133; bond for suspending sale, after indemnifying bond, upon levy of fi. fa. by sheriff, 133; bond for suspending sale on same upon levy of distress warrant, 134.

BOOKS.
See *Indecency* and *Nuisance*.

BREAKING DOORS.
For purpose of arresting felon, what course before breaking doors, 62; when doors may be broken without warrant, 62; how by constable, 62, 63; when by private individual, how justified, 61; when under a warrant justifiable after notification, &c., 63; after indictment party may be arrested wherever found, 66. See *Arrest*.

BRIBERY AND CORRUPTION.
Bribery defined, 135; statutory provisions, 135, 136; penalty on person offering bribe, 135; penalty on officer receiving bribe, 135. See *Arrest Warrants*.

BUGGERY.
See *Sodomy*.

BURGLARY.
Burglary defined, 138; what constitutes *breaking*, 139, 140; what constitutes *entering*, 141; what is the *mansion house*, 142; definition of *night*, 143; what the intent, 144; how punished, 158. See *Arrest Warrants*.

BURIAL OF THE DEAD.
Disinterment of dead a misdemeanor at common law, 147; punishment for, under statute, 147. See *Arrest Warrants*.

BURNING.
Statutory provisions relating to *felonious burning*, 149, 150; burning houses under this statute, considered, 150, 151; what constitutes a *burning*, 151; firing must be malicious, 151; "the house" what, 152; "house of another" defined, 152; not felony in wife to burn house of husband, 153; "public buildings," how laid in indictment, 153; fifth section of statute considered, 153; "stack" defined, 153; burning bridges a common law a misdemeanor, 153; offence by statute, 150, 153; value of bridge should be stated, 154. See *Arrest Warrants*.

CATTLE—(*Distempered*.)
Statutory provisions in relation to, 164; form of proceedings, 164, 165, 166; order of justice to kill distempered cattle, 166.

CERTIFICATES.
See forms of certificate under each head of offence.

CHEATS.
What cheats are misdemeanors, 166; cheat, to evade public justice by fraudulent means, 166; so is a fraud committed by public officers, 167; apprentice enlisting as soldier without consent of master, 167; selling by false weights and measures, 167; false token, 167; telling a mere lie to cheat, not indictable, 167. See *False Pretences* and *Arrest Warrants*. For forms of warrants, &c., see index, *Warrants*.

COLLEGES.
Penalty for selling, &c., to students, 169; special provision as to agent and principal, 169; proviso as to person selling with expectation of immediate payment, 169; free person violating first section, fined, 169; and compelled to give sureties, &c., 170. For forms of warrants, see index, *Warrants*.

COMMITMENT.
Order superseding commitment to be delivered to jailor, 50. See *Arrest*.

CONSPIRACY.
What is a conspiracy, 171; conspiracy to raise or depress price of labour a misdemeanor, 171; what completes offence of conspiracy, 172; merger of conspiracy in felony, if felony actually committed, 172; if one of two indicted for conspiracy be acquitted, both must be, 173; a person joining conspiracy after it is formed, equally guilty, 173. See index, *Warrants*.

CONSTABLES.
Constable may arrest for treason, &c., committed in his view, 60; in case of affray in his presence, his duty, 60; when he may justify an arrest, without warrant, though offence not committed in view, 60. See *Officers*.

CONVEYANCES.
When drivers and conductors of, guilty of misdemeanor for negligence, 177.

CONVICTS.
Penalty for bringing persons convicted of felony into this state, 180; forms of proceeding, 180.

CORONERS.
Warrant to summon inquest, 183; proclamation by constable, 189; foreman's oath, 184; proclamation, 189; oath of witness, 190; summons for witness, 190; warrant against wit-

ness for refusing to obey summons, 190; arrest warrant by coroner, 190; form of commitment by, 190; recognizance of witness taken by, 191.

COSTS.

Witnesses' attendance, 192; fees of sheriff, sergeant or coroner, 193, 194; coroner's and constable's fees, 194; to whom fees chargeable, 195; clerk's fee book, 195.

COURTS.

Warrant to summon examining court, where prisoner committed to jail, 205; warrant to summon examining court, where prisoner let to bail, 206; recognizance of bail to appear before special session of examining court, 206; same of witness, 207; form of record of court of examination, for felony, 207; same on trial of free negro for felony other than homicide or capital felony, 208; same of slave for felony, 209; warrant by two justices to transfer prisoner from county jail to jail of circuit court, 210.

CRIME.

Who are incapable of committing from want of will, occasioned by infancy, 9; because non compos mentis, 10; subjection to power of others, 13; from ignorance, 14; what are felonies, 15; what misdemeanors, 15.

DEAD BODIES.

See *Burial, &c.*

DEER.

Killing wild deer, when prohibited, 211; shooting tame deer, 211; summons for killing wild deer, 211; form of conviction, 211.

DOGS.

What dogs to be killed, 212: penalty on owner concealing them, 212; fee for killing, 212; penalty for failing to execute order of justice to kill, 212; order of justice to kill dog bitten by mad dog, &c., 212; summons for concealing dog, 212.

DRUNKENNESS.

Penalty for drunkenness, &c., 213; summons for swearing and drunkenness, 213; form of judgment, 213.

DUELLING.

Duelling defined, 214; survivor guilty of murder, 214; fighting duel a misdemeanor at common law, 214; a challenge the same, 214; messenger's guilt, 214; statutory provisions, 214, 215; warrant to arrest granted on suspicion, 215, 216; what good cause of suspicion, 216. See *Arrest Warrants.*

EMBEZZLEMENT.

Embezzlement defined, 219; distinction between larceny and embezzlement, 219; what embezzlement felony, 219, 220; what constitutes, and who may be guilty of embezzlement, 220, 221, 222; person embezzling *halves* of bank notes, how indicted, 223. See *Intent* and *Arrest Warrants.*

ESCAPES.

Escape defined, 228; what prison breaking and what rescue, 228; what voluntary escapes and when officer liable for, 230; what a negligent escape and how punished, 230, 231; retaking, when escape voluntary, 231; when negligent, 231, 232; justice's warrant to retake, how to run and be executed, 232; essential of warrant, 232.

ESCHEATS.

Duties of escheators up to conclusion of inquisition of escheat, 239, 240; form of order to summon inquest upon information of commissioner of revenue, 240; same upon written information of another, 240; form of subpœna by escheator, 241; oath administered to jurors, 241; form of inquisition, 242.

ESTRAYS.

How taken up and mode of procedure, 243; warrant to freeholder to appraise estrays, 244; oath of viewers, 244; certificate of, 244; warrant to assess compensation for keeping estrays, 245; certificate of assessors, 245.

EVIDENCE.

Parol evidence, 246; of competency of witnesses, 246; in Virginia witnesses not incapacitated by reason of religious belief, 246; on voir dire no questions touching religious opinions can be asked, 246; idiots and lunatics incompetent, 246; child's incompetency not governed by age but understanding, 246; when negro and indian competent witnesses, 246; incompetency from interest, 247; what kind of interest disqualifies, 247, 248; a release of interest restores competency, 248; husband and wife incompetent for or against each other, except in particular cases, 248; incompetency from infamy, 246; how infamy to be shewn, 248; objection to competency, how to be made, 249; examination of witness, 250; how sworn, 250; evidence confined to issue, 250, 253-4; what questions witness not bound to answer, 250; how witness's credit impeached, 250; a party cannot discredit his own witness, 251; dying declarations how admitted and when, 251; only admissible when death of deceased subject

INDEX. 695

of charge, 251; between husband and wife, 252; confessions and admissions must be free and voluntary, 252; hearsay evidence when admissible, 252-3; subscribing witness, 255; when his attendance dispensed with, 255; contents of written instrument how proven, 255; best evidence must be produced, and what *best*, 257; what allegations must be proved and what a variance, 257, 258; rule that affirmative must be proved and exceptions to it, 258; how attendance of witness enforced, 258, 259; witness's privilege as to arrest, 259; summons for witness in criminal prosecution, 260; warrant to bring witness who has refused to attend, 260; commitment of witness on civil warrant, 261; commitment of witness refusing to recognize with surety to give evidence, 261.

EXAMINATION.

By justice after arrest of complainant and witnesses, should be *on oath* in presence of party charged, 67; of justice's power to continue examination, how and for what time it may be done, 67; where jail is near, proper to commit to jail by warrant, where not, may be detained in custody by officer or committed to some near and safe place, 67.

EXTORTION.

Extortion defined, 262; statutory provision, 262. See *Arrest Warrants*.

FALSE PRETENCES AND FALSE TOKENS.

Statutory provisions, 266; false token defined, 266; counterfeit letters, 266; false pretence, 267; discussed, 268; what the intent, 268; sundry instances of these offences, 268, 269, 270.

FELONIES.

What a felony, 15; compounding or concealing of, 276. See *Arrest Warrants*.

FINES AND SUMMARY CONVICTIONS.

Statutory provisions, 279, 280; if offence not limited to twenty dollars, justice has no jurisdiction, if, over twenty, 280-81; proceedings preliminary to conviction, 281; conviction, 284, 285; proceedings subsequent to conviction, 285, 286, 287; form of complaint to justice of offence committed by negro, where punishment is corporeal, 287; arrest warrant against slave or free negro for petit larceny, 287; same against slave or free negro for using provoking language to white person, 288; same against slave for absenting himself from master's tenement without a pass, 288; same against slave or free negro for furnishing pass to slave, 288; same against slave for selling or administering medicine, 289; same for riot by slaves or free negroes, 289; same against slave or free negro for keeping fire arms, 290; judgment against slave or free negro whose punishment is whipping, 290; conviction of slave for petit larceny and an appeal from judgment, 290; recognizance for appearance of slave upon appeal, 291; conviction of free negro charged with petit larceny, where appeal asked for, 291; recognizance of same on same, 291; recognizance of witnesses to appear and give evidence on appeal, 292; commitment of free negro or slave, on appeal, offender failing to give bail, 293; summons against party to answer prosecution for penalty, 294; judgment on conviction for fines, 294; conviction for fine, where whole goes to commonwealth, 294; conviction where part or whole of fine goes to the informer, 295; appeal from judgment imposing fine, 295; warrant of commitment where delinquent is about to abscond, when part of fine goes to commonwealth, 296; conviction where party fails to pay fine instanter and corporeal punishment adjudged, 296; commitment in default of payment of fine, where no corporeal punishment, 297; do. for nonpayment of penalty in a limited time, 297; warrant to bring party before justice to hear judgment of whipping, where party is unable to pay fine, and time is allowed to pay it, 298; form of judgment upon the warrant, 298.

FISH.

Who prohibited from catching, and how catching of, regulated, 299, 300, 301. See *Arrest Warrants*.

FORESTALLING, INGROSSING AND REGRATING.

Offences defined, 306; intent the gist of these offences, 306; form of warrant, and indictment for, 307-8.

FORGERY.

Definition of time, 309; statute in relation to, 310, 311; what a false making, and counterfeiting what, 312, 316; what constitutes uttering and publishing, 316, 317; what a sufficient intent to defraud, 318. See *Arrest Warrants*.

FREEDOM—(*Suits for.*)

Suits for freedom, how instituted, 331; warrant of justice to take charge of person suing for, 331; bond given by person claiming to be owner of slave suing for, 331.

INDEX.

FUGITIVES FROM JUSTICE.
Statute in relation to, 332, 333; arrest warrant for, upon oath of complainant, 334; same upon indictment found in another state, 335; warrant to commit upon indictment found in another state, 335; same to commit on oath of a party, 336; recognizance of fugitive to appear and abide judgment of county court, 336.

GAMING.
What prohibited, 337, 338; what a place of public resort, 339; warrant against exhibitor of faro table, 339; warrant to seize money exhibited and to seize and burn table, 340; recognizance to answer presentments for keeping and exhibiting faro, 340; order to liberate prisoner upon entering into recognizance, 341.

HARBOUR MASTERS.
Statutory provisions, 341, 342, 343; arrest warrant against master of vessel for failing to obey harbour master, 343; same against harbour master for failing to do his duty, 344.

HEALTH.
Selling corrupt food, 344; adulteration of food, &c., 344; arrest warrant for selling unwholesome provisions, 345; same for adulterating liquors, 345; same for adulteration of medicine, 345.

HOMICIDE.
What murder in first degree, 347; in the second degree, 349; punishment for murder, 347; for voluntary manslaughter, 347; for involuntary manslaughter, 347; homicide defined, 347; murder defined, 347; to constitute murder there must be malice express or implied, 347, 348; who accessaries to murder, 349; manslaughter defined, 350; voluntary manslaughter, 350; involuntary manslaughter, 351; gross ignorance or culpable neglect in medical men, 352; excusable homicide by misadventure, what, 353, 354; excusable homicide in self-defence, what, 355, 357; justifiable homicide, what, 357, 360. See *Arrest Warrants*.

HORSES.
Horse afflicted with glanders to be killed, 365; forfeiture for permitting unaltered horse to go at large, 365; summons to recover penalty for suffering horse afflicted with farcy to go at large, 365; judgment, 366; notice of application to have horse killed, 366; order to kill and bury horse, 366; summons for letting unaltered horse go at large, 367; judgment, 367.

HOUSEBREAKING.
Statutory provisions, 367, 368; ourglary and housebreaking distinguished, 368; offences contained in provisions of statute, 368, 369. See *Arrest Warrants* and *Burglary*.
HUNTING, &c.
When prohibited by statute, 375; summons for, 375; judgment, 375; execution, 376; recognizance in case of third offence, 376; commitment of party failing to give recognizance, 376.

IGNORANCE.
Of law, when an excuse, 14.

INDECENCY.
Indecency, when a misdemeanor at common law, 377; instances of indecency, 377; selling or exposing to sale obscene books, 377; statutory provision, 378. See *Arrest Warrants*.

INDIANS.
Proceedings against them as white persons, 379; when competent witnesses, 246.

INDICTMENTS AND INFORMATIONS.
Indictment defined, and for what offence it lies, 379; information defined, 379; prosecutions, 379; indictments founded upon statute, how framed, 382; rule rigidly enforced, 382. For forms of indictments, see *Arrest Warrants*.

INTENT.
An essential ingredient in most cases of crime, 383; an act wilfully done necessarily presumes intention of consequences, 383.

INSURRECTION.
Insurrection by negroes, how punished, 438, 9; warrant for advising slaves to make insurrection, 448.

JURISDICTION.
Jurisdiction of justice extends no farther than limits of his county, 55; statute limiting and defining jurisdiction of offences, 384.

KIDNAPPING, &c.
Kidnapping at common law, 384; statutory provision, 384; selling free person as slave, 385; kidnapping with intent to sell, 385. See *Arrest Warrants*.

LARCENY.
Definition of, 388; what a taking and carrying away, 388; must be with intent, at the time, to steal, 388; what evidence of this intent, 388, 389; may be committed without ac-

INDEX. 697

tual trespass, 388; what constructive taking, 390; larceny by common carriers, 390; larceny of goods found, when, 391; wife not guilty of, in taking goods of husband, 391; when adulterer taking goods of husband from wife, guilty of, 391; what subjects of larceny at common law and what under statute, 392, 393; how punished, 393; how property in thing stolen may be charged, 393; goods taken in one county and carried to another, larceny in either, 393; what grand and what petit larceny, 393. See *Kidnapping*. See *Arrest Warrants*.

LEVIES AND TAXES.
Statutory provisions concerning, &c., 401-403; form of authority from justice to distrain for, 403; summons against garnishee, 403; judgment, 404; execution, 405.

LEWDNESS, &c.
Penalty for lewdly and lasciviously associating by white persons, 405; for keeping house of ill fame, 405; open and gross lewdness distinguished from lewdly and lasciviously cohabiting, 405. See *Arrest Warrants*.

LIMITATIONS.
When prosecution for perjury or subornation of perjury to commence, 409; when prosecutions for misdemeanor to commence, 409; when civil suits to be brought, 409, 410.

LOTTERIES.
What lotteries prohibited, 441; in what lottery sale of tickets prohibited, 441; what evidence in prosecutions under lottery act, 441; law concerning, remedial, 412; for warrant and indictment, see 690.

LUNATICS.
How examined, 414; questions to be asked of witnesses, 414; who lunatic, 414; how committed and how expense of, paid, 414, 419; interrogatories to be in writing, 415; an idiot how proceeded with, 416; person charged with crime found to be lunatic, 416; justice to issue warrant for lunatic who has escaped, 417; when jailor to certify confinement of lunatic to court, 418; who a lunatic, 419; form of warrant to bring lunatic before justice, 419; evidence in case of lunacy, form of taking, 420; commitment of lunatic, 420; escape warrant, 421.

MAIMING.
What at common law, 422; what under the statute, and how punished, 422, 423; distinction between unlawful and malicious maiming, 423; what is stabbing, 424; in proceedings not necessary to state an assault, 424; cutting, what, 424; instances of cutting, 424; wounding, what, 424; continuity of skin must be broken, 424; what necessary under statute to constitute maiming, 425; intents to maim, disfigure, disable or kill may be charged conjunctively, 425; if intent be to disable, must be permanent disability, 425; where two intents, sufficient though one not embraced in statute, 425; slaves protected by statute, 426. See *Arrest Warrants*.

MAINTENANCE.
What maintenance is, 119.

MANSLAUGHTER.
See *Homicide*.

MARRIAGES.
Between white persons and negroes prohibited, 432; penalty, 432; what marriages prohibited, 432; penalty if clerk issue license contrary to law, 432; penalty on party performing ceremony without license, 432.

MILLERS.
Their toll and their duty, 436.

MISPRISION.
Of treason, defined, 436; of felony, defined, 437.

MITTIMUS.
Its requisites, 69; See *Arrest*. For forms of mittimus, see under head of each offence.

NEGROES.
Who deemed slaves, 437; what slaves may be brought into state, 437; who a mulatto, 437; word 'negro' how construed, 437; statute concerning offences against white persons by free negroes, 438; when by slaves, 439; statute concerning the carrying away of slaves, &c., 440; statute concerning seditious speeches, &c. by, 441; free negroes illegally remaining or coming into state, how proceeded against and punished, 441, 442; unlawful assemblage of slaves, 443, 444; emancipator of aged, insane or infirm slave to support him, 444; selling ardent spirits to slave, 445; buying from slave, 445; master permitting slave to go at large or hire himself out, 446; clerks to deliver register to free negro, 446; second copy of register when to be delivered, 446; free negro over 12 without register to be committed, 446; second arrest, 447; jail fees, how paid, 447; punishment for employing free negro without register, 447; certificate to person of mixed blood, how granted, 447; free negro not to remove from one county to another, 447; punishment

88

for free negro bartering or selling or offering to barter or sell agricultural productions without certificate, 449. See *Arrest Warrants* and *Fines.*

NEW TRIAL.

Justice may grant new trial, when and upon what terms, 663; rules concerning new trial, 670-71.

NOTICES AND MOTIONS.

How notices are served, 468; when notice must be given for judgments, 468; motions upon judgments, upon what and where made, 468; form of notice for judgment on open account for goods sold, 469; same for work done and materials found, 469; same for money lent, 470; same for money paid by one person for another, 470; same for money received by one person for use of another, 470; same on open account, composed of items differing in character, 470; same on promissory note by payee against maker, 471; same by endorsee against maker and endorser of negotiable note, 471; same by endorsee against endorser of negotiable note, 471; same by endorsee, who is not payee, against maker of negotiable note, 472; same by assignee of bond against assignor, 472; same against obligor of bond, or other sealed instrument, for money due for hire of slave, &c., 473; same on promissory note by payee against executor of maker, 473; same by obligee against obligor of bond, or other sealed instrument for payment of money, 473; same by drawer who is payee, against acceptor of inland bill of exchange, 473; affidavits, 473, 474.

NUISANCE.

What a common nuisance, and how abated, 476; no time will legalize nuisance, 476; offending qualities of *smell, noise, danger,* indecency and *obstruction,* 476, 7; carrying on noxious trade, making noise in night, selling unwholesome food, going in public with dangerous infectious disease, keeping house of ill fame, negligently keeping powder, permitting naked slave to go in public, being common public drunkard, keeping common tippling house, obstructing rivers and highways, all nuisances, 477, 78, 79; form of warrants and indictments for, 480, 1, 2, 3.

OFFICERS.

Sheriffs and constables conservators of the peace, 484, 5; both to execute criminal warrant of justice, 484, 5; how far constable's jurisdiction extends, 484; constable officer of coroner, 485; may command aid of others, 485; penalty for refusing to aid officer, 485, 6; what property officer may levy on or distrain, and proceedings after levy, 486, 7. See *Bonds,* 126.

OYSTERS AND TERRAPINS.

When, where, how, and by whom not to be taken, sold or exported, 487, 8. For warrants, see *Arrest,* in index.

PATROLS.

County and corporation court to appoint, and who to consist of, 494; justice may appoint in vacation, 494; duty of patrol and penalty for failure to perform it, 494.

PEACE—(*Justices of.*)

Origin of justices, 496; commission void if oath not taken within six months after date, 496; general duties of, 497; not to be judge in his own cause, 497; if two necessary to do judicial act both must be present, 497; taking privy examination judicial act, 497; not bound to execute laws of United States, 498; if no coroner in county, justice to act, 499; what misdemeanors he may try, 499; jurisdiction over offence empowers him to issue warrant, 499; counsel allowed to appear before him, 500; may commit for contempt, 500; form of commitment, 500.

PERJURY.

What and how punished; oath must be wilful, false, material, and taken before competent authority, 502, 3; what is material, 503, 4; question must be lawful, 504; what evidence necessary to convict, 505; injured party competent witness, 505; how offender to be committed, 505. Warrant of arrest for, see *Arrest.*

PLEAS, &c.

Form of plea to jurisdiction of court, replication to plea, 511; plea that grand juror not a freeholder, 511; replication, 511; plea of misnomer, 512; replication, 512; plea of auterfois acquit, 512; plea of auterfois convict, 513; demurrer to indictment, 513; joinder in demurrer, 513.

POISON.

Administering or attempt to administer to person, felony, 514; administering or exposing it with intent to kill cattle, felony, 515; misdemeanor at common law, 515; what an administering, 514; warrants of arrest for, 515-16-17. See *Arrest.*

POOR.

Overseers of, how appointed and how qualified, 520-21; who poor person, and upon whose complaint and how

INDEX. 699

strolling pauper to be removed, 522; overseer to take up beggars, 523; other regulations concerning poor, 523-24-25; warrant of arrest against strolling pauper, 526; same to remove him, 526; warrant to remove pauper from another state, 527.

POSSE COMITATUS.
Power of officer to summons, 56, 485.

PROPERTY.
Title to, how tried when levied on, 127.

QUARANTINE.
How established, 527; health officer to cause vessels to be removed, 528; penalty on master of vessel for disobeying order, 528; justice to issue warrant for party escaping from, 528; form of warrant, 530; warrant against master for disobedience to order of health officer, 529.

RAILROADS.
Injuries to, where life imperilled, 531; warrants for, 532.

RAPE.
What is rape, 534; if female over 12 years, must be by force and against her will, otherwise if under that age, 534, 536; what will supply place of force, 536; carnal knowledge had by use of intoxicating liquors or narcotics, rape, 534; must be penetration, and what is sufficient penetration, 534-35; emission not necessary, 535; boy under 14 cannot be guilty of, but may be accessary at fact, 535; evidence on trial for, 536-37.

REBELLION.
See *Insurrection*.

RECEIVING STOLEN GOODS.
Offence felony, 542; distinction between stealing and receiving, 542; offences may be joined in same warrant or indictment, 543; when wife jointly charged with husband, should be acquitted, 543; what evidence of guilty knowledge, 543-44. See *Arrest Warrants*.

RECOGNIZANCE.
Recognizance defined, 548; payable to commonwealth, 549; what condition of, 549; what recognizance justice may take, 550; should not be general, 550; when void, 551; need not be signed, 551; justice to bind witnesses, 551; of minors and married women, may be taken of others, 552; party failing to give, committed, 552; to be transmitted to court, 552; bail may surrender principal, 552; recognizance of bail to appear before county court to answer for felony, 553; same to appear before special session, 206; recognizance of owner of slave for appearance before county court for felony, 553; recognizance of witnesses to appear before county court, and testify in case of felony, 558; same before special session, 207; recognizance of bail to appear and answer bill of indictment, &c., for misdemeanor, 554; recognizance for witness to appear and give evidence upon indictment for misdemeanor, 555; same in case of two witnesses, 555; recognizance for appearance of prisoner before justice during examination, &c., 556; recognizance of bail by single justice, where court, upon examination, allow bail, 557; warrant for discharge of prisoner upon giving recognizance, 558; recognizance of bail to appear and hear judgment after verdict, 558; recognizance of bail to appear and answer indictment or presentment, 559; new recognizance of bail, where party is surrendered by former bail, 559; recognizance where misdemeanor committed in one county, and offender arrested in another, 78; do. taken by coroner to answer for felony, 191; do. under duelling act, 217; do. by fugitive from justice, 336; do. by exhibitor of faro, 340; do. by person three times convicted of unlawful hunting, 376; do. by subscriber to incendiary pamphlet, 456; do. by person to answer charge of assembling with slaves, 458; do. by master of slave for permitting him to go at large, 461; by do. where slave is sentenced to be sold, 462; do. by party convicted of dealing with slave, 465; do. by non-resident to answer for unlawfully catching wild fowl, fish or oysters, 304; do. where he is convicted of catching clams, 493; do. to answer in circuit court for riot, 577; do. by person for disturbing religious assembly, 602; recognizance of the peace, 635; same where party has been committed, and afterwards finds sureties, 636; recognizance of person suspected of unlawfully retailing spirits, 643.

RECORDS.
Penalty on clerk making false entries, &c., 560; penalty for stealing or fraudulently secreting public record, 560.

RENT.
Assignee of, rights same as lessor or lessee, 562; what powers pass to grantee or devisee without express words, 562; when attornment not necessary, and when void, 562; tenancy from year to year, how termi-

nated, 562; how landlord may enter when tenant deserts the premises, 562-63; rent recovered by distress or action, 563; remedy for use and occupation, 563; who liable for rent, 563; when and by whom distress may be made, 563; what property liable to distress, 564; when property not to be removed without paying year's rent, 564; when officer may enter by force to levy, 564; distress not void for irregularity of levy, 564; proceedings after distress or attachment for, after levy, when rent reserved not in money, 565; re-entry, proceedings to establish right of, and how defendant may redeem, 565; when suit for re-entry to be brought, 565; other proceedings in relation to re-entry, 565-66; attachment for rent, when and how obtained, 566; forthcoming bond given on distress for rent, and when and how given, 567; form of bond, see No. 1, p. 129; form of affidavit for warrant of distress, 568; form of warrant of distress, 568; form of attachment for rent before property is removed, 568; same after property is removed, 569; bond to be given by landlord on attachment for rent, 569; replevy bond taken by officer levying attachment for rent, 570.

ROADS.

Statutory provisions, 584; warrant by justice to impress wagons, &c., 584; warrant to value articles obtained by surveyor of road, 584; oath administered to housekeepers, 584; certificate of two housekeepers, 585; warrant directed to three freeholders to assess damages to owner of lands, &c., 585; certificate by freeholders of damages, 585; summons and judgment for failing to work on road, 586; warrant for not keeping road passing over dam in good order, 586; summons for riding horse race in public road, 587; same for suffering horse to run race in public road, 587; summons for breaking down, &c., bridge, bench or log, across creek, 587; same for breaking down mile stone or sign board, 588; presentment against surveyor for failing to keep road in order, 588; same against owner of dam over which road passes, for not keeping the same in order, 589.

RIOT, ROUT AND UNLAWFUL ASSEMBLY.

Offences defined and distinctions between them, 572-73-74-75; by whom and how riot suppressed under statute, 571; how by the common law, 575; rioter pulling down or destroying house guilty of felony, 572; when guilty of murder, 571; no accessaries in riot, 574. See *Arrest Warrant* and *Recognizance.*

ROBBERY.

In what offence consists, 509; value of thing taken immaterial, 509; when the taking is complete, 591; must be by force or putting in fear, 591; when a taking from the person, 591, 592; what violence or fear necessary, 592; constructive force, in what it consists, 593; what fear sufficient, 593-94.

RUNAWAY SLAVES.

When apprehended to be taken before justice, 597; his duty, 597; what reward allowed and mode of payment, 598; jailor's duty in relation to, 598; when runaway may be sold and how proceeds disposed of, 599; clothes to be furnished to, 599; how fees paid if runaway die in jail, 599; certificate of arrest and endorsement, 600; order of delivered to owner, 600.

SABBATH BREAKING.

What labour on the Sabbath prohibited, 601; penalty for disturbing religious assembly, 601; each sale of goods on Sabbath not distinct offence, 602; warrant for disturbing religious meeting, 602. See *Recognizance.* Summons for working on Sabbath, and judgment and execution, 603. See *Drunkenness*, 203.

SEAMEN.

Desertion of seaman, how punished, and what remedy, 605; landing sick or disabled seamen without provision for maintenance, how punished, 605; seamen how buried, 605. See *Arrest Warrants.*

SEARCH WARRANT.

On what complaint, by whom, and for what to issue, 608; if to be executed in night, issued by two justices, 608; to whom directed, 608-9; general warrant illegal, 609; what justification to justice, 609; officer strictly to follow warrant, 609; when doors may be broken to execute it, 609; goods found not to be delivered to owner, 609-10; warrant to search for stolen goods, 610; for harboured runaway slave, 611; for fire arms in possession of negro, 611; to search for indecent books, &c., 611; to search for counterfeit coin or forged bank notes, 612; to search vessel for slave, 453.

SHIPS.

Maliciously burning ship, what offence, and how punished, 613; casting away or destroying of, when an offence and how punished, 613; when entering a ship felony, 613 ; how offender against 12th and 13th sec. chap. 192, must be committed, 613 ; when ship in body of county, 614. For warrant, see *Arrest*, and page 614-15-16.

SLAVES.—See *Negroes* and *Fines*.

SMALL POX.

Who to establish hospital, 619 ; inoculation for, must be at hospital, 619 ; not to bring it into state, 619 ; what persons justice may order to hospital, 619 ; when justice may order house, lot or vessel to be entered to remove cause of infectious disease, 620 ; how expense paid, 620 ; warrant for bringing small pox into state, 620 ; same to remove person to hospital, 621 ; same against one who has been where small pox is, 621 ; order to enter lot, house, &c., to remove cause of, 622, 23.

SODOMY AND BESTIALITY.

How punished, 622. See *Arrest Warrants*.

SUPERSEDEAS.

What commitment or recognizance a justice may supersede, and upon what terms he may do it, 626 ; one justice cannot supersede the act of another, 626 ; form of supersedeas to a commitment, 627 ; same of order to discharge recognizance, 627 ; where supersedeas and order sent, 626.

SUBPŒNA.

For witness in criminal prosecution, 260 ; in civil warrant, 261 ; commitment for disobedience of, 260-61.

SURETY OF THE PEACE AND GOOD BEHAVIOUR.

Judge, justice, and commissioner in chancery, conservator of peace, and may require surety of peace, 628 ; for what it may be required, 628, 29 ; proceedings after complaint and before arrest, 629 ; right of appeal from judgment, 629 ; in what surety of peace consists, 629, 30 ; may be required of infant as well as adult, 630 ; who has right to demand it, 630 ; parent may claim it for child, and husband for wife, 630 ; wife and husband may have it the one against the other, 631 ; how granted, 631 ; party not to be bound more than 12 months, and not to be granted where complaint malicious or frivolous, 631 ; recognizance for, where filed and how forfeited, 632 ; for good behaviour what, and distinction between good behaviour and breach of peace, 632 ; who not of good fame, 633 ; warrant of the peace, 634 ; judgment requiring sureties, 635 ; judgment dismissing complaint, 635 ; recognizance for the peace or good behaviour, 635 ; commitment for want of sureties, 636 ; same for refusing to pay costs on complaint for, 636 ; recognizance, after party has once failed to give sureties and been committed, 637 ; order to discharge upon giving recognizance, 637.

TAVERNS AND TIPPLING.

What a tavern, 640 ; not to be kept without license, and how license obtained, 638 ; license to keep house of entertainment, how obtained, 638 ; what tavern keeper to keep, 639 ; what retailing liquors prohibited, 639 ; justice suspecting party guilty of retailing may institute prosecution, 640 ; the rights and liabilities of inn keepers, 640, 41, 42 ; prosecutions for retailing spirits may be by presentment, 642 ; what necessary to prove, 642 ; retailing to two at same time and place separate offences, 642 ; summons against person suspected of retailing ardent spirits, 642 ; recognizance for good behaviour, 643 ; order to attorney to institute prosecution for retailing liquors without license, 644 ; presentment for retailing spirits to be drunk at the place where sold, without an ordinary license, 644; same for same without paying tax, 644.

THREATS.

See *Robbery*. Threats made with intent to deter from doing a lawful act, a misdemeanour at common law, 645 ; to extort money, a felony, and how punished, 645 ; when threats made by letter, what necessary to constitute offence, 645. For warrant, see page 646.

TOBACCO.

Penalty on inspector issuing or causing to be issued a receipt or note for any tobacco not received into the warehouse, 648. For warrant see 648-49.

TREASON.

Statutory provisions, 651 ; in what it consists, 651 ; what its punishment, 651 ; free persons conspiring with slaves to rebel or make insurrection, how punished, 657.

TRESPASS—(*Wilful*.)

Statutory provision, in relation to, 653 ; what constitutes offence under act, 653 ; injury to property, how stated, 654. For warrant, see *Arrest*, in index.

WARRANT.

For warrants of arrest, see *Arrest*, in index.

WARRANTS—(*Civil*.)

When and in what cases warrant may be brought, 662, 667 ; how brought and how tried, 667; justice to issue subpœna in, for witness, 667; to keep book and what to enter in it, 663; may grant new trial, 663; execution on warrant, how issued and where returnable, 664; may be suspended, how long and on what terms, 663; justice cannot try case in trespass, 668; claim cannot be divided to give jurisdiction, 668; justice has common law and equity jurisdiction, 668; when he may give judgment for defendant, 668; when warrant in detinue lies, 668; how warrant to be brought for goods claimed by married woman, 668; warrant in trover or covenant for what and how brought, 669; rules in granting new trials, 670-71; form of, on written acknowledgment or on open account, 672; form of, for debt due by wife before marriage, 673; for debt due wife before marriage, 672; form of, in debt for penalty, 672; in trover and in detinue, 674; subpœna for witness, 674; summons against witness, 674; judgment in debt for money, 675; judgment in detinue, 675; judgment in trover, 675; judgment on warrant, for penalty, 675; form of entering an appeal to county court from judgment of single justice, 676; form for suspending execution for forty or sixty days, 676; form of execution upon judgment in debt before single justice, 676; form of execution in trover, 677; form of execution in detinue, 677; form of execution against executor or administrator, 677; form of application for summons against debtor and creditor in an execution which has been levied on property claimed by another, 678; form of summons to be awarded by justice upon above application, 678; form of judgment of the justice in favour of the claimant, upon the above summons, 679; form of entering an appeal from above judgment, 679; form of record book of a justice, 680.

WILD FOWL.

Non-resident shooting, &c., wild fowl, penalty, 680; penalty on person shooting at or killing, except from land, during night, 680; penalty on person shooting at, with gun not easily discharged from shoulder, 681.

WILLS.

Penalty on person fraudulently destroying or concealing any will or codicil, 684.

WITNESSES.

See *Evidence* and *Warrants*. Subpœnas for, 620-21.

www.ingramcontent.com/pod-product-compliance
Lightning Source LLC
Chambersburg PA
CBHW071213290426
44108CB00013B/1174